The Psychology of Proof

The Psychology of Proof
Deductive Reasoning in Human Thinking

Lance J. Rips

A Bradford Book
The MIT Press
Cambridge, Massachusetts
London, England

© 1994 Massachusetts Institute of Technology

Set in Times Roman by Asco Trade Typesetting Ltd., Hong Kong. Printed and bound in the United States of America.

Library of Congress Cataloging-in-Publication Data

Rips, Lance J.
  The Psychology of proof: deductive reasoning in human thinking / Lance J. Rips.
      p.   cm.
  "A Bradford book."
  Includes bibliographical references and index.
  ISBN 0-262-18153-3
  1. Reasoning (Psychology) 2. Logic—Psychological aspects. I. Title.
  BF442.R56   1994
  160—dc20   93-5811
                                                                         CIP

Contents

Preface

Suppose some future psychologists are asked to investigate the mental faculties of a newly discovered intelligent life form. Sent to the planet that these creatures inhabit, the psychologists make observations, conduct experiments, administer tests, and finally compose a report for the *Journal of Extraterrestrial Psychology*. In reading this report, we would probably not be too surprised to find that the creatures have visual systems different from ours, and perhaps different perceptual experiences. Nor is it hard to imagine these creatures having vastly greater (or smaller) memory capacity. But suppose we are also told that the creatures reject simple, familiar inference principles in favor of equally simple but to our minds obviously incorrect principles.

To us earthlings, an intuitively straightforward inference principle is the one logicians call *modus ponens*. According to this principle, the proposition *IF so-and-so THEN such-and-such* and the proposition *So-and-so* jointly entail the proposition *Such-and-such*.[1] For example, from the propositions *IF Calvin deposits 50 cents THEN Calvin will get a coke* and *Calvin deposits 50 cents*, it follows that *Calvin will get a coke*. We can write this in the form shown in (1), where the sentences above the line are called premises and the sentence below the line the conclusion.

(1) If Calvin deposits 50 cents, Calvin will get a coke.
Calvin deposits 50 cents.
_____
Calvin will get a coke.

Now suppose that our extraterrestrials have exactly the same inference skills that we do, but with one important exception. They reject all modus ponens arguments, such as (1), and adopt instead a contrary principle we might call *modus shmonens*: From *IF so-and-so THEN such-and-such* and *So-and-so*, they conclude *NOT such-and-such*. For instance, they would say that the conclusion of (1) doesn't follow from its premises, but that the conclusion of (2) does.

(2) If Calvin deposits 50 cents, Calvin will get a coke.
Calvin deposits 50 cents.
_____
Calvin will not get a coke.

The existence of creatures who systematically deny modus ponens and accept modus shmonens would be extremely surprising—much more surprising than the existence of creatures who differ from us in basic perceptual or memory abilities. In a situation like this one, we would probably be more apt to blame the translation into English from whatever language the creatures speak than to accept the idea that they sincerely believe in modus shmonens (Davidson 1970; Dennett 1981; Frege 1893/1964; Lear 1982; Quine 1970, chapter 6). Indeed, our reluctance to attribute exotic inferences even to exotic creatures is an interesting property of *our* thought processes.[2] Modus ponens and other inference principles like it are so well integrated with the rest of our thinking—so central to our notion of intelligence and rationality—that contrary principles seem out of the question. As Lear (1982, p. 389) puts it, "We cannot begin to make sense of the possibility of someone whose beliefs are uninfluenced by *modus ponens*: we cannot get any hold on what his thoughts or actions would be like." Deep-rooted modes of thought such as these are important objects of psychological investigation, since they may well turn out to play a crucial organizing role for people's beliefs and conjectures—or so I will try to argue.

This book leads up to the conclusion that cognitive scientists should consider deductive reasoning as a basis for thinking. That is, it explores the idea—which I call the *Deduction-System Hypothesis*—that principles such as modus ponens are central to cognition because they underlie many other cognitive abilities. Part of the content of this proposal is that the mental life of every human embodies certain deduction principles— that these principles are part of the human cognitive architecture and not just the properties of people schooled in logic. This approach also views deduction as analogous to a general-purpose programming system: Just as we can use a computer language such as Basic or Pascal to keep track of our finances or to solve scientific or engineering problems, we can use deductive reasoning to accomplish a variety of mental activities.[3] In particular, we will see how deduction allows us to answer questions from information stored in memory, to plan actions to obtain goals, and to solve certain kinds of problems. The Deduction-System Hypothesis is necessarily vague at this point, but I hope to clarify it during the course of the book. In the meantime, it may help to think of deduction systems as similar to production systems but incorporating more flexible forms of representation and process.

Goals

The Deduction-System Hypothesis is controversial, both in cognitive science generally and in the psychology of reasoning in particular. Some current approaches in cognitive science deal with deduction in the same way that they deal with mundane cognitive skills such as the ability to tell time on a standard clock. According to these approaches, deduction is a similarly specialized task that is useful mainly for solving puzzles in logic or proving theorems in mathematics.

There are several possible reasons for supposing that the Deduction-System Hypothesis is false. First, the results of many psychological experiments show that subjects' performance on tasks that explicitly call for deduction is often quite poor. If deduction were a truly central cognitive ability, then one would suppose that performance would be nearly optimal. Second, one might hold that deduction is in its essentials no different from other problem-solving activities (e.g., solving chess or crossword puzzles) and can be explained according to exactly the same principles. Hence, there may be no reason to suppose that deduction has psychological primacy with respect to other such tasks. Third, there is a possibility that deduction is not sufficiently flexible to provide a reasonable basis for higher cognition. Deduction operates by adding conclusions derived from stated premises, as in (1) above. However, much of our thinking involves retracting beliefs that we now suspect are erroneous, and deduction provides us with no obvious way to do that (at least, outside of special deduction forms such as *reductio ad absurdum*—see chapter 2).

There are some short answers one could give to these objections. For example, one could point out that, although people do have trouble with certain sorts of reasoning problems, they do perfectly well with others; their accuracy on the latter rivals their accuracy on almost any cognitive task. One could also mention that many cognitive scientists—including some who think that deduction is nothing special—take production systems extremely seriously as a basis for cognitive processing. Yet these systems operate on principles that look suspiciously like modus ponens. However, a truly convincing defense of the Deduction-System Hypothesis entails setting out the details of such a theory and demonstrating that it successfully predicts mental successes and failures on a range of cognitive tasks. Developing and testing such a psychological theory is the main goal of this book.

General Plan of the Chapters

Although the study of reasoning has a long history in experimental psychology (see Woodworth 1938, chapter 30), its contribution to cognitive theory has been slight, because researchers have tended to focus on very specialized deduction tasks. Only within the last few years have cognitive psychologists come up with models that are able to describe more than a trivially small set of inferences. My first chapter examines the limitations of traditional approaches and points to some design features for more adequate models.

A key concept of the theory developed in this book is the notion of a mental proof. According to this approach, a person faced with a task involving deduction attempts to carry it out through a series of steps that take him or her from an initial description of the problem to its solution. These intermediate steps are licensed by mental inference rules, such as modus ponens, whose output people find intuitively obvious. The resulting structure thus provides a conceptual bridge between the problem's "givens" and its solution. Of course, mental proofs and mental inference rules are supposed to be similar in important respects to proofs and rules in logic and mathematics. Chapters 2 and 3 describe the logical background of these concepts and outline the role they have played in computer theorem proving. Along the way, I also try to distinguish properties of logical systems that may have psychological relevance from properties that have more to do with elegance or efficiency. Chapter 3 also develops the idea that we can use mental proofs, not only to derive theorems in formal mathematics, but also to solve more general sorts of problems.

My approach to the problem of deductive reasoning is to construct a theory in the form of a computer simulation that mimics the abilities of a person who has had no special training in formal logical methods. Along these lines, chapter 4 describes a model that is able to generate mental proofs for problems in sentential reasoning (i.e., for inferences whose correctness depends on sentence connectives such as IF, AND, OR, and NOT), and chapter 5 examines some experimental tests of this model. The complete model also handles reasoning with quantified variables, as chapters 6 and 7 show.

Like all computer models, this one contains lots of specific assumptions—too many to test in a single experiment. For that reason, chapters 4–7 describe a variety of studies that highlight different aspects of the theory. Some of these employ the traditional method of asking subjects to evaluate the logical correctness of simple arguments (premise-conclusion pairs), but in others the subjects are asked to recall the lines of a proof or to decide (while they are being timed) whether the lines follow from earlier ones. In still other experiments, subjects are asked to think aloud as they try to solve deduction puzzles.

The last four chapters deal with implications of the model. Chapter 8 points out some of the promises of a deduction-based cognitive theory, applying the model to a number of well-known cognitive tasks, including categorization and memory search. It also discusses the relation of the model to schema theories, nonmonotonic logics, and truth maintenance. As if these topics weren't controversial enough, most of the rest of the book deals with rival theories in the psychology of reasoning itself. Some of these alternative views go along with the idea of inference rules and proof but quarrel with the particular rules or proof strategies that I am advocating. I describe some of these alternatives in chapter 9, but my tendency is to try to accommodate these views in the current framework rather than to try to discriminate among them experimentally. Other alternatives, though, explicitly deny the need for rules and proofs and attempt to substitute psychological versions of Euler circles, Venn diagrams, truth tables, or similar diagram methods (see Erickson 1974 and Johnson-Laird and Byrne 1991). Chapter 10 is a critique of this position. Finally, chapter 11 deals with some general objections to deduction-based cognitive theories and tries to summarize these systems' successes and limits.

Of course, this selection of topics doesn't cover all those that might be treated in a work on reasoning, or even in one on deductive reasoning. A major omission is a systematic treatment of research on children's development of reasoning skills. The literature in this area is vast, especially when Piagetian studies are included; indeed, Piaget's logic is itself the target of several monographs, including Osherson 1974a and Seltman and Seltman 1985. Because my familiarity with developmental issues is slim, I stick mainly to adult reasoning. I mention findings from the developmental literature when they bear on the main problems, but my coverage of them is narrow. Fortunately, Braine and Rumain's (1983) review of logical reasoning in children discusses this area from a point of view similar to the one developed in these chapters.

What's New?

Chapters 1–3 are intended in part to help advanced undergraduates or graduate students in the cognitive sciences understand recent research on deduction, and they seem to have worked fairly well in the classes where I've auditioned them. Part I also contains discussions that I hope will be of interest to experts in this area, but I expect these experts to focus on the last two parts—particularly on the material that hasn't appeared elsewhere. Here is a brief guide for them to what's new: The theory of sentential reasoning in chapter 4 is a refinement of an earlier proposal (Rips 1983), but it also contains some new results on the completeness of the theory with respect to classical sentential logic. Likewise, chapter 5 reports some reaction-time data that haven't appeared previously, but also summarizes a few older experiments on the sentential model. In addition, chapter 5 applies the model for the first time to some well-known results on reasoning with negatives and conditionals. The theory for quantified variables and the supporting experiments in chapters 6 and 7 are entirely new. So, for the most part, are the extensions and comparisons in part III. Experts may be especially interested in the use of the deduction theory to handle problem solving and categorization in chapter 8 and in the discussion of pragmatic schemas and Darwinian algorithms in Chapter 9. The comments on mental models draw on earlier papers (Rips 1986, 1990b) but are updated to take into account some later developments.

The field of deductive reasoning is currently mined with controversies. Although this makes the field more intense and interesting than it had been in the last few decades, it also makes it hard to issue final judgments. I hope, however, that the perspective I develop here is a stable one, and that it will prove helpful to others in discriminating progress from polemics.

Acknowledgments

I have accumulated so many intellectual debts in writing this book that it seems no coincidence that it ends in chapter 11. My most immediate creditors are Denise Cummins, Jonathan Evans, Leon Gross, Philip Johnson-Laird, Matt Kurbat, John Macnamara, Jeff Schank, and several anonymous reviewers who did their best to get me to improve the chapters. Jeff also helped with some of the experiments reported here, as did Ruth Boneh, Fred Conrad, David Cortner, Jia Li, Sandra Marcus, and others. For conversations about psychological and logical matters, I thank especially Christopher Cherniak, Allan Collins, Dedre Gentner, William

Harper, Reid Hastie, David Israel, David Malament, Ron McClamrock, Ed Smith, Roger Tourangeau, and many others at the University of Chicago, Stanford University, MIT, and the University of Arizona. Thanks also to Olivia Parker for permission to use the jacket photo and to Jia Li for help with the index.

I used drafts of chapters 1–10 in classes at Chicago, and comments from the students are responsible for many changes. For actual monetary support I'm grateful for NIMH grant MH39633 and for a Cattell Foundation fellowship that enabled me to spend a sabbatical year at Stanford working on this project.

I also feel a deep debt to a number of teachers who have embodied for me, in different ways, the ideals of rigor and clarity in thinking. They have been an inspiration in the research and writing, though this book certainly falls far short of what they would like. But, more important, they have convinced me that clarity and rigor are what the study of reasoning is really about, rather than the details of categorical syllogisms or the four-card problem. It goes without saying that our thinking isn't always clear or rigorous; but sporadically it is, and it's important to try to understand how this is possible.

Finally, while attending an "authors' breakfast" for my seven-year-old daughter and her classmates a few months ago, I realized that I was the only member of my immediate family who wasn't the author of a book. As by far my biggest creditors, they've been remarkably helpful and remarkably patient while I've been trying to catch up with them.

I PRELIMINARIES

1 Psychological Approaches to Deduction

The great difference, in fact, between that simpler kind of rational thinking which consists in the concrete objects of past experience merely suggesting each other, and reasoning distinctively so called, is this, that whilst the empirical thinking is only reproductive, reasoning is productive.
William James (1890, pp. 329–330)

It is tempting to begin by announcing that the aim of this book is to propose a psychological theory of deductive reasoning. That is, in fact, the goal. But isn't it redundant to speak of a *psychological* theory of deductive reasoning? What other kinds of theories of deductive reasoning could there be? Isn't reasoning *by definition* a psychological process?

Although there is some redundancy in this expression, the phrase "psychological theory" emphasizes some important differences between this approach and earlier ones. On the theory to be developed here, deduction is a type of psychological process, one that involves transforming mental representations. For most of its history, however, experimental psychology has approached deduction, not as the study of a mental process, but as the study of people answering questions about a particular kind of *argument*. In this formal sense, an *argument* is a set of sentences (*the premises*) and a single additional sentence (*the conclusion*). A deductively correct argument, roughly speaking, is one in which the conclusion is true in any state of affairs in which the premises are true. Thus, argument (1) has as premises the two sentences above the line and as conclusion the sentence below the line. Moreover, argument (1) is deductively correct; in any state of affairs in which it is true both that Calvin deposits 50 cents and that *if* Calvin deposits 50 cents he will get a coke, it is also true that he will get a coke.

(1)   If Calvin deposits 50 cents, he'll get a coke.
      Calvin deposits 50 cents.

      Calvin will get a coke.

An experimenter may present subjects with a list of arguments like this and ask them to decide which are deductively correct. Or the experimenter may provide the premises of the argument along with a set of possible conclusions and have the subjects choose the conclusion that would make the argument correct (or choose "none of the above" if none of the conclusions are acceptable). Or the subjects may see just the premises and have to come up with a conclusion on their own.

Yoking deductive reasoning in this way to the study of deductively correct arguments leaves it open whether there are mental processes that are distinctive to reasoning of this sort. It is possible that whatever mental activities people go through in evaluating an argument like (1) are the same ones they use in nondeductive reasoning (Haviland 1974). It is even possible that there are no cognitive processes peculiar to *reasoning*, deductive or nondeductive. What we think of as reasoning may involve problem-solving activities much the same as those we use in balancing a checkbook or planning a menu (Newell 1990; Pollard 1982).

Whether there are distinctively deductive processes is one of the major problems to be addressed in this book, and it will not do to beg the question at the outset. In part II, I mount a full-scale attack on this question by proposing a theory of deductive reasoning that will permit us to see what is unique about thinking of this sort. In part III, I defend the idea that there are deductive processes from those who take a more homogeneous view. However, let us begin by simply trying to get a glimpse of the terrain, looking at some actual transcripts of people reasoning. These examples should prove more helpful to us than defining deductive reasoning at the start in some cooptive way. Although the cognitive processes underlying these examples may be shared with other forms of cognition, they may yet constitute the kind of stable cluster that is psychologically nonarbitrary and hence is a worthwhile target of scientific study.

The first two sections of this chapter, then, supply some instances that seem to fall under the heading of deductive reasoning, and they attempt to explain why such reasoning might be important. In general, earlier approaches within psychology have been far too limited in their scope. These older proposals contain many astute observations; but they are handicapped because they rely on overrestrictive methods and assumptions and because they insulate themselves from important developments in logic and artificial intelligence. As a result, they have relegated deduction to a quite minor role in cognitive psychology. In the rest of the chapter, I consider in more detail the two main psychological approaches to deduction: the approach that stems from psychometrics and the one that stems from experimental and social psychology. Examining the strengths and weaknesses of these prior attempts can help us in formulating a more adequate theory. What I hope will emerge from this initial discussion is the possibility that deduction may be a centrally important cognitive component, one deserving a much more thorough examination than it has typically received.

Some Examples of Deductive Reasoning

Consider what people say while they are solving problems that have traditionally come under the heading of deduction. In experiments of this sort, subjects are under instructions to "think aloud," saying whatever comes to mind during the solution process. After a little practice they usually comply with this request, particularly if the solution is fairly lengthy. Tape recordings and transcripts of their monologues can then provide some hints about the underlying mental processes. Newell and Simon's (1972) tour de force, *Human Problem Solving*, is the classic example of this method in current psychology. Controversy surrounds the claim that these transcripts are faithful traces of the subjects' mental activities (Ericsson and Simon 1984; Nisbett and Wilson 1977; Wason and Evans 1975), since some of what the subjects say may be their own theories or rationalizations rather than direct reports of their thinking. This is especially true when subjects describe a completed process rather than an ongoing one— when the protocol is "retrospective" rather than "concurrent." However, we needn't take sides in this controversy for our present purposes; even if it should turn out that the monologues are after-the-fact justifications rather than true observations, they are well worth studying in their own right. Although the subjects may initially solve the problem in some other way, the transcripts provide examples of fairly complex analysis that itself calls for explanation.

Example 1: Sentential Reasoning

The first example is taken from an experiment (Rips 1983) in which subjects received 12 arguments (from table 11.6 of Osherson 1975) and had to decide while thinking aloud whether each was deductively correct or incorrect. The subjects' exact task was to decide whether "the conclusion has to be true if the premise is true." I told the subjects to answer the question first in whatever way seemed natural; then, in order to encourage the subjects to mention all the steps in their thinking, I asked them to explain their answer again as if they were talking to a child who did not have a clear understanding of the premise and conclusion. Of the 12 problems, half were in fact deductively correct in classical sentential logic (see chapter 2 below) and half were incorrect. All the problems were described as being about a set of letters that might be "written on a blackboard in some other room of this building." Table 1.1 is a complete transcript from one

Table 1.1
Protocol from subject 7 on the argument "If is not true that there is both an M and a P, then there is an R; therefore, if there is no M, then there is an R."

Initial solution

a. The sentence above the line reads, "If it is not true that there is both an M and a P, then there is an R."

b. The sentence below the line reads, "If there is no M then there is an R."

c. If it is not true that there is both an M and a P—if you come upon a blackboard and there is an M and a P, there will always be an R.

d. If you come upon any blackboard without an M or without a P, without both of them together, there will be an R.

e. So with an M and a P, no R, and if it is not true that they're both there, then there is an R.

f. Now the sentence below says that if there is no M, then there is an R.

g. That's true.

h. Now I'm construing the top sentence a little differently, but I think that shows how I'm reasoning, correctly or otherwise.

i. If it is not true that there is both, then there is an R.

Explanation to a "child"

j. OK. Anytime you see both the letters M and P on a blackboard, then you can be sure there is no R.

k. But if one of the letters is missing or if both of the letters is missing then you'll see an R on the blackboard.

l. Now look at this blackboard here.

m. There is no M on it, so if either an M or a P is missing or both of them are missing, then there has to be an R.

n. Now what about this blackboard?

o. There is an M missing.

p. What does that say?

q. That says there has to be an R there.

---

of the subjects, a graduate student in English (with no training in formal logic) who was working on the argument shown here as (2).

(2)   If it is not true that there is both an M and a P on the
     blackboard, then there is an R.
     ―――――――――――――――――――――――――
     If there is no M, then there is an R.

In the subject's initial solution, he reads the premise and the conclusion of the argument (lines a and b in table 1.1) and then begins working over the premise by paraphrasing it in various ways, not all of which are necessarily correct (lines c–e). The most helpful of these paraphrases occurs in line d: "If you come upon any blackboard without an M or without a P ... there will be an R." From this sentence the answer seems to be self-evident because, after repeating the conclusion in line f, the subject declares the conclusion to be true. Although this last step is not elaborated in the initial solution, the subject's explanation to the imaginary child provides some insight into his reasoning. He first tries to get the child to understand that if either an M or a P is missing, or if both of them are missing, then there has to be an R—essentially a restatement of line d. He then has the child imagine a situation in which the antecedent (i.e., if-clause) of the conclusion is true: "Look at this blackboard here. There is no M on it." Because the M is missing, "there has to be an R there." We can summarize the main part of the subject's reasoning as in (3).

(3)   The premise states that if there is not both an M and a P, then there
       is an R.
       This means that if there is no M or there is no P—if either an M is
       missing or a P is missing—then there is an R.
       Suppose, as the conclusion suggests, there is no M.
       Then, according to the premise, there will be an R.
       So the conclusion must be true: If there is no M, then there is an R.

The subject transforms the premise to make it more intelligible or more useful to the task at hand. He also makes use of the conclusion to direct his thinking while he is working out the answer. Not all the subjects were as successful or as articulate as this one, but nearly all followed similar patterns of transforming the premise in a way relevant to the conclusion.

Example 2: Reasoning with Instances

Our second example deals with a puzzle about a fictitious realm whose inhabitants are called "knights" and "knaves." Knights and knaves are impossible to distinguish by appearance. In fact, there is just one characteristic that separates them: Knights always tell the truth, whereas knaves always lie. There are many puzzles concerning knights and knaves; (4), from Smullyan 1978, is typical.

(4)   Suppose there are three individuals, A, B, and C, each of whom is
       either a knight or a knave.
       Also, suppose that two people are of the same *type* if they are both
       knights or both knaves.
       A says, "B is a knave."
       B says, "A and C are of the same type."
       Question: Is C a knight or a knave?

To see how people tackle problems like these, I asked subjects to solve four knight/knave problems—problem (4) among them—while thinking aloud (Rips 1989a). They were told: "Read the problem aloud and then keep talking about it while you are trying to come up with your answer. Say everything that you are thinking about, even if it seems trivial. If you are silent for more than a few seconds, I'll remind you to keep talking." Table 1.2 contains a solution to problem (4) from one of these subjects—a college freshman who, like the subject of our earlier example, had no training in formal logic.

This subject begins by assuming that person A is a knight. Since what A says is true on this assumption and since A says that B is a knave, the subject infers that B would be a knave. B's statement that A and C are of the same type must therefore be a lie. But, by assumption, A is a knight; thus C must be a knave. So by line d of table 1.2 the subject is able to conclude that B and C are knaves if A is a knight, and she calls this her "first possibility." She then turns to the second possibility that A is a knave. This means that B is a knight, so that A and C are of the same type, namely knaves. In line g, though, the subject runs into a temporary problem: She has forgotten C's type under the first possibility. (This was not uncommon in the experiment, since the subjects were not allowed to write down their intermediate results.) In lines h and i she goes back to reconstruct the first part of her solution, and in line j she begins again on the second part. But before she develops the latter possibility she apparently has some second thoughts about the first. Finally, she reminds her-

Table 1.2
Protocol from subject 3 on knight/knave problem (4). (Ellipses indicate pauses.)

a. Well, the *type* introduction, that's a little confusing.
b. If A is knight, then B has to be lying.
c. So A and C are of, are not of the same type.
d. That would mean that B and C are knaves.
e. So that's one possibility.
f. If A is a knave, then B is a knight, and A and C are both knaves.
g. Now I've forgotten my first possibility.
h. If A is a knight, then B...if A is a knight, B is a knave and C is a knave.
i. So my first possibility is C is a knave.
j. Second possibility is if A is a knave.... Wait a minute...
k. If A is a knight, no, if A is a knight, then C is a knave.
l. Uh, if A is a knave..., then C is a knave.
m. So, either way, C is a knave.

self of the implications of the second possibility and, in line m, correctly concludes that on either possibility C is a knave.

Some Preliminary Observations

Examples 1 and 2 demonstrate that the subjects were capable of approaching such problems in a systematic way. Although they sometimes made mistakes (as in line c of table 1.1) or lost their place in the solution (line g of table 1.2), they nevertheless took into account the information given in the problem, made assumptions about unknown aspects, and drew inferences from these given and assumed facts. The overall pattern of the transcripts is similar in some respects to informal proofs in mathematics. That is, in solving these problems the subjects generated a series of statements linking the premises or givens of the problem to the solution. The steps in such a progression are intuitively sound, each step providing a justification for later steps, so the entire series forms a conceptual bridge between the parts of the problem. Furthermore, some of the steps are not only reasonable by the subjects' own criteria; they are also deductively correct, in the sense that the statement constituting the step is true whenever the given and assumed statements are true. For example, line d in table 1.1—"If you come upon any blackboard without an M or without a P ... there will be an R"—is certainly true whenever the premise of problem (2) is true. So is line d of table 1.2—"That would mean that B and C are knaves"—in the context of problem (4) and the assumption that A is a knight.

Notice, too, that the subjects could handle these problems even though the specific tasks were novel. Although the subjects may have had some training on formal proof in high school mathematics, it is very unlikely that they had faced exactly the problems they were confronting in these experiments. Despite the fact that human information-processing abilities are quite restricted, there seems to be no theoretical limit on the number of arguments we can recognize as deductively correct. This remarkable productivity is what James (1890) took to distinguish reasoning from associative thought. Consider another example: If some sentence S_1 is true and if S_2 is also true, then we can infer that S_1 *and* S_2 is true; given this new sentence, we can also infer that S_1 *and* S_1 *and* S_2 is true; this new sentence in turn permits yet another inference to S_1 *and* S_1 *and* S_1 *and* S_2; and so on. Of course, one wouldn't want to produce a stream of inferences of this trivial sort unless one had to (e.g., in support of some further theorem);

nevertheless, the fact that these inferences can be made on demand is something that a deduction theory must explain.

The analogous problem in linguistics is well known (Chomsky 1957, 1965), and the analogy itself has been elaborated by Cohen (1981), Macnamara (1986), Osherson (1976, chapter 8), Pollock (1989), Sober (1978), and others. According to Chomsky (1965, p. 15), grammatical competence includes the ability to interpret infinitely many sentences; therefore, "a generative grammar must be a system of rules that can iterate to generate an infinitely large number of structures." The ability to iterate in the proper way is equally required by a theory of reasoning, since part of the inference potential of a sentence depends on its structural composition. Although there is considerable disagreement about the extent to which this "logical form" mirrors "grammatical form," on most syntactic theories there are systematic relations between the two.[1]

The Centrality of Deductive Reasoning

The above examples suggest that deductive reasoning has some stable internal properties. It seems reasonable to suppose that subjects' utterances in these thinking-aloud experiments are the products of mental processes that represent the information contained in the problem, transform this information in a sequence of steps, and employ the transformed facts to decide on an answer to the experimenter's question. More evidence for this hypothesis will appear in later chapters (especially chapters 5 and 7), but here it provides an obvious framework for the data in tables 1.1 and 1.2.

In what follows, the terms *deductive reasoning, deduction,* and *deductive inference* will be used interchangeably for this transformation-and-decision process, and all three will be distinguished from *deductive argument* (which is a relation between sentence types, not a psychological process or entity). This conception is in fairly good agreement with ordinary usage; although people commonly apply "deductive" and "deduction" to almost any sort of reasoning,[2] they certainly think of reasoning as a kind of mental process that creates new ideas from old ones. At this point, we are not in a position to define deductive reasoning precisely. Clearly, not all mental transformations are deductive ones, and we need to leave room for obviously nondeductive transformations that can occur in image manipulation, in forgetting, and in various sorts of inductive and analogical inference. Similarly, not all of what people do when they solve deduction problems like those in (2) and (4) is deductive reasoning. It is likely that nondeductive processes (e.g., retrieving information from memory) also affect people's answers to these problems, as we will see later. However, tables 1.1 and 1.2 do exemplify the kind of process that we would eventually like to explain, and they should suffice to fix our intuition for the time being.[3]

It is not clear from the examples, however, whether there is anything important about the activity in which these subjects are engaged. People are able to solve all sorts of unusual puzzles (Rubik's cubes, retrograde chess problems, cryptarithmetic problems, and so on), but presumably the cognitive processes responsible for these solutions need not be especially important to mental life. The skills required for retrograde chess puzzles, for example, may be specialized components that have little role to play in other intellectual activities. There is evidence, however, that deductive reasoning, perhaps unlike some other problem-solving skills, is cognitively central in this respect. One source of evidence for this claim—the willingness to attribute to others simple deductive inferences (such as modus ponens) and the unwillingness to attribute contrary inferences (such as modus shmonens)—was noted in the preface. But these proclivities show up, not just in science fiction cases, but also in ordinary situations. Support for the centrality of deduction comes from theoretical accounts of how we explain others' actions and from more specific observations concerning the role of deduction in other cognitive domains.

Theoretical Evidence for the Importance of Deduction

Explaining why people perform given actions ordinarily means attributing to them a set of beliefs and goals: Adele bought a chocolate cake because she likes eating delicious things and believes that anything chocolate is delicious; Gary made a U-turn because he was in a hurry and thought a U-turn would be quicker than driving around the block. But, as Davidson (1970) and Dennett (1971, 1981) have pointed out, interpretations of this kind presuppose more than a single belief. We assume that the beliefs we explicitly attribute to others must also be melded in a coherent way to further beliefs through proper inferential links. Adele's belief about chocolate serves to explain her behavior only if we also attribute to her the belief that the cake in question is chocolate and credit her with the ability to deduce that the cake must therefore be delicious. In other words, we tend to rely on assumptions about people's inference abilities (among other abilities) as implicit parts of our explanations.

One interesting thing about this, for our purposes, is that if we find that our explanations are wrong we are more likely to call into question the beliefs or desires we attribute to others than to blame their skill at drawing deductive inferences. If we use our explanation to predict that Adele will buy a chocolate cake on her next trip to the bakery and then find that she comes back with a cheesecake, we are likely to say that she must not have liked chocolate as much as we thought or that she must have bought the cheesecake for someone else. We don't doubt her ability to perform the inference (often called *universal instantiation*) that corresponds to the argument in (5).

(5)   All chocolate things are delicious.
      This cake is chocolate.
      _____
      This cake is delicious.

Of course, there are limits to the amount of inferential power that we are willing to attribute to humans (Cherniak 1986; Stich 1981); nevertheless, assumptions about the correctness of others' reasoning are very resilient for simple deductions. The fundamental nature of these inferences is also evident if we try to envision disputes about the soundness of arguments such as (1) or (5). Although you could provide additional facts or arguments to convince someone of the truth of the premises, it is not clear what sort of evidence you could appeal to in overcoming another person's resistance to the soundness of the argument itself (Carroll 1895; Haack 1976; Quine 1936). To paraphrase Quine: If arguments like (1) and (5) are not conclusive, what is?

Empirical Evidence

The evidence so far suggests that people *believe* deduction to be a central mental activity. Whether it is in fact central is an empirical question for cognitive psychology. It is not hard to show, however, that deduction must be a component of many other psychological processes on any reasonable cognitive account of their operation. Take comprehension. Theories of how people understand discourse require deduction (as well as nondeductive inference) to generate expectations about upcoming information and to knit unanticipated input with what has gone before.

Consider as an example the mini-dialogue shown as (6), which is taken from Sadock 1977.

(6)   A: Will Burke win?
      B: He's the machine candidate and the machine candidate always
         wins.

As Sadock points out, understanding (6) involves knowing that B believes Burke will win. But B doesn't expressly state this; a hearer must infer this belief by universal instantiation from *Machine candidates always win* and *Burke is the machine candidate* to *Burke will win*, which has essentially the same form as (5). It is true that the causal relationship between comprehension and inference can sometimes be reversed, so that comprehension affects inference. For example, understanding the instructions for a reasoning problem is usually required for a correct response in any explicit test of reasoning. Similarly, in a logic class, comprehension of instructions can lead to improvements in inference skills. But these enablements are quite different from the direct dependence of comprehension on reasoning that is exhibited in (6). Comprehension seems to play a minor role, if any, during the course of reasoning itself, whereas deduction is often a proper part of ongoing comprehension.[4]

We can take planning as a second instance of a cognitive activity that presupposes deductive reasoning. To see this, suppose Adele is looking for something delicious to purchase. Since she believes that all chocolate things are delicious and notices that one of the displayed cakes is chocolate, she can use an inference corresponding to (5) to deduce that the displayed cake is delicious. Thus, from her original goal—to obtain something delicious—she can derive the subgoal of obtaining this particular cake by means of universal instantiation. It is easy to construct similar examples using other deductive patterns. For instance, any planning strategy that uses a process of elimination seems to involve the inference pattern called the *disjunctive syllogism*. Suppose Gary wants to see a movie but can't decide between *Hiroshima, Mon Amour* and *Duck Soup*. After pondering the choice, he decides he is not in the mood for *Hiroshima, Mon Amour*. He should then choose *Duck Soup* by the argument shown here as (7).

(7)   Either I will go to *Hiroshima, Mon Amour* or I will go to *Duck Soup*.
      I won't go to *Hiroshima, Mon Amour*.
      _____
      I will go to *Duck Soup*.

Gary can then amend his plan to go to a movie in favor of the more specific plan to see *Duck Soup*.

These examples are of the simplest sort, but it seems likely that more complex cases of planning will also include a deductive component with inferences such as universal instantiation and the disjunctive syllogism. The relationship between deduction and planning is somewhat less one-sided than that between deduction and comprehension. If a deduction problem is complex enough—as is, for example, proving a difficult theorem in mathematics—then planning may be necessary if one is to find a solution within a reasonable amount of time. However, for everyday instances of deduction, such as (5) and (7), explicit planning is probably minimal, whereas most episodes of planning seem to involve instantiating variables (via universal instantiation), reasoning by cases (the disjunctive syllogism), or reasoning from a conditional rule (modus ponens). (Chapter 3 contains a further discussion of the role that deduction has played in theories of planning in artificial intelligence.)

If deduction is part of higher-level mental processes, such as comprehension and planning, as these examples suggest, it is a little surprising that psychology has usually treated deduction as a relatively special-purpose mechanism (if, indeed, it has recognized deduction as a mechanism at all). The rest of this chapter offers a glimpse at how this state of affairs came about.

Main Trends in Reasoning Research

Psychology has seen two main approaches to the study of high-level cognition: psychometrics and experimental psychology. Both approaches began to deal with reasoning in the 1900s, and they have continued, at least until very recently, to pursue independent methods in this area. The theory of deduction that we will explore in this book has its roots in the experimental tradition, as does most of contemporary cognitive psychology. However, psychometrics has contributed to the study of deduction a unique perspective that also merits discussion. The review in this section is a kind of stage setting rather than an in-depth critique. Some of the experimental work will be examined in more detail when the results become pertinent in later chapters; at this point, an overview of these approaches may be helpful. Current work in psychology has also produced a number of theoretical proposals about the nature of deduction that go under the names of *natural-deduction systems* (see, e.g., Braine 1978; Braine, Reiser, and Rumain 1984; Osherson 1974b, 1975, 1976; Rips 1983, 1989a), *mental models* (see, e.g., Johnson-Laird 1983; Johnson-Laird and Byrne 1991), and *pragmatic reasoning schemas* (see, e.g., Cheng and Holyoak 1985). These will be of vital concern in later chapters; for now, however, it is useful to put the psychological study of deduction in its historical context.

The Psychometric Approach

Psychometrics concerns itself with the measurement of mental traits such as authoritarianness or paranoia, but its main quarry has been intelligence. Indeed, psychometricians' interest in deduction is traceable to the tight relationship they perceived between reasoning and intelligence (Carroll 1989). The very first intelligence tests were designed to measure ability in children and were grab-bags of problems, including some that seem to call for deduction. For example, the Binet test—the first version of which appeared in 1905—contained the item shown here as (8).

(8)   What's foolish about the following statement? "In an old graveyard in Spain, they have discovered a small skull which they believe to be that of Christopher Columbus when he was about ten years old."

Performance on such problems correlated fairly highly with global intelligence measures based on a variety of problem types. Thus, Burt (1919) claimed on the basis of some early research that, for measuring the ability of bright children, tests "involving higher mental processes, particularly those involving reasoning, vary most closely with intelligence." Burt's own test, which was designed for ages 7 through 14, contained a wide variety of reasoning problems, including problems of the type illustrated in (7) (now called *linear syllogisms* or *three-term series problems*).

(9)   Three boys are sitting in a row: Harry is to the left of Willie; George is to the left of Harry. Which boy is in the middle?

The designers of the early intelligence tests intended them to serve practical ends, such as deciding which children should go into special school programs or which enlisted men should get training for high-level positions, and they were quite unanalytic with respect to the abilities underlying the test takers' performance. Later work, particularly that of L. L.

Thurstone and his followers, stressed instead basic mental skills that were supposed to be responsible for the global results. In his monograph *Primary Mental Abilities*, Thurstone singled out reasoning as an appropriate object of these more refined analyses, since one could ask "How many reasoning abilities are there, and just what is each of them like?" (Thurstone 1938, p. 2). The general idea was to assemble pencil-and-paper tests that seemed to tap some aspect of the ability in question. In the case of reasoning, these might include syllogism tests, number-series or letter-series tests, analogy tests, arithmetic word problems, geometrical puzzles, classification problems, and so forth.[5] The investigators administered a test battery to a large number of subjects, correlated subjects' scores for each pair of tests, and factor-analyzed the correlation matrix. Factor analysis is a statistical technique whose aim is to determine the dimensions responsible for similarities and differences in performance on a test (see, e.g., Harman, 1976), and the hope of these investigators was that the revealed factors would "isolate and define more precisely primary abilities in the domain of reasoning" (Green et al. 1953, p. 135).

Thurstone identified several factors that he believed had to do with reasoning. For example, he claimed that one of the factors from the 1938 study, Factor I (for induction), tapped subjects' ability to find a rule that applied to each item in a sequence, as in a number-series test (e.g., "Find the rule in the series below and fill in the blanks: 16, 20, ___, 30, 36, 42, 49, ___"). He also tentatively identified a Factor D as having to do with some sort of deduction skill, a factor that had high loadings from tests such as nonsense syllogisms ("Good or bad reasoning?: Red-haired persons have big feet. All june bugs have big feet. Therefore, some june bugs are red haired?") Two other factors, V and R, also appeared to be connected with reasoning. Thurstone said that tests loading on V, such as verbal analogies and antonyms, are "logical in character" and have to do with ideas and the meanings of words. Factor R had high loadings from a test of arithmetical reasoning (essentially a set of arithmetic word problems) and from other tests that "involve some form of restriction in their solution."

Unfortunately, the factor-analytic studies of reasoning that followed Thurstone's yielded results that were at odds with these initial findings and with one another, casting doubt on the success of the early psychometric program. For example, on the basis of a large project devoted entirely to reasoning tests, Adkins and Lyerly (1952) suggested that there were at least three factors responsible for induction, rather than the single

I factor that Thurstone had isolated. They named these factors "perception of abstract similarities," "concept formation," and "hypothesis verification." At about the same time, Green et al. (1953) also found factor-analytic evidence that induction could be decomposed into three factors—but a different three, which they called "eduction of perceptual relations," "eduction of conceptual relations," and "eduction of conceptual patterns." The deduction factor D met a similar fate. Although some of the later investigations appeared to confirm a deductive or logical reasoning factor, Thurstone dropped the D factor in his further research on the grounds that "it has not been sustained in repeated studies" (Thurstone and Thurstone 1941, p. 6). A recent survey of factor-analytic studies (Carroll 1993) suggests evidence for a deductive or general sequential reasoning factor, an inductive reasoning factor, and a quantative reasoning factor, but concludes that the evidence for them is "hardly compelling."

The ambiguities in the results of these studies highlight some defects in the methodology (see chapter 2 of Sternberg 1977 for a review of these problems). For example, the factor pattern derived in such experiments depends crucially on the choice of the reasoning tests. Unless the investigator samples tests very broadly, there is no guarantee that the resulting factors will reappear in further testing. Moreover, even the same data can produce different results, depending on the investigator's decisions about technical matters, including the method of rotating factors and their interpretive labels (e.g., "deduction" or "hypothesis verification"). However, the major deficiency, from the present point of view, is that the method can yield only factors corresponding to processes that vary substantially across individual test takers. If there is a mental ability that is common to all the test takers (and if they exploit this ability to approximately the same extent on individual tests), then this ability cannot show up as a factor in the results. This is true whether the ability in question plays a role in all the tests or in just a subset. Since characteristics of deduction may well be universal in precisely this way, psychometric methods based on factor analysis are not appropriate for studying them.

Partly as the result of these problems, many contemporary researchers apply psychometric methods in a more refined way to a single type of reasoning test, such as verbal analogies or linear syllogisms, rather than to an assortment of tests (Embretson, Schneider, and Roth 1986; Rips and Conrad 1983; Sternberg 1980; Whitely 1980). The idea is to quantify individual differences that affect component cognitive processes within the task. Suppose, for example, that performance on linear syllogisms such as (9) depends jointly on the ability to form images of spatial arrays and the ability to perform verbal coding and decoding (to simplify the theory of Sternberg 1980). It is possible to use psychometric methods to obtain separate estimates of a subject's skill on these two aspects, using syllogisms that vary systematically in their hypothesized demands on spatial versus verbal processing. The interpretation of these estimates can then be checked by comparing them to the same subject's performance on pure spatial tests and pure verbal tests. Used in this way, however, psychometric methods are more an adjunct than an alternative to experimental methods in cognitive psychology. Carrying out this type of research means developing a substantive theory for the mental subparts of the task and testing subjects in experiments where the problems vary over trials along specific dimensions.

Psychometric methods, such as factor analysis or latent-trait analysis, can be helpful in understanding reasoning, since they provide useful tools for measuring differences in subjects' abilities or strategies. However, it has become clear that an exclusive focus on individual differences cannot tell us all we would like to know about deduction—or about other complex cognitive skills.

The Experimental Approach

Experimental efforts in the domain of deductive reasoning began about the same time as the psychometric approach, around 1900. Woodworth (1938, chapter 30) reports that Gustav Störring introduced syllogistic reasoning problems into the psychological laboratory sometime before 1908. Experiments on deduction have continued to the present, though often at the periphery of experimental and social psychology. This book is largely devoted to explaining experimental findings in this area, and specific results will be examined in part II. At this point, though, let us take a brief look at trends in the field in order to prepare for later developments. (For detailed reviews see Braine and Rumain 1983, Evans 1982, Galotti 1989, Rips 1990a, and Wason and Johnson-Laird 1972.)

The typical experiment in the psychology of deduction is very simple. As the subject, you receive a booklet containing a number of problems. Usually each problem consists of a set of premises and a conclusion, as in (1), (2), (5), and (7) above. The experimenter tells you that your job is to decide whether the conclusion "follows logically" from the premises (or whether the conclusion "must be true when the premises are true"). You check a box marked "follows" or one marked "doesn't follow" to indicate your answer, then you go on to the next problem. The basic dependent variable is usually the percentage of subjects who give the "correct" response, with "correct" defined in terms of the validity of the problem as translated into some standard system of logic. (We will need to look at this practice, since there are many different systems of logic; for now, we will simply go along with standard terminology.) In other studies, response time also serves as a dependent variable. As was mentioned above, this basic experimental task has a variation in which the experimenter asks the subjects to choose the correct conclusion from a set of alternatives. Or subjects may see just the premises and produce a conclusion on their own. However, the main idea in each case is to determine how variations in the nature of the arguments affect subjects' ability to detect (or to generate) deductively correct conclusions.

Syllogisms and Deduction by Heuristics   Nearly all the early research on deduction concerned itself with syllogisms: arguments containing exactly two premises and a conclusion.[6] Although linear syllogisms (such as (9)) and other argument forms sometimes figured in these studies, more often the problems were composed of categorical (or Aristotelian) syllogisms. For this reason, I will use the term "syllogism" to denote a categorical syllogism unless I specify otherwise. In arguments of this type, all three sentences contain explicit quantifiers—either the universal quantifier *all* or the existential (or particular) quantifier *some*. These same sentences can be negative or positive, producing four basic sentence types: *Some ... are ...*, *All ... are ...*, *Some ... are not ...*, and *No ... are ...* (the last being logically equivalent to *All ... are not ...*). Examples (10) and (11) are typical instances; the former is deductively correct and the latter incorrect in standard systems.

(10)   All square blocks are green blocks.
       Some big blocks are square blocks.
       Some big blocks are green blocks.

(11)   All square blocks are green blocks.
       Some big blocks are not square blocks.
       Some big blocks are not green blocks.

As these examples illustrate, syllogisms of this sort have three terms (in this case *green blocks, square blocks,* and *big blocks*); one term appears in the first premise and in the conclusion, another term appears in the second premise and in the conclusion, and the third (middle) term appears in both premises. The order of the terms within the premises can vary, however; thus, (12), which reverses the position of the subject and predicate terms in the premises of (10), also counts as an (incorrect) categorical syllogism.[7]

(12)   All green blocks are square blocks.
        Some square blocks are big blocks.
        Some big blocks are green blocks.

The most noticeable psychological fact about syllogisms is that subjects' performance, as measured by the percentage of subjects who produce the "correct" answer, varies greatly from problem to problem. For instance, in experiments where subjects have to choose which of a set of possible conclusions (*All ... are ..., Some ... are ..., Some ... are not ..., No ... are ...,* or no valid conclusion) follows from the premises, subjects confronted with syllogisms similar to (10) and (11) tend to select the responses shown in these examples. That is, subjects respond that the premises of (10) imply *Some big blocks are green blocks* and that the premises of (11) imply *Some big blocks are not green blocks.* However, only the first of these is correct in standard logic systems; the right answer for (11) should be that none of the conclusions is valid. In one study (Dickstein 1978a), 100% of subjects were correct on (10) but only 14% were correct on (11).

From the 1920s through at least the 1950s, experimental research on deduction was essentially an attempt to explain errors on syllogisms in terms of biases affecting subjects' responses. Following tempting short-cuts can cause subjects to deviate from the path of correct reasoning. The most famous account of this is Woodworth and Sells' (1935) atmosphere hypothesis, according to which particular or existential premises (i.e., *Some ... are ...* or *Some ... are not ...*) tend to create in the subject a dominant impression of the correctness of a particular conclusion and negative premises (i.e., *No ... are ...* or *Some ... are not ...*) to create an impression of the correctness of a negative conclusion. Hence, given a syllogism to evaluate, subjects tend to choose a particular conclusion if either premise is particular, and they tend to choose a negative conclusion if either is negative. For example, because the second premise in (11) is both particular and negative, it should create a tendency to choose the particular, negative conclusion (*Some ... are not ...*), which is indeed the usual error.

A second sort of bias depends on the content in which the syllogisms are framed. During World War II social psychologists found in syllogisms a means to explore the effects of propaganda or prejudice on reasoning by observing the effects of subjects' prior belief in a syllogism's conclusion (Janis and Frick 1943; Lefford 1946; Morgan 1945; Morgan and Morton 1944). Because the deductive correctness of an argument depends only upon the *relation* between the truth of the premises and the truth of the conclusion, the conclusion of a correct argument may happen to be false. (In deductively correct arguments, the conclusion has to be true only when all the premises are also true.) The hypothesis behind this research was that people are more critical of arguments if they have false conclusions (or conclusions they disagree with), and less critical if they have true conclusions. Although the results of these early studies tended to support this idea, these findings are difficult to evaluate because of internal flaws, including inadequate controls and dubious rewordings of the standard syllogistic forms (see Henle 1962 and Revlin and Leirer 1978 for critiques). Still, there are a few convincing examples of belief bias. For instance, in earlier research, Wilkins (1928) found that 31% of her subjects incorrectly thought the syllogism in (13) valid, whereas only 16% thought that the logically equivalent (14) was valid.

(13)   No oranges are apples.
       No lemons are oranges.

       No apples are lemons.

(14)   No x's are y's.
       No z's are x's.

       No y's are z's.

More recent experiments with tighter controls (Evans, Barston, and Pollard 1983; Revlin and Leirer 1978; Revlin et al. 1980) confirm that subjects' prior belief in the conclusion produces a significant (but often small) effect on validity judgments. For example, Evans et al. compared (15) and (16), which share the same syllogistic form.

(15)   No cigarettes are inexpensive.
       Some addictive things are inexpensive.
       Some addictive things are not cigarettes.

(16)   No addictive things are inexpensive.
       Some cigarettes are inexpensive.
       Some cigarettes are not addictive.

Prior ratings from a separate group of subjects demonstrated that the conclusion of (15) is more believable than the conclusion of (16). Accordingly, 81% of subjects decided correctly that syllogisms such as (15) were valid, whereas only 63% decided correctly that syllogisms such as (16) were valid (Evans et al. 1983, experiment 2, group 2).

Researchers have also attributed errors on syllogisms to the way subjects construe the basic sentence types. For example, subjects may interpret a sentence of the form *Some x are y* as suggesting that some x are not y and, conversely, interpret *Some x are not y* as suggesting that some x are y (Ceraso and Provitera 1971; Wilkins 1928; Woodworth and Sells 1935). These may be Gricean implicatures, arising from everyday uses of such sentences (see chapter 2). As a way of explaining errors on syllogisms like (11), several investigators have also proposed that subjects understand *Some x are not y* as entailing *Some y are not x* and understand *All x are y* as entailing *All y are x* (Ceraso and Provitera 1971; Chapman and Chapman 1959; Revlis 1975a,b; Wilkins 1928). In (11), for instance, if subjects take *All square blocks are green blocks* to imply that all green blocks are square, then the set of square blocks is the same as the set of green blocks. Thus, if some big blocks are not square (as is asserted in the second premise), it follows that some big blocks are not green—which is, again, the usual mistake.

A few of the early experimenters in this area apparently believed that error tendencies, such as those just discussed, could fully explain performance on syllogism problems. For example, Morgan and Morton (1944) began their paper on belief bias with this statement: "Our evidence will indicate that the only circumstance under which we can be relatively sure that the inferences of a person will be logical is when they lead to a conclusion which he has already accepted." Pollard (1982) gives this idea a more modern cast by invoking the findings of Tversky and Kahneman (e.g., 1974) on heuristics and biases in judgment and choice. But a pure heuristics approach to deduction is a minority position, and for good reason: The proposed heuristics seem to account for only a relatively small portion of the data. For example, if we compare the predictions of the atmosphere effect against published data sets, we find that it accounts for only 44% to 50% of responses in a multiple-choice format (Dickstein 1978a; Roberge 1970) and 43% in a fill-in-the-conclusion test (Johnson-Laird and Bara 1984). Even Woodworth and Sells (1935) saw the atmosphere hypothesis as an explanation of errors, and not as a complete theory of syllogistic reasoning.

Information-Processing Models for Syllogisms After the emergence of information-processing psychology, generative grammar, and artificial intelligence in the 1960s, theories of syllogistic reasoning began to adopt a more analytic stance. These theories specify the individual mental steps people go through in producing answers to syllogism problems, and they attempt to account quantitatively for correct responses as well as for errors (Erickson 1974; Guyote and Sternberg 1981; Johnson-Laird and Bara 1984; Revlis 1975b). These models share the notion that typical performance on such a task includes some blend of correct reasoning and mistakes (or misinterpretations), where the latter might include processing limitations (e.g., from short-term memory), inaccurate heuristics (e.g., from atmosphere), or comprehension difficulties (e.g., from conversion of *All x are y* to *All y are x*). According to Erickson's (1974, 1978) model, subjects internally represent each premise as a combination of Euler circles, as shown here in figure 1.1. Thus, an ideal subject represents the premise *All square blocks are green blocks* of (10) in two different ways: as a circle for square blocks within a circle for green blocks and as two coincident circles. The second premise, *Some big blocks are square blocks*, should be represented in four ways: as a circle for big blocks within a circle for square blocks, as a circle for square blocks within a circle for big blocks, as two coincident circles, and as two overlapping ones. To evaluate the conclusion, the subject must combine the premise representations into representations of the syllogism as a whole. In general, this can be done in more than one way (as shown at the bottom of the figure), because each premise can have several representations and because a representation of the first premise can combine with a representation of the second premise in several distinct configurations. If a potential conclusion holds in all these legal combinations, then that conclusion is deductively correct. The

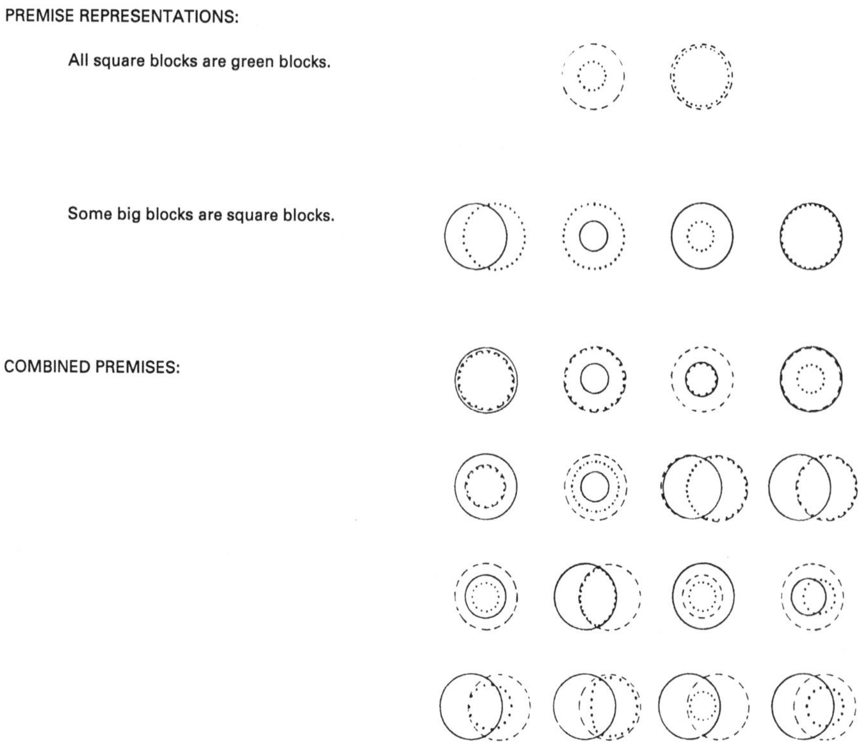

PREMISE REPRESENTATIONS:

All square blocks are green blocks.

Some big blocks are square blocks.

COMBINED PREMISES:

Figure 1.1
A representation in terms of Euler circles of the syllogism

All square blocks are green blocks.
Some big blocks are square blocks.

Some big blocks are green blocks.

The solid circles represent big blocks, the dashed circles green blocks, and the dotted circles square blocks.

model attributes errors on the syllogisms to failure to consider all relevant representations and combinations of the premises. In addition, errors can arise from bias in the way subjects represent the premises or in the way they derive conclusions from the combined diagrams.

Models such as Erickson's have been fairly successful in accounting for observed responses in syllogism experiments, and they present a deeper explanation of reasoning than one gets by cataloging biases. Their weakness lies in the difficulty of extending them to a class of inferences wider than syllogisms. Although some researchers have tried to apply their models to related deductive arguments (see, e.g., Guyote and Sternberg's (1981) treatment of conditional syllogisms), it is fair to say that these extensions have been modest.[8] You can get a feel for this limitation by trying to imagine how a model like Erickson's would handle arguments such as (2) and (4) above. One cause of this deficiency is, no doubt, the rigid form of the syllogisms: Since there are only a relatively small number of (deductively correct) syllogism types but an infinite number of deductively correct argument types, any model that is specialized for syllogisms is likely to encounter problems in generalizing to a broader class. In other words, syllogism models have difficulties in explaining the productivity of deduction, largely because syllogisms themselves are nonproductive. Although Aristotle believed that all deductive inferences could be captured by sequences of syllogisms, modern logic makes it clear that this is not the case—that more powerful deductive machinery is needed even for proofs of some of the geometry theorems that Aristotle discussed (Mueller 1974).

Why then did experimental psychologists concentrate on syllogisms rather than on the wider range of arguments generated by modern logical techniques? This may be due in part to ignorance or historical accident. As Lemmon (1965, p. 169) put it, "predicate calculus is to syllogism what a precision tool is to a blunt knife.... Nonetheless, whenever a new piece of equipment is introduced, there will always be found those who prefer the outdated machinery with which they are familiar." It is more likely, however, that syllogisms appeal to researchers because their structure lends itself to experiments. The small number of syllogistic forms makes it possible for investigators to present all of them to subjects within a single experimental session. Moreover, the combinatorics of syllogisms provide a ready-made set of dimensions to manipulate in an experimental design. In order to find out what makes syllogisms easy or difficult, we can vary the quantifiers that appear in the premises and the conclusion (the syllogistic *mood*), the order of terms in the premises (the syllogistic *figure*), the order of the premises, and the phrases that instantiate the terms. The very factors that limit syllogisms' generality are the factors that make them attractive from an experimental standpoint.

Designing experiments around modern logical systems is a more challenging task than designing experiments on syllogisms, but it is a necessary step if we want to study reasoning of the sort that the subjects of tables 1.1 and 1.2 engage in. We will return to syllogisms in chapter 7 after considering what a more general theory of deduction might be like.

Deduction in Later Cognitive Research   Although research on categorical syllogisms remains the prototype, the psychology of reasoning broadened in the 1960s and the 1970s to include studies of other forms of deduction. Some of this research centered on simple arguments—in particular, on conditional syllogisms (such as (1) above) and linear syllogisms (such as (9)). (For studies of conditional syllogisms, see Clement and Falmagne 1986; Cummins et al. 1991; Evans 1977; Marcus and Rips 1979; Markovits 1987, 1988; Rips and Marcus 1977; Taplin 1971; Taplin and Staudenmayer 1973; and Staudenmayer 1975. Studies of linear syllogisms include Clark 1969; DeSoto, London, and Handel 1965; Huttenlocher 1968; Potts and Scholz 1975; and Sternberg 1980). Other relevant studies, inspired by earlier research in psycholinguistics and concept learning, focused on people's understanding of sentences containing logical connectives such as *not* (Carpenter and Just 1975; Clark and Chase 1972; Trabasso, Rollins, and Shaughnessy 1971) and *if* (Fillenbaum 1975; Johnson-Laird and Tagart 1969; Legrenzi 1970; Wason 1968).

In research of the latter sort, subjects are not asked to assess individual arguments as such; they are asked to paraphrase sentences containing the connective, or to decide whether given information would make these sentences true or false. On one trial, for example, the experimenter might present a visual display of green dots along with the sentence *The dots aren't red* and ask the subjects to decide whether the sentence is true or false of the display. The amount of time they take to reach their decision—their *response time*—would constitute the dependent variable. But, although no argument explicitly appears, many of the investigators believed that subjects mentally represent sentences and displays in a common logical form. Thus, determining whether the display made the sentence true is clearly similar to determining the deductive correctness of (17).

(17)   The dots are green.
      The dots aren't red.

Findings from these experiments will be important in chapter 4 and 5, where we will take up propositional reasoning. For the moment, however, let us consider the general framework in which the investigators tried to explain their findings.

The theories or models that researchers proposed for these results were specialized in much the same way as the syllogism models: They provided a rigorous account of how subjects handle a particular task by specifying the elementary information-processing steps—for example, encoding and comparison operations—that subjects carry out in determining their answers. But the models were hard to extend beyond the task. Models of the way subjects compare simple affirmative or negative sentences to pictures, for example, provided accurate quantitative predictions about response time in terms of matching of constituents in the mental representations of the sentences (e.g., those in (17)). But they weren't able to explain, without new assumptions, the comparison of other proposition types (e.g., *If some of the dots are green then not all of the dots are red*). What seemed to be missing was a broader theoretical framework that could bridge between models for isolated logical connectives in isolated paradigms. Thus, Newell (1980, pp. 694–695) complained: "Theorists seem simply to write a different theory for each task. Details get filled in experimentally, but the frameworks ... are just written down.... The difficulty lies in the emergence of each of the microtheories full blown from the theorist's pen. There is no way to relate them and thus they help ensure the division of the study of human cognition into qualitatively isolated areas."

Reasoning as Problem Solving   Newell's solution to the problem is to view these specific models as special cases of general problem-solving abilities. What unites the various tasks and models, according to this framework, is the notion of a *problem space*, which Newell (1980, p. 697) defines as "a set of symbolic structures (the states of the space) and a set of operators over the space. Each operator takes a state as input and produces a state as output.... Sequences of operators define paths that thread their way through sequences of states." Problem-solving theory is the study of behavior explainable in terms of problem spaces. The idea of a problem space is illustrated most easily in a game such as chess: the set of possible configurations of pieces on the board can be taken as the states, and the legal moves in the game as operators. According to Newell, however, the problem-space concept is applicable to any "symbolic goal-oriented activity," and to deduction problems in particular. For example, we can redescribe Erickson's syllogism model in terms of a problem space by taking configurations of mental Euler circles as states and the repositionings of these circles as operators. Newell (1980, 1990) offers two rather different problem-space formulations for syllogisms.

There is no doubt, then, that problem-solving theory is applicable to clear-cut deduction tasks. Newell is also quite right in pointing to the *ad hoc* character of the reasoning models mentioned above. However, it is not clear whether problem-solving theory is the correct solution to this difficulty. The extremely general nature of the problem-space concept may itself be cause for concern, since it could turn out that the concept is too abstract to provide much insight into the nature of deduction. There are really two problems here: Problem-solving theory fails to explain some important distinctions that we need in accounting for inference, and the problem-space notion may itself be too loosely constrained to be empirically helpful.

The problem-space concept can describe an extraordinary range of cognitive tasks—not only chess puzzles and syllogisms, but also such relatively low-level processes as item recognition in short-term memory (Newell 1973b, 1990). This very flexibility creates a problem when we consider the role that deduction plays in explaining other cognitive activities. As was noted above, deduction (but not, say, solving chess puzzles) is a well-entrenched psychological concept, useful in accounting for other mental processes. The problem-space hypothesis cannot explain this contrast between central and peripheral processes, since both can be couched in terms of state-space search. What causes trouble for the idea of deduction as problem solving is the asymmetry of cognitive explanations: Although deduction may be helpful in accounting for how one solves such chess puzzles, no one would appeal to solving chess puzzles in accounting for deduction. In other words, a theory of deduction has to include, not only problem spaces for particular deduction tasks, but also an explanation of the role that deduction plays in the rest of the cognitive system.

Furthermore, some of the problems that Newell raises with respect to previous models of reasoning also occur with respect to the choice of a problem space. Since there are few limits, if any, on the states of the space or on the operators defined over them, a theorist is free to choose his problem space in a new way for each task. This means that a problem-space account of deduction can be *ex post facto* in nearly the same way as other models. In simple tasks, it might be possible to construct the problem space from surface features of the problem statement (see Newell 1990 on sentence-picture comparison); however, predicting problem spaces is difficult for complex deduction tasks. One of Newell's own theories for syllogisms (Polk and Newell 1988; Newell 1990) consists of six separate problem spaces—some containing representations of objects correspond-ing to the terms of the syllogism, others containing representations of propositions expressed by the premises, and yet others containing both sorts of representations. Perhaps these are the problem spaces that sub-jects use, but it seems unlikely that they can be predicted from nothing more than the subjects' instructions for this particular task.

In order to achieve a principled theory for deduction tasks within a problem-solving framework, investigators have to choose their problem spaces in a way that reflects subjects' general understanding of *all*, *some*, *not*, and *if*, as well as their understanding of what it means for one sentence to follow logically from another. I don't want to suggest that Newell and other researchers in problem solving have consciously adopted the view that deduction is nothing but search in a problem space. In other psycho-logical domains (e.g., parsing and object perception), they have been quite willing to accept more narrowly specified theories within the problem-space framework (Newell and Simon 1976). But the problem-space hypothesis is not sufficient, and the missing parts of the theory are not to be found in problem-solving research. The idea of a problem space gives us a generalization that applies to any rule-governed cognitive performance, including item recognition, dichotic listening, phoneme monitoring, word or picture naming, lexical decision, letter matching, and other favorite tasks. This generalization may be a useful framework for cognitive re-search; however, as I will try to show in later chapters, it is not to be confused with a theory of deduction.

Conclusions and Prospects

The psychological approaches that I have surveyed falter in explaining basic facts about deduction because of their narrow view of the subject matter. By concentrating exclusively on individual differences, psycho-metricians ignore universal aspects of deduction that may account for its productivity. Experimental psychologists tend to focus on deduction in the context of particular tasks, such as evaluating categorical or linear syllogisms. This is not necessarily a bad strategy; experimental precision may even require it. However, because the arguments that appear in these tasks have usually been nonproductive ones (and because the proposed models are tailored to the tasks), the deduction models are not productive. To make matters worse, a task-by-task approach makes it difficult to identify general properties of deduction or to understand the central role that deduction plays in supporting other mental processes.

It doesn't help very much to view these tasks within a problem-solving framework if deduction problems are treated on the same footing as chess puzzles and cryptarithmetic (Newell and Simon 1972; Newell 1990). The elements of problem-solving theory—problem states, operators, and con-trol methods—are too unconstrained to explain what is essential about deduction. If problem-solving theory merely generates a new set of states and operators for each deduction task , we are not much better off than we would be with task-tailored models.

Clearly, what is missing is a psychological theory of deduction that is broader than a model for a particular type of argument or a particular type of experiment but which captures what is characteristic of deduction with respect to other kinds of thinking. The rest of this book is devoted to developing such a theory and evaluating its empirical consequences. The main statement of the theory will appear in part II; however, as a start on this project, we will look to modern logic and artificial intelligence in the next two chapters, since these disciplines may well provide us with hints about the shape that a cognitive theory should take.

2 Reasoning and Logic

In 1926 Professor J. Łukasiewicz called attention to the fact that mathematicians in their proofs do not appeal to the theses of the theory of deduction, but make use of other methods of reasoning. The chief means employed in their method is that of an arbitrary supposition.
S. Jaśkowski (1934)

Natural deduction, however, does not, in general, start from basic logical propositions, but rather from assumptions ... to which logical deductions are applied.
G. Gentzen (1935/1969)

Traditional logic restricted research in the psychology of reasoning. Because the main instrument of traditional logic—the categorical syllogism —is a narrow type of deductive argument, experimental studies that centered on syllogisms suffered in generality. For the most part, these studies (and the models derived from them) gave no hint as to how people reason about arguments whose sentences have more than one quantifier or whose grammar is more complex than the simple *S is P* form. Since modern logic overcomes some of the syllogism's limitations, it seems a natural place to look for guidance in constructing a more adequate reasoning theory. Of course, even current logic has its limits, since there are deductive inferences that aren't represented in these formal systems. The inference from *Mike is a bachelor* to *Mike is unmarried,* is one example. Nevertheless, logic is surely the only well-developed system for assessing the deductive correctness of arguments, and it is therefore a worthwhile starting point.

The idea that formal logic bears a close relationship to human reasoning is extremely controversial within cognitive science. For example, Wason and Johnson-Laird (1972, p. 245) concluded their influential study of reasoning by stating that "only gradually did we realize first that there was no existing formal calculus which correctly modeled our subjects' inferences, and second that no purely formal system would succeed." This kind of opposition is based on evidence that subjects' judgments about an argument sometimes depart from the answer that the experimenter derived by translating the argument into some system of logic and assessing its correctness within that system. The strength of this evidence, however, clearly depends on the system the investigator uses. If the investigator's conception is too narrow, what is classified as nonlogical behavior may turn out logical after all. To evaluate the evidence, we need some clear idea of what logic has to offer.

This chapter discusses aspects of logic that have played a role in the debate on logic in reasoning and that will play an important part in the theory to be developed in later chapters. Most cognitive theories that contain a logic-like component (e.g., Braine 1978; Johnson-Laird 1975; Osherson, 1974b, 1975, 1976; Rips 1983) are based on the notion of proof, particularly the "natural deduction" proofs originally devised by Gentzen (1935/1969) and Jaśkowski (1934). The first section describes these proof methods, and the second section illustrates them in a sample system. The basic notion is familiar to anyone who has taken a high school mathematics course: If you want to know whether a particular argument is deductively correct, you can find out by taking its premises as given and then trying to derive its conclusion by applying a specified set of rules. If a proof or a derivation is possible, then the argument is deductively correct; the conclusion is *deducible* from the premises. We can also say, by extension, that the argument as a whole is deducible. The left column of table 2.1 summarizes this terminology.

Contemporary logical theory supplements the notions of formal proof and deducibility with a twin "semantic" system whose central concepts are the truth of a sentence and the validity of an argument (Tarski 1936/1956). In the semantic system the deductive correctness of an argument is a matter of the relationship between the truth of the premises and the truth of the conclusion. In particular, an argument is deductively correct if and only if the conclusion is true in all states of affairs in which the premises are true. In this case, the conclusion is *(semantically) entailed* by the premises, and the entire argument is *valid*, as shown in the right column in table 2.1. (We can also speak of a single sentence as valid if it is true in all states of affairs. This is, of course, a stronger notion of semantic correctness for a sentence than the simple truth of a sentence in the *actual* state of affairs; it is the difference between *Insects have six legs*, which is true in our present state but false in a logically possible state in which they have eight, and *Six is less than eight*, which is true in all possible states.)

Table 2.1
Summary of logical terminology.

	Proof theory	Semantics
Correctness of the relation of the conclusion to the premises	Deducibility (= conclusion provable from the premises)	Semantic entailment (= conclusion true in all states of affairs in which the premises are true)
Correctness of an argument	Deducibility	Validity

In this dual setup, then, we have two criteria of deductive correctness: deducibility and validity. We might hope that these two criteria coincide in confirming exactly the same set of arguments. For simple logical systems—for example, classical sentential and predicate logic—they do coincide; such systems are said to be *complete*. In these systems, it doesn't matter which criterion we use, as long as all we are interested in is determining which arguments are the correct ones. However, there are three reasons for keeping both criteria in mind. First, the proof-theoretic description is computationally relevant: The description contains rules that yield a finite proof of a deducible argument. By contrast, the semantic description is computationally independent, since the criterion it gives for validity does not depend on there being any finite procedure for assessing it. Second, there are more complex logical systems in which the criteria *don't* coincide—incomplete systems in which some entailments are not deducible. Third, according to an intriguing theory put forth by Johnson-Laird (1983), it is the semantic rather than the proof-theoretic criterion that is important in human reasoning (contrary to the other cognitive theories cited above). In the present chapter we will stick to concerns about deducibility; we will return to semantics and its putative role in reasoning in chapters 6 and 10.

Of course, changing the deduction rules of a logical system (or changing the way in which truth is assigned to propositions) can alter which arguments are deemed deductively correct. Logicians and philosophers of logic have in fact proposed a variety of plausible systems that differ in the elements of natural language that come in for formal treatment, and in the analysis that they give these elements. Current logics are available for concepts such as knowledge and belief, temporal precedence and succession, causality, obligation and permission, and logical necessity and possibility. For each of these concepts, there are alternative logics differing in exactly which arguments are deductively correct. Psychologists have almost completely overlooked this variety, tacitly assuming a single standard of deductive correctness. This means that, when subjects' judgments have failed to conform to the standard, psychologists have been too ready to label them illogical, or, at least, to assume that logic is of no help in understanding them. We can't begin to survey all these systems (see van Benthem 1985 and Haack 1974 for reviews), but we can consider in a preliminary way some alternatives that may be especially important for psychological purposes: alternative rules for classical logic and strengthenings of the rules that go beyond classical logic.

This chapter does not aim to settle on a single logical system that best represents human reasoning. Determining which system (if any) is best in this sense will have to await the empirical evidence presented in part II. Nevertheless, we can keep psychological plausibility in mind in examining logical techniques. On one hand, this means that certain devices (e.g., truth tables) that appear in many logic texts will receive little or no attention, since they are unlikely to play a significant role in human reasoning. (For arguments against the psychological reality of truth tables, see Osherson 1974b, 1975.) On the other hand, much of this chapter will be devoted to natural-deduction systems. The first section, in particular, describes the general properties of natural deduction and contrasts it with earlier axiomatic approaches. The second section sets out in more detail a particular natural-deduction system for classical sentential and predicate logics and considers some possible modifications that might bring it into better agreement with intuitions about deductive correctness by people with no formal training in logic. Readers who are already familiar with natural deduction from introductory logic may want to refresh their memory by glancing at the rules in tables 2.3 and 2.5 and then skip to the subsections on "possible modifications." The third section discusses an objection by Harman (1986) that rules like those of natural-deduction systems can't possibly serve as "rules of reasoning."

Formal Proof

At the most general level, a formal proof is a finite sequence of sentences $(s_1, s_2, \ldots, s_k)$ in which each sentence is either a premise, an axiom of the logical system, or a sentence that follows from preceding sentences by one of the system's rules. An argument is deducible in the system if there is a proof whose final sentence, s_k, is the conclusion of the argument. For example, consider a system that includes modus ponens among its inference rules. Modus ponens stipulates that the sentence q follows from sentences of the form *IF p THEN q* and *p*. Thus, (1) is deducible in this system.

(1) IF Calvin deposits 50 cents THEN Calvin will get a coke.
     Calvin deposits 50 cents.
     _____
     Calvin will get a coke.

The proof consists simply of the sequence of three sentences in the order listed above, since (a) each sentence in the sequence either is a premise or follows from preceding sentences by modus ponens and (b) the final sentence is the conclusion of the argument. (Capital letters are used for *IF* and *THEN* to mark the fact that these words are parts of the proof system and are not necessarily equivalent in meaning or force to English *if . . . then . . .*; this practice will continue through the book.)

In this stripped-down system, we could also prove the deducibility of (2).

(2)   IF Calvin deposits 50 cents THEN Calvin gets a coke.
      IF Calvin gets a coke THEN Calvin will buy a burger.
      Calvin deposits 50 cents.
      ───
      Calvin will buy a burger.

In this case a proof involves two applications of modus ponens, as (3) shows.

(3)   a. IF Calvin deposits 50 cents THEN Calvin gets   Premise
         a coke.

      b. Calvin deposits 50 cents.   Premise

      c. Calvin gets a coke.   Modus ponens

      d. IF Calvin gets a coke THEN Calvin will buy   Premise
         a burger.

      e. Calvin will buy a burger.   Modus ponens

Sentences (3a), (3b), and (3d) are premises of argument (2), and sentences (3c) and (3e) are derived by modus ponens from preceding ones.

To prove a more diverse set of arguments, we will clearly need greater deductive power. We can get it, within this framework, by introducing axioms or additional inference rules. An *axiomatic* (or "logistic") proof system contains a set of axioms and usually has modus ponens as its only rule. *Natural-deduction* systems contain several distinct inference rules and eliminate axioms. The two kinds of system can be equivalent in proving exactly the same set of theorems, but they possess rival advantages and disadvantages in other respects. On one hand, axiomatic systems sometimes have an advantage over natural-deduction systems when we must derive characteristics *about* the proof system itself (though natural-deduction systems have interesting metatheoretic properties of their own —see Fine 1985a,b; Gentzen 1934/1969; Prawitz 1965; Ungar 1992). On the other hand, it is usually easier to prove theorems *within* a natural-deduction system, and consequently most elementary textbooks on logic make use of natural deduction as a main proof method (e.g., Copi 1954; Fitch 1952; Lemmon 1965; McCawley 1981; Quine 1950; Suppes 1957; Thomason 1970a). For the same reason, natural deduction has been the method of choice in psychological models. Whether formal "natural-deduction" methods are natural psychologically is a major question that we will explore experimentally in part II. (The description of deduction systems in this chapter will necessarily be brisk compared to that of the textbooks just mentioned. Readers who would like a less condensed treatment should consult these sources.)

The Axiomatic Method

In this book we will focus on natural deduction, but it may be helpful to give an example of an axiomatic proof in order to highlight the differences. Of course, an axiomatic system might have generated the proof in (3); but since modus ponens was the only rule we needed, it is not very revealing. Instead, we can take as our example the somewhat similar argument shown in (4), which has the form known as *modus tollens*.

(4)   IF Calvin deposits 50 cents THEN Calvin gets a coke.
       Calvin does not get a coke.
       _____
       Calvin does not deposit 50 cents.

We will take as a sample axiom system one that contains three axiom schemas in addition to the usual modus ponens rule (Mendelson 1964, p. 31). We can spell out these schemas compactly if we allow P, Q, and R to stand for arbitrary sentences and abbreviate *IF P THEN Q* as $P \rightarrow Q$ and *NOT P* as $-P$. We then allow a sentence to count as an axiom if it is the result of substituting sentences for P, Q, and R in any of the following schemas:

(I) $(\mathbf{P} \rightarrow (\mathbf{Q} \rightarrow \mathbf{P}))$
(II) $((\mathbf{P} \rightarrow (\mathbf{Q} \rightarrow \mathbf{R})) \rightarrow ((\mathbf{P} \rightarrow \mathbf{Q}) \rightarrow (\mathbf{P} \rightarrow \mathbf{R})))$
(III) $(-\mathbf{P} \rightarrow -\mathbf{Q}) \rightarrow ((-\mathbf{P} \rightarrow \mathbf{Q}) \rightarrow \mathbf{P}).$

Table 2.2
An sample axiomatic proof of the argument $d \to c$; $-c$; therefore, $-d$.

1. $--d \to (-d \to --d)$	Axiom I
2. $(-d \to --d) \to ((-d \to -d) \to -d)$	Axiom III
3. $[(-d \to --d) \to ((-d \to -d) \to -d)] \to$ $\{--d \to [(-d \to --d) \to ((-d \to -d) \to d)]\}$	Axiom I
4. $--d \to [(-d \to --d) \to ((-d \to -d) \to d)]$	Modus ponens (from 2 & 3)
5. $\{--d \to [(-d \to --d) \to ((-d \to -d) \to d)]\} \to$ $\{[--d \to (-d \to --d)] \to [--d \to ((-d \to -d) \to d)]\}$	Axiom II
6. $[--d \to (-d \to --d)] \to [--d \to ((-d \to -d) \to d)]$	Modus ponens (from 4 & 5)
7. $--d \to ((-d \to -d) \to d)$	Modus ponens (from 1 & 6)
8. $(-d \to ((-d \to -d) \to -d)) \to$ $((-d \to (-d \to -d)) \to (-d \to -d))$	Axiom II
9. $-d \to ((-d \to -d) \to -d$	Axiom I
10. $(-d \to (-d \to -d)) \to (-d \to -d)$	Modus ponens (from 8 & 9)
11. $-d \to (-d \to -d)$	Axiom I
12. $-d \to -d$	Modus ponens (from 10 & 11)
13. $(-d \to -d) \to (--d \to (-d \to -d))$	Axiom I
14. $--d \to (-d \to -d)$	Modus ponens (from 12 & 13)
15. $[--d \to ((-d \to -d) \to d)] \to$ $[(--d \to (-d \to -d)) \to (--d \to d)]$	Axiom II
16. $(--d \to (-d \to -d)) \to (--d \to d)$	Modus ponens (from 7 & 15)
17. $--d \to d$	Modus ponens (from 14 & 16)
18. $-c \to (--d \to -c)$	Axiom I
19. $-c$	Premise
20. $--d \to -c$	Modus ponens (from 18 & 19)
21. $(d \to c) \to (--d \to (d \to c))$	Axiom I
22. $d \to c$	Premise
23. $--d \to (d \to c)$	Modus ponens (from 21 & 22)
24. $(--d \to (d \to c)) \to ((--d \to d) \to (--d \to c))$	Axiom II
25. $(--d \to d) \to (--d \to c)$	Modus ponens (from 23 & 24)
26. $--d \to c$	Modus ponens (from 17 & 25)
27. $(--d \to -c) \to ((--d \to c) \to -d)$	Axiom III
28. $(--d \to c) \to -d$	Modus ponens (from 20 & 27)
29. $-d$	Modus ponens (from 26 & 28)

Table 2.2 gives a full proof of (4), with d standing for *Calvin deposits 50 cents* and c standing for *Calvin gets a coke*. The justification for each line of the proof appears at the right; for example, "Axiom I" in the first line of the table means that this line is an instance of axiom schema I (above) when $--d$ is substituted for P and $-d$ for Q. The proof proceeds in this way by finding substitution instances for the axiom schemas and then applying modus ponens to the instances.

The point of this exercise is simply to illustrate the difficulty of finding an axiomatic proof for even a relatively brief argument such as (4). Of course, we could reduce this complexity for a given argument by choosing a different set of axioms; however, the indirection that usually accompanies axiomatic proofs suggests that other methods may be more appropriate for capturing ordinary deductive reasoning—for example, the reasoning we glimpsed in tables 1.1 and 1.2. The role that assumptions or suppositions play in human reasoning was noted in chapter 1: People often assume certain sentences are true "for the sake of argument" in order to simplify their thinking. This key notion leads to proofs that are much more lucid than the one in table 2.2 and that are presumably better candidates for human proof finding.

The Natural-Deduction Method

In table 2.2 we assumed the premises of (4) and used these premises as lines of the proof.[1] Natural-deduction methods enlarge on this idea by permitting us to make other temporary assumptions or suppositions. As an example of how suppositions can simplify a proof, consider (5)—an informal justification of (4).

(5) a. According to the first premise, if Calvin deposits 50 cents then Calvin gets a coke.

   b. Suppose, contrary to the conclusion, that Calvin *does* deposit 50 cents.

   c. Then (by modus ponens), Calvin would get a coke.

   d. But the second premise tells us that Calvin does not get a coke.

   e. Hence, Calvin must not have deposited 50 cents.

This justification embodies a typical *reductio ad absurdum* pattern: In (5b) we assume temporarily the opposite of the conclusion we wish to prove and then show that this leads to contradictory information. Since the supposition could not hold, the conclusion itself must follow from the premises. In other words, (5) tacitly appeals to an inference rule stating that if a supposition leads to a pair of contradictory sentences then the negation of that supposition must follow. This *reductio* rule, together with modus ponens, is sufficient to show that (4) is deducible.

Natural-deduction systems formalize this method of making suppositions in the service of a proof, as the quotations from Gentzen and Jaśkowski at the beginning of this chapter attest. Within these systems, we can introduce suppositions freely as lines of a proof in order to draw further inferences from them. Before the proof is complete, however, we must apply a rule that resolves or "discharges" the supposition, since the conclusion of the proof must depend on the premises alone and not on any of the arbitrary assumptions we have made along the way. In (5), for example, the supposition made in line b is resolved when we conclude that the supposition could not in fact hold (owing to the contradiction).

To state this a bit more systematically, we can use the term *domain* to refer to a designated set of lines of the proof that are associated with a supposition. Then no supposition (apart from the premises) can include the conclusion of the proof in its domain. Figure 2.1 illustrates the notion of a domain, using (5) as an example. In the figure the premises in (5) establish a domain consisting of (5a), (5d), and (5e). The supposition in (5b) establishes a second domain that comprises just (5b) and (5c). As this example illustrates, one domain can be subordinated to another: The domain of (5b) and (5c) is a subdomain of the premises' domain. If D is the smallest domain that includes a domain D′ as subordinate, then D′ is an *immediate subdomain* of D. We can also say that D is the *immediate superdomain* of D′. Thus, the domain of (5b) and (5c) is also the immediate subdomain of the premises' domain, and the latter is the immediate superdomain of the former. A sentence can be said to *hold* in the domain in which it appears, and this means that deduction rules that apply to the domain can use it freely. In the systems for classical sentential and predicate logic, which are outlined in this chapter, sentences also hold in all subdomains of their domain. According to this system, for example, (5a) holds throughout the proof in (5), including the subdomain. (Of course, (5c) holds only in the subdomain.) Other logical systems, however, place special restrictions on which sentences hold in subdomains (see the first "possible modifications" subsection below).

Superdomain D:

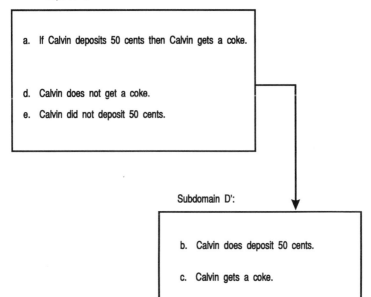

Figure 2.1
Graph of the domains in (5) for the following argument:

IF Calvin deposits 50 cents THEN Calvin gets a coke.
Calvin does not get a coke.
_____
Calvin does not deposit 50 cents.

Texts on natural deduction have used a variety of devices to indicate domains and a variety of rule systems to manipulate them. As an example, let us consider a system (similar to that of Jaśkowski 1934) that represents domains by a list of sentences, with a plus sign in front of the domain's suppositions. We indicate subdomains by indenting the list, as shown below. The system will consist of all simple English sentences (e.g., *Dogs bark*) and of more complex sentences formed in the following way: If *P* and *Q* are sentences of the system, then so are sentences of the form *IF P THEN Q* and *NOT P*. Again, *IF ... THEN* and *NOT* are capitalized to emphasize that these connectives may be somewhat different from their counterparts in natural language. The heart of the system consists of the following three inference rules.

Modus ponens (IF Elimination): If sentences of the form *IF P THEN Q* and *P* hold in a given domain, then the sentence *Q* can be added to that domain.

Reductio ad absurdum: If the sentences *Q* and *NOT Q* hold in a subdomain whose sole supposition is *NOT P*, then the sentence *P* can be added to the immediate superdomain. If the sentences *Q* and *NOT Q* hold in a subdomain whose sole supposition is *P*, then *NOT P* can be added to the immediate superdomain.[2]

Conditionalization (Conditional Proof, IF Introduction): If a sentence *Q* holds in a subdomain whose sole supposition is *P*, then *IF P THEN Q* can be added to the immediate superdomain.

The Conditionalization and Reductio rules make crucial use of suppositions and thus allow the system to emulate these characteristics of human reasoning. The rules are also compatible with the productivity of reasoning, since they can prove an unlimited number of arguments if we repeat and combine them. With this system, a formal proof of (4) would look like (6) (where a justification for each line appears at the right).

(6) a. + IF Calvin deposits 50 cents THEN Calvin   Premise
             gets a coke.

     b. + NOT Calvin gets a coke.   Premise

     c.   + Calvin deposits 50 cents.   Supposition

     d.   Calvin gets a coke.   Modus ponens

     e. NOT Calvin deposits 50 cents.   Reductio

This proof bears an obvious similarity to the informal one illustrated in (5) and in figure 2.1. We assume in (6c) that Calvin deposits 50 cents, contrary to the conclusion that we wish to prove. From this supposition, it follows that Calvin gets a coke; however, since *NOT Calvin gets a coke* is one of the premises (and therefore holds in the subdomain of (6c) and (6d)), the reductio rule applies and yields the conclusion we were hoping for. Indeed, the only differences between (5) and (6) are (6)'s more formal representation of domains and the consequent reordering of the proof's lines. Note also that the third rule, conditionalization, is not used in (6), though it *is* required to equate the power of our sample natural deduction system with that of the axiomatic system described above. (We will soon make use of conditionalization in a further example.)

This proof of (4) is not quite as simple as the corresponding proof of (1), which contains just three lines—the premises and the conclusion itself. Modus ponens is the only rule required in such a proof, whereas both modus ponens and reductio are used in (6). This accords with the results of many experiments showing that (1)'s correctness is much easier to identify than (4)'s for college-age subjects. Sandra Marcus and I (Marcus and Rips 1979) found that 98–100% of the subjects we tested (across conditions) recognized that the conclusion of arguments like (1) followed from the premises but only 57–62% recognized the conclusion of (4) as following from the premises. This provides a first hint that natural-deduction systems have properties similar to those of human reasoning, though of course the difficulty with (4) may be due to other factors as well. (See Evans 1977; Markovits 1987, 1988; Rips and Marcus 1977; Taplin 1971; and Taplin and Staudenmayer 1973 for similar findings.)

The CPL (Classical Predicate Logic) System

In this section, to illustrate natural-deduction techniques, I develop a full rule system for classical predicate logic (or *CPL*). I start in the usual way, by specifying rules for the sentence connectives AND, OR, NOT, and IF ... THEN; I then consider possible modifications to these rules that might bring them in closer touch with human inference. Next I discuss rules for the quantifiers FOR ALL and FOR SOME. The complete set of rules (connectives plus quantifiers) provides the basis of the deduction system that will be developed in succeeding chapters.

Rules for Connectives

Although the natural-deduction scheme just discussed yields fairly direct proofs for (1) and (4), it is not quite so convenient for other arguments. The only parts of the language that we can formally analyze in this system are the sentence connectives IF ... THEN and NOT. This means that in order to establish the deducibility of arguments that depend on other words we would have to show how these arguments can be translated into ones with IF ... THEN and NOT as their only operational expressions. Even an argument as elementary as (7) is not yet deducible.

(7)   Linda is a feminist AND Linda is a bank teller.
      Linda is a bank teller.

A surprising amount can be accomplished by translation. Each of the two deduction systems that we have examined so far—the axiomatic system with axiom schemas I–III and the natural-deduction system with Modus ponens, Conditionalization, and Reductio—is able to prove all the arguments that are valid in classical sentential logic, the logical system generally presented first in elementary textbooks. Valid arguments in this system containing the sentence connectives AND, OR, or IF AND ONLY IF can be proved by paraphrasing these connectives using NOT and IF ... THEN. For example, as (8) shows, if we rephrase the first premise of (7) as NOT (IF Linda is a feminist THEN NOT Linda is a bank teller), we can then show that (7) is deducible.

(8)   a.   + NOT (IF Linda is a feminist THEN
                 NOT Linda is a bank teller).   Premise
      b.   + NOT Linda is a bank teller.   Supposition
      c.   + Linda is a feminist.   Supposition
      d.   IF Linda is a feminist THEN
                 NOT Linda is bank teller.   Conditionalization
      e.   Linda is a bank teller.   Reductio

In this example, lines (8a) and (8e) form a first domain, lines (8b) and (8d) a second, and line (8c) a third, as indicated by the indentation. Line (8d) is our first example of the Conditionalization rule. The underlying idea is that we can derive a sentence of the form *IF P THEN Q* provided that we can show (in a subdomain) that Q follows from the supposition P according to the rules of the system. In the present case, we assume in line (8c) that Linda is a feminist. *NOT Linda is a bank teller* (i.e., (8b)) holds in this innermost subdomain, because of the convention of classical logic, mentioned above, that superdomain sentences hold in their subdomains. It follows by Conditionalization that *IF Linda is a feminist THEN NOT Linda is a bank teller* in the domain of lines (8b) and (8d). The conclusion of Argument (7), *Linda is a bank teller*, then follows by Reductio, since the contradictory sentences (8a) and (8d) hold in the same domain, whose supposition is *NOT Linda is a bank teller.*

Formal Rules   Even though arguments such as (7) are provable in this natural-deduction system, the proofs are more roundabout than we would like. For one thing, the translation step may not be obvious: What justifies taking *Linda is a bank teller AND Linda is a feminist* as equivalent to *NOT (IF Linda is a bank teller THEN NOT Linda is a feminist)*? For another thing, the proof in (8) seems less straightforward than the argument (7), and from a psychological point of view it seems odd to derive a trivial argument by means of a nontrivial proof. Someone who was unsure about the correctness of (7) would probably not be convinced by the proof in (8). What we require, then, are inference rules that will apply directly to arguments such as (7) and that embody the deductive potential of the connectives AND and OR. Gentzen's systems NK and NJ fulfill these requirements, and variations on these systems appear in the logic textbooks cited above. The rules in table 2.3 constitute one such variation that includes specific rules for AND, OR, IF ... THEN, and NOT. The table states them in the form of simple procedures for carrying out an individual inference step. These rules are essentially the same as those in Gentzen's NK, except for a minor modification in the rules for NOT (i.e., Double Negation Elimination and Reductio).

The system of table 2.3 derives exactly the same results as the three-rule system discussed above, but it does so in a more straightforward way. For example, the proof of argument (7) is now just a list of the premise and the conclusion, where the conclusion follows by the new AND Elimination rule. The proofs of arguments (1) and (4) are the same as before, since the expanded system also contains the Modus ponens and Reductio rules that we used in generating those proofs. We use "IF Elimination" as another name for Modus ponens and "IF Introduction" as another name for Conditionalization in table 2.3 to bring out the symmetry between them.[3] We also refer to the two forms of Reductio as NOT Introduction and NOT Elimination. As a fuller example of how these rules work, we can prove that argument (9) is deducible.

(9) (Jill is in Pittsburgh AND Robin is in Atlanta) OR ((NOT Jill is
     in Pittsburgh) AND (NOT Robin is in Atlanta))
     _____
     (IF Jill is in Pittsburgh THEN Robin is in Atlanta) AND (IF
     Robin is in Atlanta THEN Jill is in Pittsburgh)

The proof of (9), which appears in table 2.4, illustrates many of the rules from table 2.3. To make the proof more readable, *Jill is in Pittsburgh* is

Table 2.3
Inference rules for classical sentential logic.

IF Elimination (Modus ponens)
    (a) If sentences of the form IF P THEN Q and P hold in a given domain,
    (b) then the sentence Q can be added to that domain.

IF Introduction (Conditionalization)
    (a) If a sentence Q holds in a subdomain whose supposition is P,
    (b) then IF P THEN Q can be added to the immediate superdomain.

NOT Elimination (Reductio ad absurdum 1)
    (a) If the sentences Q and NOT Q hold in a subdomain whose supposition is NOT P,
    (b) then the sentence P can be added to the immediate superdomain.

NOT Introduction (Reductio ad absurdum 2)
    (a) If the sentences Q and NOT Q hold in a subdomain whose supposition is P,
    (b) then NOT P can be added to the immediate superdomain.

Double Negation Elimination
    (a) If the sentence NOT NOT P holds in a given domain,
    (b) then the sentence P can be added to that domain.

AND Elimination
    (a) If the sentence P AND Q holds in a given domain,
    (b) then the sentences P and Q can be added to the domain.

AND Introduction
    (a) If the sentence P and the sentence Q hold in a given domain,
    (b) then the sentence P AND Q can be added to that domain.

OR Elimination
    (a) If the sentence P OR Q holds in a given domain D,
    (b)   and the sentence R holds in an immediate subdomain of D whose supposition is P,
    (c)   and the sentence R holds in an immediate subdomain of D whose supposition is Q,
    (d) then R can be added to D.

OR Introduction
    (a) If the sentence P holds in a given domain,
    (b) then the sentences P OR Q and Q OR P can be added to that domain, where Q is
        an arbitrary sentence.

---

abbreviated as *p* and *Robin is in Atlanta as q*. The basic strategy of the proof is to show that the conclusion of (9) follows from either *Jill is in Pittsburgh AND Robin is in Atlanta* (i.e., *p AND q*) or *(NOT Jill is in Pittsburgh) AND (NOT Robin is in Atlanta)* (i.e., *(NOT p) AND (NOT q)*), taken separately. Thus, the conclusion follows from the disjunction of these sentences in the premise by OR Elimination. Lines b–i of table 2.4 establish the first part of this strategy, and lines j–u the second part. In line b we assume the first disjunct, *p AND q*, and we can then get *q* by AND Elimination. In line d we also assume *p*, and since *q* still holds in the subdomain created by *p* we can derive *IF p THEN q* by IF Introduction. The rest of the proof follows through repetition of roughly the same combination of steps.

Table 2.4
Sample natural-deduction proof from premise (p AND q) OR (NOT p AND NOT q) to conclusion (IF p THEN q) AND (IF q THEN p).

a.	(p AND q) OR (NOT p AND NOT q)		Premise
b.	+p AND q		Supposition
c.	q		AND Elimination (from b)
d.	+p		Supposition
e.	IF p THEN q		IF Introduction (from c, d)
f.	p		AND Elimination (from b)
g.	+q		Supposition
h.	IF q THEN p		IF Introduction (from f, g)
i.	(IF p THEN q) AND (IF q THEN p)		AND Introduction (from e, h)
j.	+NOT p AND NOT q		Supposition
k.	NOT q		AND Elimination (from j)
l.	+q		Supposition
m.		+NOT p	Supposition
n.	p		NOT Elimination (from k–m)
o.	IF q THEN p		IF Introduction (from l, n)
p.	NOT p		AND Elimination (from j)
q.	+p		Supposition
r.		+NOT q	Supposition
s.	q		NOT Elimination (from p–r)
t.	IF p THEN q		IF Introduction (from q, s)
u.	IF (p THEN q) AND (IF q THEN p)		AND Introduction (from o, t)
v.	(IF p THEN q) AND (IF q THEN q)		OR Elimination (from i, u)

The new rules for Double Negation Elimination, AND Introduction, AND Elimination, and OR Elimination all seem intuitively reasonable. Double Negation Elimination enables us to rewrite a sentence with two initial negatives (i.e., *NOT NOT P*) as a positive sentence (*P*). AND Introduction permits us to add *P AND Q* to a domain in which we already have *P* and *Q* stated separately. AND Elimination simply restates the inference that is embodied in (7). Although the OR Elimination rule has more conditions than the others, its basic task is also quite reasonable, and we have just seen an example of its usefulness in the proof of table 2.4. Assume that we have a disjunction *P OR Q* that holds in a domain and we wish to show that some further sentence *R* follows. Then one way to establish *R* is (a) to show that *R* follows from *P* and (b) to show that *R* also follows from *Q*. If both of these hold, then *R* must follow, no matter which of *P* and *Q* is the case. OR Elimination merely formalizes this idea in terms of domains and subdomains.

Other rules in table 2.3 deserve special comment, however, since they lead to inferences that many find counterintuitive. The OR Introduction rule directly sanctions arguments from a given sentence to a disjunction of that sentence and any other. For instance, argument (10) is deducible in any system that contains such a rule.

(10)   Linda is a bank teller.
       _____
       Linda is a bank teller OR Cynthia owns a deli.

Although some subjects (even those without special training in logic) find arguments like (10) acceptable, many others do not (Rips and Conrad 1983). (This problem will be discussed further in the next section.)

The IF Introduction and Reductio rules also present a problem, though a more subtle one. Although these rules came in handy for the earlier proofs, they also allow us to show that some questionable arguments, such as (11), are deducible.

(11)   Linda is a bank teller.
       _____
       IF NOT Linda is a bank teller THEN Cynthia owns a deli.

This argument has the form of one of the so-called paradoxes of implication: From any sentence one can deduce a conditional consisting of the negation of the original sentence as antecedent (if-clause) and an arbitrary sentence as consequent (then-clause). The proof of (11) proceeds as shown in (12).

(12)   a. + Linda is a bank teller.   Premise
       b.   + NOT Linda is a bank teller.   Supposition
       c.   + NOT Cynthia owns a deli.   Supposition
       d.   Cynthia owns a deli.   NOT Elimination
       e. IF NOT Linda is a bank teller THEN
           Cynthia owns a deli.   IF Introduction

Line d of (12) follows by Reductio (NOT Elimination) because the contradictory sentences *Linda is a bank teller* and *NOT Linda is a bank teller* both hold by assumption within the innermost subdomain whose supposition is *NOT Cynthia owns a deli*. Notice that arguments (10) and (11) are closely related since their conclusions are equivalent within the system: From *Linda is a bank teller OR Cynthia owns a deli* you can prove *IF NOT Linda is a bank teller THEN Cynthia owns a deli*, and from *IF NOT Linda is a bank teller THEN Cynthia owns a deli*, you can prove *Linda is a bank teller OR Cynthia owns a deli*. The premises of (10) and (11) are also the same; thus, in one sense the two arguments are equivalent, even though their proofs involve different rules. Perhaps, then, we can trace the counterintuitive nature of these arguments to a common source.

Possible Modifications   The strange character of arguments (10) and (11) is evidence that the "OR" and "IF" of the system differ from the "or" and "if" of ordinary language. This discrepancy has caused controversy within linguistics, psychology, and philosophy of logic.

One tactic is to defend the system of table 2.3 as an approximation of the everyday meaning of *if* and *or*, explaining away the oddity of these arguments on other grounds. The best-known recent defender of the classical system is Paul Grice, who argues in his 1989 lectures on logic and conversation that the conclusions in (10) and (11) are less informative than their premises. If you know that Linda is a bank teller, then it will be uncooperative of you to tell me only that either Linda is a bank teller or Cynthia owns a deli. The latter statement "carries the implication of the speaker's uncertainty of which of the two it was" (Strawson 1952, p. 91). Similarly, it would be uncooperative in the same circumstances to say that if Linda is not a bank teller then Cynthia owns a deli. On Grice's theory, people standardly use sentences containing *or* or *if* in situations where they don't already know the truth of the embedded sentences, and this is what accounts for the peculiarity of (10) and (11). On this theory there is nothing wrong with the arguments themselves; if we are playing a party game in which I have to guess the occupations of the guests, there can be no objection to your giving me the hint "Linda is a bank teller or Cynthia owns a deli, but I won't tell you which" (or "If Linda is not a bank teller, then Cynthia owns a deli") even if you already know that Linda is a bank teller. Hence, on Grice's account the meanings of *or* and *if* don't preclude the correctness of (10) and (11).[4, 5]

The other reaction to the problematic arguments is to reject the parts of table 2.3 that generate them and devise an alternative system that brings OR and IF into better conformity with everyday usage. This strategy is quite common for IF (Lewis and Langford 1932; Stalnaker 1968, 1976) and for counterfactual conditionals (Lewis 1973a), and is sometimes extended to OR (Anderson and Belnap 1975). The connectives that result from these modifications can be called *intensional* OR and *intensional* IF to distinguish them from the *extensional* OR and IF of the table. One idea along these lines is to restrict when a sentence in one domain "holds" within a subdomain. In the classical system sentences from a superdomain hold in all subdomains embedded beneath it, so we were able to use (12a) within the nested subdomains beginning in (12b) and (12c). We might consider, instead, allowing only specially designated sentences—for example, only those that are necessarily true—to hold within the subdomain mentioned in the IF Introduction rule, thus blocking the proof in (12). Intuitively, we can think of these subdomains as containing information about what would be the case in a state of affairs in which the supposition were true. Natural-deduction systems containing such restrictions are presented by Anderson and Belnap (1975), by Fitch (1952, chapter 3), and by Thomason (1970b).

The same restrictions will also block the derivation of (13), which seems dubious in much the same way as (11).

(13)   Cynthia owns a deli.
       _____
       IF Linda is a bank teller THEN Cynthia owns a deli.

As (14) shows, the conclusion follows for IF (but not for intensional IF), since the premise *Cynthia owns a deli* holds within the subdomain whose supposition is *Linda is a bank teller*.

(14)   a.   + Cynthia owns a deli.   Premise
       b.   + Linda is a bank teller.   Supposition
       c.   IF Linda is a bank teller THEN
            Cynthia owns a deli.   IF Introduction

However, if the subdomain introduced by (14b) is an intensional one, then *Cynthia owns a deli* doesn't hold within it and consequently can't be used in IF Introduction to generate the conclusion. Stalnaker (1968) discusses other examples of questionable arguments that are deducible with IF but not with intensional IF. For these reasons, it seems likely that intensional IF provides a better match than IF to at least one sense of ordinary conditionals. It is an empirical question, however, whether the facts about human inference are best explained by positing a single intensional IF connective, or by positing both IF and intensional IF, or by positing some third connective that combines the advantages of both.

Other modifications could be made in the interest of a better fit to English usage or to psychological naturalness. For example, Braine (1978) and McCawley (1981) advocate extending the AND and OR rules to allow each of these connectives to take more than two sentences as arguments. Thus, in addition to sentences of the form P_1 AND P_2 or P_1 OR P_2, we could have P_1 AND P_2 AND ... AND P_k or P_1 OR P_2 OR ... OR P_k. We could also supplement the rules in table 2.3 with others that we believe to be psychologically primitive. Consider, for instance, a rule for the so-called disjunctive syllogism that would enable us to infer Q directly from P OR Q and NOT P. Although any argument provable by means of such a rule can already be proved with the rules of table 2.3, including the disjunctive syllogism as a primitive rule may produce a proof system that corresponds more closely to human reasoning. (See Braine 1978, Johnson-Laird 1975, and Rips 1983 for proposals along these lines; see Anderson and Belnap 1975 for objections to the disjunctive syllogism.) In the chapters that follow, we will keep open the possibility of these modifications and examine subjects' judgments to see whether they warrant such a shift. Chapters 3, 4, and 6 successively alter the rules to make them both more general and more reasonable as psychological components. In the meantime, table 2.3 can usefully serve as a basic example of a natural deduction system.

Rules for Quantifiers

In addition to arguments with sentence connectives such as AND and IF, we would like to be able to deal with arguments that depend on quantifiers—for example, *all* and *some*, which we encountered in our review of syllogism research in chapter 1. Consider (15), which repeats an argument from that chapter.

(15)   All square blocks are green blocks.
       Some big blocks are square blocks.
       Some big blocks are green blocks.

To determine whether (15) is correct, we might reason: "Some big blocks are square blocks; so take an arbitrary big square block and call it 'b'. Block b must be green, since b is square and all square blocks are green. Hence, some big blocks (b, for instance) are green, as stated in the conclusion." The strategy here is to consider an arbitrary example or instantiation of the premises, test whether this example guarantees properties mentioned in the conclusion, and then generalize to the entire conclusion. This strategy is, of course, common in mathematical reasoning. For instance, to prove a theorem we often consider an arbitrary case of the hypothesis

("Suppose c is an arbitrary vector in the null space of a matrix ..."), derive some properties of the instance ("c is orthogonal to the row space"), and finally generalize over all like entities ("Since c is arbitrary, the entire set of vectors in the null space is orthogonal ...").

Formalizing this reasoning means abandoning our practice of treating simple sentences as unanalyzed wholes. We will follow the usual procedure of taking a simple (*atomic*) sentence to be composed of a descriptor (*a predicate*) and one or more *arguments*. In this notation, the sentence *"Adam's Rib" stars Katherine Hepburn* would appear as *Stars("Adam's Rib", Katherine Hepburn)*, where "Stars" is the predicate and '"Adam's Rib"' and "Katherine Hepburn" are its arguments. This example contains names of particular individuals—a movie and a person—as arguments, but we will also use arguments of two other types: variables and names of arbitrarily selected individuals. "Block b" and "vector c" in the preceding paragraph are examples of names of arbitrarily selected individuals. Thus, if b is an arbitrarily selected block, then *Green(b)* will represent the fact that b is green. We will continue to use letters from the beginning of the alphabet for these arguments, which we can call *temporary names*. By contrast, we will call names like '"Adam's Rib"' and "Katherine Hepburn" *permanent names*. Finally, we will employ *variables* in connection with quantifiers to generalize over individuals. For instance, we can express the fact that someone stars in "Adam's Rib" as *(FOR SOME x) Stars("Adam's Rib", x)*; similarly, the sentence *Everything is equal to itself* will come out as *(FOR ALL x) Equal(x,x)*, or, equivalently, *(FOR ALL x) x = x*. As in these examples, letters from the end of the alphabet will be used as variables. In this notation, then, argument (15) will have the form shown in (15') if we consider *square-block*, *big-block*, and *green-block* as single predicates.

(15')   (FOR ALL x) (IF Square-block(x) THEN Green-block(x)).
        (FOR SOME x) (Big-block(x) AND Square-block(x)).
        ───
        (FOR SOME x) (Big-block(x) AND Green-block(x)).

Formal Rules   In most natural deduction systems, a proof of an argument with quantifiers proceeds by instantiating premises with quantifiers to get new sentences with temporary names, applying the rules for sentence connectives to the instantiations, and then generalizing to the quantifiers in the conclusion. This is much like the informal method we used in discussing (15). We will therefore have to supplement our formal apparatus with rules for introducing and eliminating quantifiers, and table 2.5 offers one set of rules of this sort. These rules are essentially those proposed by Borkowski and Słupecki (1958) and by Suppes (1957), and are similar to the system of Copi (1954) and Kalish (1967). (See Fine 1985a,b for a comparison of these and other quantifier systems.) Combined with the rules in table 2.3, they allow us to derive exactly the arguments that are deductively correct in classical predicate logic.

In the new rules, $P(v)$ represents a (possibly complex) expression containing variable v—for example, *Big-block(v) AND Green-block(v)*. We say that v is *free* in this expression, since there is no quantifier to govern it. On the other hand, in the sentence *(FOR ALL v) (Big-block(v) AND*

Table 2.5
Inference rules for quantifiers in classical predicate logic. In the following rules, P(v) is a (possibly complex) formula containing variable v; t is a name (either temporary or permanent); a and b are temporary names.

FOR ALL Elimination
   (a) If (FOR ALL v) P(v) holds in a given domain,
   (b)   and P(t) is the result of replacing all free occurrences of v in P(v) with t,
   (c) then P(t) can be added to the domain.

FOR ALL Introduction
   (a) If P(a) holds in a given domain,
   (b)   and a does not occur as a subscript in P(a),
   (c)   and a was not produced by FOR SOME Elimination,
   (d)   and a does not occur in any suppositions that hold in the domain,
   (e)   and a does not occur within the scope of (FOR ALL v) or (FOR SOME v) in P(a),
   (f)   and P(v) is the result of replacing all occurrences of a in P(a) by v,
   (g) then (FOR ALL v) P(v) can be added to the domain.

FOR SOME Elimination
   (a) If (FOR SOME v) P(v) holds in some domain,
   (b)   and b has not yet appeared in the proof,
   (c)   and $a_1, a_2, \ldots, a_k$ is a list of the temporary names (possibly empty) that appear in P(v) and that first appeared in a supposition or in an application of FOR ALL Elimination,
   (d)   and $P(b_{a_1, a_2, \ldots, a_k})$ is the result of replacing all free occurrences of v in P(v) by $b_{a_1, a_2, \ldots, a_k}$.
   (e) then $P(b_{a_1, a_2, \ldots, a_k})$ can be added to the domain.

FOR SOME Introduction
   (a) If P(t) holds in a given domain,
   (b)   and t does not occur within the scope of either (FOR ALL v) or (FOR SOME v) in P(t),
   (c)   and P(v) is the result of replacing all occurrences of t in P(t) with v,
   (d) then (FOR SOME v) P(v) can be added to the domain.

Green-block(v)), *v* is *bound* by the quantifier. *P(t)* in table 2.5 corresponds to an expression containing a name *t*, such as *Big-block(t) AND Green-block(t)*, where *t* can be either a temporary or a permanent name. (For reasons that will be discussed shortly, we must sometimes subscript temporary names, such as a_b and a_{b_1, b_2}.) These rules contain a variety of conditions that we will examine after looking at an example of how the rules apply within a proof.

Given the quantifier rules, it is easy to show that the argument in (15′) is deducible. In our usual proof style, the derivation looks like (16).

(16) a. +(FOR ALL x)(IF Square-block(x)
        THEN Green-block(x)).   Premise

   b. +(FOR SOME x) (Big-block(x) AND
      Square-block(x)).   Premise

   c. Big-block(b) AND Square-block(b).   FOR SOME Elim.

   d. Big-block(b).   AND Elim.

   e. Square-block(b).   AND Elim.

   f. IF Square-block(b) THEN
      Green-block(b).   FOR ALL Elim.

   g. Green-block(b).   IF Elim.

   h. Big-block(b) AND Green-block(b).   AND Intro.

   i. (FOR SOME x) (Big-block(x) AND
      Green-block(x)).   FOR SOME Intro.

The only novel aspects of this proof are the applications of FOR SOME Elimination and FOR ALL Elimination (lines c and f) and the application of FOR SOME Introduction (line i). Line b tells us that there is a big square block, which we can then represent with the temporary name "b" in line c, using FOR SOME Elimination. Line a says that all square blocks are green; so if block *b* is square then it is green. FOR ALL Elimination gives us this result in line f. Since block *b* is big and square, it must therefore be big and green (line h). Hence according to the FOR SOME Introduction rule, there is a big, green block (line i).

Basically, the quantifier-introduction rules take us from sentences of the form *P(a)* to ones of the form *(FOR ALL v) P(v)* or *(FOR SOME v) P(v)*. The elimination rules take us in the reverse direction. However, these rules require a number of conditions to keep the proof from lapsing into error. These restrictions are particularly important for FOR ALL Introduction and FOR SOME Elimination, since these inference patterns are reasonable only in special contexts. We can't generally conclude that everything has a given property on the grounds that an arbitrarily selected thing does (FOR ALL Introduction); similarly, we can't ordinarily go from the fact that some object has a property to the conclusion that an arbitrarily selected one does (FOR SOME Elimination).

In the case of FOR SOME Elimination, we have to ensure that the arbitrarily selected object is not one to which we have already ascribed special properties (condition b in table 2.5), and we have to specify that the object may depend on earlier choices for other temporary names (condition c). Without the former condition we would be able to prove, as in (17), that there is something that is not identical to itself from the premise that there are two things that are nonidentical.

(17) a. $+$(FOR SOME x)(FOR SOME y) $x \neq y$.   Premise
      b. (FOR SOME y) $a \neq y$.   FOR SOME Elim.
    *c. $a \neq a$.   FOR SOME Elim.
      d. (FOR SOME x) $x \neq x$.   FOR SOME Intro.

The asterisk indicates the incorrect line in this "proof." Condition b blocks this line because the temporary name "a" has already appeared in line b.

To understand the reason for the third condition on FOR SOME Elimination, we need to think about the relation of this rule to FOR ALL Introduction. Consider (18), which is a pseudo-proof from the premise that everyone has a father to the conclusion that there is a particular person who is everyone's father.

(18) a. $+$(FOR ALL x)(FOR SOME y)
          (IF Person(x) THEN Father(y, x)).   Premise
      b. (FOR SOME y)(IF Person(a)
          THEN Father(y, a)).   FOR ALL Elim.
    *c. IF Person(a) THEN Father(b, a).   FOR SOME Elim.
      d. (FOR ALL x)(IF Person(x)
          THEN Father(b, x)).   FOR ALL Intro.
      e. (FOR SOME y)(FOR ALL x)
          (IF Person(x) THEN Father(y, x)).   FOR SOME Intro.

Line a states that for any person x, there is some y who is x's father. So an arbitrarily selected individual a has some y as a father, as shown in line b. At this point it might seem that if an arbitrary person a has a father, then we can also give that father a temporary name (say, "b"), as in line c. But intuitively, the named father can't be just anyone; the father in question depends on the person we are dealing with (Lauren's father is Steve, James' is Roger, and so on). To mark this dependence of b on a, conditions c and d of FOR SOME Elimination require us to subscript b with a. Thus, in a correct proof, line c would appear as *IF Person (a) THEN Father (b_a, a)*. In line d, we try to generalize over people. But since the father named by b_a depends on the previous choice of person a, this step is incorrect and is explicitly blocked by condition b of FOR ALL Introduction. So condition c of FOR SOME Elimination is motivated by the way it sets up FOR ALL Introduction.

Two conditions on FOR ALL Introduction also deserve comment (besides condition b, whose justification we have just seen). Condition c prohibits generalizing on a temporary name that FOR SOME Elimination has produced. This restriction keeps us from deriving a universal conclusion from a particular premise—in (19), the conclusion that everyone is rich from the premise that someone is rich.

(19)   a. +(FOR SOME x) Rich(x).   Premise
       b. Rich(a).   FOR SOME Elim.
      *c. (FOR ALL x) Rich(x).   FOR ALL Intro.

Since the temporary name "a" comes from applying FOR SOME Elimination, we are barred from using it in line c of (19). Similarly, condition d forbids generalizing on a temporary name that appears in a supposition— that is, from going from the supposition that there is an arbitrary object with some property to the conclusion that all objects have that property.

The remaining restrictions on FOR ALL Introduction and on the other three rules of table 2.5 are simply technical devices to ensure proper substitution of names or variables. For example, condition e of FOR ALL Introduction and condition b of FOR SOME Introduction prohibit substituting a variable for a name if that substitution results in the new variable's being accidentally bound by the wrong quantifier. If we have, for instance, *(FOR SOME x) (Big-block(a) AND Green-block(x))*, we don't want to generalize to *(FOR ALL x) (FOR SOME x) (Big-block(x) AND*

Green-block(x)). The trouble here is that *(FOR SOME x)* already governs the inner expression *Big-block(a) AND Green-block(x)*, so substituting *x* for *a* allows this new *x* to be bound by *(FOR SOME x)* rather than by *(FOR ALL x)* as desired. The region of a sentence within which a quantifier can bind a variable is called the *scope* of the quantifier. Thus, to eliminate the conflict, the conditions in question forbid substitution of a variable for a temporary name if that name already appears within the scope of a quantifier employing the same variable.

Possible Modifications   It might seem that the conditions on the quantifier rules block correct inferences as well as obviously faulty proofs such as (17)–(19). As was noted in chapter 1, many investigators believe that subjects in syllogism experiments interpret sentences of the form *Some x are y* as suggesting *Some x are not y* (or, equivalently, *Not all x are y*). Indeed, in a direct test of this argument, between 58% and 97% of subjects (across conditions) stated that it was correct (Newstead and Griggs 1983). But there is evidently no way to show that such an argument is deducible in the system of table 2.5.

Although we might try to alter the quantifier rules to accommodate the argument, this is probably not the best corrective. If *Some x are not y* were deducible from *Some x are y*, then sentences like *Some of the blocks are green–in fact, all of them are green* would be contradictory. As Horn (1973, 1989) points out, however, such sentences are perfectly consistent. Thus, most investigators have taken the Some-to-Some-not relationship as a case of Gricean conversational implicature (see, e.g., Begg and Harris 1982; Horn 1973, 1989; Newstead and Griggs 1983; McCawley 1981). In a conversational context, it would be uncooperative of a speaker who knew that all *x* are *y* to assert only that some *x* are *y*. Thus, the audience can normally assume that when a speaker sincerely says that some *x* are *y* (and is in a position to know whether all x are y), the speaker then believes that some *x* are not *y*. (See note 5 for a discussion of the inference from *All x are y* to *All y are x*.)

There are other facts about quantifiers, though, that do seem to show the limitations of our rules. Natural languages contain a much wider range of quantifiers than *all* and *some*, including (in English) *most, many, few, a few, a lot, several, any, each*, and *no*. We could paraphrase some of these using *FOR ALL* and *FOR SOME*, or we could formulate rules in the style of table 2.5 to handle them directly. (See Fitch 1973 for Introduction and Elimination rules for *no*, *any*, and *every*.) However, quantifiers such as *most* and *more than half* can't be defined in terms of *FOR ALL* and *FOR SOME* (Barwise and Cooper 1981), and valid arguments based on such quantifiers outrun what can be captured in a natural deduction system (or, in fact, in a mechanical inference method of any sort—see the discussion of Church's Thesis in the following chapter). Research on generalized quantifiers (Barwise 1987b; Barwise and Cooper 1981; Westerståhl 1989) indicates that these constructions involve resources of set theory for which there is no complete proof system. According to these proposals, for example, the generalized quantifier *most politicians* in the sentence *Most politicians whine* represents the set of all sets of objects that include most politicians, and the sentence as a whole will be true if the set of whiners is one of these sets. This complexity doesn't mean that people can't make inferences with such quantifiers; for example, from *Most politicians whine loudly* it follows intuitively that *Most politicians whine*. But it does suggest that the inferences that people recognize as correct will be only a selection of the valid ones, and how to describe these psychologically recognizable items is an open question.[6]

A final worry about the quantifier rules is that they sometimes make trivial inferences tediously cumbersome. For example, as (20) shows, the argument from *Someone is not rich* to *Not everyone is rich*, which seems straightforwardly correct, requires a five-line proof.

(20)   a. $+$(FOR SOME x) NOT Rich(x).   Premise

      b. $+$(FOR ALL y) Rich(y)   Supposition

      c.   NOT Rich(a)   FOR SOME Elim.

      d.   Rich(a)   FOR ALL Elim.

      e. NOT (FOR ALL x) Rich(x)   NOT Intro.

Although we may sometimes reason as in (20) by instantiating and then generalizing again, in many situations we seem able to move directly from one quantified expression to another (Braine and Rumain 1983). In fact, it is possible to view Aristotle's theory of syllogisms as a type of natural-deduction system comprising rules for deducing one kind of quantified expression from others in this more direct manner (Corcoran 1974; Smiley 1973). One way to attack this for psychological purposes is to supplement the rules in table 2.5 with explicit quantifier-to-quantifier rules, even though the latter are redundant (since they can be derived from the former). A rule that takes us from *(FOR SOME x) NOT P(x)* to *NOT (FOR ALL x) P(x)* might be one example of a redundant but psychologically primitive rule. Another "Aristotelian" example might be the inference from *(FOR ALL x) (IF P(x) THEN Q(x))* and *(FOR ALL x) (IF Q(x) THEN R(x))* to *(FOR ALL x) (IF P(x) THEN R(x))*. Another approach to this problem—one that we will explore in part II—is to work with a representation in which no explicit quantifiers appear and in which the work of the quantifiers is performed by names and variables. The CPL System, as formalized in the tables, provides hints about the form of a psychological model but is not the final statement of the theory.

The Place of Logic in a Theory of Reasoning

Even if we amend our natural-deduction rules in the ways contemplated in the preceding section, we may doubt that such rules are important in reasoning—or even that people use them at all. Some of the doubts have to do with computational problems that arise in incorporating rules that were originally designed for pencil-and-paper proofs. Other doubts center on the ability of the rules to predict data from psychological experiments. We will face these computational and psychological problems in later chapters, but there is a third set of theoretical difficulties that we should consider here. These difficulties threaten to show that, no matter how we tinker with rules like those in tables 2.3 and 2.5, they can never in principle explain human reasoning.

One objection of this kind—due to Harman (1986)—is based on the idea that rules of reasoning and rules of proof are entirely different types of things. The former govern the way people change their beliefs in response to evidence, whereas the latter concern the way one sentence (or group of sentences) implies another. According to this view, the rules of tables 2.3 and 2.5 are rules of proof, not rules of reasoning. Of course, Jaśkowski, Gentzen, and others designed these rules as part of a proof system—a method for showing that the conclusion of an argument follows from its premises. But these logicians also intended the rules to come close to human reasoning. What is wrong, then, with supposing that they were right—that these rules are literally part of the mental equipment we use in reasoning?

Harman's main argument against taking proof rules as rules for belief change is that doing so would yield disastrous cognitive results. One of the problems is that AND Introduction and OR Introduction, if applied blindly, can produce an avalanche of completely trivial inferences. For example, from the sentences *Tom is at work* and *Michelle is at school*, it follows by AND Introduction that *Tom is at work AND Michelle is at school*. By a second application of AND Introduction, it follows that *Tom is at work AND (Tom is at work AND Michelle is at school)*; by a third, we get *Tom is at work AND (Tom is at work AND (Tom is at work AND Michelle is at school))*; and so on. However, problems of this sort can be handled by modifications in the statement of the rules themselves, as will be shown in the next chapter.

For present purposes, a more interesting type of example is the following: Suppose you believe both that Calvin deposits 50 cents and that if he deposits 50 cents then he will get a coke. Suppose you also see nothing coming out of the coke machine and come to believe that Calvin will not get a coke. If you apply IF Elimination (modus ponens) to the first two beliefs, then you will deduce *Calvin gets a coke*; but you don't want to end up believing *that*, given what you just witnessed. Instead, you should take this result as evidence that one or more of your initial beliefs was false and cease believing it (perhaps Calvin didn't really deposit 50 cents, or perhaps it was not true that if he deposits 50 cents then he will get a coke). Hence, on Harman's account, IF Elimination can't be a rule about what sentences to believe, and therefore it is not a "rule of reasoning."

It is hard to see how any simple patching of the IF Elimination rule could escape this difficulty. Of course, we could amend the rule in table 2.3 by adding the further condition that no proposition of the form *NOT Q* holds in the domain in which *IF P THEN Q* and *P* hold. This modified IF Elimination has the advantage that it will not produce the contradictory beliefs that Calvin does and does not get a coke in the broken coke-machine example. Unfortunately, though, directly contradictory beliefs are only part of the problem. We still need to change our beliefs about Calvin in order to get rid of the source of the inconsistency, and the only way to do that is to drop one or more of the beliefs *IF P THEN Q, P,* and *NOT Q.* Perhaps we could endow mental IF Elimination with the power to delete beliefs in situations like this, but which beliefs should it delete? We have our choice of *Calvin deposits 50 cents, Calvin does not get a coke,* and *If Calvin deposits 50 cents, then Calvin gets a coke* (or any combination of these). Furthermore, our decision ought to depend on how much support we have for one belief relative to the others, where the support relation should be able to take nondeductive factors into account. You might reasonably decide to drop the belief that Calvin deposited 50 cents on the grounds that your view of his deposit was obscured and so you didn't see exactly how much money he put in, or on the grounds that you know Calvin is forgetful and thus he may not have noticed the new price increase. A modified modus ponens that can take such factors into account is no longer much like the modus ponens we started with; it is no longer a purely deductive principle.

Harman does not imply that rules such as IF Elimination play *no* role in reasoning (i.e., change of belief). Principles governing change of belief could take such proof rules into account (though Harman also believes that logical rules such as those in tables 2.3 and 2.5 have no privileged position in this respect).[7] If you realize that your beliefs *IF p THEN q* and *p* imply *q*, then that is usually a reason for believing *q*. But implication isn't always decisive, as the preceding example shows. In other words, it is consistent with Harman's view to take the rules in the tables as psychologically real components of reasoning, even though they aren't "rules of reasoning" in his sense.

The approach just contemplated demotes IF Elimination and similar rules to a cognitive position in which they don't fully determine belief change. But there is another way of attacking Harman's problem that promotes these rules. Let us assume, with Harman, that rules of belief change include a set of heuristics for resolving recognizable inconsistencies among beliefs. Harman informally describes some heuristics of this sort— for example, "Make only minimal changes (deletions and additions) to your current beliefs" and "Don't give up beliefs that you would immediately get back again (e.g., by implication from other beliefs)." These are heuristics in the sense that they don't guarantee a way around the inconsistency, since some inconsistencies may be unresolvable for practical purposes.

Let us also suppose that these heuristics can be specified as computational procedures for actually modifying beliefs. (See Pollock 1987 and 1989 for one attempt at this; see later chapters of the present work for a discussion of related work in AI.) In particular, they could be formulated as a production system for belief revision, since any computational procedure can be so formulated. (See chapter 3 of Anderson 1976 for a proof.)

The system would consist of a set of productions of roughly the following form: IF conditions $c_1, c_2, \ldots, c_k$ are met by one's current beliefs THEN modify the beliefs through (internal) actions $a_1, a_2, \ldots, a_m$. The system applies these productions by monitoring beliefs and executing the specified actions when the conditions are satisfied. But notice that this method of applying the rules is nearly identical to IF Elimination; the only important difference is that the system executes the actions in the THEN part of the conditional rather than adding a new sentence to a proof.[8] Thus, according to one way of formulating rules of belief change, the rules obey a simple variant of the IF Elimination proof rule. Promoting IF Elimination to the status of a general operating principle avoids Harman's problem because the rule no longer simply adds beliefs on the basis of others— it could very well discard some. What the principle happens to do depends on how it is "programmed"; that is, it depends on the contents of the individual productions.

Our promotional and demotional approaches to IF Elimination (and to the other rules in tables 2.3 and 2.5) offer us a choice as to how we should understand the role of logical rules in cognition. If Harman is right (as I believe he is), these rules are not methods for automatically changing beliefs. But should we think of them as general-purpose symbol manipulators, or as specific tests for determining when certain sentences logically imply others? On one hand, as demoted rules, they seem to have the better claim to the title "rules of reasoning." If we elevate logical rules to the level of production appliers then the rules are quite remote from reasoning as it is ordinarily conceived. On the other hand, the hypothesis that these rules are part of our basic cognitive architecture is inviting, because it helps explain why such principles seem so deeply embedded in thinking.

But we needn't choose between promoting and demoting the rules, since both logic-based processing rules and lower-level reasoning principles could have separate parts to play in cognition. Imagine that a suitably modified version of the rules acts as a general-purpose mental programming system along the lines of PROLOG and other logic-based languages (Clocksin and Mellish 1981; Kowalski 1979). Such rules would generalize the production applier just discussed, extending to a wider range of logical forms than the simple IF ... THEN of production systems. In addition, the system could maintain a stock of "demoted" rules for determining implications among sentences in reasoning. Some of these rules might duplicate the "promoted" ones (perhaps being derived from them by thought experiments); others could be acquired through training in mathematics and logic. The general rules, by contrast, would be a fixed component of the individual's cognitive architecture. Although positing multiple levels of logical rules may seem strange, analogies are easy to find. Most computers, after all, have a kind of logic built into their wiring and can use this logic circuitry to run theorem-proving programs that embody their own logical principles. Of course, a multilayer system may be less parsimonious than we would like, but the psychological facts may require it.

We will pursue this two-tier approach in what follows, but the present point is simply that Harman's example should not be seen as evidence that logical rules can't be cognitive rules. Harman is right that the logical rules in the tables would produce psychological havoc if we used them to change our beliefs in a purely reflexive way. He may also be right that there must be a different species of rules that govern belief change. But there *are* ways that logical rules could sensibly fit in a cognitive theory, as I will try to show in parts II and III.

3 Reasoning and Computation

Children, who have only a little experience, are nevertheless able to understand a great deal that a skilled instructor explains to them, even if he doesn't show them anything but only describes. Therefore, it is necessary that concepts of all those many things are latent in them and arise from the few with which they are already acquainted. . . .

It follows irrefutably that if somebody entered in a catalog all the primitive concepts which that child has, with a letter or character assigned to each, together with all the concepts composed of these (i.e., all the concepts which could be explained to that child without putting anything new before his eyes), he would be able to designate [all of these] with combinations of those letters or characters. . . .

Thus I assert that all truths can be demonstrated about things expressible in this language with the addition of new concepts not yet expressed in it—all such truths, I say, can be demonstrated solo calculo, or solely by the manipulation of characters according to a certain form, without any labor of the imagination or effort of the mind, just as occurs in arithmetic and algebra.
Leibniz (cited in Mates 1986)

The study of deductive reasoning is the study of a psychological process. Although logical principles may be relevant to this process, they must be embodied as mental operations if they are to exert a direct causal influence on thinking. In chapter 2 we glimpsed some of the computational issues surrounding the use of logical principles as psychological procedures. For example, we noticed that even the seemingly innocent natural-deduction rule AND Introduction (p and q entail p *AND* q) can lead to a torrent of trivial inferences that would flood our cognitive resources. Along the same lines, consider the rule of OR Introduction in the form in which it appeared in table 2.3. This rule states that a sentence p entails p *OR* q for any q. Thus, from the sentence that *James admires Pierre,* we are entitled to conclude *James admires Pierre OR Craig dislikes Julia.* But the rule can apply again to this new sentence, leading to, say, *(James admires Pierre OR Craig dislikes Julia) OR Simone approves of Alma.* In one further application we get *((James admires Pierre OR Craig dislikes Julia) OR Simone approves of Alma) OR Gaston distrusts Leslie,* and so on for as long as we care to continue. Applying the rules in an ungoverned fashion can yield an accumulation of worthless sentences.

As might be expected, this combinatorial problem is the crux of research on deduction in computer science. Any attempt to build an efficient theorem prover (or deduction-based problem solver) must find a way to guide the program toward the conclusion to be proved, avoiding runaway inferences like those of the preceding paragraph. In one of the earliest papers in computer theorem proving, Newell, Shaw, and Simon (1957) highlighted this problem in the description of what they called the *British Museum Algorithm*. Adapted to the rules of chapter 2 above, the algorithm goes like this:

To prove that a given conclusion follows from a set of premises, start by writing down a list of the premises. Apply the rules to the premises, and add any new sentences they produce to the premise list. If the conclusion is in this list, then the algorithm halts and the conclusion has been proved. Otherwise, apply the rules once again to the enlarged list of sentences, adding any new items to the premise-and-derived-sentence list. Continue in this way until the conclusion is proved.

The completeness theorems of sentential and predicate logics guarantee that the British Museum algorithm will eventually come up with a proof if the argument is valid. (If the argument is invalid, the procedure may continue indefinitely.) But the computational cost of finding a proof in this way may be enormous. Newell et al. (1957) estimated that it would require hundreds of thousands of years for the computers of that time to use the British Museum algorithm to generate proofs for just the sentential theorems in chapter 2 of Whitehead and Russell's *Principia Mathematica* (1910–1913). Since 1957 there have been big improvements in the speed with which programs can uncover logical proofs. Although these advances have not escaped the basic difficulty of exponential search time, they have made automatic theorem proving a practical matter for many kinds of problems. The advances have come from the discovery of more efficient proof methods and from the discovery of heuristic techniques for keeping the program on track. The LT (Logic Theory) program of Newell et al. was able to prove 38 of the first 52 theorems in the *Principia* through heuristic methods. Only three years later, Wang (1960) described a program that proved all of the 200 plus theorems in the first five chapters of the *Principia* in less than 3 minutes. Currently, automatic theorem provers are able to assist in answering previously open questions in matheematics. (For some examples, see chapter 9 of Wos et al. 1984.)

During the same period, the stake in finding successful theorem provers has increased, since AI investigators have turned up new ways of putting proof to use. Proof techniques have become valuable, not only in determining the correctness of arguments in symbolic logic, but also in guiding robots, parsing sentences, synthesizing computer programs, designing electronic circuits, and other problem-solving tasks. In fact, theorem proving now serves as the basis of a general AI programming language called PROLOG (short for PROgramming in LOGic), which is the chief rival to LISP (Clocksin and Mellish 1981). There is clear disagreement in the AI community about the desirability of deduction as a general problem-solving technique (see, e.g., Nilsson 1991 vs. Birnbaum 1991; see also McDermott 1987 and commentaries in the same issue of *Computational Intelligence*). But the current success of deduction systems places them in the top ranks of AI architectures.

How relevant is this progress to the study of human reasoning? On one hand, it seems extremely unlikely that ordinary people (without special instruction) can apply the newer techniques for speeding proofs, since these involve regimenting arguments in ways that are often unintuitive. To model the kind of deduction that subjects are able to carry out, it is necessary to forgo the more streamlined methods in this area. On the other hand, many of the procedures that Newell et al. (1957) and other researchers proposed in the early days of automatic theorem proving are still relevant to the study of natural reasoning. The first section of this chapter reviews some ways to improve on the British Museum algorithm and attempts to identify, in a preliminary way, which of them could be parts of everyday deduction. This review suggests some possible revisions to the deduction rules of the perceding chapter—revisions that help avoid the difficulties we have seen with the principles of AND Introduction and OR Introduction. The second section outlines some of these revisions, which will be developed in detail in part II. Of course, these revisions don't handle the combinatorial problem as well as do the more advanced techniques that we must sacrifice for psychological fidelity, but we can justify certain inefficiencies if they mimic the difficulties people experience when they engage in parallel tasks. The third section of the chapter considers some AI methods for using theorem proving to solve general problems.

Cognitive psychologists, for the most part, have ignored these efforts to solve problems through proof. Although theories of question answering in psycholinguistics took over a few of the main ideas (see the discussion of sentence-picture verification in chapter 1), deductive problem solving has usually been dismissed on the grounds that people are not very good at deduction. If ordinary people can't evaluate even simple syllogisms, why should we suppose that they use deduction as a means for dealing with other sorts of tasks? For example, in explaining why psychologists have usually not assumed that people remember information in the form of

sentences in predicate calculus, Rumelhart and Norman (1988, p. 19) comment that the two most important reasons are "issues surrounding the
organization of knowledge in memory and the notion that the logical
theorem proving processes so natural to the predicate calculus formalism
do not seem to capture the ways people actually seem to reason." As
I have already mentioned, it is true that some methods of computer
theorem proving may be out of the reach of untrained subjects. But psychologists' dismissal of theorem proving has kept them from noticing some
interesting developments that narrow the gap between automated deduction and the ways "people actually reason."

Problems of Search in Deduction

Blindly applying logical rules is a poor strategy for even simple deduction
problems. As long as the rules are stated in the unconstrained form of the
preceding chapter (as is customary in most elementary logic textbooks),
they will not automatically lead to a proof in an acceptable amount of
time. In view of the potential of the rules to produce infinite sets of irrelevant sentences, finding a short proof by randomly applying rules would be
a matter of sheer luck. If deductive reasoning is anything like a practical
process, then there must be better ways to direct the search for a proof.
The constraints that investigators in computer science have found differ in
how encompassing they are. At one extreme, there are general methods
that are applicable to all proof-finding situations; at the other, there are
special-purpose heuristics that take advantage of particular types of rules
or lines in the proof. It turns out that the heuristics are more important for
psychological research, and we will concentrate on them in this chapter.
However, the new general methods—resolution theorem proving and its
variants—are the triumphs of automated deduction, and we should try to
understand their impact.

There are some theoretical limits to what even the best general methods
or heuristics can do to simplify the proof-finding process. The best known
of these limits is the undecidability theorem of Church (1936a), which
established that there is no decision procedure for classical predicate logic
(CPL). That is, there is no procedure that, given an arbitrary argument,
will necessarily stop after a finite number of steps, correctly labeling the

argument as valid or invalid in CPL. The notion of "procedure" employed here is general enough that we can reasonably assume it to encompass any function that is computable at all, an assumption called Church's Thesis (Church 1936b; for expositions see Boolos and Jeffrey 1974, Mendelson 1990, and Rogers 1967). Thus, the undecidability result applies to all actual computers, and presumably to humans. But although *decision* procedures are out of the question for CPL, there are *proof* procedures that will exhibit a proof of an argument if that argument is valid. Proof procedures suffice for many practical purposes, as we will see in the third section of this chapter. Further, there are parts of CPL that *do* have a decision procedure—for example, classical sentential logic (the logic associated with the sentential rules in table 2.3) and monadic first-order logic (CPL restricted to predicates with at most one argument). It is possible that human reasoning can make use of such decision procedures in situations that require less than the full power of CPL. These situations include almost all the arguments that have figured in psychologists' investigations of deductive reasoning: evaluation of categorical syllogisms, evaluation of sentential arguments, verification of negative sentences against pictures, and other tasks that we glimpsed in chapter 1.

The second theoretical limitation, however, concerns the computational complexity of these decision procedures. A landmark theorem due to Stephen Cook (1971) showed that the task of deciding the validity of an arbitrary sentence in classical sentential logic belongs to the class of problems termed "NP-complete." (See chapter 2 of Garey and Johnson 1979 for a clear exposition of Cook's theorem, and chapter 4 of Cherniak 1986 for a discussion of possible implications for cognitive science.) This means that validity testing for sentential logic is equivalent in computational complexity to problems (such as the Traveling Salesman problem) for which every known algorithm requires an amount of time equal to some exponential function of the length of the problem statement.[1] In particular, suppose we have a decision procedure that takes any argument as input and returns a proof of the argument if it is valid in sentential logic, stopping (with no proof) if it is invalid. If the number of symbols in the argument is n, then the amount of time consumed by such a procedure could be, in the worst case, on the order of k^n seconds (where k is a constant greater than or equal to 1). But although an exponential increase in time seems unavoidable for a decision procedure of this sort, the implications of Cook's theorem for theories of human and machine reasoning are uncertain. First, in the case of human reasoning, we may be dealing with a deduction system that is in some ways less powerful than the full sentential logic to which Cook's theorem applies (Levesque 1988). Second, there may be decision procedures for people or computers that operate with a value of k sufficiently close to 1 that exponential complexity is no special restriction for problems of practical interest. Let us see what can be done in the way of improving proof methods.

Proof Heuristics: LT and GPS

One innovation in the Logic Theory machine of Newell et al. (1957) was to apply the system's proof rules in a backward direction. In order to spell out this idea, I will use the term *assertions of a proof* (at a given stage of the proof process) to mean the set consisting of axioms, premises, and all other sentences derived from the axioms and premises at that stage. The most obvious way to translate logical rules such as those in tables 2.3 and 2.5 into computational procedures is to fashion them as routines that take assertions as input and produce further assertions as output. On this pattern, Modus ponens would become a procedure that looks for assertions of the form *IF P THEN Q* and *P* and, if it finds them, adds *Q* to the proof. I will call such assertion-to-new-assertion routines *forward rules*. In LT, however, the logic routines worked backward from the conclusion in order to aim the proof in the right direction. Modus ponens in LT takes a conclusion *Q* as input and checks for a corresponding assertion *IF P THEN Q*; if such an assertion is available, the rule then tries to prove *P*. If it succeeds, then *Q* must follow. In this case, *P* serves as a *subgoal* for *Q*. I will call these goal-to-subgoal procedures *backward rules*. Evidence from students constructing geometry proofs suggests that these students employ both forward and backward rules (Anderson, Greeno, Kline, and Neves 1981). People with greater expertise tend to rely more on forward rules and less on backward rules, both in geometry (Koedinger and Anderson 1990) and in other areas (Larkin, McDermott, Simon, and Simon 1980).

Selective Backward Rules   The forward/backward distinction and the notions of assertions and subgoals will play essential roles in the rest of this book, so it might be helpful to have a concrete example.[2] Suppose we want to show that argument (1) is deducible.

(1)   IF Calvin deposits 50 cents THEN Calvin gets a coke.
      IF Calvin gets a coke THEN Calvin buys a burger.
      Calvin deposits 50 cents.
      _____
      Calvin buys a burger.

Using Modus ponens in the forward direction, we can combine the first and third premises in (1) to derive a new assertion: *Calvin gets a coke*. We can then apply the same rule to the second premise and the new assertion to prove the conclusion. This pure forward method is illustrated in the upper panel of figure 3.1, where the numbering of the assertions corresponds to the order in which the proof deals with them. Arrows indicate entailments among the sentences: Sentences 1 and 2 jointly entail 3, and sentences 3 and 4 jointly entail 5.

Compare this forward deduction strategy with the backward strategy, illustrated in the lower panel of figure 3.1. In the backward mode we start with the conclusion, which we can think of as the main goal of the proof. Goals and subgoals are represented in the figure with a question mark after the sentences; thus, *Calvin buys a burger?* means that the sentence *Calvin buys a burger* is one to be proved (and not that we are trying to prove a question). Assertions end with a period, as they did in the preceding diagram. Since the conclusion-goal matches the consequent of one of the premises *(IF Calvin gets a coke THEN Calvin buys a burger)*, backward Modus ponens tells us that the goal follows if we can establish *Calvin gets a coke*. This latter sentence (the antecedent of the premise) becomes our new subgoal. To fulfill this subgoal we can employ the same backward Modus ponens method. *Calvin gets a coke* matches the consequent of another premise, *(IF Calvin deposits 50 cents THEN Calvin gets a coke)*; hence, we will fulfill this subgoal if we can show that the antecedent is true. This time, though, the antecedent, *Calvin deposits 50 cents*, is already given as a premise, and this means we have succeeded in proving the subgoal and, in turn, the conclusion of the argument. The arrows again point from entailing to entailed sentences, but the order in which the sentences are considered is the opposite of figure 3.1a.

Newell et al. (1957) described two additional backward rules that are of interest in proving conditional sentences, and both of these take advantage of the transitivity of material conditionals (i.e., the IF ... THEN sentences within CPL). From *IF P THEN Q* and *IF Q THEN R*, it follows that *IF P THEN R*—an argument pattern sometimes called the

a

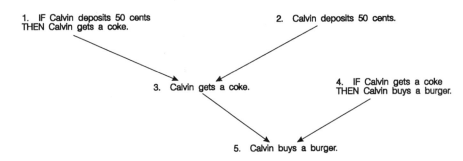

1. IF Calvin deposits 50 cents
THEN Calvin gets a coke.

2. Calvin deposits 50 cents.

3. Calvin gets a coke.

4. IF Calvin gets a coke
THEN Calvin buys a burger.

5. Calvin buys a burger.

b

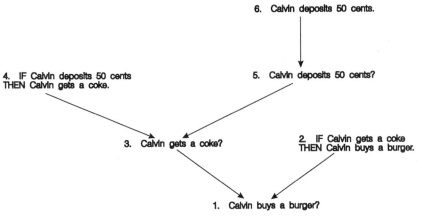

6. Calvin deposits 50 cents.

4. IF Calvin deposits 50 cents
THEN Calvin gets a coke.

5. Calvin deposits 50 cents?

3. Calvin gets a coke?

2. IF Calvin gets a coke
THEN Calvin buys a burger.

1. Calvin buys a burger?

Figure 3.1
Proof of the argument

Calvin deposits 50 cents.
IF Calvin deposits 50 cents THEN Calvin gets a coke.
IF Calvin gets a coke THEN Calvin buys a burger.

Calvin buys a burger.

using a forward strategy (a) and a backward strategy (b).

hypothetical syllogism. Thus, in the backward mode, if we are interested in proving a conclusion of the form *IF P THEN R*, it is useful to find out if there are any assertions of the form *IF P THEN Q* or *IF Q THEN R*. Four outcomes are possible here:

(a) If both of the latter conditionals are assertions, the conclusion is proved.

(b) If we have an assertion *IF P THEN Q*, we can set up *IF Q THEN R* as a subgoal, since establishing that subgoal would suffice to prove the conclusion.

(c) If we have an assertion *IF Q THEN R*, we can set up *IF P THEN Q* as a subgoal, for the same reason.

(d) If neither conditional is an assertion, LT abandons the strategy.

Newell et al. referred to outcome b as "forward chaining" and to outcome c as "backward chaining," and treated them as separate rules or "methods." But since both rules operate in the backward direction (from a conclusion or main goal to a subgoal), the terminology is somewhat awkward. For uniformity, we can refer to them as the backward *Transitivity* rules, bearing in mind the two options (b and c) for establishing the relationship.

The empirical investigation that Newell et al. carried out with the *Principia* theorems convinced them that LT's strategy of working backward was a vast improvement over the British Museum algorithm. But why should this be so? At first glance, it is not clear why working backward from the conclusion should be any more of an advantage to a theorem prover than working forward from the premises. This is particularly puzzling with Modus ponens or Transitivity, since these rules don't possess the problems that we encountered with AND Introduction or OR Introduction. These latter rules produce an unlimited number of sentences when they operate in a forward direction; Modus ponens and Transitivity do not. Once Modus ponens has produced *Calvin gets a coke* from *IF Calvin deposits 50 cents THEN Calvin gets a coke* and *Calvin deposits 50 cents*, it can produce no further conclusions from the same pair of sentences. (Of course, we could apply Modus ponens to these same sentences again to obtain a redundant token of *Calvin gets a coke*; but as long as we have some way to eliminate these duplicates, we won't have problems with runaway conclusions.) Thus, in view of the tame nature of Modus ponens and Transitivity, why should working backward help?

The reason for the improvement is that the backward-oriented rules in LT are quite selective. The British Museum algorithm applies its rules in a forward direction, with no thought of the conclusion. The rules of LT work backward but keep the premises (and other assertions) in mind. LT's backward Modus ponens, for instance, will never attempt both P and IF P $THEN$ Q as subgoals if it needs to deduce Q; rather, it attempts only P as a subgoal and only when it already has IF P $THEN$ Q as an assertion. For example, we were able to get started in the backward proof of figure 3.1b because the conclusion-goal, *Calvin buys a burger*, was the consequent of one of the premise conditionals. Similarly, backward Transitivity never tries to prove both IF P $THEN$ Q and IF Q $THEN$ R as subgoals to IF P $THEN$ R, but will attempt to prove one of them if the other is already an assertion. This *assertion sensitivity* means that LT will bother to apply a rule only when the assertions indicate that there is some reasonable chance of success; in a certain sense, the subgoals are ones that are already relevant to the assertions at a given stage of the proof.

Selective Forward and Hybrid Rules   This appraisal of LT's backward rules suggests that we might also incorporate selectivity in forward rules. We should be able to devise forward rules that are *conclusion sensitive* in a way that parallels the assertion sensitivity of the backward rules just discussed. For instance, it is easy to conceive of a forward version of AND Elimination that works as follows: Whenever P AND Q appears as an assertion, the rule checks to see whether the conclusion contains Q but not P AND Q (or P but not P AND Q). If it does, then AND Elimination is likely to be relevant to the proof of the conclusion, and the program should go ahead and apply it. If it does not, then AND Elimination is likely to be irrelevant, and the program should therefore try some other rule instead. The advantage of restricting forward AND Elimination in this way may be minimal; in fact, it could sometimes be disadvantageous. But on balance the benefits may outweigh the costs, and the benefits may be much higher for other rules—AND Introduction, for example. Selective forward rules of this type form the basis of a theory of human deduction proposed by Osherson (1974b, 1975, 1976), which we will examine in chapter 9.

It is also possible to combine forward and backward procedures in a single rule. Hybrid rules of this sort formed the core of the program that became the successor to LT: the General Problem Solver of Newell and

Simon (1972). As its name implies, GPS was a much more ambitious program than LT, since its inventors intended it not just as a theorem prover but as a model for human problem solving in many domains. Later in the book, we will look at GPS as an empirical theory of deductive reasoning, but it is useful to mention it here because of its connection with heuristic proofs. GPS's central idea was *means-ends analysis*—the notion that, in order to fulfill a goal, operators should be applied to reduce the difference between the current state of knowledge and the goal state. In the context of logic problems, this meant that GPS applied rules to assertions in order to produce further assertions that were syntactically closer to the conclusion or goal sentence. For instance, if the conclusion contained a connective that did not appear in the assertions, then GPS would seek to apply a rule that would produce a new assertion having the connective in question. Thus, GPS works forward if there is nothing to deter it. However, if such a rule did not quite apply to the current assertions, GPS would propose a subgoal of producing an intermediate assertion to which the rule in question would apply.

As an example, consider how GPS might prove argument (1) using a hybrid version of Modus ponens. The conclusion of (1), *Calvin buys a burger*, occurs as the consequent of the second premise, *IF Calvin gets a coke THEN Calvin buys a burger*; thus, in order to produce the conclusion, the program should attempt to eliminate the difference by getting rid of that premise's antecedent, *Calvin gets a coke*. Modus ponens is obviously relevant to such a task, but the rule does not directly apply to the second premise as stated. To carry out the rule, we need to have the antecedent as a separate assertion. This suggests that we should form the subgoal of proving the antecedent. But this sentence is itself the consequent of the first premise, *IF Calvin deposits 50 cents THEN Calvin gets a coke*, and hence we can derive the subgoal if we can eliminate the antecedent of *this* premise. Once again, Modus ponens is relevant to such a task, and this time there is no barrier to its application. The program can then generate the subgoal sentence, *Calvin gets a coke*, and use it to produce the conclusion. In comparing GPS to LT, Newell and Simon (1972, p. 428) speak of GPS as working forward, and in one sense this is true. In the absence of any obstacle to applying the rules, GPS produces one assertion after another until the goal is reached. But, as the Calvin example demonstrates, whenever the assertions fail to meet the rules' conditions, subgoals are created in much the same backward-oriented manner as in LT. Indeed, the order in which GPS considers the sentences in this example is the same as that of the pure backward proof in the lower panel of figure 3.1. We can therefore think of the GPS rules as hybrids—combinations of backward and forward search.

The point to be emphasized is that the sensitivity of the rules in LT and GPS to the assertions or to the conclusion simplifies proving by restricting the space within which the programs can look for a proof. But this selectivity comes at a high price—one that Newell et al. (1957) clearly identified: The restrictions on LT's or GPS's rules can keep the program from finding a proof for perfectly valid arguments. For example, it was impossible for LT to prove the valid sentence *P OR NOT NOT NOT P* from the axioms of the *Principia*. Proving this sentence would have required attempting as subgoals both premises of Modus ponens, something LT could not do without giving up its selectivity advantage. Thus, LT is not a complete proof procedure for classical sentential logic. It is in this sense that LT and GPS use "heuristic" methods; the rules forfeit the British Museum algorithm's guarantee of finding a proof for the chance of finding one within reasonable time bounds. It is natural to ask whether it is possible to have a procedure that takes no more time than LT but that ensures success for valid arguments.

Improved Algorithms for Proofs

In the 1950s—around the time of LT's birth—new techniques became available in logic (see, e.g., Beth 1955) that pointed the way to better proof algorithms. For sentential logic, LT's own domain, these techniques provided both a decision procedure and a proof procedure: For any argument at all, they could recognize whether or not the argument was valid and display a proof if it was. Moreover, these algorithms required only a small fraction of the effort that LT expended. The algorithms also generalized, in a natural way, to proof procedures for all of classical predicate logic (CPL). Two of these algorithms are of special importance for therorem proving, both based on a reductio or refutation of the conclusion to be proved. We will not pursue the details of these methods, since they lead away from psychologically plausible theories. But we need to look at them briefly in order to understand their relation to the approach we will take in part II.

Tree Proofs   As we have seen, LT's backward rules had to be restricted in order to work efficiently. That is because Modus ponens and Transitivity, when applied in the backward direction, can lead to ever-more-complex subgoals: If we want to derive a conclusion Q by Modus ponens, we can try to prove as subgoals P and *IF P THEN Q*; to prove the former we can attempt the sub-subgoals R and *IF R THEN P*; to prove the latter, we can attempt the subgoals S and *IF S THEN (IF P THEN Q)*; and so on. Exactly the same problem arises for LT's Transitivity rules. If we could get along without Modus ponens and Transitivity and rely instead on rules leading only to subgoals less complex than the original goal, then there would be no need to impose restrictions. That is, if each subgoal produces only finitely many sub-subgoals that are less complex than itself, then production of subgoals must eventually come to a halt. Gentzen (1935/1969) laid the theoretical groundwork for such an algorithm in the same paper in which he introduced the natural-deduction systems mentioned in chapter 2 above. Gentzen's main theorem (known in English as the Cut Elimination Theorem) showed that within certain related systems, the derivations could be built up from proof lines no more complex than the derivation's final line (see also Prawitz 1965 and Ungar 1992). Wang (1960) proposed some computer implementations of Gentzen's idea that yield fairly economical proofs for at least the sentential part of CPL. Both the original theorem and the algorithm, however, require basic changes in the format of the proofs themselves, making the proofs a kind of cross between axiomatic and natural-deduction techniques. We will look instead at a related technique, called the *tree* method, which produced proofs that are more similar to those we have seen. We will make use of this method in chapter 4, so it is worth examining carefully.

The tree method is based on a reductio ad absurdum strategy. We start with the premises of an argument and assume the negation of the argument's conclusion. By applying certain rules to these sentences, we can deduce simpler sentences from them—ultimately, atomic sentences (sentences with no connectives or quantifiers) or negations of atomic sentences. If the procedure shows the set of sentences to be contradictory, then the premises and negated conclusion cannot be true simultaneously. Since the premises are given, the negation of the conclusion must be false, and the conclusion itself must follow from the premises. Prawitz, Prawitz, and Voghera (1960) incorporated the tree method in a theorem-proving program. A simple exposition of the tree method can be found in Jeffrey 1967, a more advanced treatment in Smullyan 1968.

In the version of the tree system that we will look at, a proof begins with the premises and the negated conclusion in vertical list. Let us call a sentence a *literal* if it is either an atomic sentence or the negation of an atomic sentence. If some of the sentences in the initial list are not literals, we apply one of the rules in table 3.1 to the first of them. Which rule we apply is completely determined by the form of the sentence in question. For example, if the sentence is a conjunction, we apply rule 1; if a negated conjunction, rule 2; and so on. The sentences produced by the rule are written at the end of the list we are compiling. (When two sentences appear beneath the inference line in the table, as in rules 1, 4, and 6, both sentences are written at the end of the list.) We then advance to the next nonliteral sentence and apply the corresponding rule, continuing in this way until all the nonliterals (both the original sentences and the newly produced ones) have been processed.

Most of the rules in table 3.1 are variations of ones we have already encountered. The only rule that calls for comment is the one for disjunctions, rule 3. This tells us that if one of the sentences is a disjunction, *P OR Q*, we must split the vertical list we are construction into two branches, placing *P* at the beginning of one branch and *Q* at the beginning of the other. The "|" sign in the table represents this splitting. (Thus, the structure we are creating will generally be a tree structure rather than a

Table 3.1
Rules for tree proofs. (The sentence(s) below the inference line is (are) to be placed at the end of each branch in the tree. In rule 3, the "|" indicates that each branch must split in two, with P at the head of one branch and Q at the head of the other.)

Rule 1	**Rule 2**
P AND Q	NOT (P AND Q)
P	(NOT P) OR (NOT Q)
Q	**Rule 4**
Rule 3	NOT (P OR Q)
P OR Q	NOT P
P | Q	NOT Q
Rule 5	**Rule 6**
IF P THEN Q	NOT (IF P THEN Q)
(NOT P) OR Q	P
Rule 7	NOT Q
NOT NOT P	
P	

list.) If we then apply a rule to a sentence that occurs above a branch point, we must write the sentences that the rule produces at the end of each lower branch.

As an illustration, figure 3.2 shows a tree proof for argument(1). In the figure, the negation of the conclusion is written at the top, and then the three premises. Applying rule 5 to the first conditional produces *(NOT Calvin deposits 50 cents) OR Calvin gets a coke*, sentence 5 in the figure. Similarly, applying rule 5 to the second conditional premise produces sentence 6. Since these two new sentences are disjunctions, we must use rule 3 to divide the tree into branches. The first disjunction sprouts one branch headed by *NOT Calvin deposits 50 cents* and another headed by *Calvin gets a coke*. These two branches then split in turn when rule 3 is applied to the second disjunction.

A *path* in a tree is the set of all sentences that we encounter by starting at the top of the tree and following a route downward to one of the terminal sentences. For instance, if we take the left forks in the tree of figure 3.2, we obtain a path of sentences that consist of the six items along the "trunk" of the tree plus sentences 7 and 9. We can call a path *closed* if the path includes an atomic sentence and its negation; otherwise, the path is said to be *open*. Thus, the path just described is closed, because both *Calvin deposits 50 cents* and *NOT Calvin deposits 50 cents* occur in it. If all paths in a tree are closed, the entire tree is in a contradictory state, and the original argument is deducible. This is the case for the example tree, so (1) is deducible in the system. If any of the paths are open, then the argument is not deducible. There are some short-cuts that make the tree method somewhat simpler (see Prawitz et al. 1960), but we will ignore these simplifications here.

The most important property of this method for automatic theorem proving is that each step of the proof leads to successively shorter sentences. The rules in table 3.1 guarantee that we will eventually decompose all nonliteral sentences and that we can easily check the resulting literal sentences for contradictory pairs.

The tree method provides a simple algorithm for sentential logic that avoids the incompleteness of the heuristic approach of Newell et al. However, it has several clear drawbacks, both psychological and computational. On the psychological side, the new framework requires that all proofs assume a reductio form, which seems unintuitive for some arguments. As a computational method, the algorithm is problematic because

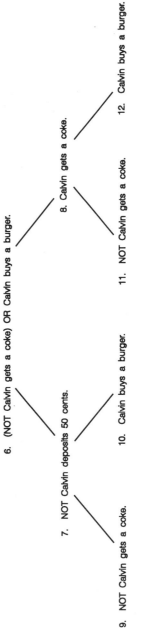

1. NOT Calvin buys a burger.

2. IF Calvin deposits 50 cents THEN Calvin gets a coke.

3. IF Calvin gets a coke THEN Calvin buys a burger.

4. Calvin deposits 50 cents.

5. (NOT Calvin deposits 50 cents) OR Calvin gets a coke.

6. (NOT Calvin gets a coke) OR Calvin buys a burger.

7. NOT Calvin deposits 50 cents.

8. Calvin gets a coke.

9. NOT Calvin gets a coke.

10. Calvin buys a burger.

11. NOT Calvin gets a coke.

12. Calvin buys a burger.

Figure 3.2
Proof of the argument

Calvin deposits 50 cents.
IF Calvin deposits 50 cents THEN Calvin gets a coke.
IF Calvin gets a coke THEN Calvin buys a burger.

Calvin buys a burger.

by means of the tree method.

it can bog down badly in proving arguments in the full CPL (see Prawitz 1960). In a CPL proof, universally quantified variables must be replaced by names. In general, the number of possible instantiations that must be produced in this way is an exponential function of the number of these variables, so the proofs rapidly become unwieldy.

The Resolution Technique Resolution theorem proving, first set out by J. A. Robinson (1965), is an attempt to overcome the multiple-instantiation problem that plagued Prawitz et al.'s (1960) algorithm and other early computational methods, such as that of Davis and Putnam (1960) and of Wang (1960). Robinson's paper was a watershed in automatic theorem proving, and much of the later progress in this field has come from refinements of the basic resolution method (see Wos and Henschen 1983 for a review). Unlike the tree method, resolution usually requires all sentences in the proof to have a special format called *clausal form.*

First, each sentence in the argument is transformed to an equivalent one in which all quantifiers appear at the beginning of the sentence, followed by a conjunction (possibly just a single conjunct). Each conjunct in this expression must itself be a disjunction (possibly just a single disjunct) of negated or unnegated atomic formulas. For example, the sentence *IF Calvin deposits 50 cents THEN Calvin gets a coke* is rewritten as a single conjunct containing the disjunction *(NOT Calvin deposits 50 cents) OR Calvin gets a coke.*

Second, all quantifiers are omitted, and existentially quantified variables are replaced by temporary names. For instance, the universally quantified sentence *All square blocks are green*, which we expressed earlier as (2a), is transformed to (2b).

(2) a. (FOR ALL x) (IF Square-block(x) THEN Green-block(x)).

  b. (NOT Square-block(x)) OR Green-block(x).

The x in (2b) retains its universal interpretation; (2b) asserts that any individual is either a nonsquare block or a green block. The existentially quantified sentence *Some big blocks are square* goes from (3a) to (3b), where a is a temporary name in the sense of the FOR SOME Elimination rule of table 2.5.

(3) a. (FOR SOME x) (Big-block(x) AND Square-block(x)).

  b. Big-block(a) AND Square-block(a).

If an existential quantifier follows one or more universal quantifiers, then the corresponding existential variable is replaced by a temporary name with subscripts for the variables of those universals. For example, the sentence *Every person has a father*, which we earlier wrote as (4a), becomes (4b).

(4)   a. (FOR ALL x) (FOR SOME y) (IF Person(x) THEN Father(y,x)).
      b. (NOT Person(x)) OR Father(a_x,x).

The subscript in (4b) reflects the fact that the identity of the father in question may depend on that of the person. (Person 1 may have father 1, whereas person 2 has father 2.)

After the quantifiers have been eliminated in this way, we are left with sentences of the form *(P_1 OR ... OR P_k) AND (Q_1 OR ... OR Q_m) AND ... AND (R_1 OR ... OR R_n)*. We can then delete the ANDs, treating the disjunctions as separate sentences called *clauses*. Genesereth and Nilsson (1987) specify an algorithm for transforming an arbitrary CPL sentence into clausal form.[3]

Once the sentences have been reexpressed, the method attempts to show that the argument is deducible through a reductio. It accepts the clausal forms of the premises as givens, adds the clausal form of the negation of the conclusion, and tries to derive a contradiction from these clauses. If it identifies such a contradiction, then the original argument must be deducible. Because of the uniform structure of the clauses, however, the method needs only a single inference rule to derive a contradiction if there is one. The rule applies to cases in which the proof contains one clause with disjunct *P* and a second with disjunct *NOT P*. That is, one clause must contain *P*, possibly with other disjuncts $Q_1, ..., Q_m$; the other must include *NOT P*, possibly with other disjuncts $R_1, ..., R_n$. In this case, the rule permits us to conclude that *Q_1 OR ... OR Q_m OR R_1 OR ... OR R_n*. In other words, we can combine the two original clauses, omitting the complementary pair *P* and *NOT P*. If repeated applications of this rule produce contradictory clauses (one clause containing *P* alone and another containing *NOT P* alone), then the reductio proof is complete and the original argument is deducible.

Figure 3.3 illustrates this method applied to the argument in (1). Sentences 1, 4, and 6 in this figure are the premises of the argument in clausal form, and sentence 2 is the negation of the conclusion. Applying the reso-

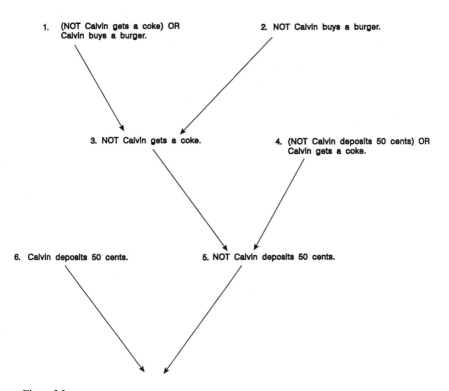

Figure 3.3
Proof of the argument

Calvin deposits 50 cents.
IF Calvin deposits 50 cents THEN Calvin gets a coke.
IF Calvin gets a coke THEN Calvin buys a burger.

Calvin buys a burger.

by the resolution method.

lution rule to sentences 1 and 2 yields sentence 3—*NOT Calvin gets a coke*—as an additional proof line. We can then use this sentence with sentence 4 in a second application of the resolution rule to get sentence 5, *NOT Calvin deposits 50 cents*. However, this last sentence contradicts one of the original premises (sentence 6), eliminating this remaining pair. The argument is therefore deducible according to this method.

The proof in figure 3.3, however, is no more impressive than some of the earlier proofs we have seen of the same argument, so the advantages of resolution must lie elsewhere. As already mentioned, resolution's crucial achievement comes in its way of dealing with quantified sentences: Instead of generating arbitrary instantiations and then checking to see if they have the properties needed to complete the proof (as in the algorithm of Prawitz et al.), the resolution technique only instantiates when this is useful in applying the resolution rule. To understand the advantage of resolution, we therefore need to consider an argument that depends on quantification. We can get a taste of the advantages by considering the argument from *Miranda is a person* and *Every person has a father* to the conclusion *There's someone who's Miranda's father*, illustrated in (5).

(5) Person(Miranda).
     (FOR ALL x) (FOR SOME y) (IF Person(x) THEN Father(y,x)).
     _____
     (FOR SOME z) Father(z,Miranda)

As we saw a moment ago, the clausal form of the second premise is (4b), and the negation of the conclusion reduces to *NOT Father(z,Miranda)*. From these clauses we then get the resolution proof (6).

(6) a. (NOT Person(x)) OR Father(a_x,x)   Premise

     b. Person(Miranda)   Premise

     c. (NOT Person(Miranda)) OR
        Father($a_{Miranda}$,Miranda)   Instantiation of line a
                                                       (substituting *Miranda* for *x*)

     d. Father($a_{Miranda}$,Miranda)   Resolution rule
                                                       (from lines b and c)

     e. NOT Father(z,Miranda)   From negation of
                                                       conclusion

     f. NOT Father($a_{Miranda}$,Miranda)   Instantiation of line e
                                                       (substituting $a_{Miranda}$ for *z*)

Lines d and f of (6) are directly contradictory, so argument (5) must be correct. The important point is that the instantiations in lines c and f of (6) match (*unify*) an atomic formula from one clause with its negation in another. The attempt to set up the resolution rule guides the instantiation and thus leads directly to the contradiction.

The resolution technique clearly improves the efficiency of proofs with quantifiers, but it also takes a large step away from cognitive concerns. Indeed, Robinson (1965, pp. 23–24) was quite clear on this split:

Traditionally, a single step in a deduction has been required, for pragmatic and psychological reasons, to be simple enough, broadly speaking, to be apprehended as correct by a human being in a single intellectual act. No doubt this custom originates in the desire that each single step of a deduction should be indubitable, even though the deduction as a whole may consist of a long chain of such steps.... Part of the point, then, of the logical analysis of deductive reasoning has been to reduce complex inferences, which are beyond the capacity of the human mind to grasp as single steps, to chains of simpler inferences, each of which is within the capacity of the human mind to grasp as a single transaction.... [But] when the agent carrying out the application of an inference principle is a modern computing machine, the traditional limitation on the complexity of the inference principles is no longer very appropriate.

The resolution rule is a principle of the latter (machine-oriented) sort, since "it condones single inferences that are often beyond the ability of a human to grasp (other than discursively)" (ibid., p. 24).

Non-Resolution Methods and Revisions to the Natural-Deduction Rules

In the opinion of some researchers, the psychological inscrutability of resolution was a hindrance even for computer-based theorem proving (Bledsoe 1977). To be useful in substantive areas of mathematics, theorem-proving programs must have access to a large set of definitions, theorems, and heuristics. But incorporating this knowledge is often easier in systems based on natural deduction than in systems based on resolution techniques, partly because this knowledge was originally produced for human consumption. Similarly, theorem-proving programs are often most profitable when they are able to interact with mathematicians, who can supply crucial bits of guidance when the program gets stuck. But this means that the mathematician must have some idea of the strategy the program is using, and natural deduction has an obvious advantage in conveying these strategies. For these reasons, Bledsoe and Bruell (1974), Nevins (1974), and others tried to adapt natural-deduction methods to automatic theorem proving. In this section we will consider some ways to recast the rules in chapter 2 above to more computationally efficient forms.

Sentential Rules

First, let us consider some possible revisions to the sentential rules of table 2.3. One thing to notice about these rules is that they divide into two classes, which we might call *self-constraining* and *self-promoting* types (see Rips 1983). Self-constraining rules are limited in the number of new sentences they can produce from a given set of assertions; by contrast, self-promoting rules can produce a potentially infinite number of sentences from the same assertion set. Modus ponens is an example of the self-constraining type, since this rule can produce only as many new assertions as there are conditional sentences. AND Introduction is an example of the self-promoting type, since it will produce any number of new conjunctions from a single assertion. An important step in taming the natural-deduction rules comes from using a rule's self-constraining or self-promoting status as a guide to whether we should apply the rule in a forward or in a backward direction.

Self-Constraining Rules   The limitation on self-constraining rules makes it possible to use them in the forward direction. As we have already seen, from premises of the form *IF P THEN Q* and *P*, Modus ponens can produce only a single new sentence *Q*; applying the rule repeatedly to the same premises will produce only new copies of the same sentence. Hence, if we can prevent the system from deriving duplicate assertions, the rule will never lead to endless looping in the proof. The forward IF Elimination (modus ponens) rule in table 3.2 illustrates this approach. The rule closely resembles its counterpart in table 2.3 but includes an extra condition. Whenever both *IF P THEN Q* and *P* are assertions, the rule checks to see whether *Q* is also an assertion in the relevant proof domain. If it finds that *Q* has not yet been produced, then it will go ahead and deduce it; however, if *Q* is already an assertion, IF Elimination will no longer apply. Clearly, the new restriction will keep the rule from producing redundant *Q*'s.

Several additional facts about this modification are also worth noticing. One is that the new condition doesn't prohibit the system from deriving assertions that it could prove without it. This is a consequence of the fact

Table 3.2
Revised inference rules for sentential logic.

Forward IF Elimination (modus ponens)
    (a) If sentences of the form IF P THEN Q and P hold in some domain D,
    (b)   and Q does not yet hold in D,
    (c) then add Q to D.
    (d) Else, return failure.

Backward IF Introduction (Conditionalization)
    (a) Set D to domain of current goal.
    (b) If current goal is not of the form IF P THEN Q,
    (c) then return failure.
    (d) Set up a subdomain of D, D′, with supposition P.
    (e) Add the subgoal of proving Q in D′ to the list of subgoals.

Backward NOT Elimination
    (a) Set P to current goal and D to its domain.
    (b) Set up a subdomain of D, D′, with supposition NOT P.
    (c) Add the subgoal of proving Q in D′ to the list of subgoals.
    (d) If the subgoal in (c) fails,
    (e) then return failure.
    (f) Add the subgoal of proving NOT Q in D′ to the list of subgoals.

Backward NOT Introduction
    (a) Set D to domain of current goal.
    (b) If current goal is not of the form NOT P,
    (c) then return failure.
    (d) Set up a subdomain of D, D′, with supposition P.
    (e) Add the subgoal of proving Q in D′ to the list of subgoals.
    (f) If the subgoal in (e) fails,
    (g) then return failure.
    (h) Add the subgoal of proving NOT Q in D′ to the list of subgoals.

Forward Double Negation Elimination
    (a) If a sentence of the form NOT NOT P holds in some domain D,
    (b)   and P does not yet hold in D,
    (c) then add sentence P to domain D.
    (d) Else, return failure.

Forward AND Elimination
    (a) If a sentence of the form P AND Q holds in some domain D,
    (b) then: If P does not yet hold in D,
    (c)   then add sentence P to D.
    (d)   If Q does not yet hold in D,
    (e)   then add sentence Q to D.
    (f) Else, return failure.

Backward AND Introduction
    (a) Set D to domain of current goal.
    (b) If current goal is not of the form P AND Q,
    (c) then return failure.
    (d) Add the subgoal of proving P in D to the list of subgoals.
    (e) If the subgoal in (d) fails,
    (f) then return failure.
    (g) Add the subgoal of proving Q in D to the list of subgoals.

Table 3.2 (continued)

Backward OR Elimination
   (a) Set P to current goal and D to its domain.
   (b) If a sentence of the form R OR S does not hold in D,
   (c) then return failure.
   (d) Else, set up a subdomain of D, D', with supposition R.
   (e) Add the subgoal of proving P in D' to the list of subgoals.
   (f) If the subgoal in (e) fails,
   (g) then return failure.
   (h) Else, set up a subdomain of D, D'', with supposition S.
   (i) Add the subgoal of proving P in D'' to the list of subgoals.

Backward OR Introduction
   (a) Set D to domain of current goal.
   (b) If current goal is not of the form P OR Q,
   (c) then return failure.
   (d) Add the subgoal of proving P in D to the list of subgoals.
   (e) If the subgoal in (d) fails,
   (f) then add the subgoal of proving Q in D to the list of subgoals.

that once IF Elimination has applied to a conditional, applying it again will produce no new information. Second, IF Elimination as a forward rule is psychologically natural. As soon as you recognize a conditional and its antecedent as true, it is hard to keep from considering the truth of its consequent (at least temporarily), no matter what goal you are working on at the time.[4] Third, having a forward rule like this doesn't preclude having a backward version too. In the context of certain proof systems, it is sensible to include a rule like the backward Modus ponens of Newell et al. (1957) in addition to the forward version just described. There may be situations, for instance, where the system needs to prove Q, has *IF P THEN Q* as an assertion, but does not yet have P. In this case, it may be necessary to propose P as a subgoal in order to finish the proof. Two examples of this sort appear later in this chapter—see argument (9) and the itinerary planner.

Other obviously self-constraining rules include Double Negation Elimination and AND Elimination. Table 3.2 sets out forward versions of these rules that are similar to Forward IF Elimination; in each case, the system can hold the rules in check by making sure that there are no repeated assertions. In certain situations backward versions of these rules can also be helpful, but there is an additional difficulty in running them in this direction. For example, a backward Double Negation rule would presumably be triggered by a conclusion P and would result in a subgoal to prove *NOT NOT P*. Assuming that this subgoal was not readily provable by other means, the same backward rule would apply, yielding *NOT NOT NOT P* and so on. Thus, we risk a cascade of subgoals in a backward direction that is analogous to the cascade of assertions in the forward direction from self-promoting rules. It is possible to avoid this problem by making backward rules for Double Negation Elimination and AND Elimination more selective, although this hasn't been done in table 3.2. (We will encounter such a formulation in the next chapter.) In general, the preferred direction for self-constraining rules is forward.

Self-Promoting Rules Whereas it is possible to control self-constraining rules by simply monitoring for duplicate assertions, self-promoting rules call for more complex solutions and (usually) backward rather than forward application. In the case of AND Introduction it would not help to check for duplicate sentence tokens, because the rule can create new sentence *types* each time it applies. That is, once *P* and *Q* have been used to produce *P AND Q*, we can prevent new copies of *P AND Q*; but we can't prevent new sentences such as *(P AND Q) AND Q, ((P AND Q) AND Q) AND Q, (((P AND Q) AND Q) AND Q) AND Q*, which the rule readily generates. Moreover, arbitrarily terminating such a sequence would keep the program from forming conjunctions that it might need in certain proofs. It thus appears that the only way to keep AND Introduction from overgenerating is to make it a backward rule or a selective forward rule of the sort we considered in connection with LT and GPS.

Table 3.2 shows how AND Introduction might look as a backward rule. In this setting, AND Introduction applies to conclusions (or subgoals) of the form *P AND Q* and then generates the separate (sub-)subgoals *P* and *Q*. Using AND Introduction in a backward direction would itself keep the rule from producing hosts of irrelevant conjunctions, since the only conjunctions it tries to prove would be needed in the proof. Furthermore, if the program first tries to fulfill subgoal *P* and fails in the attempt, there is no longer any hope of proving *P AND Q* in this manner; it can therefore skip subgoal *Q*, thus avoiding some wasted effort. If subgoal *P* is fulfilled, then the rule succeeds if it can also fulfill subgoal *Q*. The rule seems psychologically natural, in that it retains the idea that proving *P AND Q* amounts to proving both *P* and *Q* separately, avoids specialized formats, and eliminates irrelevant assertions. The table also gives a similar backward rule for OR Introduction.

Rules that involve subdomains   Of the rules in table 2.3, clear examples of
self-constraining rules are AND, IF, and Double Negation Elimination,
and equally clear examples of self-promoting rules are AND Introduction and OR Introduction. Symmetry would suggest that IF Introduction
and NOT Introduction should be self-promoting, along with the rest of
the Introduction rules, and that NOT Elimination and OR Elimination
should be self-constraining, along with the other elimination rules. This
intuition is right in the cases of IF Introduction and NOT Introduction.
Allowing these rules to operate in the forward direction will produce runaway proofs, which are typical of other self-promoting rules. For example,
(7) shows how to derive the sentences *IF P THEN P, IF P THEN (IF P
THEN P), IF P THEN (IF P THEN (IF P THEN P))*, and so on, by
means of a forward IF Introduction rule.

(7)   a.   + Linda is a bank teller   Supposition
      b. IF Linda is a bank teller THEN Linda is a
          bank teller   IF Intro.
      c.   + Linda is a bank teller   Supposition
      d. IF Linda is a bank teller THEN (IF Linda
          is a bank teller THEN Linda is a bank teller).   IF Intro.
      e.   + Linda is a bank teller.   Supposition
      f. IF Linda is a bank teller THEN (IF Linda is
          a bank teller THEN (IF Linda is a bank teller
          THEN Linda is a bank teller))   IF Intro.
          ....

Since the supposition in (7a) holds trivially in the subdomain that it defines, IF Introduction allows us to derive (7b) in the superdomain. Sentence (7b), in turn, holds in the subdomain created in (7c), yielding (7d) in
the superdomain, and so forth. A very similar proof will generate *NOT
NOT P, NOT NOT NOT NOT P, NOT NOT NOT NOT NOT NOT P,*
... from an arbitrary sentence *P* on the basis of a forward NOT Introduction rule. It seems correct, then, to handle IF Introduction and NOT
Introduction in the same way as the other self-promoting rules, using
them in the backward direction to fulfill conditional or negative goals.
Table 3.2 gives one formulation of these rules.
    This leaves NOT Elimination and OR Elimination. The first of these is
the rule that yields *P* from a contradiction derived from the supposition

NOT P. It might seem that this rule would be free from the problem of infinite assertions, since the output of this rule must be simpler than the supposition from which it is derived. But unless there are restrictions on the form of the suppositions, it is still possible to suppose sentences of any length and thereby obtain conclusions of any length. Proof (8) illustrates this difficulty.

(8) a. Linda is a bank teller.   Premise

  b.   + NOT NOT NOT Linda is a bank teller.   Supposition

  c.   NOT Linda is a bank teller.   Double Neg. Elim.

  d. NOT NOT Linda is a bank teller.   NOT Elim.

  e.   + NOT NOT NOT NOT NOT Linda is
         a bank teller.   Supposition

  f.   NOT NOT NOT Linda is a bank teller.   Double Neg. Elim.

  g. NOT NOT NOT NOT Linda is a bank
       teller.   NOT Elim.

       . . . .

The obvious way around this problem is to treat NOT Elimination as a backward rule on a par with NOT Introduction and IF Introduction, and this is the way it appears in table 3.2. Much the same considerations show that OR Elimination is also best applied as a backward rule.

   Although the rules in table 3.2 are clearly sound (i.e., will not lead from true premises to false conclusions), they will not quite do as they stand. For one thing, there are obviously valid arguments that they cannot prove. For example, there is no way in the present system to derive the conclusion of the simple argument (9).

(9)   IF Calvin is hungry AND Calvin deposits 50 cents THEN Calvin
         gets a coke.
      Calvin is hungry.
      Calvin deposits 50 cents.
      _____
      Calvin gets a coke.

AND Introduction and IF Elimination should be enough to prove (9), but the new directionality that we have imposed on these rules keeps them from cooperating in the right way. Apparently, we will have to introduce further rules if we want the system to handle all the deductive inferences that people can grasp. Furthermore, some of the rules are still too un-constrained as they stand. The Backward NOT Elimination rule, for ex-ample, is applicable to any subgoal P and directs us to try to prove any pair of contradictory sentences Q and $NOT\ Q$. But unless we have some idea of which contradictory sentences might be derived from $NOT\ P$, this is surely not a strategy that we want to employ. Thus, although table 3.2 takes us part of the way toward a more tractable natural deduction, we still face residual problems of incompleteness and inefficiency. We will cope with these in part II.

Quantifiers

Natural deduction rules for quantifiers are often cumbersome, since they ordinarily demand that we apply FOR ALL Elimination and FOR SOME Elimination at the beginning of the proof to remove the quantifiers and then apply FOR ALL Introduction and FOR SOME Introduction to replace them at the end. Derivation (16) of chapter 2 provides an example of this style. Although it is possible that some set of quantifier rules of this sort will turn out to be feasible, it is worth considering other ways of handling inferences with quantifiers. Computer-based techniques offer some suggestions along these lines, since these methods generally repre-sent quantifiers implicitly and dispense with rules for transforming them. Of course, these techniques have costs of their own; to a certain extent, they shift the burden of the quantifier rules to the process that obtains the initial representation. Nevertheless, they have the advantage of removing all the quantifiers in a single blow, including quantifiers that are deeply embedded within a premise. We have already glimpsed one method of this sort in regard to resolution proofs; however, those proofs also insist on straitjacketing other aspects of an argument's syntax. What would be desirable is a quantifier-free representation that has the expressive power of the usual CPL sentences and that stays reasonably close to surface structure.

One representation that seems to meet these requirements was proposed by Skolem (1928/1967), and it is similar to that employed in theorem-proving systems by Wang (1960), by Bledsoe, Boyer, and Henneman (1972), and by Murray (1982). It follows clausal form in eliminating quantifiers, but it doesn't insist on reducing a sentence to conjunctions of disjunctions. This format will be previewed here, since it will play an important role in later chapters.

Consider a given sentence of CPL. The sentence can contain any mix of the usual quantifiers and connectives, except for biconditionals, which must be eliminated in favor of other connectives. (For example, *P IF AND ONLY IF Q* can be rewritten as *(IF P THEN Q) AND (IF Q THEN P)*.) This restriction seems palatable, since it is possible to argue that people ordinarily understand biconditional relationships as a combination of one-way conditionals. We can transform any such sentence into a logically equivalent one in *prenex form*—that is, with all the quantifiers appearing at the beginning. To do this, we successively move the quantifiers to positions of wider scope, using the entailments in (10)–(13). (In the a and c sentences here, x must not appear in Q; in the b and d sentences, x must not appear in P.)

(10) a. ((FOR SOME x)P AND Q) $\Rightarrow$ (FOR SOME x) (P AND Q)
     b. (P AND (FOR SOME x)Q) $\Rightarrow$ (FOR SOME x) (P AND Q)
     c. ((FOR ALL x)P AND Q) $\Rightarrow$ (FOR ALL x) (P AND Q)
     d. (P AND (FOR ALL x)Q) $\Rightarrow$ (FOR ALL x) (P AND Q)

(11) a. ((FOR SOME x)P OR Q) $\Rightarrow$ (FOR SOME x) (P OR Q)
     b. (P OR (FOR SOME x)Q) $\Rightarrow$ (FOR SOME x) (P OR Q)
     c. ((FOR ALL x)P OR Q) $\Rightarrow$ (FOR ALL x) (P OR Q)
     d. (P OR (FOR ALL x)Q) $\Rightarrow$ (FOR ALL x) (P OR Q)

(12) a. IF (FOR SOME x)P THEN Q $\Rightarrow$ (FOR ALL x) (IF P THEN Q)
     b. IF P THEN (FOR SOME x)Q $\Rightarrow$ (FOR SOME x) (IF P THEN Q)
     c. IF (FOR ALL x)P THEN Q $\Rightarrow$ (FOR SOME x) (IF P THEN Q)
     d. IF P THEN (FOR ALL x)Q $\Rightarrow$ (FOR ALL x) (IF P THEN Q)

(13) a. NOT((FOR SOME x)P) $\Rightarrow$ (FOR ALL x) (NOT P)
     b. NOT((FOR ALL x)P) $\Rightarrow$ (FOR SOME x) (NOT P)

To illustrate this transformation, take a complex sentence such as (14a).

(14) a. (FOR ALL x) (IF (FOR ALL y) (P(x,y)) THEN NOT (FOR SOME z) (R(x,z) AND Q(z))).

     b. (FOR ALL x) (IF (FOR ALL y) (P(x,y)) THEN (FOR ALL z) (NOT (R(x,z) AND Q(z)))).

     c. (FOR ALL x) (FOR SOME y) (IF P(x,y) THEN (FOR ALL z) (NOT (R(x,z) AND Q(z)))).

     d. (FOR ALL x) (FOR SOME y) (FOR ALL z) (IF P(x,y) THEN NOT (R(x,z) AND Q(z))).

According to (13a), we can move the existential quantifier *(FOR SOME z)* outside the scope of the negation, switching to a universal quantifier in the process. This produces the sentence in (14b). Similarly, we can move *(FOR ALL y)* outside the conditional, using (12c). This again requires a change in quantifiers, and it yields (14c). Finally, we extract *(FOR ALL z)* by means of (12d) to get the prenex form in (14d). In general, there will be more than one choice as to which quantifier to move next. For example, we could have started by moving *(FOR ALL y)* rather than *(FOR SOME z)* in (14a). This means that prenex form for a sentence is not unique. It usually makes sense, however, to prefer a prenex form in which existential quantifiers are as far to the left as possible. For a proof that any sentence of CPL can be transformed into an equivalent in prenex form, see page 87 of Mendelson 1964.

Given the transformations in (10)–(13), we can easily derive the quantifier-free form of a CPL sentence. We first make sure that each quantifier within the sentence is associated with a unique variable. For example, *(FOR ALL x) (F(x)) AND (FOR SOME x) (G(x))*, which is acceptable in CPL, will be replaced by the equivalent sentence *(FOR ALL x) (F(x)) AND (FOR SOME y) (G(y))*. Second, we determine the prenex form, following the rules above. We then delete each existential quantifier and replace the variable it binds with a new temporary name, subscripting the name with the variables of all universal quantifiers within whose scope it appears. As the last step, all universal quantifiers are deleted. In the case of (14d), we find that the only existential quantifier in the prenex form is *(FOR SOME y)*. We must therefore replace y with a temporary name (say, a); but because *(FOR SOME y)* appears within the scope of the universal *(FOR ALL x)*, the temporary name will have x as a subscript. The remaining quantifiers are universal and can be dropped, producing the final quantifier-free form shown in (15).

(15)   IF $P(x, a_x)$ THEN NOT $(R(x,z)$ AND $Q(z))$.

Temporary names in this context are sometimes called *Skolem constants* (if unsubscripted) or *Skolem functions* (if subscripted). The form itself goes under the name *Skolem function form* (Grandy 1977) or *functional normal form* (Quine 1972). We will refer to it here simply as *quantifier-free form*. As further examples, (16)–(19) repeat some of the sentences with quantifiers from earlier parts of this chapter, along with their quantifier-free forms:

(16) a. [=(2a)] (FOR ALL x) (IF Square-block(x) THEN
          Green-block(x)).

      b. IF Square-block(x) THEN Green-block(x).

(17) a. [=(3a)] (FOR SOME x) (Big-block(x) AND Square-block(x)).

      b. Big-block(a) AND Square-block(a).

(18) a. [=(4a)] (FOR ALL x) (FOR SOME y) (IF Person(x) THEN
          Father(y,x)).

      b. IF Person(x) THEN Father(a_x,x).

(19) a. [=conclusion of (5)] (FOR SOME z) Father(z,Miranda).

      b. Father(a,Miranda).

Although the rule for going from CPL sentences to quantifier-free sentences is somewhat complex, the new sentences are not difficult to interpret; they may even have some advantages over CPL syntax in this respect. Variables continue to have universal meaning, as they did in clausal form. Temporary names stand for particular individuals, with the identity of these individuals depending on the values of any variables that subscript them. (Details of the semantics for quantifier-free form are developed in chapter 6.) For example, we can paraphrase (18b) as follows: Given any person x, there is a particular a who is the father of x. The dependencies among the quantifiers is more clearly displayed here than it is in CPL. In fact, the role of variables and temporary names in quantifier-free form is much like that of variables and symbolic constants in ordinary algebra. Algebraic equations, such as $y = 3x + k$, don't display their quantifiers explicitly; rather, they rely on conventions similar to ours to enable us to understand that (e.g.) there is a value of k such that, for any x, $3x + k = y$. Our quantifier-free sentences also present some benefits over clausal form. Whereas (17b) and (19b) are the same as their clausal representations, we have been able to hold onto the conditionals in going from (16a) to (16b) and from (18a) to (18b), instead of having to transform them to disjunctions as we must for their clausal counterparts.

A further possible advantage to quantifier-free form is that it allows us to express relationships that are impossible to represent in standard CPL. As an example (from Barwise 1979), consider the sentence *The richer the country, the more powerful one of its officials.* This seems to mean that there is some mapping from each country to an official of that country such that, if country x is richer than country y, then the indicated official of x is more powerful than the official of y. We can express this reading as *IF (Country(x) AND Country(y) AND Richer-than(x,y)) THEN (Official(b_x) AND Official(b_y) AND More-powerful-than(b_x,b_y))*, where b is the appropriate function. What makes this impossible to express in CPL is the fact that the individual selected for the first argument of *More-powerful-than(b_x,b_y)* depends only on x, whereas the individual selected for the second argument depends only on y. The closest we can come in CPL is a sentence like *(FOR ALL x) (FOR SOME u) (FOR ALL y) (FOR SOME v) (IF (Country(x) AND Country(y) AND Richer-than(x,y)) THEN (Official(u) AND Official(v) AND More-powerful-than(u,v)))*. But in this last sentence, *(FOR SOME v)* is within the scope of both *(FOR ALL x)* and *(FOR ALL y)* and so depends on the choices of both x and y. Moreover, any other plausible rearrangement of quantifiers leaves either u or v within the scope of both universal quantifiers. Intuitively, then, these CPL sentences can't be equivalent to the English original or to its rendering in quantifier-free form. (See Barwise 1979, Hintikka 1974, and Quine 1969 for discussions of such sentences.) This advantage of our quantifier-free notation is qualified, however, by the fact that NOT and similar operators do not apply freely to sentences such as our example (see chapter 6).

In part II we will make use of quantifier-free form to simplify a theory of mental theorem proving. That is, we will assume that people represent quantified sentences, at least for purposes of deduction, in this way. It will not be necessary to suppose, however, that in comprehending such sentences people translate natural language into standard CPL syntax and then translate again into quantifier-free form. There may well be a more direct route to the quantifier-free representation. Certainly, people could not understand the example sentence of the last paragraph in the intended way by translating via the indirect path. Still, the translation rules in (10)–(13) are handy because CPL notation is more familiar than quantifier-free form to many researchers, and the rules facilitate getting back and forth between them.

Solving Problems by Proving Theorems

The advances in automated deduction that were made in the 1960s and the 1970s suggested that theorem provers might be tools for more than just finding derivations in logic or mathematics. Consider, for example, the problem of designing a system to answer questions about some empirical domain, such as geographical, taxonomic, or genealogical relationships. We would like the system to be able to answer as wide a range of questions about the domain as possible when given some stock of information. Although we might try to pre-store in the system's memory answers to all questions that might arise, in most realistic situations there are far too many possibilities for this to be a practical alternative. Instead, we might store a basic set of relationships from the domain and have the system deduce others from the basic ones if it needs them in answering a query. Other intellectual tasks, such as planning and (some kinds of) game playing, have the same cognitive texture. A planner or a game player can't store in advance its responses to all contingencies that might develop. It has to remember some domain information, of course; but it must usually generate specific strategies as contingencies arise. Deduction might be an effective way of carrying out this generation step. Let us look at a few examples here, reserving more complicated instances of problem solving in a cognitive framework for chapter 8.

Sample Uses of Deduction

As a simple example of answering questions by deduction, suppose we have these geographical facts: $In(Benghazi,Libya)$, $In(Harare,Zimbabwe)$, $In(Khartoum,Sudan)$ and also $In(Libya,Africa)$, $In(Zimbabwe,Africa)$, and $In(Sudan,Africa)$. We could, of course, also store relationships like $In(Benghazi,Africa)$, but this will be unnecessarily wasteful of memory space if the number of African cities we know is relatively large. A better approach is to derive facts like the last one from our general knowledge of the transitivity of In, which we can express by $IF\ In(x,y)\ AND\ In(y,z)$ $THEN\ In(x,z)$. That is, if we are asked whether Benghazi is in Africa, we can prove that the answer is "yes" by deducing $In(Benghazi,Africa)$ from $In(Benghazi,Libya)$, $In(Libya,Africa)$, and the above conditional. In general, the answer should be "yes" if there is a proof of the conclusion, "no" if there is a proof of the negation of the conclusion, and "maybe" if neither can be proved. We can also answer Wh-questions, such as *What city is in Sudan?*, by a similar deduction procedure. In this case, we convert the question into a potential conclusion of the form $In(a,Sudan)$ and try to prove it on the basis of the remembered information. A rule analogous to FOR SOME Introduction (table 2.5) will allow us to derive $In(a,Sudan)$

from *In(Khartoum,Sudan)*; thus, by keeping track of which permanent name matched *a* in the proof, we can answer "Khartoum."

Deduction can also be used for simple planning if we express general constraints on plans through sentences with universal variables. For instance, imagine that we are planning an itinerary for a trip. We might have specific information about transportation from one city to a neighboring one (gleaned from railroad timetables, say), but no overall plan for the tour route. We can represent the domain-specific information as a series of statements asserting that there are transportation links between particular cities: *Link(Bloomington, Champaign)*, *Link(Champaign, Decatur)*, *Link(Decatur, Springfield)*, and so on. To plan the route, we also need to represent the fact that a successful route is one that links the origin and destination cities in a chain. This we can do by means of two conditionals, as in (20).

(20) a. IF Link(x,y) THEN Route(x,y)
      b. IF Link(x,u) AND Route(u,y) THEN Route(x,y)

The first conditional asserts that there is a route between two cities if they are connected by a single link, and the second states that there is a route between two cities if there is a link from the origin to an intermediate city and a route from there to the destination. (Of course, there may be other constraints on a desirable route, such as bounds on total distance and time, but these are all we need for the purposes of the example.) We can thus derive a plan, by asking our system to prove that there is a route from the origin to the destination. If we wanted to plan a route from Bloomington to Springfield, we would propose the conclusion *Route(Bloomington, Springfield)* and trace the derivation from the sentences in memory. A theorem prover might attempt to prove such a conclusion by a backward Modus ponens strategy. It would first try to prove that *Link(Bloomington, Springfield)*, since (20a) guarantees a route between two locations if there is a single link between them. Failing this, the theorem prover would try to establish *Link(Bloomington,a) AND Route(a,Springfield)* on the basis of (20b). The facts listed earlier would permit the first of these subgoals to be fulfilled by *Link(Bloomington, Champaign)*, and the system would then attempt to prove *Route(Champaign, Springfield)*. By applying the same strategy recursively to this *Route* subgoal and later ones, the system would eventually complete the proof by working backward, link by link. Reading off the intermediate cities from the proof would then give us the itinerary we sought.

Methods in Deductive Problem Solving

The idea that theorem proving could be used for planning and other problem-solving situations seems to have begun with McCarthy (1968) and has been elaborated by Kowalski (1979) and others. AI researchers who have explored these possibilities have followed one of two approaches, which line up with our earlier distinction between resolution and natural-deduction methods. The central dilemma on both approaches is that solving a problem means proving a conclusion from premises that are not usually fixed in advance. In the context of question-answering, the question corresponds to the conclusion that the system must try to prove, but the user of the system does not generally specify the premises. Any memory sentence is a potential premise; but unless the amount of stored information is small, most of this information will be irrelevant and searching through it will drastically slow the proof. One approach to this difficulty is to employ resolution methods and related strategies to speed the proof process. Another uses natural-deduction rules, but surrounds these rules with control strategies to make them more practical.

The resolution approach is illustrated by Green's (1969, 1969/1980) QA3, one of the early deduction problem solvers. This program divided sentences into two sets: a Memory set, which contained all the information in the system's database, and a Clauselist, which contained only the sentences currently participating in the resolution proof. Initially, the Clauselist included just the clausal form of the negation of the conclusion. The program then transferred sentences from Memory to the Clauselist according to resolution-based heuristics. For example, it included only Memory sentences that resolved with items already on the Clauselist, giving priority to resolutions in which one of the input sentences was atomic or was the negation of an atomic sentence. QA3 also placed bounds on the number of intermediate steps; that is, it deduced only sentences that could be obtained in fewer than a fixed number k of applications of the resolution rule. If the procedure exceeded these bounds without finding a proof, the program switched from the attempt to prove the conclusion true to an attempt to prove it false. If the second attempt also exceeded the bounds, QA3 noted that no proof had been found and gave the user the option of increasing the bounds on intermediate steps.

The second approach originated at about the same time and is exemplified by Hewitt's (1969) PLANNER. The distinctive feature of this program (or programming language) is that, instead of encoding general relations as sentences, PLANNER encoded them as procedures. In our earlier example, we expressed the transitivity of *In* as a universal sentence—*IF In(x,y) AND In(y,z) THEN In(x,z)*—and let the inference procedures decide how this fact would be used during the course of a proof. But it is also possible to specify the use of the relation directly. For instance, we could write a procedure that asserted *In(x,z)* whenever two statements of the form *In(x,y)* and *In(y,z)* appeared in the database. Or we could write a routine that produced the subgoals of proving *In(x,y)* and *In(y,z)* whenever *In(x,z)* was a goal. Essentially, the first procedure (called an "antecedent theorem" in PLANNER) has the effect of forward Modus ponens applied to the above conditional, whereas the second (a "consequent theorem") has the effect of backward Modus ponens. By expressing the transitivity relation in one of these two ways, we control how the theorem prover will use this information during a proof, rather than leaving it up to the inference rules. PLANNER also provided a facility for recommending which procedures the program should try first in proving a given goal or subgoal, thereby focusing the search for a proof.

These two approaches to solving problems by deduction have spawned separate research traditions. The resolution approach has been incorporated in the STRIPS program (Fikes and Nilsson 1971) for robot manipulation and in PROLOG, a general-purpose AI language (Clocksin and Mellish 1981). PLANNER was adopted as part of Winograd's (1972) language understander SHRDLU, and can be seen as the ancestor of CONNIVER (Sussman and McDermott 1972) and later truth-maintenance systems (de Kleer 1986; Doyle 1979; Forbus and de Kleer 1993; McAllester 1978). It is common to view these two approaches as taking opposite stands on the issue of whether general relations, such as the transitivity of *In*, should be represented as sentences ("declaratively," as in QA3) or as routines ("procedurally," as in PLANNER)—see Winograd 1975. This, in turn, is probably a reflection of the fact that natural-deduction systems must have more elaborate control processes than resolution systems. The proposal developed in the following chapters takes an intermediate position on this question, since it represents generalities in a declarative way but retains natural-deduction methods.

For present purposes, the differences between the QA3 and PLANNER traditions are of less interest than their shared belief in deduction as a central part of question answering, planning, and other forms of symbolic computation. These programs achieved some notable successes, but they also met with criticism from other AI researchers. Marvin Minsky, in an appendix to his influential paper on frames (1975/1985), takes the deduction approach to task on several grounds. Minsky's most forceful comments concern the alleged inflexibility of this approach in everyday reasoning and decision-making. We will return to these arguments in detail in chapter 8, where we will consider recent "nonmonotonic" reasoning systems that are intended to address them. It is possible, however, to view many of the difficulties that Minsky raised as boiling down to the idea that purely deductive systems can't account for ordinary nondeductive inference and decision making (e.g., deciding on the best time to cross a busy intersection); thus, an approach to AI based solely on deduction, with no means for nondeductive inference, will be too restrictive (see also McDermott 1987). This point is undoubtedly correct; however, for the reasons mentioned at the end of chapter 2, it doesn't preclude the hypothesis that deduction plays a superordinate role in governing other intellectual processes, including nondeductive ones. Since the research we have reviewed in psychology, logic, and AI has given us a rich base of knowledge about deduction, it seems worthwhile to explore this hypothesis in the context of both artificial and natural intelligence.

II A PSYCHOLOGICAL THEORY OF DEDUCTION

4 Mental Proofs and Their Formal Properties

Much virtue in 'if'.
As You Like It (V, iv)

Everything only connected by "and" and "and."
Open the book.
Elizabeth Bishop, "Over 2000 Illustrations and a Complete Concordance"

Part I offered a glimpse of deduction in some of the forms it assumes in psychology, logic, and artificial intelligence. The aim of the following chapters is to draw on insights from these fields to shape a theory that accounts for the deductive reasoning of ordinary people—people who have no training in formal logic. The survey in part I suggests that natural-deduction systems provide a good starting point for the development of such a theory. Alternatives such as axiomatic systems in logic and resolution systems in artificial intelligence, though they have certain mathematical or computational advantages, are psychologically out of reach for most of us.

This chapter develops a theory for sentential reasoning along natural-deduction lines. The next chapter will demonstrate that the theory can explain data from several kinds of reasoning experiments in which subjects evaluate the deducibility of arguments or solve certain deduction puzzles.

The central notion in the theory will be that of a mental proof. I assume that when people confront a problem that calls for deduction they attempt to solve it by generating in working memory a set of sentences linking the premises or givens of the problem to the conclusion or solution. Each link in this network embodies an inference rule somewhat similar to those of table 3.2, which the individual recognizes as intuitively sound. Taken together, this network of sentences then provides a bridge between the premises and the conclusion that explains why the conclusion follows. Of course, people are not always successful in producing a mental proof of this sort for every deductively correct argument (relative to some logic system). They may not possess or may not be able to apply an inference rule that is crucial for a particular proof. Resource limitations—for example, capacity restrictions in working memory—may keep them from completing a proof. They may even possess nonstandard rules of inference that lead them to conclusions not sanctioned in classical predicate logic. Nevertheless, the claim is that people will at least *attempt* a mental proof during their problem-solving process.

The first sections of this chapter outline the main assumptions of the theory: the way it represents proofs in memory and the way it assembles these proofs on the basis of rules of inference. These assumptions are similar to those that I have proposed in earlier works (Rips 1983, 1984; Rips and Conrad 1983), but with a number of modifications that grew out of my experience in translating the theory into a computer model and in exploring its formal properties. The essential idea of the theory is that we can get a satisfactory account of human deduction by marrying the notion of a supposition from formal natural-deduction systems in logic with the notion of a subgoal from models of problem solving in artificial intelligence. Suppositions and subgoals are, in a way, conceptual duals, and they provide the twin columns to support the theory. In the remainder of the chapter, I take a more abstract look at this system. I prove that when this system is given an argument to evaluate it always halts either in a state in which it has found a proof for the argument or in a state in which it has unsuccessfully tried all available subgoals. I also show that the system as outlined is incomplete with respect to classical sentential logic but can easily be extended to a complete system through the addition of two forward rules for conditionals. In a sense, these proofs locate the difference between the psychological system proposed here and standard logical systems in the way that conditional sentences are handled.

In this chapter and the next we will explore the idea of mental proof by asking how *sentential* proofs are produced. But of course this is only one of the challenges that a theory of deduction faces. We don't want to stop with sentential reasoning, since much of deduction's power depends on its ability to bind variables. To take advantage of this power, we need to expand the theory to handle quantification. Chapters 6 and 7 will deal with this. However, let us first consider proof production in sentential logic, since it provides the basis for these further developments.

Overview of the Core Theory

The basic inference system consists of a set of deduction rules that construct mental proofs in the system's working memory. If we present the system with an argument to evaluate, the system will use those rules in an attempt to construct an internal proof of the conclusion from the premises. If we present the system with a group of premises and ask for entailments of those premises, the system will use the rules to generate proofs of possible conclusions. The model comes up with a proof by first storing the input premises (and conclusion, if any) in working memory. The rules then scan these memory contents to determine whether any inferences are possible. If so, the model adds the newly deduced sentences to memory, scans the updated configuration, makes further deductions, and so on, until a proof has been found or no more rules apply. Thus, the inference routines carry out much of the work in the basic system, deciding when deductions are possible, adding propositions to working memory, and keeping the procedure moving toward a solution. In what follows, I will refer to the system as PSYCOP (short for Psychology of Proof).[1] The system exists as a PROLOG program for personal computers that includes the procedures described in this chapter and in chapter 6.

PSYCOP's strategy in evaluating arguments is to work from the outside in, using forward rules to draw implications from the premises and using backward rules to create subgoals based on the conclusion. (See chapter 3 for the forward/backward distinction.) The forward rules operate in a breadth-first way, and create a web of new assertions. The backward rules operate depth-first: PSYCOP pursues a given chain of backward reasoning until it finds assertions that satisfy the required subgoals or until it runs out of backward rules to apply. In the first case, the proof is complete, since there is a logical pathway that connects the premises to the conclusion. In the second case, PSYCOP must backtrack to an earlier choice point where some alternative subgoal presented itself and try to satisfy it instead. If all the subgoals fail, PSYCOP gives up. In situations where PSYCOP is expected to produce conclusions rather than to evaluate them, it can use only its forward rules to complete the task, since there is no conclusion-goal to trigger the backward rules.

As an example of how the system operates, consider (1)—a simple argument that it can evaluate using the rules of table 3.2.

(1)   IF Betty is in Little Rock THEN Ellen is in Hammond.
      Phoebe is in Tucson AND Sandra is in Memphis.
      _____
      IF Betty is in Little Rock THEN (Ellen is in Hammond AND
      Sandra is in Memphis).

At the start of this problem, working memory will contain just these three sentences, as shown in figure 4.1a. The conclusion appears with a question

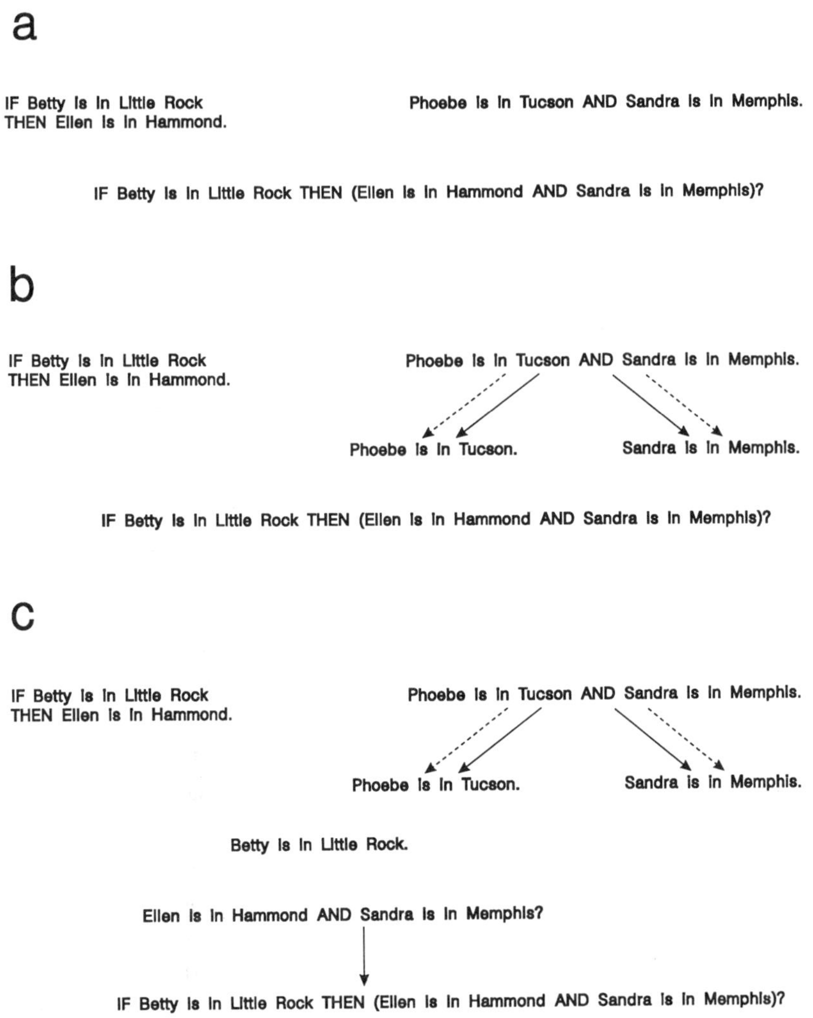

a

IF Betty Is In Little Rock   Phoebe Is In Tucson AND Sandra Is In Memphis.
THEN Ellen Is In Hammond.

IF Betty Is In Little Rock THEN (Ellen Is In Hammond AND Sandra Is In Memphis)?

b

IF Betty Is In Little Rock   Phoebe Is In Tucson AND Sandra Is In Memphis.
THEN Ellen Is In Hammond.

Phoebe Is In Tucson.   Sandra Is In Memphis.

IF Betty Is In Little Rock THEN (Ellen Is In Hammond AND Sandra Is In Memphis)?

c

IF Betty Is In Little Rock   Phoebe Is In Tucson AND Sandra Is In Memphis.
THEN Ellen Is In Hammond.

Phoebe Is In Tucson.   Sandra Is In Memphis.

Betty Is In Little Rock.

Ellen Is In Hammond AND Sandra Is In Memphis?

IF Betty Is In Little Rock THEN (Ellen Is In Hammond AND Sandra Is In Memphis)?

Figure 4.1
Development of PSYCOP's working-memory representation for the proof of

IF Betty is in Little Rock THEN Ellen is in Hammond.
Phoebe is in Tucson AND Sandra is in Memphis.
_____
IF Betty is in Little Rock
   THEN Ellen is in Hammond AND Sandra is in Memphis.

Solid arrows are deduction links, dashed arrows are dependency links, and double lines represent a match between a subgoal and an assertion. Sentences ending with periods are assertions; those ending with question marks are goals.

d

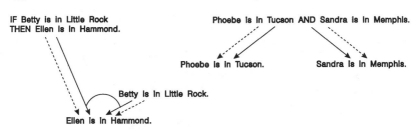

e

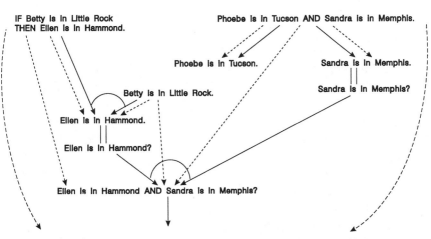

Figure 4.1 (continued)

mark to indicate its status as a goal, and the premises end with periods to show that they are assertions. To begin, PSYCOP notices that the second premise is a conjunction and is therefore subject to Forward AND Elimination. Applying this rule creates two new sentences, *Phoebe is in Tucson* and *Sandra is in Memphis*, which it stores in working memory (figure 4.1b). (The solid and dashed arrows in the figure show how these two sentences are deduced; this will be discussed in the next section.)

At this stage of the proof no other forward rules apply, but it is possible to begin some work in the backward direction. Since the conclusion (and goal) of the argument is a conditional, Backward IF Introduction is appropriate here. According to this rule (table 3.2), we should try to deduce the conclusion by setting up a new subdomain whose supposition is *Betty is in Little Rock* (the antecedent of the conditional conclusion) and attempting to prove *Ellen is in Hammond AND Sandra is in Memphis* in that subdomain. Figure 4.1c shows this supposition and the resulting subgoal in the developing memory structure. (The structure represents subdomains by means of the pattern of dashed arrows, as will be explained below.) Since we are now assuming both *Betty is in Little Rock* and *IF Betty is in Little Rock THEN Ellen is in Hammond*, the forward IF Elimination (i.e., Modus ponens) rule will automatically deduce *Ellen is in Hammond* (figure 4.1d). However, we must still satisfy the subgoal of proving *Ellen is in Hammond AND Sandra is in Memphis*. The relevant rule is, of course, Backward AND Introduction, which advises us to set up subgoals corresponding to the two halves of this conjunction. The first of these, *Ellen is in Hammond*, is easy to fulfill, since it matches the assertion that we have just produced. (Double lines are used in the figure to represent the match between assertion and subgoal.) The second subgoal can also be fulfilled by an earlier assertion. Satisfying these two subgoals satisfies the conjunction, and this in turn satisfies the main goal of the problem. Thus, figure 4.1e is a complete proof of argument (1).

PSYCOP's proof of argument (1) is more direct than is often the case when it evaluates arguments. One reason for this is that the set of rules in table 3.2 is quite small, so it is clear which rule PSYCOP should apply at any stage of the proof. In fact, as was noted above, the rules in the table are too limited and would keep the model from proving many arguments that people find obviously correct (e.g., argument (9) of chapter 3). But adding further rules complicates the search for a proof, since it makes it easier for the model to run into dead ends by following subgoals that it cannot satisfy. With a richer set of inference routines, PSYCOP can be faced with a choice of which backward rule to try first, where a poor choice can mean wasted effort. For these reasons, PSYCOP contains some heuristics to point along the most promising path.

PSYCOP's core system fulfills some of the criteria that were discussed in chapter 1 for an adequate deduction theory in psychology. The productivity of the system, in particular, is ensured by the productivity of the inference rules and their modes of deployment. Even with the limited rule set in table 3.2, PSYCOP can prove an infinite set of theorems in sentential logic. Of course, we also need to be careful that the model isn't too productive, generating irrelevant inferences when it should be focusing more narrowly on the task at hand. The combination of forward and backward rules, however, helps eliminate irrelevancies while ensuring that the model will be able to derive needed sentences. Rules such as IF Introduction also allow PSYCOP to manipulate suppositions in order to advance its proof of complex arguments. This characteristic matches subjects' use of suppositions in some of our earlier examples (see tables 1.1 and 1.2). In figure 4.1, for instance, the system used the supposition *Betty is in Little Rock* as a crucial element in the proof. The memory links shown in the figure provide a way of keeping track of these suppositions and the sentences that depend on them.

Core Assumptions

Assumptions about Memory

The PSYCOP model possesses a standard memory architecture that is divided into long-term and working-memory components. (The distinction between the two memory systems will become important when we consider PSYCOP's ability to accomplish cognitive tasks that require long-term memory search.) The two systems are similar in structure, the main difference between them being working memory's smaller capacity. Both memory systems contain internal sentences connected by labeled links, as in earlier memory models proposed by Anderson (1976, 1983), Collins and Loftus (1975), and others. We can examine the main features of both memory systems by returning to the working-memory proof in figure 4.1.

The links connecting memory sentences are probably of a large variety of types, but there are two that are especially relevant to the deduction process. Let us call them *deduction links* and *dependency links*. The deduction links—represented as solid arrows in the figure—run from memory sentences to any other sentences that they immediately entail. For example, in figures 4.1b–4.1e there is a deduction link that connects the sentence *Phoebe is in Tucson AND Sandra is in Memphis* to *Phoebe is in Tucson*, indicating that PSYCOP deduced the latter sentence from the former in a single inference step. Each deduction link is the product of a particular rule (AND Elimination, in this example), and I will sometimes tag the links with the name of that rule. In many cases two sentences combine to produce a third. In the present example, the sentence *Ellen is in Hammond* is deduced by IF Elimination from both *IF Betty is in Little Rock THEN Ellen is in Hammond* and *Betty is in Little Rock*. To indicate that sentences like these are jointly responsible for an inference, I use an arc to connect the deduction links emanating from them, as in figures 4.1d and 4.1e. Thus, deduction links give us a record of the individual steps in a derivation, each link (or set of arc-connected links) corresponding to the application of a single deduction rule.[2]

The dependency links in memory (dashed lines) represent the way the sentences depend on premises or suppositions in the mental proof. In the natural-deduction systems that we surveyed in previous chapters, the same sort of dependency was captured by indenting sentences within their subdomains. The deductive status of any of these indented sentences depends on the supposition of the subdomain in which it appears, as well as on the suppositions or premises of any superdomains in which it is embedded. For example, in our old system a natural-deduction proof of argument (1) would look like (2).

(2)   a. IF Betty is in Little Rock THEN Ellen is in
          Hammond.   Premise
      b. Phoebe is in Tucson AND Sandra is in Memphis.   Premise
      c. Phoebe is in Tucson.   AND Elim.
      d. Sandra is in Memphis.   AND Elim.
      e.   + Betty is in Little Rock.   Supposition
      f.   Ellen is in Hammond   IF Elim.
      g.   Ellen is in Hammond AND Sandra is in
              Memphis   AND Intro.
      h. IF Betty is in Little Rock THEN (Ellen is in
          Hammond AND Sandra is in Memphis)   IF Intro.

In the context of this proof, *Ellen is in Hammond AND Sandra is in Memphis* in line g is ultimately derived from the supposition *Betty is in Little Rock* and the two premises of the argument. If we were to withdraw the supposition or premises, then we could no longer derive line g. I indicate this in the memory representation by directing three dependency links from the supposition and premises to *Ellen is in Hammond AND Sandra is in Memphis* in figure 4.1e. The conclusion of the argument in line h, however, depends only on the premises; in the language of formal natural-deduction systems, the supposition is "discharged" when the conclusion is drawn. The corresponding sentence in the figure therefore has incoming dependency links from the premises alone. In general, the indented sentences in (2) are those that receive a dependency link from the supposition *Betty is in Little Rock*, whereas the unindented sentences are those that are not linked to that supposition. The dependency links thus partition the proof sentences in the same way as the indentation, marking the same distinction between superdomain and subdomain. This is important because subdomain sentences usually do not hold in their superdomains, and confusion about a sentence's domain could lead to logical inconsistencies in memory.

PSYCOP's dependency links also fulfill a function similar to that of truth-maintenance systems in AI research (de Kleer 1986; Doyle 1979; Forbus and de Kleer 1993; McAllester 1978). These systems monitor the relation between sentences in a data base and the assumptions from which the sentences have been derived. Roughly speaking, they ensure that the currently believed sentences rest on logically consistent assumptions, identifying any assumptions that lead to contradictions in the data base (see chapter 8). This provides the system with a way of returning directly to problematic assumptions and revising them, rather than reviewing in chronological order all the assumptions that the system has made. Truth-maintenance systems also provide a record of the sentences for which each assumption is responsible; thus, if an assumption must be withdrawn, all the dependent sentences can be withdrawn too. This facility is important for PSYCOP in problem-solving situations where it must make arbitrary choices of suppositions that may later turn out to be incorrect.

In earlier versions of the deduction system (Rips 1983, 1984), working memory was divided into two parts, one concerned with assertions and the other with subgoals. Each of these two parts contained separate segments corresponding to subdomains in the proof. To indicate that a particular subgoal was satisfied under a given set of suppositions, links connected segments in the subgoal structure to corresponding segments in the assertion structure. The present revision simplifies memory by merging these two parts. The subgoal or assertion status of a sentence is now part of the sentence's representation (the periods and question marks in figure 4.1), so there is no need to store them in separate memory locations. The newer method also eliminates some duplication of sentences between structures and therefore achieves a more compact proof.[3] Notice, too, that the dependency links make it unnecessary to place subdomains in different parts of memory. Because there seem to be no empirical data that would favor the earlier representation over the newer one, we settle on the revised version on grounds of simplicity.

We assume, of course, that working memory has a limited capacity. If mental proofs exceed this capacity, a person will usually have to recompute and recode information in order to avoid making mistakes. This is in line with demonstrations by Hitch and Baddeley (1976) and by Gilhooly et al. (1993) that a working-memory load from an unrelated task can produce errors on deduction problems. One of the initial examples in chapter 1 above (table 1.2) is evidence for this forgetting effect.

Assumptions about Inference Routines

The core system consists of inference routines from table 3.2, supplemented by additional rules that are intended to reflect people's primitive inference patterns. The additional rules are of two types: forward rules that capture intuitively obvious deductions and backward versions of some of the previously specified forward rules. We must also consider how the system should control these rules, since (as we saw in chapter 3) some of them would cause problems if applied blindly.

Additional Forward Rules   Exactly which inferences are immediate or primitive is an empirical matter, and so it is not possible to enumerate them before the evidence is in. Nevertheless, theoretical considerations and previous experiments suggest some plausible candidates for rules to add to PSYCOP's repertoire. Table 4.1 lists some of them (along with the earlier forward rules), in their conventional argument form (on the left side of the table) and then in the form of inference routines (on the right). These rules come from the theories of Braine, Reiser, and Rumain (1984), Johnson-Laird (1975), Osherson (1975), Rips (1983), Sperber and Wilson (1986), and

Table 4.1
PSYCOP's forward routines.

Forward IF Elimination

IF P THEN Q
P
———————
Q

(a) If a sentence of the form IF P THEN Q holds in some domain D,
(b) and P holds in D,
(c) and Q does not yet hold in D,
(d) then add Q to D.

Forward AND Elimination

P AND Q
———————
P

P AND Q
———————
Q

(a) If a sentence of the form P AND Q holds in some domain D,
(b) then if P does not yet hold in D,
(c)   then add P to D,
(d)   and if Q does not yet hold in D,
(e)   then add Q to D.

Forward Double Negation Elimination

NOT NOT P
———————
P

(a) If a sentence of the form NOT NOT P holds in some domain D,
(b) and P does not yet hold in D,
(c) then add P to D.

Forward Disjunctive Syllogism

P OR Q
NOT Q
———————
P

P OR Q
NOT P
———————
Q

(a) If a sentence of the form P OR Q holds in some domain D,
(b)   then if NOT P holds in D and Q does not yet hold in D,
(c)   then add Q to D.
(d) Else, if NOT Q holds in D and P does not yet hold in D,
(e)   then add P to D.

Forward Disjunctive Modus Ponens

IF P OR Q THEN R
P
———————
R

IF P OR Q THEN R
Q
———————
R

(a) If a sentence of the form IF P OR Q THEN R holds in some domain D,
(b) and P or Q also holds in D,
(c) and R does not yet hold in D,
(d) then add R to D.

Forward Conjunctive Modus Ponens

IF P AND Q THEN R
P
Q
———————
R

(a) If a sentence of the form IF P AND Q THEN R holds in some domain D,
(b) and P holds in D,
(c) and Q holds in D,
(d) and R does not yet hold in D,
(e) then add R to D.

Forward DeMorgan (NOT over AND)

NOT (P AND Q)
———————
(NOT P) OR (NOT Q)

(a) If a sentence of the form NOT (P AND Q) holds in some domain D,
(b) and (NOT P) OR (NOT Q) does not yet hold in D,
(c) then add (NOT P) OR (NOT Q) to D.

Table 4.1 (continued)

Forward DeMorgan (NOT over OR)	
NOT (P OR Q) ―――――― NOT P	(a) If a sentence of the form NOT (P OR Q) holds in some domain D,
NOT (P OR Q) ―――――― NOT Q	(b) then if NOT P does not yet hold in D (c) then add NOT P to D. (d) and if NOT Q does not yet hold in D, (e) then add NOT Q to D.

Forward Conjunctive Syllogism	
NOT (P AND Q) P ―――――― NOT Q	(a) If a sentence of the form NOT (P AND Q) holds in some domain D, (b) then if P also holds in D
NOT (P AND Q) Q ―――――― NOT P	(c) and NOT Q does not yet hold in D, (d) then add NOT Q to D. (e) Else, if Q holds in D, (f) and NOT P does not yet hold in D, (g) then add NOT P to D.

Forward Dilemma	
P OR Q IF P THEN R IF Q THEN R ―――――― R	(a) If a sentence of the form P OR Q holds in some domain D, (b) and IF P THEN R holds in D, (c) and IF Q THEN R holds in D, (d) and R does not yet hold in D, (e) then add R to D.

others. (Not all rules from these sources necessarily appear in the table. The names given these rules are not standard ones in all cases, but they may help in keeping the rules in mind.)

Many of the inference patterns embodied in the rules of table 4.1 could be derived in alternative ways (possibly with help of the backward rules in the following section). For example, we can capture Disjunctive Modus Ponens—the inference from *IF P OR Q THEN R* and *P* to *R*—by means of the regular Modus ponens rule (IF Elimination) together with OR Introduction. Psychologically, however, Disjunctive Modus Ponens appears simpler than OR Introduction. In research to be discussed in chapter 5, I estimated the probability that subjects correctly applied each of these rules when it was appropriate for them to do so in evaluating a sample of sentential arguments. According to this measure, subjects applied the Disjunctive Modus Ponens rule on 100% of relevant trials, but applied OR Introduction on only 20%. If these estimates are correct, the subjects could not have been using OR Introduction to achieve the effect of Disjunctive Modus Ponens. Thus, it seems reasonable to suppose that Disjunctive Modus Ponens functions as a primitive inference rule on its own, despite its logical redundancy. Braine et al. (1984) and Sperber and Wilson (1986) present further reasons for favoring Disjunctive Modus Ponens as a primitive.

Psychological models of deduction differ in which rules they consider to be the primitive ones. These differences are not merely notational, since some arguments are provable in one system but not in others. For example, the present model is able to prove argument (3), which could not be proved in the model of Osherson (1975).

(3)   (p OR q) AND NOT p.

    q.

But the choice of rules is not the most important point of comparison between models. This is because most investigators have been cautious about claiming that the particular rules incorporated in their models exhaust the primitive ones. (The work by Braine (1978) and Braine, Reiser, and Rumain (1984) is an exception.) The usual claim (Osherson 1975; Rips 1983) is that the incorporated rules are a subset of the primitive ones. It is also worth noting that the evidence on the status of a rule is sometimes ambiguous, particularly if primitive rules can vary in how easy they are to deploy. It is not always clear, for example, whether subjects are proving a given argument by means of two very efficient primitives or by means of one more global but not-so-efficient primitive. The problem becomes even more complex if we allow for individual differences and for the learning or the compiling of new primitive rules. For these reasons, it seems wise to concentrate on other criteria in comparing and evaluating deduction systems. In developing PSYCOP, I have tried to include most of the rules that earlier models have taken as primitive, so the model's current repertoire is fairly large. We will return to the question of model comparison in chapters 9 and 10, after finishing our tour of PSYCOP's inference abilities.

Additions and Changes to Backward Rules   The system described so far is psychologically incomplete in that it is unable to prove some arguments that subjects find fairly easy. One reason for this is that we have been too restrictive in confining IF Elimination and other principles to forward inference routines. Although these rules should be used as forward rules, we sometimes need them as backward routines in order to motivate the search for subgoals. For example, we currently have no way to show that (4) is deducible.

Table 4.2
PSYCOP's backward rules.

Backward IF Introduction (Conditionalization)

+P	(a) Set D to domain of current goal.
⋮	(b) If current goal is of the form IF P THEN Q,
Q	(c) and neither D nor its superdomains nor its immediate
‾‾‾‾‾‾‾‾‾‾‾	subdomains contain supposition P and subgoal Q,
IF P THEN Q	(d) and IF P THEN Q is a subformula of the premises or
	conclusion,
	(e) then set up a subdomain of D, D′, with supposition P.
	(f) Add the subgoal of proving Q in D′ to the list of
	subgoals.

Backward NOT Elimination

+NOT P	(a) Set P to current goal and D to its domain.
⋮	(b) If P is a subformula of the premises or conclusion,
Q AND (NOT Q)	(c) and Q is an atomic subformula in the premises or
‾‾‾‾‾‾‾‾‾‾‾‾‾‾‾	conclusion,
P	(d) and neither D nor its superdomains nor its
	immediate subdomains contain supposition NOT P
	and subgoal Q AND (NOT Q),
	(e) then set up a subdomains of D, D′, with supposition
	NOT P,
	(f) and add the subgoal of proving Q AND (NOT Q) in
	D′ to the list of subgoals.

Backward NOT Introduction

+P	(a) Set D to domain of current goal.
⋮	(b) If current goal is of the form NOT P,
Q AND (NOT Q)	(c) and P is a subformula of the premises or
‾‾‾‾‾‾‾‾‾‾‾‾‾‾‾	conclusion,
NOT P	(d) and Q is an atomic subformula of the premises or
	conclusion,
	(e) and neither D nor its superdomains nor its
	immediate subdomains contain supposition P and
	subgoal Q AND (NOT Q),
	(f) then set up a subdomain of D, D′, with supposition P,
	(g) and add the subgoal of proving Q AND (NOT Q) in
	D′ to the list of subgoals.

Backward OR Elimination

P OR Q	(a) Set D to domain of current goal.
+P	(b) Set R to current goal.
⋮	(c) If a sentence of the form P OR Q holds in D,
R	(d) and both P and Q are subformulas or negations of
+Q	subformulas of the premises or conclusion,
⋮	(e) and R is a subformula or negation of a subformula of
R	the premises or conclusion,
‾‾‾‾‾‾‾‾‾‾‾	(f) and neither D nor its superdomains nor its immediate
R	subdomains contain supposition P and subgoal R,
	(g) and neither D nor its superdomains nor its immediate
	subdomains contain supposition Q and subgoal R,
	(h) then set up a subdomain of D, D′, with supposition P,
	(i) and add the subgoal of proving R in D′ to the list of
	subgoals.
	(j) If the subgoal in (i) succeeds,

Table 4.2 (continued)

| | (k) then set up another subdomain of D, D″, with supposition Q, |
| | (l) and add the subgoal of proving R in D″ to the list of subgoals. |

Backward AND Introduction

P	(a) Set D to domain of current goal.
Q	(b) If current goal is of the form P AND Q,
P AND Q	(c) and D does not yet contain the subgoal P,
	(d) then add the subgoal of proving P in D to the list of subgoals.
	(e) If the subgoal in (d) succeeds,
	(f) and D does not yet contain the subgoal Q,
	(g) then add the subgoal of proving Q in D to the list of subgoals.

Backward OR Introduction

P	(a) Set D to domain of current goal.
P OR Q	(b) If current goal is of the form P OR Q,
Q	(c) and D does not yet contain the subgoal P,
P OR Q	(d) then add the subgoal of proving P in D to the list of subgoals.
	(e) If the subgoal in (d) fails,
	(f) and D does not yet contain subgoal Q
	(g) then add the subgoal of proving Q in D to the list of subgoals.

Backward IF Elimination (modus ponens)

IF P THEN Q	(a) Set D to domain of current goal.
P	(b) Set Q to current goal.
Q	(c) If the sentence IF P THEN Q holds in D,
	(d) and D does not yet contain the subgoal P,
	(e) then add P to the list of subgoals.

Backward AND Elimination

P AND Q	(a) Set D to domain of current goal.
P	(b) Set P to current goal.
Q AND P	(c) If the sentence P AND Q is a subformula of a sentence that holds in D,
P	(d) and D does not yet contain the subgoal P AND Q,
	(e) then add P AND Q to the list of subgoals.
	(f) If the subgoal in (e) fails,
	(g) and the sentence Q AND P is a subformula of a sentence that holds in D,
	(h) and D does not yet contain the subgoal Q AND P,
	(i) then add Q AND P to the list of subgoals.

Backward Double Negation Elimination

NOT NOT P	(a) Set D to domain of current goal.
P	(b) Set P to the current goal.
	(c) If the sentence NOT NOT P is a subformula of a sentence that holds in D,
	(d) and D does not yet contain the subgoal NOT NOT P,
	(e) then add NOT NOT P to the list of subgoals.

Table 4.2 (continued)

Backward Disjunctive Modus Ponens

IF P OR Q THEN R
P
———————
R

IF P OR Q THEN R
Q
———————
R

(a) Set D to domain of current goal.
(b) Set R to current goal.
(c) If the sentence IF P OR Q THEN R holds in D,
(d) and D does not yet contain the subgoal P,
(e) then add P to the list of subgoals.
(f) If the subgoal in (e) fails,
(g) and D does not yet contain the subgoal Q,
(h) then add Q to the list of subgoals.

Backward Disjunctive Syllogism

P OR Q
NOT P
———————
Q

Q OR P
NOT P
———————
Q

(a) Set D to domain of current goal.
(b) Set Q to the current goal.
(c) If a sentence of the form P OR Q or Q OR P holds in D,
(d) and NOT P is a subformula of a sentence that holds in D,
(e) and D does not yet contain the subgoal NOT P,
(f) then add NOT P to the list of subgoals.

Backward Conjunctive Syllogism

NOT (P AND Q)
P
———————
NOT Q

NOT (Q AND P)
P
———————
NOT Q

(a) Set D to domain of current goal.
(b) If the current goal is of the form NOT Q
(c) and either of the sentences NOT (P AND Q) or NOT (Q AND P) holds in D,
(d) and D does not yet contain the subgoal P,
(e) then add P to the list of subgoals.

Backward DeMorgan (NOT over AND)

NOT (P AND Q)
———————
(NOT P) OR (NOT Q)

(a) Set D to domain of current goal.
(b) If current goal is of the form (NOT P) OR (NOT Q),
(c) and NOT (P AND Q) is a subformula of a sentence that holds in D,
(d) then add NOT (P AND Q) to the list of subgoals.

Backward DeMorgan (NOT over OR)

NOT (P OR Q)
———————
(NOT P) AND (NOT Q)

(a) Set D to domain of current goal.
(b) If current goal is of the form (NOT P) AND (NOT Q),
(c) and NOT (P OR Q) is a subformula of a sentence that holds in D,
(d) then add NOT (P OR Q) to the list of subgoals.

---

(4)   IF NOT NOT Calvin deposits 50 cents THEN Calvin gets a coke.
      Calvin deposits 50 cents.

      Calvin gets a coke.

We would like to apply IF Elimination to derive the conclusion. But since
IF Elimination is a forward routine, we must wait until the antecedent of
the first premise (*NOT NOT Calvin deposits 50 cents*) comes along. Although there is a way to deduce the antecedent from the second premise,
it requires NOT Introduction—a backward rule. Thus, before we can
bring NOT Introduction into play, we must have a subgoal that asks the
system to derive *NOT NOT Calvin deposits 50 cents*. We are stuck in the
present situation because the system has no way to propose this subgoal.
One solution is to add a backward version of IF Elimination (similar to
the Modus ponens rule in LT (Newell et al. 1957)) that can handle subgoals.[4] Table 4.2 states this rule (along with similar ones for backward
disjunctive modus ponens and conjunctive syllogism). The right column of
the table gives the operational format; the left column gives the nearest
analogue in traditional natural-deduction style.

The new backward IF Elimination is triggered when a subgoal Q
matches the consequent of some conditional assertion *IF P THEN Q*. The
rule then proposes the further subgoal of proving P, since if this subgoal
can be fulfilled then Q itself must follow. PSYCOP's internal proof of (4)
would then proceed as shown in figure 4.2. As the first step, backward IF
Elimination notices that the main goal of the proof *Calvin gets a coke*
matches the consequent of the first premise. The antecedent of that conditional is the double-negative sentence mentioned above, and Backward IF
Elimination turns it into the next subgoal. Once we have this subgoal,
however, NOT Introduction can apply, positing *NOT Calvin deposits 50
cents* as a supposition and looking for a contradiction as a subgoal. Since
the supposition itself contradicts the second premise, the subgoal is easily
fulfilled, and this completes the proof.

In addition to Backward IF Elimination, we also add to PSYCOP
backward versions of some of the other forward rules. For example, it
seems reasonable to use AND Elimination and Double Negation Elimination in a backward direction in order to show that (5) and (6) are
deducible.

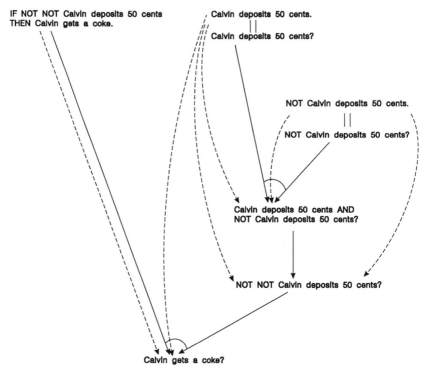

Figure 4.2
PSYCOP's working-memory representation for the proof of

IF NOT NOT Calvin deposits 50 cents THEN Calvin gets a coke.
Calvin deposits 50 cents.
_____
Calvin gets a coke.

(5) IF NOT NOT Calvin deposits 50 cents, THEN (Calvin gets a coke
     AND Calvin buys a burger).
     Calvin deposits 50 cents.
     _____
     Calvin gets a coke.

(6) IF NOT NOT Calvin deposits 50 cents THEN NOT NOT Calvin
     gets a coke.
     Calvin deposits 50 cents.
     _____
     Calvin gets a coke.

A proof of (5) is blocked because Forward IF Elimination doesn't apply to
the premises as stated, for the reasons we have seen in connection with (4).

However, the new Backward IF Elimination rule will not work here either: To trigger that rule, some subgoal must match the consequent of the conditional (*Calvin gets a coke AND Calvin buys a burger*), but the only subgoal in play is the conclusion (*Calvin gets a coke*). The proof procedure ought to realize that the consequent entails the goal and that it is therefore worthwhile trying to prove the antecedent; yet it has no way of knowing this. Backward AND Elimination would be helpful in this context; it would tell us that we can prove *Calvin gets a coke* if we can show that *Calvin gets a coke AND Calvin buys a burger*. From that subgoal, we can then use Backward IF Elimination and NOT Introduction, as in figure 4.2, to show that (5) is deducible. Much the same strategy, coupled with a backward Double Negation rule, will handle (6).

The difficulty with backward versions of AND Elimination and Double Negation Elimination is that they can lead to an infinity of subgoals, as was observed in chapter 3. For example, if we use AND Elimination backward on goal P to produce subgoal $P\ AND\ Q$, then we should be able to use it again on $P\ AND\ Q$ to obtain the subgoal *(P AND Q) AND R*, and so on. Perhaps the most reasonable solution, under these circumstances, is to restrict the rules so that no subgoal can be produced that isn't already a "part" of the current set of assertions. To pin down this notion of part more precisely, let us use the term *subformula* to denote any consecutive string of symbols in a sentence (including the entire sentence) that would also qualify as a grammatical sentence on its own. Thus, *Calvin gets a coke AND Calvin buys a burger* is a subformula of the first premise of (5), but *(Calvin gets a coke AND Calvin buys a burger) AND Calvin deposits 50 cents* is not. Since the proposed backward AND Elimination rule can only produce subgoals that are subformulas of an assertion or conclusion, we can generate a subgoal for the first of these sentences (thus allowing PSYCOP to prove (5)) but not the second. A similar restriction can be placed on Backward Double Negation Elimination and the DeMorgan rules. Table 4.2 gives one formulation of these backward rules as they are incorporated in PSYCOP.[5]

We must also confront the problem of controlling the rules that produce subdomains—IF Introduction, OR Elimination, NOT Introduction, and NOT Elimination. Although it is not really difficult to find ways to prevent these rules from leading to infinite backward searches, it is not at all obvious whether these restrictions will also reduce the overall power of the system. We could stipulate, for instance, that OR Elimination can apply only once per derivation, but this type of arbitrary limitation would almost certainly prevent PSYCOP from showing that some simple valid arguments are deducible. The version of these rules in table 4.2 gives one possible solution to this difficulty. The most general of the restrictions we impose on these rules is that new subdomains must have a supposition and a subgoal distinct from its superdomains. This prohibits infinite embedding of subdomains. Some of the rules also have unique restrictions. For example, we require that the supposition created by NOT Introduction be a subformula of the premises or of the conclusion of the argument. Later it will be proved that there is a certain sense in which these restrictions do not reduce PSYCOP's deductive power: We can include the restricted rules in a system quite similar to PSYCOP that is in fact complete with respect to classical sentential logic.

Assumptions about Control

The rules as formulated in tables 4.1 and 4.2 leave room for some further decisions about the order in which PSYCOP should deploy them. We need to specify, for example, when PSYCOP should apply forward rules and when backward rules, as well as which rules in each class it should try first. In making these choices, we need to consider the internal characteristics of the rules. Clearly, PSYCOP can apply its forward rules in a nearly automatic way, since their self-constraining nature requires little external monitoring and will never lead to infinite forward searches (as will be shown below). It therefore seems reasonable to activate them as soon as possible whenever a triggering assertion appears in the database. Backward rules, however, present more of a control problem. Although the constraints we have placed on the backward rules keep them from producing infinite loops, they nevertheless have the potential to produce extremely inefficient searches. This means that we might want to adopt a flexible approach to using these rules, allowing the system to profit from heuristic advice about which subgoals to follow up.

Currently, when PSYCOP has to evaluate an argument it begins by applying its forward rules to the premises until no new inferences are forthcoming. It then considers the conclusion of the argument, checking to see whether the conclusion is already among the assertions. If so, the proof is complete; if not, it will treat the conclusion as a goal and attempt to apply one of the backward rules, as in the example of the previous section. PSYCOP tests each of the backward rules to see if it is appropriate in this situation, and it does this in an order that is initially determined by the complexity of the backward rules. The idea is that simple rules should be tried first, since less work will have been lost if these rules turn out to lead to dead ends. PSYCOP prefers backward rules that can be satisfied by a single subgoal and that do not require new subdomains; thus, it tries Backward IF Elimination and similar rules first. If none of these rules is applicable, it next tries Backward AND Introduction, which requires two subgoals to be satisfied but which does not use subdomains. Finally, it will resort to the subdomain-creating rules IF Introduction, OR Elimination, NOT Introduction, and NOT Elimination. In later phases of the proof, PSYCOP revises this initial ordering in such a way that any rule it used successfully is given first priority in the next round of deduction. Thus, PSYCOP incorporates a simple procedure for learning from practice—a procedure that can give rise to a kind of "set" effect in deduction (cf. Lewis 1981).

Once a backward rule has been activated and has produced a subgoal, PSYCOP checks whether the new subgoal matches an assertion. If not, PSYCOP places the subgoal on an agenda, reruns the forward rules in case some assertions were added, and repeats its cycle. In principle, PSYCOP could try the subgoals on the agenda in any order—for instance, according to a heuristic measure of how "easy" these subgoals seem. In the absence of other instructions, however, it will follow a depth-first search; that is, it first tries to fulfill the conclusion-goal, then a subgoal to the conclusion that a backward rule has proposed, then a sub-subgoal to the first subgoal, and so on. If it reaches a subgoal to which no backward rules apply, it backtracks to the preceding subgoal and tries to fulfill it another way via a different backward rule. There is also a provision in PSYCOP for a bound on the depth of its search, limiting the length of a chain of subgoals to some fixed number. Finally, PSYCOP halts with a proof if it has found assertions to fulfill all the subgoals along some path to the conclusion. It halts with no proof if it can complete none of the subgoal paths. As will be proved later in this chapter, even without a depth bound it will always end up, after a finite number of steps, in one of these two conditions.

Formal Properties

For the most part, psychologists have not been concerned with the properties of deduction systems that are of most interest to logicians. All the psychological deduction systems for sentential reasoning cited earlier in this chapter are *sound* in the logician's sense of *only* producing proofs for arguments that are valid in classical sentential logic (see chapters 2 and 6 for the notion of validity). But there are no proofs that these systems are *complete*—that they generate proofs for *all* arguments that are valid. Since completeness is one of the first properties that a logician would want to know about a logical system, it is surprising at first glance that psychologists have paid it so little attention. There is some justification, however, for the psychologists' indifference. After all, the purpose of these cognitive proposals is not to capture inferences that are valid according to some abstract standard, but to capture the ones that untrained people can accept in ideal circumstances. The systems should be *psychologically* complete (since we want the systems to find a proof for all the sentential arguments to which people will agree in ideal situations), but not necessarily *logically* complete (since people may not, even in ideal situations, accept all the sentential inferences sanctioned by a given logical system). Psychological completeness, in contrast to logical completeness, is for the most part an empirical matter, to be settled by observation and experiment rather than by mathematics. (See Osherson 1975 for the distinction between logical and psychological completeness.)

There are, nevertheless, some reasons for exploring the formal properties of PSYCOP. Since the classical sentential calculus is a landmark system in logic and philosophy, it is appropriate to wonder whether the sort of reasoning that people do lives up to this standard. Of course, the fact (if it is one) that human sentential reasoning isn't equivalent to classical logic doesn't imply that humans are irrational; there are logical systems other than the classical one, and these could be viewed as providing alternative criteria of rationality. However, a divergence with classical logic would be interesting, particularly if we could spot the source of the discrepancy. This would help us locate human-style reasoning within the space of possible logical theories.

In this section, I proceed with the following agenda. I first show that PSYCOP is not complete with respect to classical logic, by exhibiting as a counterexample an argument that is valid in classical logic but which PSYCOP is unable to prove. I then supplement the set of rules by adding two new forward rules whose purpose is to transform conditional sentences into ones without conditionals. It is then possible to prove several related facts about this enlarged system, which I call PSYCOP+. First, the system always halts when given an argument to evaluate. (This establishes that PSYCOP itself always halts, since PSYCOP's routines are a subset of PSYCOP + 's.) Second, any proof in a demonstrably complete system of classical sentential logic (one similar to that of Jeffrey (1967) or to that of Smullyan (1968)) can be mapped into a natural-deduction proof of a certain type. This mapping means that any valid argument has a proof in what I will call a *canonical* natural-deduction format. Finally, I establish that PSYCOP + will always find this canonical proof if it hasn't found a simpler one instead. This guarantees that PSYCOP + will find a proof for any valid argument—that is, that the system is complete. Since the rules of the system are sound, and since it always halts, PSYCOP + is in fact a decision procedure for classical sentential logic. Thus, although PSYCOP is not complete, we can make it complete by endowing it with the ability to paraphrase conditional sentences in a particular way.

The upshot of these results is somewhat appealing, since classical logic's handling of conditional sentences has always seemed its most unintuitive aspect. This intuition, however, might seem hard to reconcile with the fact that the rules for conditionals in most natural-deduction systems—IF Elimination (modus ponens) and IF Introduction (conditionalization)—seem entirely acceptable. One way of viewing the results, then, is that a deduction system can contain versions of both IF Introduction and IF Elimination (as indeed PSYCOP does) and still not force one to recognize all inferences involving conditionals that are valid in classical logic. In proving these results, I have tried to keep the development in the text simple; the more involved aspects of the proofs are given in the appendix to this chapter. Readers with no patience for formalizing should skip to the final section for a summary.

PSYCOP's Incompleteness with Respect to Classical Logic

Consider the following argument (from Adams 1965):

(7) NOT (IF Calvin passes history THEN Calvin will graduate).
     Calvin passes history.

This argument is valid in classical logic (i.e., when IF is interpreted as CPL's material conditional), since any negated conditional semantically entails its antecedent. The argument nevertheless seems suspect and has the form of one of the "paradoxes" of implication. Of course, it is derivable in the formal deduction systems surveyed in the previous chapters, since these systems are complete; but PSYCOP cannot derive it. In what follows, I work with a "vanilla" PSYCOP that excludes special heuristics on the rules and that adopts the depth-first strategy (without depth bounds) for backward search that I discussed in the subsection on control. I also assume that there are no limitations on the size of working memory. That is, I focus on a slightly idealized PSYCOP in order to study the nature of its rules.

To see that PSYCOP is unable to prove (7), notice that the only rule in table 4.1 or table 4.2 that will apply to this premise-conclusion pair is the rule for NOT Elimination. Thus, PSYCOP's first move in trying to find a mental proof for this argument is the attempt shown in figure 4.3a, where p has been substituted for *Calvin passes history* and q for *Calvin will graduate*. The supposition $NOT\ p$ in the figure begins a new subdomain, which I have indicated by indenting the supposition and its subgoal as in the earlier natural-deduction notation. According to the formulation of the NOT Elimination rule in table 4.2, the subgoal the rule produces must be the conjunction of an atomic sentence and its negation, where the atomic sentence is one that appears in the premise or in the conclusion. PSYCOP could begin with either p or q as the atomic sentence; however, for definiteness we can assume that PSYCOP always tries the atomic sentences in the order in which they appear in the argument (in this case, p before q), although this ordering will not affect the results. So we now need to prove $p\ AND\ NOT\ p$, and the only rule we can apply in this context is backward AND Introduction. (Another instance of NOT Elimination is blocked at this point by part b of that rule.) AND Introduction instructs PSYCOP to attempt to prove p, with the result shown in figure 4.3a.

At this stage, backward NOT Elimination is again the only applicable rule, and using it (together with AND Introduction) produces the memory structure in figure 4.3b. Note that part d of NOT Elimination keeps PSYCOP from setting up supposition $NOT\ p$ with subgoal $p\ AND\ NOT\ p$ once again; so this time PSYCOP is forced to try subgoal $q\ AND\ NOT\ q$.

From this point, PSYCOP's only course is to continue with NOT Elimination and AND Introduction. After two further applications of these rules, its memory structure looks like figure 4.3c. No further progress is possible, even with NOT Elimination, since part d of the rule prohibits any further subdomains. This structure activates none of the other backward or forward rules; hence PSYCOP must back up to the last point at

a
                    NOT (IF p THEN q).

                        NOT p.

                            p?

                            p AND NOT p?

                  p?

b
                    NOT (IF p THEN q).

                        NOT p.

                              NOT p.

                                q?

                                q AND NOT q?

                            p?

                            p AND NOT p?

                  p?

c
                    NOT (IF p THEN q).

                        NOT p.

                            NOT p.

                                NOT q.

                                    NOT q.

                                  q?

                                  q AND NOT q?

                              p?

                              p AND NOT p?

                          q?

                          q AND NOT q?

                      p?

                        p AND NOT p?

                p?

Figure 4.3
PSYCOP's unsuccessful attempt to prove

NOT (IF p THEN q).
_____
p.

which choice of a subgoal was possible. It returns to the place where it supposed *NOT q* with the intent of proving *p AND NOT p* and tries subgoal *q AND NOT q* instead. After several more futile attempts of this sort, it finally backs up to the initial goal of proving *p* from *NOT (IF p THEN q)*. But, since it has now exhausted all its resources, it halts, deciding that the conclusion is not deducible from the premise. Thus, it is clear that PSYCOP is unable to prove all arguments that are valid in classical logic. Since (7) seems questionable on psychological grounds, this result seems reasonable. But of course there is still a long way to go to show that PSYCOP is a correct psychological model, so not too much should be read into this finding. There may be further arguments that PSYCOP fails to prove that seem intuitively correct, and others that PSYCOP proves that are psychologically marginal or unacceptable. A possible example of the first kind is the argument in note 5. As a possible example of the latter sort, PSYCOP has no trouble with (11) of chapter 2, another of the paradoxes of implication.

A Halting Theorem for PSYCOP and PSYCOP+

Although PSYCOP is not itself complete with respect to classical sentential logic, it is quite easy to extend it to a complete proof procedure while keeping all its current rules and its control structure intact. All that is needed, in fact, is the addition of the two forward rules shown in table 4.3. The first of these rules allows us to deduce both *P* and *NOT Q* from a sentence of the form *NOT (IF P THEN Q)*; the second allows us to deduce *(NOT P) OR Q* from *IF P THEN Q*. In effect, these rules translate conditional and negated conditional sentences into sentences without conditionals. Obviously, the negated conditional rule makes the proof of (7) trivial, since the conclusion follows from the premise in one forward step. Also, these rules seem to be the sort that one would *not* want to include in a cognitively realistic deduction system, for exactly the same reason that makes (7) itself dubious. I call the PSYCOP system that includes the table 4.3 rules "PSYCOP+" to mark its departure from the official system.

The proof that PSYCOP+ is complete is somewhat lengthy, so I will take it in several steps. In this subsection, I first show that, given any list of assertions and any subgoal, PSYCOP+ will always come to a stop after a finite number of steps. We will need this result later, but it is important in its own right since it implies that PSYCOP (without the plus) also never attempts endless searches. The next subsection demonstrates

Table 4.3
New forward rules for PSYCOP +.

Negated Conditional Transformation

NOT (IF P THEN Q)	(a) If a sentence of the form NOT (IF P THEN Q) holds in
P	some domain D,
	(b) then if P does not yet hold in D,
NOT (IF P THEN Q)	(c) then add P to D,
NOT Q	(d) and if NOT Q does not yet hold in D,
	(e) then add NOT Q to D.

Conditional Transformation

IF P THEN Q	(a) If a sentence of the form IF P THEN Q holds in some
(NOT P) OR Q	domain D,
	(b) and (NOT P) OR Q does not yet hold in D,
	(c) then add (NOT P) OR Q to D.

---

how any proof in a complete tree-style proof system (such as that of Smullyan 1968) can be turned into a proof in a natural-deduction system containing a subset of PSYCOP +'s rules. Finally, I will show that PSYCOP + will eventually discover this proof.

Proving that PSYCOP + halts entails showing that its ensemble of rules never leads to infinite forward or backward searches or to infinite loops. For this purpose, it is useful to consider the different types of rules separately, beginning with the rules that create subdomains.[6]

Halting Proof I: PSYCOP +'s rules create only finitely many domains for a given argument. Clearly, one way that a system such as ours could fail to halt is if rules that create subdomains (i.e., IF Introduction, OR Elimination, NOT Introduction, and NOT Elimination) create an infinite number of them. Is this possible? Notice that each of these rules produces only subdomains whose supposition and goal are chosen from a fixed set of sentences (subformulas of the premises and the conclusion, or restricted combinations of these subformulas). Moreover, the conditions on these rules require the supposition-goal pairs that initiate nested subdomains to be unique. (See figure 4.3 for an example of nesting.) Since only a finite number of unique pairs can be formed from the finite set of candidate suppositions and goals, only a limited set of subdomains is possible for a particular argument. The proof of proposition HP-I in the appendix gives the details of this result.

Halting Proof II: The backward rules produce only a finite number of subgoals within a domain. Having eliminated the possibility that infinite searches could occur through an infinite number of subdomains, we are left with the possibility that an infinite search could occur *within* a single domain. This could happen either because of the forward rules from tables 4.1 and 4.3 or because of the backward rules of table 4.2 (excluding the four domain-creating backward rules just examined). Notice, though, that the forward and backward processes are independent inside a domain, in the sense that once the forward rules have run in that domain then further application of the backward rules can't trigger any more forward inferences. This is a consequence of the fact that the backward rules that operate within a domain don't produce any new assertions, so there are no further sentences for the forward rules to operate upon. Thus, to prove that PSYCOP+ converges it suffices to show, first, that the backward rules produce only finitely many subgoals within a given domain and, second, that the forward rules can produce only finitely many new assertions when applied to a fixed set of assertions.

The backward case is quite easy. An infinite backward search in a domain would mean that the rules would have to produce an infinite sequence of subgoals $G_0, G_1, G_2, \ldots$, where G_1 is a subgoal of G_0, G_2 a subgoal of G_1, and so forth. However, the conditions of the within-domain backward rules (i.e., those that follow OR Elimination in table 4.2) restrict the possible subgoals to those formed from subformulas of the assertions or from subformulas of preceding goals in the series. This means that only a finite set of distinct subgoals are possible within a domain. And since the conditions of the rules prohibit duplicate subgoals in this situation, there can be no infinite sequence of them. (See proof HP-II in the appendix.)

Halting Proof III: The forward rules produce only a finite number of assertions within a domain.   The only remaining way that PSYCOP+ could get stuck in an endless search is for its forward rules (in tables 4.1 and 4.3) to continue producing assertions indefinitely. Because these rules have varied forms, it is not obvious at first that this can't happen. However, several factors conspire to limit the number of assertions. First, the rules produce only sentences that contain no more atomic sentences than appear in the set of sentences to which they applied. For example, IF Elimination produces a sentence Q on the basis of the sentences P and *IF P THEN Q*, so any atomic sentences in Q must already be in *IF P THEN Q*. Second, the conditions on the rules limit the number of NOTs in the assertions they produce. Proof HP-III in the appendix demonstrates that these conditions restrict the forward rules to producing only finitely many new sentences within a domain.

Taken together, the results on domain-creating backward rules, within-domain backward rules, and forward rules that appear in HP-I, II, and III lead directly to our main conclusion that PSYCOP+ must always halt. HP-I establishes that PSYCOP+ can produce only a finite number of domains, and HP-II and III show that within the domains there can be only a finite number of subgoals and assertions. PSYCOP+ can continue only as long as new subgoals or assertions are generated, and so it must always come to a stop. Recall, too, that PSYCOP+ differs from PSYCOP only by the addition of the two forward rules in table 4.3. Removing these two rules would clearly lead to shorter, not longer, searches, since there are fewer opportunities for new inferences. Thus, PSYCOP, like its cousin PSYCOP+, never ventures beyond a finite number of rule applications.

Canonical Proofs

Of course, it is one thing to show that our program always halts and another to show that it halts with a correct answer. To get the latter result, I take a somewhat indirect path that makes use of the tree method, which we examined in chapter 3. This method has a simple algorithmic character and is also known to be complete. Tree proofs, as it turns out, can be reexpressed in a natural-deduction system like PSYCOP+'s, and we will call these reexpressed versions *canonical* proofs. Since any valid argument has a tree proof (by the completeness of the tree method), any valid argument also has a canonical natural-deduction proof in a PSYCOP-like system. The final section of the chapter shows that PSYCOP+ (but not PSYCOP, of course) will actually hit on this proof if it hasn't found a simpler one. (See Prawitz 1965 and Smullyan 1965 for other canonical natural-deduction systems.)

The Tree Method of Proof   The tree method yields a proof by contradiction. In the version of chapter 3, inference rules break down the premises and negated conclusion into atomic sentences and negations of atomic sentences. An argument is deducible just in case all of the paths in the tree that is created in this way contain both an atomic sentence and its negation. Both Jeffrey (1967) and Smullyan (1968) give proofs of the soundness and completeness of the tree method. The tree proofs summarized here use

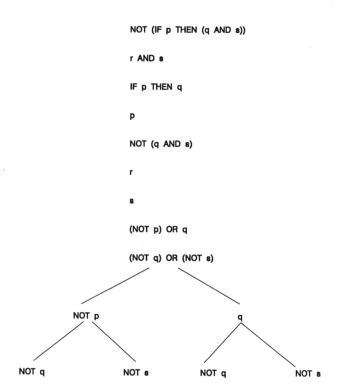

NOT (IF p THEN (q AND s))

r AND s

IF p THEN q

p

NOT (q AND s)

r

s

(NOT p) OR q

(NOT q) OR (NOT s)

NOT p   q

NOT q   NOT s   NOT q   NOT s

Figure 4.4
A tree proof of the argument

IF p THEN q.
r AND s.
_____
IF p THEN (q AND s).

a somewhat different set of rules than are found in these two sources, but the differences do not affect either of these properties.

As an illustration, figure 4.4 shows a tree proof for (8) (which is equivalent to (1)), using the rules from table 3.1.

(8)   r AND s.
       IF p THEN q.
       _____
       IF p THEN (q AND s).

In the figure, the negation of the conclusion is written at the top, and then the two premises. Applying rule 6 to the negated conclusion yields p and NOT $(q$ AND $s)$, and applying rule 1 to r AND s produces the two additional sentences *r* and *s*. *(NOT p) OR q comes* from *IF p THEN q* by rule 5, and *(NOT q) OR (NOT s)* from *NOT (q AND s)* by rule 2. When we get to *(NOT p) OR q*, however, we must split the tree into two branches, according to rule 3. Finally, each of these branches must divide when we apply rule 3 to *(NOT q) OR (NOT s)*. Each of the paths in this tree are closed (i.e., contains a pair of contradictory sentences). For example, the path that follows the left branches of the tree contains both *p* and *NOT p*. Since all paths are closed, argument (8) is deducible.

Canonical Proofs: An algorithm for translating trees to natural-deduction structures. Tree proofs such as that in figure 4.4 can be mimicked by means of natural-deduction proofs in PSYCOP+. Most of the tree rules in table 3.1 correspond to forward rules in the program: rule 1 to AND Elimination, rule 2 to DeMorgan (NOT over AND), rule 4 to DeMorgan (NOT over OR), rule 5 to Conditional Transformation, rule 6 to Negated Conditional Transformation, rule 7 to Double Negation Elimination. These are the only forward rules that we will need in mimicking tree proofs, and we can call them the *key* forward rules. (This is where the use of the conditional transformation rules is crucial; without them, we can't find natural-deduction proofs that correspond to arbitrary tree proofs.) One exception to the correspondence between the tree rules and PSYCOP+'s forward rules is rule 3. The forward rules don't give us a way of dividing the proof into parts on the basis of a disjunction. However, there is a backward rule—OR Elimination—that we can use for this purpose. The OR Elimination rule produces from a disjunctive assertion *P OR Q* two subdomains, one with supposition *P* and the other with supposition *Q*. This is analogous to the way rule 3 operates on *P OR Q* to divide a tree into two branches.

Given this correspondence, we can turn a tree proof **T** into a natural-deduction structure **N** in roughly the following way: The original premises of the argument become the premises of **N**, and the conclusion of the argument becomes the conclusion of **N**. Following the reductio strategy imposed by the tree proof, we next set up a subdomain in **N** whose supposition is the negation of the conclusion. If this subdomain leads to contradictory sentences, then the conclusion must follow by NOT Elimination. We can then use the key forward rules to decompose the premises and the supposition in **N**, in the way that rules 1–2 and 4–7 of table 3.1 decompose the premises and the negated conclusion in **T**. In general, this will leave us with some undecomposed disjunctions. For any such disjunction,

P OR Q, we can use OR Elimination to form two subdomains within the domain of the negated conclusion, one with supposition *P* and the other with supposition *Q*. The subgoal of these subdomains will be a contradictory sentence, *R AND NOT R*, formed from one of the contradictory literals in **T**. Further disjunctions will result in additional pairs of subsubdomains embedded in both of those just formed. Procedure CP-I in the appendix gives an algorithm for mapping any tree proof to a naturaldeduction structure. Sometimes the structure produced by CP-I will not quite be a proof as it stands, but it can be made into one by inserting one extra level of subdomains (as shown in CP-II of the appendix).

As an illustration of this mapping between tree proofs and naturaldeduction proofs, table 4.4 shows the natural-deduction proof that corresponds to the tree in figure 4.4. The premises of argument (8) appear at the beginning of the proof along with the sentences derived from them by the key forward rules. The first subdomain has as supposition the negation of the conclusion, *NOT (IF p THEN (q AND s))*, with the sentences that the forward rules produced from it directly beneath. The last sentence of this domain (line 34 in the table) is *p AND (NOT p)*. The rationale for this domain lies in an application of NOT Elimination, an attempt to show that the conclusion follows by a reductio. Within the domain of the negated conclusion are two immediate subdomains, the first with supposition *NOT p* and the other with supposition *q*, each of which has *p AND (NOT p)* as its final line. We can think of these domains as the result of applying OR Elimination to the sentence *(NOT p) OR q*, which appears above in line 5. The intent is to show that *p AND (NOT p)* follows from the disjunction by showing that it follows from *NOT p* and also from *q*. Most of the remaining subdomains are related to OR Elimination in the same way.

The innermost subdomains of table 4.4 (lines 18–19, 21–22, 26–27, and 29–30) are not part of the structure produced by the mapping procedure CP-I, but have been added to this structure to justify the line that follows. The natural-deduction proof that we construct from a tree in this way is the canonical proof (referred to as **N′** in the appendix). Each line of the canonical proof in table 4.4 can be justified using PSYCOP + 's rules, though it remains to be shown that this is possible in the general case. The justifications appear in the rightmost column. The canonical proof is not the most elegant proof of argument (8) within our system; figure 4.1 shows

Table 4.4
The canonical natural-deduction proof for argument (8).

1. IF p THEN q.	Premise
2. r AND s.	Premise
3. r	AND Elim. (from 2)
4. s	AND Elim. (2)
5. (NOT p) OR q	Cond. Transformation (1)
6. +NOT (IF p THEN (q AND s)).	Supposition
7. p	Neg. Cond. Transformation (6)
8. NOT (q AND s)	Neg. Cond. Transformation (6)
9. (NOT q) OR (NOT s)	DeMorgan (NOT over AND) (8)
10. +NOT p	Supposition
11. +NOT q	Supposition
12. p AND (NOT p)	AND Intro. (7, 10)
13. +NOT s	Supposition
14. p and (NOT p)	AND Intro. (7, 10)
15. p and (NOT p)	OR Elim (9, 11–14)
16. +q	Supposition
17. +NOT q	Supposition
18. +p	Supposition
19. q AND (NOT q)	AND Intro. (16, 17)
20. NOT p	NOT Intro. (18, 19)
21. +NOT p	Supposition
22. q AND (NOT q)	AND Intro. (16, 17)
23. p	NOT Elim. (21, 22)
24. p AND (NOT p)	AND Intro. (20, 23)
25. +NOT s	Supposition
26. +p	Supposition
27. s AND (NOT s)	AND Intro. (4, 25)
28. NOT p	NOT Intro. (26, 27)
29. +NOT p	Supposition
30. s AND (NOT s)	AND Intro. (4, 25)
31. p	NOT Elim. (29, 30)
32. p AND (NOT p)	AND Intro. (28, 31)
33. p AND (NOT p)	OR Elim. (9, 17–32)
34. p AND (NOT p)	OR Elim. (5, 10–33)
35. IF p THEN (q AND s)	NOT Elim. (6–34)

the way PSYCOP would normally prove an argument of this form. So the lengthy nature of the proof in table 4.4 should not be taken as an argument for the tree method over natural deduction. Our goal at this point is a purely theoretical one: to find a uniform procedure for getting from tree proofs to natural-deduction proofs, not to find a quick one.

Canonical Proofs II: Canonical proofs are deducible via PSYCOP+'s rules. Of course, in order to show that the structure **N** that our translation method produces can be turned into a legitimate proof in PSYCOP+, we must show that each of its sentences is either a premise or a supposition, or else that it follows from the premises and the suppositions by one of the rules in this system. What enables us to do this, of course, is the correspondence between the tree rules and PSYCOP+'s rules.

As a preliminary, it is helpful to recognize that if a sentence is copied from the tree proof to the natural-deduction structure by the algorithm then all the sentences that were used to derive that sentence in the tree are also available for its derivation in the natural-deduction proof. This result is called the *Inheritance Lemma* in the appendix, where a proof of it is given. As an example, the eighth line of figure 4.4, *(NOT p) OR q*, is derived in the tree proof by applying rule 5 to the premise *IF p THEN q*. *(NOT p) OR q* also appears in the natural-deduction proof of table 4.4 at line 5, where it is shown as derived from the same premise by the Conditional Transformation rule.

Given the Inheritance Lemma, we can easily see that any sentence S in tree **T** that our algorithm copied to the natural-deduction structure **N** is either a supposition or a premise in **N**, or else that it follows from the suppositions and the premises by one of the key forward rules. That is, each of these sentences can be legitimately derived in **N** by a rule in PSYCOP+. However, as was remarked above, the structure **N** is not yet a canonical proof. The canonical proof **N'** contains some lines that are not in **T**: the last lines of the various domains. For example, the conclusion of the proof in table 4.4 and the sentences *p AND (NOT p)* are not part of the tree proof. To justify these lines, we need to employ the backward rules OR Elimination, AND Introduction, NOT Elimination, and NOT Introduction. (Examples of the uses of all four occur in table 4.4.) As was noted above, this justification process can involve the addition of one further level of subdomains (e.g., that in lines 18–19 of table 4.4). However, proof CP-II in the appendix shows that each line of the canonical proof so constructed follows by PSYCOP+'s rules.

Completeness and Decidability of PSYCOP+

Any proof that PSYCOP or PSYCOP+ produces will be sound: If it can find a proof for an argument, then that argument will be valid in classical sentential logic. This is a consequence of the fact that all the rules in tables 4.1–4.3 are special cases of rules that are known to be sound in the classical system. What we saw in the previous subsection also goes a long way toward showing that PSYCOP+ is a complete proof procedure. Since every valid argument has a tree proof and since every tree proof corresponds to a canonical proof of the same argument, all that is missing for completeness is to show that PSYCOP+'s control structure allows it to discover the canonical proof. Of course, it is perfectly all right if PSYCOP+ happens to find a simpler proof of a valid argument. All we require is that PSYCOP+ be able to find the canonical proof if it hasn't found an easier one.

Suppose PSYCOP+ is given a valid argument to evaluate, and let N' denote a canonical proof of this argument. PSYCOP+'s first step is to run its forward rules on the premises. If it is lucky, this first step will yield the conclusion, and this will amount to a proof of the argument (though, of course, it will not be proof N'). In the general case, however, the conclusion won't be forthcoming. As has already been shown, forward rule application must eventually stop, and at that point PSYCOP+ will try a backward rule. The rule that leads to N' is NOT Elimination, but another of the rules may apply first in this situation. This rule will lead either to a different proof of the argument or to a situation in which no further rules apply. (Infinite searches are barred by the halting theorem proved above.) In the latter case, PSYCOP will apply another of its backward rules, continuing in this way until it either finds a novel proof or attempts to apply NOT Elimination. A check of the conditions on NOT Elimination in table 4.2 shows that there are no barriers to the rule in this situation.

NOT Elimination itself allows a choice of which contradiction it will attempt to prove. (See step c in table 4.2.) However, since there are only a finite number of candidates, it will eventually hit on the critical one—say, $R\ AND\ (NOT\ R)$—if it hasn't already found a proof on the basis of some other contradiction. At this point, PSYCOP+ will set up a new domain whose supposition is the negation of the conclusion and whose subgoal is $R\ AND\ (NOT\ R)$, and it will then apply its forward rules to the new set of assertions. Repeating the argument of the last two paragraphs at each stage of the proof shows that PSYCOP+ will (if it has found no earlier proof) eventually apply the right sequence of backward rules to yield proof N'. This implies that PSYCOP+ is indeed a complete proof procedure. Moreover, we have proved that PSYCOP+ will halt for any argument whatever. If the argument happens to be invalid, it must halt without achieving a proof, since its rules are sound. This means that PSYCOP+ is also a decision procedure for classical sentential logic.

Summary

The PSYCOP model is a set of representational and processing assumptions that attempts to explain deductive reasoning. This chapter has surveyed PSYCOP's core theory: its memory, sentential inference rules, and control structure. In essence, PSYCOP has a working memory and a long-term memory containing sentences that are interrelated by deduction links and dependency links. The former connect sentences to their direct entailments; the latter connect premises or suppositions to direct or indirect entailments. The entailment relation is established by the inference rules, which divide into our now-familiar forward and backward types. These rules include many natural-deduction principles well known from elementary logic, but they are specialized in a way that keeps them from spawning irrelevant inferences. PSYCOP applies these rules in the context of a fairly simple control structure: The forward rules create (breadth first) a web of assertions in working memory, while the backward rules generate (usually depth first) a succession of subgoals aimed at the web. The program halts if it finds a match between assertions and subgoals that suffices for a proof or if its rules no longer apply.

Our investigation of PSYCOP's mathematical properties demonstrated that if we give the program an argument to evaluate it will always halt, but not necessarily with the answer sanctioned in classical logic. Although PSYCOP produces no false alarms, its hit rate for classically valid arguments isn't perfect. For certain sorts of conditional arguments, such as (7), PSYCOP will stop without having found a proof. This means that PSYCOP is incomplete for classical logic, but there is a sense in which it is close: By adding a pair of rules that translate conditionals into truth-functionally equivalent expressions (i.e., the rules of table 4.3), we get both completeness and decidability. Accepting these somewhat unintuitive rules, then, is one measure of the cost of achieving classical completeness. This result must be interpreted cautiously, though, since completeness could be achieved by other means. For example, we can get a complete system by relaxing some of the conditions on PSYCOP's rules in tables 4.1 and 4.2, and it is possible that some such alteration could yield a computationally and psychologically plausible theory. In the absence of an acceptable alternative, however, we will assume that human reasoners may not be perfect classical-logic machines, even when we abstract over time and memory limitations, as we have in the present chapter.

Appendix: Proofs of the Major Propositions

HP-1: PSYCOP+'s rules create only finitely many domains for a given argument.

Proof A perusal of the IF Introduction, OR Elimination, NOT Introduction, and NOT Elimination rules shows that any subdomain that they produce has a supposition S and an initial goal G that are tightly constrained. For example, the IF Introduction rule produces a subdomain where both S and G are subformulas of the premises and the conclusion of the argument. In general, across all four rules, S and G are either (a) subformulas of the premises and conclusion, (b) the negation of such a subformula, or (c) a sentence of the form *Q AND NOT Q*, where *Q* is such a subformula. However, there are only a finite number of premises, and the conclusion and premises are each of finite length. Thus, there are only a finite number of sentences of type a, and for this reason sentences of types b and c must be finite too.

Consider a particular domain D in some proof. The conditions of the four domain-creating rules require that D's immediate subdomains have distinct pairs of supposition and goal. (See chapter 2 for the definition of *immediate subdomain.*) That is, if D_1 is an immediate subdomain of D with supposition S_1 and goal G_1, and D_2 is another immediate subdomain with supposition S_2 and goal G_2, then it cannot be the case that both $S_1 = S_2$ and $G_1 = G_2$. We have just seen that the set of possible sentences that can serve as supposition or goal is finite; hence, the number of possible pairs (S_i, G_i) is finite too. It follows that there can be only finitely many immediate subdomains in D.

This limitation on the number of *immediate* subdomains means that if the rules produce an infinite number of domains then this can occur only through embedding one subdomain within another. The initial domain D must have immediate subdomain D_1, which itself has immediate subdomain D_2, which has immediate subdomain D_3, and so on. Figure 4.3c illustrates embedding of subdomains to five levels. (The fact that there must be an infinite nesting of subdomains in an infinite backward search follows from König's lemma, which states that any infinite tree in which each point has only finitely many branches must have at least one infinite path. See Smullyan 1968 for a proof.) However, the conditions on the rules make this infinite nesting impossible. As above, the rules require each domain in such a series to have a distinct pair of supposition and goal; but since there are only finitely many candidates for these pairs, the sequence of nested domains must end. Thus, PSYCOP+ can produce only a finite number of domains in attempting to prove any given argument.

HP-II: The backward rules produce only a finite number of subgoals within a domain.

Proof Consider a situation in which PSYCOP+ is given a (finite) set of assertions Σ that hold in some domain D and a goal G_0 in that domain. An infinite backward search within D means that PSYCOP+ would produce a succession of subgoals $G_1, G_2, \ldots$, where G_1 is a subgoal of G_0, G_2 is a subgoal of G_1, and so on, all within D. (We are again relying on König's lemma.) Each G_i must be unique, since the rules do not allow duplicate subgoals. Notice that Backward IF Elimination, AND Elimination, Double Negation Elimination, Disjunctive Modus Ponens, Disjunctive Syllogism, Conjunctive Syllogism, and the DeMorgan rules can apply only a finite number of times in this situation. This is because any subgoal they produce must be a subformula of some assertion in Σ (see table 4.2), and there are only a finite number of subformulas from that set. The only remaining single-domain rules are Backward AND Introduction and OR Introduction. Thus, after some stage k, all the subgoals $G_{k+1}, G_{k+2}, \ldots$, would have to be produced by one of these two rules. However, a glance at the statement of these rules in table 4.2 shows that the subgoals they generate must be subformulas of the preceding goal. Thus, G_{k+1} must be a subformula of G_k, G_{k+2} must be a subformula of G_{k+1}, and so on. Since the subformula relation is transitive, $G_{k+1}, G_{k+2}, \ldots$, must all be unique subformulas of G_k. But this is impossible, since G_k has only finitely many unique subformulas.

HP-III: *The forward rules produce only a finite number of assertions within a domain.*

Proof Call a sentence produced by one of the forward rules (tables 4.1 and 4.3) a *conclusion* for that rule, and the sentence or sentences that trigger the rule its *premises*. (E.g., Forward IF Elimination has as premises *IF P THEN Q* and *P* and has as conclusion *Q*.) We also need to distinguish between an atomic sentence *token* that might occur in a complex sentence and an atomic sentence *type*. The former is a specific appearance or occurrence of an atomic sentence; the latter is the class to which these occurrences belong. Thus, there are two tokens of the atomic sentence type *Calvin deposits 50 cents* in the complex sentence *IF Calvin deposits 50 cents AND Calvin is hungry THEN Calvin deposits 50 cents.*

In these terms, the number of atomic sentence tokens in the conclusion of a forward rule is no greater than the number of tokens in the set of its premises. (In the case of IF Elimination, for example, the conclusion *Q* appears in the premise *IF P THEN Q*. For this reason, the number of atomic sentence tokens in *Q* must be less than or equal to the number in *IF P THEN Q* and thus less than or equal to the number in the set of its premises $\{P, IF\ P\ THEN\ Q\}$.) Furthermore, the forward rules don't introduce any new atomic sentence types, because the conclusions of these rules contain only atomic sentence types that are already contained in the premises. (For example, the conclusion of IF Elimination is *Q*, which is already part of *IF P THEN Q*, so any atomic sentence type in the former is also in the latter.)

Now consider a particular domain D, and the finite set of sentences Σ that hold in that domain before application of the forward rules. Let m be the number of atomic tokens in Σ and n the number of atomic types ($n \leq m$). From the first of the two observations above it follows that any sentence produced by the forward rules in D can contain no more than m atomic sentence tokens, and from the second observation it follows that the number of types from which these tokens can be drawn is n. For example, if there are a total of three atomic tokens in Σ, each belonging to one of two types (say, p and q), then the forward rules can produce a sentence that is at most three tokens long, each token being either p or q. If our language contained only the binary connectives AND, OR, and IF ... THEN, this would be sufficient to prove the theorem: Each sentence contains at most m atomic tokens, and hence at most $m - 1$ binary connectives. Thus, there are only a finite number of distinct sentences that can be produced by using these connectives to bind the tokens into sentences. (In our three-token, two-type example, there are 144 distinct sentences that are three tokens long, 12 sentences that are two tokens long, and two that are one token long.)

However, the connective NOT introduces a complication. Unless the number of NOTs is limited, new sentences can continue to be produced even when these sentences have a constant number of atomic tokens (e.g., $NOT\ p$, $NOT\ NOT\ p$, etc.). Inspection of the rules shows, though, that they can produce sentences with only a finite number of NOTs. The only forward rules that contain NOT in their conclusion are DeMorgan (NOT over OR), Conjunctive Syllogism, Negated Conditional Transformation, Conditional Transformation, and DeMorgan (NOT over AND). The first three of these generate conclusions that have no more NOTs than appear in their premises. Conditional Transformation and DeMorgan (NOT over AND) are the only forward rules that allow PSYCOP+ to produce a sentence with more NOTs than any sentence that appears in Σ. The first of these applies to sentences of the form IF P THEN Q and the second to sentences of the form $NOT(P\ AND\ Q)$. Notice, however, that none of the forward rules produce sentences that add an AND or an IF ... THEN. Thus, the total number of NOTs that can be produced by Conditional Transformation is limited to the number of IF ... THENs contained in Σ, and the total number of NOTs that can be produced by DeMorgan (NOT over OR) is limited to the number of ANDs in Σ. Thus, if x is the number of NOTs in Σ, y the number of ANDs, and z the number of IF ... THENs, no sentence produced by the forward rules can have more than $x + y + z$ NOTs.

Thus, any sentence produced by the forward rules can have no more than m atomic sentence tokens, $m - 1$ binary connectives, and $x + y + z$ NOTs. But the number of distinct sentences meeting these upper bounds must be finite. Hence, the forward rules can produce only finitely many new sentences.

CP-I: An algorithm for translating tree proofs to natural-deduction structures.

In general, the tree method leads to a structure similar to that shown at the top of figure 4.5, where $P_1, P_2, \ldots, P_k$ are the premises of the argument to be evaluated, $NOT\ C$ is the negation of its conclusion, and the Qs are the result of applying the rules in table 3.1. In particular, each branch

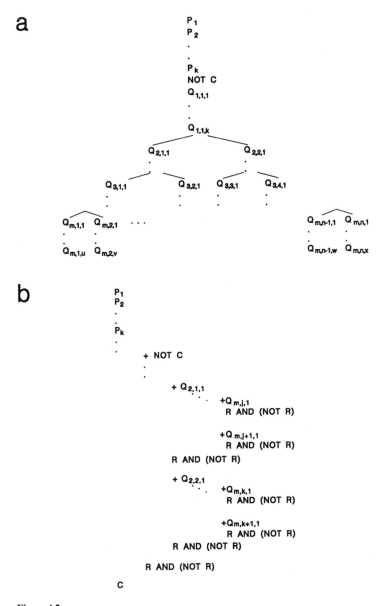

Figure 4.5
The general form for tree proofs (a) and for the analogous natural-deduction structure (b).

in the tree is the result of applying rule 3 to a disjunction that occurs higher up. Define a *branch sentence* to be one that appears immediately beneath the points where the tree splits; thus, $Q_{2,1,1}$, $Q_{2,2,1}$, and $Q_{3,1,1}$ are all branch sentences. Let *pivot sentence* refer to any sentence that is either a branch sentence, a premise, or the negated conclusion. A final piece of terminology: By *derivation of a sentence Q in tree* T, we mean the sequence of sentences S_1, S_2, ..., S_k, where S_1 is a premise or the negated conclusion, $S_k = Q$, and S_{i+1} was derived in tree T from S_i by the application of one of the rules in table 3.1

Suppose we have an arbitrary tree T for some deducible argument. All paths of T will be closed, and it will have the general form shown in figure 4.5. The algorithm below constructs a natural-deduction structure N that is analogous to T. The bottom half of figure 4.5 shows the basic details of N in our old indented notation for natural deduction, and the steps in constructing it are these:

(1) Let the outermost (most superordinate) domain of N include the premises P_1, P_2, ..., P_k of T as the first k lines and the conclusion C as the last line.

(2) Let the first subdomain include the negated conclusion, *NOT C*, as its supposition. As the last line, put the conjunction *R AND (NOT R)*, where R is an atomic proposition and both R and *NOT R* appear in some path in T. (Since T is closed, there must be such an R.)

(3) Insert in the subdomain created in step 2 two further subdomains: one with supposition $Q_{2,1,1}$ and the other with supposition $Q_{2,2,1}$ from T. The last line of each of the new subdomains is again *R AND (NOT R)*. (See figure 4.5b.)

(4) Continue embedding subdomains in this way: If $Q_{i,j,1}$ is the supposition for some domain D in N and if the first branch in T below $Q_{i,j,1}$ leads to the branch sentences $Q_{i+1,k,1}$ and $Q_{i+1,k+1,1}$, then place two new subdomains within D. $Q_{i+1,k,1}$ will be the supposition of the first, and $Q_{i+1,k+1,1}$ will be the supposition of the second. Both will have *R AND (NOT R)* as the last line.

(5) Take the first sentence in T that is not a pivot. The derivation of this sentence must have begun with either a premise or the negated conclusion, and may have included one or more branch sentences. We

then have the following (mutually exclusive) possibilities: (a) If the derivation included a premise but no branch sentence, copy the sentence in the outermost domain of N (i.e., the main proof) beneath any sentences in its derivation. (b) If the derivation included the negated conclusion but no branch sentence, copy the sentence into the second domain (i.e., the one whose supposition is *NOT C*) beneath any sentences in its derivation. (c) If the derivation involved a branch sentence, copy the sentence into the domain whose supposition corresponds to the lowest branch sentence in its derivation, again beneath any sentences in that derivation. Repeat this step for each of the remaining nonpivots.

Inheritance Lemma Suppose sentence Q is copied by the above algorithm from tree **T** to some domain D in the natural-deduction structure **N**. Then all sentences in the derivation of Q in **T** also hold in D.

Proof The proof is by induction on the length of the derivation of Q in **T**: In the first place, the derivation must begin with one of the premises or with the negated conclusion, and steps 1 and 2 ensure that these sentences hold in D. Let us assume, then, that the first k sentences of the derivation hold in D. If sentence $k + 1$ is a pivot, then it also holds in D, given the procedure in steps 3 and 4. If $k + 1$ is a nonpivot, step 5 will have placed it in **N** in a domain whose supposition is a pivot among the first k sentences. Since this pivot holds in D, so does a nonpivot within the same domain.

CP-II: Canonical proofs are deducible via the rules of PSYCOP+.

Proof Algorithm CP-I, above, is a procedure for mapping a tree proof **T** into a natural-deduction structure **N**. However, to turn **N** into the final canonical proof **N'**, we must usually add a few additional lines. To show that **N'** is a legitimate proof, we first demonstrate that each line in **N** that came from **T** follows by one of PSYCOP+'s rules. We then specify the remaining lines of **N'** and show that these lines also follow by the rules.

Let **T** be a tree proof and **N** be the natural-deduction structure created from it by algorithm CP-I. Any sentence S in **N** that was copied from **T** is deducible in **N** by the PSYCOP+ rules. If the sentence is a pivot in **T**, steps 1–4 guarantee that it will be a premise or a supposition in **N**, and hence its deductive status is not in question. If the sentence is not a pivot, it must have been derived in **T** from a higher sentence by one of the rules in table 3.1. The rule in question cannot be rule 3, since this would make the sentence a pivot; hence, the rule must correspond to one of the key natural-deduction rules mentioned earlier. By the Inheritance Lemma, all the sentences in the derivation of S must also hold in S's domain. Thus, we can rederive S in **N** using a rule of PSYCOP+.

The canonical proof **N**' also contains sentences that were not in **T**— including, each domain's final line. We still need to show that these lines follow according to the natural-deduction rules. For this purpose, we will use just four of the backward rules from table 4.2: AND Introduction, NOT Introduction, NOT Elimination, and OR Elimination.

Take the most embedded pair (or pairs) of domains in **N** constructed in steps 3 or 4 above. (The special case in which **N** contains no such pairs will be considered below.) The final sentence of these domains is R AND $(NOT$ $R)$. By construction, the sentences that hold in each of these domains correspond to those on some complete path through **T**. Since all paths in **T** are closed, this path contains some atomic sentence S and its negation NOT S. If $S = R$, then the sentence R AND $(NOT$ $R)$ can be derived in this domain by AND Introduction. If $S \neq R$ in one of the domains D, then we embed one further pair of subdomains in D. One of these subdomains consists of just two sentences, supposition R and goal S AND $(NOT$ $S)$; the other consists of supposition NOT R and goal S AND $(NOT$ $S)$. Since both S and NOT S hold in these subdomains, S AND $(NOT$ $S)$ can be derived in them (by AND Introduction again). Because of the first subdomain, we can derive NOT R in D by NOT Introduction; because of the second, we can derive R in D by NOT Elimination. (Inspection of the statement of these rules in table 4.2 shows that all their conditions are satisfied.) Hence, R AND $(NOT$ $R)$ holds in D, too, by AND Introduction. The structure derived from **N** by the possible addition of these subdomains is the *canonical proof*, **N**'.

Thus, the final lines follow in each member of the most embedded domain pairs constructed in steps 3–5. It remains to be shown that this is also true for the rest of the domains. We do this by working outward from the most embedded subdomains just considered. That is, take the domain D*, which is the immediate superdomain of the most embedded pairs. The suppositions in the subdomains, say $Q_{i,j,1}$ and $Q_{i,j+1,1}$, must have been branch sentences in **T**, derived by rule 3 from the disjunction $Q_{i,j,1}$ OR $Q_{i,j+1,1}$. This disjunction was copied to **N** along with the rest of the **T** sentences, and by the Inheritance Lemma the disjunction must also hold in D*. Thus, since the sentence *R AND (NOT R)* follows in both subdomains, this same sentence must be derivable in D* by OR Elimination.

We can repeat this reasoning with all embedded domain pairs. For example, if D* itself happens to be a member of such a pair, then *R AND (NOT R)* must also be deducible in the other member of the pair; hence, it will follow by OR Elimination in D*'s immediate superdomain. By iterating this process, we will eventually be able to derive *R AND (NOT R)* in the outermost pair of domains (i.e., the ones whose suppositions are $Q_{2,1,1}$ and $Q_{2,2,1}$ in figure 4.5b). Thus, with one more application of OR Elimination, *R AND (NOT R)* must follow in the domain of the negated conclusion. (In the special case in which there are no embedded pairs of subdomains created in steps 3 and 4, **T** has no branches and consists of a single path. Since *R* and *NOT R* are both in **T**, they must be in the path and thus hold in the subdomain of the negated conclusion. Therefore, *R AND (NOT R)* follows in this domain by AND Introduction.) Finally, *C* itself must follow in the premises' domain by NOT Elimination. The construction **N'** is then a correct proof of *C* from $P_1, P_2, \ldots, P_k$ via PSYCOP +'s rules.

5 Mental Proofs and Their Empirical Consequences

This chapter is devoted to experimental results that compare the model's performance to that of human reasoners. If the general theory is right, mental proofs may figure in many different kinds of cognitive tasks. As we saw in the third chapter, deduction may play a central role in planning or in question answering, which at first glance are not specifically deduction problems. Theoretically, then, we could use findings about such cognitive skills to test our theory of mental proofs.

There is something to be gained, however, from beginning with experiments that focus on more obviously deductive tasks—for example, tasks in which subjects evaluate the deductive correctness of arguments. In the first place, these tasks are the traditional ones in the psychology of reasoning (see chapter 1) and so provide some common ground for comparing our theory with alternative proposals. Second, these tasks allow us some flexibility in testing the theory, since we can single out particular inferences for examination. Of course, we need to proceed cautiously. I assume that subjects bring to bear rules that they judge appropriate for solving math-type puzzles of this sort (the ones I called demoted rules in chapter 2). These derive from the abstract rules in tables 4.1 and 4.2, but exactly which of these rules subjects actively employ may be open to individual differences and pragmatic pressures. Moreover, instructing subjects to decide whether an argument is "logically valid" or whether the conclusion "necessarily follows" from the premises doesn't guarantee that they will understand these instructions in the intended way. We can't always rule out the possibility that processes other than deduction interfere with the results. Still, these deduction tasks are probably as close as we can come to pure tests of the theory, and so they provide a good empirical base from which to begin.

In the first section of this chapter, I review a number of experiments that I designed to test the theory of chapter 4 (or a closely related theory). In these experiments subjects attempted to evaluate the validity of arguments, or to follow proofs or remember proofs presented to them. Taken as a group, the experiments provide a fairly broad test of the core assumptions. In the second section, I consider whether the PSYCOP theory is consistent with earlier research on simpler problems involving conditional and negative sentences, which were briefly encountered in chapter 1. Although I will discuss some additional experiments with PSYCOP in chapter 7, the present set of findings should provide a "consumer report" on the model's empirical strengths and weaknesses.

Some Tests of the Proof Model

PSYCOP consists of too many assumptions to test with any precision in a single experiment or type of experiment. The following studies therefore highlight different aspects of the model—inference rules, real-time processing, and memory structure—that combine to produce subjects' responses. Although some of these studies were designed as specific tests of PSYCOP, we can begin with a look at an older experiment that was conceived as a test of an earlier version of the model. The PSYCOP theory grew out of a somewhat more restricted model of propositional reasoning called ANDS (for A Natural-Deduction System), which I developed in the early 1980s (Rips 1983; Rips and Conrad 1983). To a certain extent, PSYCOP can be considered an extension of that earlier theory, and so some of the experiments based on ANDS will also serve as tests of PSYCOP.

Evidence from Evaluation of Arguments

The traditional experiment in the psychology of reasoning is one in which subjects study a set of arguments and decide which of them are valid. This paradigm dates at least as far back as Störring's (1908) experiments; in view of this long history, it might be useful to show that the model can predict its results.

In order to conduct such a test, I assembled the 32 problems listed in table 5.1. (The table uses "&" for AND, " ∨ " for OR, " − " for NOT, and "→" for IF ... THEN.) These problems are all deducible in classical sentential logic and are also deducible in the model by means of rules very similar to PSYCOP's. The critical rules for these problems (see tables 4.1 and 4.2) are IF Elimination, DeMorgan (NOT over AND), Disjunctive Syllogism, Disjunctive Modus Ponens, AND Elimination, AND Introduction, OR Introduction, NOT Introduction, and OR Elimination. The reason for singling out these rules was that they constituted the inference schemas for the earlier ANDS theory; however, all of them also appear among PSYCOP's rules. Although the experiment does not test the full range of PSYCOP's inference skills, it does test an important subset. The arguments were constructed so that each could be proved by means of three rules selected from the above list. In addition to these deducible arguments, there were also 32 nondeducible ones, created by recombining the premises and conclusions of the first set. Finally, 40 filler arguments were added to the ensemble; most of these were simple deducible problems.

Table 5.1
Predicted and observed percentages of "necessarily true" responses to deducible arguments.

Argument	Observed	Predicted
A $(p \lor q) \& -p$ $\overline{}$ $q \lor r$	33.3	33.3
B s $p \lor q$ $\overline{}$ $-p \rightarrow (q \& s)$	66.7	70.2
C $p \rightarrow -(q \& r)$ $(-q \lor -r) \rightarrow -p$ $\overline{}$ $-p$	16.7	32.4
D $--p$ $-(p \& q)$ $\overline{}$ $-q \lor r$	22.2	30.6
E $(p \lor r) \rightarrow q$ $\overline{}$ $(p \lor q) \rightarrow q$	83.3	79.9
F $-p \& q$ $\overline{}$ $q \& -(p \& r)$	41.7	40.5
G $(p \lor q) \rightarrow -r$ $r \lor s$ $\overline{}$ $p \rightarrow s$	61.1	70.2
H $(p \rightarrow q) \& (p \& r)$ $\overline{}$ $q \& r$	80.6	76.6
I $(p \lor q) \rightarrow -s$ s $\overline{}$ $-p \& s$	55.6	41.2
J q $\overline{}$ $p \rightarrow ((p \& q) \lor r)$	33.3	36.0
K $(p \lor -q) \rightarrow -p$ $p \lor -q$ $\overline{}$ $-(q \& r)$	22.2	35.6
L $(p \lor q) \rightarrow -(r \& s)$ $\overline{}$ $p \rightarrow (-r \lor -s)$	75.0	70.4
M $-p$ q $\overline{}$ $-(p \& r) \& (q \lor s)$	22.2	26.4
N $(p \lor r) \rightarrow -s$ $\overline{}$ $p \rightarrow -(s \& t)$	50.0	38.1
O $-(p \& q)$ $(-p \lor -q) \rightarrow r$ $\overline{}$ $-(p \& q) \& r$	77.8	75.8
P $(q \lor r) \& s$ $\overline{}$ $-q \rightarrow r$	69.4	68.5

Table 5.1 (continued)

	Argument	Observed	Predicted
Q	p $(p \lor q) \to -r$ ――――――――― p & $-(r \& s)$	33.3	40.5
R	$p \to r$ ――――――― $(p \& q) \to r$	58.3	69.1
S	s $p \to r$ ――――――― $p \to (r \& s)$	75.0	70.9
T	$p \lor q$ ――――――――― $-p \to (q \lor r)$	33.3	32.2
U	p $(p \lor q) \to r$ $r \to s$ ――――――― $s \lor t$	38.9	33.9
V	$p \& q$ ――――――――― $q \& (p \lor r)$	47.2	37.6
W	$-(p \& q)$ $(-p \lor -q) \to -r$ ――――――――――― $-(r \& s)$	23.0	35.5
X	$(p \lor s) \to r$ s ――――――――― $-(r \to -s)$	50.0	36.1
Y	$p \to -q$ ――――――――― $p \to -(q \& r)$	36.1	33.9
Z	$-(p \& q) \& r$ $(-p \lor -q) \to s$ ――――――――――― s	66.7	73.9
A′	$(p \lor q) \to (r \& s)$ ――――――――――――― $p \to r$	91.7	86.9
B′	$-r$ $q \lor r$ ――――――― $r \to - -q$	36.1	38.7
C′	$-(p \& q)$ $- -q$ ―――――――――― $-p \& -(p \& q)$	72.2	62.2
D′	$(p \lor q) \& ((r \lor s) \to -p)$ r ―――――――――――――――――― q	83.3	75.8
E′	$p \lor s$ $(p \lor r) \to s$ ――――――――― $s \lor t$	26.1	36.0
F′	t $-(r \& s)$ ―――――――――――――― $((-r \lor -s) \& t) \lor u$	36.1	33.8

The subjects in this study saw the arguments in a single randomized list. For each argument, they were to circle the phrase "necessarily true" beneath the problem if the conclusion had to be true whenever the premises were true, and the phrase "not necessarily true" otherwise. Subjects responded to each problem in this way even if they had to guess. For half of the subjects, the arguments appeared in instantiations having to do with the location of people in cities. For example, argument E in table 5.1 would have looked like (1).

(1)   If Judy is in Albany or Barbara is in Detroit, then Janice is in Los Angeles.

If Judy is in Albany or Janice is in Los Angeles, then Janice is in Los Angeles.

The remaining subjects saw the same problems rephrased in terms of the actions of hypothetical machines. Thus, for these subjects, the sample argument appeared in the following guise:

(2)   If the light goes on or the piston expands, then the wheel turns.

If the light goes on or the wheel turns, then the wheel turns.

The subjects in both groups were students or nonstudents of approximately the same age. None of them had taken a formal course in logic. (This holds true, as well, for all the experiments reported in this book.)

According to our theory, subjects should correctly respond that the conclusion of such an argument is necessarily true if they can construct a mental proof of that conclusion, and success in doing so will obviously depend on whether they can muster all the inference rules needed to complete the proof. As a working assumption, we will suppose that errors on these problems are due to a failure to apply the rules. The failure may be due to retrieval difficulties, slips in carrying out the steps of the rule, failure to recognize the rule as applicable in the current context, or other factors. In general, we can think of each rule R_i as associated with a probability p_i that the rule will be available on a given trial. This means that there will be some occasions on which R_i would be useful in completing a proof but is not available to the subject. On these occasions, the subject will have to search for an alternative proof that uses rules other than R_i. (Such alternatives are sometimes possible because of the redundancy of the system.) If no such alternative exists, we will assume that the subject either guesses at the answer (with probability p_g) or simply responds incorrectly that the conclusion does not necessarily follow (with probability $1 - p_g$).

For example, when all the rules listed above are available, the model will prove (1) or (2) using a combination of IF Introduction, OR Elimination, and Disjunctive Modus Ponens. If these rules are available with probabilities p_1, p_2, and p_3, respectively, then (assuming independence) the probability of a correct "necessarily true" response might be (3) where the first term is the probability of a correct mental proof and the second term reflects a correct guess after failure to find the proof.

(3) $P(\text{"necessarily"}) = p_1 p_2 p_3 + 0.5 \, p_g (1 - p_1 p_2 p_3)$,

This equation is not quite right, however, since the model can still find a proof of these arguments even if Disjunctive Modus Ponens is missing. OR Introduction and IF Elimination can combine to fill the same role played by the unavailable rule. (All the remaining rules are necessary for the problem, since omitting them keeps the model from producing any proof at all.) To correct for this alternative derivation, we must add some new terms to the equation. If p_4 is the probability that IF Elimination is available and p_5 is the probability that OR Introduction is available, then the proper expression is (4).

(4) $P(\text{"necessarily"}) = p_1 p_2 p_3 + (1 - p_3) p_1 p_2 p_4 p_5$

$$+ 0.5 \, p_g [1 - p_1 p_2 p_3 - (1 - p_3) p_1 p_2 p_4 p_5].$$

The first term is again the probability of finding a proof by the original method, the second term is the probability of finding the alternative proof, and the third is the probability of a correct guess.

To derive predictions from the model, then, we need two pieces of information about each of the arguments in table 5.1: the rules that are used in a proof of that argument, and the probability that each of these rules will be available. We can obtain the first type of information by simulation, giving the model the argument and inspecting the proof to find which rules it employs. These rules can then be omitted (singly and in combination) to determine whether there are alternative proofs. The process is then repeated until no new proofs are forthcoming. This simulation allows us to formulate an equation like (4) for each of the arguments. The rule availabilities can be estimated by treating them as parameters when fitting the resulting equations to the data.

Table 5.1 gives the obtained and predicted percentages of correct "necessarily true" responses for the critical deducible problems. An analysis of variance of the data turned up no effect of the problem content (people in locations vs. machine actions) and no interaction of this factor with scores on the individual problems. Hence, the data from the two groups of subjects are combined in the table. The overall rate of correct responses is fairly low (50.6%), though there is obviously a very wide range across individual problems—from 16.7% correct on the hardest problem to 91.7% correct on the easiest. The percentage of incorrect "necessarily true" responses to the nondeducible problems (i.e., false alarms) was 22.9%. Thus, despite the low hit rate, subjects were distinguishing the deducible from the nondeducible items. In experiments like this one involving choice of alternative responses, the absolute response rate depends not only on subjects' accuracy but also on the criterion they adopt for a "necessarily true" response. Cautious subjects, for example, are likely to give somewhat low rates of positive responses, even though they are able to discriminate correct from incorrect arguments with reasonable accuracy. In accounting for these results, we therefore need to concentrate on the relative scores across the set of problems.[1]

The predicted scores in the table are the result of fitting equations similar to (4) to the data. The full model requires a large number of availability parameters, since we need a distinct parameter for each inference rule. To reduce this number somewhat, we have collapsed forward and backward versions of a given rule, using the same parameter for both members of a pair. For example, the same parameter represented the availability of backward and forward IF Elimination. We also set the guessing parameter, p_g, using the data from the nondeducible problems: If subjects respond "necessarily true" to these nondeducible items only because of bad guesses, then the guessing rate (after failure to find a proof) should be twice this value, or 45.8%. (This is not the overall probability of guessing; it is the conditional probability of guessing rather than saying "not necessarily true" given that no proof was forthcoming.) These economy moves still leave 10 parameters, but there are 21 remaining degrees of freedom for a test of the model.[2]

Although the fit of the model is difficult to summarize because of the varied nature of the problems, table 5.1 shows that the predictions are reasonably accurate. The correlation between predicted and observed scores, 0.93, yields a significant proportion of variance accounted for when tested against the Problem × Subject interaction from an analysis of variance:

$F(10, 1054) = 26.43, p < 0.01.$

The residual variance is fairly small, but it is also significant because of the large number of residual degrees of freedom:

$F(21, 1054) = 1.88, p < 0.05.$

The parameter estimates are those in table 5.2. For the most part, these parameters are what we might expect on the basis of the intuitive nature of the rules. The easiest rules are those that seem obviously correct, including AND Introduction, AND Elimination, and Disjunctive Modus Ponens. The most difficult rule is OR Introduction, which allows us to deduce sentences of the form P OR Q from P. Many subjects apparently fail to apply this rule, probably for pragmatic reasons (Grice 1989; Gazdar 1979; McCawley 1981; Pelletier 1977): The conclusion of such an inference contains information that may seem to be irrelevant to the premise on which it is based and thus to violate conversational conventions, as was discussed in chapter 2.[3] (For more empirical evidence on the difficulty of OR Introduction, see Rips and Conrad 1983.)

   One puzzling aspect of these estimates is the very low availability for NOT Introduction versus the relatively high availabilities for OR Elimination and IF Introduction. The routines for these rules in table 4.2 make them seem about equally complex: All three are backward rules that involve subdomains. So why should NOT Introduction be so much harder to apply? The difficulty might be explained as an artifact of the particular

Table 5.2
Parameter estimates for model as applied to argument-evaluation experiment.

Rule	Estimate
Disjunctive Modus Ponens	1.000
AND Introduction	1.000
AND Elimination	0.963
IF Introduction	0.861
OR Elimination	0.858
IF Elimination	0.723
DeMorgan (NOT over AND)	0.715
Disjunctive Syllogism	0.713
NOT Introduction	0.238
OR Introduction	0.197

sample of problems, but in fact we can also find evidence for such difficulty in other paradigms, as we will see in later subsections of this chapter ("Evidence from Proof Comprehension" and "Inferences with Conditionals") and in the chapters that follow. Evidently, the reductio strategy of assuming the opposite of what one wants to prove is not an obvious move for subjects who haven't had extensive mathematics training.[4] A plausible guess is that this difficulty is related to the conceptual distance between the main goal of proving $NOT\ P$ and the subgoal of proving a contradiction Q and $NOT\ Q$ on the basis of P. By contrast, OR Elimination and IF Introduction seem more direct, more intimately tied to the goals and assertions that trigger them.

One way to see what the model buys us is to compare the fits just mentioned against what we can obtain using other possible measures of problem difficulty. We might expect, for example, that the greater the number of premises in an argument, the more difficult that argument would be to evaluate. Similarly, the greater the number of atomic sentences in the argument, the harder it should be. For instance, argument F' in table 5.1 contains four types of atomic sentences (r, s, t, and u), and seven atomic sentence tokens or occurrences. It should therefore be more difficult than B', which contains only two atomic sentence types and five tokens. In general, however, these measures of surface complexity fail to provide a good account of the data. The correlation between the percentage of correct responses and the number of premises is -0.23, and the correlations with number of types and tokens of atoms are -0.04 and 0.10, respectively. This suggests that the true difficulty of the arguments is associated with the inference patterns they display, where these patterns are close to those specified in PSYCOP.

Evidence from Proof Comprehension

Argument-evaluation experiments, such as the one just discussed, allow us to gather data quickly on a broad sample of problems. However, in these experiments each subject proceeds at his or her own pace, and hence the studies can't tell us much about the real-time properties of the model. To get a better test of these processing characteristics, we need an experiment in which we can time subjects as they carry out their inferences. One type of task that is useful for this purpose involves presenting subjects with consecutive parts of a proof and having them respond to each part under timed conditions. In general, the hypothesis is that those parts of the proof that require more effort from PSYCOP should also be the parts producing the slowest response times from subjects. To understand the details of the predictions, though, we need to step back for a moment and consider some further features of the model. So far, we have discussed the way that PSYCOP evaluates arguments by constructing proofs. The present task, however, requires PSYCOP to deal with proofs that arrive from external sources.

Proof Comprehension in PSYCOP   At first glance, we might expect proof comprehension to be no problem at all for the model. After all, PSYCOP can construct its own proofs in working memory; thus, if a proof is simply given to it in input, the model shouldn't have much difficulty understanding it. In fact, though, comprehending proofs is no small matter, as you will probably agree if you recall struggling to understand proofs in difficult mathematics texts. One reason for this is that most mathematical proofs (outside of elementary logic and geometry) don't present every step in the inference chain. Instead, they are usually "gappy proofs" or "enthymemes" that give only the main landmarks on the route to the conclusion, leaving the reader to fill in the rest. The problem that PSYCOP faces is the same: It must translate the externally presented proof into one that contains all the missing details and therefore shows explicitly how each of the proof's lines follows from the preceding ones. To avoid confusion, we can call the proof that is given to PSYCOP the *external proof* and the proof that the model creates in response—the one that it stores in working memory— the *internal proof*. One difference between them is that, whereas the external proof can be extremely gappy, the internal proof of the same argument will have all the inference steps intact if PSYCOP is successful in comprehending it. (See Singer et al. 1990 and 1992 for evidence that people also deduce information from their general knowledge in order to close the gaps in ordinary text.)

How does PSYCOP manage to fill the gaps in an external proof? As each sentence of the proof appears, PSYCOP makes a decision about how to handle it and reports that decision to the user. For example, the model may decide that the new sentence is a restatement of one it has already deduced; in that case, it will print out the message "I already know this to be true on the basis of these sentences ...," filling the blank with the names of the working-memory sentences from which it had earlier deduced the item. Or it may judge that the input sentence is some new consequence that it hasn't yet inferred, and then try to deduce it from what it currently knows, using its stock of inference rules. If it succeeds, it will print out "I have deduced [the new sentence] ...," specifying the working-memory sentences immediately involved in the inference and the suppositions that were in effect at the time. PSYCOP can recall this information about memory sentences and assumptions, since it is represented in its deduction and dependency links (see chapter 4). If the model fails to deduce the new sentence, it will note "This doesn't seem to follow" and will hold the sentence in a pending state, trying to deduce it again after more information from the proof has appeared.

In coming to these decisions, PSYCOP makes use of phrases (discourse markers) in the input such as "suppose that," "under these circumstances," "this is because," and "therefore," as well as input cues that a new sentence "follows by" a certain rule or "follows from" an earlier theorem. These cues can often speed up PSYCOP's performance; however, the model will often make the right decisions in the absence of these cues, using its default assumptions. In the special case where the input consists of just the premises and the conclusion of an argument, PSYCOP will treat the text as a maximally gappy proof—one in which all the intermediate steps are omitted—and will proceed to try to deduce the conclusion in just the way discussed in chapter 4.

We can get a feel for how PSYCOP's proof interpretation works by considering how it responds to a simple external proof. The example we will use (which figures in the reaction-time experiment to be described later) concerns the argument shown here as (5), which is deducible by means of the rules in tables 4.1 and 4.2.

(5)   IF q THEN NOT p.

    p.
    _____

    IF (IF NOT q THEN s) THEN s.

An external proof of this argument is shown in boldface in the "dialogue" (6). After each line, PSYCOP tries to figure out how the line fits into its internal proof and indicates its actions by printing the responses shown in lightface.

(6)   a. **Suppose IF q THEN NOT p.**

    b. Okay, I'll suppose IF q THEN NOT p.

   c. **Suppose p.**

   d. Okay, I'll suppose p.

   e. **Suppose IF NOT q THEN s.**

   f. Okay, I'll suppose IF NOT q THEN s.

   g. **Under these circumstances, NOT q.**

   h. I have deduced NOT q ... under assumptions IF q THEN NOT p, p, and IF NOT q THEN s.

   i. **Under these circumstances, s.**

   j. I already know that s is true on the basis of IF NOT q THEN s and NOT q ...

   k. **Therefore, IF (IF NOT q THEN s) THEN s.**

   l. I have deduced IF (IF NOT q THEN s) THEN s ... under assumptions IF q THEN NOT p and p.

In lines a and c the external proof asks us to suppose that the premises of the argument are true, and PSYCOP follows this advice by placing these sentences in working memory, typing "Okay ... " when it has done so.[5] The same goes for the extra supposition in line e. In some situations, as we will see momentarily, the supposed sentences will be sufficient to trigger PSYCOP's forward rules, producing some unprompted assertions in memory; but at the beginning of this proof no inference routines operate. Thus, the state of working memory is that shown in figure 5.1a, containing just the three suppositions.

When line g of (6) appears, PSYCOP must do some work to figure out why $NOT\ q$ is supposed to hold. An impasse like this one causes the model to try to prove the new line from previous information in essentially the same way that it would prove a conclusion from a set of premises in an argument-evaluation task. In this case, the new sentence, $NOT\ q$, triggers PSYCOP's Backward NOT Introduction rule. This routine tells PSYCOP to suppose q (see sentence 5 in figure 5.1b) and attempt to deduce a contradiction. Part of this contradiction is immediately forthcoming, since the new supposition q together with the premise $IF\ q\ THEN\ NOT\ p$ yields $NOT\ p$ by Forward IF Elimination. Because PSYCOP is already assuming p (sentence 2 in the figure), the contradiction is complete. At this point PSYCOP prints out the message in line h, noting the assumptions that are in effect after it infers $NOT\ q$. (Supposition q is not mentioned, since this

a

1. IF q THEN NOT p.   2. p.

3. IF NOT q THEN s.

b

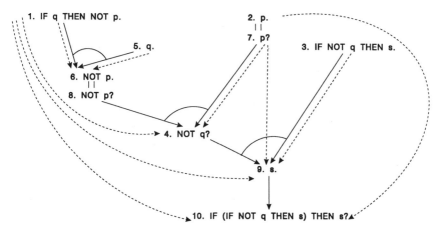

c

Figure 5.1
Development of PSYCOP's internal proof in comprehending (6).

supposition is discharged by NOT Introduction when the conclusion is drawn.) However, this is not quite all that the model does in response to line g. Since it is assuming *IF NOT q THEN s*, and since it now knows *NOT q*, it can also derive *s* by a second application of Forward IF Elimination. Hence, when the external proof gets around to saying that *s* follows in line i, PSYCOP can respond that it "already knows" this is true. (See figure 5.1b.)

Finally, the external proof asserts the main conclusion—one that the model has not anticipated. To see whether the conclusion follows, PSYCOP again turns to its backward rules, specifically to IF Introduction, since the conclusion is a conditional. This routine asks PSYCOP to assume the antecedent, *IF NOT q THEN s*, and attempt to deduce the consequent, *s*. However, before doing any deductive work on its own, PSYCOP always checks to see if the necessary inferences are already in working memory. In this case it notices that it is already assuming the antecedent (as sentence 3) and that it has deduced the consequent on this basis (as sentence 9). Thus, all the conditions on IF Introduction have been carried out, and the conclusion follows just as asserted in the external proof. The state of the internal proof in working memory is that of figure 5.1c, and this allows PSYCOP to announce in line l of (6) that it has deduced the conclusion "under the assumptions" *IF q THEN NOT p* and *p*. (The supposition *IF NOT q THEN s* is discharged by IF Introduction.) Since these are the premises of the original argument in (5), the internal proof is complete.

The key point of this example is that PSYCOP progresses through a proof by fits and starts, sometimes anticipating a line before it appears in the external proof and sometimes pausing to see how a line follows by means of its backward rules. This pattern of hesitations and anticipations provides the basis for our reaction-time test.

Reaction-Time Predictions The experiment compared subjects' performances on pairs of external proofs, such as the example in table 5.3. The B proof (labeled "more difficult") is exactly the same as the one we took up in (6). The A proof ("simpler proof") is identical to B with the exception of the very first line, which substitutes *IF p THEN NOT q* for *IF q THEN NOT p*. Since these two lines are logically equivalent, the two proofs differ minimally in surface form and in logical structure. However, PSYCOP handles these two proofs in very different ways, yielding a somewhat surprising set of predictions.

Table 5.3
Sample proof pair from comprehension experiment.

A. Simpler proof	B. More difficult proof
1. Suppose IF p THEN NOT q.	1. Suppose IF q THEN NOT p.
2. Suppose p.	2. Suppose p.
3. Suppose IF NOT q THEN s.	3. Suppose IF NOT q THEN s.
[4. Under these circumstances, NOT q.]	[4. Under these circumstances, NOT q.]
5. Under these circumstances, s.	5. Under these circumstances, s.
6. Therefore, IF (IF NOT q THEN s) THEN s.	6. Therefore, IF (IF NOT q THEN s) THEN s.

The first point to notice about these proofs is that PSYCOP is able to anticipate the fourth line in A but not in B. After PSYCOP reads lines A1 and A2, it will immediately deduce *NOT q* using Forward IF Elimination; so when A4 eventually comes in, PSYCOP will respond "I already know *NOT q* is true...." By contrast, we have already noticed that PSYCOP has no way of anticipating B4 and must rely on its backward rules to determine why it is supposed to follow. Assuming that this difference also holds for human reasoners, we ought to predict that subjects would take longer in assimilating B4 than A4.

A second point of difference concerns the relationship between lines 4 and 5. Given proof A, PSYCOP can deduce *s* immediately after reading line 3: lines 1 and 2 yield *NOT q* by Forward IF Elimination, as just explained, and line 3 and *NOT q* produce *s* by the same inference rule. This means that we could omit line 4 entirely, and PSYCOP would still be able to deduce *s* before it appears in line 5. Not so, however, in proof B. Although PSYCOP can also deduce *s* before line 5 in B, this depends crucially on line 4. As we noticed in connection with the dialogue above, line 4 sets up the string of inferences leading to *s*. Thus, if line 4 were omitted in B, PSYCOP would have to pause and conduct a lengthy backward search when it came upon line 5. This yields an interaction prediction for response times: Processing should be relatively fast for line A5, whether line A4 is present or absent. But processing of B5 should be fast if line B4 is present, slow if it is absent.

In the experiment, each subject studied proofs that appeared one line at a time on a CRT display. The subjects had been instructed to assume that lines beginning with "Suppose" were true, and that they could take as much time as they liked in understanding them. When a subject felt ready to continue he or she was to press an "advance" button, which then displayed the next line of the proof on the screen. Old lines stayed on the screen after new ones appeared. Each subject continued in this way until he or she had studied all the "Suppose" lines. At that point, a row of asterisks was displayed on the screen as a "ready" signal, and the subject pushed the advance button once more when prepared to go on. This brought up a line beginning "Under these circumstances," and the subjects were under instructions to decide whether this line necessarily followed from preceding lines or did not necessarily follow. Subjects pressed one of two buttons on the response panel to indicate their decisions, and the computer recorded their response times from the point at which the sentence appeared until the button was pressed. This sequence was repeated until the subjects had responded to all the remaining lines in the proof.

The critical proofs follow the pattern of those in table 5.3: Although we constructed the eight proof pairs using different inference rules, they were all similar to A and B. The within-pair differences were confined to the early "Suppose" lines; the critical "Under these circumstances" and "Therefore" lines were identical from one member of the pair to the other. The proof pairs were also similar to A and B with respect to which lines PSYCOP could deduce in advance and which it had to wait to derive. In the simpler member of the pair, there were two consecutive lines—a *Preparatory* line analogous to A4 and a *Succeeding* line analogous to A5—both of which PSYCOP could derive before reading them. In the more difficult member of the proof pair, PSYCOP could anticipate the Succeeding line only if it had processed the Preparatory line.

Each proof occurred in two versions: one in which the Preparatory line (e.g., line 4) was present and one in which it was absent. Thus, subjects viewed 32 critical proofs: eight proof pairs with two versions of each member. In addition, there were 32 additional proofs that contained a "Therefore" or "Under these circumstances" line that was not a logical consequence of the "Suppose" lines. We included these proofs as fillers to keep subjects honest. Without them, subjects could have responded with perfect accuracy by always pressing the "necessarily follows" button.

Subjects saw instantiations of the proofs, rather than the schematic forms shown here in table 5.3. The instantiations all employed people-in-places sentences like those of the preceding experiment; for example, the first sentence in A would have appeared to subjects as *Suppose that if Martha is in Boston, Claire is not in LA.* The two versions of a proof were differently instantiated to disguise their logical similarity, and the

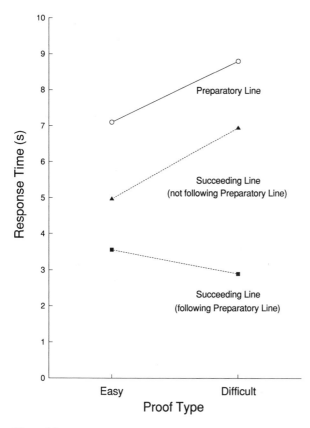

Figure 5.2
Mean correct response time for preparatory and succeeding lines in simpler and more difficult proofs.

computer presented the entire set of 64 proofs to each subject in a distinct
random permutation.

Figure 5.2 displays the mean correct reaction times that are relevant to
our predictions. Consider first the data for the Preparatory line, represented by the top curve of the figure. Clearly, when this line is present,
subjects take longer to process it in the context of the more difficult proof
than in the simpler proof ($F(1,27) = 6.48$, $p = 0.02$). This is consistent with
the idea that subjects were able to infer beforehand the contents of the line
in the simpler proof, but not in the more difficult one. (See Lea et al. 1990
for further evidence on sentential inferences during comprehension.)

The more interesting prediction concerns the Succeeding line, which is indicated by the bottom two curves in the figure. According to our predictions, when the Preparatory line is omitted, the times should once again increase for the more difficult proof. However, when the Preparatory line is present, subjects should be able to anticipate the Succeeding lines in both proofs, eliminating the difference. The results show that this prediction is correct, as evidenced by a significant interaction between proof type (simple or difficult) and the presence or absence of the Preparatory line ($F(1,27) = 6.78$, $p < 0.01$). The figure also shows that responses were faster overall for the Succeeding than for the Preparatory line. This is probably the result of a difference in the complexity of these sentences: In all but two of the eight proof pairs, the Preparatory line contained more logical connectives and atomic propositions. The error rates for these data were 14% for both the Preparatory and Succeeding lines, and they showed only a main effect of difficulty.

These results help confirm the forward/backward distinction that is an integral part of PSYCOP. It is the forward rules that account for the model's ability to foresee the upcoming Preparatory and Succeeding lines in the simpler proofs. When the forward rules are unable to derive the upcoming lines (as in the case of the Preparatory line of the difficult proofs, or the Succeeding line of the same proofs when the Preparatory line is omitted), PSYCOP must wait until these target lines appear and verify them by backward inference. The response times therefore suggest that our division of inferences into forward and backward sets may reflect a similar split in subjects' deductive processes.

Evidence from Memory for Proofs

The PSYCOP theory assumes that working memory holds the mental proofs that people use in dealing with deductive questions, but so far there has been little to say about working memory apart from its role as a container. The design of the previously described experiments deliberately reduced memory limitations by giving subjects free access to the premises and the conclusion of the problem (in the argument-evaluation study) or to the individual proof lines (in the reaction-time study). This strategy was motivated by the fact that the experiments were tests of the inference rules rather than of the memory assumptions. Nevertheless, the natural-deduction structure of mental proofs makes some predictions about memory that deserve a closer look. One test of this structure comes from an experiment in which Marcus (1982) studied people's recall of individual lines from simple arguments. Although this experiment addressed hypotheses that Marcus derived from a generic natural-deduction framework, they apply to PSYCOP as a specific instance.

What Marcus observed was that lines from subdomains of proofs may have a different memory status than lines from superdomains. Subdomain sentences result from rules such as IF Introduction and NOT Introduction, and they play a supporting role in the proof, helping to establish superdomain inferences. These sentences are also hypothetical, in the sense that they hold only within the confines of the subdomain, and not in the larger proof. By contrast, sentences that belong to the main proof— that is, to the outermost domain—have the same status as the premises and the conclusion. Although these sentences may act as subgoals during the proof process, their position is guaranteed if the proof is successful, and they hold in every subdomain embedded beneath them. Experiments on text comprehension (Kintsch et al. 1975; Meyer 1975) have demonstrated that subjects are better able to recall sentences from higher levels in the organization of a passage than those from subordinate levels, and a parallel logic would predict higher recall scores for superdomain than subdomain lines in a proof.

By manipulating the top-level assertions and suppositions, Marcus was able to construct pairs of proofs in which essentially the same sentence appeared either in the top domain or in a subdomain. For example, one of Marcus's proofs reads as shown here in (7).

(7) a. Suppose the runner stretches before running.

   b. If the runner stretches before running, she will decrease the chance of muscle strain.

   c. Under that condition, she would decrease the chance of muscle strain.

   d. If she decreases the chance of muscle strain, she can continue to train in cold weather.

   e. In that case, she could continue to train in cold weather.

   f. Therefore, if the runner stretches before running, she can continue to train in cold weather.

In this passage, lines b and d are assertions at the top level of the proof, and line f is the conclusion (also at the top level). However, lines a, c, and e are all parts of a subdomain, which justifies the conclusion via IF Introduction.

Compare the proof in (7) with that in (8), in which the sentence about the runner stretching is elevated to the status of a premise.

(8) a. The runner stretches before running.

  b. If the runner stretches before running, she will decrease the chance of muscle strain.

  c. Therefore, she will decrease the chance of muscle strain.

  d. If she decreases the chance of muscle strain, she can continue to train in cold weather.

  e. Thus, she can continue to train in cold weather.

  f. If she did not decrease the chance of muscle strain, she would ruin her chance of running in the Boston Marathon.

Proof (8) contains no subdomains, so all its lines are equally factual. In particular, sentences (8a), (8c), and (8e) are now part of the premises' domain, rather than being embedded in a subdomain as their counterparts in (7) are. We can refer to (7a), (7c), and (7e) as *embedded sentences* and to (8a), (8c), and (8e) as *unembedded controls*. In these terms, then, we should predict that subjects will recall the unembedded controls better than the embedded sentences, for the reasons just discussed. Of course, we need to be sure that such a difference is actually due to embedding and not to other variables associated with (7) and (8). One way to check this possibility is to compare the *superordinate* sentences (7b) and (7d) with the analogous sentences (8b) and (8d), which we will call *superordinate controls*. Since these sentences don't differ with respect to embedding, we should observe no difference in their recall.

In Marcus' (1982) experiment the subjects heard five passages similar to (7) and (8) and then attempted to write them down in as much detail as possible. The same procedure was then repeated with another five passages. Marcus constructed the proofs with embedded sentences using the rules IF Introduction (as in (7)), OR Elimination, and NOT Introduction. She created the control proofs (e.g., (8)) from the experimental ones by changing the supposition to a premise and altering the concluding line. For a given subject, an experimental proof and its control were instantiated with different content; however, the assignment of content to proof type was balanced across subjects.

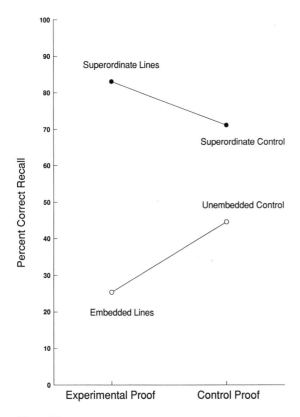

Figure 5.3
Percent correct recall of proof lines as a function of proof type and line status, from Marcus 1982.

Figure 5.3 shows the main recall proportions from Marcus' study. As predicted, the subjects were significantly more accurate in recalling unembedded controls than embedded sentences. Thus, sentences in subdomains are less well remembered than those in superdomains, even when the form and content of the lines are the same. However, the comparison between superordinate sentences in the experimental and control passages shows a trend in the opposite direction, with superordinate experimental sentences (such as (7b)) recalled slightly but not significantly better than controls (such as (8b)). This supports the idea that the embedding effect is not attributable to the greater complexity of proofs like (7) or to other incidental factors associated with the global proof structure.[6] The recall deficit for embedded sentences, together with the absence of a deficit for superordinate sentences, produced a significant interaction for the data in figure 5.3.

Marcus' results demonstrate that we can predict memory for natural-deduction proofs like (7) in terms of the underlying configuration of these proofs—in particular, the subdomain-superdomain relations. Of course, the experiment gives us no information about whether natural deduction is more "natural" psychologically than other possible proof methods, since it didn't include such a comparison. But the results are important, never-theless, in establishing that subjects' recall is sensitive to properties central to PSYCOP's own memory structure.

Summary

We are not done with experiments based on PSYCOP; chapter 7 will describe further tests. However, the three experiments that we have just glimpsed provide us with initial evidence about the core theory. The first of these showed that we can predict the likelihood with which subjects correctly evaluate an argument if we assume that they behave like PSYCOP in constructing mental proofs. Most of the rules are apparently obvious to subjects, and they find it possible to evaluate arguments that these rules can prove. However, a few of the rules cause difficulties, perhaps because of interfering pragmatic or strategic factors. The second experiment em-ployed a reaction-time design that let us test the model without having to fit a large number of free parameters. This study used PSYCOP's distinc-tion between forward and backward rules to predict how quickly subjects can assimilate the lines of an explicit proof. We found that when PSYCOP could anticipate a line through a forward rule, subjects' response times were relatively fast; however, when PSYCOP needed a backward rule to determine that a line followed, subjects' times were correspondingly slow. This accords with what we would expect if the human proof-following ability is similar to PSYCOP's, employing forward rules on an automatic basis and backward rules in response to specific goals. Finally, Marcus' experiment buttresses the idea that PSYCOP's superdomain-subdomain structure also describes subjects' memory for simple proofs. While these three experiments are by no means a complete test of the model, we have some support for its basic tenets.

However, the studies discussed in this section are rather atypical, since they employ stimulus items that are much more complex than is usual in reasoning experiments. The ability to handle complex arguments of this sort is one of the advantages I would claim for the PSYCOP approach, but it is nevertheless important to show that the theory can also handle the simpler arguments that pervade earlier research. This is because there is now a wealth of data about these simple arguments and because some of the earlier experiments have turned up surprises.

Consistency with Earlier Findings

Most research on sentential reasoning has centered on arguments containing a single connective, usually *if* or *not*. The goal of these experiments has been to locate the sources of difficulty associated with the connectives—the problems subjects have in comprehending them and in combining them with further information. As was noted in chapter 1, this has led to the development of a large number of mini-models, each specific to a connective and a task— models of conditional syllogisms, for example, or of verifying negative sentences against pictures. It would be useful to show that these data and models are consequences of more general assumptions, and in this section I try to show that the PSYCOP theory allows us to do this. Of course, each type of experiment poses special demands that go beyond pure reasoning. In sentence-picture verification, for instance, subjects must be able to represent the picture in some suitable format. Still, PSYCOP should be helpful in providing the central deductive machinery. (It might shed some light on other aspects of the tasks as well, following the "promotional" strategy discussed in chapter 2. I will return to this possibility in chapter 8 after introducing PSYCOP's handling of variables.)

Inferences with Negatives

The most detailed findings on negatives come from experiments in which subjects decide whether individual sentences correctly describe accompanying pictures. (See, e.g., Carpenter and Just 1975; Clark and Chase 1972.) In their classic study, Clark and Chase (1972) presented on each trial a display consisting of a sentence at the left (e.g., *Star isn't above plus*) and a picture to the right (either a "star" (asterisk) directly above a plus sign or a plus directly above a star). The sentences varied in whether or not they contained a negative and whether they were true or false of the picture. On a given trial, subjects might have seen a picture of a star above a plus, together with one of the sentences *Star is above plus*, *Plus is above star, Star isn't above plus, Plus isn't above star.* The time between the presentation of the display and the subjects' true/false decision was the basic dependent variable.

On average, Clark and Chase's subjects took longer to verify the negative sentences than the positive ones, as we might expect from the added complexity involved in encoding the negative items. The more interesting result, however, was that for positive sentences the reaction times were longer when the sentence was false, whereas for negative sentences the times were longer when the sentence was true. Figure 5.4 illustrates these results. For example, if the picture showed a star above a plus, then times were shorter for the true positive sentence *Star is above plus* than for the

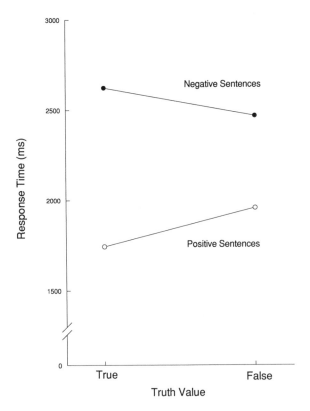

Figure 5.4
Mean response times for correctly verifying positive and negative sentences with the relation *above* against picture of a star above a plus or a plus above a star (from Clark and Chase 1972, experiment 1).

false positive *Plus is above star*; however, times were shorter for the false negative *Star isn't above plus* than for the true negative *Plus isn't above star* (Clark and Chase 1972, experiment 1).

In order to account for this interaction between the truth of a sentence and its polarity (positive or negative), let us suppose along with Clark and Chase that subjects were encoding both the sentence and the picture into a common sentential format. We can then think of the task as one of deciding whether the picture representation entails the sentence representation, as was noted in chapter 1. But in order to perform correctly on this task, subjects need to know more than just what was given in the display. They must also bring into play semantic information about the spatial relation *above*. They must recognize, in particular, that *above* is asymmetric, so that, for example, if the star is above the plus then the plus isn't above the star. We might represent the asymmetry in this experimental setup by the premise *(IF star is above plus THEN NOT plus is above star) AND (IF plus is above star THEN NOT star is above plus)*. With this addition, determining whether the sentence is true of the picture in the four conditions is equivalent to determining whether the conclusions of the arguments in (9) follow from their premises.

(9) a. Star is above plus.   Encoded picture
         (IF star is above plus THEN NOT plus is
           above star)
         AND (IF plus is above star THEN NOT
           star is above plus).
         _____
         Star is above plus.   True positive

     b. Star is above plus.   Encoded picture
         (IF star is above plus THEN NOT plus is
           above star)
         AND (IF plus is above star THEN NOT
           star is above plus).
         _____
         Plus is above star.   False positive

     c. Star is above plus.   Encoded picture
         (IF star is above plus THEN NOT plus is
           above star)
         AND (IF plus is above star THEN NOT
           star is above plus).
         _____
         NOT plus is above star.   True negative

d. Star is above plus.   Encoded picture
(IF star is above plus THEN NOT plus is
 above star)
AND (IF plus is above star THEN NOT
 star is above plus).
_____
NOT star is above plus.   False negative

It seems safe to assume that subjects can respond with an immediate "true" response if there is a direct match between the conclusion and one of the premises and can respond with an immediate "false" if the conclusion directly contradicts one of the premises. Thus, arguments (9a) and (9d) will be disposed of quickly. However, arguments (9b) and (9c) require further inferences. These arguments, unlike (9a) and (9d), depend on the extra premise concerning *above*, and hence subjects must unpack this premise. Applying Forward AND Elimination will produce *IF star is above plus THEN NOT plus is above star*, from which we can derive *NOT plus is above star* by Forward IF Elimination. This last assertion directly contradicts the conclusion of (9b) and directly matches the conclusion of (9c), correctly yielding a "false" response to the former and a "true" response to the latter. Thus, the additional inferences account both for why false positive sentences take longer to verify than true positive ones and for why true negative sentences take longer to verify than false negative ones. (Of course, since forward rules carry out the extra inferences, subjects should make these deductions in all four conditions. However, the decision for true positive and false negative sentences needn't wait for these inferences to appear, whereas they must be present before subjects can respond to false positives and true negatives.)

Although our assumptions about the representations of the picture and sentence are the same as those of Clark and Chase (1972), the rest of the account differs. On their view, the response-time increments for false positive and true negative sentences are due to changes in a special truth register or index whose value depends on a comparison between subparts of the sentence and picture representations. According to the Clark-Chase theory, the representations can be divided into an inner string (*plus above star* or *star above plus*) and an outer string (which contains *NOT* in the case of a negative sentence and is otherwise empty). For example, the sentence *NOT star above plus* has *NOT* as its outer string and *star above plus* as its inner string. To make their decisions, subjects are supposed to begin with the truth index set to the value True. They then compare the inner strings of the sentence and picture representations, and then the two outer strings. Mismatches on either comparison cause the truth index to switch its value from True to False or from False to True, each switch producing a constant increase in time. In the case of a true positive trial, for instance, the sentence and the picture match on both strings (see the first premise and the conclusion in (9a)), so the response time should be minimal. However, for false positive trials, the inner strings mismatch (see (9b)), causing the truth index to change from True to False and increasing the decision time. Carpenter and Just (1975) and Trabasso, Rollins, and Shaughnessy (1971) present related models that retain the notion of a comparison between segments of the sentence and picture encodings.

My account predicts Clark and Chase's results. In both models, the main effect of negation is attributed in part to encoding the negative particle. But the interaction, which Clark and Chase explain through extra changes to the truth index, is here the result of extra inference steps. One reason to prefer the present account is that it provides a better rationale for the subjects' performance. If we look at the task as involving a simple comparison between parts of the representations, then it is difficult to see why a mismatch should produce a change in truth value, as it does on the Clark-Chase theory. After all, if the sentence was *star is near plus* and the representation of the picture was *plus is near star*, then a mismatch between these inner strings would not mean that the sentence was false of the picture. The truth index would have to remain unchanged to yield the right answer. On the theory just outlined, the reason why *star is above plus* conflicts with *plus is above star* is that subjects know that *above* is an asymmetric relation, as captured in the second premise of (9a)–(d). No such information is available for *near*, since this relation is a symmetric one. Another way to see this is to notice that the first premise in (9a) would imply its conclusion and the first premise of (9d) would contradict its conclusion, even if we knew nothing about the properties of *above*. For example, substituting a nonsense relation for *above* would not affect the correct answer. However, the first premise of (9c) does not entail its conclusion and the first premise of (9b) does not contradict its conclusion without the extra information about *above*. Our account locates the difficulty of false positives and true negatives in the need to derive these facts.

A complaint about models like Clark and Chase's is that they seem overly specialized to the demands of the task (Newell 1973a; Tanenhaus,

Carroll, and Bever 1976); they do not offer a clear understanding of how subjects manage to go from their general knowledge and skills to the specific processing strategy that the model postulates. The approach we have been pursuing may have an advantage over older models in this respect, since our explanation of the data largely follows from the general representational and processing assumptions of the core PSYCOP model.[7]

Inferences with Conditionals

Reasoning with conditional sentences has been a popular topic within the psychology of reasoning, second only to Aristotelian syllogisms. This research has also been the one with the greatest impact on investigators in other fields, since the results seem to show that subjects are prone to serious mistakes on problems whose logical requirements are purportedly very simple. It is easy to interpret such data as proving that people are inherently irrational, or that, at best, their reasoning abilities are extremely limited. In this subsection we will look at this evidence from the perspective of the PSYCOP model in the hope that it might clarify the source of the difficulty with *if*. Although subjects probably do make errors in handling conditionals, part of the trouble may turn out to be a consequence of the structure of the deduction system. Most of this research has focused on conditional syllogisms and on Wason's selection task. Let us consider these two kinds of experiments in turn.

Conditional Syllogisms Conditional syllogisms are arguments that consist of a conditional first premise, a second premise containing either the antecedent or consequent of the conditional, and a conclusion containing the conditional's remaining part (the consequent if the second premise contained the antecedent; the antecedent if the second premise contained the consequent). The second premise and the conclusion can appear in either negated or unnegated form, yielding a total of eight argument types.[8] Table 5.4 exhibits these types along with some data from experiment 2 of Marcus and Rips (1979), in which subjects attempted to decide whether the conclusion of the argument "followed" or "didn't follow" from the premises. The table gives the arguments in schematic form, but the subjects saw the arguments in three instantiated versions. Thus, the conditional in the first premise might have appeared in any of the following ways: *If there's a B on the left side of the card, then there's a 1 on the right*

Table 5.4
Percentages of "follows" and "doesn't follow" responses and mean response times to eight conditional syllogisms (from Marcus and Rips 1979). (n = 248 responses.)

Syllogism	Response proportions		Mean response time (ms)	
	"Follows"	"Doesn't follow"	"Follows"	"Doesn't follow"
1. IF A, C A — C	0.98	0.02	1907	2119
2. IF A, C A — NOT C	0.03	0.97	2145	2177
3. IF A, C NOT A — C	0.08	0.92	3001	2628
4. IF A, C NOT A — NOT C	0.21	0.79	2412	2640
5. IF A, C C — A	0.33	0.67	1813	2437
6. IF A, C C — NOT A	0.08	0.92	3141	2514
7. IF A, C NOT C — A	0.03	0.97	2086	2483
8. IF A, C NOT C — NOT A	0.52	0.48	2882	2245

side; *If the ball rolls left, then the green light flashes*; *If the fish is red, then it is striped*. These different versions are collapsed in the percentages and reaction times in the table.

In classical logic and in the PSYCOP system of chapter 4, the only arguments that are deducible are the first and last in the table. It is clear, however, that subjects were much more apt to accept argument 1 (corresponding to the modus ponens form) than argument 8 (corresponding to modus tollens). Our subjects responded "follows" 98% of the time on the former but only 52% of the time on the latter. Performance on the remaining nondeducible problems also varied widely. For arguments 2, 3, 6, and 7 over 90% of the responses were "doesn't follow," which is the response that both classical logic and PSYCOP dictate. This same response is also appropriate for arguments 4 and 5, but only 79% of subjects said that the conclusion of argument 4 didn't follow and only 67% said that the conclusion of argument 5 didn't follow. These last two arguments are sometimes labeled fallacies in textbooks on elementary logic (argument 4 as the "fallacy of denying the antecedent" and argument 5 as the "fallacy of affirming the consequent")—and, taken at face value, the data suggest that subjects are often ready to commit them. Evans (1977) and Taplin and Staudenmayer (1973) have reported similar results.

An account of these findings based on an intensional interpretation of IF, similar to the one discussed in chapter 2, is given in Rips and Marcus 1977. The PSYCOP system suggests a simpler explanation: The difference between arguments 1 and 8 can be ascribed to the fact that the model contains a rule for modus ponens (IF Elimination) but not one for modus tollens. As a consequence, subjects would have to derive the conclusion of the latter argument by means of an indirect proof, using both NOT Introduction and IF Elimination. This is, in fact, exactly the difference that I noted between these arguments at the beginning of chapter 2. On this account, the longer times and lower response rates for "follows" in argument 8 are both due to the extra inference step (Braine 1978).

However, the tendency of some subjects to respond "follows" to arguments 4 and 5 must also be explained. Clearly, if subjects interpret the conditional sentences in this experiment using the IF of the model, then no proof is possible for either argument; so where are these responses coming from? In modeling the data of table 5.1, we assumed that "follows" responses could sometimes be due to guessing by subjects who had failed to find a proof for a particular argument. But mere guessing would not explain why arguments 4 and 5 attract so many more "follows" responses than the other invalid argument schemas in table 5.4 (i.e., arguments 2, 3, 6, and 7). A more reasonable suggestion is that some subjects treated the conditional premise as suggesting its converse (for example, interpreting *If p then q* as implicating *IF q THEN p* as well as *IF p THEN q*). This interpretation would yield the same results as if subjects had taken the conditional as a biconditional (*p IF AND ONLY IF q*), and therefore it is consistent with earlier research by Taplin (1971; see also Taplin and Staudenmayer 1973). On this reading arguments 4 and 5 (but not arguments 2, 3, 6, and 7) are deducible, yielding the elevated response rates. Note, too, that PSYCOP could deduce argument 5 in this case by the same IF Elimination strategy that it would use with argument 1, which explains the relatively fast responses for these two arguments.

This propensity to consider both the conditional and its converse might well have been encouraged by the nature of one of the conditionals we employed: *If the ball rolls left, then the green light flashes.* This sentence was supposed to refer to a pinball-machine-like device containing differently colored lights and different channels along which a ball could travel. There seems to be a natural tendency in this situation for subjects to assume a one-to-one relationship between channels and lights, which leads them to think that if the green light flashes then the ball must have rolled left (Cummins et al. 1991; Legrenzi 1970; Markovits 1988; Rips and Marcus 1977). In the experiment reported in Marcus and Rips 1979, 36% of the subjects consistently accepted arguments 1, 4, 5, and 8 (and rejected the remaining arguments) when the problems were phrased in terms of the conditional about the pinball machine, but less than 10% of subjects produced this response pattern when the conditional was about a deck of cards or the markings on tropical fish. This sensitivity to content appears to be a hallmark of subjects' performance with conditionals, and it will recur in a more extreme form in the following subsection. The present point is that, although PSYCOP does not by itself explain why subjects bring this extra information into the problem (see note 5 to chapter 2), the model can use it to yield the observed results by means of the same mechanisms that we have used to account for other tasks.

The Selection Task   A more popular type of experiment with conditionals concerns a problem invented by Wason (1966). Imagine a display of four index cards that (in a standard version of the problem) show the characters E, K, 4, and 7 on their visible sides (one character per card). Each card has a number on one side and a letter on the other. The problem is "Name those cards, and only those cards, which need to be turned over in order to determine whether the [following] rule is true or false": If a card has a vowel on one side, it has an even number on the other.

According to Wason and Johnson-Laird (1972), the two most popular answers to this *selection task* are that one must turn over both the E and 4 cards (46% of subjects respond in this way) and that one must turn over just the E card (33%). But neither of these answers is right. Certainly the E card must be checked, since an odd number on its flip side would be inconsistent with the rule. The K card, however, is consistent with the rule no matter whether it is paired with an even or an odd number, so this card cannot discriminate whether the rule is true or false. Likewise, if the 4 card has a vowel on its flip side it is consistent with the rule, and if it has a consonant it is also consistent. The 4 card is therefore irrelevant to the test. This leaves the 7 card. If its flip side contains a vowel this card contradicts the rule, whereas if the flip side contains a consonant it conforms to the rule. Therefore, the E and 7 cards must be turned over. Wason and Johnson-Laird found that only 4% of their subjects discovered this. In later replications, the percentage of correct responses on similar tasks varied from 6% to 33% (Evans 1982).

To determine "whether the rule is true or false" in this context means to find out whether the rule applies to all four cards or whether it fails to apply to one or more cards. And there are several ways that subjects could go about choosing which cards must be checked. The simplest possibility, however, might be to find out for each card whether the character on its face-up side, together with the rule, implies the vowel/consonant or even/odd status of the character on the flip side. If such an implication can be drawn, then the card must be turned over, since the rule is false of this card when the implication is not fulfilled. If no such implication can be drawn, the card need not be turned over. In the case of the E card, the fact that E is a vowel, together with the rule *IF vowel THEN even*, implies that the flip side contains an even number, so this card must be checked. We can represent the inferential tasks that correspond to the four cards as in (10) assuming that the K is encoded as *NOT vowel* and the 7 as *NOT even* in this context.

(10)   E card: IF vowel THEN even.
                 Vowel.
                 ―――――――
                 ?

        4 card: IF vowel THEN even.
                 Even.
                 ―――――――
                 ?

        K card: IF vowel THEN even.
                 NOT vowel.
                 ―――――――
                 ?

        7 card: IF vowel THEN even.
                 NOT even.
                 ―――――――
                 ?

Viewed in this way, the selection task bears an obvious similarity to the conditional syllogisms in table 5.4. The difference is that the present task provides no conclusions, so subjects must produce the conclusions on their own.

PSYCOP is able to deduce *Even* from the first of these sets of premises by means of its Forward IF Elimination rule; however, for the other three sets it draws a blank. The reason is that, with no explicit conclusion, PSYCOP relies solely on its forward rules, and the only forward rule that is applicable in this situation is Forward IF Elimination. In particular, nothing follows from the premises corresponding to the 7 card, because PSYCOP lacks a forward rule for modus tollens and lacks a subgoal to trigger a backward search for the same inference. (Backward search by means of NOT Introduction is how PSYCOP managed to handle the comparable argument in the syllogism task.) Thus, the difference between the E card and the 7 card is much like the difference between the two proofs in table 5.3. Given the simple strategy outlined above, we would therefore expect PSYCOP to respond by turning over just the E card, which is the response given by about a third of the subjects. The other popular response—both the E and 4 cards— may be the result of subjects' assuming the converse of the conditional, as was discussed above. When the converse conditional *IF even THEN vowel* is added to the premises above, PSYCOP will draw a conclusion for the premise sets corresponding to the E and 4 cards (using Forward IF Elimination again) but to neither of the other sets.[9]

Of course, a small percentage of subjects do manage to solve this problem, and we need to be able to explain how this is possible on the present theory. A reasonable guess is that the successful subjects explicitly consider potential letters or numbers that might be on the flip sides of the cards, corresponding to conclusions for the premise sets in (10). This means thinking about the possibility that there might be an even number or a noneven number on the back of the E card, a vowel or a nonvowel on the back of the 4 card, and so on. Considering these explicit possibilities would invoke backward rules and allow thorough logical processing. In terms of the arguments in (10), this translates into filling in the conclusions *Even* and *NOT even* for both the E and K premises and filling in the conclusions *Vowel* and *NOT vowel* for both the 4 and 7 premises. If a subject determines that any of these conclusions is deducible, then he or she should check the corresponding card. Enumerating possible conclusions on a case-by-case basis this way will produce the same responses for the E, K, and 4 cards as did the simpler strategy; the 7 card, however, will now be selected, since subjects can determine (via Backward NOT Introduction) that *IF vowel THEN even* and *NOT even* imply *NOT vowel*. This more complex strategy obviously requires extra effort and presumably is something that subjects will not do except in unusual circumstances. Even then they may fail to deduce the *NOT vowel* conclusion because of the difficulty of the backward inference.

If a correct answer to the selection task requires projecting possible values for the conclusions in (10), we should expect factors that encourage this projection to improve performance. Some experimental variations on the task are consistent with this prediction. First, it is possible to highlight possible conclusions by telling subjects exactly which symbols might appear on each card's back (e.g., that the E card might have an 8 or a 9 on its back, that the 4 card could have a U or a V, and so on). Smalley (1974) found improved choices after such a manipulation. Second, integrating the values of the antecedent and the consequent as parts of a unified object, rather than segregating them on different parts of a card, should make it easier for subjects to imagine possible conclusions. In line with this, Wason and Green (1984) found more correct answers when the problem was about differently colored shapes than when the problem was about cards that had a shape on one half and a color patch on the other. Third, projection should be simpler if subjects' choice is limited to the values of the consequent (even vs. odd numbers in the above example) and if subjects actually get to view possible completions for the missing value. In selection-task variants of this sort (Johnson-Laird and Wason 1970; Wason and Green 1984), the instructions specify that there are several cards containing odd numbers and several cards containing even numbers. On each of a series of trials, subjects must choose to examine an odd or an even card in an effort to determine whether the rule (e.g., *IF vowel THEN even*) correctly applies to the entire pack. The results of these studies show that subjects learn quite quickly to examine every card whose value contradicts the consequent (cards with odd numbers) and to disregard every card whose value is the same as the consequent (cards with even numbers).

PSYCOP can therefore capture the main aspects of subjects' responses in the standard version of the selection task and in some of its variations. However, much of the recent work on this problem has focused on some dramatic effects of the conditional rule's content. For example, if the rule is phrased in terms of police checking compliance with a drinking regulation (*If a person is drinking beer, then the person must be over 19*) and the cards represent ages (e.g., 15 and 25) and the beverages (Coca-Cola and beer), performance can run as high as 70% correct (Griggs and Cox 1982; Pollard and Evans 1987). Similarly, improvement on the selection task has been observed when the problem is phrased in terms of authorities checking compliance with rules that emphasize permission or obligation (e.g., *If one is to take action 'A,' then one must first satisfy precondition 'P'*) (Cheng and Holyoak 1985; Cheng et al. 1986). However, not all types of content benefit performance. Pollard and Evans (1987) report little facilitation when the problem is stated in terms of secret police checking compliance with a regulation about identity cards (*If there is a B on the card, then there is a number over 18 on it*). And there seems to be no benefit for a rule such as *If I eat haddock, then I drink gin* when the cards indicate "what I ate" and "what I drank" at a particular meal (Manktelow and Evans 1979).

These results may be due to subjects' memories of situations involving the same or similar information, rather than to a change in the way the subjects reason (Griggs 1983). For instance, if subjects already know that violators of the drinking rule are underage people and beer drinkers (or know of an analogous situation), then they can determine the correct answer from their previous knowledge. Similarly, a rule phrased in terms of necessary preconditions may remind subjects of a prior situation in which violators were those who had taken the action and had not satisfied the preconditions. A complete account would, of course, have to explain this retrieval step; however, the present point is that subjects' performance is a function, not only of the inferences that PSYCOP sanctions, but also of the information that the subjects include in their working-memory representation of the problem. The cover stories that experimenters tell to set up the contentful versions of the selection task may invite subjects to rely on background information, and this will, in turn, enable them to make inferences that go beyond what can be derived in the more pristine form of the task. (See chapters 9 and 10 for further discussion of these content effects. In these chapters we also explore the possibility that facilitation in the selection task is due to use of modal operators.)

Summary

The experiments reviewed in this chapter provide some evidence for the generality and accuracy of the model. PSYCOP seems generally able to account for the way subjects follow and remember proofs, verify sentences against pictures, and evaluate propositional arguments (conditional syllogisms, as well as more complicated argument forms). For many of these results, it is PSYCOP's distinction between forward and backward reasoning that provides the major explanatory tool. Subjects have an easier time following proofs based on forward rules, since this allows them to predict what lies ahead; in addition, performance on conditional syllogisms and the Selection task is better when only forward reasoning is required. However, several other factors come into play in predicting subjects' inference ability. The more difficult problems are those that require more inference steps, more complex rules, and more embedded proof structures.

In the second section of the chapter, we focused on PSYCOP's consistency with some prior results on negative and conditional sentences. The model gives us a new way of looking at these results and a uniform perspective on the kinds of inference skills that they require. Most earlier explanations of these findings took the form of information-processing models that the investigators had tailored to the specific task. Although the fits of these models are often excellent in quantitative terms, they require many "hidden parameters" in the form of assumptions about representation, processing components, and order of processing operations. Of course, no model can entirely avoid some specific presuppositions about the task. PSYCOP's goal, however, is to reduce the number of these *ad hoc* assumptions, attempting to account for these results with a common set of representations and inference mechanisms. To a first approximation, the model seems successful in this respect; it appears to capture the basic effects, including the interaction between truth and polarity in verifying sentences against pictures, the relative difficulty of conditional syllogisms, and the most common pattern of responses in the selection task.

The findings we have just considered certainly don't exhaust the previous data on propositional reasoning. For example, Braine et al. (1984) and Osherson (1974–1976) have claimed that several experiments similar to the argument-evaluation task reported at the beginning of this chapter confirm their own deduction models. However, the findings reviewed in the second section of this chapter are surely the best-known and best-replicated ones and are therefore a good place to begin assessing PSYCOP's adequacy. We will return to the other models in chapter 9.

6 Variables in Reasoning

The momentum of the mind is all toward abstraction.
Wallace Stevens, "Adagia"

At this point, we need to return to the discussion of quantifiers and variables that we began in chapter 3 and see how we can incorporate them in our framework. Chapter 3 described a representation that allows us to express quantified sentences without explicit quantifiers, such as the logician's ∃ (for some) and ∀ (for all). This "Skolemized" representation simplifies the deduction system to some extent, since we don't need to manipulate quantifiers, but it still forces us to consider the variables $(x, y, \ldots)$ and temporary names $(a, b, a_x, b_y, \ldots)$ that the quantifiers leave in their wake. Recall that, in this notation, universally quantified sentences, such as *Everything is equal to itself*, are represented in terms of variables, $x = x$; existentially quantified sentences, such as *Something is fragile*, are represented in terms of temporary names, *Fragile(a)*; and sentences with combinations of universal and existential quantifiers, such as *Every satellite orbits some planet*, are represented in terms of combinations of variables and temporary names, with subscripts to indicate dependencies, *IF Satellite(x) THEN (Planet(a_x) AND Orbits(x, a_x))*. The first section of this chapter proposes a way for PSYCOP to deal with these variables and temporary names—a method that gives it most of the power of predicate logic. The second section looks at some formal results concerning the correctness of the system. The following chapter takes up experimental data on reasoning with classical syllogisms and on reasoning with more complex arguments containing multi-variable sentences.

   The importance of extending the core system to variables lies partly in its ability to express general rules. We would like a deduction system to be able to carry out cognitive operations over a range of examples without having to fix these examples in advance. For instance, the system should be able to store the definition that any integer that is evenly divisible by 2 is an even number and to use this definition to realize that 752, for example, is even. PSYCOP must recognize new instances as something about which it has general knowledge, and the obvious way to do this in the current framework is to have it instantiate variables to the names of the instances or generalize the instances to match the variables. The problem-solving illustrations in chapter 3 provide a taste of the advantages of this approach; some additional cases with more of a cognitive-psychology flavor appear in part III. It is worth emphasizing, however, that instantiation or generalization is a feature of any reasonable cognitive system. Production systems (e.g., Newell 1990), schema theories (Brachman and Schmolze 1985), and network theories (Ajjanagadde and Shastri 1989; Smolensky 1990) all need some technique for binding variables in their data structures to specific examples. Results on generalizing and instantiating are likely to have implications, then, beyond the PSYCOP system itself.

Moreover, variables have a close relationship to pronouns in natural language. Understanding the sentence *Calvin gave the clock to the woman who fixed it* presupposes a way of correctly associating *who* with *the woman* and *it* with *the clock*. Variables allow us to make these relationships explicit; for example, we can translate this sentence as *Calvin gave the clock x to the woman y such that y fixed x*. Thus, variables, or indexing devices very similar to them, are independently needed to represent the products of the comprehension process.

Extending the Core System to Variables

By working with quantifier-free representations, we can avoid some of the problems of quantifier introduction and elimination rules that were noted in chapter 2. But in order to incorporate these representations in our proofs we must make some additional provisions. First, we confine our attention to sentences in our quantifier-free notation that are logically equivalent to sentences in classical predicate logic. As was noted in chapter 3, quantifier-free form provides some extra degrees of freedom, allowing us to express dependencies among temporary names and variables that CPL outlaws. However, the very same dependencies create difficulties if we want to manipulate quantifier-free sentences with the types of natural-deduction rules we have used so far. Some of these rules require us to negate an arbitrary sentence or extract an antecedent from an arbitrary conditional, and these operations aren't expressible in quantifier-free form if the unnegated sentence or the antecedent is not also representable in CPL. (See Barwise 1979 on similar logics with branching quantifiers.) We will therefore work with quantifier-free sentences that are also expressible in CPL. Second, as already mentioned, we need some regulations for matching or unifying the variables and temporary names that the quantifiers leave behind. We need to be able to deduce, for example, a specific conclusion from a more general premise. Third, we must modify parts of the sentential rules in order to pass variable bindings from one part of the rule to another. These modifications will be considered informally in this section; some more rigorous justifications will be offered in next.

A Sample Proof with Variables and Temporary Names

To see what is needed to adapt the system, let us consider what a proof with variables and names should look like. We can take as an example the following simple syllogism from chapter 2: *All square blocks are green blocks*; *Some big blocks are square blocks*; *Therefore, some big blocks are green blocks*. For reasons that we will consider later, we must first make sure that no sentence in the argument shares variables or temporary names with any other. Also, temporary names in the premises must be distinguished from temporary names in the conclusion; we will do this by placing a caret over the former. Thus, the quantifier-free form of our syllogism is as shown in (1).

(1)   IF Square-block(x) THEN Green-block(x).
       Big-block(â) AND Square-block(â).
       _____
       Big-block(b) AND Green-block(b).

The proof of this argument is shown in figure 6.1. As before, double solid lines indicate that matching has taken place; but this time matching will couple, not only identical propositions, but also certain propositions whose variables and names differ. Initially, the proof consists of just the two premises and the conclusion (sentences 1, 2, and 5 in the figure). As the first deductive step, we can split the second premise, *Big-block(â) AND Square-block(â)*, into its two conjuncts by means of Forward AND Elimination; these appear as sentences 3 and 4. No other forward rules are applicable at this point, though, so we must try using a backward rule on the conclusion. Backward AND Introduction is the obvious choice, since the conclusion has the form of a conjunction (i.e., *Big-block(b) AND Green-block(b)*), and this rule therefore proposes *Big-block(b)?* as a subgoal (sentence 6). This subgoal asks whether there is a big block, and as it happens we already know there must be one because of the assertion *Big-block(â)* in sentence 3. Hence, the subgoal should match (i.e., be fulfilled by) this assertion, as the double lines indicate in the figure.

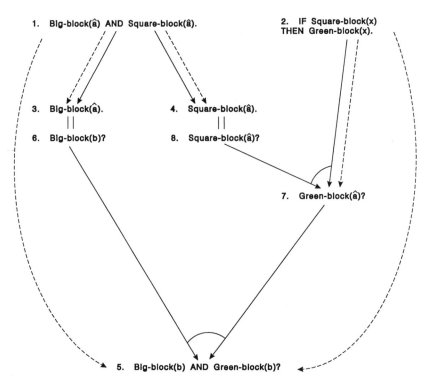

Figure 6.1
PSYCOP's proof of the syllogism

IF Square-block(x) THEN Green-block(x).
Big-block(â) AND Square-block(â).
_____
Big-block(b) AND Green-block(b).

At this stage of the proof, Backward AND Introduction has done half its job of proving the conclusion. The conclusion of (1) demands that we prove that some block is both big and green, and AND Introduction has so far succeeded in showing that there is a big block (namely, â). It remains to be shown that this *same* block is also green. (We can't prove the conclusion merely by showing that some block is big and some block green, since two different blocks might be involved.) For this reason AND Introduction must ensure that the second subgoal it sets is *Green-block(â)?*, as shown in sentence 7 of figure 6.1. That is, AND Introduction must substitute the new temporary name â for b in the second part of the conclusion. This illustrates one of the ways in which we will need to modify the backward rules.

We have no assertion that states outright that *â* is a green block, but we do have a conditional premise that tells us that if something is a square block then it is green. This suggests that we should use a variation on our old backward IF Elimination strategy: Since we want to show *Green-block(â)?* and since we know *IF Square-block(x) THEN Green-block(x)*, it makes sense to try to prove *Square-block(â)?*. Backward IF Elimination makes the relevant substitution in the antecedent of the conditional and produces this subgoal as sentence 8. However, this subgoal is easy to fulfill, for we have already deduced *Square-block(â)* at the beginning of the proof—it's just sentence 4. Since *â* is square, IF Elimination tells us it must be green, and this completes the second half of the proof of the syllogism. (Further examples of proofs using the newly modified rules appear in chapters 7 and 8.)

Matching

In the proof of figure 6.1, we needed the fact that the subgoal *Big-block(b)?* could be fulfilled by the assertion *Big-block(â)*, despite the fact that these sentences have different temporary names. This raises the general question of when we can deduce one sentence from another that has the same predicates and logical constants but may have different variables and names.

To see the issue associated with matching, consider the subgoal *Red(a)?* (i.e., Is anything red?), and suppose that the assertions of our proof include *Red(y)* (i.e., Everything is red). Intuitively, this assertion suffices to prove the subgoal, since *Red(y)* means that everything is red and *Red(a)* means that there is a particular individual that is red. Hence, if *Red(y)* is true, so is *Red(a)*. By contrast, if *Red(y)?* were the subgoal, we could not fulfill it by means of an assertion *Red(a)*, since the first of these sentences is more general than the second. We clearly need an explicit policy for deciding when we can match variables and temporary names in assertions and subgoals.

Let us call two sentences *isomorphic* if they are alike except for their variables and names. Thus, isomorphic sentences must have exactly the same predicates and logical constants in the same structural relations, but can differ in their arguments. (For example, *Red(a)* is isomorphic to *Red(x)*, but not to *Green(a)*.) Our example suggests that we should be allowed to match subgoals to some isomorphic assertions, but not to all. The simplest way to proceed might be to consider the variables and names of the subgoal one at a time. If the variable or name can be matched to one in a corresponding position in the assertion (according to the rules we are about to state), then we can produce a new subgoal that is also isomorphic to the original but that has the new variable or name from the assertion substituted for the old one in the subgoal. We continue in this way until we either create a subgoal that is identical to an assertion or fail in the matching process. For example, suppose we have *Similar(x,y)* as a premise (everything is similar to everything), and *Similar(Kathleen Turner, Lauren Bacall)* as a conclusion (Kathleen Turner is similar to Lauren Bacall). To show that the premise implies the conclusion, we can generalize the latter sentence to *Similar(x,Lauren Bacall)* (i.e., everything is similar to Bacall) and then generalize again to obtain the premise.

In effect, this process generalizes the original subgoal incrementally in order to mate it with an assertion. The rules in table 6.1 specify the conditions that govern this generalization process. Basically, these rules permit variables in subgoals to match variables in assertions, permanent names in subgoals to match variables in assertions, and temporary names in subgoals to match variables, permanent names, or temporary names. However, we need to impose some restrictions on matching to avoid fallacious proofs, just as we had to restrict the quantifier introduction and elimination rules in chapter 2.

As a preliminary step in carrying out proofs in quantifier-free form, we must make sure that each sentence in the argument to be proved contains distinct variables and temporary names. For example, if one premise states that some integer is even and another states that some integer is odd, we don't want to symbolize the former as *Integer(a) AND Even(a)* and the latter as *Integer(a) AND Odd(a)*. The usual AND Introduction and Elimination rules would then permit us to conclude *Integer(a) AND Even(a) AND Odd(a)*, which is to say that some integer is both even and odd. We must also take the further precaution of differentiating the temporary names that appear in the premises from those that appear in the conclusion, using carets over all temporary names in the premises as we did earlier. Hence, if *Integer(a) AND Even(a)* is a premise it will appear as *Integer(â) AND Even(â)*, but if it is a conclusion it will appear as plain *Integer(a) AND Even(a)*. In a sense, temporary names in the premises

Table 6.1

Matching rules for predicate logic. In these rules, P(n) represents an arbitrary quantifier-free sentence that contains argument n. P and P' are said to be isomorphic if they are identical except for the particular variables and temporary names that they contain (i.e., they must have the same predicates and connectives in the same positions). Some backward rules (e.g., IF Elimination) require a subgoal to match a subformula of an assertion, and in that case the phrase "target formula" in the following rules refers to that subformula. Otherwise, the target formula is a complete assertion.

Matching 1 (variables in subgoal to variables in assertion)

Conditions: (a) P(x) is a target formula and P'(y) is an isomorphic subgoal.

           (b) x and y are variables.

           (c) wherever x appears in (a nonsubscript position in) P(x) either y or a temporary name t_y with y as subscript appears in P'(y).

           (d) if t_y appears in the same position as x, then t_y appears only in positions occupied by variables.

           (e) wherever x appears as a subscript in P(x), y appears as a subscript in P'(y).

Action: Add the subgoal of proving P'(x) to the list of subgoals, where P'(x) is the result of:

           (a) substituting x for all occurrences of y in P'(y).

           (b) substituting x for all occurrences of t_y in P'(y) if t_y appeared in some of the same positions as x.

           (c) substituting x for y in P'(y) at each remaining subscript position that y occupies in P'(y).

Matching 2 (temporary names in subgoal to temporary or permanent names in assertion)

Conditions: (a) P(n) is a target formula and P'(t) is an isomorphic subgoal.

           (b) t is a temporary name, and n is a (temporary or permanent) name.

           (c) any subscripts of n are included among the subscripts of t.

           (d) t is not of the form â.

           (e) either n or a variable appears in P(n) in all positions that t occupies in P'(t).

Action: Add the subgoal of proving P'(n) to the list of subgoals, where P'(n) is the result of substituting n for t in P'(t) at all positions that t occupies in P'(t).

Matching 3 (permanent names in subgoal to variables in assertion)

Conditions: (a) P(x) is a target formula and P'(m) is an isomorphic subgoal.

           (b) x is a variable and m is a permanent name.

           (c) m appears in P'(m) in each nonsubscript position that x occupies in P(x).

           (d) if a temporary name t appears in P'(m) in the same position that an x-subscripted temporary name t_x appears in P(x), then any additional tokens of t also appear in positions occupied by t_x.

Action: Add the subgoal of proving P'(x) to the list of subgoals, where P'(x) is the result of:

           (a) substituting x for m in P'(m) at each nonsubscript position that x occupies in P(x).

           (b) substituting t' for t in P'(m) wherever t occurs in the same position as an x-subscripted temporary name in P(x) and where t' is a new temporary name with subscripts consisting of x and all subscripts of t.

Table 6.1 (continued)

Matching 4 (temporary names in subgoal to variables in assertion)

Conditions: (a) $P(x_1,\ldots,x_k)$ is a target formula and $P'(t)$ is an isomorphic subgoal.

(b) $x_1,\ldots,x_k$ are variables and t is a temporary name.

(c) x_1 or x_2 or ... x_k appears in nonsubscript positions in $P(x_1,\ldots,x_k)$ at each position that t occupies in $P'(t)$.

(d) if a temporary name t' appears in $P'(t)$ in the same position that an x_i-subscripted temporary name t_{x_i} appears in $P(x_1,\ldots,x_k)$, then any additional tokens of t' also appear in positions occupied by t_{x_i}.

Action: Add the subgoal of proving $P'(x_1,\ldots,x_k)$ to the list of subgoals, where $P'(x_1,\ldots,x_k)$ is the result of:

(a) substituting x_i for t wherever t occupies the same position in $P'(t)$ that x_i occupies in $P(x_1,\ldots,x_k)$.

(b) substituting t'' for t' in $P'(t)$ wherever t' occurs in the same position as an x_i-subscripted temporary name in $P(x_1,\ldots,x_k)$ and where t'' is a new temporary name whose subscripts consist of x_i and all subscripts of t'.

behave like permanent names, whereas temporary names in goals behave more like variables.

The main thing to observe about the matching rules in table 6.1 is that we must be careful about differences in the distribution of arguments in the assertion and the subgoal.

First, if we are matching a variable y in a subgoal to another variable x in the assertion, then we need to be sure that y occurs at each position in the subgoal that x appears in the assertion. We might say that the subgoal variable must "cover" the assertion variable. Without this restriction we could end up with (2), which proves that everything is identical to everything else from the premise that everything is self-identical.

(2) a. x = x   Premise

*b. x = y   Matching

*c. z = y   Matching

In constructing this proof, we work backward trying to match the conclusion in (2c) to the premise in (2a) by first substituting x for z (thus obtaining (2b)), and then substituting x for y. But the restriction in question blocks this attempt. We can't go from subgoal (2c) to (2b), because z does not appear in all positions in (2c) that x does in (2a); z doesn't cover x. The same is true of the step from (2b) to (2a). Note that the converse argument, with (2c) as premise and (2a) as conclusion, is perfectly valid and is permitted by the matching rule. (It says that everything is equal to everything, therefore everything equals itself.)

Second, we must observe the opposite distribution requirement when matching a temporary name such as b in the subgoal to a name (permanent or temporary) in the assertion. In this case, the assertion name (or some variable) must cover each position in which b appears in the subgoal. As (3) shows, breaking this rule would allow us to prove that there is something that is not identical to itself from the premise that there are two things that are nonidentical.

(3) a. $\hat{a} \neq \hat{c}$ Premise
      b. $\hat{a} \neq b$ Matching
  *c. $b \neq b$ Matching

Again, the converse argument is valid and is not blocked by the rules of table 6.1. (In the following section, we will return to these rules in order to show that they never lead to invalid inferences.)

The matching rules are for subgoal-to-assertion matching, which is the most important kind. But there may be situations when we need to match one assertion (or part of an assertion) to another. For example, it follows from the assertions *IF Aardvark(x) THEN Mammal(x)* and *Aardvark(Ginger)*, that *Mammal(Ginger)*. As currently formulated, however, the obvious rule for generating this sentence, Forward IF Elimination, does not apply, since *Aardvark(Ginger)* isn't the same as the antecedent *Aardvark(x)*. To get around this problem, we could modify the Forward IF Elimination rule, allowing it to match a conditional's antecedent to another assertion. Setting x to *Ginger* would give us *IF Aardvark(Ginger) THEN Mammal(Ginger)*, which would lead to the right conclusion. The trouble is that the self-constraining nature of IF Elimination no longer holds under this type of matching. If the conditional contains a subscripted temporary name in the consequent, then matching of this type can produce an infinite number of new assertions. For instance, suppose we have the conditional assertion *IF Integer(x) THEN (Successor(x,$\hat{a}_x$) AND Integer($\hat{a}_x$))*, which states that every number has a successor. If the proof also contains *Integer(0)*, then matching and Forward IF Elimination will produce *Successor(0,$\hat{a}_0$) AND Integer($\hat{a}_0$)* and, hence, *Integer($\hat{a}_0$)* by AND Elimination. This latter sentence, however, can also be matched to the antecedent of the conditional, leading to *Integer($\hat{a}_{\hat{a}_0}$)*, and so forth.

There may be ways around this problem,[1] but one obvious possibility is to leave well enough alone: We may not want to make inferences such as *Mammal(Ginger)* on the fly, for reasons of cognitive economy, especially if we have many other assertions—*Aardvark(Marie)*, *Aardvark(Fred)*, and so on. If we really need to prove *Mammal(Ginger)*, we can always do so by means of the Backward IF Elimination rule (in the modification discussed in the next subsection). Of course, Church's Theorem (see chapter 3) makes it inevitable that there will be some infinite searches in any deduction system that is complete with respect to CPL, and it is possible to construct examples in which Backward IF Elimination can produce a subgoal that can be taken as input to a second application of the same rule, and so on (Moore 1982). However, it seems reasonable to shield the forward rules from these difficulties, given the automatic way in which these rules operate in our present formulation. Backward rules allow more opportunity for controlling these problems, since we can choose to abandon a series of subgoals if it appears to be leading nowhere. In special contexts where there is no danger of unconstrained production, we might find a place for a Forward IF Elimination rule of the sort envisioned in the preceding paragraph; in general, however, the difficulties with this rule seem to outweigh its advantages. For the time being we will keep the forward rules in their old versions, which don't include an instantiation step.

Modifications to Rules

Some New Forward Rules   In addition to carrying over the old forward rules from table 4.1, we increase our stock with new ones that seem well adapted to predicate-argument structure. These rules do not involve instantiation and so do not present the problems that beset the modifications to the forward rules we just considered. In particular, Braine and Rumain (1983) and Guyote and Sternberg (1981) suggest rule schemas similar to the ones listed here in table 6.2.

The Transitivity rule allows us to conclude that *IF F(x) THEN H(x)*, provided that *IF F(x) THEN G(x)* and *IF G(x) THEN H(x)*. In other words, this rule licenses the simple universal syllogism from *all F are G* and *all G are H* to *all F are H*. The Exclusivity rule captures a similar intuition that if all F are G and no G are H, then no F are H either. In our notation, this becomes *NOT(F(x) AND H(x))*, provided that *IF F(x) THEN G(x)* and *NOT(G(x) AND H(x))*. Finally, the Conversion rule

Table 6.2
New forward inference rules for predicate logic.

Transitivity

IF F(x) THEN G(x) IF G(y) THEN H(y) IF F(z) THEN H(z)	(a) If sentences of the form IF F(x) THEN G(x) and IF G(y) THEN H(y) hold in some domain D, (b) and IF F(z) THEN H(z) does not yet hold in D, (c) then add IF F(z) THEN H(z) to D.

Exclusivity

IF F(x) THEN G(x) NOT(G(y) AND H(y)) NOT(F(z) AND H(z))	(a) If sentences of the form IF F(x) THEN G(x) and NOT(G(y) AND H(y)) hold in some domain D, (b) and NOT(F(z) AND H(z)) does not yet hold in D, (c) then add NOT(F(z) AND H(z)) to D.

Conversion

NOT(F(x) AND G(x)) NOT(G(y) AND F(y))	(a) If a sentence of the form NOT(F(x) AND G(x)) holds in some domain D, (b) and NOT(G(y) AND F(y)) does not yet hold in D, (c) then add NOT(G(y) AND F(y)) to D.

---

allows us to conclude that no G are F on the grounds that no F are G, which amounts to reversing the order of the conjuncts under negation: $NOT(F(x) \ AND \ G(x))$ entails $NOT(G(x) \ AND \ F(x))$. All three rules seem obvious and are self-constraining in the sense of chapter 3. As will be shown in chapter 7, they appear to play a crucial role in the way subjects handle Aristotelian syllogisms.

Modifications to Backward Rules   The use of quantifier-free form forces some revamping in the backward rules of table 4.2. For one thing, many of the backward rules require the theorem prover to coordinate several sentences, and this means that the rules must check that any matching that takes place for one sentence carries over to the others. For example, suppose we want to prove the conclusion *Child-of(Ed,a) AND Child-of(Ann,a)*—that is, there is someone who is the child of Ed and Ann. Backward AND Introduction tells us that we can prove this conclusion if we can prove each conjunct. But if we fulfill the subgoal *Child-of(Ed,a)* by matching to an assertion like *Child-of(Ed,Benjamin)*, we must then try to show that *Child-of(Ann,Benjamin)*. We can't get away with matching *a* to one child in fulfilling the first conjunct and to another child in fulfilling the second. The proof of figure 6.1 presented a similar problem for AND Introduction, since we had to show that the same item was both a big block and a green block. Coordination of this sort is also necessary for other rules that require both locating an assertion and fulfilling a subgoal (e.g., Backward IF Elimination).

One way to coordinate matching is to keep a record of the substitutions that occur when one condition of a rule is satisfied and to impose these same substitutions on sentences that appear in later conditions. In the preceding example, we matched *a* to *Benjamin* in fulfilling the first subgoal of Backward AND Introduction and then substituted *Benjamin* for *a* in the second subgoal. We can think of each match as producing an ordered pair, such as ⟨*a,Benjamin*⟩, in which the first member is the "matched" argument and the second member the "matching" argument. In carrying out later parts of the rule, these pairs must be used to produce new versions of subgoals or assertions in which each occurrence of a previously matched argument is replaced by its matching argument. A reformulated AND Introduction rule that includes this substitution step appears in table 6.3 .

A related point concerns the consequences of matching one temporary name to another. Suppose we again want to prove *Child-of(Ed,a) AND Child-of(Ann,a)*. We certainly want the subgoal *Child-of(Ed,a)* to match an assertion such as *Child-of(Ed,b̂)*: The subgoal asks whether anyone is the child of Ed, and the assertion states that someone is indeed the child of Ed. But once we have matched these sentences and substituted *b̂* for *a* to obtain *Child-of(Ann,b̂)*, we are no longer free to match *b̂* to other temporary or permanent names. In particular, we can't at this point satisfy *Child-of(Ann,b̂)* by matching to *Child-of(Ann,ĉ)*, since *ĉ* may denote someone other than the person denoted by *b̂*. There may be someone who is the child of Ed and someone who is the child of Ann without Ed and Ann's having any children in common. In effect, temporary names that come from premises and other assertions act like permanent names with respect to matching. For that reason, the matching rule in table 6.1 will not permit matching of tented temporary names in subgoals to names in assertions; and this provides the rationale for distinguishing temporary names that originate in the premises from those that originate in the conclusion.

Another modification concerns rules that deal with conditional and negative sentences. As we noticed in defining quantifier-free form, we must be careful in dealing with variables and temporary names when they are within the scope of a negative or in the antecedent of a conditional. For example, the sentence written as *(∃x) Rich(x)* in standard predicate logic will be symbolized *Rich(a)* in quantifier-free form, whereas its opposite or

Table 6.3
Backward inference rules for predicate logic. In these an asterisk indicates the result of reversing arguments by means of the procedure described in the text. P and P' denote isomorphic sentences (ones which are identical except for their variables and names). P* is the result of applying the Argument Reversal procedure to P, unless otherwise indicated. Notational variants are isomorphic sentences that differ only by substitution of variables for other variables or temporary names for other temporary names. Conditions for matching isomorphic sentences are described in table 6.1. Procedures for Argument Reversal and Subscript Adjustment appear in table 6.4.

Backward IF Elimination (Modus ponens)
(a) Set R to the current goal and set D to its domain.
(b) If R can be matched to R' for some sentence IF P' THEN R' that holds in D,
(c) then go to Step (e).
(d) Else, return failure.
(e) If P' and R' share variables and one or more names or variables in R matched these variables,
(f) then set P to the result of substituting those names or variables for the corresponding variables in P'. Label the substituting arguments, the matched arguments of P and the residual arguments the unmatched arguments of P.
(g) Else, set P to P'. Label all its arguments as unmatched.
(h) Apply Argument Reversal to unmatched arguments of P.
(i) Apply Subscript Adjustment to output of Step h. Call the result P*.
(j) If D does not yet contain the subgoal P* or a notational variant,
(k) then add the subgoal of proving P* in D to the list of subgoals.

Backward IF Introduction (Conditionalization)
(a) Set D to domain of current goal.
(b) If current goal is of the form IF P THEN R,
(c)   and neither D nor its superdomains nor its immediate subdomains contains both supposition P and subgoal R (or notational variants),
(d)   and IF P THEN R is a subformula of the premises or conclusion,
(e) then let P' be the result of substituting in P new tented temporary names for any variables that P shares with R,
(f)   and label substituting arguments matched arguments and the residual arguments unmatched,
(g)   and set up a subdomain of D, D', with supposition P* (where P* is the result of applying the Argument Reversal procedure to any unmatched arguments in P').
(h) Add the subgoal of proving R in D' to the list of subgoals.

Backward NOT Elimination
(a) Set P to current goal and D to its domain.
(b) If P is a subformula of the premises or conclusion,
(c)   and Q is an atomic subformula in the premises or conclusion,
(d)   and neither D nor its superdomains nor its immediate subdomains contains both supposition NOT P* and subgoal Q or supposition NOT P* and subgoal NOT Q* (or notational variants),
(e) then set up a subdomain of D, D', with supposition NOT P*,
(f)   and add the subgoal of proving Q AND NOT Q* in D' to the list of subgoals.
(g) If the subgoal in (f) fails,
(h)   and neither D nor its superdomains nor its immediate subdomains contains both supposition NOT P* and subgoal Q* or supposition NOT P* and subgoal NOT Q (or notational variants),
(i) then set up a subdomain of D, D'', with supposition NOT P*, and add the subgoal of proving Q* AND NOT Q in D'' to the list of subgoals.

Table 6.3 (continued)

Backward NOT Introduction

(a)   Set D to domain of current goal.

(b)   If current goal is of the form NOT P,

(c)   and P is a subformula (or notational variant of a subformula) of the premises or conclusion,

(d)   and Q is an atomic subformula of the premises or conclusion,

(e)   and neither D nor its superdomains nor its immediate subdomains contains both supposition P* and subgoal Q, or supposition P* and subgoal NOT Q* (or notational variants),

(f)   then set up a subdomain of D, D', with supposition P*,

(g)   and add the subgoal of proving Q AND NOT Q* in D' to the list of subgoals.

(h)   If the subgoal in (g) fails,

(i)   and neither D nor its superdomains nor its immediate subdomains contains both supposition P* and subgoal Q* or supposition P* and subgoal NOT Q (or notational variants),

(j)   then set up a subdomain of D, D'', with supposition P*, and add the subgoal of proving Q* AND NOT Q in D'' to the list of subgoals.

Backward AND Introduction

(a)   Set D to domain of current goal.

(b)   If current goal is of the form P AND Q,

(c)   and D does not yet contain the subgoal P

(d)   then add the subgoal of proving P in D to the list of subgoals.

(e)   If the subgoal in (d) succeeds,

(f)   and P is matched to P', and P and Q share temporary names,

(g)   then set Q' to the result of substituting in Q any names that were matched to those temporary names.

(h)   Else, set Q' to Q.

(i)   If D does not yet contain the subgoal Q',

(j)   then add the subgoal of proving Q' in D to the list of subgoals.

Backward OR Elimination

(a)   Set R to current goal and set D to its domain.

(b)   If a sentence of the form P OR Q holds in D,

(c)   and both P and Q are subformulas or negations of subformulas of the premises or conclusion (or notational variants of a subformula),

(d)   and neither D nor its superdomains nor its immediate subdomains contains both supposition P and subformula R (or notational variants),

(e)   and neither D nor its superdomains nor its immediate subdomains contains both supposition Q and subformula R (or notational variants),

(f)   then replace any variables that appear in both P and Q with temporary names that do not yet appear in the proof. Call the result P' OR Q'.

(g)   Set up a subdomain of D, D', with supposition P'.

(h)   and add the subgoal of proving R in D' to the list of subgoals.

(i)   If the subgoal in (h) succeeds,

(j)   then set up a subdomain of D, D'', with supposition Q',

(k)   and add the subgoal of proving R in D'' to the list of subgoals.

Table 6.3 (continued)

Backward OR Introduction

(a) Set D to domain of current goal.
(b) If current goal is of the form P OR Q,
(c) then if D does not yet contain the subgoal P or a notational variant,
(d)   then add the subgoal of proving P in D to the list of subgoals.
(e)   If the subgoal in (d) fails,
(f)   and D does not yet contain subgoal Q or a notational variant,
(g)   then add the subgoal of proving Q in D to the list of subgoals.

Backward AND Elimination

(a) Set D to domain of current goal.
(b) Set P to current goal.
(c) If P can be matched to P' in some subformula P' AND Q' of a sentence that holds in D,
(d)   and D does not yet contain the subgoal P' AND Q' or a notational variant,
(e) then add P' AND Q' to the list of subgoals.
(f) Else, if P can be matched to P' in some subformula Q' AND P' of a sentence that holds in D,
(g)   and D does not yet contain the subgoal Q' AND P' or a notational variant,
(h) then add Q' AND P' to the list of subgoals.

Backward Double Negation Elimination

(a) Set D to domain of current goal.
(b) Set P to the current goal.
(c) If P matches P' in a subformula NOT NOT P' of a sentence that holds in D,
(d)   and D does not yet contain the subgoal NOT NOT P' or a notational variant,
(e) then add NOT NOT P' to the list of subgoals.

Backward Disjunctive Syllogism

(a) Set D to domain of current goal.
(b) If the current goal Q matches Q' in a sentence (P' OR Q') or (Q' OR P') that holds in D,
(c) and NOT P' is isomorphic to a subformula of a sentence that holds in D,
(d) then go to Step(f).
(e) Else, return failure.
(f) If P' shares variables with Q' and one or more names or variables in Q matched these variables,
(g) then set P to the result of substituting those names or variables for the corresponding variables in P'. Label the substituting arguments, the matched arguments of P, and the residual arguments the unmatched arguments of P.
(h) Else, set P to P', labeling all its arguments as unmatched.
(i) Apply Argument Reversal to unmatched arguments of P and then Subscript Adjustment. Call the result P*.
(j) If D does not yet contain the subgoal NOT(P*) or a notational variant,
(k) then add the subgoal of proving NOT(P*) in D to the list of subgoals.

Backward Disjunctive Modus Ponens

(a) Set D to domain of current goal.
(b) Set R to current goal.
(c) If R can be matched to R' for some sentence IF P' OR Q' THEN R' that holds in D,
(d) then go to Step (f).
(e) Else, return failure.
(f) If P' shares variables with R' and one or more names or variables in R matched these variables,

Table 6.3 (continued)

(g)   then set P to the result of substituting those names or variables for the corresponding variables in P′. Label the substituting arguments, the matched arguments of P, and the residual arguments the unmatched arguments of P.

(h)   Else, set P to P′, labeling all its arguments as unmatched.

(i)   Apply Argument Reversal and then Subscript Adjustment to P. Label the result P*.

(j)   If D does not yet contain the subgoal P* or a notational variant,

(k)   then add the subgoal of proving P* in D to the list of subgoals.

(l)   If the subgoal in (k) fails,

(m)   and Q′ shares variables with R′ and one or more names or variables in R matched these variables,

(n)   then set Q to the result of substituting those names or variables for the corresponding variables in Q′, labeling the arguments as in Step (g).

(o)   Else, set Q to Q′, labeling all its arguments as unmatched.

(p)   Apply Argument Reversal and then Subscript Adjustment to Q. Label the result Q*.

(q)   If D does not yet contain the subgoal Q* or a notational variant,

(r)   then add the subgoal of proving Q* in D to the list of subgoals.

Backward Conjunctive Syllogism

(a)   Set D to domain of current goal.

(b)   If the current goal is of the form NOT Q,

(c)   and Q matches Q′ in a sentence NOT(P′ AND Q′) or NOT(Q′ AND P′) that holds in D,

(d)   then go to Step (f).

(e)   Else, return failure.

(f)   If P′ shares variables with Q′ and one or more names or variables in Q matched these variables,

(g)   then set P to the result of substituting those names or variables for the corresponding variables in P′. Label the substituting arguments, the matched arguments of P, and the residual arguments the unmatched arguments of P.

(h)   Else, set P to P′, labeling all its arguments as unmatched.

(i)   Apply Argument Reversal to unmatched arguments of P and then Subscript Adjustment. Call the result P*.

(j)   If D does not yet contain the subgoal P* or a notational variant,

(k)   then add the subgoal of proving P* in D to the list of subgoals.

Backward DeMorgan (NOT over AND)

(a)   Set D to domain of current goal.

(b)   If current goal is of the form (NOT P) OR (NOT Q),

(c)   and some subformula of a sentence that holds in D is of the form NOT(P′ AND Q′),

(d)   and P AND Q matches P′ AND Q′,

(e)   and D does not yet contain the subgoal NOT (P′ AND Q′) or a notational variant,

(f)   then add NOT (P′ AND Q′) to the list of subgoals.

Backward DeMorgan (NOT over OR)

(a)   Set D to domain of current goal.

(b)   If current goal is of the form (NOT P) AND (NOT Q),

(c)   and some subformula of a sentence that holds in D is of the form NOT(P′ OR Q′),

(d)   and P OR Q matches P′ OR Q′,

(e)   and D does not yet contain the subgoal NOT (P′ OR Q′) or a notational variant,

(f)   then add NOT (P′ OR Q′) to the list of subgoals.

---

contradictory, NOT $(\exists x)$ $Rich(x)$ $(\equiv (\forall x)$ NOT $Rich(x))$, will become NOT $Rich(x)$. Variables are interpreted as if they were attached to quantifiers having wide scope. The procedure for translating sentences from classical predicate logic to quantifier-free form (chapter 3) mandates this interpretation, since it first converts the CPL sentence to prenex form before dropping the quantifiers. This means that if we want to deduce two sentences that are contradictory, as we must for the NOT Introduction and NOT Elimination rules, we must prove $Rich(a)$ and NOT $Rich(x)$. These sentences are truly contradictory, despite their appearance, since they mean that someone is rich and no one is rich. By contrast, the pair $Rich(a)$ and NOT $Rich(a)$, as separate sentences, are not contradictory, since together they merely assert that someone is rich and someone is not rich. These sentences are "subcontraries" in scholastic logic.

The same sort of adjustment must be made for IF Elimination and other rules that handle conditionals. Take the sentence IF $Rich(a)$ $THEN$ $Famous(y)$, which means that someone is such that if she is rich then everyone is famous. If we want to use IF Elimination with this sentence in order to derive $Famous(y)$, we must also have $Rich(x)$ and not just $Rich(a)$. To prove that everyone is famous, it is not enough to show that there is one rich person (since that person might not be the one relevant to the conditional). We must show instead that everyone is rich.

For these reasons, we sometimes need to reverse the roles of variables and temporary names in sentences on which the rules for IF and NOT operate. Usually, this is simply a matter of transforming some sentence P into an isomorphic sentence P^* in which temporary names in P are replaced by new variables in P^* and variables in P are replaced by new temporary names in P^*. The main complication is due to subscripts, since we have to determine which of P^*'s temporary names should be subscripted by which of its variables. The procedures in table 6.4, called Argument Reversal and Subscript Adjustment, yield the correct pattern of subscripts for the backward deduction rules. Some of the rules (e.g., NOT Introduction) require just Argument Reversal. Other rules (e.g., IF Elimination) require both Argument Reversal and Subscript Adjustment in order to deal with variables and temporary names that have been substituted from an earlier subgoal. The next section of this chapter gives proofs of the soundness of some of these rules—proofs that also show why the procedures of table 6.4 are necessary. Table 6.3 collects the changes to all the backward rules.

Table 6.4
Argument Reversal and Subscript Adjustment for backward rules.

Argument Reversal
Let P be an arbitrary sentence in quantifier-free form. Then the following steps produce the argument-reversed, isomorphic sentence P_r:

    1. Assign to each temporary name a_i that appears in P a variable y_i that has not yet appeared in the proof.

    2. Assign to each variable x_i in P a temporary name b_i that has not yet appeared in the proof.

    3. Let $\{a_i\}$ be the set of all temporary names in P that do not have x_i as a subscript. Let $\{y_i\}$ be the set of variables assigned in step 1 to the a_i's in $\{a_i\}$. Subscript b_i with the variables in $\{y_i\}$.

    4. Replace each a_i in P with the y_i assigned to it in step 1. Replace each x_i in P with the b_i assigned to it in step 2, together with the subscripts computed in step 3. The result is P_r.

Subscript Adjustment
Let P be a sentence in quantifier-free form, and let P_r be the result of applying the Argument Reversal procedure above to unmatched arguments of P (i.e., arguments that do not arise from substitution). The following operations yield the subscript-adjusted sentence P_s when applied to P_r:

    1. Let c_j be a temporary name in P_r that derives from reversing an unmatched variable x_j in P. For each such c_j, add to its subscripts any variable y_i in P_r, provided either of the following conditions is met:

        (a) y_i was matched to a variable x_i in P or y_i is a subscript of a temporary name that matched x_i in P, and no temporary name in P contains x_j but not x_i.

        (b) y_i is a subscript of a temporary name that matched some temporary name b_i in P, and b_i does not have x_j as subscript.

    2. Let d_j be a temporary name in P_r that derives from matching to some variable x_j of P. Then for each such d_j, add to its subscripts any variable x_i in P_r, provided all the following conditions are met:

        (a) x_i derives from reversing a temporary name b_i from P.

        (b) b_i does not have x_j as subscript.

        (c) b_i does not have x_k as subscript, where y_k matched x_k and y_k is not a subscript of d_j.

Formal Properties

In examining the sentential rules, we stressed questions of completeness and decidability. In scrutinizing the way PSYCOP deals with variables, however, we need to give more emphasis to soundness—the system's ability to produce only valid inferences. The main reason for this is that the matching rules in table 6.1 and the deduction rules in table 6.3 are more complex than the sentential rules and not as obviously correct. The methods introduced for handling variables are not as closely linked to earlier methods in formal logic and stand in need of verification. Completeness is less of an issue here. We already know that PSYCOP is not complete with respect to classical sentential logic on the basis of the counterexample of chapter 4, and a similar counterexample is enough to show that PSYCOP in its updated version will also be incomplete with respect to classical predicate logic. For these reasons, the bulk of this section is devoted to finding out whether the system gets into trouble by producing proofs, such as (2) and (3), that are not valid. However, we will look briefly at completeness at the end of the chapter. If you don't need reassurance about soundness, you can skip the proofs in the appendix to this chapter; but it might be helpful, even if you skip those proofs, to look at the material on semantics in the subsection just below, since we will compare semantic models of this sort with mental models in chapter 10.

Soundness of Matching

In order to prove that the rules of table 6.1 are sound, we need a standard of correctness with which to compare them. One way to do this is to link the matching rules directly to a semantic interpretation for our quantifier-free sentences. If we can specify what it means for such a sentence to be true, then we can establish the soundness of the rules by showing that they produce only true conclusions from true premises. In terms of table 2.1, we can try to establish that any argument deducible by these rules is also valid. In using this direct method, however, we should bear in mind that our semantics for quantifier-free sentences is not supposed to be a proposal about how people understand them. "Semantics" here is used in the logician's sense of a formal, set-theoretic method for specifying truth and validity. I will try to argue in chapter 10 that this sense of "semantics" is inappropriate for cognitive purposes, and that it should be sharply distinguished from psycholinguists' use of "semantics" to describe the inferential role of meaningful sentences. Nevertheless, logical semantics is valuable for our present concerns since it provides an abstract norm against which to test our rules.

Semantics for Quantifier-Free Sentences Descriptions of formal semantics appear in many logic textbooks (see, e.g., Bergmann et al. 1980 and Thomason 1970a); more advanced treatments can be found in Chang and Keisler 1973 and van Fraassen 1971. The point of this endeavor is to make precise the sense in which the validity of an argument depends on the truth of its premises and its conclusion. We defined validity informally in chapter 2 by saying that an argument is valid if and only if its conclusion is true in all states of affairs in which the premises are true. Formal semantics proceeds by defining a *model*, a set-theoretic entity that might represent a state of affairs in this definition. Given the concept of a model, we can then restate the definition of validity in mathematically precise terms by substituting "models" for "states of affairs": An argument will be valid if and only if the conclusion is true in every *model* in which the premises are true. I will first define what it means for a sentence to be true in a model, and then give an example of how the definition works.

A model **M** for a logical system like ours is simply a pair $\langle D, f \rangle$, in which D is a nonempty set (the domain of entities to which the names and variables in the language refer). The second part of the model, f, is an *interpretation function* that designates for each permanent name in the language an individual element in D and for each predicate a set of "tuples" of elements in D: If P is a one-place predicate, f assigns to it a set of elements from D; if P is a two-place predicate, f assigns to it a set of ordered pairs of elements from D; if P is a three-place predicate, f assigns to it a set of ordered triples from D; and so on. These tuples contain the elements that bear the relation specified by the predicate. For example, suppose D is the set of all people. Since *Swedish* in the sentence *Swedish(x)* is a one-place predicate, $f(Swedish)$ will be a subset of elements of D (i.e., Swedes in the intended model); since *Similar* in the sentence *Similar(x,y)* is a two-place predicate, $f(Similar)$ is the set of all ordered pairs $\langle x, y \rangle$ of elements of D such that (in the intended model) x is similar to y.

To determine the truth of a sentence in our quantifier-free language with respect to a model, we also need to specify possible assignments of the variables and temporary names to elements of D. Let g be such a function that designates for each variable (x, y, etc.) an element of D. For example, if D consists of all people, then $g(x)$ might equal Napoleon, $g(y)$ Madonna, and $g(z)$ William Estes. For temporary names ($a, b_x, c_{x,y}$, etc.), we will employ a second function, h, defined in the following way: If a temporary name b has no subscripts, then h assigns it to a single element of D. If a temporary name $b_{x_1, \ldots, x_n}$ has n subscripts, then h assigns it to a *function* from n-tuples of D elements to D elements. So, for example, $h(b)$ might be Napoleon again; however, $h(b_x)$ would be a function from each element in D to a second (possibly identical) element in D; $h(b_{x,y})$ would be a function from all ordered pairs of D elements to an element in D; and so on. For example, $h(b_x)$ might have as its value the function from each person to his or her father.

Given a model $\mathbf{M} = \langle D, f \rangle$ and functions g and h, we can specify the truth of an arbitrary sentence S in the model. We do this by defining what it means for g and h to *jointly satisfy* a sentence in the model and then generalizing over different choices of g and h. Thus, suppose we have an atomic sentence consisting of an n-place predicate P followed by a sequence of n arguments (variables, temporary names, or permanent names) $t = \langle t_1, t_2, \ldots, t_n \rangle$. Let t' be the sequence formed by replacing each variable x in t by $g(x)$, each permanent name m in t by $f(m)$, and each temporary name $b_{x_1, x_2, \ldots, x_k}$ by $h(b)(g(x_1), g(x_2), \ldots, g(x_k))$. (This last expression is the function picked out by $h(b)$ applied to the k-tuple of elements picked out by $\langle g(x_1), g(x_2), \ldots, g(x_k) \rangle$.) For example, consider the sentence *Child-of*(x, b_x), which says intuitively that every individual is the child of some individual. Then $t = \langle x, b_x \rangle$ and $t' = \langle g(x), h(b)(g(x)) \rangle$. If g and h are the sample functions mentioned in the last paragraph, then $t' = \langle$ Napoleon, Napoleon's father $\rangle$. In the intended model, this pair ought to be among those that the predicate *Child-of* refers to, and if it is we can say that g and h *jointly satisfy* the sentence *Child-of*(x, b_x). In symbols, g and h jointly satisfy *Child-of*(x, b_x) if and only if $t' \in f($ *Child-of* $)$.

In general, g and h *jointly satisfy* a sentence S in $\mathbf{M}$ if and only if the following hold:

(a) S is an atomic sentence Pt and $t' \in f(P)$.

(b) S has the form S_1 AND S_2, and g and h jointly satisfy S_1 and S_2.

(c) S has the form S_1 OR S_2, and g and h jointly satisfy S_1 or S_2.

(d) S has the form NOT S_1, and g and h do not jointly satisfy S_1.

(e) S has the form IF S_1 THEN S_2, and g and h do not jointly satisfy S_1 or g and h jointly satisfy S_2.

Finally, a sentence S *is true* in a model $\mathbf{M}$ iff there is a function h such that, for every function g, h and g jointly satisfy S.

To see how this apparatus works, take the sentence *IF Satellite*(x) *THEN Orbits*(x, b_x)—that is, every satellite orbits some object. The intended model for this sentence might have D as the set of all astronomical objects and $f($Satellite$) = \{x : x$ is a satellite$\}$ and $f($Orbit$) = \{\langle x, y \rangle : x$ orbits $y\}$. Suppose g assigns x to the moon and h assigns b_x to the function from each individual in D to the object it orbits, if any, and otherwise to Alpha Centauri. Then g and h jointly satisfy the sentence with respect to the model: Clause e above states that the sentence is satisfied if its consequent $Orbits(x,b_x)$ is. But g and h map the arguments $\langle x,b_x \rangle$ of the consequent to $\langle g(x),h(b)(g(x)) \rangle = \langle$ moon,earth $\rangle$. Since $\langle$ moon,earth $\rangle \in \{\langle x,y \rangle : x$ orbits $y\}$, the consequent is satisfied according to clause a. Furthermore, this sentence is true in the model. No matter which object g assigns to x, g and h will jointly satisfy the sentence. On one hand, if g assigns x to a satellite, $h(b)(g(x))$ will be the object it orbits, and clause e will satisfy the whole sentence. On the other hand, suppose g assigns x to a nonsatellite. Then the antecedent $satellite(x)$ will not be satisfied, since a nonsatellite is not a member of $\{x : x$ is a satellite$\}$. So the whole sentence will again be satisfied for any choice of g by clause e.

With the notion of truth in a model in hand, we can go on to define semantic entailment and validity, the crucial semantic concepts in table 2.1. A finite set of premises $P = \{P_1, P_2, \ldots, P_n\}$ *semantically entails* a conclusion C iff in all models for which each sentence in P is true C is also true. (This implies that the empty set of premises semantically entails a conclusion whenever the conclusion is itself true in all models, because it is vacuously true in this special case that all sentences of P are true in all models.) We can also take an argument with premises P and conclusion C to be *valid* iff C is semantically entailed by P.

Semantics and Argument Reversal When we discussed the deduction rules for negative and conditional sentences, we found that we sometimes had to reverse arguments (temporary names and variables) to preserve inference relationships. For example, to obtain the opposite of a sentence like $NOT(Bird(x))$ (i.e., nothing is a bird) we had to go to $Bird(a)$ (i.e., something is a bird). However, the semantics never explicitly mentions reversing arguments for negatives and conditionals. For example, clause d of the definition of satisfaction relates the sentence $NOT\ S_1$ to S_1 rather than to a similar sentence with variables replacing temporary names and temporary names replacing variables. This may seem puzzling at first, but the reason is that the notion of joint satisfaction defined by clauses a–e depends on the relation between specific elements of D (as given by the functions g and h) and formulas of the language; it doesn't directly relate whole sentences. If $g(x)$ is an element of D, for example, then we want $g(x)$ to satisfy a sentence like $NOT(Bird(x))$ just in case it is not an element of the subset that *Bird* denotes (i.e., is not a bird, does not satisfy *Bird(x)*), because any individual element of *D* must be either a *Bird* or a non-*Bird*. But this satisfaction relation does not imply that *NOT(Bird(x))* is true if and only if *Bird(x)* is false. It had better not, since the first says that everything is a nonbird, whereas the second says that everything is a bird. Thus, *NOT(Bird(x))* and *Bird(x)* can both be false provided some member of *D* is a bird while another is a nonbird.

To see that the semantics and the Argument Reversal procedure agree in this example, we need to show that *NOT(Bird(x))* and *Bird(a)*, which are contradictory according to Argument Reversal, also have opposite truth values according to the semantics. To do this, notice that if *NOT(Bird(x))* is true in some model then, by the definition of truth, $g(x)$ must satisfy *NOT(Bird(x))* for all g. That is, no matter which element we pick from *D*, that element satisfies *NOT(Bird(x))*. By clause d of the definition of satisfaction, this means that, for all g, $g(x)$ does not satisfy *Bird(x)*. In other words, there is nothing (no element of *D*) that satisfies *Bird(x)*—nothing is a bird. But this means that there can be no h such that $h(a)$ satisfies *Bird(a)*, and this implies that *Bird(a)* is false according to our truth definition. So if *NOT(Bird(x))* is true, then *Bird(a)* is false. Since this relationship also holds in the opposite direction, *NOT(Bird(x))* is true if and only if *Bird(a)* is false: These sentences are contradictories, as we claimed earlier.[2] We prove later in this chapter that the Argument Reversal procedure is correct in general, not just in this simple example.

Are the Matching Rules Sound?   The satisfaction conditions give us the truth of a complex sentence containing any mix of connectives. However, for purposes of testing the matching rules in table 6.1 we needn't worry about a sentence's internal structure. Each of the matching rules states the conditions for generalizing a given sentence to another isomorphic one: The two sentences have exactly the same pattern of connectives and predicates, and they differ only in the arguments to those predicates. We can therefore regard the entire sentence and its generalization as if they were atomic propositions whose arguments consist of all their names and variables. For example, we can represent the sentence *IF Satellite(x) THEN Orbits(x,b_x)* from our earlier example as *P(x,x,b_x)*. We note, too, that some of the conditions of the matching rules are irrelevant for soundness. The overall purpose of these rules is to generalize a subgoal until it exactly matches an assertion, and some of the conditions are intended to "aim" the generalization toward a likely target. For example, if we have *Similar(Kathleen Turner, Lauren Bacall)?* as a subgoal and *Similar(x, y)* as an assertion, we want to generalize the former sentence to produce something identical to the latter. However, all that is required for the rules to be sound is that, at each generalization step, the more specific sentence is semantically entailed by the more general one. That is, if the rule produces a new generalized subgoal P_1 from the original subgoal P_2, we need only show that P_1 semantically entails P_2. Soundness does not depend on whether we eventually achieve a match to the assertion.

Our strategy for proving soundness proceeds in the way illustrated in figure 6.2. We assume that the generalization P_1 is true in some model **M**. In terms of the semantics for our language, this means that there is a function for temporary names, h_1, such that, for any function g_1 for variables, h_1 and g_1 will jointly satisfy P_1. We also assume, for purposes of exposing a contradiction, that the original subgoal P_2 is false in the same model **M**. Thus, for every function h_2, there is a function g_2 such that h_2 and g_2 do *not* jointly satisfy P_2. We can define h_2 in a way that makes its assignments quite similar to those of h_1, and then consider a g_2 that fails to satisfy sentence P_2. Finally, we show that there is a g_1 that, in conjunction with h_1, gives to the terms of P_1 the same denotations that h_2 and g_2

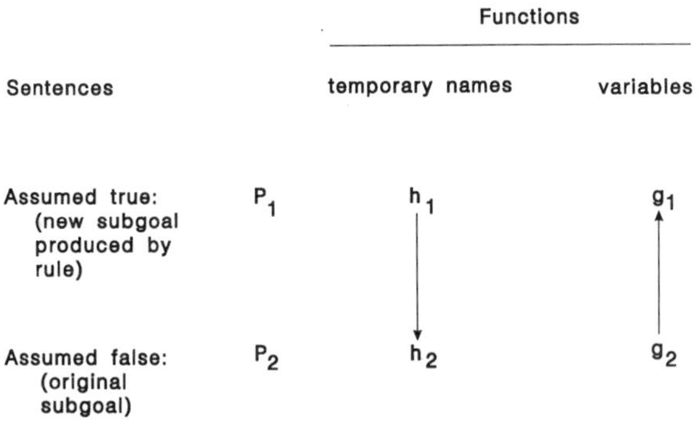

Figure 6.2
Proof strategy for soundness of matching rules: (a) We assume P_1 true in **M** so that there exists an assignment h_1 that satisfies P_1 for any g. (b) We construct h_2 so that h_2 and h_1 make similar assignments to temporary names. (c) We assume for reductio that P_2 is false in **M**; thus, there exists a g_2 such that h_2 and g_2 do not satisfy P_2. (d) We construct g_1 so that h_1 and g_1 give the same denotations to terms of P_1 that h_2 and g_2 give to P_2. Thus, h_1 and g_1 must fail to satisfy P_1 in **M**, contrary to (a).

give to the terms of P_2. Since P_1 and P_2 differ only in their terms, h_1 and g_1 must not satisfy P_1, contrary to our initial assumption. This contradiction implies that P_2 must also be true in **M**, and therefore that P_1 semantically entails P_2. The appendix to this chapter contains proofs of soundness along these lines for each of the rules in table 6.1.

Soundness of Deduction Rules

The proofs for the matching rules verify PSYCOP's method for deducing a conclusion from a premise that differs from it only in its terms. But, in general, PSYCOP must also deduce conclusions from premises whose forms differ also in the predicates and connectives they contain. For this purpose, it relies on the forward rules of tables 4.1 and 6.2 and the backward rules of table 6.3. Most of these rules are variations on the usual introduction and elimination rules in natural-deduction systems for CPL; however, the backward rules that deal with conditionals and negatives are rather unusual, since they require Argument Reversal, which flips temporary names and variables. So it might be a good idea to show that the reversal procedure gives us the right results.

Soundness with Respect to CPL: Rules for Negation   Although we can establish the soundness of the deduction rules directly through the semantics, as we did with the matching procedures, it might be more revealing to show that the negation rules yield the same inferences we would get had we applied standard CPL rules to the equivalent sentences. If so, then, since the CPL rules are sound, the rules for quantifier-free form must be sound too. To see this, consider first the rules for negatives: Backward NOT Introduction and Backward NOT Elimination. These rules use the argument-reversal procedure as part of a proof by contradiction: They show that some supposition leads to a pair of contradictory sentences and that therefore the opposite of the supposition follows. What the argument-reversal procedure does is ensure that the pair of sentences is contradictory and that the supposition contradicts the rule's conclusion. In other words, Argument Reversal should take as input a quantifier-free sentence P and produce as output another quantifier-free sentence P^* such that P and $NOT(P^*)$ (or, alternatively, P^* and $NOT(P)$) are contradictory. The procedure delivers the right result, relative to CPL, if P and $NOT(P^*)$ are the translations of two contradictory CPL sentences. Proving the soundness of the negation rules thus amounts to proving the soundness of the argument-reversal procedure.

As an example, the CPL sentence $(\forall x)(\exists y)(\forall z)P(x,y,z)$ becomes $P(x,b_x,z)$ in quantifier-free form, according to the translation procedure in chapter 3. The contradictory of the original sentence is $NOT((\forall x)(\exists y)(\forall z)P(x,y,z)) \equiv (\exists x)(\forall y)(\exists z)NOT(P(x,y,z))$, which becomes $NOT(P(a,y,c_y))$ in our notation. Thus, we want the argument-reversal rule to map $P(x,b_x,z)$ to $P(a,y,c_y)$, or some notational variant. To check that it does, we follow the steps of the procedure in table 6.4: (a) We assign b to a new variable, say y'. (b) We assign x and z to new temporary names, a' and c'. (c) The set of temporary names in $P(x,b_x,z)$ that do not have x as subscript is empty, and the set of temporary names that don't have z as subscript is $\{b\}$. The variable assigned in step a to b is y'. Hence, we must subscript c' with y'. (d) We therefore replace b_x with y', x with a', and z with $c'_{y'}$ in $P(x,b_x,z)$ to get $P(a',y',c'_{y'})$, which is indeed a notational variant of $P(a,y,c_y)$.

In general, then, we would like to prove the following proposition: Let P be a sentence in quantifier-free form that has been derived from a CPL sentence F, according to the procedure of chapter 3. (Recall that the rules in table 6.3 apply only to sentences that can be derived from CPL formulas in this way.) Let P^* be the sentence we get by applying the argument-reversal rule to P. Then $NOT(P^*)$ can be derived from a CPL sentence that is logically equivalent to $NOT(F)$. Figure 6.3 illustrates these relationships, and a proof of the proposition appears in the appendix.

Soundness with Respect to CPL: Conditionals   Like negative sentences, conditionals require special handling in our quantifier-free format, and for much the same reason. In CPL a conditional sentence such as *IF* $(\forall x)$ $F(x)$ *THEN* $(\forall y)$ $G(y)$ is equivalent to $(\exists x)(\forall y)$ *IF* $F(x)$ *THEN* $G(y)$, and this goes into quantifier-free form as *IF* $F(b)$ *THEN* $G(y)$. In this case, we simply switch the universal quantifier that is embedded in the antecedent to an existential quantifier when it is brought out front. But there is an additional complication with conditionals that we didn't have to face in dealing with negatives: Some of the variables or temporary names that appear in the antecedent may also be shared by the consequent, and reversing these latter arguments in the antecedent will not do. Rules like Backward IF Elimination must distinguish these global (or

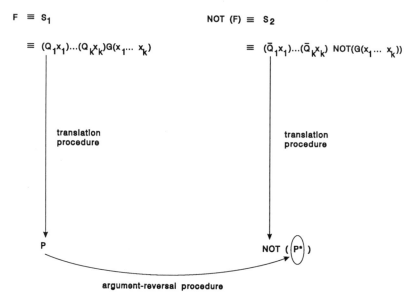

$F \equiv S_1$ $\qquad\qquad\qquad\qquad$ NOT (F) $\equiv S_2$

$\equiv (Q_1 x_1)...(Q_K x_K) G(x_1 ... x_k)$ $\qquad\qquad \equiv (\bar{Q}_1 x_1)...(\bar{Q}_K x_K)$ NOT$(G(x_1 ... x_k))$

translation $\qquad\qquad\qquad\qquad\qquad\qquad$ translation
procedure $\qquad\qquad\qquad\qquad\qquad\qquad$ procedure

P $\qquad\qquad\qquad\qquad\qquad\qquad\qquad\qquad$ NOT (P*)

argument-reversal procedure

Figure 6.3
Proof strategy for soundness of Argument Reversal. Assume P is a quantifier-free sentence that derives from a sentence F that is logically equivalent to the prenex sentence S_1. Let P^* be the result of applying the Argument Reversal procedure of table 6.4 to P. We then show that $NOT(P^*)$ is the translation of a CPL sentence equivalent to $NOT(F)$.

matched) arguments from the arguments that are local to the antecedent in order to carry out the deduction correctly.

Let us study this situation more carefully in the case of the Backward IF Elimination rule in table 6.3. We are given a conditional assertion *IF P' THEN R'* and a subgoal R that we can match to the consequent R'. By the results proved earlier, we know that if we can deduce R' then R must follow validly. The IF Elimination strategy is to deduce the consequent R' by deducing the antecedent; but we shouldn't just attempt to prove P' itself. We may have to adjust some of the arguments in P' for the reasons just mentioned. The steps of the rule in table 6.3 spell out how these arguments should be changed. Essentially, we apply the argument-reversal procedure to just the *local* arguments of the antecedent and then add subscripts to ensure that global variables correctly govern local temporary names. The subscript-adjustment procedure in table 6.4 is responsible for this latter change.

As an example, we can consider a problem related to the African cities database that we looked at in chapter 3. In that context, our domain consisted of locations in Africa, and we used *In(Khartoum, Sudan)* to mean that Khartoum is in Sudan and *In(Sudan, Africa)* to mean that Sudan is in Africa. To express the transitivity of the *In* relation, we relied on the generalization: *IF In(x,y) AND In(y,z) THEN In(x,z)*. Now, suppose we want to prove, for some reason, that all locations in the database are in Africa, given the transitivity generalization and the fact that any such location is in some place that is in Africa. This amounts to a proof of (4).

(4)   IF In(x,y) AND In(y,z) THEN In(x,z)
$$\frac{\text{In}(w,a_w) \text{ AND } \text{In}(a_w,\text{Africa})}{\text{In}(u,\text{Africa})}$$

To prove this by Backward IF Elimination, we must match the conclusion to the consequent of the first premise (steps a–d of the IF Elimination rule in table 6.3). In this process, u will be matched to x and *Africa* to z. According to steps e–g, we must also substitute the same terms in the antecedent, producing *In(u,y) AND In(y,Africa)*. This is sentence P in the statement of the rule, with u and *Africa* as matched arguments and y as the sole unmatched argument. In step h, argument reversal applies to this unmatched argument, changing the antecedent to *In(u,b) AND In(b,Africa)*. But this last sentence isn't quite what we want as a subgoal, for it says that there is some particular location b in Africa that everyplace is in. The proper subgoal should instead say that each location is in some place or other in Africa: *In(u,b_u) AND In(b_u,Africa)*. The subscript adjustment in step i yields precisely this result, which is called $P*$ in the rule. (See table 6.4 for the details of subscript adjustment.) It is easy to see that this subgoal matches the second premise of (4).

In order to show that this adjustment produces valid results in the general case, we can again demonstrate that the IF Elimination rule yields exactly the same result we get using standard Modus ponens in CPL. More formally, what we would like to prove is this: Suppose *IF P' THEN R'* derives from a CPL sentence S_1 and R from a CPL sentence S_3. Let $P*$ be the result of applying the Argument Reversal and Subscript Adjustment procedures of table 6.4 to P', subject to the other conditions listed in the Backward IF Elimination rule. Then $P*$ is a translation of a CPL sentence S_2 such that S_1 and S_2 entail (in CPL) S_3. (The use of primes and asterisks here corresponds to the way the rule is stated in table 6.3.) A proof of this proposition is given in the appendix to this chapter.

Of course, the proofs we have given here of the matching rules, the negation rules, and IF Elimination do not show that the entire system is sound. However, they do establish the soundness of some of its main parts—parts that may not be as intuitively obvious as PSYCOP's other principles.

Incompleteness

As we have seen, PSYCOP is unable to prove some valid propositional arguments that involve transforming conditional sentences to nonconditionals. Similarly, our extended model for predicate-variable sentences is unable to prove arguments like (5), which is valid according to the semantics outlined above (and whose CPL counterpart is, of course, also valid).

(5) $\underline{\text{NOT(IF P(x) THEN Q(x))}}$
     P(a)

The cause of this incompleteness is the same as before: By design, PSYCOP doesn't possess rules that are capable of deducing the conclusion from the premise.

However, there are some issues concerning completeness that are relevant to our choice of quantifier-free form and that merit our attention. On one hand, as long as we stick to quantifier-free sentences that are equivalent to sentences of CPL, the form itself does not pose a barrier to completeness. The trouble with (5), for example, has nothing to do with the fact that we have eliminated explicit quantifiers in its premise and in its conclusion. There are complete proof systems in logic that make use of quantifier-free form—systems that originated in the work of Skolem (1928/1967) (see also Quine 1972, chapter 34). Along the same lines, resolution systems in AI are complete even though they operate (after some stage) on quantifierless representations (see chapter 3). These systems have many advantages: They are more elegant than PSYCOP, since they are based on a uniform reductio procedure. Also, the problems associated with argument reversal don't arise for such systems. After the first step (in which the conclusion is negated), they get along without rules such as IF Elimination (or they use these rules in ways that don't require switching quantifiers).

But what such systems gain in simplicity they lose in psychological fidelity, since they don't correctly reflect human proof strategies.

On the other hand, if we take full advantage of quantifier-free form and use sentences that have no equivalents in CPL, completeness is impossible no matter which finite set of rules we choose. This is a consequence of the fact that we can create sentences in this form with temporary names that have distinct sets of variables as subscripts. For example, in chapter 3 we used *IF (Country(x) AND Country(y) AND Richer-than(x,y)) THEN (Official(b_x) AND Official(b_y) AND More-powerful-than(b_x,b_y))* to represent Barwise's (1979) example *The richer the country, the more powerful one of its officials.* In this sentence, the identity of official b_x depends on the country we choose as the value of *x*, and that of official b_y on *y*; but b_x does not depend on choice of *y*, and b_y does not depend on *x*. It is known, however, that logics that can encode such relationships are incomplete (Westerståhl 1989).

Psychologists and philosophers have sometimes taken this theoretical incompleteness as indicating a defect in proof-based approaches. If there are valid arguments that it is impossible for such a system to prove, doesn't that mean that humans aren't proof-based (or "syntactic") systems after all but instead operate on the basis of other (perhaps "semantic" or even "pragmatic") principles? (See Lucas 1961 for related arguments; see Benacerraf 1967 and Dennett 1978 for refutations.) The trouble with this conclusion is that it presupposes that the alternative methods for evaluating arguments are ones that humans can use to do what proof systems can't. Although it is true that model-theoretic semantics can describe valid arguments that can't be proved, these methods do not automatically yield *procedures* by which people can recognize such arguments. On the contrary, what the incompleteness theorems establish is that any procedure within a very broad class (i.e., those that can be carried out by Turing machines) is incapable of recognizing all valid arguments. Such a procedure will be incomplete whether it uses standard proof rules or not. For example, "mental model" theories (Johnson-Laird 1983), which are advertised as "semantic" methods, are also supposed to be Turing computable; if so, they are subject to incompleteness just as proof-based systems are. (See chapter 10 below for further discussion of mental models.) Moreover, even if an alternative method can correctly recognize valid arguments that slip by a specific proof system, it remains to be shown that there isn't a further valid argument that slips by the alternative method. It is possible that humans really do have abilities that outstrip the algorithmic procedures to which the incompleteness theorems apply. But no psychological proposal that I'm aware of comes close to being both sound and complete over the range of arguments that can be expressed in quantifier-free form.

Perhaps objections based on incompleteness have more point if they focus on the specific difficulties that PSYCOP has in proving arguments like (5). As just mentioned, there are many well-known systems that are complete with respect to CPL; but PSYCOP is incomplete even in this narrower domain. Nor is this incompleteness limited to extremely lengthy problems: Any student of elementary logic should be able to show that (5) is correct. However, whether this is a defect in PSYCOP is an empirical matter. The theory is supposed to represent the deductive abilities of people untutored in logic; thus, we are on the wrong track if *these* people can correctly assess arguments that PSYCOP can't. We need data from such people to determine the plausibility of PSYCOP's restrictions.

Appendix: Proofs of the Major Propositions

In the proofs of soundness for the matching rules, β, γ, and δ range over temporary names, and σ ranges over variables.

Matching rule 1 of table 6.1 (variables in subgoal to variables in assertion) is sound.

Proof For this rule, we take P_1 to be the new subgoal $P'(x)$ and P_2 to be the original subgoal $P'(y)$ (see table 6.1). As in figure 6.2, we assume that P_1 is true in **M** and choose an assignment h_1 that satisfies P_1 for all g. If P_2 is false in **M**, then for *any* h there is a g such that h and g fail to satisfy P_2. In particular, we can define h_2 in the following way: Let $h_2(\beta) = h_1(\beta)$ for all temporary names β that do *not* appear in P_2 in the same position in which x appears in P_1. For temporary names $\gamma_{...y...}$ that *do* appear in the same position as x, let h_2 assign $\gamma_{...y...}$ to the function $f_2(...g(y)...) = g(y)$. In other words, $\gamma_{...y...}$ denotes the function whose value is the same as its argument $g(y)$. (Because of condition d and action b in rule 1, $\gamma_{...y...}$ cannot appear in P_1; so we are free to define $h_2(\gamma)$ as we like.) We can then let g_2 be an assignment to variables so that h_2 and g_2 do not jointly satisfy P_2.

Define $g_1(\sigma) = g_2(\sigma)$ for all $\sigma \neq x$, and $g_1(x) = g_2(y)$. The conditions of rule 1 imply that there are only three ways in which P_1 and P_2 can differ: (a) P_2 has y where P_1 has x; (b) P_2 has $\gamma_{...y...}$ where P_1 has x; and (c) P_2 has $\beta_{...y...}$ where P_1 has $\beta_{...x...}$. Since $g_1(x) = g_2(y)$, terms in positions covered by case a have the same denotations. Moreover, in case c, h_1 and h_2 assign β to the same function (say, f_β). Since $f_\beta(...g_1(x)...) = f_\beta(...g_2(y)...)$, these terms too have the same denotations. Finally, in case b, h_2 assigns $\gamma_{...y...}$ to $g(y)$ by definition of h_2, and $g_2(y) = g_1(x)$ by definition of g_1. So, once again, x in P_1 and $\gamma_{...y...}$ in P_2 denote the same element of the model. This means that each term in P_1 has exactly the same denotation as the analogous term in P_2. Since P_1 and P_2 are otherwise identical, h_1 and g_1 cannot satisfy P_1. This contradicts our assumption that h_1 satisfies P_1 for all g.

Matching rule 2 of table 6.1 (temporary names in subgoal to temporary or permanent names in assertion) is sound.

Proof To prove rule 2 sound, we let P_1 equal $P'(n)$, the generalized subgoal, and let P_2 equal $P'(t)$, the original subgoal. Again, assume P_1 true in $\mathbf{M} = \langle D, f \rangle$, and for the reductio suppose P_2 is false in $\mathbf{M}$. Let h_1 be an assignment that satisfies P_1 for all g, and define h_2 as follows: $h_2(\beta) = h_1(\beta)$ for all $\beta \neq t_{x_1,...,x_i,...,x_k}$, where $t_{x_1,...,x_i,...,x_k}$ is the one temporary name that appears in P_2 in the same position that n occupies in P_1. Because n replaces all occurrences of $t_{x_1,...,x_i,...,x_k}$, when P_1 is formed, $t_{x_1,...,x_i,...,x_k}$ itself does not appear in P_1. Hence, no conflict can arise over the assignment for $t_{x_1,...,x_i,...,x_k}$. If the name n mentioned in the rule is a permanent name, we can let h_2 assign $t_{x_1,...,x_i,...,x_k}$ to the function

$$f_2(g(x_1),...,g(x_i),...,g(x_k)) = f(n)$$

(that is, to the constant function whose value is the element of D that the model gives to proper name n). If n is a temporary name, say $\hat{a}_{x_1,...,x_i}$, then by condition c of the rule its subscripts are a subset of those of $t_{x_1,...,x_i,...,x_k}$. So we can let h_2 assign $t_{x_1,...,x_i,...,x_k}$ to the function

$$f_2(g(x_1),...,g(x_i),...,g(x_k)) = f_1(g(x_1),...,g(x_i)),$$

where f_1 is the function that h_1 assigns to $\hat{a}$. (That is, the value of f_2 is just the value that f_1 gives to the subset of arguments $g(x_1),...,g(x_i)$.)

Because of condition e and the action of rule 2, the terms of P_1 and P_2 are identical, except that the former has n where the latter has

$t_{x_1,\ldots,x_i,\ldots,x_k}$. But by the above construction the denotation of n under h_1 must be the same as the denotation of $t_{x_1,\ldots,x_i,\ldots,x_k}$ under h_2 for any choice of g. Hence, if h_2 does not satisfy P_2 for some g_2, then h_1 will not satisfy P_1 for all g. But this contradicts the hypothesis that h_1 satisfies P_1 for every g.

Matching rule 3 of table 6.1 (permanent names in subgoal to variables in assertion) is sound.

Proof This time let $P_1 = P'(x)$ and $P_2 = P'(m)$, from rule 3. Following the usual procedure of figure 6.2, we assume P_1 true in $\mathbf{M} = \langle D, f \rangle$, so there is an h_1 that satisfies this sentence for any g. We also suppose P_2 false in $\mathbf{M}$ and define h_2 as follows: $h_2(\beta) = h_1(\beta)$, for all temporary names β, except those that appear in P_2 in the same positions occupied by x-subscripted temporary names in P_1. In the latter case, if $\delta_{y_1,\ldots,y_k}$ appears in the same position as $\gamma_{x,y_1,\ldots,y_k}$, let h_2 assign δ to the function

$$f_2(g(y_1),\ldots,g(y_k)) = f_1(d,g(y_1),\ldots,g(y_k)),$$

where f_1 is the function that h_1 assigns to γ and $d = f(m)$ (i.e., the constant element of the model associated with the permanent name m). Since P_2 is supposed to be false, there must be a g_2 such that h_2 and g_2 do not jointly satisfy P_2.

Let $g_1(\sigma) = g_2(\sigma)$, for all $\sigma \neq x$ and let $g_1(x) = f(m)$. Rule 3 ensures that the terms of P_1 and P_2 are the same except when (a) P_2 has m where P_1 has x and (b) P_2 has $\delta_{y_1,\ldots,y_k}$ where P_1 has $\gamma_{x,y_1,\ldots,y_k}$. But terms in positions covered by (a) have the same denotation, since $g_1(x) = f(m)$. And the same is also true of the terms covered by (b), since, under h_2 and g_2, $\delta_{y_1,\ldots,y_k}$ refers to

$$f_2(g_2(y_1),\ldots,g_2(y_k)) = f_1(d,g_2(y_1),\ldots,g_2(y_k))$$

$$= f_1(g_1(x),g_1(y_1),\ldots,g_1(y_k)),$$

which is the denotation of $\gamma_{x,y_1,\ldots,y_k}$ under h_1 and g_1. Since analogous terms in P_1 and P_2 have the same referents, h_1 and g_1 must fail to satisfy P_1 if h_2 and g_2 fail to satisfy P_2, contradicting the premise that h_1 satisfies P_1 for all g.

Matching rule 4 of table 6.1 (temporary names in subgoal to variables in assertion) is sound.

Proof In this case, $P_1 = P'(x_1,\ldots,x_k)$ and $P_2 = P'(t)$. Suppose that P_1 is true and, for contradiction, that P_2 is false in some model $\mathbf{M}$. Let h_1 be an assignment for temporary names that satisfies P_1 for any g. We can then define h_2 so that $h_2(\beta) = h_1(\beta)$ for all temporary names β, with the following exceptions: First, if t is the temporary name mentioned in rule 4 that appears in the same positions as $x_1,\ldots,x_k$, then let h_2 assign t to a constant function whose value is an arbitrary member, d, of the model's domain. Second, suppose $\gamma_{y_1,\ldots,y_j}$ is a temporary name in P_2 that appears in the same position as a temporary name $\beta_{x'_1,\ldots,x'_i,y_1,\ldots,y_j}$ in P_1, where the subscripts $x'_1,\ldots,x'_i$ are chosen from among $x_1,\ldots,x_k$. Then let h_2 assign $\gamma_{y_1,\ldots,y_j}$ to the function

$$f_2(g(y_1),\ldots,g(y_j)) = f_1(d,\ldots,d,g(y_1),\ldots,g(y_j)),$$

where f_1 is the function that h_1 assigned to $\beta_{x'_1,\ldots,x'_i,y_1,\ldots,y_j}$, and where the first ith arguments of f_1 are d. We also let g_2 be a variable assignment, such that h_2 and g_2 do not jointly satisfy P_2.

Define $g_1(\sigma) = d$ if $\sigma = x_1$ or x_2 or ... or x_k, and $g_1(\sigma) = g_2(\sigma)$ otherwise. Conditions c–d, together with the action portion of rule 4, force P_1 and P_2 to be identical, except in cases where (a) P_2 has t where P_1 has x_1, $x_2,\ldots$, or x_k, or (b) P_2 has $\gamma_{y_1,\ldots,y_j}$ where P_1 has $\beta_{x'_1,\ldots,x'_i,y_1,\ldots,y_j}$. By the definitions of h_2 and g_1, however, $h_2(t) = d = g_1(x_1) = \cdots = g_1(x_k)$. So terms in positions covered by (a) have the same denotations. Similarly, the denotation of $\gamma_{y_1,\ldots,y_j}$, as defined above, is

$$f_1(d,\ldots,d,g_2(y_1),\ldots,g_2(y_j)) = f_1(d,\ldots,d,g_1(y_1),\ldots,g_1(y_j))$$
$$= f_1(g_1(x'_1),\ldots,g_1(x'_i),g_1(y_1),\ldots,g_1(y_j)),$$

which is the denotation of $\beta_{x'_1,\ldots,x'_i,y_1,\ldots,y_j}$. For this reason, if h_2 and g_2 fail to satisfy P_2, then h_1 and g_1 must fail to satisfy P_1, contradicting our original assumption.

Soundness of Argument-Reversal Procedure (table 6.4)   Let P be a sentence in quantifier-free form that has been derived from a CPL sentence F, according to the procedure of chapter 3. Let P^* be the sentence we get by applying the argument-reversal rule to P. Then $NOT(P^*)$ can be derived from a CPL sentence that is logically equivalent to $NOT(F)$.

Proof According to the translation method of chapter 3, P comes from F via a logically equivalent CPL sentence in prenex form:

$$(Q_1x_1)(Q_2x_2)\cdots(Q_kx_k)G(x_1,x_2,\ldots,x_k),$$

where each Q_i is an existential or universal quantifier. Call this prenex sentence S_1 (see figure 6.3). Hence,

$NOT(F) \Leftrightarrow NOT(S_1)$

$$\Leftrightarrow NOT((Q_1 x_1)(Q_2 x_2) \cdots (Q_k x_k) G(x_1, x_2, \ldots x_k))$$

$$\Leftrightarrow (\overline{Q}_1 x_1)(\overline{Q}_2 x_2) \cdots (\overline{Q}_k x_k) NOT(G(x_1, x_2, \ldots, x_k)),$$

where $\overline{Q}_i = \forall$ if $Q_i = \exists$ and $\overline{Q}_i = \exists$ if $Q_i = \forall$. It then suffices to show that $NOT(P^*)$ is a translation of this last expression, which we can label S_2. (See figure 6.3.)

First, suppose that a is a temporary name (possibly subscripted) in P. The argument-reversal procedure (table 6.4) will replace a with a novel variable y in P^* in steps 1 and 4. But note that, by the translation method of chapter 3, a must have come from some existentially quantified variable in S_1. When S_1 is negated to produce S_2, the same variable will be universally quantified (owing to the switch in quantifiers). Thus, we can choose y to stand for this variable when S_2 is translated into quantifier-free form.

Second, suppose x is a variable in P. The argument-reversal procedure will assign x to some new temporary name b in step 2. In step 3 the procedure gathers the set of all temporary names $\{a_j\}$ in P that do *not* have x as a subscript, and then subscripts b with the variables in $\{y_j\}$ that have been assigned to these temporary names in step 1. Step 4 replaces x with the temporary name $b_{\{y_j\}}$ in P^* (where $b_{\{y_j\}}$ is b subscripted with each variable in $\{y_j\}$). Now, x must have originally been derived from a universally quantified variable in S_1. Similarly, the temporary names in $\{a_j\}$ must have been derived from a set of existentially quantified variables $\{z_j\}$ in S_1—in particular, from those existential quantifiers that precede $(\forall x)$ in S_1, given the translation method. (If they followed $(\forall x)$, they would have received x as a subscript.) Thus, when S_1 is negated to produce S_2, x will become existentially quantified, and the z_js will be those universally quantified variables whose quantifiers precede x in S_2. To translate S_2 into quantifier-free form, we must select a temporary name for x and subscript it with this same set of universally quantified variables. In the preceding paragraph, we saw that elements of $\{z_j\}$ will appear as the elements of $\{y_j\}$ in P^*. If we choose b as the temporary name to replace x, then x will become $b_{\{y_j\}}$ in translation.

The translation of S_2 must be of the form $NOT(P')$, where P' is identical to P^*, with the possible exception of P' and P^* terms. However, we have just seen that each variable in P' corresponds to a like variable in P^*, and each temporary name in P' to a like temporary name in P^*. This means that $P' = P^*$, which is what we set out to prove.

Soundness of Backward IF Elimination   Suppose $IF\ P'\ THEN\ R'$ derives from a CPL sentence S_1, and R from a CPL sentence S_3. Let P^* be the result of applying the argument-reversal and subscript-adjustment procedures of table 6.4 to P', subject to the other conditions listed in the Backward IF Elimination rule. Then P^* is a translation of a CPL sentence S_2 such that S_1 and S_2 entail (in CPL) S_3.

Proof   We tackle this proof in three parts. The first two parts show that S_1 entails a further CPL sentence, shown in (8) below. The third part completes the proof by demonstrating that P^* is the translation of a sentence S_2, which, together with (8), entails S_3. Since S_1 entails (8), it follows that S_1 and S_2 entail S_3. Here are the details:

1. Suppose $IF\ P'\ THEN\ R'$ is the translation of S_1, which we can write as in (6).

(6) $(Q_1 x_1) \cdots (Q_k x_k)(IF\ F\ THEN\ G)$.

Then P' will be the translation of $(Q_1 x_1) \cdots (Q_k x_k)F$, and R' is a translation of $(Q_1 x_1) \cdots (Q_k x_k)G$. To simplify matters, we need some preliminary transformations of (6). Note that when IF Elimination is carried out variables and names in R will be matched to the variables and names in R' (see step b of the rule in table 6.3). Consider, first, those universal quantifiers in (6) that correspond to matched variables in R'. (For example, $(Q_i x_i)$ will be such a quantifier if $Q_i = \forall$, x_i appears in R', and x_i is matched by a variable or temporary name from R.) By moving some of these universals leftward in (6), we can arrange it so that any universal $(\forall x_i)$ whose variable x_i matches a variable y_i from R precedes universals and existentials whose variables match temporary names containing y_i as subscript. (Suppose R' is $G(x_1, x_2)$ and R is $G(c_y, y)$, so that c_y matches x_1 and y matches x_2. Then we want $(\forall x_2)$ to precede $(\forall x_1)$ in (6), and we can write $(\forall x_2) < (\forall x_1)$ to denote this ordering.) In this rearrangement we must also make sure that $(\forall x_i)$ follows universals and existentials whose variables match temporary names that do not contain y_i as subscript. In other words, the ordering of the quantifiers should copy the ordering of the corresponding quantifiers in S_3.

What justifies this rearrangement? In the first place, such an ordering is possible, since its analogue already appears in S_3. Second, if we can achieve this ordering by moving the universal quantifiers in (6) leftward over existentials or other universals, then the rearranged sentence is logically entailed by (6): In CPL $(\forall x_{i-1})(\forall x_i)H$ entails (in fact, is equivalent to) $(\forall x_i)(\forall x_{i-1})H$, and $(\exists x_{i-1})(\forall x_i)H$ entails $(\forall x_i)(\exists x_{i-1})H$ (see Reichenbach 1966, pp. 134–135, or Suppes 1957, p. 115). Thus, to move a universal quantifier leftward in CPL we can strip preceding quantifiers by means of $\forall$-Elimination or $\exists$-Elimination from table 2.5, apply one of these entailments, and then restore the preceding quantifiers by $\forall$-Introduction or $\exists$-Introduction. Sentence 6 entails this result. Third, we can indeed achieve the desired ordering by leftward movement of universals alone. To see this, suppose that whenever $(\forall x_i) < (\exists x_j)$ in (6) then $(\forall y_i) < (\exists y_j)$ in S_3, where x_i corresponds to y_i and x_j to y_j. Then a series of left shifts of universal quantifiers is sufficient to achieve the correct ordering. (Suppose (6) is $(\exists x_2)(\exists x_4)(\forall x_5)(\forall x_3)(\exists x_6)(\forall x_1)(IF\ F\ THEN\ G)$ and S_3 is $(\forall y_1)(\exists y_2)(\forall y_3)(\exists y_4)(\forall y_5)(\exists y_6)G$, where y_1 matches x_1, y_2 matches x_2, and so on. Then by jumping the universal quantifiers in (6) leftward we can obtain the correct ordering. One algorithm would be to start with the universal quantifier that should appear in leftmost position, $(\forall x_1)$, moving it in front of the others by a series of leftward steps, and then to move the universal that should appear next, $(\forall x_3)$, into position.) The only barrier to complete alignment occurs if $(\forall x_i) < (\exists x_j)$ in (6) but $(\exists y_j) < (\forall y_i)$ in S_3, for in this case it would be necessary to move the universal in (6) to the right rather than to the left to achieve the proper ordering. But this situation is not consistent with our hypothesis that R matches R', because in such a case the arguments of R' would include x_i and $b_{...x_i...}$ and the arguments of R would include y_i and c (where c's subscripts do not include y_i). The first two matching rules of table 6.1 would then prohibit matching y_i to x_i and $b_{...x_i...}$ to c.

An additional change is needed in (6), however. Within unbroken strings of universals $(\forall x_i)...(\forall x_j)$ in the newly rearranged sentence, we can move universals whose variables match terms in R in front of universals whose variables are not matched (i.e., variables that appear only in P'). This further reshuffling is justified by the same CPL principles mentioned above, so that the new sentence is also entailed by (6). Let us denote the result of these changes as in (7).

(7) $(Q'_1 x_1) \cdots (Q'_k x_k) (IF\ F\ THEN\ G).$

The sentence $(Q_1'x_1)\cdots(Q_k'x_k)G$ translates into a quantifier-free sentence that is similar to R, except that the former sentence may have variables in some of the positions where R has temporary names. Hence, if we substitute existential quantifiers in corresponding positions in $(Q_1'x_1)\cdots(Q_k'x_k)G$, we get a sentence that translates into R itself. In particular, S_3 is $(Q_1'x_1)\cdots(\exists x_i)\cdots(Q_k'x_k)G$, where we have set any universal quantifiers $(\forall x_i)$ to existentials if R has a temporary name in place of x_i. Thus, in order to prove our main theorem, if suffices to show that (7) entails a sentence of the form shown in (8) and that P^* is the translation of (8)'s antecedent.

(8)   IF $(Q_1''x_1)\cdots(Q_k''x_k)F$ THEN $(Q_1'x_1)\cdots(\exists x_i)\cdots(Q_k'x_k)G$.

2. To show that (8) follows from (7), we need a few more facts from CPL. First, if $(Q_kx_k)(IF\ F\ THEN\ G)$ entails $IF\ (Q_k''x_k)F\ THEN\ (Q_k'x_k)G$, then $(Q_1x_1)\cdots(Q_{k-1}x_{k-1})(Q_kx_k)(IF\ F\ THEN\ G)$ entails $(Q_1x_1)\cdots$ $(Q_{k-1}x_{k-1})(IF\ (Q_k''x_k)F\ THEN\ (Q_k'x_k)G)$. (To show this, we can strip away the first $k-1$ quantifiers using $\forall$-Elimination and $\exists$-Elimination from table 2.5, make use of the entailment, and then restore the quantifiers with $\forall$-Introduction and $\exists$-Introduction.) This means that we can move the quantifiers in on a step-by-step basis, so that $(Q_1x_1)\cdots(Q_kx_k)$ $(IF$ $F\ THEN\ G)$ entails $IF\ (Q_1''x_1)\cdots(Q_k''x_k)F\ THEN\ (Q_1'x_1)\cdots(Q_k'x_k)G$. Second, in CPL, $(\exists x)(IF\ F\ THEN\ G)$ entails $IF\ (\forall x)F\ THEN\ (\exists x)G$; $(\forall x)(IF\ F\ THEN\ G)$ entails $IF\ (\forall x)F\ THEN\ (\forall x)G$; $(\forall x)(IF\ F$ $THEN\ G)$ entails $IF\ (\exists x)F\ THEN\ (\exists x)G$; and if x does not appear in G, then $(\forall x)(IF\ F\ THEN\ G)$ entails $IF\ (\exists x)F\ THEN\ (\forall x)G$. (See Reichenbach 1966, pp. 134–135.)

These facts allow us to perform the following transformation on (7): (a) If $Q_i' = \exists$, move the quantifier inward with $\forall$ in the antecedent and $\exists$ in the consequent; (b) if $Q_i' = \forall$ and x_i in R' is matched by a variable in R, then move in the quantifier with $\forall$ in the antecedent and $\forall$ in the consequent; (c) if $Q_i' = \forall$ and x_i does not appear in G, move in the quantifier with $\exists$ in the antecedent and $\forall$ in the consequent; (d) If $Q_i' = \forall$ and x_i in R' is matched by a temporary name in R, then move in the quantifier with $\exists$ in the antecedent and $\exists$ in the consequent.

The final product of this transformation follows from (7) in CPL on the basis of the entailments mentioned above. Moreover, the consequent of this product is the same as the consequent of (8). Thus, let us take the transformation as fixing the quantifiers in the antecedent of (8) and attempt to prove that this antecedent translates into quantifier-free form as P^*.

3. Figure 6.4 summarizes our current state of affairs. We have seen that $S_1 = (6)$ entails (8), as indicated at the top of the figure. The consequent of (8) itself entails S_3, so if we take S_2 to be the antecedent of (8) then S_1 and S_2 will entail S_3. It remains to show that P^* is the translation of S_2.

Consider an arbitrary quantifier $(Q_j'' x_j)$ in the antecedent of (8). If $Q_j'' = \forall$, it must have derived from clause a or clause b of part 2 of this proof. If from clause a, then Q_j'' was originally an existential quantifier in (6) and (7). Since existentially quantified variables in CPL become temporary names in quantifier-free sentences, this variable will become a temporary name in $IF\ P'\ THEN\ R'$, which is the translation of (6) (see the left side of figure 6.4). However, the argument-reversal procedure will change this (unmatched) temporary name back to a variable when P' is converted to P^* (along the bottom half of figure 6.4). So in this case the antecedent of (8) agrees with P^*: The variable in P^* correctly translates $(\forall x_j)$ in the antecedent of (8).

Similarly, if $(\forall x_j)$ derives from clause b, then it was also a universal quantifier in (6) and (7), and its variable matched a variable in R. Because of this match, it will remain a variable in P^*. (Argument reversal applies only to *unmatched* arguments, as stipulated in the IF Elimination rule.) So again P^* agrees with the antecedent of (8).

Suppose, however, that $Q_j'' = \exists$. Then it must have derived from either clause c or clause d of part 2. If it comes from clause c, then Q_j'' was originally a universal quantifier in (6) and (7) and corresponds to an unmatched variable in P'. Argument reversal will therefore change it to a temporary name, say c, in P^*. This agrees with (8) (i.e., an existentially quantified variable is translated as a temporary name), but we must also check to see whether c's subscripts also agree. Suppose there is some $(\forall x_i)$ that precedes $(\exists x_j)$ in the antecedent. If x_i is unmatched (i.e., comes from clause a), then $(\exists x_i) < (\forall x_j)$ in (7). Since both variables are unmatched, they must have been in the same order in (6). (Only matched universals are moved in the rearrangement that turned (6) into (7).) This means that x_i is translated into a temporary name in P', one that will not have x_j as a subscript. Argument Reversal will then change this temporary name into a variable, as we saw earlier, and will also add the variable as a subscript to c. (Under the same conditions, if $(\forall x_j) < (\exists x_i)$ in (6) and (7), the temporary name corresponding to x_i will have x_j as subscript, so the converse also holds.)

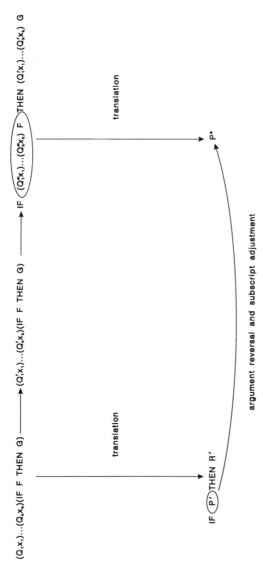

Figure 6.4
Proof strategy for soundness of Backward IF Elimination. At left is the conditional *IF P' THEN R'* in quantifier-free form and its equivalent in prenex form. Argument Reversal and Subscript Adjustment (see table 6.4) take the antecedent *P'* into *P**. The transformation described in parts 1 and 2 of the proof takes the prenex conditional into the conditional shown at the upper right. Part 3 of the proof shows that the antecedent of the transformed conditional translates as *P**.

On the other hand, suppose that x_i is matched to a variable in R (i.e., comes from clause b). Then $(\forall x_i) < (\forall x_j)$ in (7). If this same order appeared in (6), then there can be no temporary name in P' that contains x_j but not x_i as subscript, in view of the translation rules for quantifier-free form in chapter 3. Hence, the variable that matched x_i will become a subscript of c because of Subscript Adjustment in step i of the IF Elimination rule (see tables 6.3 and 6.4). It is possible, though, that $(\forall x_j) < (\forall x_i)$ in (6). If both quantifiers come from the same unbroken string of universals, then again there will be no temporary name in P' that has x_j but not x_i as subscript, and the variable matching x_i will be added to c's subscripts. However, if $(\forall x_j)$ and $(\forall x_i)$ come from different strings in (6), then in order to prompt the movement of $(\forall x_i)$, there must have been a third quantifier $(Q_k x_k)$ in (6) such that $(Q_k x_k) < (\forall x_j) < (\forall x_i)$, where x_k matched a temporary name $b_{...y_i...}$ and x_i matched y_i. If $Q_k = \forall$, then there is no temporary name in P' that has x_j but not x_k as subscript; so y_i will become a subscript of c in step i. If $Q_k = \exists$, then in P' there is a matched temporary name that does not contain x_j as subscript, and y_i will again be added as a subscript to c by Subscript Adjustment. (Conversely, if $(\exists x_j) < (\forall x_i)$ in the antecedent of (8), with x_i matched and x_j unmatched, then $(\forall x_j) < (\forall x_i)$ in (7). Since universal quantifiers with matched variables in (7) precede any that are unmatched in the same string of universals, there must be some existential quantifier between the two: $(\forall x_j) < (\exists x_k) < (\forall x_i)$. This same order must be preserved in (6), since existentials and unmatched quantifiers like $(\forall x_j)$ don't move and matched universals like $(\forall x_i)$ can move only to the left. So x_k will translate as a temporary name containing x_j but not x_i as a subscript, and the variable matching x_i will not be a subscript to c.)

We must backtrack, however, to consider the case in which $Q_j'' = \exists$ but this existential derives from clause d. Here the quantifier originated as a universal in (7) that was matched by a temporary name, c. This temporary name will be substituted in P' and will be maintained in P^*. This conforms to the antecedent of (8), since $(\exists x_j)$ must also translate as a temporary name. However, we must again check to make sure that the subscripts of c also coincide with (8). Suppose that in (8) $(\forall x_i) < (\exists x_j)$. If the universal quantifier comes from clause a, then in (7) we have $(\exists x_i) < (\forall x_j)$. The ordering must have been the same in (6), since universals can move only from right to left. P' will therefore contain a temporary name corresponding to $(\exists x_i)$ that does not have x_j as subscript. Argument Reversal will turn this temporary name back into a variable, and Subscript Adjustment will add it as a subscript of c. (And conversely: If $(\exists x_j) < (\forall x_i)$ in (8), then $(\forall x_j) < (\exists x_i)$ in (7), with x_j matched to c and x_i unmatched. If the same ordering holds in (6), then $(\exists x_i)$ becomes a temporary name in P' that has x_j as subscript. This temporary name becomes a variable in P^*, but Subscript Adjustment prohibits it from subscripting c. If $(\exists x_i) < (\forall x_j)$ in (6), then in order to trigger the shift we must have $(\forall x_k) < (\exists x_i) < (\forall x_j)$, where x_k matches a variable y_k from R and c does not have y_k as subscript. In this case, too, Subscript Adjustment prohibits subscripting c—see line 2c of table 6.4.)

Finally, if $(\forall x_i)$ is the result of clause b, then in (7) $(\forall x_i) < (\forall x_j)$, where x_i matched a variable in R and x_j matched a temporary name. Because of the way we constructed (7) from (6), this ordering occurs iff the variable matching x_i is already a subscript of c. In all cases, then, c receives a subscript in P^* iff $(\forall x_i) < (\exists x_j)$ in the antecedent of (8). Since all terms agree, P^* must be a translation of the same antecedent.

7 Reasoning with Variables

Experiment. Make that your fashion motto for 1991. When times are tough, it's not the time to retreat into old safe and sure styles.
Carrie Donovan, *New York Times*

It is an odd fact that psychologists who favor natural deduction mostly support their theories with experiments on sentence connectives, whereas psychologists who lean toward images or diagrams or "mental models" mostly experiment with quantifiers, usually syllogisms. Perhaps this is because the natural-deduction rules for connectives have an appeal that some of the rules for quantifiers lack. As was noted in chapter 2, the introduction and elimination rules for quantifiers (table 2.5) sometimes make the proof of an argument more roundabout than it should be.

But natural-deduction theories aren't necessarily stuck with quantifier introduction and elimination. In chapter 6 we came up with a way to represent quantifiers implicitly in terms of the variables they bind, letting the rules for connectives pass these variables from premise to conclusion. One point in favor of this approach is that it explains some similarities in the ways people reason with connectives and quantifiers. Independent variables that affect inferences with conditional sentences, for example, also tend to affect inferences with universals (Revlis 1975a)—a fact that is easy to account for if a universal such as *All psychologists are batty* is represented as *IF Psychologist(x) THEN Batty(x)* and is manipulated by the same rules that govern other conditional sentences.

However, we need to take a more systematic look at the experimental results on variables and quantifiers in order to tell whether the principles of chapter 6 handle them adequately. Research on quantifiers in psychology has concentrated on the categorical sentences: *All F are G, Some F are G, No F are G*, and *Some F are not G*. We will therefore begin with these sentences and the syllogistic arguments in which they appear. However, the system described in chapter 6 covers a much wider set of arguments than syllogisms, and this means that we must come up with new experiments in order to get a fair test of the extended model.

Empirical Predictions for Sentences with a Single Variable

We can translate the four categorical sentences into our system, using *IF F(x) THEN G(x)* for *All F are G*, *NOT(F(x) AND G(x))* for *No F are G*, *F(a) AND G(a)* for *Some F are G*, and *F(a) AND NOT G(a)* for *Some*

F are not G.[1] These correspond to the standard ways of expressing the propositions in classical predicate logic, and within this framework none of these sentences implies any of the others. The same is, of course, true within our own quantifier-free system. For example, if we try to show that *All F are G* entails *Some F are G*, our proof will stall almost immediately. If we use Backward AND Introduction to establish that $F(a)$ *AND* $G(a)$, we must then fulfill both of the subgoals $F(a)$ and $G(a)$. But both of these fail. We have nothing to match $F(a)$ against, given only *IF* $F(x)$ *THEN* $G(x)$. None of the other rules help us out of this jam. We could use Backward IF Elimination to try to get $G(a)$, but this rule then requires us to satisfy $F(a)$ again.

Scholastic logic differs from CPL in identifying two entailment relations among the four categorical sentences. In the older logic, *All F are G* entails *Some F are G*, and *No F are G* entails *Some F are not G*. In their standard representation in CPL, however, both *All F are G* and *No F are G* are true when there are no *F*s at all, and in this same situation both *Some F are G* and *Some F are not G* are false. Hence, the former statements can't entail the latter ones. (For example, if we represent *All unicorns are white* as *IF Unicorn(x) THEN White(x)* and *Some unicorns are white* as *Unicorn(a) AND White(a)*, then the former sentence will be vacuously true and the latter false.) In order to get the scholastic inferences, we have to supplement the representation of the All and No sentences to include the assertion that there are some *F*s. If we translate the All sentence as *(IF F(x) THEN G(x)) AND F(a)*, and the No sentence as *NOT (F(x) AND G(x)) AND F(a)*, we can then derive Some from All and Some-not from No in CPL and in PSYCOP. Subjects' judgments sometimes go along with these inferences.[2] Begg and Harris (1982) and Newstead and Griggs (1983) found that 56–80% of their subjects agreed that All implies Some and 48–69% that No implies Some-not.

Presuppositions and Implicatures of Categorical Sentences

One way to understand the scholastic inferences (and subjects' willingness to draw them) is to interpret All and No statements as involving a presupposition about the existence of members of the set named by the subject term (Strawson 1952, chapter 6). On this view, the existence of members of this set is a condition on All or No sentences having a truth value. If there are no unicorns, for example, then the question of the truth or falsity of *All unicorns are white* and *No unicorns are white* simply doesn't arise. Thus, if subjects are told to accept such a premise as true (as they were in the experiments just cited), they must also accept the related existential presupposition, and the scholastic inference will follow. For example, if we assume that *All unicorns are white* is true, we are also presupposing that there are unicorns. And because these unicorns must be white on the original assumption, then it must also be true that *Some unicorns are white*. Parallel reasoning yields *Some unicorns are not red* from *No unicorns are red*. It is possible to contend that these presuppositions are in force only when the All or No sentences contain other phrases, such as definite descriptions or proper names, that independently presuppose the existence of a referent (Vendler 1967, chapter 3). Thus, *All the unicorns are white* will, but *All unicorns are white* will not, presuppose that there are unicorns. Although this may well be correct, the difference between these two universal forms may be sufficiently subtle that subjects overlook it in typical experiments and adopt existential presuppositions for both cases.

Some subjects also go beyond both CPL and scholastic logic in assuming that *Some F are G* implies *Some F are not G* and conversely. In the Begg-Harris and Newstead-Griggs experiments, 58–97% of subjects agreed to the inferences for Some to Some-not and 65–92% for Some-not to Some. As was noted in chapter 2 above, most researchers have ascribed these inferences to Gricean conversational implicatures (Begg and Harris 1982; Horn 1973, 1989; Newstead 1989; Newstead and Griggs 1983; McCawley 1981). If a speaker knows that all F are G, then it would be misleading, though not false, to say that some F are G. On the assumption that the speaker is being cooperative, then, we should be able to infer that *not* all F are G—in other words, some F are not G. The conversational implicature operates in the opposite direction too. A speaker who knows that no F are G would mislead us by saying that some F are not G. Hence, from the sincere assertion that some F are not G, we can assume that it is not the case that no F are G (equivalently, that some F are G).

This Gricean view seems quite reasonable and extends to the scholastic cases. For example, it is misleading to assert that all the pencils on a table are yellow when there are in fact no pencils on the table at all. Strawson (1952, p. 179) recognized the possibility of this kind of explanation for the existential presuppositions:

Certainly a 'pragmatic' consideration, a general rule of linguistic conduct, may perhaps be seen to underlie these points: the rule, namely, that one does not make the (logically) lesser, when one could truthfully (and with equal or greater linguistic economy) make the greater, claim. Assume for a moment that the form 'There is not a single ... which is not ...' were *introduced* into ordinary speech with the same sense as '~(∃x)(fx ~ gx)' [≡ (∀x)(f(x) ⊃ g(x))]. Then the operation of this general rule would inhibit the use of this form where one could say simply 'There is not a single ...' (or '~(∃x)(fx)'). And the operation of this inhibition would tend to confer on the introduced form just those logical presuppositions which I have described.... The operation of this 'pragmatic rule' was first pointed out to me, in a different connexion, by Mr. H. P. Grice.

On this view, sentences of the form *All F are G* have *F(a)* as an implicature, and *G(a)* follows as well, since this last sentence is entailed by *IF F(x) THEN G(x)* and *F(a)*. Similarly, *No F are G* might appear misleading, though perhaps not as obviously so, when nothing at all is an F. In that case, we can treat both *F(a)* and *NOT G(a)* as implicatures of the No sentence in the same way. In some recent pragmatic theories conversational implicatures and presuppositions are treated as distinct entities, whereas in others presuppositions reduce to conversational implicatures plus ordinary entailments (see Levinson 1983 for a review). Although we will treat them similarly in what follows, we needn't take a stand on whether purported presuppositions (e.g., the inference from All to Some) and purported implicatures (e.g., the inference from Some to Some-not) ultimately have the same source.

We can summarize all four of the non-CPL inferences just discussed in a more uniform way if we assume that each categorical statement has both an asserted and an implicated component. The asserted part corresponds to the usual CPL interpretation, which appears in the b sentences of (1)–(4). The implicated part is an assumption about the existence of Fs that are either Gs or not Gs, and these appear as the c sentences.

(1)   a.   All F are G.

    b.   IF F(x) THEN G(x).

    c.   F(a) AND G(a).

(2)   a.   No F are G.

    b.   NOT (F(x) AND G(x)).

    c.   F(a) AND NOT G(a).

(3)   a.   Some F are G.

    b.   F(b) AND G(b).

    c.   F(a) AND NOT G(a).

(4)   a. Some F are not G.

      b. F(b) AND NOT G(b).

      c. F(a) AND G(a).

The c components are similar to presuppositions in that they meet the usual criterion of being unaffected by negation of the original sentence. Thus, the implicature of the All sentence in (1c), $F(a)$ AND $G(a)$, is the same as that of Some-not, its negation, in (4c). Similarly, the implicature of the Some sentence in (3c), $F(a)$ AND NOT $G(a)$, is the same as that of No in (2c).[3]

Note, too, that when we consider the implicature and the assertion together the representation for Some and that for Some-not will be equivalent, in accord with a hypothesis of Begg and Harris (1982). However, we must distinguish the roles of the b and c sentences if we want to preserve all four of the non-CPL inferences. The assertion and implicature of a Some sentence jointly entail both the assertion and implicature of a Some-not sentence (i.e., (3b) and (3c) jointly entail both (4b) and (4c)). But the relation between All and Some sentences works differently, since (1b) and (1c) do not jointly entail both (3b) and (3c). What is true of all the non-CPL inferences is that the implicature of the premise yields the assertion of the conclusion. That is, for All to Some (1c) = (3b), for No to Some-not (2c) = (4b), for Some to Some-not (3c) = (4b), and for Some-not to Some (4c) = (3b). Thus, the non-CPL inferences require the implicature of the premise, but sometimes require overriding the implicature of the conclusion. (Along similar lines, the non-CPL inferences can't be transitive; for if they were we could derive Some-not from All (All → Some → Some-not) and Some from No (No → Some-not → Some).) These facts will become important when we consider syllogisms. Of course, not all subjects accept the extra information in the c sentences; thus we also need to bear in mind the stricter b readings in predicting how subjects will reason about arguments that contain categorical sentences.

Categorical Syllogisms

A categorical syllogism consists of two categorical premises and a categorical conclusion, but with some additional restrictions on the form of the argument. In traditional syllogisms, one of the terms from the first ("major") premise reappears as the predicate of the conclusion, and one of the terms from the second ("minor") premise serves as the subject of the conclusion. The premises share the one additional ("middle") term. Thus, argument (5), which was used in chapter 6 to illustrate PSYCOP's proof procedure, is a syllogism in good standing.

(5) IF Square-block(x) THEN Green-block(x).
     Big-block(â) AND Square-block(â).
     _____
     Big-block(b) AND Green-block(b).

There is an opaque medieval code that researchers use to denote syllogisms and to intimidate readers. When I have to talk about the surface forms of individual syllogisms, I will use a somewhat less compressed but more comprehensible notation in which *All(F,G)* stands for *All F are G*, *No(F,G)* for *No F are G*, *Some(F,G)* for *Some F are G*, and *Some-not(F,G)* for *Some F are not G*. We can then name the syllogism simply by listing the form for the premises and conclusion. For example, in this notation syllogism (5) is

⟨All(S,G), Some(B,S), ∴ Some(B,G)⟩,

where S is square-blocks, G is green-blocks, and B is big-blocks. In this example, B is the subject of the conclusion, G is its predicate, and S is the middle term. There are plenty of wrangles about the nature of the syllogism from a historical perspective (see, e.g., Adams 1984 and Smiley 1973), but our concern here is whether our extended model is consistent with the way subjects reason about these argument forms.

Syllogism Experiments   To see how well PSYCOP does with syllogisms, we need information about the difficulty of the individual problems. Although there have been many experiments with syllogisms as stimuli, only a few of these have both included the full set of items and have reported data for each item separately. The main exceptions are the studies of Dickstein (1978a) and Johnson-Laird and Bara (1984a), and we will examine both of these data sets. There are some aspects of these studies, however, that make them less than ideal for our purposes. Johnson-Laird and Bara gave their subjects pairs of syllogistic premises and asked them to produce conclusions that logically followed. This method puts a premium on subjects' ability to formulate natural-language sentences to represent the inferences they have derived, and therefore it is open to biases in this formulation step. Subjects may be more likely to consider conclusions that are prompted by the form of the premises, that seem more natural in the premises' context, or that are simpler or more salient. All experiments are liable to interference from response factors, but these problems seem especially acute for production tasks (as we will see later).

Dickstein employed the more usual method of presenting subjects with the premises and asking them to choose one of the conclusions $All(S,P)$, $No(S,P)$, $Some(S,P)$, and $Some\text{-}not(S,P)$ or to say that none of these conclusions is valid. This avoids the formulation problem, since the range of potential conclusions is available for the subjects to inspect. However, forced choice also means that, for a given pair of premises, subjects' responses to the different conclusions are not independent. For example, a subject who receives the premises $All(G,H)$ and $All(F,G)$ cannot respond that both $All(F,H)$ and $Some(F,H)$ follow, even though he or she may believe this is the case. Any factor that increases the frequency of one of these responses must automatically decrease the frequency of the others. Moreover, the combinatorics of syllogisms are such that only 15 of the 64 possible premise pairs have deducible categorical conclusions in CPL (a slightly larger number in Aristotelian and scholastic logic). Thus, the correct choice will be "none of these" on most trials. As Revlis (1975a) has pointed out, this can encourage subjects to give incorrect categorical conclusions (All, No, Some, or Some-not) rather than "none of these" in order to balance the frequency of the five response types over trials.

Jeffrey Schank and I have carried out a new syllogism experiment that attempts to avoid these difficulties. Subjects received a list of all 256 traditional syllogisms—the 64 premise pairs combined with the four possible categorical conclusions—and they decided for each of these items whether the conclusion "would *have* to be true in every situation in which the first two sentences are true." We also informed subjects that the conclusion would be true for only about 10% of the problems, since we wanted to discourage subjects from adopting a response bias of the sort just discussed. There were no special instructions, however, about the meaning of the quantifiers. Although every subject judged all 256 syllogism types, the content of the syllogisms varied from one subject to the next. For each subject, we constructed the syllogisms by randomly assigning one of 256 common nouns (e.g., *doors, ashtrays, stockings*) to each syllogistic form. To generate the three terms of the syllogism, we combined this noun with three adjectives (*red* or *blue, large* or *small*, and *old* or *new*), and these noun phrases were then randomly assigned to the subject, predicate, and middle term of the syllogism. Thus, argument (6) was a possible item in our set.

(6)   All red stockings are old stockings.
       Some old stockings are large stockings.
       Some large stockings are red stockings.

We randomized the order of the syllogisms for each subject and then split the list in half. Subjects received a booklet containing the first 128 items in one session and received the remaining items in a second session one to four days later. The subjects were 20 University of Chicago students, none of whom had taken a course in logic.

The table in the appendix to this chapter gives the percentage of the subjects that judged each of the syllogisms valid. A glance at this table reveals a fair degree of accuracy. On the 15 syllogisms that are deducible in CPL, subjects said the conclusion followed on 72.3% of trials; on the 241 syllogisms that are not deducible in CPL, they said the conclusion did not follow on 88.5%. The lower rate on deducible problems may be due to our warning that only a small number of the syllogisms had categorical conclusions. Nevertheless, it is clear that the subjects were able to discriminate deducible from nondeducible syllogisms in the aggregate: The hit and correct-rejection rates just mentioned correspond to a d' of 1.79. In what follows, we will rely most heavily on the data from this experiment and on those from sample 2 of Dickstein 1978a.[4] However, Johnson-Laird and Bara's production task will be discussed at the end of this section.

Syllogism Performance: Deducible Arguments   Our look at the categorical statements suggests that a subject's response to a syllogism should depend in part on whether he or she accepts the implicatures of the premises and conclusion. There are 15 syllogisms that are deducible when the premises and conclusions are represented as in the b sentences of (1)–(4), and of these items only six remain deducible when we add both the premises' and conclusion's implicatures. Table 7.1 identifies these two groups of arguments, along with the percentages of "follows" responses in Dickstein's experiment and our own. The table shows that subjects tend to offer more "follows" responses for syllogisms that are unaffected by the implicatures. In our experiment, subjects gave 85.8% "follows" responses to these syllogisms, but only 63.3% "follows" responses to the nine remaining problems. In Dickstein's study, the corresponding percentages are 89.4 and 70.8. This difference is, of course, confounded by factors other than the status of the implicatures, but the data hint that implicatures may have played a role in the subjects' reasoning.

Table 7.1
Percentage of "follows" responses and inference rules for each of the deducible syllogisms.

Syllogism	Inference rules	% "follows" responses	
		Schank-Rips	Dickstein
Deducible with or without implicatures			
All(G,H) All(F,G) All(F,H)	Transitivity	90.0	94.7
No(G,H) All(F,G) No(F,H)	Exclusivity	85.0	92.1
No(H,G) All(F,G) No(F,H)	Exclusivity Conversion	90.0	92.1
All(H,G) No(F,G) No(F,H)	Exclusivity Conversion	90.0	94.7
Some(G,H) All(G,F) Some(F,H)	AND Elim. (forward) AND Intro. (back) IF Elim. (back)	80.0	84.2
Some-not(G,H) All(G,F) Some-not(F,H)	AND Elim. (forward) AND Intro. (back) IF Elim. (back)	80.0	78.9
Deducible without implicatures			
All(G,H) Some(F,G) Some(F,H)	AND Elim. (forward) AND Intro. (back) IF Elim. (back)	80.0	89.5
All(G,H) Some(G,F) Some(F,H)	AND Elim. (forward) AND Intro. (back) IF Elim. (back)	75.0	89.5
All(H,G) No(G,F) No(F,H)	Exclusivity Conversion	65.0	89.5
Some(H,G) All(G,F) Some(F,H)	AND Elim. (forward) AND Intro. (back) IF Elim. (back)	70.0	89.5
No(G,H) Some(F,G) Some-not(F,H)	AND Elim. (forward) AND Intro. (back) Conj. Syll. (back)	60.0	68.4
No(H,G) Some(F,G) Some-not(F,H)	AND Elim. (forward) AND Intro. (back) Conj. Syll. (back)	60.0	57.9

Table 7.1 (continued)

Syllogism	Inference rules	% "follows" responses	
		Schank-Rips	Dickstein
No(G,H) Some(G,F) Some-not(F,H)	AND Elim. (forward) AND Intro. (back) Conj. Syll. (back)	60.0	55.3
No(H,G) Some(G,F) Some-not(F,H)	AND Elim. (forward) AND Intro. (back) Conj. Syll. (back)	65.0	23.7
All(H,G) Some-not(F,G) Some-not(F,H)	AND Elim. (forward) AND Intro. (back) NOT Intro. (back) IF Elim. (back)	35.0	73.7

If we take into account the implicatures of the syllogisms and the rules that are needed to derive the conclusions, we can begin to understand the range of difficulty of these problems. Consider first the arguments at the top of table 7.1, which are deducible even when their implicatures are included. We have just seen that these syllogisms are easier to verify than the remaining ones, but the table also shows that, within this group, syllogisms that PSYCOP can prove via forward rules (see table 6.2) have higher scores than those that also require backward rules (Backward AND Elimination and IF Elimination). The percentage of "follows" responses was 88.8% for the first group and 80.0% for the second group in our experiment, and 90.8% vs. 81.6% in Dickstein's.

Scores also vary with rules among the syllogisms in the bottom part of table 7.1. Among this group, the more difficult syllogisms all require either the backward NOT Introduction or the backward Conjunctive Syllogism rule. The overall percentage of "follows" responses for this subset of problems is 56.0% (Schank and Rips) and 55.8% (Dickstein). By contrast, the remaining four syllogisms require either Exclusivity and Conversion or AND Introduction, AND Elimination, and IF Elimination. These problems are decidedly easier, with overall scores of 72.5% and 89.5% in the two experiments. In general, then, we can account for these data if we assume that the rules for NOT Introduction and Conjunctive Syllogism are more difficult for subjects to deploy than the rules for AND and modus ponens. This assumption seems intuitively right, and it also accords with the results of chapter 5. (See table 5.2: AND Introduction, AND

Elimination, and IF Introduction all received higher parameter estimates than NOT Introduction. Conjunctive Syllogism did not figure in the earlier problems.) In fact, the only anomaly in the table is that the syllogism $\langle \text{All(H,G)}, \text{No(G,F)}, \therefore \text{No(F,H)} \rangle$, which requires only Exclusivity and Conversion, is no easier than the syllogisms that PSYCOP proves with AND Introduction, AND Elimination, and IF Elimination.

In earlier research, much was made of the fact that the difficulty of a problem varies with the order of the terms in the premises. Premises of the form $\langle Q_1(\text{G,H}), Q_2(\text{F,G}) \rangle$ tend to be easier than those of the form $\langle Q_1(\text{H,G}), Q_2(\text{F,G}) \rangle$ or $\langle Q_1(\text{G,H}), Q_2(\text{G,F}) \rangle$, and the latter premises are themselves easier than $\langle Q_1(\text{H,G}), Q_2(\text{G,F}) \rangle$, where Q_1 and Q_2 are the usual quantifiers (All, No, Some, or Some-not). This "figure effect" also holds in the data of table 7.1: In our study, the scores for these three groups were 78.8% for $\langle Q_1(\text{G,H}), Q_2(\text{F,G}) \rangle$, 71.3% for $\langle Q_1(\text{H,G}), Q_2(\text{F,G}) \rangle$ and $\langle Q_1(\text{G,H}), Q_2(\text{G,F}) \rangle$, and 66.7% for $\langle Q_1(\text{H,G}), Q_2(\text{G,F}) \rangle$; in Dickstein's experiment the comparable figures are 86.2%, 78.3%, and 67.6%. It is possible, however, that this difference is a by-product of implicatures and rule use, as just discussed, rather than due to the order of the terms *per se*. When these rules and implicatures are held constant, the figure effect becomes more equivocal. Thus, there is no advantage of $\langle \text{No(G,H)}, \text{All(F,G)}, \therefore \text{No(F,H)} \rangle$ over $\langle \text{No(H,G)}, \text{All(F,G)}, \therefore \text{No(F,H)} \rangle$ in either study. In our study, $\langle \text{All(G,H)}, \text{Some(F,G)}, \therefore \text{Some(F,H)} \rangle$ has a higher score than $\langle \text{All(G,H)}, \text{Some(G,F)}, \therefore \text{Some(F,H)} \rangle$, in accord with the figure effect, but in Dickstein's there is no such difference. And although Dickstein found a figure effect for $\langle \text{No, Some}, \therefore \text{Some-not} \rangle$ syllogisms, it disappears in our experiment (see items 11–14 in table 7.1). Although it is possible to reformulate PSYCOP's rules to make them more sensitive to the order of the terms in a problem, it is not clear from the present data that such a move is necessary. (Figure effects might be more prominent in experiments in which subjects produce their own conclusions, since subject may have a tendency to consider conclusions that are similar in surface features to the premises. They may also be more prominent for nontraditional syllogisms in which the subject of the conclusion comes from the first premise and the predicate from the second premise—e.g., $\langle \text{All(F,G)}, \text{All(G,H)}, \therefore \text{All(F,H)} \rangle$.)

Syllogism performance: Nondeducible Arguments According to the present approach, subjects test syllogisms (and other argument forms) by attempting to prove the conclusion. For nondeducible arguments, of course, no such proof is possible, and subjects must determine how to interpret this negative evidence. From a subject's point of view, failure to find a proof may mean that the argument is not deducible and that no proof is available; however, it is also possible that a perfectly good proof exists, but one that the subject was unable to derive because of information-processing limits.

What subjects do when they can't find a proof may depend on properties of the experimental setup. In the mathematical model of chapter 5, we simply assumed that subjects in this situation respond "doesn't follow" with probability $(1 - p_g)$ and guess at random between the two alternatives with probability p_g. Thus, $(1 - p_g)$ represented the subjects' certainty that no proof is possible. For syllogisms, however, there is a large body of research suggesting that subjects' decisions on nondeducible problems are not entirely random but are biased by features of the syllogisms and of the presentation method. We considered some of these—atmosphere and belief bias—in chapter 1, and a response-frequency effect was mentioned earlier in this section. (See Chapman and Chapman 1959, Dickstein 1978b, and Evans 1989. Chapter 10 contains a further discussion of bias.) For the experiment of the appendix, we took steps to neutralize belief bias and response frequency. But there are two other factors that may play a role in these results. One of these depends on the implicatures of categorical statements; the other is related to atmosphere.

We noticed earlier that the implicatures of the premises and the conclusion can turn a deducible syllogism into a nondeducible one. It is therefore pertinent to ask whether the opposite can also happen: Can a syllogism that is nondeducible when the premises and the conclusion are represented as in the b sentences of (1)–(4) become deducible if we add the implicatures in the c sentences? The answer is that this does occur, though it is rare. In fact, only 2 of the 241 nondeducible syllogisms become deducible when the implicatures supplement the usual representations of the premises and the conclusion. (The two syllogisms in question are $\langle \text{Some(G,H)}, \text{All(G,F)}, \therefore \text{Some-not(F,H)} \rangle$ and $\langle \text{Some-not(G,H)}, \text{All(G,F)}, \therefore \text{Some(F,H)} \rangle$.) Subjects can get a more liberal crop of new deducible syllogisms, however, if they are willing to accept the implicatures of the premise without those of the conclusion. In this case, 18 previously nondeducible syllogisms become deducible, including many of those that

Aristotelian and scholastic logic sanctioned (see Adams 1984). The appendix identifies these items. Subjects may be tempted to accept just the premise implicatures as a kind of opportunistic strategy. If they fail to find a proof on a stricter interpretation, then including the premise's implicatures will sometimes give them a second chance.

There is evidence that these premise implicatures influence the way subjects appraise the syllogisms. In our own data set, subjects judged that these items followed on 41.7% of trials, versus 9.0% for the remaining nondeducible syllogisms. This difference is much narrower in Dickstein's data (15.1% vs. 12.1%), perhaps in part because of the forced-choice format of that experiment. When subjects judge the premise pair $\langle All(G,H), All(F,G) \rangle$, for example, they can't check both of the alternatives All(F,H) and Some(F,H), since only one response is allowed. Because the first of these conclusions is deducible whether or not the subjects take the implicatures into account, it should dominate the second, which is deducible only if subjects add the premises' (but not the conclusion's) implicatures.

However, it is clear that implicatures can't be the whole story behind responses to the nondeducible syllogisms. A glance at the appendix shows a much larger proportion of Some and Some-not conclusions than of All or No conclusions, particularly for syllogisms that contain a Some premise or a Some-not premise. This tendency might suggest an atmosphere explanation (Sells 1936; Woodworth and Sells 1935), but the responses don't always mesh well with the classical atmosphere predictions. For example, atmosphere predicts that when both premises are Some subjects should reach a Some conclusion; but the results show about equal proportions of Some and Some-not responses. Similarly, syllogisms that contain two Some-not premises or one Some and one Some-not premise should produce Some-not responses; but again there are about equal numbers of Some and Some-not conclusions. Rather than atmosphere, these data suggest that our subjects may have been trying to hedge their bets, on the assumption that it is more likely that some F are H or that some F are not H than that all F are H or no F are H. Subjects may believe that the Some and the Some-not conclusions take less information to establish and that they are therefore more likely to be the correct answers than their universal counterparts, All and No. If this is right, it seems closer to what Woodworth and Sells called the principle of caution than to their much-better-known atmosphere effect.

Summary and Model Fitting   We are supposing that subjects in syllogism experiments are guided by the rules of chapter 6. However, they also have some options about the way they should interpret the premises and conclusion and about how to respond when no proof of the interpreted syllogism is forthcoming. On the interpretation side, they can choose to adopt the implicatures of the premises, the conclusion, or both, where accepting the premises' implicatures will tend to increase their chance of finding a proof and accepting the conclusion's implicatures will decrease it. On the response side, if subjects fail to find a proof they may be more likely to hazard a guess at the answer with a Some or a Some-not conclusion than with an All or a No conclusion. These assumptions are admittedly *ad hoc*, motivated as they are by our survey of the available syllogism data sets. Nevertheless, it is of interest to see how close they come to providing an accurate fit to the data: Systematic departures from the model can indicate mistakes in our assumptions or places where further factors are playing a role.

Figure 7.1 summarizes the assumptions in a way that shows how they lead to a "necessarily true" or "not necessarily true" response to a given syllogism. We suppose that subjects will accept the premises' implicatures with probability p_{prem}, and that they will accept the conclusion's implicatures with probability p_{conc}. Then they seek a proof for the interpreted syllogism, where the probability of finding such a proof depends on the availability of the deduction rules in their repertoire. The rules that are necessary in constructing a proof will, of course, differ depending on the implicatures adopted; in general, more rules will be needed if the subjects have to prove the conclusion's implicatures as well as the conclusion itself. We can abbreviate the availability of the rules, using p_{r1} as the probability of having available all rules needed to prove the conclusion when subjects adopt both sets of implicatures, p_{r2} as the comparable probability when subjects adopt the premises' implicatures but not the conclusion's implicatures, p_{r3} as the probability when subjects adopt the conclusion's implicatures but not the premises', and p_{r4} as the probability when subjects adopt neither set of implicatures. (In fact, none of the syllogisms are deducible when only the conclusion's implicatures are present; thus, $p_{r3} = 0$.)

The values of the p_r parameters are functions of the availabilities of the individual deduction rules. For example, if a syllogism is provable on the basis of Forward AND Elimination, Backward AND Introduction, and

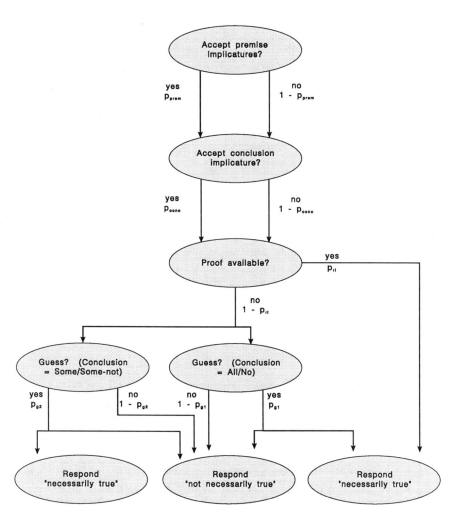

Figure 7.1
Summary of the application of the PSYCOP model to syllogisms.

Backward IF Elimination when both sets of implicatures are accepted, then p_{r1} will be a function of the probabilities associated with each of these rules. The rules that appear in the proofs of the syllogisms are Transitivity, Exclusivity, Conversion, Forward AND Elimination, Backward AND Introduction, Backward Conjunctive Syllogism, Backward IF Elimination, and Backward NOT Introduction. To keep the model simple, we can assume that the availabilities of these rules are independent, as in the simulations of chapter 5. We also assume that the chance of deriving an alternative proof is negligible if the model's initial proof of the argument fails. Finally, to reduce the number of rule parameters, we can take the probabilities of the three rules in table 6.2 to be equal, since they are all forward rules of about equivalent complexity. A further reduction in rule parameters occurs because AND Elimination and AND Introduction always appear together in a proof, so we can estimate a single parameter to represent their joint availability.

The overall probability that subjects will find a proof for the syllogism is therefore

(7) $P(\text{proof}) = p_{\text{prem}} \, p_{\text{conc}} \, p_{r1} + p_{\text{prem}} \, (1 - p_{\text{conc}}) \, p_{r2}$

$$+ (1 - p_{\text{prem}}) \, p_{\text{conc}} \, p_{r3} + (1 - p_{\text{prem}}) \, (1 - p_{\text{conc}}) \, p_{r4}.$$

(As was mentioned earlier, p_{r3} is 0 for these problems, so the third term disappears.) If subjects find a proof in this way, they should respond "necessarily true"; if there is no proof, they may either respond "not necessarily true" or guess at the correct answer. As figure 7.1 shows, we assume that the probability of guessing is p_{g1} when the conclusion is either All or No and p_{g2} when the conclusion is Some or Some-not. This allows for (though it doesn't enforce) the possibility that subjects will guess more often with the "safer" Some or Some-not conclusions. If subjects choose "necessarily true" on half of their guesses, then the probability of a "necessarily true" response for syllogisms with All or No conclusions is

(8) $P(\text{"necessarily true"}) = P(\text{proof}) + 0.5(1 - P(\text{proof}))p_{g1},$

and that for a syllogism with a Some or a Some-not conclusion is

(9) $P(\text{"necessarily true"}) = P(\text{proof}) + 0.5(1 - P(\text{proof}))p_{g2}.$

To evaluate these assumptions, we have fitted these equations to the data from our experiment using nonlinear least-squares regression. The predictions from the model appear beneath the observed data in the appendix. The model fits fairly well overall, although there are some clear deviations. The correlation between the 256 observed and predicted responses is 0.879, and the root-mean-square deviation is 9.55. The rule parameters estimated from these data are very much in accord with intuition and with the earlier model fitting in chapter 5. These estimates appear in table 7.2 and show that rule availabilities are highest for the simple forward rules from table 6.2 and for the AND Elimination/Introduction pair. Of the backward rules, IF Elimination receives higher availability scores than the Conjunctive Syllogism rule, and NOT Introduction has quite low availability just as it did in the experiment discussed in chapter 5. The interpretation and response parameters are also close to what we anticipated from our look at the data in the appendix. Subjects appear more willing to accept the implicatures of the premises than those of the conclusion, and they are more likely to guess at a response when the conclusion begins with Some or Some-not than with All or No.[5]

The most serious departures from the predictions appear in nondeducible syllogisms containing two All premises or an All and a No premise. The model clearly underestimates the frequency of All conclusions in the former case, and to a lesser extent it underestimates the frequency of No conclusions in the latter. In the present context, it seems natural to attribute these discrepancies to mistakes in applying the Transitivity and Exclusivity rules. If subjects reversed the order of the terms in the All premises on some portion of the trials, these rules would lead to exactly

Table 7.2
Parameter estimates for the model of equations (7)–(9), fitted to the data of the appendix.

Parameter	Interpretation	Estimate
Presupposition parameters		
P_{prem}	Probability of accepting premise implicatures	0.50
P_{conc}	Probability of accepting conclusion implicatures	0.12
Response parameters		
P_{g1}	Probability of guessing with All/No conclusions	0.08
P_{g2}	Probability of guessing with Some/Some-not conclusions	0.31
Rule parameters		
$P_{tr} = P_{ex} = P_{con}$	Probability of forward rules' being available for proof	0.95
P_{and}	Probability of AND Introduction and Elimination	0.93
P_{ie}	Probability of IF Elim.	0.85
P_{cs}	Probability of Conjunctive Syllogism	0.70
P_{ni}	Probability of NOT Intro.	0.30

the conclusions that pose difficulties for the model. If this tendency exists it will be quite similar to the traditional notion of "illicit conversion," in which subjects are supposed to interpret *All F are G* as equivalent to (or as inviting the inference that) *All G are F* (Ceraso and Provitera 1971; Chapman and Chapman 1959; Revlis 1975a,b). This reversal of arguments must be relatively infrequent, however, since in these data no more than 40% of the subjects respond that these deductively incorrect syllogisms are necessarily true (see also Begg and Harris 1982 and Newstead and Griggs 1983). In this context, it seems better to regard conversion as an occasional tendency than as a dominant part of subjects' understanding of All statements.

It is possible to revise the model in order to take this tendency into account, but I have not tried to do so. The point of fitting equations (7)–(9) is not to give a complete account of syllogism responses but to show how PSYCOP can be extended in that direction. It is clear that specific interpretation and response processes have to supplement PSYCOP's basic tenets in order to reproduce details in the response profiles. But it is also important to see that subjects' handling of syllogisms is part of a broader deductive scheme that can encompass many other sorts of sentential and variable-based problems.

Producing Conclusions to Syllogistic Premises

As has been mentioned, it is possible to present just the premises of a syllogism and have the subjects fill in a conclusion. Johnson-Laird and Bara (1984a) have reported experiments of this sort and have given the production frequency for each of the 64 pairs of syllogistic premises. We can therefore ask whether a model like the one we are developing can also account for these data. This question is an especially interesting one, since Johnson-Laird (1983; see also Johnson-Laird and Byrne 1991) has expressly denied that syllogistic reasoning is accomplished by mental rules like those PSYCOP incorporates. In the present subsection we will see whether the syllogism results justify this denial; we will consider Johnson-Laird's other reasons for skepticism about rules when we take up his theory in chapter 10.

PSYCOP already has a mechanism for generating conclusions to premises: its forward rules. Since these rules don't need a conclusion or subgoal to trigger them, they can apply directly to syllogistic premises to generate a correct answer. In the case of categorical syllogisms, we would expect the forward rules in table 6.2 to be the important ones, and we should predict that the deducible conclusions produced by these rules will be much more frequent than deducible conclusions that require backward processing. This is easily confirmed by the data of Johnson-Laird and Bara[6]: There are six premise pairs that yield conclusions by the forward rules alone, and for these pairs 77.5% of subjects produced one of these conclusions as a response. By contrast, there are 16 pairs that yield conclusions by backward rules, and for these pairs only 31.6% of subjects produced such a conclusion.[7]

Suppose, however, that subjects are confronted with a premise pair for which no forward conclusions are possible. How should they proceed? One simple strategy might be to select tentative conclusions from the possible categorical sentences linking the end terms and then test these possibilities to see if any are deducible. (We proposed a similar strategy for the Selection task in chapter 5.) For example, with a pair such as ⟨Some-not(A,B), All(C,B)⟩ no forward conclusion will be forthcoming; so subjects may generate possible categorical conclusions like Some-not(A,C) or All(C,A) and check if there is a proof for them. This generate-and-test strategy seems quite reasonable in the context of an experiment like this, where all the stimulus sentences have a common categorical format and where there is an implicit demand to link the end terms (i.e., A and C) of the premises. The strategy is a powerful one, since it allows subjects to bring their backward rules into play.

Of course, not all subjects will have the inclination to test each of the possible conclusions—All(A,C), All(C,A), Some(A,C), Some(C,A), and so on. This is especially true since, on the majority of trials, subjects would have to test exhaustively all eight conclusions; only 22 of the 64 premise pairs have conclusions that can be deduced in this fashion (see note 6). The subjects may therefore settle for checking just one or two salient possibilities. If they find a proof for one of these items, they can then produce the conclusion as their response; if they don't find a proof, they can either guess or respond that nothing follows, just as in the syllogism-evaluation model that we discussed earlier. In deciding which conclusions to test, subjects are probably influenced by the form of the premises they are considering. If they are studying a premise pair such as ⟨Some-not(A,B), All(C,B)⟩, then the conclusions Some-not(A,C), Some-not(C,A), All(A,C), and All(C,A) naturally come to mind, since the quantifiers in these sentences are the same as those of the premises. Newell (1990) incorporates a similar assumption in his account of Johnson-Laird and Bara's results. (This may qualify as a kind of "matching" bias, related to that discussed in Evans and Lynch 1973, or it may be the result of an availability heuristic such as that documented in Tversky and Kahneman 1973. See chapter 10 for further discussion of these biases.)

A look at the data of Johnson-Laird and Bara shows that this correspondence between premise quantifiers and response quantifiers is clearly present. Of the 743 categorical conclusions produced by subjects in their experiment, 87.9% had quantifiers that were the same as those in the premises. The percentage expected by chance is 43.8%. (The chance percentage is slightly less than 50% because 16 of the premise pairs—e.g., $\langle \text{All(A,B)}, \text{All(C,B)} \rangle$—contain just one type of quantifier; for these items, the probability that a randomly generated categorical conclusion will have the same quantifier is, of course, 0.25.) In some instances, conclusions with the same quantifiers as the premises are deducible; but even if we confine our attention to syllogisms with no deducible conclusion, the effect is about the same. There were 567 (incorrect) categorical conclusions that Johnson-Laird and Bara's subjects generated for these items, and 91.9% had a quantifier that duplicated one of the premises'.

One further fact about this congruence between the quantifiers of the premises and those of the conclusion-response is worth noticing: For pairs in which the premise quantifiers differ (e.g., $\langle \text{All(A,B)}, \text{Some(B,C)} \rangle$), there are two possible choices for the premise quantifier (All or Some in the example). In these cases, the responses seem to follow a systematic pattern in which No dominates Some-not, Some, and All; Some-not dominates Some and All; and Some dominates All. Given $\langle \text{All(A,B)}, \text{Some(B,C)} \rangle$, for example, the modal response is Some(A,C); with $\langle \text{Some-not(B,A)}, \text{Some(C,B)} \rangle$, the modal response is Some-not(C,A). Gilhooly et al. (1993; see also Wetherick and Gilhooly 1990) have independently noted the same pattern. The ordering clearly differs from an atmosphere bias and from the penchant for Some and Some-not conclusions that we met in studying the syllogism-evaluation experiments. Instead, it seems to reflect the notion that the best responses are ones that posit the least overlap between the terms. If we have to find a relation between terms A and C, we might start with the minimal one in which A and C have least in common.

We can then summarize the subjects' production strategy in the following way: When they receive a premise pair, they first see whether any conclusion follows spontaneously via forward rules. If so, they produce that conclusion as a response. If not, they consider as a tentative conclusion a categorical statement that links the end terms and whose quantifier is grafted from one of the premises. In most cases, the premises will have two different quantifiers, and the one they choose apparently follows the ordering just described. (When the premises have only a single type of quantifier, then of course that quantifier is the one they select.) Subjects attempt to determine whether this tentative conclusion follows, this time employing their full repertoire of rules, and they will again respond with the conclusion if a proof is available. However, should the search for a proof turn out to be unsuccessful, subjects follow a procedure similar to that of figure 7.1, either guessing about the validity of the conclusion, responding that no conclusion follows, or persevering in checking other possible conclusions. The data suggest that only a small number of subjects persevere; for simplicity, we can assume that most subjects stop after checking just the first possibility, a small minority continuing until they have found a deducible conclusion or exhausted all the possibilities.

This procedure is consistent with the qualitative features of Johnson-Laird and Bara's results. For any pair of premises, the responses should consist of (a) any conclusions that follow from forward rules; (b) conclusions that share the dominant quantifier of the premises, based either on guesses or on backward processing; (c)"no conclusion follows" responses; and (d) a small number of correct conclusions with nondominant quantifiers, based on backward processing by the persistent subjects. This predicts the possibility of 200 different response types across all pairs of premises. In fact, 165 of these appear in the data, accounting for 90.3% of the reported response tokens (see note 6). Conversely, there are 376 response types that are predicted *not* to appear, only 27 of which occur (and which constitute the residual 9.7% of the response tokens). This seems an extremely high success rate, in view of the relatively unconstrained nature of the production task.[8]

Of course, we are again relying on *post facto* assumptions that go beyond the basic PSYCOP framework, the most serious of which is the dominance ordering among the quantifiers. But even if we forget about dominance and assume simply that subjects attend first to a conclusion containing one of the premise quantifiers, we still do quite well. We now predict the possibility of 296 response types, 175 of which appear in the data, capturing 93.1% of the reported response tokens. In the other direction, there are 280 response types that are not predicted, and only 17 of these actually occur. In other words, even with very simple response assumptions we can account for the major qualitative properties of the production data. We would have to refine these assumptions in order to produce a quantitative model of the sort we worked up in the previous section. But our aim is accomplished if we can show that PSYCOP is consistent with these previous syllogism data, and the statistics already reported suggest that this is the case. To get a firmer grip on the strengths and weaknesses of the model, we need to generate new empirical and theoretical results for the wider domain of inferences that PSYCOP can prove, and this is the goal that we take up in the following section.

Predictions for Multi-Variable Contexts

As further tests of the extended model, we need problems with variables that are not confined to the All, Some, No, Some-not categorical format. We look at two such tests in this section, the first centered on PSYCOP's matching rules and the second based on textbook problems in predicate logic.

An Experiment on Matching Time

The essential components in PSYCOP's treatment of variables are the matching rules of table 6.1 that enable the system to recognize when one sentence is a generalization of another. These rules ensure, for example, that PSYCOP can derive instances like *Calvin = Calvin* from the abstract premise $x = x$. Generalization and instantiation are at the heart of all symbolic cognitive theories, and we want our system to account for them. We would like the theory to be able to predict the relative difficulty people have in coping with terms at different levels of abstraction, and we can make some headway toward a test by considering the number of different types of rules that PSYCOP must employ when matching sentences.

   As an example of how we could frame such a test, consider argument (10) (with the variables x and y ranging over people).

(10) $\underline{\text{Dazzles}(x,y)}$
       Dazzles(Fred,Mary)

This argument says that *Fred dazzles Mary* follows from the premise *Everyone dazzles everybody*; it seems quite obvious, since the only rule we need to derive it is the one relating permanent names to variables. It takes a bit more thought, however, to deal with (11).

(11)   Dazzles(x, Mary)
       ─────────────────
       Dazzles(Fred, b)

We can paraphrase (11) as: Everyone dazzles Mary; therefore, Fred dazzles somebody. In this case, we need two distinct rules: one relating variables and permanent names (*x* and *Fred*) and the other relating permanent and temporary names (*Mary* and *b*).

Figure 7.2 surveys some of the possibilities for matching in a sentence that contains two arguments (variables or names). Here *m* and *n* stand for permanent names; *x* and *y* stand, as usual, for variables; *a* and *b* stand for temporary names. So *P(m,b)* in the figure corresponds to a sentence

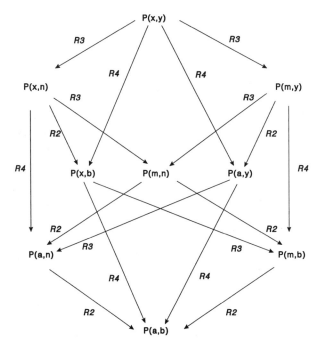

Figure 7.2
Deducibility relations for sentences containing two terms. Arrows connect one sentence to another that can be deduced by means of a matching rule from table 6.1. Labels on the arrows correspond to the order of the rule in the table. *m* and *n* denote permanent names, *a* and *b* temporary names, and *x* and *y* variables in quantifier-free notation.

like *Dazzles(Fred,b)*. The arrows indicate the matching relations. For example, the arrow connecting $P(x,y)$ to $P(m,y)$ at the top right of the figure means that PSYCOP can match these sentences on the basis of one of the matching rules—in this case, the third rule in table 6.1. The labels on the arrows represent the rules that are responsible for the matches: R2 stands for the second rule in table 6.1 (the rule matching temporary to permanent names), R3 for the third rule (permanent names to variables), and R4 for the fourth (temporary names to variables). Pathways of arrows indicate derivations involving combinations of rules. For example, the path from $P(x,y)$ through $P(m,y)$ to $P(m,n)$ shows one way to derive $P(m,n)$ from $P(x,y)$ via two applications of matching rule 3, and the path from $P(x,n)$ through $P(m,n)$ to $P(m,b)$ shows the derivation of $P(m,b)$ from $P(x,n)$ via matching rules 2 and 3. The first of these pathways corresponds to a proof of argument (10), the second to a proof of argument (11).

The heuristics in the matching rules guarantee that PSYCOP always takes one of the shortest paths when there is more than one route available. In matching $P(a,b)$ at the bottom of figure 7.2 to $P(x,y)$ at the top, for example, PSYCOP traverses the path through $P(x,b)$ rather than any of the more circuitous routes, although those routes are also valid generalizations. Second, the figure shows a single arrow (labeled R3) connecting sentences like $P(x,y)$ and $P(m,y)$, but most of these adjacent sentences can't appear together as the premise and conclusion of an argument. As was noted earlier, each sentence in an argument must have distinct variables and temporary names; so if $P(x,y)$ were a premise, it could not have $P(m,y)$ as a conclusion, but might have $P(m,z)$ instead. The inference from $P(x,y)$ to $P(m,z)$ requires R1 to match z to y and R3 to match m to x. However, this will not affect the predictions that we derive below. Third, there are other types of atomic sentences containing two variables that do not appear in the figure (e.g., $P(x,a_x)$ or $P(y,y)$). These sentences also entail (or are entailed by) some of the depicted sentences, but since these items don't occur in the present experiment I have omitted them to keep the diagram simple.

Our main prediction concerns arguments, such as (10) and (11), in which PSYCOP must change two terms in order to obtain a match between the conclusion and the premise: It should take subjects longer to determine the correctness of an argument like (11) that requires the use of two different rules than to determine the correctness of an argument like (10) that requires two applications of a single rule. Double application of a single rule should be simpler since PSYCOP will find the rule quicker after its first success (see chapter 4)—a type of priming effect. There are three arguments of this simpler type with sentences from figure 7.2: the arguments from $P(x,y)$ to $P(m,n)$, from $P(x,y)$ to $P(a,b)$, and from $P(m,n)$ to $P(a,b)$. Table 7.3 lists these under the heading "One rule, two steps," together with the rule that each requires. There are a larger number of arguments that depend on two distinct rules (six in all), but the experiment included just three of them in order to equate the frequency of the argument types. These appear under "Two rules, two steps" in table 7.3. Notice that within these two groups of arguments the same rules are used equally often; what differs between the groups is the distribution of the rules to the individual items. Thus, any difference in the internal complexity of the matching rules should not affect the results of the experiment. The same is true of the numbers of variables, temporary names, and permanent names

Table 7.3
Reaction times and error rates for two-place arguments involving matching rules.

Argument forms	Rules	Mean correct response time (ms)	Error rate (%)
Two rules, two steps			
P(m,y)	R2, R4	4018	3.4
P(a,b)			
P(x,n)	R2, R3	4190	30.6
P(m,b)			
P(x,y)	R3, R4	3439	2.1
P(a,n)			
One rule, two steps			
P(x,y)	R4, R4	3435	2.1
P(a,b)			
P(m,y)	R2, R2	3062	2.8
P(a,b)			
P(x,y)	R3, R3	3207	2.8
P(m,n)			
Additional arguments			
P(x,y)	R1, R3	3948	7.6
P(z,n)			
P(a,n)	R2, R2	3357	1.4
P(c,b)			
P(m,y)	R4	3283	0.7
P(m,b)			

that appear in the premises and conclusions. For example, variables appear four times in the premises of the two-rule-two-step arguments and four times in the one-rule-two-step arguments; permanent names appear twice in the premises of each argument type; and so on. So sheer frequency of the different types of terms does not confound the comparison.

We also included three additional deducible arguments that correspond to sentences connected by a single arrow in figure 7.2. For reasons already mentioned, we sometimes have to alter these sentences when they appear together in an argument, and in that case they require two rules for a match. Table 7.3 shows the corrected arguments and rule sets. Only the third of these "additional arguments" can PSYCOP actually deduce in one step.

The experiment mixed the nine types of deducible arguments just described with nine nondeducible ones that interchanged the premises and the conclusions of the items in table 7.3. So, for example, in addition to the deducible argument $P(x,y)$, *Therefore*, $P(a,b)$, subjects also received the nondeducible argument $P(a,b)$, *Therefore*, $P(x,y)$. As a result, half of the arguments were deducible and half nondeducible.

In this study, 24 University of Chicago students were told that they would see problems concerning groups of people and that each problem concerned a separate group. The problems appeared on a monitor, each argument consisting of a premise written above a line and a conclusion beneath the line. The subjects were supposed to assume that the premise was true of the group of people and decide whether the conclusion was necessarily true of the same group on the basis of this information. Each subject indicated his or her decision by pressing a key labeled "follows" or one labeled "does not follow" on a keyboard, and a computer measured the response time from the presentation of the argument to the key press. The computer provided each subject with feedback on his or her performance after every block of 18 arguments. The feedback consisted of the subject's average response time and the percentage of correct responses during that block, but there was no feedback on individual problems.

There were six blocks of trials in this experiment, each block consisting of one instance of each of the deducible arguments in table 7.3 and one instance of each of the nondeducible arguments. To frame the problems, we compiled six sets of 18 transitive verbs, so that the mean word frequency of the verbs was approximately the same per set. One set was then assigned to the six main groups of arguments: the two-rule-two-step group, the one-rule-two-step group, the additional group, and their three nondeducible counterparts. Within these groups, we randomly assigned the verbs to the argument instances. In constructing the stimulus items, we used *everyone* or *everybody* to translate variables, *someone* or *somebody* for temporary names, and common male and female first names for the permanent names. Thus, subjects might have seen (12) as one instance of the first argument in table 7.3.

(12) Janet rewards everybody.

  Someone rewards somebody.

Universal and existential quantifiers never appear together in any of the sentences in this experiment, so none of the sentences exhibit scope ambiguities.

Table 7.3 gives the average times for correct responses and the error rates for the deducible arguments. Each mean represents 144 observations (24 subjects × 6 repetitions of each argument type), less the number of errors. Overall, subjects took 3882 milliseconds to decide that the two-rule-two-step arguments followed, 3235 ms for the one-rule-two-step arguments, and 3529 ms for the additional arguments. An analysis of variance indicates that the main effect of argument type is significant ($F(2,46) = 24.03$, $p < 0.001$), and Newman-Keuls tests confirm that each mean differs from the others. The difference between two-rule and one-rule arguments is exactly what the PSYCOP theory predicts. And although we had no direct hypothesis about the relation of the additional problems to the other two groups, the times for the separate additional arguments also fit what we would expect from the rule breakdown in the table: The argument that takes two rules and two steps is slower than the argument that takes one rule and two steps, and the latter argument is, in turn, slower than the argument that takes only one step.

The error rates in this experiment generally follow the pattern of the response times. Errors are highest for the two-rule-two-step problems (12.0%) and lowest for the one-rule-two-step problems (2.6%), in accord with our prediction about their relative difficulty. For the additional arguments, the error rate is 3.2%. The main effect of argument type is significant ($F(2,46) = 18.61$, $p < 0.001$), with the two-rule-two-step arguments differing from the other two groups. Within the additional group, the errors agree with the response time differences that we just examined. The only surprise in the error data is the very high error rate (30.6%) for one of the two-rule-two-step arguments, the problem corresponding to argument (11). The reason for the large number of errors is unclear, although this argument is the only one that has different permanent names in the premise and the conclusion. It may have confused subjects to have to generalize *from* one permanent name while generalizing *to* another.

For the most part, however, the results of this experiment provide support for PSYCOP's method of handling variables and names. The matching rules differ in the requirements they impose on subgoals and assertions, and these distinctions among the rules evidently affect people's facility with them. Arguments that require two sorts of matching are more difficult than arguments that require only one. In this experiment we have highlighted the matching process by keeping other features of the arguments as simple as possible. But the simplicity of the arguments is a bit deceptive, since the deductive operations must be fairly sophisticated to avoid difficulties of the type we studied in chapter 6 (e.g., the incorrect proofs in examples (2) and (3) of that chapter). It may be, in general, that much of the deductive work that we carry out from day to day consists of steps of this kind—steps so routine that they seem not to require deduction at all. The seeming transparency of these inferences may also account for why (to my knowledge) no previous experiments on deduction have focused directly on the process of abstraction or that of instantiation.

Complex Multi-Variable Arguments

In the experiment discussed above, we examined PSYCOP's method for matching variables and temporary names in a pure context where there were no other logical operators to worry about. However, our system can handle inferences that depend on both sentential connectives and terms. We have seen a simple example of this dual capacity in the case of syllogisms, but the arguments that PSYCOP can deal with have much greater variety. To get a better idea of the system's adequacy, we ought to apply it to a larger range of arguments.

For this purpose, I collected a set of argument exercises from introductory textbooks on predicate logic that might form the basis of a stimulus set. The textbooks were Bergmann et al. 1980, Copi 1973, Guttenplan and Tamny 1971, and Leblanc and Wisdom 1976; the arguments selected were all items that PSYCOP could prove by means of the rules of chapter 6 and that seemed short enough to be comprehensible to subjects.[9] Moreover, in order to obtain stable parameter estimates and to avoid capitalizing on chance, the key arguments were ones whose proofs used rules that also figured in the proof of at least one other argument in the group. Thus, none of the proofs required a unique rule. The final set of arguments (in quantifier-free form) appears in table 7.4. The subjects saw these 25 valid arguments randomly mixed with an equal number of invalid ones, created by re-pairing premises and conclusions. The stimuli also included 30 filler arguments (14 valid and 16 invalid), for a total of 80 arguments.

All the arguments were presented to subjects in the form of sentences about members of a club, and the predicates of the sentences therefore referred to human characteristics or relationships. The one-place predicates were selected randomly from the phrases *has blue eyes, is tall, has glasses, has long hair*, and *is cheerful*; the two-place predicates from *praises* and *helps*; and the three-place predicates from *introduces ... to ...* and *talks about ... to ...* (No predicates with more than three places were used.) For example, one of the problems (argument 1 in table 7.4) is shown in (13).

(13)   There's a person A such that for any person B: if B is cheerful then A has glasses.
_____
There's a person C such that: if C is cheerful then C has glasses.

The subjects read the problems in printed booklets, with the order of problems in a different random permutation for each subject.

The instructions were generally similar to those used in the earlier experiments we have reviewed, but with special warnings about the nature of the variables. The subjects were told that each club had at least one member and that the different letters in the arguments could refer to the same individual: "A person labeled 'A' in one sentence might also be labeled 'B' in another sentence in the same problem.... Exactly the same goes for letters that occur within a single sentence. For example, the sentence 'There are people A and B such that A likes B' would be true if there is a club member George who likes himself. The A's and B's can refer independently to anyone in the club. It's not necessary that there be two distinct club members for 'A' and 'B' to refer to." The instructions included several sample arguments to clarify these points. The subjects, 20 Stanford undergraduates, were asked to respond to each of the experimental arguments by circling "follows" or "does not follow" in their booklets.

The percentage of "follows" responses for each of the valid arguments appears in table 7.4. Overall, the subjects said that these valid arguments

Table 7.4
Predicted and observed percentages of "follows" responses for arguments with multi-variable sentences.

	Observed	Predicted
1. IF F(x) THEN G(a) ⎯⎯⎯⎯⎯⎯⎯⎯⎯ IF F(b) THEN G(b)	75.0	79.6
2. NOT(F(x)) IF (G(m,y) OR H(y,y)) THEN F(a) ⎯⎯⎯⎯⎯⎯⎯⎯⎯ NOT(G(m,z) OR H(z,z))	40.0	45.3
3. IF (F(x) AND G(x)) THEN H(x) G(y) AND NOT(J(a,m)) ⎯⎯⎯⎯⎯⎯⎯⎯⎯ IF F(z) THEN H(z)	45.0	54.0
4. F(x) AND (G(x,x) AND H(x)) ⎯⎯⎯⎯⎯⎯⎯⎯⎯ G(a,m) AND H(y)	50.0	47.6
5. IF F(x) THEN G(x) ⎯⎯⎯⎯⎯⎯⎯⎯⎯ IF F(a) THEN G(y)	55.0	58.9
6. F(x,y,z) ⎯⎯⎯⎯⎯⎯⎯⎯⎯ IF F(u,v,w) THEN F(w,v,u)	55.0	61.7
7. IF F(x) THEN G(x,y,m) IF G(n,u,v) THEN H(v,u,u) ⎯⎯⎯⎯⎯⎯⎯⎯⎯ IF F(n) THEN H(a,o,o)	50.0	51.4
8. IF (F(m,x) AND F(y,m)) THEN F(y,x) IF G(z) THEN F(m,z) G(a) AND F(a,m) ⎯⎯⎯⎯⎯⎯⎯⎯⎯ G(b) AND (IF G(u) THEN F(b,u))	75.0	55.9
9. F(a) AND (IF F(x) THEN G(x,a)) ⎯⎯⎯⎯⎯⎯⎯⎯⎯ F(b) AND G(b,b)	60.0	60.1
10. IF F(x,y) THEN F(x,a) F(z,b_z) ⎯⎯⎯⎯⎯⎯⎯⎯⎯ F(u,c)	75.0	75.0
11. IF F(x) THEN G(x) ⎯⎯⎯⎯⎯⎯⎯⎯⎯ IF (F(y) AND H(z,y)) THEN (G(y) AND H(z,y))	55.0	54.0
12. IF F(x,y) THEN G(m,x) F(z,w) ⎯⎯⎯⎯⎯⎯⎯⎯⎯ G(a,a)	60.0	59.9
13. IF F(x) THEN G(y) ⎯⎯⎯⎯⎯⎯⎯⎯⎯ IF NOT(G(z)) THEN NOT(F(z))	40.0	45.8
14. IF F(x,m) THEN G(y) F(n,z) ⎯⎯⎯⎯⎯⎯⎯⎯⎯ IF H(u,o) THEN G(u)	15.0	—
15. IF F(x,y) THEN F(z,x) F(m,n) ⎯⎯⎯⎯⎯⎯⎯⎯⎯ F(u,v)	60.0	59.9

Table 7.4 (continued)

	Observed	Predicted
16. F(a) AND G(x) —————— F(b) AND G(b)	60.0	79.6
17. F(a) G(b) —————— F(c) AND G(d)	100.0	94.6
18. IF F(x) THEN G(x) IF (G(y) AND H(z,y)) THEN J(z) K(a) AND (F(b) AND H(a,b)) —————— K(c) AND J(c)	57.9	54.8
19. IF F(x,m) THEN F(x,n) —————— IF (G(y,z) AND F(z,m)) THEN (G(y,a_y) AND F(a_y,n))	35.0	55.9
20. IF (F(x) AND G(y)) THEN H(x,y) (F(a) AND NOT(F(b))) AND NOT(H(a,b)) —————— NOT(F(c)) AND NOT(G(c))	60.0	44.8
21. IF F(x) THEN G(a_x) —————— IF F(y) THEN G(b)	90.0	77.2
22. F(a,b) OR G(x,y) —————— F(c,d) OR G(c,d)	90.0	79.6
23. IF F(x) THEN G(x) IF G(y) THEN H(y) —————— IF F(z) THEN H(a)	50.0	61.3
24. IF F(x,y) THEN F(y,z) —————— IF F(u,v) THEN F(v,u)	70.0	75.6
25. IF F(m,x) THEN G(x,n) IF G(y,n) THEN G(n,a) —————— IF F(m,z) THEN G(n,b)	70.0	61.3

In these arguments, letters near the end of the alphabet (x, y, z, u, v, w) are variables, letters near the beginning of the alphabet (a, b, c, d) are temporary names, and letters near the middle (m, n, o) are permanent names.

followed on 60% of the trials and that the matched group of invalid arguments did not follow on 79% of trials. Thus, their performance was roughly comparable to the performance on other argument-evaluation experiments discussed above: Although the success rate on valid problems was low, subjects were able to discriminate reasonably well between valid and invalid items. As was also true of those earlier experiments, the percentage of correct responses varied greatly over individual arguments. For example, all subjects responded "follows" to argument 17 of table 7.4 ($F(a)$, $G(b)$; Therefore, $F(c)$ AND $G(d)$), whereas only 15% of subjects responded "follows" to argument 14.

Argument 14 is, in fact, something of an outlier among the problems in the set, and it suggests a difficulty with our formulation of the IF Introduction rule. The argument looked as follows in the guise in which our subjects saw it:

(14)   For any people A and B: if A helps Linda then B is cheerful.
       For any person C, Rob helps C.
       _____
       For any person D, if D praises Ben then D is cheerful.

Notice that the antecedent of the conclusion, *D praises Ben*, has a predicate that is not in the premises, and so the suggested relationship between praising Ben and being cheerful is not one that the premises establish directly. The conclusion does follow, however, by IF Introduction: This rule tells us to assume that D praises Ben and to prove that D is cheerful, and this goes through on a technicality. Since Rob helps everyone (according to premise 2), he helps Linda in particular, thus making everyone cheerful (according to premise 1). So D must be cheerful too. This reasoning seems a bit suspicious, though, for exactly the same reasons as in argument (13) of chapter 2. The fact that the conclusion's consequent is deducible seems too weak a reason to accept the entire conditional. The various pragmatic and logical accounts of conditionals mentioned in chapter 2 suggest ways of accommodating subjects' intuitions.

Although the model clearly fails with argument 14, it is still interesting to ask how it fares with the remaining problems. To find out, I fitted equation 8 to the response proportions under assumptions similar to those I have discussed for syllogisms. As in the earlier experiment, the model assumes that the probability of finding a proof for an argument is equal to the product of the probabilities that each of the rules in the proof is available. (PSYCOP proves the arguments of table 7.4 with rules drawn from the following set: Forward AND Elimination, Backward AND Introduction, Backward IF Introduction, Backward IF Elimination, Backward NOT Introduction, and the four matching rules of table 6.1.) The model also assumes that the likelihood is negligible that subjects will find an alternative proof if their first attempt has failed. However, there are two differences between the syllogism model and the model for these multi-variable problems. One is that no assumptions are made in the latter model about presuppositions. The experimental instructions and the wording of the problems were supposed to minimize effects of these factors; although this may not have been completely successful, it is likely that presuppositions play a smaller role than they do in syllogism experiments. The second difference between the models has to do with the matching rules. In fitting the syllogism data, I tacitly assumed that these rules were always available to subjects; but preliminary model fitting suggested that this assumption was unlikely for the new problems. A possible reason for this is that the rules are more difficult to apply to a sentence that contains more than one variable or temporary name. In a syllogism, where there is only one variable or name per sentence, there can be no subscripted names; hence, there is never any need to carry out the b parts of the actions in matching rules 1, 3, and 4 (see table 6.1). The model therefore included parameters for the matching rules as well as for the deduction rules.

The predictions from this model appear next to the observed responses in table 7.4, and the parameter estimates are listed in table 7.5. The corre-

Table 7.5
Parameter estimates for the model of equation (8), fitted to the data of the multi-variable experiment.

Parameter	Interpretation	Estimate
Rule parameters		
p_{ande}	Probability of Forward AND Elim.	0.96
p_{andi}	Probability of Backward AND Intro.	0.83
p_{ife}	Probability of Backward IF Elim.	0.90
p_{ifi}	Probability of Backward IF Intro.	0.66
p_{ni}	Probability of Backward NOT Intro.	0.31
Matching parameters		
$p_{m1} = p_{m3} = p_{m4}$	Probability of matching to variables	0.62
p_{m2}	Probability of matching to names	1.00
Response parameters		
p_g	Probability of guessing	0.70

lation between predicted and observed values is 0.806, and the root-mean-square deviation is 9.57—values that are comparable to those for the syllogism experiment. The rule parameters are also what we would predicted from the earlier experiments: high availabilities for the AND rules and for IF Elimination, intermediate availability for IF Introduction, and low availability for NOT Introduction. In fact, the parameter estimates come very close to duplicating those of the syllogism experiment for rules that overlap the two sets of arguments (see table 7.2). For IF Elimination the parameter values are 0.90 for the present arguments and 0.85 for syllogisms; for NOT Introduction they are respectively 0.31 and 0.30. The current values for AND Elimination (0.96) and AND Introduction (0.83) are also close to the combined parameter for the AND rules in the syllogism study (0.93). The remaining deduction parameter, the one for IF Introduction, has no counterpart in the previous experiment.

The rest of the parameters also tell an intelligible story about these arguments. Preliminary model fitting indicated that, under a variety of assumptions, values for matching rules 1, 3, and 4 were always quite close to one another and were considerably lower than that for matching rule 2. (This is also consistent with the response-time differences among the one-rule-two-step arguments in the previous experiment; see table 7.3.) For that reason, I have fitted a single value for the former rules in the model reported in tables 7.4 and 7.5. Notice that matching rules 1, 3, and 4 are the ones responsible for generalizing subgoal terms to assertion variables, whereas matching rule 2 generalizes terms to names. Part of the reason for the difference in parameter values may be that the matching-to-variable rules require subjects to keep track, not only of the main term that the variable will replace, but also of other temporary names in the subgoal (see condition d and action b of rules 1, 3, and 4 in table 6.1). Rule 2 is simpler in this respect, and it tends to be used in the present proofs to match a subgoal to an assertion that is a notational variant (e.g., to match $G(b)$ to $G(\hat{a})$ in problem 8).

The only clear disparity between the two experiments is that the parameter for guessing in this experiment (0.70) is larger than the parameters for guessing in the syllogism experiment (0.08 and 0.31). This disparity may be due to differences in the sample of arguments or, perhaps, to our having warned the subjects in the previous study that only a small percentage of the syllogisms were valid. In that situation, subjects may have been more willing to think that an argument for which they had no proof simply didn't follow. The subjects in the present experiment lacked such assurance and may have been more likely to hazard a guess.

Summary

We have been aiming for a unified account of deductive reasoning, one that can explain how people handle arguments that depend on sentential connectives and on predicate-variable structure. Most previous cognitive models have concentrated on just one of these argument types, and so explanations for inferences with connectives tend to look quite different from explanations of inferences with syllogisms. This is a state of affairs we should avoid, if we can, since it misses some generalizations. It is an empirical fact that variables that affect reasoning with conditionals have similar effects on reasoning with universals—something that is hard to understand if your theory says that people represent universals with Euler circles and conditionals with truth tables. Moreover, it is obvious that many arguments depend jointly on connectives and variables. The arguments in table 7.4 are examples of just this sort, and it is not at all clear how earlier disparate representations can hybridize to yield a mechanism that would explain these problems. Ideally, we would like a theory that can handle arguments with connectives (e.g., those of table 5.1), categorical arguments (e.g., those of table 7.1), and arguments with mixed structure (e.g., those of table 7.4).

The theory of chapter 6 gives us an approach that may help us explain all these problem types. The basic representation uses connectives explicitly and captures quantifiers implicitly through the structure of the quantified terms. The basic mechanisms are the rules for connectives, which also pass along terms during the proof. The experimental results of this chapter provide some support for the theory. It does reasonably well with syllogisms—psychologists' favorite argument forms—provided that we allow for presuppositions of the categorical sentences. Of course, we don't have an explanation for every effect that researchers have demonstrated in experiments with syllogisms. (We will return to some of these additional effects in chapter 10.) But the theory does seem to account for much of the variation among syllogisms whose subject matter isn't strongly biased, and it operates fairly accurately both in contexts in which subjects evaluate conclusions and in contexts in which they produce conclusions from premises. Furthermore, the results of the last two experiments suggest that the same model applies to nontraditional arguments that contain more than one term per sentence.

The parameter estimates from these studies enhance our hopes for a unified theory. Parameter values for the same deduction rules are quite consistent from the syllogisms to multi-variable arguments, and there is also substantial agreement with the parameters from our study of sentential reasoning in chapter 5. In all three sets of estimates, the introduction and elimination rules for AND have highest availabilities, followed by the rules for IF. NOT Introduction has consistently low availability in each experiment (see tables 5.2, 7.2, and 7.5). The stability of the parameters across different types of problems, different wording conventions, and different groups of subjects suggests that the success of our model is not merely due to local features of the data sets, but rather that it reflects deeper properties of inference.

Appendix: Syllogism Results

Table 7.6 gives the percentages of "yes" responses for all classical syllogisms. (Bold entries are observed responses; lightface entries are predictions from the model described in the text; $n = 20$.)

Table 7.6

Premises	Conclusion			
	All(F,H)	No(F,H)	Some(F,H)	Some-not(F,H)
⟨All(G,H),All(F,G)⟩	**90.0**[a,b,c]	**5.0**	**65.0**[b]	**0.0**
	89.1	5.0	43.7	15.0
⟨All(H,G),All(F,G)⟩	**40.0**	**0.0**	**0.0**	**0.0**
	5.0	5.0	15.0	15.0
⟨All(G,H),All(G,F)⟩	**25.0**	**5.0**	**45.0**[b]	**15.0**
	5.0	5.0	43.7	15.0
⟨All(H,G),All(G,F)⟩	**30.0**	**0.0**	**75.0**[b]	**5.0**
	5.0	5.0	43.7	15.0
⟨All(G,H),No(F,G)⟩	**0.0**	**15.0**	**0.0**	**25.0**
	5.0	5.0	15.0	15.0
⟨All(H,G),No(F,G)⟩	**0.0**	**90.0**[a,b,c]	**0.0**	**50.0**[b]
	5.0	84.4	15.0	38.9
⟨All(G,H),No(G,F)⟩	**0.0**	**40.0**	**0.0**	**10.0**
	5.0	5.0	15.0	15.0
⟨All(H,G),No(G,F)⟩	**5.0**	**65.0**[a,b]	**0.0**	**50.0**
	5.0	81.3	15.0	15.0
⟨All(G,H),Some(F,G)⟩	**5.0**	**0.0**	**80.0**[a,b]	**25.0**
	5.0	5.0	72.5	15.0
⟨All(H,G),Some(F,G)⟩	**0.0**	**0.0**	**15.0**	**20.0**[b]
	5.0	5.0	15.0	23.6
⟨All(G,H),Some(G,F)⟩	**5.0**	**0.0**	**75.0**[a,b]	**25.0**
	5.0	5.0	72.5	15.0
⟨All(H,G),Some(G,F)⟩	**0.0**	**0.0**	**40.0**	**30.0**
	5.0	5.0	15.0	15.0
⟨All(G,H),Some-not(F,G)⟩	**0.0**	**5.0**	**30.0**[b]	**10.0**
	5.0	5.0	43.7	15.0
⟨All(H,G),Some-not(F,G)⟩	**0.0**	**0.0**	**5.0**	**35.0**[a,b]
	5.0	5.0	15.0	32.2
⟨All(G,H),Some-not(G,F)⟩	**5.0**	**0.0**	**35.0**[b]	**10.0**
	5.0	5.0	43.7	15.0
⟨All(H,G),Some-not(G,F)⟩	**0.0**	**5.0**	**20.0**	**5.0**
	5.0	5.0	15.0	15.0
⟨No(G,H),All(F,G)⟩	**5.0**	**85.0**[a,b,c]	**0.0**	**60.0**[b]
	5.0	88.6	15.0	40.2
⟨No(H,G),All(F,G)⟩	**0.0**	**90.0**[a,b,c]	**0.0**	**60.0**[b]
	5.0	84.4	15.0	40.2
⟨No(G,H),All(G,F)⟩	**0.0**	**35.0**	**5.0**	**50.0**[b]
	5.0	5.0	15.0	40.2
⟨No(H,G),All(G,F)⟩	**0.0**	**15.0**	**0.0**	**35.0**[b]
	5.0	5.0	15.0	40.2
⟨No(G,H),No(F,G)⟩	**0.0**	**25.0**	**15.0**	**10.0**
	5.0	5.0	15.0	15.0

Table 7.6 (continued)

Premises	Conclusion			
	All(F,H)	No(F,H)	Some(F,H)	Some-not(F,H)
⟨No(H,G),No(F,G)⟩	**5.0**	**15.0**	**0.0**	**5.0**
	5.0	5.0	15.0	15.0
⟨No(G,H),No(G,F)⟩	**5.0**	**15.0**	**5.0**	**10.0**
	5.0	5.0	15.0	15.0
⟨No(H,G),No(G,F)⟩	**0.0**	**30.0**	**0.0**	**10.0**
	5.0	5.0	15.0	15.0
⟨No(G,H),Some(F,G)⟩	**0.0**	**5.0**	**10.0**	**60.0**[a,b]
	5.0	5.0	15.0	65.3
⟨No(H,G),Some(F,G)⟩	**0.0**	**5.0**	**5.0**	**60.0**[a,b]
	5.0	5.0	15.0	65.3
⟨No(G,H),Some(G,F)⟩	**0.0**	**10.0**	**10.0**	**60.0**[a,b]
	5.0	5.0	15.0	65.3
⟨No(H,G),Some(G,F)⟩	**0.0**	**5.0**	**10.0**	**65.0**[a,b]
	5.0	5.0	15.0	65.3
⟨No(G,H),Some-not(F,G)⟩	**0.0**	**0.0**	**5.0**	**30.0**[b]
	5.0	5.0	15.0	40.2
⟨No(H,G),Some-not(F,G)⟩	**5.0**	**5.0**	**20.0**	**20.0**[b]
	5.0	5.0	15.0	40.2
⟨No(G,H),Some-not(G,F)⟩	**0.0**	**5.0**	**5.0**	**35.0**[b]
	5.0	5.0	15.0	40.2
⟨No(H,G),Some-not(G,F)⟩	**0.0**	**5.0**	**0.0**	**35.0**[b]
	5.0	5.0	15.0	40.2
⟨Some(G,H),All(F,G)⟩	**0.0**	**5.0**	**40.0**	**20.0**
	5.0	5.0	15.0	15.0
⟨Some(H,G),All(F,G)⟩	**0.0**	**5.0**	**25.0**	**20.0**
	5.0	5.0	15.0	15.0
⟨Some(G,H),All(G,F)⟩	**5.0**	**5.0**	**80.0**[a,b,c]	**40.0**[b,c]
	5.0	5.0	76.4	47.3
⟨Some(H,G),All(G,F)⟩	**5.0**	**0.0**	**70.0**[a,b]	**25.0**
	5.0	5.0	72.5	15.0
⟨Some(G,H),No(F,G)⟩	**0.0**	**15.0**	**5.0**	**10.0**
	5.0	5.0	15.0	15.0
⟨Some(H,G),No(F,G)⟩	**0.0**	**5.0**	**15.0**	**25.0**
	5.0	5.0	15.0	15.0
⟨Some(G,H),No(G,F)⟩	**0.0**	**5.0**	**5.0**	**5.0**
	5.0	5.0	15.0	15.0
⟨Some(H,G),No(G,F)⟩	**0.0**	**0.0**	**10.0**	**20.0**
	5.0	5.0	15.0	15.0
⟨Some(G,H),Some(F,G)⟩	**0.0**	**0.0**	**30.0**	**35.0**
	5.0	5.0	15.0	15.0
⟨Some(H,G),Some(F,G)⟩	**0.0**	**0.0**	**20.0**	**25.0**
	5.0	5.0	15.0	15.0
⟨Some(G,H),Some(G,F)⟩	**5.0**	**0.0**	**25.0**	**20.0**
	5.0	5.0	15.0	15.0

Table 7.6 (continued)

Premises	Conclusion			
	All(F,H)	No(F,H)	Some(F,H)	Some-not(F,H)
⟨Some(H,G),Some(G,F)⟩	**0.0** 5.0	**0.0** 5.0	**30.0** 15.0	**30.0** 15.0
⟨Some(H,G),Some-not(F,G)⟩	**0.0** 5.0	**0.0** 5.0	**20.0** 15.0	**25.0** 15.0
⟨Some(G,H),Some-not(F,G)⟩	**0.0** 5.0	**5.0** 5.0	**20.0** 15.0	**10.0** 15.0
⟨Some(H,G),Some-not(G,F)⟩	**5.0** 5.0	**0.0** 5.0	**15.0** 15.0	**20.0** 15.0
⟨Some(G,H),Some-not(G,F)⟩	**0.0** 5.0	**0.0** 5.0	**15.0** 15.0	**10.0** 15.0
⟨Some-not(G,H),All(F,G)⟩	**0.0** 5.0	**5.0** 5.0	**20.0** 15.0	**30.0** 15.0
⟨Some-not(H,G),All(F,G)⟩	**0.0** 5.0	**5.0** 5.0	**25.0** 15.0	**35.0** 15.0
⟨Some-not(G,H),All(G,F)⟩	**0.0** 5.0	**0.0** 5.0	**35.0**[b,c] 47.3	**80.0**[a,b,c] 76.0
⟨Some-not(H,G),All(G,F)⟩	**5.0** 5.0	**0.0** 5.0	**30.0**[b] 43.7	**25.0** 15.0
⟨Some-not(G,H),No(F,G)⟩	**0.0** 5.0	**10.0** 5.0	**5.0** 15.0	**10.0** 15.0
⟨Some-not(H,G),No(F,G)⟩	**0.0** 5.0	**5.0** 5.0	**5.0** 15.0	**10.0** 15.0
⟨Some-not(G,H),No(G,F)⟩	**5.0** 5.0	**0.0** 5.0	**10.0** 15.0	**15.0** 15.0
⟨Some-not(H,G),No(G,F)⟩	**0.0** 5.0	**5.0** 5.0	**25.0** 15.0	**10.0** 15.0
⟨Some-not(G,H),Some(F,G)⟩	**0.0** 5.0	**0.0** 5.0	**15.0** 15.0	**30.0** 15.0
⟨Some-not(H,G),Some(F,G)⟩	**0.0** 5.0	**0.0** 5.0	**25.0** 15.0	**15.0** 15.0
⟨Some-not(G,H),Some(G,F)⟩	**0.0** 5.0	**0.0** 5.0	**20.0** 15.0	**15.0** 15.0
⟨Some-not(H,G),Some(G,F)⟩	**0.0** 5.0	**0.0** 5.0	**25.0** 15.0	**15.0** 15.0
⟨Some-not(G,H),Some-not(F,G)⟩	**0.0** 5.0	**0.0** 5.0	**20.0** 15.0	**25.0** 15.0
⟨Some-not(H,G),Some-not(F,G)⟩	**0.0** 5.0	**0.0** 5.0	**15.0** 15.0	**20.0** 15.0
⟨Some-not(G,H),Some-not(G,F)⟩	**0.0** 5.0	**0.0** 5.0	**20.0** 15.0	**30.0** 15.0
⟨Some-not(H,G),Some-not(G,F)⟩	**0.0** 5.0	**0.0** 5.0	**15.0** 15.0	**15.0** 15.0

a. Valid in CPL.
b. Valid with premise implicatures (but not conclusion implicatures)
c. Valid with premise and conclusion implicatures

III Implications and Extensions

8 The Role of Deduction in Thought

Our texture of belief has great holes in it.
M. F. K. Fisher, *How to Cook a Wolf*

One reason that deduction has played a rather minor role in cognitive psychology is that it has been hard for psychologists to envision what purpose deduction serves. If there are no specifically deductive mechanisms and if what pass for deductions are just the results of general-purpose heuristics, then of course deduction has no proper use; it has been explained away. Similarly, if it is just a matter of diagram manipulation, then again deduction is only a special case of a more general-purpose mechanism. What is really of interest is the general mechanism, not deduction itself. I will argue in a later chapter that both the heuristics approach and the diagram/model approach fail, for internal reasons, to give a correct explanation of inference. If this is right, then deduction may have a bigger part to play in cognitive theory.

I touched on the theme that deduction has a role in other cognitive skills back in part I, and I'd like to return to it here. The crucial ingredient that we need to realize this potential is the ability of our model to bind values to variables, because that gives it the power to manipulate symbols in memory and thus to perform cognitively useful tasks. It seems clear, at least in retrospect, that the inability of previous deduction theories to instantiate variables is what makes them so anemic and useless.

In the first section of this chapter, we will look at some ways in which the instantiating of variables can be combined with other logical operations to provide a model for cognitive processes such as simple problem solving and categorization. Categorization poses an especially interesting problem for the present theory, since beliefs about category membership —for example, the decision that a perceived object is a birthday present— usually aren't deducible from the evidence available to us. More often, the evidence provides inductive warrant for categorizing, just as in more obviously judgmental situations (e.g., whether I should bring red or white wine to a dinner party, whether Harry Aleman is guilty or innocent, or whether a particular scientific theory is true or false). But if so, how can we handle such decisions on our deduction-based approach?

AI has faced very similar questions about how to handle nondemonstrative (i.e., nondeductive) inferences, and we will examine some of its responses in the second section. The problem comes up most clearly in reasoning with defaults or typical properties. For example, we know that, by and large, cups have handles. (Perhaps this information is part of a mental schema or frame or mini-theory that we have about cups.) Thus, if we are told that Calvin sipped tea from a cup, we assume quite reasonably that the cup had a handle. If we later learn that the cup was Chinese or styrofoam, however, we are likely to reverse our decision, and this "defeasibility" strongly suggests that our original conclusion can't have been deduced from a fixed set of axioms. Defeasible inferences must be extremely common in everyday thinking, and any general theory in AI or psychology must accommodate them. One possibility is to pass the buck to schemas, frames, or similar data structures and let them do the inferencing. Another is to revise the logical system in order to take these inferences into account—a possibility that has motivated "nonmonotonic" logics in AI. In what follows I will try to suggest, though, that schemas don't provide any special inference abilities, and that nonmonotonic logics are suspect as psychological theories. In contrast, the monotonic system developed in part II, although it certainly doesn't provide a general theory for inductive inferences, is at least consistent with them and can supply all the purely logical machinery that they require.

Deduction as a Cognitive Architecture

It is worth exploring how our extended model could be useful in tasks that go beyond those of standard reasoning experiments. At the end of chapter 3, we looked at some ways in which deduction might come into play in general problem solving. PSYCOP's new ability to manipulate variables gives it everything it needs to implement these examples. Rather than replay these illustrations, however, it might be more instructive to see whether PSYCOP can handle tasks that cognitive psychologists have investigated directly, such as fact retrieval and classification. The aim is not to provide a new detailed model of how people accomplish these activities: PSYCOP is abstract enough to be consistent with many alternative models. Instead, the point is simply to be sure PSYCOP is capable of carrying out these processes in a human-like way. I have picked these two examples, out of the many tasks that cognitive psychologists have studied, on the grounds that enough facts are known about them to provide some constraints on theorizing and that they don't obviously embody deductive reasoning. To the extent that PSYCOP can provide a framework for these tasks, it seems likely that it can do the same for many other cognitive processes.

Problem Solving by Deduction

Let us take as an initial example PSYCOP's performance on an experimental task, devised by J. R. Hayes (1965, 1966), that calls for memorizing and retrieving information. In Hayes' study, subjects first memorized a list of paired associates, which were supposed, according to the experiment's cover story, to represent code names of pairs of spies. Each pair designated two spies who were able to communicate; thus, the pair *Tango–China* meant that the spy named *Tango* could talk to the one named *China*. Figure 8.1 shows a possible list of pairs of this sort. Notice that the pairs, taken together, form a "spy network"; for example, the pairs on the left in figure 8.1 constitute the network in the diagram on the right (though the subjects saw only the pairs, not the network). In the test phase of the experiment, subjects received instructions like "Get a message from Tango to Larynx," and they were to solve the problem by saying aloud the path that the message would take (e.g., "Tango to China, China to Shower, Shower to Larynx").

Problem Representation   To represent Hayes' problem in the PSYCOP framework, the program must know both the relevant pairs and the definition of a message pathway. We can use the predicate *Talk-to* as a way of expressing the fact that two spies can communicate directly; thus, let us assume that the elements of the paired-associate list are stored in memory as the assertions *Talk-to(Tango,China)*, *Talk-to(China,Shower)*, and so on. To record the fact that there is a pathway between two spies along which a message can travel, we need a second predicate (say, *Path*); so *Path(Tango,Larynx)* will mean that there is a path between Tango and Larynx. PSYCOP can then use this predicate to represent the experimental problem as a goal; for example, *Path(Tango,Larynx)?* represents *Is there a path between Tango and Larynx?*

Solving the problem amounts to searching the *Talk-to* pairs to satisfy the goal, and this requires an explicit way to recognize which pairs constitute a path. Clearly, if one spy can *Talk-to* another then there is a trivial, one-link path between them. PSYCOP can represent this simple case by the conditional assertion (1a).

(1)   a. IF Talk-to(u,v) THEN Path(u,v)

     b. IF Talk-to(x,y) AND Path(y,z) THEN Path(x,z)

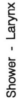

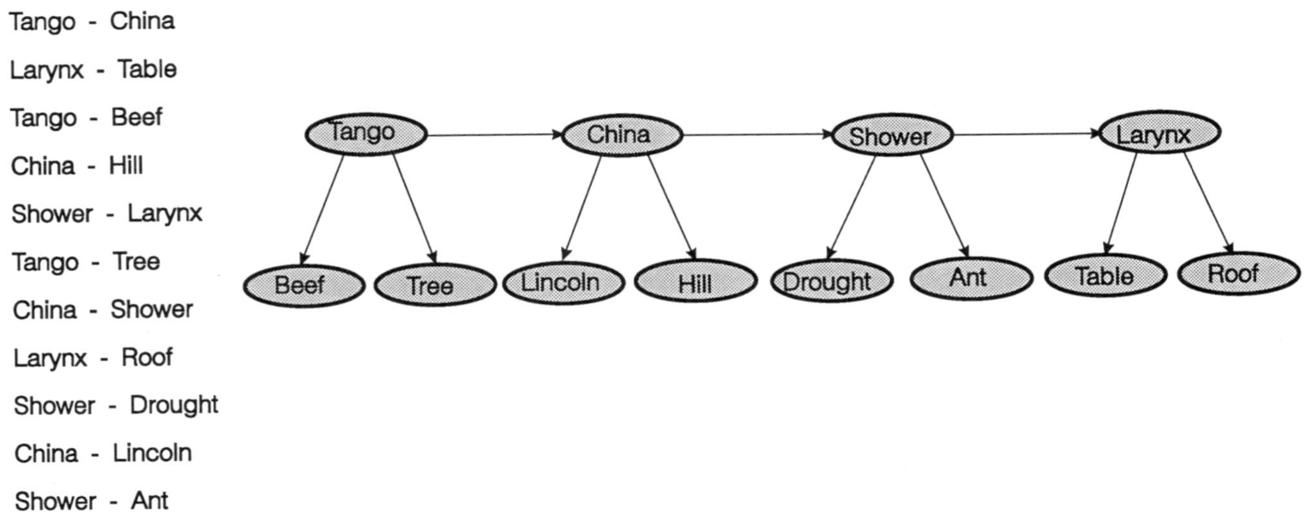
Tango - China
Larynx - Table
Tango - Beef
China - Hill
Shower - Larynx
Tango - Tree
China - Shower
Larynx - Roof
Shower - Drought
China - Lincoln
Shower - Ant
Tango
China
Shower
Larynx
Beef
Tree
Lincoln
Hill
Drought
Ant
Table
Roof

Figure 8.1
A sample stimulus list for the Hayes experiment, and a network representation of the same stimulus items. Each item represents a "spy," and spy pairs in the list can communicate with each other.

Of course, a path will usually consist of more than one pair, but we can simplify the problem by taking it a step at a time. We can find a path from Tango to Larynx, for example, by first finding someone Tango can talk to and then finding a path from that intermediate spy to Larynx. Assertion (1b) represents this stepwise method: There is a path between any two spies x and z if x can talk to a third spy y and if there is a path from y to z. In order to solve the spy problem, all PSYCOP needs are the Talk-to pairs (i.e., the paired-associate list), the goal, and the assertions in (1) about the relation between *Talk-to* and *Path*. To handle this problem we need make only minimal assumptions about memory storage. It is enough to suppose that the *Talk-to* relations are accessible in long-term or short-term memory, and that PSYCOP can retrieve them as part of the process of looking for matches to its subgoals. For example, a subgoal like *Talk-to(Shower,c)?* should be able to retrieve any *Talk-to* sentence in which *Shower* is the first argument. This is similar to Norman and Bobrow's (1979) notion of retrieval by partial description.

Problem Solution   Given the assertions and the goal, PSYCOP looks for a way to derive the goal from the assertion, using its general rules. Figure 8.2 shows the steps it takes in solving the problem when the spy pairs have the configuration of figure 8.1. As we will see, the order of the system's search depends on the order in which the assertions are found in memory. For purposes of this illustration, we have assumed that the order of the *Talk-to* assertions is the same as the ordering of the pairs in figure 8.1, and that (1a) occurs before (1b). Changing the order of the *Talk-to* relations will affect the order in which PSYCOP searches the links, but will not keep it from solving the problem. The same is true of (1a) and (1b); PSYCOP will solve the problem when these assertions are reversed, though the solution will be much less direct. (In the next example, order will be more crucial.) The numbered subgoals in figure 8.2 give the order in which PSYCOP considers these subgoals as it solves the problem; figure 8.2a is the initial segment of the solution and figure 8.2b is the finale. The figure shows the assertions only when they directly match the subgoals (as indicated by double lines).

The main goal of the problem is the one shown at the bottom of figure 8.2a: Is there a path between Tango and Larynx? There is no direct assertion about any such path; so PSYCOP has to use its inference rules to see if it can find one. In the present case, Backward IF Elimination notices

Figure 8.2
PSYCOP's solution to the problem of tracing through the spy network of figure 8.1 from
Tango to Larynx. Panel a is the initial part of the solution. Panel b shows the continuation,
after the program has returned to subgoal 8.

that the goal *Path(Tango,Larynx)?* matches the consequent of the conditional assertion (1a). The rule recognizes that in this situation the goal will be fulfilled if the antecedent of the conditional holds; that is, if *Talk-to(Tango,Larynx)* holds, it must be the case that *Path(Tango,Larynx)* holds. The IF Elimination rule stipulates that the main goal is fulfilled if PSYCOP can establish the subgoal of proving *Talk-to(Tango,Larynx)?*, which becomes subgoal 2 in the figure. Unfortunately, though, *Talk-to(Tango,Larynx)* isn't among the pairs PSYCOP knows, and there is no indirect means of establishing it. So subgoal 2 fails outright.

PSYCOP needs some alternative way to get at subgoal 1, and assertion (1b) suggests a second possibility. The same IF Elimination rule notices that it can also fulfill the goal by showing that there is a third spy *c1* to whom Tango can talk (i.e., *Talk-to(Tango,c1)*) and from whom there is a path to Larynx (*Path(c1,Larynx)*). Subgoal 3 represents this conjunctive subgoal, an instantiated version of the IF part of assertion (1b). (IF Elimination substitutes the temporary name *c1* for *y* when it applies the argument-reversal procedure to the antecedent; see table 6.3.) PSYCOP splits this two-part goal in half using backward AND Introduction. It first tries subgoal 4: *Talk-to(Tango,c1)?*. This subgoal succeeds easily, since it matches several of the *Talk-to* pairs. The first one it finds is *Talk-to(Tango,China)*, which takes it one link along the correct solution path. However, PSYCOP must still establish that there is a path between China and Larynx, and it takes this as subgoal 5.

At this point, then, PSYCOP must deal with *Path(China,Larynx)?*, which has the same form as the main goal that it started with, *Path(Tango,Larynx)?*. In doing this, it follows exactly the same procedure it used before, first checking unsuccessfully for a one-link connection between China and Larynx (subgoal 6) and then looking for an indirect path (subgoal 7). This involves finding someone to whom China can talk (subgoal 8). But this time PSYCOP unluckily finds Hill as a possibility, since *Talk-to(China,Hill)* is the first such pair it locates in memory. As is apparent in figure 8.1, however, this choice leads to a dead end: Apart from China, there is no one to whom Hill can talk; thus, there is no way to show that Hill can talk directly to Larynx (subgoal 10) and no way to find a path from Hill to Larynx (subgoals 11–13). Since all these subgoals fail, PSYCOP must back up and try another route.[1]

Figure 8.2b illustrates PSYCOP's progress when it gets back on track. (The unsuccessful subgoals from figure 8.2a are omitted to give a clearer view of the solution strategy.) The system returns to subgoal 8, the point at which it last retrieved a *Talk-to* assertion. This time, it satisfies *Talk-to(China,c2)?* by finding *Talk-to(China,Shower)*, and then attempts *Path(Shower,Larynx)?* (subgoal 14 in figure 8.2b). For the earlier subgoals, assertion (1a) was of no help, since there were no one-link pathways among the spies that these subgoals mentioned. For *Path(Shower,Larynx)?*, however, that assertion turns out to be crucial; it allows PSYCOP to satisfy the subgoal if it can show that *Talk-to(Shower,Larynx)?* (subgoal 15). Because this is one of the pairs that PSYCOP studied, it can satisfy the new subgoal with a direct match. At this point, then, the solution is complete in that PSYCOP has found a connected path from Tango to Larynx. Reading from top to bottom in figure 8.2b, we find that *Talk-to(Shower,Larynx)* satisfies *Path(Shower,Larynx)?*; this in turn satisfies *Path(China,Larynx)?* in view of the fact that China can talk to Shower; finally, we can conclude that *Path(Tango,Larynx)*, since we have found that Tango can talk to China. PSYCOP can stop, its task accomplished.

Adequacy Hayes' (1965) data are in reasonable agreement with the way in which PSYCOP solves such problems. First, solution time increased with the length of the correct pathway, and this is obviously consistent with PSYCOP's step-by-step method. Second, solution time also increased with the number and length of the dead ends (e.g., the one from China to Hill) that run from the junction points along the correct route. This is analogous to Anderson's (1976, 1983) "fan effects" and to other interference phenomena in memory. PSYCOP exhibits the same behavior, since it simply chains from its current position to a neighboring one, sometimes entering the dead ends. Once it heads down a dead end, it will continue until it reaches the terminus and is forced to back up. Third, Hayes' subjects carried out the final step of the problem more quickly than the preceding steps. PSYCOP does too: On each step it first tries for a quick solution via (1a) and then resorts to (1b); on each step but the last, the quick solution fails.[2] The purpose of our example, however, is not to model the results precisely but simply to demonstrate the main features of PSYCOP's performance in a cognitive task.

Deduction in Classification

Hayes' experiment is conceptually simple, since the definition of the problem and the information that subjects need to solve it are mostly specified as part of the task. Matters become less clear-cut, however, when we turn from fact retrieval to categorization. Categorization (or classification) is the process of recognizing something as part of a larger category. This includes assigning individual entities (or pictures of them) to specified groups—for example, deciding whether a particular object is an apple. However, psychologists also use "categorization" to include judgments about subset-superset relations, such as whether apples are fruits. In these examples the categories are ones that subjects know before the experiment, but investigators can, of course, construct artificial categories that subjects must learn during the task session. Theories in this area focus on the way people represent information about categories in memory and the processes they use to decide on category membership. In looking at categorization from the PSYCOP perspective, we will focus on a situation in which a person classifies a perceived object as a member of a well-known category, since this case seems central to the field and preserves nearly all its interesting issues.

Classification as Deduction?   Suppose you believe that an object is a bird if it has feathers. If you need to determine whether a feathered creature named George is a bird, you can then use the argument shown here as (2).

(2)   IF Feathered(x) THEN Bird(x)
       Feathered(George)
       _____
       Bird(George)

The argument is simple, and PSYCOP can easily categorize George in this way. But of course the first premise of (2) isn't strictly true, since arrows, pillows, dusters, and other objects can have feathers without thereby being birds; thus, the conclusion of (2) needn't be true either, despite the evident validity of the argument. If we want to ensure that this deductive method categorizes things correctly, we need premise information that is sufficient for category membership. However, sufficient properties are notoriously hard to find for all but a handful of natural-language categories (see, e.g., Fodor 1981; Rosch 1978; Smith and Medin 1981).[3]

These considerations, however, aren't enough to show that there is anything wrong with (2) as a description of how people classify birds. All they show is that people will sometimes make incorrect classifications (false alarms) if they accept the corresponding inference. And making mistakes in categorizing is not that uncommon; it is exactly what we would expect from nonexperts. What *would* cast doubt on a deductively correct argument like (2) as a classification method is, not the absence of sufficient properties, but the absence of people's belief in them. In order to use (2) in classifying George, people would have to accept the conditional premise. If they don't believe the premise, then (2) is useless for classification, despite its validity.

Do people believe there are sufficient properties for ordinary categories? Of course, people aren't likely to accept something as obviously faulty as the first premise of (2) and be duped into thinking that arrows are birds; but then (2) doesn't give a very realistic set of properties. By adding other bird characteristics to the antecedent of the first premise, we might be able to cut the false-alarm rate to a more reasonable size. We are not concerned with the conditional in (2) itself, but with the possibility that there is some conditional that could fill its role. If there is any nontrivial conditional with $Bird(x)$ as its consequent that people take as true, then we might be able to use a deductive argument as a classification device in situations where the antecedent of the conditional is fulfilled. (The conditional must be nontrivial, since there are obviously sentences (e.g., *IF Bird(x) THEN Bird(x)*) that are of no help in categorizing.)

Some evidence from McNamara and Sternberg (1983) suggests that people do think they know sufficient properties. These investigators asked subjects whether they could identify individual properties or sets of properties that are sufficient for membership in eight natural-kind and eight artifact categories. As it turned out, the subjects named properties they deemed sufficient for each of the natural kinds and nearly all the artifacts. Examples are "bird that appears on quarters" for eagle and "light source that has a shade" for lamp. This suggests that in some circumstances an inference along the lines of (2) might not be implausible as a classifying mechanism. These circumstances must be rather limited, however. We may be able to use *light source with shade* to determine that something is a lamp if we hear or read this description; however, it isn't going to be much help in perceptually classifying objects, because it relies on *light source*—a category whose members are probably no easier to classify than lamp itself. Ditto for eagle, which relies on *bird*. So we must impose additional restrictions on the antecedent in (2) to make it useful for perceptual classification.

Classification as Induction   It is certainly not impossible that deductively correct arguments along the lines of (2) could play a part in categorization.

The discussion so far suggests that whether they do is a more subtle question than it might at first appear. Of course, if they do, then we have all we need to explain how PSYCOP could simulate categorization. But consider the alternative possibility. Suppose that, on at least some occasions, people categorize things on the basis of evidence that they themselves consider inconclusive (Rips 1989b; Smith 1989). We take the feathered object on the sill to be a bird, even though we're quite aware that the feathers (and the other properties we have noticed) don't guarantee birdhood—that there are objects that have these properties but aren't birds at all. Still, feathers make it likely that the object is a bird, and this may be all the certainty we demand in this situation. It seems undeniable that people sometimes engage in this kind of plausible inference, especially in contexts where the information and the time available for the decision are limited. We therefore need to ask how a deductive model like PSYCOP can handle these nondeductive judgments.

Maybe we can salvage this situation if we turn (2) on its head. Although we may not be able to deduce directly that George is bird, we may be able to deduce the observable properties of George on the assumption that he is a bird. This is illustrated by (3).

(3)   IF Bird(x) THEN Feathered(x)
       Bird(George)
       _____
       Feathered(George)

The strategy here is similar to the "hypothetico-deductive" theory in the philosophy of science. If we can *de*duce the facts about George from the hypothesis that he is a bird, then we can *in*duce the truth of that hypothesis. In order for this strategy to work, of course, people would have to believe that the properties in question are necessary for category membership. The conditional in (3) makes *feathered* necessary in exactly the same way that the conditional of (2) made *feathered* sufficient. But perhaps necessary properties aren't as difficult to find as sufficient ones; for example, it seems more reasonable to attribute to people the belief that all birds are feathered than the belief that all feathered things are birds. (There is some resemblance here to the use of deduction in AI systems for "explanation-based learning" (see, e.g., DeJong 1988 and Minton et al. 1990). However, in these systems proof is used, not to classify instances directly, but to determine why a given category member—a training example—satisfies the prespecified criteria for that category. These systems then generalize the derived explanation on an inductive basis to classify further instances.)

However, this second categorization strategy suffers from the same defects as the hypothetico-deductive method. Being able to deduce a true proposition from a hypothesis generally isn't enough to show that there is good evidence for that hypothesis (see, e.g., Osherson et al. 1986 and Salmon 1967). In (4), for example, we can correctly conclude that the property of being cold is true of Siberia from the "hypotheses" in the premises.

(4)   IF Bird(x) THEN Cold(Siberia)
      Bird(George)
      _____
      Cold(Siberia)

Moreover, *Cold(Siberia)* is something we can observe to be true. But (4) clearly gives us little confidence in *Bird(George)*, even though we can use this premise to deduce a true conclusion.

Another possible solution to the categorization problem would be to show that a deduction system like PSYCOP can indirectly implement the types of models that already exist in the categorization literature. In this case, we have an array of possibilities to choose from. (See Smith and Medin 1981 and Medin 1989 for reviews.) Most of these models are based on the idea that categorizing is a matter of computing the similarity between the item to be classified and representatives of its potential categories. For example, we might classify the object on the sill as a bird if it is sufficiently similar to a prototypical bird (Posner and Keele 1968; Reed 1972) or to previously encountered bird instances (Brooks 1978; Hintzman 1986; Medin and Schaffer 1978; Nosofsky 1986), or if it has sufficient "family resemblance" to these instances (Rosch 1978). There is little doubt that PSYCOP could duplicate the behavior of such theories; the problem is that none of these similarity-based models is completely satisfactory for natural categories (Rips 1989b, 1991). There are demonstrations that subjects will classify an instance as a member of category A rather than category B even when they judge the very same instance more similar to B than A (Rips 1989b; Rips and Collins, in press). Carey (1985), Gelman and Markman (1986), and Keil (1989) have produced related evidence that subjects will sometimes overlook similarity in making category judgments.

Unless the notion of similarity is gerrymandered in such a way that any attempt to consult the properties of the category and of the to-be-classified instance counts as determining their "similarity," similarity can't be the only relevant factor in categorizing.

Although I believe that neither the pure deductive approach (in either its direct or its inverse version) nor the similarity approach will work for natural categories, there is something right about each of them. On one hand, similarity-based theories seem right in supposing that classification depends in part on the goodness of fit between the category and the instance. Goodness of fit in this case may be relative to a contrast class of mutually exclusive categories. For example, in classifying George the contrast class might consist of the categories of things commonly found on sills; in other situations, it might be the set of basic-level animal categories (*bird, mammal, fish*, etc.) that this specimen might fall under. On the other hand, what is right about the deduction theories is that deductive inference may play a role in directing the classification process. This role must be more indirect, however, than either deducing category membership from known properties or deducing properties from the category.

Classification as Explanation   What both the deductive and the similarity theories are missing is that classifying the instance in the way we do helps us solve a problem. The instance confronts us with an array of properties in a particular combination that we have likely never experienced. By classifying the instance as a member of a category, we can explain many of these properties and many more that are unobserved or unobservable. This idea of classification as explanation is akin to the thought that classifying things is a matter of predicting their behavior or seeing how they might serve practical goals (see, e.g., Anderson 1990 and Holland et al. 1986). But I doubt that most of the classifying we do is tied to prediction or goal satisfaction to any significant extent, unless of course the goal is simply to know more about the instance. Classifying a plane figure as an isosceles triangle, for example, tells us something of its properties, but it would be odd to say that it allows us to predict them or to use them to serve our goals. The same goes for classifying a piece of music as eighteenth-century or a painting as abstract expressionist. Even classifying George may be mainly a theoretical enterprise on our part. Of course we do sometimes classify things for practical purposes, but this seems unlikely to be the basic motive.

Thinking about classification as explanation doesn't take us very far without some way of explaining explanation, and adequate general theories of explanation are not much in evidence. (See Salmon 1989 and chapter 5 of Van Fraassen 1980 for reviews of previous theories of scientific explanation.) Still, I think some headway can be made if we look at simple cases of categorization for natural kinds such as *bird*. For these categories, it is reasonable to suppose that what is in back of many of the instances' manifest properties are causal relations to whatever qualifies the instances in the first place as members of the kind. Obviously the details of the causal story are mostly unknown to us nonbiologists, and before the advent of modern genetic theory any available stories may have been largely false. But the fact that we believe there is a causal connection between being a member of a species and manifesting certain properties may itself be enough to go on (Medin 1989). Determining which natural kind an instance belongs to seems to entail (a) finding out whether there are causal links between membership in one of these kinds and some of the manifest properties of the instance and (b) making sure no other kind in the same contrast class provides a better causal account.

Perhaps we could dig deeper and attempt to determine what people believe about how membership in a category causes the properties of interest, but I won't pursue that project here. Since our focus is on categorization rather than on recognition of causality, we can take the causal links as given in long-term memory and see how PSYCOP might use them in determining category membership.

A Causal Approach to Categorizing   Categorization, according to our causal theory, is relative to a set of manifest properties and to a contrast class. Thus, to construct a simple example of a causal model, suppose we observe George's feathers and seek to classify him in a situation where the relevant contrast categories are birds, mammals, and fish. Long-term memory tells us that membership in the bird category leads to feathers, versus fur for mammals and scales for fish; therefore, this information can help us make the decision about George. Argument 5 produces one sort of procedure that results in the information that *Isa(George,bird)*. I am not assuming, however, that this information is represented in memory in the form of an argument. Listing it in this way merely highlights the crucial sentences. (Representational issues will be taken up in the following section.) In essence, the method works by checking which categories in the contrast class are "Possible" for the object (i.e., which ones can cause the object's properties), and then asserting that the object "Isa" member of a category if that category is the only possible one. The conditional premises in (5) specify the method for carrying out the categorization, the *Cause* premises give the long-term memory information about the links between categories and their properties, and the *Concat* and *Notequal* premises provide the facts about the contrast class. Although the procedure is essentially self-contained, it makes use of the special predicate *Assert* (similar to the PROLOG predicate of the same name), which places its argument—for example, the sentence *Isa(George,bird)*—in working memory whenever *Assert* is encountered during a proof.

(5)   IF (Test(xinst1,xprop1) AND Trouble(xinst1)) THEN
          Categorize(xinst1,xprop1).
      IF (Possible(xinst2,xcat2) AND Assert(Isa(xinst2,xcat2))) THEN
          Categorize(xinst2,xprop2).
      IF (Concat(xcat3) AND (Cause(xcat3,xprop3) AND
          (Assert(Possible(xinst3,xcat3)) AND False(m)))) THEN
          Test(xinst3,xprop3).
      IF True(m) THEN Test(xinst4,xprop4).
      IF (Possible(xinst5,xcat5) AND (Possible(xinst5,xcat6) AND
          Notequal(xcat5,xcat6))) THEN Trouble(xinst5).
      True(x).
      Cause(bird,feathers).
      Cause(mammal,fur).
      Cause(fish,scales).
      Concat(bird).
      Concat(mammal).
      Concat(fish).
      Notequal(bird,mammal).
      Notequal(bird,fish).
      ⋮
      Notequal(mammal,fish).
      _____
      Categorize(George,feathers).

How does this work? Notice, first, that the conclusion of this argument sets up the goal to categorize George on the basis of his feathers, and the first two premises give two alternative methods of fulfilling the *Categorize* goal: The top one checks whether any categorization is possible, and it aborts further processing if any "Trouble" occurs. The second premise comes into play only if the first fails, and it is the one that actually classifies by adding an *Isa* sentence to memory (e.g., *Isa(George,bird)*). Premises 3 and 4 exhaustively check the categories in the contrast class to see which of them can cause the given property, and they add the sentence *Possible(x)* to memory for each category *x* that can do so. The final conditional notes trouble in case there is more than one category in the contrast class that is possible for this instance.

Figures 8.3–8.6 show how this procedure applies to George's case. As in the earlier example, the figures depict only the sequence of goals that PSYCOP places in working memory; assertions appear only if they directly match a goal (indicated by double lines). Since PSYCOP's main goal is *Categorize(George,feathers)?*, it begins by applying Backward IF Elimination to the first premise, which has a predicate of this type as its consequent. This leads it to set up the subgoals *Test(George,feathers)?* and *Trouble(George)?* via AND Introduction (figure 8.3, goals 3 and 4). To handle the first of these subgoals, it tries the third premise of (5), which initiates exhaustive search of the contrast categories. To satisfy the *Test* subgoal with this premise, we need to find one of the contrast categories *a* (i.e., one that satisfies *Concat(a)?*), show that this category causes feathers (*Cause(a,feathers)?*), assert that George is possibly a member of this category (*Assert(Possible(George,a))?*), and finally satisfy the subgoal *False(m)?*. In fact, this last subgoal can never be satisfied, but the failure to fulfill it causes PSYCOP to cycle back through all the categories in the contrast class. Figure 8.3 represents the effect of trying these subgoals (subgoals 6–11) when Category *a* = *bird*. In this case, PSYCOP easily determines that birdhood causes feathers (because of the seventh premise in (5)) and then asserts that George is possibly a bird. (Notice that the AND Introduction rule that is reponsible for these subgoals is also in charge of communicating the fact that *a* has been instantiated to *bird*.) But because the *False* subgoal fails, PSYCOP must go back and try another possibility from the contrast categories. The point of this is to make sure no rival categories also cause feathers.

In figure 8.4, we try Category *a* = *mammal*. Subgoals 1–7 in this figure are the same as in the previous diagram; PSYCOP does not rederive them. The only new activity is shown at the top, where the program tries to fulfill subgoals 6 and 7 again, using *mammal* instead of *bird*. This means trying

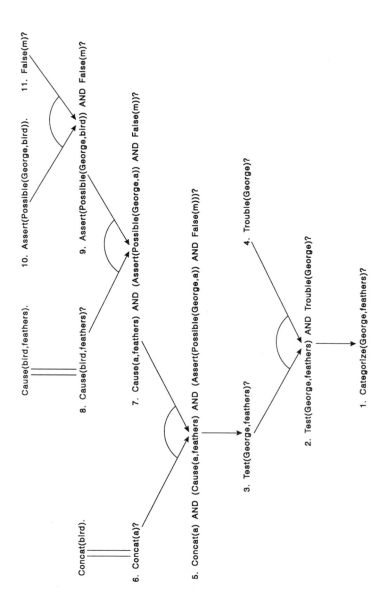

Figure 8.3
PSYCOP's simulation of categorizing an object, George, on the basis of one of his properties (feathers), given the contrast class {bird, mammal, fish}. The procedure followed is the one in (5). In this part of the example, PSYCOP decides that George is possibly a bird.

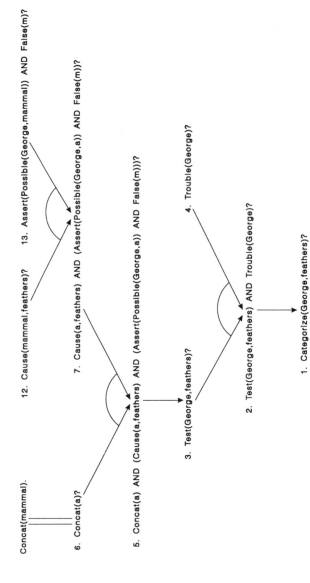

Figure 8.4
The categorization example continued. PSYCOP rejects the possibility that George is a mammal, since being a mammal doesn't lead to having feathers.

to show that mammals cause feathers (subgoal 12); of course the attempt fails immediately, since we have no way to prove anything of the kind. Thus, PSYCOP skips subgoal 13; that is, it is not tempted to assert that George is possibly a mammal. An identical failure—not shown in the figures—occurs when Category $a = fish$.

This inability to satisfy the antecedent of the third premise of (5) means that PSYCOP needs to find another way to fulfill the subgoal *Test(George,feathers)?*. The fourth premise offers the only other possibility: The *Test* subgoal follows if we can show *True(m)?*. Figure 8.5 indicates this as subgoal 16, and it is easily satisfied because of the *True(x)* premise. The purpose of this device is simply to allow computation to resume after examining the contrast categories. Even after satisfying the *Test* subgoal, however, we still have to deal with *Trouble(George)?* (subgoal 4 in figure 8.5). The point of this latter goal is to ensure that any category we have found for our to-be-classified object is unique. The fifth premise, together with our usual IF Elimination–AND Introduction pair, generates subgoals 17–22, which ask whether there are categories b and c such that *Possible(George,b)*, *Possible(George,c)*, and $b \neq c$. This could happen only if we had found in the previous step that more than one of the contrast categories could cause feathers. As it is, the only relevant assertion is *Possible(George,bird)*, which we derived in fulfilling subgoal 10 (figure 8.3). This means that there is no way to show *Trouble(George)*; subgoal 22 fails, and so does subgoals 4 and 2. If PSYCOP had succeeded in finding more than one possible category for George, we would be finished, and the procedure would stop, having noted the possibilites but not having asserted that George "isa" member of either category.

At this point, the procedure has failed all the way back to the main goal *Categorize(George,feathers)?*, and PSYCOP therefore needs some other way of handling it. The second premise of (5) allows us to finish up, since it tells us that the *Categorize* goal will be fulfilled if we can prove *Possible(George,d)?* and *Assert(Isa(George,d))?* for some category d. These appear as subgoals 24 and 25 in figure 8.6. The first of these matches *Possible(George,bird)*, which PSYCOP now knows to be the only such match. It then asserts *Isa(George,bird)* and stops, having completed the classification.

Adequacy Although the above example is a simplified one, it does seem to capture some of what we want from a categorization theory. It avoids

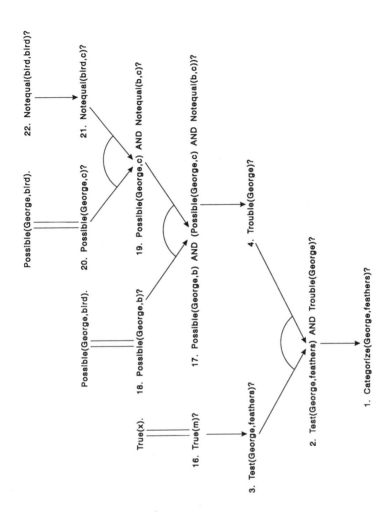

Figure 8.5
The categorization example continued. PSYCOP determines that *bird* is the only category in the contrast class that could possibly include George.

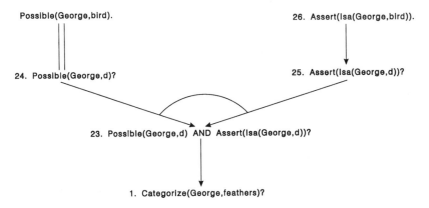

Figure 8.6
The categorization example concluded. PSYCOP asserts that George is a bird.

reliance on an unconstrained notion of similarity. It also provides more flexibility in categorizing than either the deductive method in (2) or the hypothetico-deductive approach in (3). Although PSYCOP derives the conclusion of (5) in a deductively correct manner, this conclusion is *not* that the instance is a member of a specific category. PSYCOP can prove the conclusion of (5) while remaining undecided about the instance's category membership; the conclusion is merely a dummy proposition that triggers the classification process. The point at which the process decides on membership is the point at which it asserts the *Isa* proposition, and this proposition does not follow deductively from anything in (5). Of course, it is possible to rewrite (5) so that the *Isa* sentence does follow whenever there is a unique causal connection between a category and the instance's properties. But this would mean reworking the premises in the argument, and these revised premises would presumably correspond to beliefs that seem questionable in precisely the same way as the conditional premises of (2) and (3). We need to distinguish carefully between two different claims: (a) that people's belief that there are causal relations of a certain sort produces their belief that George is a bird and (b) that people believe that if there are causal relations of a certain sort then George is a bird. What (5) commits us to is (a), not the less plausible (b).[4]

The limitations of (5) are not hard to see. For example, the causal relations are much too simple. The bird species doesn't cause feathers, even in folk biology. Rather, something about being a bird—maybe having the right genetic structure—causes the properties. Moreover, we often classify objects on the basis of second-hand information—say, because someone informs us that an instance is a bird. In that case, if there are causal relations involved, those relations must run through our informant's ability to recognize and communicate facts about the category. These indirect connections are also apparent in classifying instances as members of artifact categories, such as *pajamas* and *chairs*. Being a chair doesn't cause an object to have a back or seat. If we ask why a particular chair has a back, the answer might be a causal story, but it would reflect design decisions on the part of whoever was responsible for the chair's manufacture. Clearly, then, a procedure like (5) needs to be elaborated with a theory of how people derive causal relations and which of these indirect relations qualify instances as category members. (Of course, for definitional categories, such as *prime number* or *isosceles triangle*, causal relationships may be entirely irrelevant. For these categories, however, we already have a method for classification via arguments like (2).)

There are also questions about specifying the contrast class in the *Concat* premises of (5). This information must be peculiar to the situation in which the classifying occurs, whereas the conditional premises are parts of long-term generic memory. But, of course, the contrast class isn't given in the external situation in the way that George and his properties are. People must infer the relevant contrast class from other facts. If one is touring a zoo then bird, mammal, and fish might be relevant, whereas if one is glancing at a windowsill then bird, vase, and leaf might be the right categories. It might be possible to treat such inferences on a par with (5), where we narrowed the contrast set of categories to those that are "possible" and then narrowed further to the final category. We might start instead with an even larger set of categories and cull the contrast categories on the basis of the situation we are in. An alternative possibility, however, is that the contrast categories depend on the way long-term memory is organized. People may represent coherent facts about specific settings, such as zoos, so that, when they recognize the setting, related information (including the contrast categories) becomes available automatically (Tversky and Hemenway 1983). This is the idea that, in the mid 1970s, prompted many AI and memory researchers to propose larger-scale memory representations—frames (Minsky 1975/1985), scripts (Schank and Abelson 1977), or schemas (Rumelhart 1975). Indeed, many investigators believe that categorizing is just a matter of applying a script or a frame; thus, we should examine how our assumptions about reasoning sit with these proposals.

Frames, Schemas, Theories, and Deduction

The motive behind frames, schemas, and scripts was the idea that skilled cognition depends on integrated packages of information. The usual example is that in comprehending stories we do more than string together the individual sentences of the text; we elaborate these sentences into a coherent structure by bringing to bear our background knowledge about the story's events and objects. The story produces a higher-level memory representation if we are successful in understanding it; but the background facts are parts of higher-level representations, too, according to these theories. They are something like mental encyclopedia entries that we can consult to make predictions or fill in missing information. In fact, we might think of the whole of our long-term memory for generic information as composed of encyclopedia-entry chunks of this sort. The entries would specify facts that are constant across instances; the entry for *bird* would mention egg laying, and the entry for *restaurants* would note that they serve food. Cross-references to schemas for these subconcepts—see *egg*, or see *food*—would also appear, in the form of memory pointers. In addition, the schemas would specify facts that are usually but not invariably associated with the relevant instances: default values that should be assumed unless specifically contravened (birds fly; restaurants have menus). Finally, the entries would have variables that can be instantiated when the schemas are applied to a specific example (the color of a bird, or the location of a restaurant). (See Brachman and Schmolze 1985 for a worked-out version of this idea.)

Research on concepts and categories has also pointed to the need for higher-level representations. Murphy and Medin (1985; see also Medin 1989) invoke lay theories to explain why some sets of instances constitute coherent categories, while others (e.g., the set of all things that are either parts of Atlas missiles or ingredients for cheesecake) appear to be arbitrary assemblages. Similarly, Carey (1985) appeals to children's theories of psychology and biology to explain how they generalize properties from one instance to related ones. I have used the same idea to explain why adults'

category decisions sometimes override their judgments of similarity between instance and category (Rips 1989b, 1991; Rips and Collins, in press).
There is a quibble about whether the sets of beliefs that children, or even
adults, have about such domains are large enough and coherent enough to
qualify as "theories" in the sense in which this term is used in science
or in philosophy of science. But call it what you will; people seem to draw
on a set of beliefs about a category in order to explain why the category
has the instances and the properties it does. Although the emphasis may
be slightly different, these mini-theories seem quite close to schemas or
frames, and it will probably do no harm to identify them.[5] I will use
schema as the cover term for these sorts of structures.

Although I emphasized the logical form of individual mental sentences
in spelling out the details of the theory in part II, there are several reasons
to think that there is no real incompatibility between schema theory and
our deduction system. In the first place, Patrick Hayes (1979) has convinc-
ingly argued that the inferential powers of schemas are all available in
first-order logic. In particular, PSYCOP's representations have all the
important features of schemas identified by Rumelhart (see Rumelhart and
Norman 1988, p. 537): They allow the use of variables; they can express
knowledge at any level of abstraction; they can spell out encyclopedic
information (rather than simple necessary and sufficient features); and they
can serve as classification devices.[6] In fact, these properties were illustrated in the categorization example of the preceding section. The only
inferential property of schemas that goes beyond what I have discussed is
the use of default values to express typical characteristics. Hayes believes
that defaults, too, can be handled in a first-order system if we admit names
that refer to the state of the system's own knowledge base. (I will return to
the problems posed by defaults in the following section.)

The importance of schemas seems to lie, not in their inference powers
(which are quite simple), but in the way they organize long-term memory
and guide retrieval. Schemas are methods for bundling related facts in
long-term memory. From this perspective, however, there is no reason
why the organized information can't itself appear in logical form *à la*
PSYCOP. In fact, the PSYCOP system is already committed to schema-
like structures that relate individual sentences. First, the deduction and
dependency links (e.g., those pictured in figures 8.2–8.6) associate the mental sentences within a proof. The proof itself can be considered a type of
schema, with the links providing retrieval pathways. Second, the routine

for categorization that we considered above also presupposes higher-level organization to ensure that PSYCOP uses the conditional sentences in the order in which they appear in (5). The classification routine operates correctly only if the system tries the third premise before the fourth premise of (5) in attempting to satisfy a *Test* goal. Otherwise, *Test* could be fulfilled without any evaluation of the causal relationships that are supposed to be the key parts of the process. There is some flexibility in the way the sentences in (5) are ordered, but we usually have to observe the given sequence for conditionals that share the same consequent. We could get around this, if we wanted to, by disjoining the antecedents in a single complex conditional. This would force the correct ordering of antecedents, because the Disjunctive Modus Ponens rule that processes such conditionals observes a left-to-right ordering of the disjuncts. If we want to keep the conditionals in their simpler form, however, we need to regard them as parts of a partially ordered structure.

As originally conceived, schemas were permanent units in long-term memory. But the inventors of schemas no longer seem to regard permanence as an important property. Schank (1982) thinks of scripts as structures created on the fly from more fundamental units called "memory organization packets," and Rumelhart, Smolensky, McClelland, and Hinton (1986) view schemas as emerging from temporary activation patterns in a connectionist network. Whether we should regard schemas as static or as dynamic structures in human memory seems to be partly an empirical question—one whose answer might depend on the system's state of learning or on the schema's subject matter. It is also an issue on which we can afford to be neutral. If schemas must be assembled from more elementary units, we can do so by taking the units to be our usual mental sentences. As long as a cognitive system can put together information about a key object or event for purposes of retrieval and can instantiate variables for purposes of inference, then it has nearly all it needs to account for the phenomena usually attributed to schemas.

Natural Deduction, Nonmonotonic Logic, and Truth Maintenance

Schemas appear to be consistent with deduction-based approaches, with one potential exception: default values. The problem is that we often want to make simple inferences on the basis of typical or normal cases. By and large, birds fly, mammals live on land, fruit is sweet, chairs have legs, cars burn gas, cups have handles, and crimes have victims. If we learn that something is a member of one of these categories, then we should conclude, all things being equal, that the typical properties hold. But of course things aren't always equal. We have to acknowledge the existence of flightless birds (ostriches, penguins), aquatic mammals (whales, dolphins), nonsweet fruits (olives, lemons), legless chairs (beanbag chairs, booster chairs), gasless cars (electric cars, bumper cars), handleless cups (styrofoam cups, Chinese teacups), and victimless crimes (littering, jaywalking). These exceptions don't mean that people are wrong to make the default assumptions (in most cases, the inferences are reasonable), but they do make life more difficult for deduction systems.

Minsky (1975/1985) pointed out this problem and stimulated a great deal of research in AI aimed at solving it. Minsky's own solution, and that of many other schema theorists who followed him, was to let the schemas themselves perform the default inferences. If we learn that object$_1$ is a fruit, then the fruit schema provides the information that object$_1$ is sweet. Of course, if we then learn that object$_1$ is an olive, both the olive schema and the fruit schema are activated, and we will get conflicting inferences about the sweetness of this item. In such conflict situations, these theories usually decide in favor of the default from the more specific schema; thus, object$_1$ will be judged not sweet. This specificity principle is simple enough to make it seem plausible that schemas can handle default reasoning on their own, without the support of an external inference engine.

It is not hard to see, however, that there are severe difficulties for schema-based default reasoning. Although we can rely on the specificity rule for simple cases of conflicting defaults, there are other situations in which rival information comes from schemas at roughly the same level of abstraction. To combine an example of Reiter's (1987; see also Reiter and Criscuolo 1981) with one of Tversky and Kahneman (1983), suppose we believe that bank tellers are typically conservative and that feminists are typically not conservative. If we then meet Linda, the famous feminist bank teller, we are left with a situation in which our defaults collide but there is no hope of determining the best inference—conservative or not conservative—on the ground of specificity alone. Conflicts of this sort defy our stereotypes or schemas and call for either withholding the inference (Touretzky 1984) or using some outside strategy to adjudicate it (Hastie et al. 1990; Kunda et al. 1990; Reiter 1980). But if schemas can't resolve the conflict, what can?

Nonmonotonic Logic

A different response to Minsky's problem is to remedy it by modifying the logic responsible for default inferences. (See Ginsberg 1987 and Reiter 1987 for reviews.) Traditional logics are "monotonic" in the sense that the entailments of any set of sentences are also entailments of any superset of those sentences. For example, if an entailment of $\{P_1, P_2, \ldots, P_k\}$ is C, then C is also an entailment of $\{P_1, \ldots, P_k, \ldots, P_n\}$. But, intuitively, this seems wrong. If we deduce $Sweet(object_1)$ from $Fruit(object_1)$, we don't want the result about sweetness once we learn that the object is an olive. To fix this problem, several groups of AI researchers attempted to construct "nonmonotonic logics" that could retract entailments as new information appeared in the database.

One way to proceed, for instance, is to include in the relevant conditionals a provision that the defaults hold as long as the object in question is not abnormal. In the case of sweet fruit, this might take the form of the *default condition* (6).

(6)   IF Fruit(x) AND NOT(Abnormal(x)) THEN Sweet(x).

We would then list the kinds of things we consider abnormal, the *abnormality conditions*. For instance, as (7) notes, olives and lemons are abnormal with respect to sweetness.

(7)   a. IF Olive(x) THEN (Fruit(x) AND Abnormal(x)).
      b. IF Lemon(x) THEN (Fruit(x) AND Abnormal(x)).

Next we would stipulate that the set of objects that are *Abnormal* must be the smallest set satisfying the default and abnormality conditions. We would also stipulate that the objects that are *Sweet* can be any set satisfying the same default and abnormality conditions, plus the restriction just mentioned on *Abnormal*. These stipulations are what McCarthy (1980, 1986) calls the *circumscription* of (6) and (7), with respect to the predicate *Abnormal* and with the variable predicate *Sweet*. For example, suppose the domain of interest contains just three objects—$object_1$, $object_2$, and $object_3$—and suppose we know that $Fruit(object_1)$, $Lemon(object_2)$, and $Olive(object_3)$. Under the default and abnormality conditions in (6) and (7), the extension of *Fruit* is $\{object_1, object_2, object_3\}$, the extension of *Lemon* is $\{object_2\}$, and the extension of *Olive* is $\{object_3\}$. Moreover, the extension of *Abnormal* must include at least $object_2$ and $object_3$, since we declared lemons and olives abnormal in (7). To circumscribe the *Abnormal* predicate in this case means taking its extension to include *no more* than these two objects, so that *Abnormal* = {object$_2$, object$_3$}. What about *Sweet*, the main predicate of interest in this example? Well, since object$_1$ is in *Fruit* and not in *Abnormal*, it must be in *Sweet* by the default condition (6).

Circumscription gives the intuitively correct result in our example. If all we know of object$_1$ is that it is a fruit, then we should take it to be sweet on the basis of our beliefs. However, if we should later find out that object$_1$ is an olive, then our conclusion must change. Since olives are abnormal by (7a), the extension of *Abnormal* is now forced to include object$_1$ as well as object$_2$ and object$_3$. But the default condition says only that normal fruits are sweet. So object$_1$ is not necessarily sweet in this case, and this blocks the default inference. Circumscription produces nonmonotonic inferences, because new knowledge about abnormal cases reduces the number of instances eligible for default conclusions. In this example, of course, we are using the predicate *Abnormal* in a way that is tacitly linked to sweetness. Lemons and olives are abnormal fruits with respect to sweetness, but they are perfectly normal fruits in other ways (say, in having seeds and in growing on trees). So we need to distinguish different abnormality predicates for different typical characteristics of fruits: one for being sweet, another for having seeds, a third for growing on trees, and so on.

In our sweet fruit example, we followed the usual practice of discussing default reasoning as proceeding from knowledge of category membership (i.e., object$_1$ is a fruit) to the conclusion that the instance has typical properties of the category (object$_1$ is sweet). However, default assumptions might be made in the opposite direction as well. This seems to be exactly what we did in reasoning from *George has feathers* to *George is a bird* in the category decision of the preceding section: If George has feathers, then, unless George is abnormal in some way, he is a bird. We can make the circumscription trick that yielded the default inference above apply to categorizing just by reversing the position of the predicates representing the category and its property, since the logic is indifferent to which predicate is which. In place of (6), we would have *IF Feathered(x) AND NOT(Abnormal(x)) THEN Bird(x)*, and in place of (7) we would have sentences like *IF Arrow(x) THEN Abnormal(x)*. This suggests that circumscription and other forms of nonmonotonic logic might succeed where we failed earlier; they might provide a purely deductive solution to the problem of categorizing.

Unfortunately, though, nonmonotonic logics are less than ideal for cognitive purposes. First, despite the fact that they have been developed by AI investigators, nonmonotonic logics don't lend themselves to simple implementations. Circumscription, in its general form, can be stated only in second-order logic. But second-order logic is not complete—there are no algorithms that can determine whether an arbitrary argument is valid. Much the same is true for other forms of nonmonotonic logic: There are no general ways to compute the proper nonmonotonic conclusions from a given database of beliefs. As we saw in the case of PSYCOP, incompleteness is not necessarily a problem. It may be possible to implement a significant fragment of nonmonotonic logic that achieves much of what this logic was intended for, but this remains to be shown.[7] (See Lifschitz 1985 for some special cases where circumscription can be reduced to first-order sentences.) Second, these logics don't seem to reflect the deliberations that actually underlie human reasoning with defaults (Harman 1986; Israel 1980; McDermott 1987). In these situations we seem to go along with the main conclusion (e.g., object$_1$ is sweet) even while acknowledging that the range of potential exceptions (nonsweet fruits) is open-ended—fruit may be rotten, unripe, injected with quinine, and so on. But then we must also believe that the result of circumscription is false, since circumscription forces the conclusion that abnormal cases are restricted to those explicitly stated. Although there is a perfectly valid deductive argument from the circumscription of (6) and (7) and $Fruit(object_1)$ to $Sweet(object_1)$, we cannot use this argument to sanction our belief that $Sweet(object_1)$, because we don't believe that the circumscription of (6) and (7) is true. Instead, we regard $Sweet(object_1)$ as a plausible or inductively strong conclusion from our general knowledge.[8]

The same negative lesson applies to categorizing. In deciding that feathery George is a bird, we do so in the face of the fact that there is an open class of feathery nonbirds (arrows, pillows, hats, people who have been tarred and feathered, etc.). Since we regard the result of circumscription as false (it is not the case that feathery nonbirds are confined to an explicit list of exceptions), we can't use circumscription as a deductive ground for our belief that George is a bird. What this means is not that deduction has no role to play in producing this conclusion, but rather that the conclusion doesn't follow by a deductively correct inference from other beliefs. Even in deduction systems, there is no need to suppose that every belief in the database either is an axiom or follows deductively from axioms.

There is, however, a remaining problem for deduction systems. If we conclude *Isa(George,bird)* by some nondemonstrative means (as in (5)) and then on closer inspection decide *NOT(Isa(George,bird))*, how do we avoid troubles caused by the contradiction? A possible solution comes from another AI innovation: truth-maintenance systems.

Truth Maintenance

A truth-maintenance system (TMS) is a routine for maintaining the logical consistency of a database for an AI problem solver (de Kleer 1986; Doyle 1979; Forbus and de Kleer 1993; McAllester 1978, 1982). Strictly speaking, these systems have little to do with the actual truth value of the data, and "database consistency maintenance" would be a more accurate way to describe what they do. "Truth maintenance," however, is the term that has stuck. In a typical application, the problem solver plugs along independently, making assumptions and applying its own set of inference rules to derive further information. The problem solver, for example, might be solving the Towers of Hanoi or troubleshooting an electronic circuit. The TMS monitors the assumptions and consequences that the problem solver draws. If a contradiction arises, the TMS identifies the set of assumptions responsible and the consequences that depend on them. Thus, the TMS makes it easy to retract assumptions (and dependent information) once it becomes clear that they are faulty. In addition, the TMS inspects the database to ensure that there are no circular beliefs in which the problem solver uses assumption A to derive B and also uses B to derive A. In carrying out these tasks, the TMS doesn't care how the problem solver arrives at its consequences; it might do so by means of deductively correct inferences, inductively strong inferences, or mere guesses. The TMS simply guarantees that these processes, whatever they are, will not lead to an incoherent set of beliefs.

Since TMSs are in charge of ridding databases of contradictions, they seem to be exactly what we need to take care of the problem of second thoughts about George's birdiness or object$_1$'s sweetness. But they provide less help than we might expect, even though they provide an important method for managing assumptions. Notice, first, that many of the benefits of truth maintenance already exist in PSYCOP in virtue of its natural-deduction framework. As we saw in chapter 4, PSYCOP's dependency links connect the assumptions and premises of a proof to the sentences that depend on them. PSYCOP also keeps a record of the converse relation. Every sentence in a proof contains pointers to the assumptions on which it depends, and every assumption contains pointers to the consequences that depend on it. Thus, it is a simple process to identify the assumptions that produce a contradiction; all that is necessary is to follow the (converse) dependency links from the contradictory sentences. The union of these assumptions is the set that is responsible. (For example, if P has converse dependency pointers to assumptions Q and R, and $NOT\ P$ has converse dependency pointers to assumptions R and S, then the set $\{Q, R, S\}$ is itself faulty—a *nogood*, in TMS terminology.) Clearly, we also need to extend this facility to assertions that PSYCOP produces by nondeductive means. For example, when the sentence $Isa(George,bird)$ is entered in memory as the result of the classification procedure in (5), PSYCOP will need to record the fact that it depends on some of the assumptions that appear as (5)'s premises. Then, if later inferences lead us to conclude $NOT(Isa(George,bird))$, we can reexamine the assumptions that landed us in this mess.

More important, truth maintenance doesn't grapple with the crux of the problem that we started with: Of two contradictory propositions, which one should we believe? If we have managed to infer that object$_1$ is both sweet and not sweet, how do we resolve this contradiction? Although these systems can identify the assumptions that cause the contradictory result, they leave open how these assumptions should change. Ruling out inconsistent assumptions usually isn't enough to determine which of the consistent sets warrant our belief. For purposes of philosophy (and perhaps AI), we need normative rules about how to change our minds in the face of conflicting evidence (Goldman 1986; Harman 1986; Israel 1980); for purposes of psychology, we also need descriptive information on how people deal with the same sort of conflict. Implementing these rules amounts to placing a priority ordering on sets of assumptions, but coming up with the rules, both normative and descriptive, is a core problem of cognitive science.

Open Questions

In this chapter we have tried to gain some perspective on our model by viewing it in a larger cognitive context. The effort has been to show that a deduction system like PSYCOP can serve as a type of cognitive architecture—one much on a par with production-based systems such as ACT*

(Anderson 1983) and Soar (Newell 1990). That this is possible should come as no surprise, since production systems are a kind of special case of the logical approach we are considering—one in which the only rules are modus ponens and universal instantiation. The fact-retrieval and categorization examples that we developed at the beginning of this chapter demonstrate how a deduction-based system can account for these typically cognitive operations. Of course, there are many types of cognitive skills, and our two examples don't represent all of them. Nevertheless, it is not too hard to extrapolate these examples to other cognitive tasks that require symbol manipulation. Whether this exhausts the domain of cognition—whether there are "subsymbolic" processes that are properly cognitive—is a delicate and controversial issue (see, e.g., Rumelhart et al. 1986 and Fodor and Pylyshyn 1988). By most estimates, however, the progress in adapting nonsymbolic models to higher tasks—inference, problem solving, decision making, language processing—hasn't been startling, and for these tasks it doesn't seem too outlandish to pin our hopes on a symbol manipulator like PSYCOP. The most successful connectionist systems for inference (see, e.g., Ajjanagadde and Shastri 1989) encode predicate-argument structures, bind variables, and operate according to principles such as modus ponens.

But if deduction really has this directorial role, we seem to be left with a puzzle. How do inductively generated beliefs come about if the cognitive system operates on deductive principles? This puzzle arises because we think of a belief as the conclusion of some supporting argument. Since by hypothesis the argument can't be deductively correct, it must be an argument of some other sort—an inductive argument. But, of course, the only arguments that a system like PSYCOP can handle are deductively correct ones; so it looks as if inductively generated beliefs are impossible in PSYCOP.

The considerations in this chapter suggest that the way out of this dilemma is to suppose that there are ways of creating and justifying a belief other than making it the conclusion of a special sort of argument (Harman 1986). The categorization example is a case in point, since the critical belief that George is a bird was not the conclusion of the argument that produced it. From the point of view of the system, the belief was a side effect of the deduction process. This doesn't mean that the belief was unjustified; on the contrary, it was justified by a kind of causal theory about the properties of category members. However, the example does suggest that critical beliefs need not be *represented* as conclusions, and this allows us to reconcile the presence of these beliefs with our overall framework.

Of course, it is one thing to admit beliefs with inductive support and quite another to give a general explanation for them. I have tried to argue here that, for psychological purposes, neither schema theory nor non-monotonic logics give a satisfactory account of these beliefs. Similarly, Osherson et al. (1986) have examined a number of psychological proposals about inductive support and found all of them lacking (see also Rips 1990a). It may be, as Osherson et al. suggest, that no general theory of induction is possible and that inductive support can take a variety of forms for different purposes. We may have to content ourselves with a number of smaller-scale theories like the one sketched for categorization. For our purposes, though, we can reserve judgment about this issue. If our project can provide a reasonable cognitive framework for specifying possible forms of inductive support, we will have done well enough.

Alternative Psychological Theories: Rule-Based Systems

Rules always come right if you wait quietly.
Kenneth Grahame, *The Reluctant Dragon*

Psychological theories of deduction seem to divide into those that are based on rules that are sensitive to an argument's logical form and those that are based on other properties of the argument or its context. I will use this split to organize the discussion in this chapter and the next, describing rule-based systems here and non-rule-based alternatives in chapter 10. It is convenient to do this, and much of the debate in the research literature has been fought under these banners. But this distinction shouldn't be pushed too far. In PSYCOP we have a clear example of what a rule-based system is like, and there are several other proposals with much the same character. It is also clear that a theory stipulating that people decide about the correctness of arguments on a purely random basis wouldn't qualify as rule-based. Although rules may be involved (e.g., "valid" if a coin lands on heads and "invalid" if on tails), this sort of rule obviously isn't sensitive to logical form. But the distinction is rarely this clear-cut.

In distinguishing rule-based and non-rule-based theories, investigators tend to have in mind prototype rules, such as IF Elimination and AND Introduction, that operate on linguistically structured representations, that center on the usual connectives and quantifiers, and that are parts of standard logical systems such as classical predicate logic. If an investigator devises a system whose principles deviate from this prototype, then there is a temptation to say that the system is not based on "rules." For example, it is easy to come up with principles that implement the atmosphere effect in syllogisms (Begg and Denny 1969). These principles depend on the presence of SOME and NOT (or NO), just as standard rules do, but they produce conclusions that are far from acceptable in either scholastic or CPL systems. (See chapters 1 and 7 for discussions of atmosphere.) Likewise, some psychologists have proposed that there are principles that capture inferences based on expressions of permission or obligation, such as the modal *must* in the sentence *She must be 16 before she can legally drive* (Cheng and Holyoak 1985; Cheng et al. 1986). These principles seem to be defined over linguistic structures, at least on some views, but they go beyond the logical connectives in CPL.[1] It is also possible to find psychological theories whose principles yield exactly the same valid arguments as in the sentential portion of CPL, and whose representations include the logical constant "$\neg$"(i.e., *NOT*) and proposition symbols analogous to *P* and Q but don't otherwise have typical structure. Johnson-Laird et al. (1992) fiercely defend theories of the latter kind as not based on formal rules.

If the principles of a deduction theory differ from more typical rules, it is seductive to claim that the principles aren't rules (or aren't formal rules, or aren't logical rules). In the same vein, because the more typical rules operate on syntactically structured logical form, it is tempting to say that the new principles aren't "syntactic" but something else; "pragmatic" (Cheng and Holyoak 1985) and "semantic" (Johnson-Laird 1983) are the obvious alternatives. There are differences among these theories, but neither the rule/non-rule distinction nor the syntactic/semantic/pragmatic distinction conveys them appropriately (see Stenning 1992). It is important to keep in mind, as we examine these theories, that all the serious ones operate according to principles (i.e., routines, procedures, algorithms) that inspect the format of the argument's mental representation. Each of them depends indirectly on some method (usually unspecified) for translating natural-language sentences into the chosen format. Each retains options for consulting background information from long-term memory and selecting responses in accord with the systems' goals. With a clear view of these common properties, it becomes easier to see that the main differences among the theories lie in the interaction of the principles and the representational format. In this chapter we will consider deduction theories that are similar to PSYCOP in sticking fairly close to the prototype of principles keyed to logical constants. Chapter 10 strays further afield in examining theories based on heuristics and diagrams.

Alternative Theories Based on Natural Deduction

PSYCOP has a number of ancestors and siblings that rely directly on natural-deduction rules, and in some ways they provide the clearest comparison to what has been done in previous chapters. However, it is not always easy to devise experimental tests that discriminate cleanly among these theories. Although there is no shortage of research in this area, contrasts are difficult, both because the theories cover somewhat different domains and because they continue to evolve as the result of new findings. There are no theories that cover both sentential and general predicate-argument structures in the way that PSYCOP does, but Osherson's (1976) theory handles certain modal arguments (with operators for time, necessity, and obligation) to which PSYCOP does not extend. Thus, the overlap between the domains of the theories is only partial. Braine et al. (1984) have reported several experiments that may help in discriminating among the natural-deduction models; however, the message from these studies is somewhat mixed.

Despite the difficulty in contrasting the models, it is informative to look at the array of options available within the natural-deduction approach. In addition to Osherson's and Braine's models, we should examine some early research by Newell and Simon (1972), who can claim to be the first to study an entire deduction system experimentally. The only remaining proposal along these lines is one by Johnson-Laird (1975); but since Johnson-Laird no longer regards this theory as correct, I will skip over it here, returning to his current approach in chapter 10. (See Rips 1983 for comments on the earlier theory.)

GPS Revisited

As was noted in chapter 3, Newell and Simon's goal was broader than developing a theory of deduction; their concern was to formulate and test a general model of human problem solving. Their book concerns itself with a computational theory called GPS (the General Problem Solver). According to the GPS approach, problem solvers represent internally the overall goal that would constitute a solution to the problem at hand. They also describe their own present state of knowledge in terms that are commensurate with the goal state. By comparing their current state to the goal state, they are able to detect differences that they must eliminate in order to solve the problem. For example, in the logic problems that Newell and Simon looked at, the goal state was a description of the conclusion of an argument, the initial state was a description of the premises of the argument, and the relevant differences were the structural discrepancies between the premises and the conclusion. One such difference might be that the atomic sentences occur in a different order in the premises than in the conclusion; another might be that a particular atomic sentence appears more often in the conclusion than in the premises; a third possibility could be that there is a connective in the conclusion that isn't in the premises; and so on.

GPS reduces the discrepancies between the current state and the goal state by what Newell and Simon call "operators," which are triggered by

the differences they are qualified to eliminate. Applying one of these operators to the current state causes the problem solver to advance to a new
state. Differences between the new state and the goal state are then re-
assessed, and new operators are called into play to reduce these residual
differences. This process continues until the problem is solved or aban-
doned. In the logic context, the operators are deduction rules that allow
one sentence to be rewritten as another, just as in the sort of model
discussed above. Thus, OR Introduction might be used as an operator to
eliminate the difference between a premise S and a conclusion $S \; OR \; T$. If
these operators don't quite apply as they stand, subgoals may be set up to
achieve some state to which the original operators do apply. This may
involve applying other operators, which may invoke other subgoals, and
so on. The general principle of solving problems by applying operators in
order to reduce differences is *means-ends analysis*.

Newell and Simon's interest in logic was confined to its use in testing the
GPS theory; they weren't concerned with how people naturally tackle
reasoning problems, or with the rules or operators that people intuitively
know. As a consequence, the logic experiments they report are extremely
artificial. In fact, although the questions that the subjects answered in
these experiments were standard sentential logic problems, the subjects
were probably unaware that the problems had anything to do with *and, or,
if,* and *not,* because all the problems appeared in symbolic form rather
than as English expressions. Instead of asking the subjects to decide
whether, for example, *(IF R THEN NOT P) AND (IF NOT R THEN
Q)* implies *NOT ((NOT Q) AND P)*, they phrased the problem as in (1).

(1) $\quad \dfrac{(R \supset \sim P) \cdot (\sim R \supset Q)}{\sim (\sim Q \cdot P)}$

In some logic systems, "$\cdot$" is an alternative notation for AND, "$\sim$" for
NOT, and "$\supset$" for IF ... THEN. But the subjects were not told about
these equivalences. They were told only that they were to "recode" the first
string into the second one.

Newell and Simon conducted their experiments by giving the subjects a
list of 12 rules for transforming one expression into another. The subjects
could consult these rules whenever they wanted. One of the rules, for
example, was stated in the form shown here in (2).

(2) $\quad A \supset B \leftrightarrow \sim A \vee B$

This meant that the subjects could recode a string that matched the right- or the left-hand side into one that matched the other side. The subjects were then given a set of starting strings and a target string, with instructions that they should try to transform the starting strings into the target string using only the rules on their list. (This experimental method had originally been suggested by Moore and Anderson (1954).) The problems that Newell and Simon presented to their subjects were very difficult ones, involving as many as 11 steps in their derivations. The subjects were asked to think aloud, and the transcripts of their monologues constitute the data from the experiment. Thus, the subjects' task wasn't just to determine if a derivation was possible; they had to produce explicitly each intermediate step. (They were not allowed to write anything down; the experimenters wrote down the steps for them.)

The nature of the data makes it very difficult to summarize them neatly. Newell and Simon broke down their protocols into individual problem-solving episodes that centered around the application of one of the rules. They then qualitatively compared the sequence of these episodes for each individual subject with the sequence that the GPS program had generated for the same problem. Although it is not always clear how the investigators determined that a subject was trying to apply a certain rule at a given moment, the protocols do seem to support the GPS orientation. It seems true, for example, that the subjects tried to achieve the goal state by applying rules that looked relevant on the basis of superficial differences between the premise strings and the conclusion strings. For example, they talk about applying the rule shown here as (2) if the premises contained a formula with a horseshoe ($\supset$) and the conclusion contained a formula with a wedge ($\vee$). If these rules did not apply to the strings as given, the subjects tried to make the strings fit the rules, taking this as a subgoal and achieving it with additional rules.

This research served Newell and Simon's purposes in demonstrating that GPS could be applied to symbol-pushing problems of this sort. But, of course, it is much less clear whether these results are representative of the subjects' deductive reasoning. It is easy to imagine that the subjects would have employed different strategies if the meaning of the symbols had been explained to them. This could have made the true relevance of particular rules much more apparent, allowing more direct solutions and less dependence on the surface appearance of the rules and formulas. A related problem is that the rules that Newell and Simon handed their

subjects may not be the ones that the subjects would have employed naturally had they been permitted to justify the correctness of the arguments
according to their own logical intuitions. The rules on their list might not
correspond to psychologically primitive rules. Rule 2 in particular is one
that we have rejected as part of the PSYCOP system.

Some evidence of the generality of Newell and Simon's results comes
from a pair of experiments by Reed, McMillan, and Chambers (1979). In
the second of their studies, subjects were given six of Newell and Simon's
problems under conditions approximating those of the original experiment. Half of these subjects saw the rules and problems in the form of
uninterpreted symbols, as in the original study. In fact, Reed et al. went
further in disguising the connectives, using novel symbols—* for AND, ¢
for OR, and # for IF ... THEN—to eliminate the possibility that subjects
would recognize the symbols from math courses they had taken. The other
half of the subjects saw the same rules and problems, but were told about
the meaning of the connectives. They knew, in other words, that ¢ meant
OR and so on. Thus, if there was any benefit to understanding the natural-
language counterparts for these strings of symbols, the subjects in the
second group should have turned in better performances than those in the
first group. The results of this experiment were quite surprising, however,
since they indicated that, if anything, knowing the meaning of the symbols
hurt rather than helped the subjects. Overall, the two groups of subjects
were equally able to solve the problems: 74% of the subjects in the Meaning group and 75% in the No Meaning group were successful. Among the
successful subjects, however, those in the No Meaning group reached their
solutions faster. The average solution time for the No Meaning group was
410 second, versus 472 seconds for the Meaning group—a difference of
about a minute. An analysis of the derivations showed that the No Meaning subjects applied fewer irrelevant rules in the course of their problem
solving. In this respect, then, Newell and Simon's conclusions appear to be
more general than might be expected: Merely knowing the interpretation
of the symbols did not improve the subjects' strategies. It is still possible
to object, though, that the Meaning group's relatively poor performance
could have been due to the unnaturalness of the rules. To take an extreme
case, suppose that to subjects in the Meaning group the rules made no
sense at all as ways of drawing inferences from sentences containing *and*,
or, *if*, and *not*. For these subjects, the rules would have been just as arbitrary with respect to English connectives as with respect to the meaning-

less symbols. Forcing the subjects to apply intuitively inappropriate rules to these familiar connectives might even have confused them.

Reed et al. provide some data on the latter point, too. In a separate experiment, subjects were given arguments formed from each of Newell and Simon's rules. For example, rule 2 above would have appeared as the two arguments: shown in (2').

(2') $\dfrac{A \# B}{-A \notin B}$ $\dfrac{-A \notin B}{A \# B}$

Like the subjects in the Meaning group, these subjects were informed about the nature of the connectives. The subjects then decided whether the conclusions followed from the premises and rated their confidence on a scale from -3 (for "very certain that the conclusion doesn't follow") to $+3$ (for "very certain the conclusion follows"). As a control, invalid arguments were included among those that the subjects rated. Reed et al. found that, although most of the arguments corresponding to Newell and Simon's rules received positive confidence, there were three arguments whose average ratings were negative. The two arguments in (2') were among these, consistent with PSYCOP's rejection of this conditional transformation principle. This rule was also the one subjects were most likely to misapply in the derivation task that we considered earlier. The third negatively rated item had $-(-A * -B)$ (i.e., *NOT (NOT A AND NOT B)*) as premise and $A \notin B$ (i.e., *(A OR B)*) as conclusion, an argument that PSYCOP also fails to deduce with its current stock of inference rules. So there seems to be warrant for the suggestion that inferences made with some of Newell and Simon's rules might have seemed quite foreign to the subjects and might have promoted problem-solving strategies that aren't typically used in deduction.

Newell and Simon's original experiment was, of course, never intended as a study of psychologically natural inference making. Their focus was on symbol transformation strategies, and for this purpose there is a tremendous advantage in controlling the rules that subjects use. Problem-solving strategies are much easier to spot in thinking-aloud (or any other) data when you know the elementary operations that subjects have available than when you have to infer simultaneously both the operations and the strategies. But something like this more complex process seems to be necessary in domains such as this, since there appears to be no simpler method to guide us toward the right choice of psychological primitives.

Osherson's Models of Deduction

If we abandon Newell and Simon's experimental task, we face the method-ological problem of studying deduction under conditions where we have no prior assurance about the psychological reality of either the inference rules or the manner in which they are applied. There may be several ways to proceed in these circumstances. One possibility is to construct a model including both kinds of assumptions, draw predictions from the model, and hope that the predictions will be sufficiently accurate to lend credibil-ity to the whole package. The first person to adopt this approach in study-ing deduction was Daniel Osherson, who used it in his work *Logical Abilities in Children* (1974b, 1975, 1976).

The details of Osherson's theory change slightly from volume to vol-ume, but in essence he proposes that people have a stock of mental infer-ence rules that apply in fixed order to the premises of an argument. Thus, unlike Newell and Simon, Osherson assumes that people have internal natural deduction rules, not merely that they can use externally presented rules. One of Osherson's (1975, table 11.1) rules for sentential reasoning is the DeMorgan rule, shown here in (3), with the provision ("helping condi-tion") that neither *P OR Q* nor *Q OR P* appear in the conclusion of the argument.

(3) $\dfrac{\text{NOT (P OR Q)}}{\text{(NOT P) AND (NOT Q)}}$

Another example is a rule for contraposing conditionals shown here as (4).

(4) $\dfrac{\text{IF P THEN Q}}{\text{IF NOT Q THEN NOT P}}$

Here the helping condition stipulates that the rule applies only if a sub-formula of *P* and a subformula of *Q* appear in the conclusion of the argument as a whole; moreover, these subformulas must be negated in the conclusion if they are unnegated in the sentence to which the rule applied (or they must be unnegated in the conclusion if negated in the original sentence).

According to this model, subjects mentally check the rules in a fixed order until they find one that is relevant to the premise. (Osherson's model operates only with single-premise arguments.) This first relevant rule is then applied to produce a single new sentence. Subjects then begin again from the top of their internal list of rules, scanning to see if any apply to the new sentence. This process continues until either the conclusion is produced or no rule is relevant. In the first case the subjects will declare that the argument follows, in the second that it doesn't follow. Thus, rules like (3) and (4) should be understood to mean that if the last sentence in the proof is of the form shown at the top and if the helping condition holds, then the next sentence in the proof should be the one on the bottom. Osherson's rules all operate in a forward direction, but the helping conditions check the conclusion as well as the last assertion. This sensitivity to the conclusion keeps the model's derivations from drifting in the wrong direction (see chapter 3). However, unlike GPS and PSYCOP, Osherson's model has no provision for subgoals (other than the conclusion itself). This means that it is impossible for the system to return to a previous point in the proof if it has applied a rule that branches away from the conclusion. Osherson's theory also has no place for suppositions; each sentence of a derivation either is the premise or follows from it by means of an inference rule.

The rigid structure of this procedure means that Osherson's model sometimes misses inferences that seem no more complex than ones it handles. For example, the model easily copes with the argument from *IF P THEN Q* to *(IF P THEN (Q OR R)) OR (S AND T)*, but it fails with the formally similar one from *IF P THEN Q* to *(IF P THEN (Q OR R)) OR (P AND T)* (Rips 1983). To prove the first argument, the system transforms the premise to *IF P THEN (Q OR R)* and then transforms this last sentence into the conclusion. It is possible to prove the second argument in precisely the same way, but the model overlooks it. Because of the presence of *P AND T* in the conclusion, the model rewrites the premise as *IF (P AND T) THEN Q*, which throws it off the track of the correct proof. This mistake is a fatal one, since there is no possibility of returning to a previous choice point.

To assess this model, Osherson asked his subjects—who were in upper-level grade school, junior high, or high school—to evaluate relatively simple arguments expressed in English. A typical argument (from Osherson 1975, table 15.2) reads as in (5).

(5)   If Peter is ice skating, then Martha either goes to a movie or she
       visits a museum.

       If Martha does not go to a movie and she does not visit a museum,
       then Peter is not ice skating.

The stimulus arguments were ones whose proofs were fairly short, usually two to four lines long in Osherson's system. The conclusion of (5), for example, follows from the premise via one application of rule 4—to get *IF NOT (Martha goes to a movie OR she visits a museum) THEN NOT Peter is ice skating*—and then one application of rule 3. In addition, the stimuli included one-step arguments that corresponded to the individual deduction rules, much as in the experiment of Reed et al. For example, Osherson's rules given here as (3) and (4) were associated with arguments (3′) and (4′), respectively.

(3′)   It is not true that Bill either mows the lawn or rakes the leaves.

Bill does not mow the lawn and Bill does not rake the leaves.

(4′)   If Martha is the apartment manager, then the tenants are satisfied.

If the tenants are not satisfied, then Martha is not the apartment manager.

As we will see, these one-step arguments are crucial in testing the theory. For each argument, the subjects indicated either that the conclusion followed from the premises, that it didn't follow, or that they couldn't decide. They then rated the difficulty of all the arguments they had said were correct.

In order to evaluate his model, Osherson makes use of two predictions that he calls the "inventory" and the "additivity" requirements. The inventory prediction rests on the idea that a subject's correct acceptance of one of the multi-step arguments must be due to his possessing all the rules needed to derive it. For this reason, we would expect the same subject to accept all the one-step arguments based on those rules. Conversely, if a subject incorrectly rejects a multi-step argument, then he must be missing one or more of the rules that figure in its proof. So we should expect the subject to reject one or more of the one-step arguments that correspond to these rules. For instance, since a proof of argument (5) involves rules (3) and (4) according to Osherson's theory, subjects who judge (5) correct should also say that the two single-step arguments (3′) and (4′) are correct. But subjects who judge (5) to be incorrect should say that at least one of (3′) and (4′) is also incorrect.

Osherson's additivity requirement also makes use of the relationship between the multi-step and the single-step arguments. It seems reasonable to suppose that the difficulty of deciding whether an argument is correct should be related to the difficulty connected with the rules in its proof. The difficulty of (5), whose proof involves rules (3) and (4), should depend on the difficulty of the latter rules. So the judged difficulty of (5) should vary positively with that of the one-step arguments (3') and (4'). To test this relationship, Osherson simply correlated the difficulty rating of the multi-step arguments with the sum of the difficulty ratings of the relevant single-step arguments.

At least at first sight, the inventory and additivity predictions seem quite reasonable; but the experiments Osherson conducted offered somewhat limited support for them. In his third volume (Osherson 1975), which is concerned with sentential reasoning, the percentage of inventory predictions that are true of the data ranges from 60 to 90 across experiments, and the additivity correlations vary between 0.57 and 0.83. In volume 4 (Osherson 1976), which is devoted to reasoning with quantifiers and modals, the inventory predictions vary from 61% to 77% correct, and the additivity correlations vary from 0.29 to 0.90.

In an epilogue to the final volume, Osherson himself regards the additivity and inventory predictions as "bad ideas." The basis of his criticism is that the predictions depend on the idea that evaluating a rule embodied in a single-step argument is equivalent to applying that rule in the context of a larger proof. But this needn't be the case. It may be easier for subjects to recognize a rule as applicable, for instance, if that rule applies to the premise of a problem than if it applies to an intermediate line in the proof. After all, the premise is actually written out for the subjects, whereas the intermediate lines are present, according to the theory, only in the subjects' memory. If that is the case, an inventory prediction may easily fail for the wrong reason. Subjects might be very good at recognizing that rules (3) and (4) are appropriate when each of those rules is embodied in an argument of its own. However, the same subjects may fail to see that rule (3) is applicable in a multi-step argument in which rule (4) also appears. If they reject the multi-step argument on this basis, then they will have violated the inventory prediction.

This suggests that the inventory and additivity requirements may have underestimated the worth of Osherson's model, but there is also a possibility that the predictions give us too rosy a picture of the model's success. Suppose that part of the difficulty of a reasoning problem is simply due to parsing the premises and the conclusion. In fact, when subjects think aloud as they solve one of Osherson's problems, they often repeat the premises over and over as if trying to comprehend them (Rips 1983). Of course, it is difficult to tell how much of this is due to difficulty in parsing the sentences and how much is part of the reasoning process itself; but assume that there is at least some component due to parsing alone. But notice that parsing difficulty for a multi-step argument will probably be shared by some of the corresponding single-step arguments. In the earlier example, the premise of the multi-step argument (5) has much the same syntactic form as the premise of the single-step argument (4'), since both are conditionals. Thus, if subjects' difficulty ratings in part reflect the difficulty of parsing, this will tend to inflate the additivity correlations for reasons that have little to do with inference.

There are some grounds, then, for thinking that Osherson's tests were too stringent, and others for thinking they were too lax. Unfortunately, there is no way to determine the relative seriousness of these problems, and this leaves us uncertain about the strength of Osherson's models. Nevertheless, Osherson's general ideas of mental rules and mental proof were groundbreaking, and they were certainly the main inspiration for the project reported in part II and for the work of Braine and his colleagues on similar natural-deduction systems.

Natural Logic According to Braine, Reiser, and Rumain

Braine's theory is an attempt to specify the natural-deduction schemas that underlie sentential reasoning; thus, it falls squarely within the tradition of mental rules. The schemas themselves exhibit a few changes from one presentation to the next (e.g., Braine 1978, 1990; Braine and O'Brien 1991; Braine and Rumain 1983); but we can concentrate here on the theory as Braine, Reiser, and Rumain (1984) set it out, since this appears to be its most complete statement.

The rules of Braine et al. include versions of what I have called AND Introduction, AND Elimination, Double Negation Elimination, Disjunctive Modus Ponens, Disjunctive Syllogism, Conjunctive Syllogism, Dilemma, IF Elimination, IF Introduction, and NOT Introduction. (See tables 4.1 and 4.2.) Braine et al. generalize some of these rules to operate with conjunctions and disjunctions of more than two sentences; for example, the AND Introduction rule operates on sentences $P_1, P_2, \ldots, P_n$ to yield the sentence P_1 AND P_2 AND $\ldots$ AND P_n. The multi-place connectives, however, do not play a role in the predictions for their experiments. There are also three technical rules for introducing suppositions and recognizing contradictions. And finally, there are three rules that do not play a part in the theory of chapter 4. One of these allows sentences of the form *P OR NOT P* to appear at any point in a proof. The other two are a rule for distributing AND over OR and a variation on Dilemma, as shown here in (6) and (7).

(6) a. $\dfrac{P \text{ AND } (Q_1 \text{ OR } \ldots \text{ OR } Q_n)}{(P \text{ AND } Q_1) \text{ OR } \ldots \text{ OR } (P \text{ AND } Q_n)}$

    b. $\dfrac{(P \text{ AND } Q_1) \text{ OR } \ldots \text{ OR } (P \text{ AND } Q_n)}{P \text{ AND } (Q_1 \text{ OR } \ldots \text{ OR } Q_n)}$

(7) $\begin{array}{l} P_1 \text{ OR } \ldots \text{ OR } P_n \\ \text{IF } P_1 \text{ THEN } Q_1 \\ \quad \vdots \\ \underline{\text{IF } P_n \text{ THEN } Q_n} \\ Q_1 \text{ OR } \ldots \text{ OR } Q_n \end{array}$

PSYCOP handles inferences like (7) with a combination of OR Elimination and IF Elimination, and it handles (6) by means of AND Introduction, AND Elimination, OR Introduction, and OR Elimination. Rules (6b) and (7) could be incorporated in PSYCOP as forward rules, which is roughly how they function in the theory of Braine et al. However, (6a) would create difficulties for PSYCOP as a forward rule, and we will see that it is also a trouble spot for Braine et al.

The theory proposes that people apply the deduction rules in a two-part procedure (Braine et al. 1984, table III). The first (*direct*) part applies a subset of the rules in a forward direction to the premises of an argument. (If the conclusion of the argument happens to be a conditional sentence, then the process treats the antecedent of the conditional as a premise and its consequent as the conclusion to be proved.) The rules included in the direct part are AND Elimination, Double Negation Elimination, IF Elimination, Disjunctive Modus Ponens, Conjunctive Syllogism, Disjunctive Syllogism, and Dilemma, plus (6) and (7). This step can also use AND Introduction if it enables one of the other direct rules. If the conclusion of the argument is among the sentences produced in this way, then the process stops with a "true" decision. If the conclusion of the argument contradicts one of these sentences, then the process stops with a "false" decision. Otherwise, the direct process is repeated, much as in the British Museum algorithm (chapter 3), until a decision is reached or it produces no new sentences. During a repetition, the process cannot apply a rule to the same sentences it has used on a previous round, and it cannot produce a sentence that it has already deduced. If the direct process fails to reach a "true" or a "false" decision, then an indirect process begins, implementing strategies (such as NOT Introduction) that call for suppositions. Braine et al. believe that the direct process is common to all or most subjects, whereas the indirect process may require more problem solving and produce some individual differences. Although Braine et al. give examples of indirect strategies, they do not provide a complete description.

Even if we confine our examination to the direct process, however, the model of Braine et al. can't be quite correct as currently stated, since it leads to infinite loops. Consider, for example, any argument with premises that include P and Q OR R. Then the derivation shown in (8) is consistent with the direct schemas of Braine et al.

(8) a. P   Premise

   b. Q OR R   Premise

   c. P AND (Q OR R)   AND Intro. (from a,b)

   d. (P AND Q) OR (P AND R)   Rule (6) (from c)

   e. (P AND (Q OR R)) AND ((P AND Q)
        OR (P AND R)   AND Intro. (from c,d)

   f. ((P AND (Q OR R)) AND (P AND Q))
        OR ((P AND (Q OR R)) AND
        (P AND R))   Rule (6) (from e)

   ⋮

As was noted above, the direct procedure limits the use of AND Introduction, but permits it in situations (such as (8c) and (8e)) where it is necessary for applying a further rule (in this case, the distribution rule (6a)). Furthermore, neither of these rules duplicates sentences in the derivation, nor do they apply more than once to the same sentence. Hence, there appears to be no way to block such an infinite derivation without either altering the direct reasoning process or excising one or more of the rules. In general, it appears that the direct reasoning procedure (as presented by Braine et al. in table III) exerts too little control on inference.

The main concern of Braine et al., however, is to provide evidence for the proposed inference rules, rather than the reasoning procedure. Toward this end, they report several experiments that use the sum of rated difficulties of individual rules to predict the difficulties of arguments they can derive. These predictions (a modified version of Osherson's additivity requirement) are applied to response times, errors, and ratings over sets of problems whose proofs require from one to four steps. The model produced a correlation of 0.73 between the error rates and the sums of the weighted rules. In fitting response times and ratings of difficulty, Braine et al. found a fairly strong correlation with argument length (in number of words). After partialing out the length effect, the sum-of-rules measure correlated between 0.83 and 0.91 with ratings and 0.41 with response times. These correlations are vulnerable to the same uncertainties as Osherson's additivity idea, but they provide some support for the proposed rules over a fairly large database of arguments.

It is clear that PSYCOP's predictions for these data would be fairly similar to those of Braine et al., owing to the overlap in the systems' rules. This is no accident, since I canvased the rules of Braine et al. in designing PSYCOP, as mentioned in chapter 4.[2] The distinctive feature of the theory of Braine et al. is the commitment to the rules in (6) and (7). The distinctive features of PSYCOP are the residual rules in tables 4.1, 6.2, and 6.3 (e.g., the DeMorgan rules), the use of subgoals to control inference, and the ability to perform inferences based on variables and names. Further experimental evidence might be helpful in deciding about the status of particular rules; however, global comparisons between the models are extremely difficult because of the lack of details in Braine et al.'s description of their indirect reasoning procedure.

Summary

PSYCOP has benefited from the lessons of the earlier efforts just reviewed. As positive lessons from this prior work, PSYCOP inherited many of its inference rules, plus a methodological imperative to test the model over a variety of inference forms. The negative lessons were the need to improve the control structure and to handle variables and names. PSYCOP's ancestors were simply too inflexible in the manner in which they wielded their rules (a common failing among ancestors generally). The symptoms of inflexibility were a tendency to produce assertions that are obviously irrelevant to the proof or the contrary tendency to ignore obviously relevant ones. Lack of facility with variables also limited the types of inferences that these earlier models could handle. Osherson (1976) extended his theory to one-place predicates and names, and Braine and Rumain (1983) suggested rules for certain operations on sets. Neither theory, however, handles multiple-place predicates or individual variables in a general way. I tried to make the case for variables in the last three chapters, and it may be that the pursuit of methods for handling variables will be the principle line of progress for future work in this tradition.

There remain a few substantive differences in the sets of rules that the natural-deduction models adopt. But the overlap in rule choice is more impressive than the disparities. Moreover, emphasizing rule distinctions is likely to seem a kind of narcissism of small differences when compared to the sorts of alternative theories that will be discussed in chapter 10.

Pragmatic Schemas

The theories that we looked at in the last section are the only general rule-based accounts of deduction and are by far PSYCOP's closest relatives. Investigators have proposed more specialized rule models, however —mainly to explain performance on Wason's selection task. I discussed the selection task in connection with sentential reasoning in chapter 5, and I offered a tentative explanation within the PSYCOP framework for the typically poor performance on this problem. Recall that in this task subjects receive a conditional sentence, such as *If there's a vowel on one side of the card, there's an even number on the other*, and must decide which of a set of exemplars they must check (e.g., cards showing E, K, 4, or 7) in order to determine whether the conditional is true or false of the set as a whole. As was also noted, it is possible to improve performance on the task markedly by rephrasing the problem while retaining the IF ... THEN format. A clear example of such improvement occurs when the conditional is *If a person is drinking beer, then the person must be over 19* and the instances to be checked are cards representing people drinking beer, people drinking coke, people 16 years of age, and people 22 years of age (Griggs and Cox 1982). In this guise, the conditional becomes a clear-cut regulation, and subjects usually spot the cards indicating possible rule violators (i.e., the beer drinker and the 16-year-old). Investigators have proposed new rule-based models in order to explain the benefit that this wording conveys.

A main difficulty in reviewing this research is keeping one's perspective. The effects of content in the selection task have produced several ongoing controversies (e.g., Cheng and Holyoak (1985, 1989) vs. Cosmides (1989); Cheng and Holyoak (1985) vs. Jackson and Griggs (1990)), and these controversies have the effect of drawing attention away from questions about deductive reasoning to questions about the details of the selection task. This tendency seems to be amplified by properties of the selection task itself: In discussing some of their own results, Jackson and Griggs (1990, p. 371) remark that their experiments "mirror those observed throughout the past 20 years of research on the selection task in that a result can be changed dramatically by only a subtle change in problem presentation." This raises obvious questions about the suitability of the selection task as an object of intense scientific theorizing. Furthermore, subjects' lackluster performance on the usual version of the task has tempted investigators, especially in other areas of cognitive science, to conclude that people are generally unable to reason to deductively correct conclusions. This neglects the fact that subjects solve many other deduction problems with near-perfect accuracy. Braine et al. (1984), for example, found less than 3% errors for one-step arguments involving AND Introduction, AND Elimination, Double Negation Elimination, IF Elimination, Disjunctive Modus Ponens, Dilemma, and Disjunctive Syllogism. We also noted minimal errors for all but one of the generalization problems in the response-time study of chapter 7 (see table 7.3). In looking at theories of content effects in the selection task, we must be careful to ask how likely it is that they will extend to other findings in the reasoning domain.

Schemas According to Cheng and Holyoak

Prompted by results like those from the selection problem on drinking, Cheng and Holyoak (1985, p. 395) proposed that people typically make inferences based on "a set of generalized, context-sensitive rules which, unlike purely syntactic rules, are defined in terms of classes of goals (such as taking desirable actions or making predictions about possible future events) and relationships to these goals (such as cause and effect or precondition and allowable action)." Cheng and Holyoak refer to these rule sets as *pragmatic reasoning schemas*, where "pragmatic" refers to the rules' usefulness or goal-relatedness, rather than to the Gricean notion of pragmatics that we encountered in previous chapters. (See also Holland et al. 1986.) As an example of a pragmatic reasoning schema, Cheng and Holyoak offer the four production rules shown here in (9), which constitute the basis of a schema for dealing with permission.

(9)   a. If the action is to be taken, then the precondition must be
         satisfied.

      b. If the action is not to be taken, then the precondition need not be
         satisfied.

      c. If the precondition is satisfied, then the action may be taken.

      d. If the precondition is not satisfied, then the action must not be
         taken.

To explain the selection task, Cheng and Holyoak assume that the usual
versions (e.g., the one based on arbitrary pairings of letters and numbers)
don't reliably evoke pragmatic schemas, and so performance is poor.
However, the drinking-age problem (and similarly modified problems)
do evoke the permission schema: Because of the match between (9a) and
the conditional rule in the selection instructions (*If a person is drinking
beer* ...), the pragmatic schema is activated, and the schema then makes
the rest of the items in (9) available to the subjects. These rules point
subjects to the need to check the cards representing beer drinking (the
action is taken, so rule (9a) applies) and being underage (the precondition
is not satisfied, so rule (9d) applies). The other two cards—representing
the cola drinker and the 22-year-old—are covered by the antecedents of
rules (9b) and (9c). But since the consequents of these rules state only that
something may or may not be the case, the "cola" and "22" cards need not
be checked. This choice is the conventionally correct one, so the permission schema yields the correct answer. Cheng and Holyoak suggest, however, that schemas based on other pragmatic conditions (e.g., schemas for
causation or covariation) would not necessarily have the same facilitating
effect. Thus, good performance on the drinking-age problem is due to
the fact that the schema it triggers—the permission schema—happens to
have testing rules that coincide with those of the material conditional (i.e.,
the IF ... THEN connective of CPL).

   In discussing the pragmatic schemas, it is helpful to distinguish two
facets of their operations, especially since the notion of an "inference rule"
seems to apply in different ways within the theory. Cheng and Holyoak
refer to the items in (9) as production rules, and they believe these items
are directly responsible for the selection-task choices. The pragmatic-
schema theory, however, also presupposes a mechanism that supplies
(9b)–(9d) whenever (9a) matches the conditional in the task, and this

relationship constitutes an inference of its own. For example, the theory assumes that people infer *If the precondition is not satisfied, then the action must not be taken* ($=$(9d)) from *If the action is to be taken, then the precondition must be satisfied* ($=$(9a)). In comparing the pragmatic-schema idea to other theories, we will usually be concerned with the latter *schema-based inferences*. It might also be helpful to repeat a warning from chapter 2: Which answer is deductively correct depends on the analysis of the structure of the problem. Early research on the selection task assumed that the correct answer is given by the definition of the material conditional (chapter 6) applied to the selection rule. But part of what is at issue in current work is whether this analysis is appropriate for conditionals like the drinking regulation. I will use "correct answer," in regard to the selection task, as an abbreviation for the choice of the cards corresponding to the antecedent and the negated consequent, since that is how it is used in the literature. However, this is not meant to create prejudice against rival theories of the nature of the problem. Ditto for "better performance," "higher scores," and the like. I will take up the question of what constitutes a "true" error in detail in the final chapter.

To bolster their explanation, Cheng and Holyoak (1985; see also Cheng et al. 1986) report experiments in which permission contexts enhance selection performance. In one experiment, for example, subjects were told they were immigration officials checking a form in order to make sure the following rule applied: *If the form says 'ENTERING' on one side, then the other side includes cholera among the list of diseases.* Giving subjects a rationale for this rule (that the rule was to make sure passengers had been inoculated against the listed disease) boosted their performance from about 60% correct to 90% correct on the corresponding selection task. The claim is that the jump in scores is due to the rationale suggesting the permission schema. A second experiment showed that the rule *If one is to take action 'A,' one must first satisfy precondition 'P'* also produced an advantage over the standard selection task (61% vs. 19% correct) despite the absence of concrete descriptions for the action and the precondition.

The Status of Pragmatic Schemas

There is no doubt that contexts like the drinking-age and cholera problems promote much better performance in the selection task, but how convincing is the evidence for pragmatic schemas as Cheng and Holyoak define them? In discussing these content effects in chapter 5, I noted that

Griggs (1983) takes the position that the effects are due to the content's reminding subjects of specific incidents in which rule violations correspond to the right choice of cards. Subjects may not have experience with cholera inoculations, of course; however, they may well have had analogous experiences (e.g., other sorts of vaccinations required for entering a country, for going to school, or for going to summer camp), and these experiences could yield the correct answer (Pollard 1990). Cheng and Holyoak intended their abstract version of the permission rule (*If one is to take action 'A,' one must first satisfy precondition 'P'*) to address this concern. The theory is that this conditional is "totally devoid of concrete content" (Cheng and Holyoak 1985, p. 409) and should therefore not trigger retrieval of specific experiences. But it is open to a critic to claim that "satisfying preconditions" and "taking actions" have enough residual content to prompt retrieval of specific episodes (Cosmides 1989).[3] Since the schemas themselves are supposed to apply on a "context-sensitive" basis (see the earlier quotation from Cheng and Holyoak 1985), it would seem there must be enough context to evoke the permission schema even in the abstract permission rule. But if this context is sufficient to evoke the schema, why shouldn't it also be able to evoke specific experiences involving preconditions and actions?[4]

Despite this uncertainty about the source of content effects in the selection task, there is no reason to doubt that people sometimes make inferences about permissions, obligations, causes, covariation, and other important relationships. It seems very likely, for example, that people can reason from *It is obligatory that P given Q* to *It is permissible that P given Q*, and from *It is obligatory that (P AND Q) given R* to *It is obligatory that P given R* (Lewis 1974). We can represent these examples as in (10).

(10)   a.   <u>OBLIGATORY(P | Q)</u>
            PERMISSIBLE(P | Q)

       b.   <u>OBLIGATORY(P AND Q | R)</u>
            OBLIGATORY(P | R)

Specific remembered experiences seem less helpful in these cases than in the selection task. In the latter, particular experiences can serve as a cue about cases that could potentially violate a rule. It is not clear, though, how a memory for a circumstance R in which P *AND* Q is obligatory would show that P must be obligatory in that same circumstance. Intuitively, the truth about the memory seems to be warranted by the inference, not vice versa. For these reasons, it seems to me that Cheng and Holyoak are probably right about the existence of rules for permission and obligation, even if these rules aren't responsible for selection-task performance. What is in question, however, is the nature of these rules (Rips 1990a). It is striking that the very concepts that are supposed to constitute pragmatic schemas—permission, obligation, and causality—are the targets of well-studied systems of modal logic (e.g., see Lewis (1973b) on causality and Føllesdal and Hilpinen (1971), Lewis (1974), and von Wright (1971) on permission and obligation). Fitch (1966) gives a natural-deduction system for obligation, and Osherson (1976, chapter 11) proposes mental inference rules for permission and obligation that operate in much the same way as his rules for monadic quantifiers. This suggests that the schema-based inferences might be mental deduction rules defined over modal operators such as *PERMISSIBLE* and *OBLIGATORY*.

Cheng and Holyoak don't discuss either the logical or the psychological deduction systems for permission and obligation—*deontic* systems, as they are usually called. But they do give some characteristics of pragmatic schemas that they believe distinguish them from deduction rules. One point they mention (1985, p. 396) is that the schema in (9) "contains no context-free symbols such as *p* and *q* [as in rules of logic]." Instead, they continue, "the inference patterns include as components the concepts of possibility, necessity, an action to be taken, and a precondition to be satisfied." It is unlikely, however, that the lack of schematic letters is crucial here. The sentences in (9) refer to individual actions and preconditions; so we need to use individual variables or names to formulate them (not just sentence letters like *p* and *q*). But within such a predicate-argument framework, we can rephrase a rule like (9a) as *If x is an action to be taken and y is a precondition of x, then y must be satisfied*, where the variables are "context free" in applying to any entity in the domain of discourse. In fact, if the items in (9) are production rules (as Cheng and Holyoak assert), then the introduction of variables or some similar device seems to be required in order to instantiate them to specific cases.

A more critical difference between pragmatic schemas and deduction rules is that, according to Cheng and Holyoak (1985, p. 397), "the rules attached to reasoning schemas are often useful heuristics rather than strictly valid inferences.... Because reasoning schemas are not restricted to strictly valid rules, our approach is not equivalent to any proposed formal or natural logic of the conditional." As an instance they note that (9c) does not follow validly from (9a): Since there may be more than one precondition, the statement *If the action is to be taken, then the precondition must be satisfied* needn't imply *If the precondition is satisfied, then the action may be taken.* But the pragmatic schema makes (9c) available whenever a conditional sentence matches (9a); so it looks as though the permission schema draws invalid inferences. However, there doesn't appear to be any strong experimental evidence for (9c) (or for (9b), which may also not be entailed by (9a)). Support for the permission schema comes from improved selection-task choices, but to explain the correct answers we don't need (9b) or (9c). These rules are supposed to tell us that there is no reason to choose the "action not taken" card and the "precondition satisfied" card. But subjects who avoid these cards may do so simply because they have no incentive to choose them. Not having a rule that covers these cards seems as reasonable an explanation as having a rule that says they are irrelevant. If this is true, then the Cheng-Holyoak findings are consistent with a valid deduction principle based on deontic logical operators— one that produces an analogue of (9d) from an analogue of (9a).

Of course, to explain the data we need to understand *OBLIGATORY(P|Q)* and *PERMISSIBLE(P|Q)* as expressions of duties and privileges. There is no reason to think that the broader senses of these terms would be successful in the selection experiments. But even with this restriction, there may be an advantage to representing the (9a)–(9d) relationship in terms of deontic operators, since deduction principles with these operators seem to be needed independently to capture inferences like (10a) and (10b).[5]

The general point is that, when we look at them carefully, proposals based on "pragmatic schemas" may have little more to offer than theories based on deduction rules. This coincides with the conclusion in chapter 8 above that we can usually capture inferences from schemas and similar structures by ordinary deduction machinery (Hayes 1979). As long as the deduction system can include modal operators for such concepts as obligation, the system can be exactly as sensitive to context as the proposed schemas. And to the extent that the schemas depend on production rules that match to propositions in memory, the schemas are exactly as "syntactic" as deduction rules. Thus, drawing distinctions between the "pragmatic" and the "syntactic" is far more confusing than illuminating in this context.

Morals Concerning Standard Deduction Rules

In addition to championing pragmatic schemas, the Cheng-Holyoak position tends to disparage deduction rules like those in part II. Cheng et al. (1986) do not deny that "*some* people may in fact reason with this syntactic rule [modus ponens]," but they believe that such rules are not typically used if a pragmatic schema is available. These conclusions rest mainly on the results of training experiments that appear to show that instruction on the material conditional is not as effective as instruction on pragmatic schemas in promoting good performance on the selection task. Cheng et al. (1986, p. 298) express the key idea this way: "Since in our view the rule system is not used in natural contexts, people lack the requisite skills to interpret problems in terms of the material conditional, and hence would profit little from instruction in it." They don't discuss either the logical or the psychological systems that incorporate other types of conditionals,[6] so it is conceivable that these conditionals would profit from instruction in a way that the material conditional doesn't. But let's consider the training results in their own terms and see what morals we can draw from them.

The training results of Cheng et al. (1986) are complex, but at a summary level they showed that neither a semester's logic course nor brief training on equivalences for *if p then q* (e.g., telling subjects that it can be reformulated as *If not q, then not p*, but not as *If q, then p* or *If not p, then not q*) has much effect on the selection task. We need to observe, however, that training does help on other deduction tests. For example, Cheng et al. found that their training procedure aided subjects in identifying the equivalence of conditionals and their contrapositives. In fact, this appears to be among the biggest effects reported in their paper; it boosted performance from 27% correct to 81% correct. Conrad and I reported (Rips and Conrad 1983) that a quarter's course in elementary logic improved subjects' ability to evaluate propositional arguments like those in table 5.1, many of which contained conditionals and which the students had probably never encountered in a class or in a textbook. Moreover, other forms of training do benefit selection scores. Cheng et al. found that when they told subjects how to *use* the reformulations to check whether an *if ... then* sentence had been violated, the subjects were then able to perform the selection task more accurately. Explaining the answers to an initial problem sometimes also aids in the solution of subsequent ones (Klaczynski, Gelfand, and Reese 1989). Furthermore, although Cheng et al. found no advantage for a logic course, Lehman, Lempert, and Nisbett (1988) show that two years of graduate training in law, medicine, or psychology (but not chemistry) help students on a set of selection problems (see also Nisbett et al. 1987). Morris and Nisbett (1993) also report that graduate training in psychology (but not philosophy) improves performance on the same problems, while Lehman and Nisbett (1990) found that majors in humanities and natural sciences (but not social sciences or psychology) improve over their undergraduate years.

What can we conclude from this complicated group of results? The underlying logic of Cheng et al.'s training experiments can be paraphrased as in (11a), and Cheng et al. also seem to imply the associated principle shown in (11b).

(11) a. If X is a problem that subjects ordinarily find difficult, and
          If abstract training aids in the solution of X,
          Then subjects must have an intuitive basis for understanding the abstract principles underlying X's solution.

      b. If X is a problem that subjects ordinarily find difficult, and
          If abstract training does *not* aid in the solution of X,
          Then subjects do *not* have an intuitive basis for understanding the abstract principles underlying X's solution.

Along these lines, Nisbett et al. (1987, pp. 625 and 629) state: "Rules that are extensions of naturally induced ones can be taught by quite abstract means. This description does not apply to formal, deductive logical rules or to most other purely syntactic rule systems, however.... We believe that abstract logical training by itself was ineffective [in Cheng et al. 1986] because the subjects had no preexisting logical rules corresponding to the conditional. (Or, more cautiously, any such rules are relatively weak and not likely to be applied in meaningful contexts)." The negative conclusions about logical rules clearly depend on (11b) or some closely analogous idea. (Fong, Krantz, and Nisbett (1986) appeal to (11a) to support an intuitive basis for statistical principles like the law of large numbers.) But (11b) seems much less compelling than (11a). It is easy to imagine a person who has an intuitive understanding of an abstract principle in physics, and who appreciates abstract training on the principle, but who still fails to solve a difficult problem in which that principle applies. Perhaps the problem also depends on additional principles that weren't part of the lesson, or perhaps the problem requires extensive calculation, or perhaps the formulation of the problem is somehow tricky or ambiguous. In view of the susceptibility of the selection task to "subtle changes in problem presentation" (Jackson and Griggs 1990), lack of transfer to this task seems doubtful evidence for the position that people have no strong subjective grasp of logical principles. At the very least, such a position seems to require showing that subjects fail to transfer to other sorts of problems.

The training evidence also tells us nothing about the ability of people to grasp logical principles for connectives other than *if*. There are genuine reasons to question whether people use material conditionals to interpret conditional sentences in natural language (see chapter 2), and the deduction theory of part II refuses to sanction inferences with IF that would follow from unrestricted material conditionals. However, as I have also noted, people are clearly able to recognize other principles (including AND Introduction, AND Elimination, and matching rules for names and variables) as deductively correct. For deduction rules like these, "pragmatic schema" explanations seem to fall apart; there simply doesn't seem to be anything about the inference from (say) *P AND Q* to *P* that would make it more pragmatically useful than the sorts of conditional rules that Cheng et al. criticize. Surely no one believes that to appreciate AND Elimination we need to tie it to permission, causality, or other "pragmatic" contexts. Thus, in light of the evidence on AND Elimination and similar inferences, pragmatic criteria can't be sufficient for determining whether something is an intuitively acceptable inference principle.

The upshot, at a specific level, is that the pragmatic-schema theory leaves us without a satisfactory account of why subjects usually fail on the standard selection task. If the reason were simply the pragmatic uselessness of rules for conditionals, then equally useless rules (such as AND Elimination) should also be unavailable in arbitrary contexts, contrary to fact (Braine et al. 1984). More important, the pragmatic-schema theory lacks a general account of deductive inference, since it gives us no hints about how people reason with the full range of logical operators.

Social Contracts

Cosmides (1989) has proposed a variation on pragmatic schemas in which rules of social exchange, rather than general permissions and obligations, determine successful performance on the selection task. According to this notion, the selection rules that produce the conventionally correct choices are of the form *If you take the benefit, then you pay the cost*—for example, *If Calvin brings food to your table, then you must tip Calvin 15%*. Rules of this sort evoke algorithms that are specialized for dealing with social exchanges, including algorithms that identify "cheating" in the exchange. Cheaters are those who take the benefit without bothering to pay the cost (e.g., getting the advantage of table service without tipping); so, in the context of the selection task, cheater detectors would help focus attention on the cards associated with taking the benefit (getting service) and not paying the cost (stiffing the waiter). Thus, the cheater detectors are responsible for the correct selections.

To handle the Griggs-Cox drinking-age problem or the Cheng-Holyoak cholera problem, the notion of social exchange has to be enlarged to more general social contracts of the type *If you take the benefit, then you must meet the requirement* (e.g., *If you are drinking beer, then you must be over 19*). Within a selection task that features a social contract, the cheater detector would prime the cards representing the person taking the benefit (a beer drinker) and the person not meeting the requirement (a 16-year-old), yielding the correct answer. Since no such procedure for identifying violations is connected with the rules in the standard selection task, performance should be correspondingly poor. The difference between social exchanges and social contracts may be important in determining whether Cosmides' approach is justified. The theory comes with an evolutionary rationale that is supposed to motivate the existence of innate, modular cheater detectors. Adaptive selection of these detectors, however, seems more plausible for social exchanges than for social contracts, since individual exchanges must have existed long before full-blown social regulations in human history: "While social exchange was a crucial adaptation for hunter-gatherers, permission from 'institutional authorities' was not ..." (Cosmides 1989, p. 255). Yet the contracts are what one needs to explain much of the data on content effects, as Cheng and Holyoak (1989) have pointed out. Cheng and Holyoak have other criticisms of the evolutionary approach, but in this overview I will mostly ignore this aspect (except for a few comments at the end of this section) and concentrate instead on whether contracts are helpful in clarifying subjects' performance.

According to Cosmides (1989, p. 235), the social-contract theory is supposed to share with the pragmatic-schema theory both the idea that "people lack a 'mental logic'" and the idea that "in solving the selection task, people use rules of inference appropriate to the domain suggested by the problem." Where it differs is its specificity: "All social contract rules involve permission (or, more strictly, entitlement), but not all permission rules are social contract rules" (p. 236). This difference provides a possible route for testing the two theories: Some permissions are social contracts and some permissions are not; hence, if the contract theory is right, only the former should help subjects on the selection task. Cosmides' experiments are devoted to testing this hypothesis, as well as to testing the specific-memory view. From our perspective, however, social contracts share most of the advantages and disadvantages of pragmatic schemas.

Costs-and-Benefits' Costs and Benefits

In discussing pragmatic schemas, we found some openings for the alternative idea that the advantages of schemas might be due instead to memory for specific incidents that highlight rule violations. Cosmides also criticizes Cheng and Holyoak's (1985) experiments for failing to eliminate this memory-cuing hypothesis. She believes that the earlier study failed to equate the permission versions and the control versions of the selection task for the total amount of content they contained; hence, any advantage for permissions could be set down to the sheer number of retrieval cues available. To overcome this potential confounding, Cosmides compared social contracts with what she calls "descriptions" (as well as with more standard selection tasks). Both conditions involved lengthy stories about fictional native peoples, and both centered on the same conditional sentence (e.g., *If a man eats cassava root, then he must have a tattoo on his face*). In the social-contract story, however, the conditional conveys a regulation (cassava root is a precious aphrodisiac that ought to be eaten only by tattooed men, all of whom are married); in the descriptive story, the conditional conveys a generalization (no costs or benefits attach to eating cassava root or to having a tattoo). In line with predictions, subjects made 75% correct selections for social contracts, versus 21% correct for descriptions.

It is difficult to tell, however, whether the experiment succeeds in its objective of ruling out possible effects of specific experiences. Although the social-contract and descriptive stories are roughly similar in complexity, they also differ in several respects that could cue differing numbers of specific incidents. (See the appendix to Cosmides 1989 for the texts of the problems.) More important, the differences in the cover stories that changed the conditional from a contract to a description may well evoke recall of different types of incidents—ones involving assessing regulations versus assessing descriptions (Pollard 1990). These memories may, in turn, cause subjects to attend differentially to the rule-breaking cards if, as might be the case, the retrieved incidents contain more vivid information about regulation violators than about exceptions to descriptive generalizations. Cosmides points out quite correctly that explanations of this sort have to include a substantive theory of how subjects manage to map the relevant aspects of the selection task onto those of the remembered incident.[7] But it is not clear why a defender of the specific-experience view couldn't develop a theory of this sort, perhaps along the lines of the failure-driven remindings of Schank (1982) and Schank, Collins, and Hunter (1986).[8] I will argue in the following chapter that there are legitimate reasons for rejecting a theory of deduction based solely on specific experiences (or "availability"); the present point is that such a view is hard to eliminate within the confines of explanations for content effects. This spells trouble for the social-contract theory and for the pragmatic-schema theory, which are founded entirely on such evidence.

Cosmides' other main goal is to show that the social-contract theory better explains the data on content effects than pragmatic schemas. Cosmides and Cheng and Holyoak agree that social contracts are a subset of permissions; so the social-contract theory ought to predict no advantage for permissions that don't happen to be contracts, whereas the pragmatic-schema theory ought to predict an advantage for these same noncontract permissions. But although this prediction seems straightforward, there appears to be evidence on both sides of the issue. In the social-contract corner, Cosmides attempted to construct pairs of stories that implied either social contracts or noncontract permissions. One pair concerned the conditional *If a student is to be assigned to Grover High School, then that student must live in Grover City*. The social-contract story described Grover High as a much better school than its alternatives and attributed this to the higher taxes that Grover City residents pay. The noncontract-permission story said nothing about the quality of schools or towns, but described the rule as one adopted by the Board of Education to ensure that all schools had the right number of teachers. Cosmides found 75% "correct" selection choices for the contract version, but 30% for the noncontract-permission version.

In the pragmatic-schema corner, there is evidence that permission rules can produce content effects even when they are not associated with contracts or exchanges. Manktelow and Over (1990) and Cheng and Holyoak (1989) both report good performance for conditionals that express the need to take a precaution—for example, *If you clean up spilt blood, then you must wear rubber gloves*—in a context where failure to take the precaution can have dire consequences, such as spreading disease. Since cleaning up blood doesn't seem to qualify as a benefit, it doesn't clearly fall under Cosmides' definition of a social contract. Yet it is expressible as an obligation (e.g., *OBLIGATORY(x wears rubber gloves | x cleans up spilt blood)*), and so it seems consistent with the pragmatic-schema theory.

This evidence, taken at face value, suggests that some kinds of noncontract permissions (precautions, as in the rubber-gloves example) facilitate performance whereas other kinds (e.g., permission to attend one of two equivalent high schools) do not. If this is right, then the conclusion must be that both the social-contract theory and the pragmatic-schema theory are incorrect or at least incomplete, since neither correctly describes the full range of phenomena that it should address. Of course, it is possible that some of the evidence is flawed. Cheng and Holyoak (1989) contend, for example, that Cosmides' noncontract stories were too unclear to engage the permission schema; so this is a place where some clarifying experiments might be helpful. But it is interesting to speculate that some other principle might underlie the content differences.

One possibility along these lines is that the contexts that seem to produce the strongest facilitation are those that focus on the obligatory nature of an event or a state.[9] Being over 19 is clearly an obligation of the beer drinker, having a cholera vaccination is an obligation of the deplaning passenger, and wearing rubber gloves is an obligation of the person cleaning up blood. Each of these fits the *OBLIGATORY(P | Q)* framework. Further, the content effect seems to break down when the cover story fails to guide subjects to this interpretation of the conditional. For example, Cosmides' noncontract story can be read as a conditional permission, as in (12a), rather than as the stronger obligation in (12b).

(12)   a. PERMISSIBLE(Student x is assigned to Grover High | Student x lives in Grover City).

      b. OBLIGATORY(Student x lives in Grover City | Student x is assigned to Grover High).

The same is true of Cheng and Holyoak's cholera problem when it is presented to subjects without a rationale. Cheng and Holyoak's rationale about inoculation and Cosmides' discussion of better schools for higher taxes emphasize that the story characters are incurring a serious obligation and encourages a stronger reading like that of (12b). Notice that when the conditional is interpreted as (12a) none of the selection cards can show that the rule has been broken (e.g., it is possible that students from other cities also have permission to attend Grover High). On the (12b) reading, however, both the "Grover High" card and the "Doesn't live in Grover City" card are relevant, and these cards correspond to the standard "correct" selection.

This way of looking at the content results isn't by any means a complete explanation (especially in view of the wording effects discussed in note 4), but it may help us understand the relative strengths and weaknesses of social contracts and pragmatic schemas. Social contracts may be effective because the notions of costs-in-exchange-for-benefits and requirements-in-exchange-for-privileges are direct forms of conditional obligation (in the sense of $OBLIGATORY(P \mid Q)$). However, there are other forms of obligation (e.g., precautions, and maybe threats) that social-contract theory seems to miss. Pragmatic schemas are better adapted to handling the full range of effects. But it may be that not every conditional that embodies a permission will produce a content effect, since not every such conditional implies $OBLIGATORY(P \mid Q)$.

Morals Concerning Standard Deduction Rules

We need to consider one further aspect of Cosmides' experiments that bears on claims about mental-deduction rules. In addition to the social-contract stories and conditionals just discussed, some of her studies concerned "switched" conditionals of the form *If you pay the cost, then you take the benefit.* For example, Cosmides presented the cassava-root story mentioned above, together with the conditional *If a man has a tattoo on his face, then he eats cassava root* (in place of *If a man eats cassava root, then he must have a tattoo on his face*). Despite the change in the conditional, individuals who violate the rule (within the context of the story) are still those who indulge in cassava without having a tattoo. Thus, if Cosmides' subjects were monitoring for cheaters, they should have continued to choose the "cassava" and "no tattoo" cards. In fact about 67% of them did, versus 4% for the matched generalization. Cosmides argues that these results show that the social contracts were not simply stimulating subjects to reason "logically." The correct "logical" answer for the switched problems would be the "tattoo" and "no cassava" cards, which correspond to the antecedent and the negation of the consequent in the switched conditional; but only 4% of subjects chose these items.

These findings are susceptible to the criticism that the lengthy background story convinced subjects that the intended meaning of the switched conditional was the same as before: $OBLIGATORY(x \text{ has tattoo} \mid x \text{ eats cassava root})$. (Johnson-Laird and Byrne (1991) and Manktelow and Over (1990) raise similar points.) There is some flexibility in how to represent sentences in natural language within a given context, and this means that people must use their judgment in mapping the text onto an underlying interpretation. There are many ways of conveying a conditional permission or obligation, including surface conjunctions (*Get a tattoo and you can have cassava root*) and surface disjunctions (*Get a tattoo or you can't have cassava root*), in addition to surface conditionals (G. Lakoff 1970; R. Lakoff 1971; Springston and Clark 1973), so it is not surprising to find subjects overriding a literal sentence in order to achieve consistency with background information. The social-contract theory, of course, requires an analogous procedure of recasting the stimulus material into a form to which the cost-benefit algorithms apply. According to the theory, "[an] interpretive component must then map all explicitly described elements in the situation to their social exchange equivalents (cost-benefit relationship, the entitlement relationship, and so on)," and "to do this, implicit inference procedures must fill in all necessary steps—even those that have not been explicitly stated" (Cosmides 1989, p. 230).

More recent research has also obtained flipped content effects—selection of the cards for the consequent and the negated antecedent of the target conditional—by giving subjects instructions regarding which of the parties to an obligation might be breaking it (Gigerenzer and Hug 1992; Manktelow and Over 1991). For example, Manktelow and Over told their subjects that a shop had given customers the promise *If you spend more than £100, then you may take a free gift.* When the instructions indicated that the shop might not have given customers what they were due and asked them to check the cards they would need to find out, the subjects tended to select the "more than £100" and "no free gift" cards. By contrast, when the instructions stated that the customers might have taken more than they were entitled to and asked the subjects to check, they tended to select the "free gift" and "less than £100" cards. These results seem easy to understand on the assumption that the conditional promise places obligations on both the shop and the customer. We could represent these as *OBLIGATORY(shop gives free gift | shop receives > £100)* and *OBLIGATORY(customer spends > £100 | customer gets free gift)*, where the first spells out the onus on the shop and the second the requirements on the customer.[10] Which of these obligations the subjects attended to naturally depended on which one they had been told to check. It therefore seems that neither Cosmides' "switched" contracts nor changed obligations pose any greater difficulty for deduction rules than did the original finding of Cheng and Holyoak.

Cosmides briefly considers the possibility of explaining her results using deontic logic, but she ends up arguing against this possibility. The first reason for this is the same as her case against pragmatic schemas: Deontic logics apply in all permission-obligation settings and hence should incorrectly predict facilitation on the selection task for noncontract-permission rules. We have already noted, however, that subjects may have understood the noncontract problems as conditional permissions (as in (12a)) that had no implications for the choice of cards. But a bigger difficulty for this argument is that inferences about obligations and permissions *do* arise outside social contracts. The arguments in (10) are one instance; the precaution results of Cheng and Holyoak (1989) and Manktelow and Over (1990) are another. To capture these inferences we need a more general theory, and deontic inference rules might be one component of such an account.[11]

Cosmides' second reason for preferring contracts over deontic logics is that "there is an explanation of why the mind should contain social contract algorithms, while there is no explanation of why it should contain a deontic logic.... Social contract theory is directly derived from what is known about the evolutionary biology of cooperation, and it is tightly constrained as a result." (1989 p. 233) However, evolutionary considerations don't by themselves make the case for "cheater detectors" over more general forms of inference. Sober (1981, p. 107) shows that evolution can favor standard deduction rules on grounds of their relative simplicity:

... let me suggest that deductive logics which are truth-functional will be informationally more fit than those which are not. In a truth-functional logic, the truth value of a sentence depends on just the truth values of its components, while in a non-truth-functional system, the valuation of a string will turn on the truth value of its components, and on other considerations as well. The informational advantages of a truth-functional system will thus resemble the advantages noted before of an instruction which triggers healing processes when a wound occurs, without regard to the shape of the wound. No shape detector is needed; all that is necessary is that the organism be able to pick up on when a wound has occurred.... Truth-functional logics are similarly austere; relatively little information about a sentence needs to be acquired before a computation can be undertaken.

Even if there is some adaptive pressure to recognize cheaters, there may well be an evolutionary advantage to accomplishing this through more general inference mechanisms. This would be the case if the more specific solutions required a greater drain on internal resources or otherwise impractical implementations. The complexity of such an algorithm seems an especially pressing problem when one considers the elaborate legal definitions of cheating on contracts. Similarly, the more restricted procedure might be at a disadvantage if people need more general principles for independent reasons. Of course, deontic deduction rules are not purely truth-functional either, since the truth of $OBLIGATORY(P|Q)$ and that of $PERMISSIBLE(P|Q)$ are not completely determined by the truth of P and Q. But I am not arguing that evolution selected deontic deduction rules over cheater detectors. The point is, rather, that evolutionary theory by itself provides no reasons for preferring more narrowly formulated inference algorithms over more general ones. (See Sober 1981 for an informed discussion of other evolutionary constraints on inference. Stich (1990, chapter 3) questions claims that particular inference strategies are necessarily under genetic control, and Lewontin (1990) provides reasons to doubt that there is any convincing evidence to back particular evolutionary theories of cognition.)

Summary

The aims of the pragmatic-schema theory and the social-contract theory obviously differ from those of the deduction systems discussed in the first section of this chapter. Schemas and social contracts give us primarily accounts of content effects in the selection task. Although they generalize to other situations where schemas like (9) apply or to situations where people need to detect cheaters, they are useless in handling even simple inferences such as AND Elimination or instantiation. We have no trouble realizing that it follows from *Everyone gaxes everybody* that *Someone gaxes somebody*, even if we haven't the faintest idea what *gaxes* means. What pragmatic schema or Darwinian algorithm could account for this? Moreover, the inferences that pragmatic schemas and Darwinian algorithms *do* promote are not necessarily deductively valid (Cheng and Holyoak 1985). A pluralistic conclusion would therefore be that deduction theories such as PSYCOP account for deductive reasoning whereas schema and contract theories account for certain nondeductive inferences —for example, ones for permission, causality, and covariation. Specific rules of the latter sort seem closer to practical human concerns in a historical or a contemporary context, and so it is easy to justify them within the framework of a general learning theory or of an evolutionary approach.

One might try for a more unified account by extending pragmatic schemas or evolutionary modules to encompass rules in deduction systems— general-purpose schemas or modules with IF Elimination, AND Introduction, and the rest. But general-purpose schemas or modules defeat the rationale behind these theories: Inferences of this sort aren't directly linked to practical goals and have no direct adaptive advantage; thus, one can no longer explain where they came from or why people don't employ them to solve the selection task. It is not clear that proponents of schemas or contracts are prepared to swallow these consequences.

Another route to a unified theory is to adapt the deduction systems to handle obligation, causality, necessity, and other modal concepts. These concepts engender inferences that don't reduce to the rules presented above in chapters 4–7. But it is interesting to contemplate the possibility of extending such systems in this direction, taking advantage of related research on modal logic. This is the path that Osherson (1976) pursued in modeling children's evaluation of modal arguments, and our look at the recent literature on the selection task suggests that it might also accommodate those findings. However, this clearly entails more than just adding a few rules. Criticisms of "logical" or "syntactic" rules in this literature boil down to the observation that subjects' responses aren't predictable from the mere presence of the words "if ... then." The obvious reply to the criticism is that deduction rules apply not to the surface form of the sentences in a reasoning problem, but to the mental representations of the sentences as people interpret them. But saying this doesn't solve the problem of how such interpretation occurs, and the problem becomes more pressing the greater the distance between the surface form and the representation to which the rules apply (Evans 1989). The same must be true for rival proposals, of course, since the surface sentences don't explicitly display costs and benefits or permissions and obligations either.

Nevertheless, theories like PSYCOP have a certain advantage here, since the underlying form they posit is closely related to Logical Form in current linguistic theories (e.g., Higginbotham 1987; May 1985). Research on language understanding within this framework provides a natural counterpart to the theory proposed here.

10 Alternative Psychological Theories: Ruleless Systems

In the world of mules,
There are no rules.
Ogden Nash

Rule-based theories such as those discussed in chapter 9 are certainly not the only approach to the psychology of deduction, and we can gain insight by comparing them with rival approaches. The natural-deduction rules that form the heart of PSYCOP and similar systems apply to most of the research in this area, as I have tried to demonstrate. But the very generality of rule-based theories has provoked criticisms from many investigators who believe that human reason proceeds by more concrete methods. It is hard for these researchers to take seriously the idea that ordinary people have access to rules that are sensitive only to the logical form of a sentence—rules that apply no matter what the sentence happens to be about. How could such principles be learned in the first place? How could they be consistent with the evidence of error and of context-sensitivity in reasoning? One could very reasonably retort that these difficulties are no more problematic for deduction rules than they are for grammatical rules. Before the development of formal linguistics, it must have seemed mysterious how people could have grammatical principles sensitive only to the syntactic form of a sentence and how such principles could comport with evidence on learning and on speech errors. It seems fair to say, however, that these problems have well-defined answers within current linguistic theory, and it is unclear why they should pose any additional difficulty for deduction systems.[1] Still, the persistence of these questions in the context of deduction suggests that we should take them seriously. We have already seen that even those who go along with rules in principle often opt for ones that are less abstract and more closely tailored to the task domain.

Those who reject rules as a basis for deduction have the opposite problem of explaining the seemingly systematic performance that subjects exhibit on many tasks. One obvious approach is to explain such performance by reducing it to simple heuristics or "natural assessments" that arise automatically in the course of perception or comprehension (Tversky and Kahneman 1983). These might include assessments of similarity or of availability, or other rules of thumb. Part of the appeal of this kind of explanation is that it goes along with the impressive body of research on probabilistic inference (see, e.g., the papers collected in Kahneman et al. 1982). But although there is plenty of evidence that heuristics sometimes affect performance on deduction tasks, there have been few proponents of the idea that deduction is solely a matter of heuristics. Instead, the anti-rule forces have claimed that people solve deduction problems by manipulating "mental models" or other diagrammatic representations of the problem domain (Erickson 1974, 1978; Johnson-Laird 1983, 1989). Like heuristics, mental models are supposed to arise from perception or from comprehension; however, they differ in requiring much more active operations—typically, a search for counterexamples to a given conclusion.

Heuristic-Based Theories and "Content" Effects

There is a very general sense in which nearly all cognitive activity is "rule governed." Cognitive psychologists generally assume that people are able to perform intellectual tasks in virtue of mental programs or strategies that control lower-level activities, such as search or comparison operations. All contemporary psychological theories of deduction are rule based in this sense, since they assume that people have systematic internal routines for solving problems. The differences among the theories lie in the types of routines they postulate. In this context, those who criticize the use of rules in deduction have in mind rules of a special sort: those of inference systems that are sensitive to logical form. These rules apply to internal sentence tokens whenever they contain specified arrangements of logical connectives or quantifiers, and they produce further tokens whose form is similarly defined. PSYCOP's rules (chapter 6 above) are of exactly this type.

The nature of the alternative "ruleless" theories is not so clear. Although such theories try to avoid "logical" rules like PSYCOP's, the operations that take their place are not always easy to characterize. The simplest case of a theory without logical rules is one in which decisions about the correctness of an argument are made by consulting some property that is independent of its logical constants. For example, Morgan and Morton (1944) proposed that people ordinarily evaluate an argument in terms of how believable the conclusion is: If you already think that the conclusion is true, you will believe that the argument is correct. But radical theories of this sort have few partisans these days, since they have trouble accounting for the data on elementary inferences. The theory closest to this pure approach may be Pollard's (1982) proposal that deduction is a matter of availability.

Deduction and Availability

In the literature on decision making, "heuristics" has come to denote short-cut strategies that people use to assess the probability of an uncertain event. Tversky and Kahneman's well-known work (e.g., 1974) suggests that people's probability estimates do not obey the standard axioms of the probability calculus, and that instead they employ simple, accessible properties of events to provide a rough answer. One type of event might be deemed more probable than another if the first is more easily brought to mind (is more *available* than the second) or if the first event is more similar on average to other members of its class (is more *representative*, in Tversky and Kahneman's terminology).

Pollard (1982) has claimed that the availability heuristic can also explain many of the research results on deduction. The general idea is that subjects select responses that correspond to familiar information or familiar associations. In evaluating arguments, for example, subjects choose the conclusion that seems most prevalent, much as in the Morgan-Morton hypothesis. For this reason, the availability heuristic works best as an explanation of experiments that use problems about familiar situations, rather than with the more austere stimuli that we concentrated on in part II. Most of those who have conducted research on reasoning with sentential connectives and with quantifiers have selected their test items so as to avoid confoundings with subjects' pre-experimental knowledge, and this means that correct and incorrect responses are usually equivalent in availability. There is no reason to suppose, for example, that the patterns of subjects' answers in the experiments presented in chapters 5 and 7 were due to differential familiarity. How could subjects have used availability to choose some of the arguments in table 5.1 over others, for example, when all of them were framed in similar sentences (e.g., *If Judy is in Albany or Janice is in LA, then Janice is in LA*)? Thus, the availability hypothesis is at best extremely incomplete. Those who want to explain all reasoning as heuristic processing must pin their hope on the possibility that new heuristics will be discovered that can account for performance on problems with unfamiliar content.

Despite this incompleteness, it is worth considering how availability might explain studies that look at effects of subjects' preexisting knowledge of the materials, especially since these are among the best-known experiments.

"Content" in Deduction

The basic results on familiar content in categorical syllogisms were apparent in an early study by Minna Wilkins (1928), who presented her subjects with problems having the same logical form but ranging in content from everyday activities and objects (*Some of the boats on the river are sailboats*) to scientific jargon and nonsense terms (*Some Ichnogobs are Rasmania*) to meaningless letters (*Some x's are y's*). Considering just the problems subjects actually attempted, Wilkins found a small benefit for everyday wording: 82% correct, versus 75% for jargon and 76% for letters. In addition, the subjects were slightly more accurate with everyday syllogisms whose conclusions were neutral (85%) than with ones whose conclusions were "misleading" (80%). Wilkins considered a conclusion misleading if it followed from the premises but was clearly false or if it didn't follow but was true. An example of one of Wilkins' misleading syllogisms (of the form $\langle No(G,H), No(F,G), \therefore No(F,H) \rangle$) was given in chapter 1 and is repeated here as (1). Syllogism (2) is the counterpart with familiar wording and a neutral conclusion.

(1)   No oranges are apples.
      No lemons are oranges.
      No lemons are apples.

(2)   None of the Smiths' money is invested in real estate.
      None of this money belongs to the Smiths.
      None of this money is invested in real estate.

Only 5% of subjects thought the conclusion of (2) followed from the premises, whereas 31% went along with (1).

Effects of Prior Likelihood   Since Wilkins' time, there has been a long history of attempts to replicate the finding that the prior likelihood or believability of the conclusion affects subjects' evaluation of syllogisms (see, e.g., Evans et al. 1983; Janis and Frick 1943; Lefford 1946; Morgan 1945; Morgan and Morton 1944; Oakhill and Johnson-Laird 1985; Oakhill et al. 1989; Revlin et al. 1980). As was noted in chapter 1, most of these studies confirmed the effect, though its magnitude was often quite small. Moreover, there is evidence that even when the effect is relatively large it does not fully account for subjects' choices. For example, Evans et al. (1983) varied independently the validity of the stimulus syllogisms and the believability of their conclusions and found clear evidence of believability: Subjects accepted syllogisms with believable conclusions on 80% of trials and ones with less believable conclusions on only 33% across three experiments. Nevertheless, with believability controlled, subjects still accepted valid syllogisms more often than invalid ones (72% vs. 40%). There was also an interaction between these factors, with believability exerting a larger influence on invalid items.

Pollard (1982) takes the believability results as support for the availability heuristic, on the assumption that the more believable a conclusion the more available it is as a response alternative. There may be reason to wonder, however, if this equivalence isn't too simple. Although believable sentences might be easier to remember or produce than less believable ones, it is not so clear that believable sentences are necessarily more available when subjects must evaluate them in the context of syllogisms. In the choice between a believable conclusion such as *Some addictive things are not cigarettes* and a less believable one such as *Some cigarettes are not addictive*, it is not at all obvious that the first is more available. Couldn't the surprising quality of the second sentence make it the more available of the two? Yet the former conclusions are the ones that elicited more positive responses in the experiment of Evans et al. (1983) (see examples (15) and (16) in chapter 1 above). In other words, there is little reason to suppose that availability mediates the effect in question.

The important point of the experiment of Evans et al., however, is that no matter how we explain the believability effect, it cannot by itself account for the results on syllogisms with familiar wording. Unless a pure heuristics theory can explain the overall difference between valid and invalid familiar syllogisms, it is no more cogent than it was in the case of arguments with unfamiliar terms.

Effects of Elaboration   The framing of a conditional sentence can affect the conclusions subjects derive from it (see chapter 5). The generalization seems to be that if a conditional suggests a one-to-one relation between the domains associated with its antecedent and its consequent, subjects will sometimes treat the sentence as if it implicates a biconditional (Fillenbaum 1975, 1977; Legrenzi 1970; Li 1993; Marcus and Rips 1979; Markovits 1988; Rips and Marcus 1977; Staudenmayer 1975). In one of the experiments in the Rips-Marcus paper, for example, subjects inspected a pinball machine with several alleys for ball bearings to roll down and several differently colored lights. We told subjects in one condition that each alley was connected to a distinct light and in a second condition that an alley could be associated with more than one light. We then asked them to classify different contingencies (e.g., the ball rolls left and the green light flashes; the ball rolls right and the red light flashes) as logically consistent or inconsistent with an explicit conditional sentence such as *If the ball rolls left then the green light flashes*. When subjects thought the alleys and lights were paired, most of them (67%) evaluated the contingencies as if they were comparing each one to both the conditional and its converse. For example, they tended to judge as inconsistent with the above sentence a situation in which the ball rolls right and the green light flashes, but to judge as consistent a situation in which the ball rolls right and the red light flashes. Only 4% of the subjects exhibited this tendency when there was no one-to-one correlation.

The effect of content in these studies of conditional reasoning is different from that in the believability experiments. The present results don't depend on the prior likelihood of the conclusion, since in some of the experiments just cited the conclusion is completely neutral. For example, as was noted in the discussion of conditional syllogisms in chapter 5, subjects accept argument (3) below more readily than Argument (4). However, it is not very credible that they do so because *The ball rolls left* is more likely on the basis of experience than *The card has an A on the left*.

(3) If the ball rolls left, the green light flashes.
     The green light flashes.
     _____
     The ball rolls left.

(4) If the card has an A on the left, it has a 7 on the right.
     The card has a 7 on the right.
     _____
     The card has an A on the left.

The difference is much more plausibly due to subjects' willingness to elaborate the information conveyed in the conditional. Pre-experimental beliefs are coming into play, all right, but the relevant beliefs have to do with the usual relationship between antecedent and consequent in situations where the conditionals are appropriate. In the light of knowledge of devices like our pinball machine with paired alleys and lights, the first premise in (3) conveys the notion that if the ball doesn't roll left then the green light will not flash. Similarly, on the basis of your knowledge of the purpose of promises, you can conjecture that *If you drink your milk, you can have a snack* also means that if you don't drink your milk you will not have a snack (Fillenbaum 1977). In accord with this, the elaboration effects increase when instructions tell subjects to regard the task not as a matter of logic but rather as "a set of problems directed to your understanding ... when you are figuring out what is implicit or implied in sentences that you might encounter" (Fillenbaum 1975, p. 250).

If availability is to have any chance of explaining these results, we must presumably shift our focus from availability of the conclusion to the availability of the relationship implicit in the conditional. However, this relationship cannot be just a brute association between words in the antecedent and the consequent or an association between their referents. The association between balls rolling left and green lights flashing is certainly no stronger than the one between having an A on the left of a card and a 7 on the right. To account for the difference between (3) and (4), what must be available is some type of constraint specifying which combinations of antecedent and consequent values are normally possible in the type of situations that the problems refer to (cf. Barwise 1986). Once some of these combinations are specified, pinball machines place different restrictions on the rest of them than cards.

To describe these results as effects of availability, however, is more a play on words than a serious explanation. Obviously, these constraints must be "available" to the subjects if they are to influence the decisions: Subjects must be able to retrieve the information before they can use it. But this doesn't mean that subjects employ availability itself as the basis for their responses, which is what the availability heuristic is supposed to be. According to Tversky and Kahneman's (1973) account, subjects make their probability decisions by assessing how available—how easily brought to mind—the to-be-judged event is. By contrast, nothing about these results appears to depend on *how easily* information can be found. Instead, what matters is the nature of the information obtained: the antecedent-consequent constraints themselves. Stretching the meaning of "availability" to cover these constraints throws no new light on the nature of these experiments.[2]

Content Effects in the Selection Task   The best-known content manipulations are the ones associated with Wason's selection task, reviewed in chapter 9 above (see also Evans 1989, chapter 4). Can we ascribe the improvement in performance on the selection task to an availability heuristic? If we can, then it is presumably because content makes the correct choices more available. Perhaps in the context of the drinking-age regulation and similar rules it is potential violators—for example, people who are drinking beer and people who are underage—that are the most obvious choices. However, as Pollard (1982) points out with respect to a related issue, it is not clear why violators should be more available than law-abiding citizens (adults and cola drinkers), who are undoubtedly more frequent. To make the availability idea work, one must suppose that availability depends not just on the frequency or familiarity of the exemplars but also on the manner in which they are considered. The nature of the problem must somehow suggest that the rule violators, and not the rule abiders, are relevant.

Although the correct cards may be in some sense the more available ones in the drinking problem and in similar facilitating contexts, availability could hardly be the sole cause of the results. Subjects must first recognize the problem as one in which it makes sense to consider exceptions or counterexamples to the rule before beer drinkers and underage patrons can become relevantly "available." As in the other examples of conditional and syllogistic reasoning, the availability heuristic must be supplemented by more complex processes in order to explain the nature of the content effect.

Can Availability Explain Deduction?

The availability heuristic is the only heuristic that has been claimed to be a general explanation of performance in deduction experiments. The attraction of the claim is that it could reduce a large number of separate findings—in both deductive and probabilistic reasoning—to a single psychologically simple principle: The more available a response, the more likely subjects are to make it. A closer look at this claim, however, suggests that it is unfounded. In the first place, there is no hope that availability can explain the results with unfamiliar problems, since experimenters customarily control this very factor. But second, even in the realm of problems with more familiar wording, availability rarely seems the crucial determinant. In order to make the availability heuristic work in these cases, we must either stretch the notion of "availability" to the point of triviality or hedge it with other principles that themselves call for deeper explanations.

Particularly in the case of conditional reasoning, we need to appeal to fairly abstract constraints (correlations between the antecedent and consequent domains, or circumstances that highlight counterexamples) before the availability heuristic makes sense. Moreover, in both categorical syllogisms and conditional problems there are large residual effects when the purported availability factors are held constant.

Of course, there are many possible heuristics other than availability; so these difficulties with availability don't mean that heuristics can't capture the reasoning results. But most researchers seem agreed that an explanation (especially for unfamiliar problems) must lie in processes that are much more systematic than what the usual notion of a heuristic is able to capture.

Reasoning by Diagrams and Models

If the goal is to avoid logical rules like those of PSYCOP and yet account for the reliably correct intuitions that people have about some deduction problems, then it seems reasonable to look to diagrammatic representations such as Venn diagrams or Euler circles. There is a long history of proposals for logic diagrams or logic machines that automatically check the correctness of categorical syllogisms (Gardner 1958). Such devices have contributed little to logical theory but have served as helpful teaching tools in introducing students to the notions of sets and quantifiers. Diagrams of this sort appeal to students because they rely on simple perceptual-geometric properties, such as overlap and disjointness, to represent relations among more abstract entities.

Diagrams appeal to many psychologists for similar reasons. Those who believe that perception provides a more primitive representational medium than sentential structures may also feel that reasoning with diagrams is more "natural" than reasoning with sentences or formulas (see, e.g., Rumelhart 1989). This idea is especially tempting in the case of reasoning about information that is itself spatial. If you must deduce implicit information about a spatial array or a geographical area from explicitly stated relations, you may try to develop mental maps and read the required facts from them in something like the way you read route information from a physical map of terrain (see, e.g., Bower and Morrow 1990). Similarly, problems that require subjects to deduce order relations (e.g., If

Fred is taller than Mary and Charles is shorter than Mary, who is tallest?) also seem to call for some sort of internal array to represent the sequence. (See the research on linear syllogisms cited in chapter 1; also see Byrne and Johnson-Laird 1989.[3]) There are questions about how literally we can take these claims about mental maps and diagrams (Pylyshyn 1984), but we can grant their existence for current purposes. The problem for us is to decide how plausible they are as explanations of more complex inferencing. Are they really competitors as theories for the sorts of deductive inferences that we studied in part II?

Diagrammatic Approaches

Many psychological diagram theories aim at explaining reasoning with categorical syllogisms. Erickson's (1974, 1978) theory, mentioned in chapter 1, illustrates the basic features of this approach. To determine whether a syllogism is correct, people are supposed to translate each premise into Euler diagrams that exemplify the possible set relations that the premise implies. In the example of figure 1.1, the premise *All square blocks are green blocks* appears as two separate Euler diagrams, one with a circle representing square blocks inside another representing green blocks. The second diagram contains two coincident circles representing the same two classes. Similarly, the premise *Some big blocks are square blocks* is represented in terms of the four diagrams that appear in the second row of figure 1.1. Erickson's model assumes that subjects never actually consider more than one possible diagram per premise, and that some of the errors they commit are therefore due to incomplete representations.

In order to determine the validity of the syllogism, subjects must combine these two premise representations. There are usually several ways in which this can be done (see the combined diagrams at the bottom of figure 1.1), and Erickson (1974) proposes several variant models that differ in the thoroughness of the combination process. A correct procedure, of course, would be to combine the representations in all possible ways that are set-theoretically distinct. Finally, subjects must check whether the syllogism's conclusion holds in all combinations (in the case of a syllogism-evaluation task), or must generate a conclusion that holds in all of them (in the case of a production task). Erickson assumes that when more than one conclusion is possible on this basis, subjects' decisions are determined by biases like that of the atmosphere effect (see chapter 7). Thus, predictions about the difficulty of syllogisms depend on assumptions about which Euler diagram represents a premise, how thoroughly subjects combine the diagrams, and which conclusions they use to express the combinations. Of course, these predictions are supposed to apply to people without any formal knowledge of Euler circles. There is little doubt that people can form mental images of Euler circles if given sufficient training with them; however, the model is directed not at experts but at the intuitions of naive subjects.

It would be of interest to compare Erickson's predictions with those of our own model, but there are problems in doing this that stem from parameter estimation. Erickson's most tractable models are ones that combine the premise diagrams in all possible ways or that combine them in just one randomly chosen way. But, as he shows, these two models give an incorrect account of those syllogistic premises that have no valid conclusion (constituting the majority of problems). The random-combination model tends to underpredict the number of correct responses to these premise pairs, since single combinations always allow some incorrect categorical conclusion; but the complete-combination model overpredicts correct ("no valid conclusion") responses. It is therefore necessary to assume that subjects consider only some premise combinations and to specify which combinations these will be. Since the number of potential combinations is large, this means specifying a large number of parameters, one corresponding to the probability that each type of combination is considered. Because of this difficulty, it is not clear that this intermediate model can be fitted in a statistically meaningful way to the full set of syllogisms. Erickson himself has attempted to do so only for small subsets of problems. It may be possible to constrain the number of Euler combinations to make the theory easier to handle, but no such modification has yet been formulated.

Models and Mental Models

Johnson-Laird (1983) and his colleagues (Johnson-Laird and Bara 1984a; Johnson-Laird and Byrne 1991) have advocated a very similar approach to categorical syllogisms, using somewhat more compact diagrammatic representations. The model for syllogisms, however, is part of a more comprehensive theory of what Johnson-Laird calls "mental models." Before returning to syllogisms, let us get a grip on the intuition underlying this approach.

The idea of "mental models" rests on an analogy with model theory in logic. Traditional treatments of logic distinguish proof systems for a formal language from the semantics of the language, a distinction that we have already discussed in chapters 2 and 6. Proof theory concerns problems of deducibility—which sentences of the language can be derived from others. Model theory has to do with notions of semantic entailment and validity (see table 2.1). As we have seen, a sentence is semantically entailed by others if it is true in all models in which the others are true, and an argument is valid if its conclusion is semantically entailed by its premises. In this book we have focused mainly on deducibility, since our principal objective has been to formulate a deduction system based on proof.

However, several points about formal semantics are important in comparing logical models to mental models. One is that the models of a sentence (or of a set of sentences) need not be confined to the intended model, the one that the sentence seems to be about. In discussing the sentence *IF Satellite(x) THEN Orbits(x,b_x)* in chapter 6, we took the model to be one containing astronomical objects and defined the predicates *Satellite* and *Orbits* to coincide with their natural denotations. But we could also come up with a completely legitimate model $\mathbf{M} = \langle D,f \rangle$ in which the same sentence is true but D (the model's domain) consists of the set of natural numbers and f (the interpretation function) assigns the predicates to the following sets: $f(\text{Satellite}) = \{x: x \text{ is odd}\}$ and $f(\text{Orbits}) = \{\langle x,y \rangle: y = x + 1\}$. The same conditional sentence will be true in this model and in an infinite number of other models as well. This also means that a sentence can be true in some model even though it is false. For example, the sentence *IF Person(x) THEN Child-of(x,b_x)* (i.e., every person has a child) is false even though it is true in both of the models just constructed when $f(\text{Person}) = f(\text{Satellite})$ and $f(\text{Child-of}) = f(\text{Orbits})$, as defined above. Of course, any true sentence must be true in at least one model, namely the intended model for that sentence.

A related point is that model theory gives us no way to *compute* the validity of an argument. To determine whether an argument is valid, we need to consider the relation of the truth of the premises and the conclusion in *all* models, not just the intended one. Since there are generally an infinite number of models, there is obviously no possibility of checking them one by one. Part of the importance of model theory, as a branch of logic, is that it gives us a means of precisely characterizing correctness of arguments in a way that doesn't depend on computational considerations.

It is in proof theory that computation gets its due, since the deduction procedures of proof theory are always ones that we can carry out in a purely mechanical way. Thus, the comparison between the proof-theoretic and model-theoretic descriptions of a logical system (as in the results of chapter 6) gives us an idea of the extent to which the validity of an argument outstrips our ability to recognize it through mechanical means. This is true not only for the sorts of proof systems we considered in part II, but also (if Church's thesis is correct) for any procedure that is mechanically realizable.

If we restrict the domain of inferences, however, it is possible to give an algorithm that uses models to test arguments. A simple example is the truth-table method for testing propositional arguments in elementary logic (see, e.g., Bergmann et al. 1980 and Thomason 1970a). In this case, we can think of each line of the truth table as a model in which the function f assigns to each atomic sentence in the argument a value T (for true) or F (for false). Within each line, rules for AND, OR, NOT, and IF (similar to those in our definition of joint satisfaction in chapter 6) then assign T or F to each premise and to the conclusion on the basis of the truth of the atomic sentences. Separate lines represent different models—that is, the different possible assignments of T or F to the atomic sentences. As a simple example, the truth table for the sentences p OR q and p AND q would have this form:

p	q	p OR q	p AND q
T	F	T	F
F	T	T	F
T	T	T	T
F	F	F	F

The table shows, for example, that p AND q has the value T only when both p and q have T. In the general case there will be 2^n truth-table lines in all, where n is the number of atomic sentence types in the argument. We can say that the premises semantically entail the conclusion (and that the argument is valid) if the conclusion gets the value T in every model (i.e., line of the table) in which all the premises have the value T. Thus, an argument with p AND q as premise and p OR q as conclusion would be valid, since whenever p AND q is true so is p OR q. Although the procedure for evaluating an argument in this way can be extremely lengthy if the number of atomic sentence types is large, we can always carry out the test mechanically.

Euler circles also present a special case in which we can use models algorithmically to check arguments of a restricted type, namely arguments such as syllogisms containing only categorical sentences (i.e., *IF P(x) THEN Q(x)*, *P(b) AND Q(b)*, *NOT(P(x) AND Q(x))*, and *P(b) AND NOT(Q(b))*). The idea is to let the domain *D* be points in a plane and to let the interpretation function *f* assign predicates (*P*, *Q*, etc.) to regions that contain a set of these points. Since all that matters for satisfaction of these sentences are relations between regions, all interpretations that preserve these relations (inclusion, overlap, and nonoverlap) are equivalent, and we can represent the entire class of interpretations by the usual circles or ellipses.

Truth tables, Euler circles, and similar devices give us a decision procedure for arguments, but at the price of severely limiting the range of arguments we can test. For less constrained languages, model theory will give us a description of what it means for an argument to be valid, but not a method for recognizing valid and invalid ones.

The Mental-Models Hypothesis

With this background, let us look at a proposal for a psychologized version of model theory. Philip Johnson-Laird has described mental models for several types of arguments (see, e.g., Johnson-Laird 1983; Johnson-Laird, Byrne, and Tabossi 1989; Johnson-Laird and Byrne 1991; Johnson-Laird, Byrne, and Schaeken 1992); however, the theory for categorical syllogisms is a good place to begin studying them, since it provided the main theoretical and empirical starting point for Johnson-Laird's approach. Different versions of the syllogism model are presented in different publications (Johnson-Laird 1983; Johnson-Laird and Bara 1984a; Johnson-Laird and Byrne 1991; Johnson-Laird and Steedman 1978); we will use the most recent formulation (Johnson-Laird and Byrne 1991). (For critiques of an earlier version of the syllogism theory, see Ford 1985 and Rips 1986.)

Mental Models for Categorical Syllogisms   Although the representation is a bit more abstract than Euler circles, the basic features of the "model" model are much the same as in Erickson's theory. As a first step, people are supposed to translate the individual syllogistic premises into diagrams like those in figure 10.1. The idea is that these diagrams represent the terms of the premises as tokens standing for specific instances of the corresponding sets. For example, the premise *All square blocks are green blocks* would appear as a diagram in which there are tokens standing for individual square blocks (the xs in the top diagram in figure 10.1) and other tokens standing for individual green blocks (the ys). The former tokens are aligned horizontally with the latter, indicating that each square block is identical to some green block. The ellipsis at the bottom is a part of the model and means that additional rows of xs and ys can be added. However, the brackets around the xs stipulate that members of the set cannot occur elsewhere in the model (the xs are "exhausted" with respect to the ys in mental-model terminology). Because the ys are not bracketed, further rows of the model could contain ys with either xs or non-xs (where the latter are symbolized $\neg x$). Similarly, *No square blocks are green blocks* would be represented by a diagram containing a sample of xs and a sample of ys segregated in different rows, as in the third diagram in figure 10.1.

Premise Type	Diagram	
All X are Y	[x]	y
	[x]	y
	. . .	
Some X are Y	x	y
	x	y
	. . .	
No X are Y	[x]	
	[x]	
		[y]
		[y]
	. . .	
Some X are not Y	x	
	x	[y]
		[y]
	. . .	

Figure 10.1
Representations for categorical premises, according to Johnson-Laird and Byrne (1991).

The brackets mean that no *x*s can appear with a *y* and no *y*s can appear with an *x* in further rows of the model.

In order to determine the validity of a syllogistic conclusion (or to produce a conclusion to a pair of premises), people must combine the diagrams for the individual premises to produce a representation for the premise pair as a whole. For example, consider how the model would deal with the sample syllogism that was used in earlier chapters (e.g., chapter 6, example (1)). For reasons that we will take up later, Johnson-Laird and Byrne's model applies most easily to situations where subjects must produce a conclusion from a pair of premises. Thus, suppose the task is to find a conclusion for (5) that will make the syllogism valid.

(5)   All square blocks are green blocks.
      Some big blocks are square blocks.
      ―――――――――――――――――――――――――
                      ?

Figure 10.2 illustrates the mental-model approach to this problem in a form comparable to the Euler-circle representations of figure 1.1. The premise diagrams at the top are the same as those in figure 10.1, with *s*s representing individual square blocks, *g*s green blocks, and *b*s big blocks. The initial combined diagram is the one Johnson-Laird and Byrne (1991, table 6.1) give as the representation for the premises of syllogism (5). This combined diagram preserves the premise relationships in one possible way, with the ellipsis again allowing us to add further rows to the model. If you interpret the implied relation between the *b*s and the *g*s according to the convention about the meaning of the rows, you can see that in this combination some big blocks are green blocks.

Before one can be sure that the conclusion is correct, however, one must check whether there are alternative combined diagrams that also represent the premises but in which the tentative conclusion is false. If such a counterexample exists, one must select a new tentative conclusion that is true of all combined diagrams found so far and then continue to search for further counterexamples. If no counterexample exists, then the tentative conclusion must be a valid consequence of the premises. (When there is no categorical conclusion containing the end terms that holds in all models of the premises, one should respond that no valid conclusion is possible.) In the present example, further combinations can be formed by adding new *b*, *s*, and *g* tokens. Figure 10.2 shows possible ways of "fleshing out" the

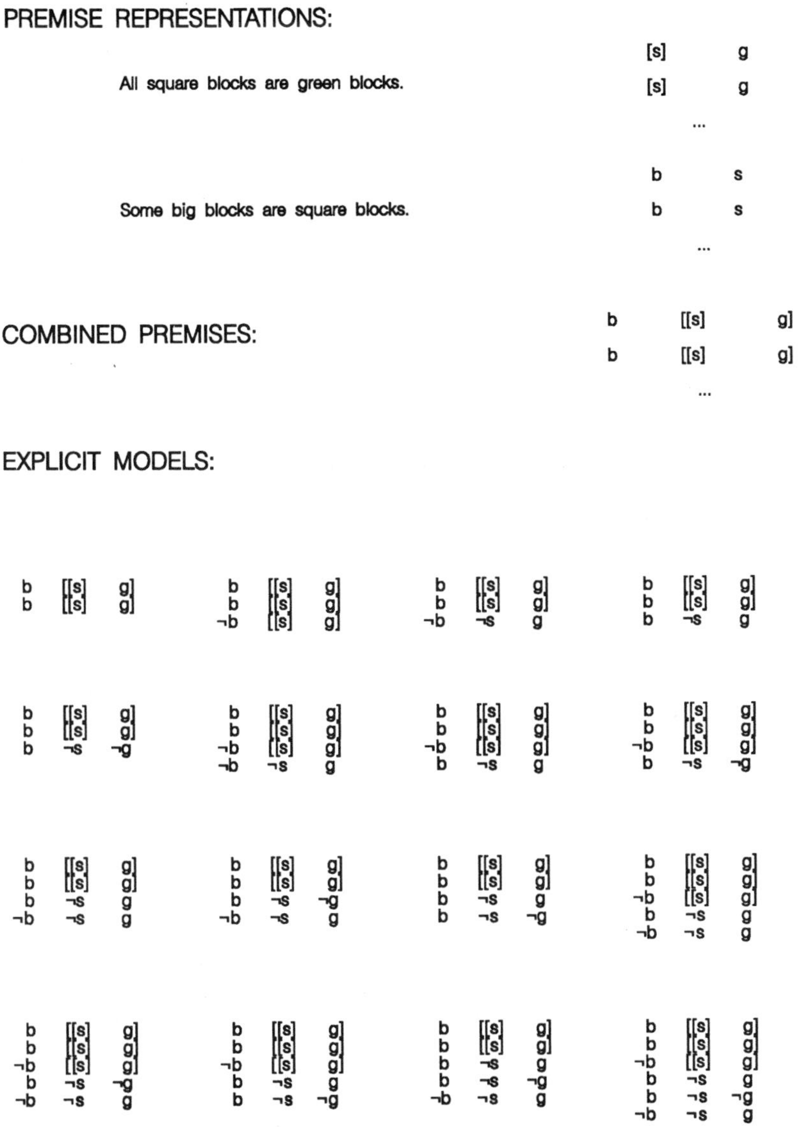

PREMISE REPRESENTATIONS:

	[s]	g
All square blocks are green blocks.	[s]	g
	...	

	b	s
Some big blocks are square blocks.	b	s
	...	

COMBINED PREMISES:

b	[[s]	g]
b	[[s]	g]
	...	

EXPLICIT MODELS:

Figure 10.2
A representation in terms of Johnson-Laird and Byrne's (1991) diagrams of the syllogism

All square blocks are green blocks.
Some big blocks are square blocks.
_____
Some big blocks are green blocks.

initial model that correspond to the 16 Euler circle combinations in figure 1.1. However, the same conclusion, *Some big blocks are green blocks*, remains true in these explicit models. Since there are no counterexamples to this conclusion, it is a correct completion for the premises in (5).

Predictions about the difficulty of syllogisms depend on the number of counterexamples. Syllogism (5) is an especially easy one, according to Johnson-Laird and Byrne, since there are no counterexamples to the conclusion reached in the initial model. Argument (6) presents more of a challenge.

(6)   Some square blocks are not green blocks.
      All square blocks are big blocks.
      _____
                        ?

Figure 10.3 shows the premise models and the two combined models that Johnson-Laird and Byrne give for the premises in (6). In the first of the combined diagrams, it is true that some green blocks are not big and that some big blocks are not green blocks, so we have two potential conclusions to deal with. The second combined model provides a counterexample to one of them (*Some green blocks are not big*), since all the green blocks are now big; hence, the only categorical conclusion relating the big and green blocks is *Some big blocks are not green blocks*. Since there are no further diagrams of the premises that make this conclusion false, it must be the correct completion for (6). On Johnson-Laird and Byrne's account, the difficulty of solution is a function of the number of models that a person must form before reaching the correct conclusion. This implies that syllogism (5), which requires only one model, should be easier than syllogism (6), which requires two—and this prediction clearly holds in the data.

An Appraisal of Mental Models for Syllogisms   Johnson-Laird and Byrne (1991) report that "it is a striking fact that the rank order of difficulty of the problems is almost perfectly correlated with the predictions of the theory." The theory predicts a total of 205 different types of conclusions across the syllogistic premises, 159 of which actually appeared in the data of Johnson-Laird and Bara's (1984a) third experiment. (See chapter 7 above for a discussion of this data set.) These conclusions accounted for 87.3% of the response tokens that the subjects produced. In the opposite direction, there are 371 response types that are predicted not to appear; of these, 46 types did in fact occur, contrary to prediction. These make up the

PREMISE REPRESENTATIONS:

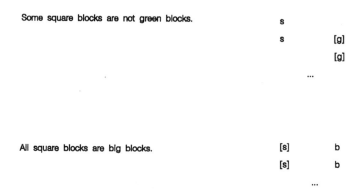

COMBINED PREMISES:

Figure 10.3
A representation in terms of Johnson-Laird and Byrne's (1991) diagrams for the syllogism
Some square blocks are not green blocks.
All square blocks are big blocks.
_____
?

remaining 12.7% of the responses.[4] (Johnson-Laird and Bara explain some of these on the basis of a Gricean implicature from sentences of the form *Some X are not Y to Some X are Y*.) Thus, the model performs about as well as the one described in chapter 7. A closer examination of the theory and the data, however, suggests some problems concerning the logical adequacy of mental models and the relation between the theory and its predictions.

Notice, first, that Johnson-Laird and Byrne's mental models differ from standard logical models in several ways. Whereas standard models consist entirely of sets, mental models also possess such devices as negation signs, ellipses indicating the potential for further models, brackets representing subset relationships, and rows depicting equality among the tokens. The procedures for constructing and revising mental models and the procedures for generating conclusions from them must preserve the meanings of these symbols. For example, the procedures must govern the brackets so that if *[a] b* exists in a model it will not be fleshed out with a new row pairing *a* with ¬*b*. Newell (1990, p. 394) points out that, as these devices increase in scope, they "become indistinguishable from full propositional representations." It is easy to overlook these constraints, but they must exist in the mental-model apparatus in order to guarantee correct results. Thus, mental models and the procedures defined over them have a lot in common with rule-based proof systems. Not only do both contain negation signs and other operators, both also employ routines for transforming strings of these symbols into other strings that preserve the truth of the premises. This means that it is at best extremely misleading to regard mental models as a "semantic" theory distinct in kind from "syntactic" approaches (Rips 1986). The strings in a mental model have a syntax as well, and are as much in need of semantic interpretation as any other representation. As Soames (1985, p. 221) puts it, "the 'mental models' hypothesis is, in effect, a proof procedure inspired by semantic ideas."

Along the same lines, mental models, like Euler circles, have built-in limitations when compared with formal models. For example, since predicates are represented by a small number of tokens, it will be impossible to represent correctly sentences with predicates or quantifiers that depend on an infinite number of objects. If *k* is the largest number of tokens that can appear in a mental model, then there is no apparent way to represent sentences like *There are more than k natural numbers*. Although Johnson-Laird (1983) mentions such sentences, his treatment suggests that mental models are not the way people represent them. "Scaled-down" models with only a few tokens might go some way toward dealing with such sentences, but in general the information from them "can be grasped without having to construct a mental model containing the complete mapping. One way of thinking of the representation of the sentence is therefore ... a propositional representation that is set up but never actually used in a procedure to construct a mental model." (ibid., p. 443) Reasoning with such sentences, Johnson-Laird believes, forces "a distinction between naive or intuitive reasoning based on mental models and mathematical reasoning, which relies on other mechanisms" (p. 444). There is little elaboration on what these other mechanisms might be.

Further, Johnson-Laird and Byrne's syllogism theory is inexplicit in ways that make it difficult to understand the basis of their predictions. This is easiest to see in the case of syllogisms such as those in (7).

(7) a. All green blocks are square blocks.
         All square blocks are big blocks.
         _____
                        ?

     b. All green blocks are square blocks.
         Some square blocks are big blocks.
         _____
                        ?

Suppose you are a subject in an experiment and you have to produce a conclusion that follows from each of these syllogisms. According to mental-model theory, you must first produce an initial model of the combined premises. In the case of (7), it turns out that these initial models are identical (see Johnson-Laird and Byrne 1991, pp. 121 and 126):

(8) [[g]   s]   b
     [[g]   s]   b
             . . .

Now, from this representation you can read off the tentative conclusion *All green blocks are big blocks.* This is, of course, the correct conclusion for syllogism (7a), which is one of the easiest problems. Johnson-Laird and Byrne state that "there is no way of fleshing out the model to refute this conclusion: it is valid and depends on the construction of just one model" (ibid., p. 121). If you produced this same conclusion to (7b), however, you would be wrong. There is no categorical conclusion that follows from (7b), and the correct response should be that "nothing follows." It must be possible to revise the initial model in (8) to show that *All green block are big blocks* isn't an entailment of (7b), and Johnson-Laird and Byrne suggest (9).

(9) [[g]   s]
     [[g]   s]
             s   b
             s   b
             . . .

Syllogism (7b) is a multiple-model problem, since both (8) and (9) are required to show that there is no valid conclusion.

The troublesome aspect of this example is this: How does the reasoner know to stop with model (8) in the case of (7a) and to continue revising the model in the case of (7b)? Model (8) itself can't supply the answer, since this model is precisely the same for the two syllogisms. Nor is it true that there are no further models of the premises in (7a); the model in (10), for example, is also consistent with the same premises.

(10) [[g]   s]   b
      [[g]   s]   b
              s   b
                     b
              . . .

Somehow reasoners needs to determine that revised models like (10) will not refute the tentative conclusion whereas models like (9) will; but it is not clear how this is possible in mental-model theory unless one actually inspects these models. On one hand, suppose the reasoners can infer from the premises of (7a) and (8) alone that no further models will refute *All green blocks are big* and, likewise, can infer from the premises of (7b) and (8) alone that further models would refute this conclusion. Then they would appear to be engaging in a form of inference that goes far beyond what is provided in the mental-model approach. The ability to make such inferences is entirely unexplained. In fact, for someone who is able to reason in this way, there would be no point whatever in constructing (9), and both (7a) and (7b) would be one-model problems, contrary to what Johnson-Laird and Byrne assert. On the other hand, suppose the reasoners must actually construct models like (10) in order to determine that no further models of (7a) refute the conclusion, just as they must construct

(9) to reject the conclusion for (7b). Then it is very misleading to say that (7a) "depends on the construction of just one model." Moreover, it is not clear exactly how many models reasoners must consider before deciding that the tentative conclusion must be correct.

A similar gap in the theory has to do with forming the initial combined model. On Johnson-Laird and Byrne's account, syllogism (6) is a "two-model" problem, since one of the potential conclusions that holds in the initial model in figure 10.3 (*Some green blocks are not big*) can be refuted by the second. According to Johnson-Laird and Byrne, this predicts that *Some green blocks are not big* should be a common error, committed by subjects who fail to keep track of the second model. But this relationship is not symmetric. Suppose that, instead of starting with the former model, you start with the latter. In that case, the model is consistent with the conclusion *All green blocks are big* as well as with the correct conclusion, *Some big blocks are not green*. Thus, *All green blocks are big* should be a common error. (In fact, although a few subjects do respond erroneously with *Some green blocks are not big*, none of them say *All green blocks are big*, according to the data of Johnson-Laird and Bara (1984a).) Thus, the predicted response to a syllogism depends on the order in which you generate the models. But Johnson-Laird and Byrne give no details on how this ordering is determined. (See Rips 1986 for further discussion.[5])

Difficulties like these become especially acute when we try to apply the mental-model hypothesis to other experimental procedures involving syllogisms. Consider the problem of predicting the difficulty of syllogisms in the task we studied in chapter 7, where subjects see a complete syllogism and must assess its logical correctness. Suppose the syllogism is a valid one. Then if subjects begin by mentally constructing a model in which the premises are true, as Johnson-Laird and Byrne hypothesize, the conclusion of the syllogism will also be true in that model. Moreover, further revisions of the model that preserve the truth of the premises will, of course, also allow the same conclusion, since by definition a conclusion that is semantically entailed by its premises is true in all models of the premises. But notice that what makes a syllogism a one-, two-, or three-model problem seems to be the number of models necessary to eliminate rival conclusions that are consistent with the initial model but that are not entailed by the premises. For example, syllogism (6) is a two-model problem because the model on the right side of figure 10.3 is necessary to eliminate the incorrect conclusion *Some green blocks are not big*. In the

case of evaluating syllogisms, however, there are no rival categorical conclusions that a subject need consider; the only relevant conclusion is the
one explicitly stated. This seems to imply that all valid syllogisms are
one-model problems in the argument-evaluation task. But these problems
are far from equivalent in difficulty for subjects, varying from 35% to 90%
correct in the Schank-Rips data and from 24% to 95% in the Dickstein
data (see chapter 7). One factor that might explain these differences is the
figure of the syllogism (i.e., the arrangement of its terms), since according
to Johnson-Laird and Byrne's account it is easier to construct models in
some figures than in others. But even if we hold figure constant, there is
still an enormous range in the difficulty of valid syllogisms. For example,
syllogisms of the second figure (i.e., of the form $\langle Q_1(H,G), Q_2(F,G)\rangle$) vary
from 35% to 90% correct in our data and from 58% to 95% correct in
Dickstein's. Without further assumptions, there seems to be no way to
predict these differences within the mental-model framework.[6]

Extended Mental Models: Multiple Quantifiers   Johnson-Laird has tried
in more recent work to address some of the limitations of mental models
by attempting to show that mental models can handle all the arguments
that rule-based theories can and, at the same time, to provide a better fit
to the data.

One extension is to a class of two-premise arguments that contain sentences with a single relation and two separately quantified terms. Arguments (11) and (12) are examples of this sort from table 5 of Johnson-Laird
et al. 1989.

(11)   None of the grocers are related to any of the violinists.
       Some of the violinists are related to all of the dancers.
       _____
       None of the grocers are related to any of the dancers.

(12)   None of the grocers are related to any of the violinists.
       All of the violinists are related to some of the dancers.
       _____
       None of the grocers are related to some of the dancers.

In these arguments, *related to* is supposed to be understood "in the simple
consanguineal sense that subjects naturally treat as being transitive and
symmetric" (ibid., p. 665). Both of these arguments are deductively correct,
according to Johnson-Laird et al., but subjects find it easier to generate a
correct conclusion to the premises of (11) than to those of (12).

The mental models for these problems are somewhat similar to those for categorical syllogisms in containing tokens for individual members. Instead of relating the tokens by aligning them in separate rows, however, Johnson-Laird et al. display them in regions of the model, with all the individuals who are "related" to one another in the same region. For example, Johnson-Laird et al.'s model for *Some of the violinists are related to all of the dancers* is

| v v v d d | 0v 0v | ,

where the vs represent violinists, the ds dancers, and the $0v$s violinists who may or may not exist.[7] The model for *All of the violinists are related to some of the dancers* is

| v d d | v d | v d d | 0d | .

As in the case of the models for categorical syllogisms, subjects are supposed to combine the models for individual premises, formulate a conclusion from the combined model, and attempt to refute the conclusion by constructing further models of the premises in which the conclusion is false. Predictions again depend on the number of models that provide counterexamples. Johnson-Laird et al. don't tell us exactly how many models each syllogism requires, however; they simply divide them into one-model and multiple-model problems. Argument (11) calls for one model and argument (12) for multiple models, according to this account.

The experiments of Johnson-Laird et al. confirm that subjects have a more difficult time producing conclusions to their multiple-model premises. But Greene (1992) has raised a serious question about the adequacy of these results. The basic contrast in the data is between one-model and multiple-model problems with valid conclusions,[8] but the conclusion that Johnson-Laird et al. count as correct for all the latter problems is the one they express as "None of the X are related to some of the Y," as in argument (12). For this response to be deductively right, however, it must be interpreted as if *some* has wide scope. That is, it must be understood to mean that there are some Y such that no X is related to them (i.e., $(\exists y)NOT((\exists x)Related(x,y)) \equiv (\exists y)(\forall x)NOT(Related(x,y))$, or, in our quantifier-free notation, $NOT(Related(x,b)))$. Greene shows that few subjects accept this reading for the sentence in question. Moreover, when given diagrams that embody the intended relationship, no subject (out of 40) was able to formulate a sentence describing them that meant the same as *NOT(Related(x,b))*. This is not because these subjects were producing a more obvious description that blocked the sentence of interest; only 9 of the 40 subjects managed to respond with *any* true description. These findings imply that the difficulty of these multiple-model problems has to do with how the sentences are interpreted or produced rather than with the number of models that the subjects must form during reasoning.

Greene's results tally nicely with an experiment of my own in which Stanford undergraduates received complete syllogisms (premises plus conclusions) similar to (11) and (12) above. Half of the subjects saw the valid one-model and the valid multiple-model problems used by Johnson-Laird et al. (The conclusions for these syllogisms were the ones Johnson-Laird et al. suggest are entailed by the premises.) These valid items appeared randomly mixed with an equal number of invalid ones formed by permuting the premises and the conclusions. The other half of the subjects saw the same problems, but with each sentence rephrased to make its intended meaning more explicit. Thus, problems (11) and (12) would have appeared as (11′) and (12′) in the revised versions.

(11′)   No grocer is related to any violinist.
        There's a violinist who every dancer is related to.
        _____
        No grocer is related to any dancer.

(12′)   No grocer is related to any violinist.
        Every violinist is related to a dancer (but not necessarily the same
           dancer).
        _____
        There's a dancer who no grocer is related to.

Subjects were to decide whether the conclusion of each syllogism followed from the premises.

The results of this study show that the difference between one- and multiple-model syllogisms depends strongly on the wording. With the wording of Johnson-Laird et al., the subjects correctly evaluated 86.1% of the valid one-model problems but only 41.6% of the valid multiple-model problems. With the revised wording, the difference was significantly reduced; the repective percentages were 83.3 and 72.2. Thus, clarifying the premises and conclusions largely eliminates the effect of number of models. The residual difference between one-model and multiple-model syllogisms is probably due to the inclusion of very simple one-model items (e.g., *All of the X are related to all of the Y*; *All of the Y are related to all of the Z*; *Therefore, all of the X are related to all of the Z*), which can be handled by simple forward rules and for which performance was perfect in the experiment. The best test cases are the syllogisms in (11)–(12) and (11′)–(12′), since these items control for most other factors, as Johnson-Laird et al. acknowledge. The results for these pairs showed a large difference with the original wording: 92.0% correct on (11) and 42.0% correct on (12). But with the revised wording, the difference vanished entirely: Subjects were correct on 75.0% of trials with both (11′) and (12′). Like Greene's results, these suggest that the effect Johnson-Laird et al. attribute to the number of models subjects form during reasoning is more likely the result of difficulty subjects had in grasping the meaning of the premises and potential conclusions.

Extended Models: Propositional Arguments.[9] Johnson-Laird, Byrne, and Schaeken (1992) have also attempted to enlarge the mental-models hypothesis to cover reasoning with propositional connectives. However, although the mental models that they propose in this domain bear a surface resemblance to those for categorical syllogisms, they must be interpreted quite differently, in a way that closely approaches the entries in a truth table. For example, a sentence of the form *p OR q* would appear as

$$
\begin{array}{ll}
p & \neg q \\
\neg p & q \\
p & q
\end{array}
$$

where each row is a separate "model" and where the *p*s and *q*s represent propositions. The first row or model represents the possibility that *p* is true and *q* is false, the second model the possibility that *p* is false and *q* is true, and so on. The models represent all the separate contingencies in which the entire sentence is true. Thus, the three "models" correspond to three lines of the standard truth table that we looked at earlier, namely those lines that assign T to *p OR q*. (Johnson-Laird et al. also allow *p OR q* to be represented "implicitly" by just the first two lines above, until the task requires that subjects "flesh out" the representation by adding the third line.) This choice of representation also brings out a point that I made earlier about the syntax of mental models. As Johnson-Laird et al. mention, one can turn any of their models for sentential reasoning into an isomorphic sentence in standard logical notation simply by placing an AND between each of the elements in the rows and then joining the rows with OR. For example, the models for *p OR q* above can be expressed as *(p AND (NOT q)) OR ((NOT p) AND q) OR (p AND q)*. Sentences like these—composed of disjunctions, each of which is a conjunction of atomic sentences or negations of atomic sentences—are said to be in *disjunctive normal form*. Thus, any mental model can be translated into an isomorphic sentence in disjunctive normal form.

As in the earlier studies, Johnson-Laird et al. (1992) use the number of models (i.e., rows) to predict the difficulty of a deduction problem. For example, premises that require three models should be more difficult for subjects than premises that require only one or two. However, these modified truth tables lead to some dubious predictions. Consider the sentential arguments shown in (13) and (14).

(13)   p AND q
       IF p THEN r
       IF q THEN r
       ──────────
       r

(14)   p OR q
       IF p THEN r
       IF q THEN r
       ──────────
       r

These two arguments vary only in their first premise, and both are clearly valid. However, they differ in the number of models in their representation. The first premise of (13) is just a single line or model consisting of *p* and *q*. But the first premise of (14) would appear as the three lines in our earlier example (or as just the first two lines in the case of the "implicit" representation). The conditional premises don't reduce this difference. The full set of premises in (13) has the model (13'), whereas the full set of premises in (14) has the model (14').

(13')   p   q   r

(14')   p   ¬q   r
          ¬p   q   r
          p   q   r

We are assuming that the OR in (14) is inclusive; but even if we were to interpret it as an exclusive disjunction, (14) would still require more models than (13). The representation would change only by deleting the last line of (14′). Thus, on any plausible assumptions (implicit vs. explicit representation, inclusive vs. exclusive OR), the mental-model theory must predict that (13) is easier for subjects to evaluate than (14).

Similar predictions hold for the pairs of arguments that form the rows in table 10.1. The first row of the table simply repeats (13) and (14). The second row contains related arguments that switch the polarity of the atomic sentences in the premises from p to *NOT* p and from q to *NOT* q. These two arguments are also valid, of course, and their models are like (13′) and (14′) except that the positions of p and $\neg p$ (q and $\neg q$) are reversed. The arguments in the third row of the table are logically equivalent to those of the second row and have exactly the same models. Thus, the argument on the left in all three rows is associated with just a single model, whereas the argument at the right is associated with more than one model. It follows from the mental-models theory that the arguments on the left should be easier than the corresponding ones on the right. However, although the arguments in rows 2 and 3 are logically equivalent, they differ in the scope of the negation. The arguments in row 2 have narrow scope (the negation is within the conjunction or disjunction), while those in row 3 have wide scope.

Table 10.1
Percentage of "necessarily true" responses for one-model and multiple-model problems. ($n = 37$).

One model		Multiple models	
Argument	% Correct	Argument	% Correct
p AND q IF p, r IF q, r —————— r	89.2	p OR q IF p, r IF q, r —————— r	89.2
(NOT p) AND (NOT q) IF NOT p, r IF NOT q, r —————— r	94.6	(NOT p) OR (NOT q) IF NOT p, r IF NOT q, r —————— r	81.1
NOT(p OR q) IF NOT p, r IF NOT q, r —————— r	64.9	NOT(p AND q) IF NOT p, r IF NOT q, r —————— r	64.9

To test the prediction of the mental-models theory, I asked subjects to decide whether the conclusions of the arguments in table 10.1 were "necessarily true" or "not necessarily true" on the basis of their premises. There were three groups of subjects in this experiment; each received the two arguments in one of the rows of the table. Each group also received two filler arguments that were not valid. The arguments were phrased in terms of simple sentences about the location of people in places, as in the experiments discussed in chapter 5 (see Rips 1990b).

Table 10.1 shows the percentages of the subjects that responded that the conclusion was necessarily true for the six critical arguments. The overall accuracy for these problems was fairly good (80.6%), in accord with their intuitive simplicity. However, contrary to the predictions of the mental-model theory, there was no difference whatever in subjects' accuracy for (13) and (14) (as can be seen in the first row). The same is true for the arguments in row 3, which have wide-scope negatives. Only the arguments with narrow-scope negatives (row 2) produced a trend in the direction of greater accuracy for one-model problems, though this difference did not result in a significant effect for number of models. There are, however, obvious differences in difficulty among these six problems. Comparing the three rows, we find that subjects have more trouble with the arguments involving wide-scope negation (only 64.9% correct) than for arguments with narrow-scope or no negation (87.8% and 89.2% correct, respectively).

These results suggest that the need to keep track of multiple models was not the source of the subjects' difficulties. Subjects must follow up the consequences of just one model to evaluate argument (13), but two or three models for argument (14); yet there is no difference in how easy it is to recognize them as deductively correct. This is not just a matter of a ceiling effect, since the same goes for the problems in row 3 of table 10.1, where performance is relatively poor. What makes for complexity in reasoning with these problems is not multiple models but wide-scope negatives. These results are generally consistent with PSYCOP's approach to these arguments. PSYCOP deduces the conclusion of argument (13) by means of its Forward AND and IF Elimination rules, and it deduces the conclusion of (14) by means of Forward Dilemma (see table 4.1). Although more rules are necessary for the proof of (13), it is quite possible that the Dilemma rule is somewhat harder for subjects to apply than the AND and IF Elimination sequence; Dilemma requires coordination of three premises, whereas AND and IF Elimination require one or two. There is no reason to think that one of these methods should be much easier than the other. The same is true for the arguments in the second row of table 10.1. However, both problems in the third row also require distributing the *NOT* via one of the forward DeMorgan rules. Since this extra distribution step requires extra work on PSYCOP's part, accuracy should decrease.

How Plausible Are Mental Diagrams and Models as Explanations of Reasoning?

If people use mental models for reasoning, these models are unlikely to be much like formal models. There are ordinarily an infinite number of formal models for any consistent set of sentences; thus, there is no hope that people could evaluate the deductive correctness of arguments by sorting through all formal models for a set of premises. To make a psychologized version of model theory plausible, you have to introduce some limitations in the nature of the models and in the kinds of arguments they can handle. In the case of Erickson's Euler-circle theory the limitations are clear. Even if there were no psychological limits on generating and manipulating Euler circles, the theory would apply only to a restricted set of arguments. There is no way to represent arguments that contain five or more terms with Euler circles (Quine 1972), and this means that we can deal effectively with categorical syllogisms and not much more.

In the case of Johnson-Laird's mental models, the restriction to finite numbers of exemplars leads to problems with even fairly simple inferences. The difficulties in reasoning with sentences like *There are more than k natural numbers*, when k is the largest number of tokens that can appear in a mental model, have already been noted. Our survey of the mental-models literature points up another sort of restriction. Since arguments that depend on propositional connectives are handled by one sort of model and arguments with quantifiers by another, there is no apparent way to explain reasoning that depends on both. This includes the type of arguments that we studied in chapter 7 (e.g., *Someone is rich and everyone pays taxes; therefore, someone is rich and pays taxes*). The models for quantifiers and the models for propositions all contain similar-looking tokens, but they must be interpreted in completely different ways when we move from one type of task to another. The mental model

a   b

can mean that some artists are beekeepers, that one artist is a beekeeper, that Alfred is in Albany AND Ben is in Boston, that an aardvark is to the left of a baboon, and presumably many other things. Hence, distinct processes have to operate on this model in these varied contexts in order to enforce the hidden logical differences among them. We have also seen that the mental-models hypothesis depends on a large number of unspecified assumptions about how people form and revise mental models, and it runs into serious problems in accounting for the experimental results.

In view of these deficiencies, why should we believe the mental-model hypothesis? Johnson-Laird (1983, chapter 2) lists six problems about reasoning that he believes mental models can solve, but which he believes create difficulties for approaches based on mental inference rules. Perhaps these problems could tip the balance in favor of models, despite the difficulties we have scouted. The first three of these problems are addressed in part II of this book: Which logics are to be found in the mind, how is mental logic formulated, and why do people sometimes make fallacious inferences? The theory outlined in chapters 4 and 6 provides answers to the questions about the nature and the form of mental logic, as well as some reasons why deduction sometimes breaks down. The results in chapters 5 and 7 confirm these hypotheses. I have also offered an answer to the fourth of Johnson-Laird's problems: How can we explain the inferences people spontaneously draw from the potentially infinite number that follow from a set of premises? The solution is that the spontaneous inferences are ones that follow from forward rules, where the distinction between forward and backward rules is in turn explained by the self-constraining property of the former (as discussed in chapter 3). People can use forward rules spontaneously because the output of these rules will never lead to runaway inferences. The remaining two points of Johnson-Laird deserve comment, however, since they might provide a reason to hang onto mental models despite their flaws. We will also consider a matter that Johnson-Laird takes up elsewhere concerning the ability of models to explain truth and falsity.

Models, Inference Rules, and Content Effects

One of Johnson-Laird's remaining points has to do with the content effects discussed in the first section of this chapter: Perhaps mental models are better able to deal with these effects than logical rules, which are tied to the logical form of sentences. But our examination of mental models shows that their ability to take "content" into account is no different from that of systems based on logical rules. For example, there is nothing in Johnson-Laird and Byrne's theory of syllogistic reasoning that depends on what the tokens in their models (the little gs, ss, and bs in figures 10.2 and 10.3) stand for. The mental-model theory would work in exactly the same way if the terms of the syllogism were switched from green, square, and big blocks to grocers, squires, and barristers, or to any other triple. Of course, you could change mental models to coincide with further information you have about these classes. For example, if you happen to know on the basis of experience that all green blocks are square, then you might alter the representation of the first premise in figure 10.2 (*All square blocks are green blocks*) by bracketing the gs to indicate that there are no green blocks that aren't square. This would, in turn, have a subsequent effect on the conclusions you draw from the syllogism.

As Politzer and Braine (1991) have noted, however, proponents of mental models have offered no account of how such an interpretive process takes place beyond saying that it depends on "world knowledge." Moreover, even if one grants such a process, this method of dealing with content is also open to inference-rule approaches. Prior information about the terms of a syllogism can be added to the premises in the form of additional mental sentences, where this extra information is then open to manipulation by rules in the usual way. For example, the premises in figure 10.2 could be supplemented by a sentence stating that all green blocks are square, and the outcome would presumably be the same as in the case of mental models.

For these reasons, mental models do not seem especially well suited to explain the sorts of findings that I called elaboration effects above; and much the same is true of effects of believability. There is nothing about mental models to explain why subjects sometimes think arguments with believable conclusions are more likely to be correct than ones with less believable conclusions. A proponent of mental models might stipulate that people don't work as hard at finding counterexamples when the tentative conclusions are more believable (see Oakhill et al. 1989). But proponents of inference rules could equally well assert that people slack off when searching for proofs for arguments with *less* believable conclusions.[10] In short, mental models are no better equipped than inference rules to explain either elaboration or believability effects, though both kinds of theory are probably consistent with such effects under further assumptions.

Models, Inference Rules, and Truth

In Johnson-Laird's framework, mental models are fundamentally different from the more usual formalisms in cognitive psychology, such as mental sentences and mental networks. The idea is that, whereas mental sentences and mental networks are just syntactically arranged strings of symbols, mental models could go beyond syntax in order to determine the truth or falsity of sentences:

> Theories based solely on linguistic representations do not say anything about how words relate to the world.... Until such relations are established, the question of whether a description is true or false cannot arise. Mental models are symbolic structures, and the relation of a model to the world cannot simply be read off from the model. So how is the truth or falsity of an assertion judged in relation to the world? The answer is that a discourse will be judged true if its mental model can be embedded in the model of the world. Thus, for example, you will judge my remark about the table being in front of the stove as true if it corresponds to your perception of the world, that is, a model based on the assertion can be embedded within a perceptual model of the situation.... (Johnson-Laird 1989, pp. 473–474)

The first thing to notice about this argument is that the term "linguistic representation" is ambiguous, since it could refer to representations derived from specifically linguistic material (such as spoken or written sentences) or to any mental representation that itself has the structure of a sentence. If we understand "linguistic representation" in the first way, then there are obviously situations in which our judgments of whether something is true or false depend on something other than these linguistic representations. If I tell you that the table is in front of the stove, then you might judge that to be true on the basis of your perception of the table's being in front of the stove. On this reading, a representation derived from perception isn't a linguistic representation; so we need something more than linguistic representations to make judgments about truth.

However, the difficulty with understanding "linguistic representation" in this way is that you then can't use the argument to show that you need mental models in addition to mental sentences in order to account for such judgments. To see why, let us go back to the experiment by Clark and Chase (1972) that we discussed in chapter 5. Recall that on Clark and Chase's theory the sentence *The star is above the plus* is represented as the mental sentence *Above(star,plus)*. A picture of a star above a plus is also represented as a mental sentence of the same form. In order to judge the truth or falsity of a sentence with respect to a picture, one compares the two mental sentences. No further entity, such as a mental model, is necessary, on this theory, to account for the true/false decision. Mental sentences are sufficient to account for these judgments because you can use mental sentences to represent the information derived from perception as well as the information derived from a spoken or written sentence.

Thus, in order for Johnson-Laird's argument to establish that mental models are necessary, "linguistic representation" must be understood more broadly. "Linguistic representation" has to mean something like a mental sentence or some similar structure. If mental sentences can't by themselves account for judgments of truth or falsity, then maybe we need some other mental entity—perhaps mental models. But in that case there is no reason at all to accept Johnson-Laird's premises. If a linguistic representation is just a mental sentence, then mental sentences can account for judgments of truth and falsity at least as well as mental models. That is exactly what we just noticed in the star-plus example, where we can judge truth or falsity by comparing mental sentences. In other words, neither reading of "linguistic representation" allows the argument to establish that mental sentences aren't perfectly sufficient for truth judgments.

There may be another way to take Johnson-Laird's argument, however. In the preceding discussion, mental models were supposed to account for the belief that *The table is in front of the stove* is true: One might believe that this is true because one can compare a representation of the sentence with a representation based on perception of a scene. For these purposes, it seems as though the representation of the scene could as easily be a mental sentence as a mental model. But perhaps what Johnson-Laird means is that we need mental models in order to establish whether the sentence is really true, not just whether we believe it is. The sentence *The table is in front of the stove* is true because of the way the world is, not because of the way our representations are. To establish truth in this sense, a comparison of mental sentences clearly isn't sufficient. Maybe Johnson-Laird thinks mental models are necessary because they can put us in touch with the world in a way that mental sentences can't. This sort of interpretation is suggested in the passage quoted above by the assertion that linguistic representations do not say anything about how words relate to the world.

But consider *The table is in front of the stove*. This sentence is true, Johnson-Laird suggests, if there is a mental model for it of the right sort.

As he says, mental models are themselves symbolic structures; so we can't simply read off the truth of the sentence from the model. However, the sentence will be true if its mental model can be "embedded in the model of the world." It is completely obvious, though, that if this "model of the world" is also a mental model—another symbolic structure—then we need to ask how it is that we know that this model of the world is true. Even if one's model of the world is some sort of image derived from perception, there is no guarantee that it is true, since it is notorious that perception is subject to all sorts of illusions. Thus, if the model of the world that Johnson-Laird has in mind is another mental representation, being embedded in such a model is no guarantee of truth.

Could Johnson-Laird mean that a sentence is true if it has a mental model that can be embedded in a *non*mental model of the world? If so, then we need some sort of explanation of what it means to embed a mental model in a nonmental one. Moreover, at this point it is no longer clear what the concept of a model is buying us. Instead of saying that *The table is in front of the stove* is true if its mental model can be embedded in a nonmental model of the world, couldn't we say more simply that the sentence is true if the table is in front of the stove? Johnson-Laird and Byrne (1991, p. 213) suggest that, although their computer simulations operate in a purely syntactic way, the models become semantic when they are embodied in people because of causal links between models and the world. However, if that is true for mental models, it could equally well be true for other forms of mental representation. The mental-model hypothesis is at its weakest when it claims for itself representational powers that go beyond those of sentences.[11]

Mental Models, Inference Rules, and Acquisition

Johnson-Laird's final point is that there is no obvious way that mental inference rules can be learned, whereas mental models pose no such problem. It is possible to suppose, of course, that inference rules for specific connectives or quantifiers are learned along with the words to which they correspond. AND Elimination and AND Introduction are acquired, on this account, while children are mastering the meaning of *and* in their native language. This seems quite reasonable, in some respects, in view of the close connection between a connective's meaning and its use in performing inferences (Dummett 1973; Sundholm 1986); in some cases, exactly this sort of learning may occur. But, as Fodor (1975, 1981) has pointed out, the child needs some logical base even to begin formulating hypotheses about the meaning of such a word. If the child acquires *and* by learning that *and* means "...", then he or she must already have a language that is logically rich enough to fill in the blank. This seems to entail that some logical principles are innate. Johnson-Laird (1983, p. 25) objects to this conclusion on the ground that "there is no direct evidence for it whatsoever, merely the lack of any alternative that proponents find convincing." Moreover, he argues that mental models avoid this problem, since there are no inference rules to acquire. Instead, "what children learn first are the truth conditions of expressions: they learn the contributions of connectives, quantifiers, and other such terms to these truth conditions" (p. 144).

The innateness of basic logical abilities is not a bitter pill, however. These abilities are exactly the sort of things one might expect to be innate, if anything is, given the central role of reasoning in cognition and learning. (See Macnamara 1986 for a development of this point of view.) And, of course, the presence of innate logical abilities doesn't imply that people never make mistakes in deduction, or that they are incapable of improving their inference skills, any more than the presence of innate grammatical abilities implies that people never make grammatical errors, or that they can't improve their grammar through learning. Mistakes can come about through limits on rule availabilities or memory capacity, improvements can occur (in logic class, say) through the learning of short-cuts that compress long chains of inferences into single steps.

What is important in this context, however, is that, even if we are dubious about the innateness of logical rules, Johnson-Laird's truth conditions are not going to be more palatable. The truth conditions for the logical connective *and* are standardly given in the form in which they were stated in chapter 6: S_1 AND S_2 is satisfied (or is true) iff both S_1 and S_2 are satisfied (are true). Within this framework, we can think of S_1 AND S_2 as the expression to be learned and of the material on the right-hand side of the biconditional as part of the child's preexisting language. But this makes it completely obvious that any such learning is impossible unless the child already understands what it means for both S_1 and S_2 to be true—that is, unless the child already knows the meaning of some expression that is logically equivalent to AND. Recasting this in terms of mental models, rather than formal models, doesn't avoid this consequence. Then the truth condition is presumably that S_1 AND S_2 is true in a mental model iff both S_1 and S_2 are true in the mental model. And this formulation, too, transparently requires prior knowledge of *and*'s meaning. Fodor's problem applies in spades to the learning of truth conditions, and it leads to exactly the same innateness hypothesis. The basic argument for innateness is the difficulty of conceiving a learning mechanism that doesn't already contain basic logical operations.

Problems about acquisition of logical knowledge, like problems about effects of content on reasoning, are difficult, and any theory that could give a convincing explanation of them would certainly be welcome. But mental models come no closer to this ideal than do rule-based approaches. This is probably traceable to the fact that both types of theories are, at heart, methods for transforming configurations of (syntactically structured) symbols in ways that preserve truth. In order for this to be done in a general way—a way that avoids the need to restate the same inference pattern for every new domain—both theories must be quite abstract, and their abstractness is what makes content effects and acquisition thorny issues. To decide between the theories, we need to consider other properties, such as explicitness, generalizability, and empirical accuracy. The results in part II should help decide the issue with respect to these characteristics.

11 Perspectives on Reasoning Ability

Galileo, you are traveling the road to disaster.... A moment ago, when you were at the telescope, I saw you tied to the stake, and when you said you believed in proof, I smelt burning flesh.
Brecht, *Galileo*

We have been after a psychological theory of deductive reasoning that can be defended on the basis of experiments and that has advantages over rival accounts. I hope that part II successfully carried the experimental burden of the theory and that the earlier chapters of part III established some of its advantages. But we also need to look from a higher position at the theory's adequacy, since we want to ensure that its assumptions don't clash with global facts about cognition or with secure principles from philosophy or AI. We have already bumped against such high-level principles in considering the place of deduction among inference types, but it is worth gathering some of these general issues here to get an overview of the theory's commitments. I would like to prevent misreadings of the theory's claims, if I can, and to indicate what questions the theory currently leaves open.

Most of the critiques of rule-based, psychological theories of deduction fall into two opposing camps. One camp consists mainly of psychologists to whom such theories seem to make people out to be far more logical or rational than they are in practice. If people really come equipped with inference rules, how come they have such trouble with seemingly trivial problems in deduction? The other camp consists mainly of philosophers who feel that these theories make people out to be much more irrational than is possible. This camp believes that, on a proper analysis of the very concepts of deduction and rationality, people can't be systematically in error about basic logical matters. These two camps have clearly conflicting positions, and the present theory's intermediate stance places it in the crossfire. To see whether the theory is defensible, I therefore need to consider both camps and find out how much of the theory remains intact. Let me start with the view that our theory is "too rational," reserving discussion of the "too irrational" position till the end.

Aren't You Making People Out to Be More Logical or Rational Than They Really Are?

It is obvious, at this late stage, that the PSYCOP theory allows certain types of errors, since much of the evidence that supports the theory comes from data on the percentage of "incorrect" responses from subjects. Yet the question of what qualifies as an error in reasoning isn't straightforward. In early research on the psychology of reasoning, experimenters counted as an error any deviation from a standard logical system— generally Scholastic doctrine in the case of syllogisms or classical sentential logic in the case of sentential arguments. However, if an "error" of this sort is something for which we can actually criticize a subject, rather than just a convenient label for classifying the subject's responses, then the logical systems themselves must be correct norms of appraisal. Some early researchers may have accepted the standard systems as normatively appropriate simply out of ignorance of rival ones, but the variety of contemporary logics raises questions about the correctness of Scholastic and of classical logic. Inferences that follow the pattern of Double Negation Elimination, for example, are valid in classical logic but not in intuitionistic logic (Dummett 1977; Fitch 1952; Fitting 1983; Heyting 1956). Similarly, the syllogism ⟨All(G,H), All(G,F), ∴Some(F,H)⟩ is valid according to Scholastic logic but not according to classical logic (see the appendix to chapter 7 above). This means that attributing errors to subjects can be a delicate matter that depends on how we justify the logical systems themselves. Let us call justifications of this sort "system justifications," since they determine the entire system's correctness or incorrectness.

Once we have fixed on a system that we can justify, there is a further question of how closely people's decisions conform to it. Whether people's reasoning is correct or not is most clear-cut if the justification of the system doesn't itself depend on facts about human reasoning. Things become more complex if the system's criteria are themselves based on people's intuitions about correct inferences. It is reasonable to hold, for example, that a correct deduction system is one that squares with primitive intuitions about what follows from what (Cohen 1981; Goodman 1965; Harman 1986; Peacocke 1987). In that case the correctness of a particular inference depends on how it fits with the deduction system, and the correctness of the deduction system depends on how it fits with primitive judgments. Theories of this sort place a limit on how badly people reason, since the primitive judgments partially define correct reasoning. However, these theories generally leave some room for errors. Distractions can keep people from tapping their primitive intuitions for simple arguments, and their intuitions may not extend directly to more complex argument forms.

The problem of errors in reasoning is also complicated by the different computational levels in PSYCOP. This model comes with a stock of inference rules (the rules of part II), which I take to constitute part of the architecture of human cognition. It is possible to raise questions about whether these rules are correct, much as one can raise questions about the correctness of classical logic. *If* I am right about empirical matters (that these rules really are embodied in the architecture), and *if* these rules are incorrect, then the inference rules could be committing people to a type of irremediable error. Human thinking would then contain a basic flaw that could never be entirely eradicated.

I am assuming, however, a second level of deduction, in accord with the promotional/demotional approach introduced in chapter 2. When people face a concrete deduction problem (e.g., those in the experiments of part II), they make use of deduction rules that they can employ strategically and can emend or supplement. I have assumed that these rules resemble the built-in ones, since built-in structure governs the way people learn and deploy the lower-level rules. But there may be disparities between levels, just as there can be disparities between programs in PASCAL and in the assembly language to which the PASCAL programs are translated. Errors arise naturally with respect to these lower-level rules, since individuals' processing limits and biases, competition from other nondeductive strategies, uncertainties about the correctness of a rule, and assumptions about the appropriateness of a rule can all interfere with the way people use them.[1]

One must keep these distinct levels of deduction in mind when discussing whether PSYCOP is "too logical." Some of the questions about errors are best directed to the architectural level, whereas others are more appropriately directed to the strategic level. It is much more difficult (though perhaps not impossible) to convict human deduction of mistakes in architecture than to convict it of mistakes in strategic use of rules. Let us consider some of the possible issues about errors in relation to this dual approach.

Aren't You Asserting the Discredited Doctrine of Psychologism (or that the Laws of Logic Are the Laws of Thought)?

Psychologism is the thesis that a logical or a mathematical system is a description or a generalization of how people reason. According to this thesis, whether Double Negation Elimination (for example) is deductively correct can be decided only in terms of whether people agree (perhaps under ideal circumstances) to the inference from *NOT NOT P* to *P*. Psychologism appears to be the result of an expansionist tendency of some nineteenth-century philosophers and psychologists to try to explain all facets of intellectual life in empirical psychological terms. Not surprisingly, this tendency provoked a strong backlash by members of other disciplines, who saw these psychological explanations as essentially trivial. As a result of this backlash, it has come to be a truism that logical principles are not merely redescriptions of psychological ones: "If we could accept as good psychology the old idea that logic teaches the laws of thought, we should be far ahead in our knowledge of the process of thinking. Recent students of logic and psychology agree that logic, or at least the formal logic which has come down from Aristotle, is not psychology to any great extent." (Woodworth 1938, p. 807) It may seem at first glance that theories like PSYCOP are throwbacks to the earlier psychologistic tradition, but that would reflect a misunderstanding of the aims of these approaches.

Frege's (1893/1964, 1918/1977) well-known attack on psychologism emphasized the fact that truths of logic and arithmetic hold whether or not anyone has managed to discover them. Moreover, such truths are constant, in contrast with people's fluctuating psychological awareness of them. These subsistence and stability properties are fundamental to doing logic and math, and it is impossible to explain them in purely psychological terms. (See chapter 1 of Macnamara 1986 for a discussion of the psychologism/anti-psychologism controversy.) Logical and mathematical truths also seem to be necessary truths that hold across all possible worlds or states of affairs. By contrast, empirical facts about human psychology are only contingently true, on the assumption that in other possible worlds our psychological makeup would be different. This tension between logical necessity and psychological contingency (see Stroud 1981) again suggests that the latter can't be entirely responsible for the former. If a logical truth depended solely on contingent psychological properties of ours, then in some other world in which that property failed to apply—in which we reasoned in ways that we don't now—the logical truth presumably would also have to fail. But since logical truths can't fail, logic can't be psychological at heart.

It might be possible to defuse some of these anti-psychologistic arguments. For example, Sober (1978) claims that Frege's contrast between logical stability and psychological variability was due to his taking introspectionist psychology as a guide. Current information-processing theories posit mental mechanisms that are stable enough to allow logical principles to be psychologically real. (Sober believes, however, that full-blown psychologism still falls prey to Frege's subsistence thesis.) One might also argue that any such psychologically real logical principles must be essential aspects of the human mental makeup and hence true in all possible worlds. Such a position would contend that, just as a correct chemical theory of a natural kind such as water identifies properties of water that are necessarily true (Kripke 1972; Putnam 1975), so a correct theory of psychology identifies properties of reasoning that are necessarily true. If this is correct, then there need be no conflict in the status of logical principles and their psychological embodiments across possible worlds.

The theory of part II, however, doesn't depend on the outcome of the debate between psychologism and anti-psychologism. The theory needn't claim that logic exists only as a psychological object or activity, and thus it doesn't entail psychologism as defined above. It is consistent with the possibility that logics are wholly or partly mind-independent entities and with the possibility that a logic system is justified by non-psychological standards. A complete divorce beween logic and psychology creates puzzles about how people could apprehend a logic system, but these are puzzles for anti-psychologism itself and not for the particular reasoning theory I have proposed.

The PSYCOP theory simply means to be descriptive of the mental processes that people go through when they engage in deductive reasoning, and nothing in Frege's argument contradicts the possibility that this is right (Notturno 1982). What Frege (1918/1977, p. 2) denied is that these mental processes *constitute* logical truths: "... an explanation of a mental process that ends in taking something to be true, can never take the place of proving what is taken to be true. But may not logical laws also have played a part in this mental process? I do not want to dispute this, but if it is a question of truth this possibility is not enough. For it is also possible that something non-logical played a part in the process and made it swerve from the truth." On Frege's view, logical laws might inform mental processes, though the two can't be identical.

The robustness of Frege's logical truths suggests that, instead of trying to reduce logical principles to psychological ones, it would be more reasonable to move in the opposite direction. Perhaps if it were possible to show that Fregean laws did all the work required of a theory of mental inference rules, we could dispense with these rules as superfluous. But this would probably be a mistake. Mental rules are supposed to be part of a *causal* account of the way people evaluate arguments, produce conclusions, and solve other types of deduction problems. How Fregean logical truths could accomplish these things is, to say the least, perplexing.

Aren't You Assuming That People Can't Possess "Incorrect" Deduction Rules?

PSYCOP clearly admits the possibility that people don't always reason correctly. But how deep do the errors go? In the simulations of part II, we assumed that subjects have a certain pool of inference rules at their disposal but sometimes fail to apply them correctly, which causes their judgments to deviate from what they are ideally capable of. But what about the inference rules themselves? All the rules posited in chapters 4 and 6 appear to be sound with respect to classical logic, so people who stuck to these rules couldn't reach classically invalid conclusions. Any errors that occurred in their reasoning would have to be errors of omission (essentially, failures to find some mental proof) or errors due to guessing or to interference from other factors. However, one might try to argue that people also make errors of commission, applying some unsound rules that get them into trouble. (Goldman (1986) raises the issue of unsound rules in discussing cognitive models of deduction, though he doesn't necessarily advocate including them.)

As examples of possible errors of commission, consider the "formal fallacies" that appear in textbooks on informal logic and rhetoric. These books warn against reasoning in certain rule-like patterns that are unsound in standard logic systems. For instance, the fallacy of "denying the antecedent" is an unsound argument of the form *IF P THEN Q; NOT P*; therefore, *NOT Q*. It would be easy enough to formulate a deduction rule along the lines of those in table 4.1 that would produce such a fallacy if faced with the appropriate task. There is nothing about the mechanics of the inference-rule system that would forbid it. Moreover, subjects sometimes affirm arguments of just this type (see chapter 5). So there seems to be some motivation for taking these unsound rules to be psychologically real. Along the same lines, it is possible to specify an "atmosphere rule" for syllogisms that would cause subjects to affirm arguments like $\langle \text{All}(G,H), \text{All}(G,F), \therefore \text{All}(F,H) \rangle$, as was noted in chapter 9. In the area of probabilistic reasoning, claims for the presence of fallacious rules are common (see, e.g., Kahneman et al. 1982). For example, some individuals seem to operate under the "law of small numbers" (Tversky and Kahneman 1971) or "gambler's fallacy," giving higher odds to a coin's landing "heads" the longer the string of preceding flips that landed "tails." If people possess such normatively inappropriate rules for reasoning with uncertainty, it seems a short step to assuming that they have similarly inappropriate rules for reasoning deductively.

Strategic Errors   The possibility of incorrect deduction rules has different implications for the strategic levels and the architectural levels of the theory, because these levels vary in how easy it is to change them. At the strategic level, it seems reasonable to suppose that people could have incorrect routines that they mistakenly take to be correct deduction rules. We could imagine, for example, a devious instructor who persuaded his students to use a particular rule for solving deduction problems that didn't happen to be correct and that produced incorrect proofs of arguments. Nothing in the model would prohibit such a possibility, and from the standpoint of proponents of nonclassical logics that is what most logic teachers actually do. (See, for example, Anderson and Belnap's (1975) discussion of the "Official View" of IF.) Of course, the methods that people use in reasoning are probably not ordinarily ones they explicitly learned in class, and deliberate professorial brainwashing is unlikely to be the source of many incorrect rules. But if people can learn incorrect rules through direct training, it seems highly likely that they can also learn them in indirect ways, abstracting them from the speech or the writing of others. So why not take incorrect rules such as these to be the basis for some of the mistakes that people make in reasoning experiments?

   Whether to include Denying the Antecedent and similar principles among the deduction rules can't be decided without evidence. PSYCOP excludes them because it seems possible to construct within this framework better explanations for the phenomena that they are supposed to explain. I have suggested that when subjects affirm an argument of the form of Denying the Antecedent they may do so on the basis of extra information that they import from background knowledge, using legitimate inductive inferences (see chapters 5 and 10). Since these inductive strategies are needed anyway, a Denying the Antecedent rule seems redundant. Similarly, we get a better account of the syllogism data on the assumption that people reason by applying the rules of chapter 6 to the premises and their implicatures. The implicatures are again needed on independent grounds to explain other facts about communication and inference, so this assumption seems sensible. It was also assumed that subjects are more willing to guess with Some or Some-not conclusions than with All or No conclusions, since the former seem "safer" to them. This assumption, too, makes more sense of the data than an Atmosphere rule that automatically produces a particular (Some or Some-not) conclusion if either premise is particular and a negative conclusion if either premise is negative. Excluding incorrect deduction rules on the basis of explanatory inadequacy, however, leaves the door open to including them if the evidence tips in the opposite direction.

Architectural Errors   What about errors at the architectural level? If intuitionistic logic is correct, for example, then there must be something wrong with the rules we are currently assuming to be part of the architecture, since they include Negation Elimination, Double Negation Elimination, and other principles that aren't valid in intuitionistic logic. But the situation here is different from that at the strategic level. Although we can try out strategic rules, discarding those that get us into trouble, we are stuck with architectural rules, since by definition architectural properties are fixed parts of the cognitive system (Newell 1990; Pylyshyn 1984). There is no way for us to get outside the particular architectural rules with which we are endowed. And since it is through these rules that we learn about and make sense of the mental capacities of other creatures, the rules place limits on the extent to which we can identify reasoning that proceeds according to principles that are very different from our own. This is one of the lessons of the philosophical work on rationality by Davidson, Dennett, and others cited in the preface and in chapter 1.

   The concept of a deduction system itself limits the scope of architectural errors, since deduction systems commit us to constraints on what can qualify as a rule. For example, as Belnap (1962) pointed out, potential rules for a new connective have to be consistent with old ones. The new rules can't sanction arguments not containing the connective that weren't previously derivable; otherwise, it is possible to have rules (e.g., the *-Introduction and *-Elimination rules mentioned in note 3 to chapter 2) that prove any sentence on the basis of any other. Systems that violate such constraints no longer seem to have much to do with deduction. Of course, the deduction-system hypothesis may itself turn out to be a false account of the psychology of thinking. People may not operate according to deduction rules at all; we may operate solely on the basis of probabilistic or connectionist principles, contrary to the evidence presented in part II. (See Rips 1990a for a discussion of this point of view.) However, if the deduction-system hypothesis is correct, there are going to be bounds to the erroneous rules that can be part of people's mental architecture. Although we can live with an operating system that has an occasional bug, it has to meet some minimal functional standards in order to be an operating system at all.

Doesn't the Account of Performance Beg the Question about the Source of Subjects' Errors on Deduction Tasks?

A related criticism of the theory is that, although it may provide a place for reasoning errors, it doesn't explain them in a principled way. According to this objection, if errors are simply the result of an arbitrary failure to apply a rule or of a haphazard collection of interfering strategies, then it seems that we haven't made much progress in accounting for why people commit them. This is especially true, of course, if we appeal to these error-producing factors in an *ad hoc* way. Similarly, estimating parameters from the data to produce the error distributions, as was sometimes done in the experiments, may give us reason to think that the model is *consistent* with the results; but it doesn't seem to provide much insight, since it doesn't generate *predictions* or explanations about the difficulty of the problems (Johnson-Laird and Byrne 1991).

A preliminary point to make in regard to this objection is that we need to be careful about adopting unrealistically simple ideas about the source of subjects' mistakes. The successful performance of any complex skill obviously depends on the coordination of a large number of internal components and external enabling conditions, and the failure of any of these factors can lead to errors. For this reason, a unified account of errors seems extremely unlikely. This doesn't mean that errors are unimportant or irrelevant for studying mental abilities; on the contrary, much of cognitive psychology is premised on the idea that errors can reveal something of the structure of skills. There are even classes of errors that have intrinsic interest and deserve study on their own. However, it is unlikely that we will make much progress in studying reasoning unless we recognize that there are diverse sources of mistakes. Working-memory limitations, time limitations, attention limitations, response biases, interpretation difficulties,

Gricean pragmatic factors, number of required steps in the problem, and complexity of individual steps are all known to affect performance on a wide range of cognitive tasks, and it would be extremely surprising if they didn't affect reasoning performance as well. The study of errors in reasoning is important precisely because different types of errors pinpoint different aspects of reasoning. Thus, if having a principled account of reasoning errors means discovering a single factor that explains all of them, no such account is apt to be forthcoming.

Why Errors Happen Our handling of errors could be unprincipled in another sense if it appealed to errors in order to hide defects in the deduction theory. Evidence that subjects' responses fail to conform to the predictions of the model could obviously be due to the model's deficiencies. If it is, then to explain these deviations by claiming them to be subjects' errors is to blame the subjects for the theorist's mistake. Ascribing errors to subjects in this way threatens to make the theory vacuous unless there are good independent grounds for these error tendencies.

But I don't think it is fair to describe the use of errors in the experiments reported here as merely an *ad hoc* attempt to make the theory fit the data. In explaining some of the earlier results in this field, the analysis was necessarily *ad hoc*; there is no way to test the theory in this context short of redesigning the original studies. We did, in fact, redesign the categorical-syllogism experiments for this reason in order to eliminate what we thought were error tendencies (e.g., bias caused by response frequency) that obscured the syllogism findings. But there are so many different types of deduction experiments that one cannot do this in all cases, and for many of these studies we have to be content with plausibility arguments to the effect that the theory is consistent with the findings. When we move from earlier research to the new studies of part II, however, we no longer have to rely on *ad hoc* methods. Most of these experiments derive predictions from the model on the basis of well-established assumptions about how errors come about. These studies employ the straightforward notions that, other things being equal, errors are more likely if the problem contains more required steps, if the complexity of each step is relatively great, or if the types of steps are more varied. It is hard to think of more fundamental assumptions than these in the cognitive psychology tradition. Using these assumptions in a predictive way to evaluate a theory is as clear-cut a methodology as cognitive psychology has to offer. The proof-following experiment in chapter 5 and the matching experiment in chapter 7 are nearly pure examples of this methodology.

Parameters and Model Fitting. Parameter estimation in theory testing introduces some further complications because the parameter values seem to many people to be devoid of predictive or explanatory power: The values appear to be derived entirely from the data rather than from the theory. Thus, fitting the model in this way, as we did in several of the studies in part II, again raises questions about whether our explanations aren't *ad hoc*.

The reason for estimating parameters, however, is to provide a quantitative analysis of errors and other response measures. As long as we are content with qualitative predictions, we can rely solely on what the theory says about the relative number of steps and the relative complexity of the steps in a problem. But in order to obtain quantitative predictions, we need exact measures of how likely it is that a reasoning step will go awry or how long such a step will take. Although there are several ways of estimating these measures, none of them entirely eliminates free parameters. Moreover, alternative methods are also based in part on the data and are sometimes subject to confoundings, as was noted in chapter 9.[2]

Although it is certainly possible to abuse parameter estimation in model fitting, "free" parameters in models like that of part II are constrained by the theory. First, the values of these parameters depend in part on the structure of the equations in which they appear, and the equations are themselves based upon what the theory says about the relation between internal processes and external responses. This contrasts with the case of fitting an arbitrary polynomial to the data, in which the values of the coefficients aren't tied to any substantive theory. An incorrect theory will, of course, come closer to fitting the data as the result of optimizing the values of its free parameters. Nevertheless, there are upper limits to how good the fit can be when the theory dictates the form of the equations, as one quickly learns from practical experience in model fitting.

Second, the estimates gain credence when similar values appear from one experiment to the next, as they did in the studies reported in chapters 5 and 7. Stability of the estimates across different sets of subjects and different types of deduction problems suggests that the parameters are capturing permanent aspects of people's reasoning ability and not just superficial features of the experiment. It is a remarkable fact that very similar values of the rule parameters show up when subjects are reasoning about sentential arguments, categorical syllogisms, and general multi-variable arguments.

Third, the theory assigns an interpretation to the parameters, and this too constrains the role they play in the explanation of reasoning errors. In general the theory predicts that more structurally complicated rules should be associated with lower parameter values in our studies, since the more complex the rule the more difficult it should be to use correctly. For example, rules that create and manipulate subdomains should be more difficult than rules that don't, other factors being equal. Parameter values that accord with this complexity ordering help confirm the theory. The experiments on syllogisms and multi-variable arguments in chapter 7 support this prediction, since estimates are invariably lower for rules that create subdomains (e.g., NOT Introduction) than for rules that don't (e.g., AND Introduction or AND Elimination). (See tables 7.2 and 7.5.) Parameter values for the argument-evaluation experiment in chapter 5 (table 5.2) are not as clear-cut. For example, the Backward OR Introduction rule (which yields *P OR Q* from *P*) is fairly simple internally, but it has the lowest availability value in that experiment. This finding must be treated with caution, and my tentative explanation for it (that Gricean factors made subjects unwilling to go along with inferences of this type) is indeed *ad hoc*. However, deviations like these are no different from deviations from other predictions; parameter estimation plays no special role.

In short, PSYCOP has a well-motivated account of how and when subjects make errors in reasoning. These predictions arise naturally from the form of the theory—the type and the structure of the rules—together with some very general and widely accepted assumptions about performance breakdown. In the studies reported here, we have mainly relied on the notion that a problem is error prone to the extent that it requires many rules (types or tokens) or more complicated rules in its solution. The data confirm this notion in most cases.

Aren't You Assuming a "Logicist" Approach That Has Already Proved Unwieldy in AI? (Aren't You Assuming That Everything Is a Matter of Deductive Reasoning?)

Aside from errors, a second source of uneasiness about linking reasoning with natural-deduction rules is the question how such rules could be responsible for the variety of inferences that people engage in. There are obviously lots of perfectly good inferences that aren't deductively valid. I infer from my previous beliefs that the french fries at the university cafeteria come from potatoes rather than from recycled newspaper, even though there is no valid argument from my evidence to my conclusion; it is not logically, or even causally, inconsistent with these beliefs that someone has discovered that paper pulp can serve as a cheap potato substitute. Furthermore, these nondeductive inferences occur continually in comprehension, planning, problem solving, and decision making. Giving deduction rules a crucial role in thinking—making them part of cognitive architecture—seems to deny the cognitive importance of other inference types and seems to leave us without any way of explaining them. This amounts to a kind of deduction chauvinism whose only excuse is the fact that logical theory has given us a neat set of rules to work with.

Logicism in AI   A related issue has been played out in artificial intelligence as a debate between "logicist" researchers (who employ proof-theoretic and model-theoretic methods) and others who favor non-logic-based approaches. (See, e.g., McDermott 1987 vs. Hayes 1987 and other papers in the same issue of *Computational Intelligence*, and Nilsson 1991 vs. Birnbaum 1991.) Of course, neither party to this controversy believes that the only interesting inferences are those that correspond to theorems of classical logic. Rather, the crux is the extent to which we can fruitfully capture the commonsense information needed for skills like planning or problem solving in a theory composed of explicit sentences and of a logic for unpacking the entailments of these sentences. There are some obvious advantages to a logicist research program, since representing commonsense beliefs as an explicit theory makes it much easier to determine the adequacy of these beliefs (e.g., whether they are consistent and cover all of the intended domain) and to use the knowledge in situations that the researcher didn't foresee. The purported disadvantage is that this strategy seems to exalt deduction at the expense of other, equally interesting forms of inference: "... logicists tend to ignore other sorts of reasoning that seem quite central to intelligent behavior—probabilistic reasoning, reasoning from examples or by analogy, and reasoning based on the formation of faulty but useful conjectures and their subsequent elaboration and debugging, to name a few...." (Birnbaum 1991, p. 59)[3] In psychology, Kahneman and Varey (1990) have recently expressed similar anti-logic views with respect to reasoning about counterfactual situations, and their viewpoint is probably widely shared.

Logicists have some room to maneuver in this controversy. It is possible to claim, for purposes of AI or even cognitive psychology, that formalizing commonsense knowledge in the logicist manner is a necessary preliminary step. Formalizing makes clear the content of commonsense beliefs by specifying the entities and relations that it presupposes. Once this job has been completed and it is clear what the domains of the beliefs are, we can then turn to implementing the theory in a computer program or discovering how it happens to be implemented in humans. Thus, the logicist needn't claim that people actually represent knowledge in a logic-based theory, or that they use deduction to draw inferences from it. A logicist could even agree that other forms of representation and process are more practical for building computer programs. The formalizing step is a way of doing a kind of "natural-language metaphysics" by teasing out the basic components of our everyday talk and thought (Bach 1986; Hayes 1985; McCarthy 1977); simulation and experimentation can take over from there. Moreover, logicists can point, with some justification, to the excessive vagueness of alternative ways of developing theories of commonsense knowledge in both AI and psychology.

But although this line of defense is congenial in many respects, it depends on a certain way of partitioning these domains of human knowledge. The logicist program allows us to focus on the information that the axioms make explicit, leaving it to the logic to flesh out the axioms' implicit (but derivable) consequences. As long as the logic itself is well understood, this strategy seems realistic, and the logicist can afford to ignore probabilistic reasoning, analogical reasoning, and the rest. But in practice such proposals have had to incorporate powerful logics (e.g., the higher-order intentional logic of Montague (1973), or the nonmonotonic logics discussed in chapter 8) whose properties aren't as clear or as elegant as those of standard systems. Once the logics become complex, it is no longer clear what advantage the logicist approach has over other forms of theorizing that include nondeductive inferences in their artillery.

The Place of Nondeductive Reasoning   No matter how this debate turns out, it is clear that the present theory doesn't have the luxury of claiming that implementing reasoning is someone else's business. Our goal is describing the ways people reason, and the theory is incorrect if it ascribes to deduction inferences that people carry out by other means. It would be a mistake, however, to view the theory as taking the position that all inference is deduction. There is a place in this framework for nondeductive inference at exactly the same level as the strategic use of deductive reasoning. For example, we found in our discussion of categorizing (chapter 8) that the belief that an instance belongs to a particular category is generally not deducible from available evidence. We were able to accommodate this form of nondeductive reasoning by implementing it indirectly, placing the relevant sentence (that the instance is in the category) in memory when supporting evidence becomes available. The supporting evidence needn't logically entail the belief in order to trigger this process. PSYCOP can include other forms of reasoning in the same or similar ways. That is, we can express procedures for probabilistic reasoning or analogical reasoning that search memory for relevant support and produce inferences when the support meets given conditions for strength and simplicity. Of course, working out the details of these reasoning theories isn't a simple matter. But since many prior psychological theories of probabilistic reasoning (see, e.g., Collins and Michalski 1989; Osherson et al. 1991) and analogical reasoning (see, e.g., Gentner 1983; Gick and Holyoak 1983) can be implemented using sentences in the language of chapter 6, they seem to be perfectly consistent with our framework.

At the strategic level deductive and nondeductive reasoning are on a par, but at the architectural level the theory works solely according to the deduction rules of part II. This helps explain the theoretical and empirical evidence for the centrality of deduction that we encountered in chapter 1. It helps account for why elementary deductive inferences such as IF Elimination, AND Elimination, and instantiation are so hard to deny and yet so hard to justify in more basic terms. But in making these assumptions, we are not attempting to reduce all forms of reasoning to deduction or to portray such reasoning as deduction in disguise. It is easy to see how we could use a computer language such as PROLOG, which employs a form of resolution theorem proving, to write a program that reasons in a very different manner—say, according to the Tversky-Kahneman heuristics. In exactly the same way, it is possible to use an architecture that runs on natural deduction to carry out nearly any sort of nondeductive inference. This means that a theory of the psychological principles that govern nondeductive inference can proceed along independent lines, and the principles themselves will have an independent scientific interest. If this is a case of deduction chauvinism, it is a very mild one.

Aren't You Making People Out to Be More Illogical or Irrational Than They Really Are?

Once one has admitted the possibility that people can make mistakes in reasoning, one is open to doubts and criticisms from the opposite point of view. As I have already acknowledged, there appear to be theoretical limits on ascribing illogical thinking to people. The aim of this scientific enterprise is to explain ordinary people's inferences, where part of what it means to explain them is to view these thought patterns as obeying certain psychological laws or generalizations. But the generalizations at work in cognitive psychology are ones that presuppose a healthy dose of rationality: that people have sufficient mental aptitude to be able to fashion strategies to achieve their goals, that they can select among the strategies those that are more likely to be successful on the basis of their beliefs, that they can recognize when a strategy is in fact successful, and so on. Creatures who behave in a thoroughly irrational manner don't conform to these cognitive platitudes and hence aren't easily explained from a cognitive point of view. Of course, creatures who do conform to these platitudes needn't have perfect rationality; for example, people's ability to achieve goals doesn't mean that they always reason optimally in attaining them. But, having glimpsed these underlying rational principles, one can easily become skeptical of any alleged instances of reasoning errors (see, e.g., Cohen 1981, 1986; Henle 1978). For example, with respect to errors in experiments on deduction, Cohen (1986, p. 153) claims that "it looks as though the data are inevitably inconclusive. To be sure that the subjects understood the exact question that the investigators wished to ask them, it would be necessary to impose on them such an apparatus of clarifications and instructions that they could no longer be regarded as untutored laymen and the experiment would then become just a test of their educational progress in the field of philosophical logic."

Whether PSYCOP is too illogical or irrational depends, of course, on how "reasoning errors" are defined. Many of the types of error tendencies that we considered earlier don't count as reasoning errors for purposes of this debate, even though these tendencies may lead to judgments that differ from those sanctioned by some logic system. Both parties to the debate agree that many factors can be responsible for such deviations. If Q follows from P according to some logical theory T but subjects fail to affirm that Q follows from P, that could be because (a) T isn't the appropriate normative standard; (b) subjects interpret the natural-language sentences that are supposed to translate P and Q in some other way; (c) performance factors (e.g., memory or time limits) interfere with subjects' drawing the correct conclusion; (d) the instructions fail to convey to subjects that they should make their responses on the basis of the entailment or deducibility relation rather than on some other basis (e.g., the plausibility or assertibility of the conclusion); (e) response bias overwhelms the correct answer; or (f) the inference is suppressed by pragmatic factors (e.g., conversational implicatures). If Q does not follow from P according to T but subjects affirm that Q follows from P, that could be because (a)–(e) hold as above; (g) subjects are interpreting the task as one in which they should affirm the argument, provided only that P suggests Q, or P makes Q more likely, or P is inductive grounds for Q; (h) subjects treat the argument as an enthymeme that can be filled out by relevant world knowledge; (i) subjects ascribe their inability to draw the inference to performance factors and incorrectly guess that P entails Q; or (j) subjects are misled by a superficial similarity to some valid inference from P' to Q' into supposing that there is a valid inference from P to Q. Any of these factors might, in the right circumstances, provide a plausible reason for why subjects' judgments depart from what is prescribed by a logic system—and this is not an exhaustive list.

The question about "reasoning errors" is whether PSYCOP posits mistakes that go *beyond* factors like (a)–(j) and implicates a "true" failure in people's thinking apart from lapses of interpretation, attention, or response. Needless to say, it isn't easy to identify such errors in an actual sample of data. Armed with factors (a)–(j) and others like them, a determined skeptic can usually explain away any instance of what seems at first to be a logical mistake. (The opportunistic use of these factors is behind the earlier complaints about unprincipled accounts of errors.) To determine whether we are giving people too little credit for correct reasoning, we therefore need to get straight about what would count as a true reasoning error and whether it makes conceptual and empirical sense to postulate such errors.

Aren't You Assuming That People Are Programmed to Be Irrational?

Some of those who believe that theories like PSYCOP paint too grim a picture of human reasoning seem to suggest that these theories doom people to faulty inferences. For example, Rescher (1988, pp. 194–195) writes that "recent psychological studies have sought to establish with experimental precision that people are generally inclined to reason in inappropriate ways. One investigation [Rips 1984], for example, concludes that people systematically commit the well-known fallacy of denying the antecedent.... But it is far from clear that an error is actually committed in the cases at issue. For, people often use 'If p, then q' in everyday discourse as *abbreviation* for 'if but *only* if p then q'. ('If you have a ticket they will let you board', 'If you pass the course, you will get four credits'.) What seems to be happening in the cases at issue is not *misreasoning*, but mere conclusion-jumping by tacitly supplying that 'missing' inverse." Similarly, Rescher remarks a bit later (p. 196), "to construe the data [from experiments on deductive and probabilistic reasoning] to mean that people are systematically programmed to fallacious processes of reasoning—rather than merely indicating that they are inclined to a variety of (occasionally questionable) substantive suppositions—is a very questionable step." Rescher doesn't deny that human irrationality is possible: "Irrationality is pervasive in human affairs. While all (normal) people are to be credited with the capacity to reason, they frequently do not exercise it well." (ibid., p. 198) What seems to be at issue is whether incorrect reasoning is a "systematically programmed" part of thinking rather than just a peccadillo.

One type of systematically programmed reasoning error, on this account, would be the incorrect rules discussed in the preceding section. Thus, if people had a Denying the Antecedent rule that operated alongside the rules of chapter 6, there would be a natural tendency for them to conclude *NOT Q* from premises of the form *IF P THEN Q* and *NOT P*, and this would constitute the kind of inherently fallacious thinking that Rescher deems questionable. It is quite true that subjects sometimes affirm the correctness of arguments that are of the denying-the-antecedent type (see Marcus and Rips 1979, and other studies cited in chapter 5). And it is also true that psychologists have, at times, posited systematic error patterns of this general sort; the atmosphere rules for syllogisms would probably qualify, at least under some interpretations. However, it would be a misreading of the present theory (and of earlier versions, such as that in Rips 1984) to suppose that it builds in such error tendencies. As has already been noted, there is no Denying the Antecedent rule in PSYCOP or its ancestors, nor is there any other rule that is not sound in classical logic. Although the theory does not exclude incorrect rules on *a priori* grounds, a better account can often be provided through the kind of alternative factors that Rescher mentions. For instance, the idea that a conditional sometimes suggests its converse is essentially what I used to explain the data on conditional syllogisms in chapter 5.

As PSYCOP is currently constructed, any "systematically programmed" errors must be due to failures to apply its rules. For example, the probability that subjects correctly apply the NOT Introduction rule is fairly low, according to the model. But should we take this as evidence of a built-in prohibition against this type of inference (i.e., as a "true" reasoning error), or instead as a proclivity that often affects reasoning performance? I claimed earlier that the stability of the parameters indicates that these tendencies are themselves stable characteristics of reasoning, and this might incline someone to view them as preprogrammed. However, the point of making these rule failures probabilistic parts of the model is to acknowledge variability in the use of a rule over occasions in which it is relevant. Rules like NOT Introduction are relatively difficult for subjects to apply, at least partly as a result of their internal complexity, and this gives rise to stable estimates. But this added complexity doesn't mean that people are inherently *incapable* of applying such rules. It is doubtful, for this reason, that the errors predicted by the availability parameters are instances of programmed irrationality of the sort that Rescher warns against.

In this respect rules like NOT Introduction, which the model claims are difficult for subjects to use, differ from rules like Conditional Transformation (table 4.3), which are not part of the model's repertoire at all. Thus, if it turned out that a normatively appropriate theory of reasoning included inferences that could be derived only via Conditional Transformation, then PSYCOP could be said to be systematically unable to reason in a normatively correct manner. But convicting PSYCOP of this type of error would require evidence of the missing inferences.

Aren't You Assuming That People Should Interpret Connectives in a Truth-Functional Manner and Then Accusing Them of Errors When They Don't Do So?

Another way in which we could be making people out to be too illogical is by holding them to an inappropriate standard of logic. Cohen (1986) has raised this possibility in discussing the evidence regarding the rule of OR Introduction. We found in chapter 5 that subjects tend not to affirm arguments whose proofs rely on this rule, according to our proof system. And beginning logic students tend to find this rule counterintuitive, at least in the way it is usually presented. But perhaps people's reluctance to use this rule merely indicates that they do not understand the English *or* as the OR of classical logic: "Rips is assuming that the layman always uses and understands the elementary connectives of natural language in a purely truth-functional sense, so that a proposition of the form '*p* or *q*' is true if and only if *p* and *q* are not both false. And, if we are not prepared to take this notoriously controversial assumption for granted, we can just as well construe Rips's result as revealing individual differences in how people use and understand such connectives...." (Cohen 1986, p. 151)

Cohen's aim in suggesting this possibility is to ward off what he sees as a threat to human rationality. He construes the theory's account of arguments with OR as attributing to people a logical defect—as exemplifying the sort of built-in error that I have just discussed: "Very many papers have appeared which claim to have established that logically or statistically untutored adults are inclined to employ one or another of a variety of fallacious procedures in their reasonings or not to employ the correct procedures. The normal person's intuitions on these issues, it is claimed, tend to be persistently irrational." (Cohen 1986, p. 150) We have already seen in connection with Rescher's comments that this is a misunderstanding of the present theory. Nothing about the model implies that subjects are somehow "persistently irrational" in connection with OR Introduction or in connection with other rules that received low availability values in the studies discussed in part II. We interpreted the results on OR Introduction, in particular, as probably due to sensitivity to pragmatic factors (such as the pointlessness of asserting *P OR Q* when the stronger statement *P* is known to be true). Since Cohen himself uses the same kind of conversational factors to explain other findings in the literature on deductive reasoning (1986, p. 152), he presumably doesn't view them as irrational.[4]

Although Cohen aims his comments about irrationality at the wrong target, the point about truth-functional connectives is worth considering. Our account would simply be wrong if people reasoned solely with non-truth-functional connectives and PSYCOP solely with truth-functional ones. We need to be a bit careful in examining this issue, however, since it is not necessarily true that the model implies that the layman always uses and understands the elementary connectives of natural language in a purely truth-functional sense. Truth-functionality means that the truth of any sentence that PSYCOP handles is completely determined by the truth of its constituent sentences. But since PSYCOP is a proof system and doesn't determine the truth of its working-memory sentences directly, only in a derivative sense could it qualify as truth-functional. One possibility along these lines would be to say that if $*$ is a logical connective then the system should be able to prove $S * T$ from the premises consisting of its component sentences (S, T) or their negations $(NOT\ S, NOT\ T)$. Standard deduction systems for classical sentence logic are truth-functional in this sense (e.g., they can prove $IF\ S\ THEN\ T$ from $NOT\ S$ or T). But the results of chapter 4 show that the system is incomplete with respect to classical logic, and this means that the system will sometimes fail to recognize certain truth-functional relationships. Thus, if using sentence connectives in a truth-functional sense entails being able to derive compound sentences from their components, then PSYCOP isn't a purely truth-functional system.[5]

Whether or not the system is fully truth-functional, however, the rules of part II provide for only a single version of the connectives. It is easy to agree that natural language includes a wide variety of logical operators, not currently included in PSYCOP, that are worthy of psychological investigation. For example, there is little doubt that natural language contains *ifs* that differ from the IF of our system—perhaps along the lines of the intensional IF of chapter 2. We also discussed giving PSYCOP (non-truth-functional) rules for OBLIGATORY and PERMISSIBLE to explain recent results on the selection task. PSYCOP in its current form isn't supposed to be an exhaustive theory of the logical operators that humans can comprehend; the model is psychologically incomplete with respect to this wider field of operators. From this perspective, the possibility that some subjects understood the connectives in our problems in an alternative way is one of the many factors that, like (a)–(j) above, can affect their responses. What the theory does claim is that its rules for AND, OR, NOT, and IF are psychologically real, and that they are among the basic deductive processes in cognition. Thus, what would cast doubt on the theory is, not the presence of alternative connectives, but the absence of the specified ones.

Summary

One way to think about the theory developed here is as a merger of two main ideas about the human nature of deductive reasoning. One of these ideas is that reasoning involves the ability to make suppositions or assumptions—that is, to entertain propositions temporarily in order to trace their consequences. This idea comes from formal natural-deduction systems in logic, but it is clearly psychological at root. Nothing about deduction *per se* forces suppositions on us, since there are perfectly good deduction systems that do without them; we could start with a set of axioms and derive all the same theorems. But human styles of reasoning aren't like that, as both Gentzen and Jaśkowski observed. We tend to assume propositions for the sake of the argument in order to focus our efforts in exploring what follows.

The second of the key ideas is that reasoning includes subgoals. People are able to adopt on a temporary basis the desire to prove some proposition in order to achieve a further conclusion. This idea seems more mundane than the one about suppositions, since we are accustomed to the use of subgoals in cognitive and computer science. Even the simplest AI programs use subgoaling to reduce the amount of search. But, again, deduction itself doesn't require subgoals. Even natural-deduction systems, as logic textbooks formulate them, don't have subgoals. Instead instructors in elementary logic have to provide informal hints about strategies for applying the rules, generally in the form of advice about working backward from the conclusion to more easily achievable lemmas. If these subordinate conclusions don't pan out, we can abandon them for others that may prove more successful. Our theory gives this purposefulness a status equal to that of suppositions.

Although I have borrowed suppositions from logic and subgoals from computer science, these concepts are closely interrelated. Suppositions are roughly like provisional beliefs, and subgoals roughly like provisional desires. In something like the way beliefs and desires about external states guide external actions, provisional beliefs and desires guide internal action in reasoning. According to the current theory, what gives human reasoning its characteristic tempo is the way these suppositions and subgoals coordinate: Can we show that some sentence C follows from another sentence P? Well, C would follow if we can show that C' follows from P'; so let's assume P' for now and try to find out whether C' holds; and so on. From one perspective, this sequence helps to simplify the problem at hand by lemma-izing it into manageable parts. But reasoning of this type also presupposes some fairly sophisticated cognitive apparatus for keeping track of the nesting of suppositions within suppositions and sub-subgoals en route to subgoals.

In the present theory, most of the responsibility for handling suppositions and subgoals devolves on the deduction rules. The rules in the model are a conservative choice of principles that seem psychologically (though not always logically) primitive. Research in this area should consider expanding this set of principles, and perhaps emending the current set, to achieve better coverage of the logical resources of natural language (see, e.g., Dowty 1993). But the present rules seem to provide a good starting point, both because they account for much of the data from the experiments reviewed here and because they are capable of supporting other cognitive tasks. A main innovation in the current model, with respect to previous deduction theories in psychology, is that the rules also handle variables and names in a general way. This means that the system achieves most of the power of predicate logic, and without having to include additional rules for quantifiers. This accords with the mathematical practice of omitting explicit quantifiers in equations and instead using distinct variables and constants, for ease of manipulation. Although this capability comes at the price of additional complexity in the rules, the payoff is a single model that applies to all, or nearly all, of the tasks that psychologists have studied under the heading of deductive reasoning. It seems surprising that, despite fairly wide agreement about the importance of variables and instantiation, no previous psychological theories of deduction have addressed this problem in a global way and no previous experiments have looked at the details of how people match variables and names.

The ability to deal with variables and names greatly expands the utility of deductive reasoning. Instantiating and generalizing variables allow the model to swap information in memory and thereby carry out many higher-level cognitive tasks within the same supposition/subgoal framework. Binding variables gives the model the power of a general symbol system, and this raises the possibility that deduction might serve as the basis for other higher cognitive tasks. This proposal will seem wildly improbable to many cognitive scientists, who are used to thinking of deduction as a special-purpose, error-prone process, but I hope that the examples in chapter 8 will help soften them up. A couple of examples, of course, are hardly sufficient to establish the proposal as adequate for the full range of higher cognitive tasks; we need a great deal of further experience with the system in order to understand its strengths and weaknesses. However, the idea that cognition has deductive underpinnings shouldn't be any harder to swallow than the idea of a production system as a cognitive theory. In fact, we could get quite a close approximation to a production system by modifying the rule we called Conjunctive Modus Ponens and applying it to conditional sentences (i.e., "production rules") in a special partition of long-term memory. The examples in chapter 8 also make it clear that deduction doesn't replace other forms of reasoning in this theory but supports these forms by supplying mechanisms for keeping track of assumptions, exploring alternative cases, conditional branching, binding, and other necessities. It may help those who boggle at the deduction-system idea to recognize that these processes are essentially deductive ones.

This perspective on deduction does not resolve the debate about the scope of human rationality, but it may help us to bring some of the complexities of this issue into focus. If the outlines of the model are correct, then reasoning takes place on at least two mental levels, perhaps each with its own distinctive forms of rationality. We would expect reasoning at the architectural level to be relatively free of interference from response bias or from conversational suggestion, and equally immune to facilitation in learning. Reasoning at the strategic level may have the opposite susceptibilities: Explicit training could enhance it, but disturbances from neighboring processes could have it at their mercy. The present theory provides an account of how errors can occur during reasoning, based on the length of a chain of reasoning and on the strength of its individual links, and it acknowledges further sources of errors. But at the same time, the theory doesn't mandate reasoning errors through unsound rules. In this way the theory tries to steer between the extremes of asserting that people can't reason correctly and asserting that they can't *but* reason correctly. It attempts to portray human reasoning, instead, in both its intricacies and its frailties.

Notes

Preface

1. *Modus ponens* means "affirming mode," since we are affirming the IF part of the orginal sentence in order to affirm the THEN part. Modus ponens contrasts with *modus tollens* ("denying mode"), which is the argument from *IF so-and-so THEN such-and-such* and *NOT such-and-such* to *NOT so-and-so*. These terms come from traditional logic.

Of course, even earthlings will forego a modus ponens inference under special circumstances—for example, when other information shows that the argument is elliptical. (See chapter 3, note 4, below.)

2. Cross-cultural research might throw light on these issues, but conclusions in this area have been inconsistent, at least on the surface. For example, on the basis of his research in rural Russia, Luria (1971, p. 271) suggested that "these facts indicate that the operation of reaching a logical conclusion from the syllogism is certainly not a universal character as one might have thought." However, Hamill (1990, p. 60) suggests that his own, more recent "syllogism tests were strikingly consistent across language boundaries. Consultants considered the same kinds of argument valid and invalid, and in no case did they draw conclusions that were invalid according to the rules of textbook logic." The safest conclusion might be that any difference in performance between cultures on tests of deductive reasoning are probably attributable to translation difficulties (Au 1983; Liu 1985) or to relative familiarity with Western test-taking conventions (e.g., restricting consideration to explicitly stated premises; see Scribner 1977).

3. In fact, the comparison between deduction and programming languages is more than just an analogy. There are now general-purpose languages that use deduction to carry out their activities. The best-known language of this sort is PROLOG (short for PROgramming in LOGic), which has receive publicity because of its connection with the Japanese Fifth Generation computer project. For more on PROLOG, see Clocksin and Mellish 1981 and Sterling and Shapiro 1986. Kowalski 1979 contains a more general discussion of the idea of deduction as programming.

Chapter 1

1. For example, within the current Government-Binding framework, the logical form of a sentence is a level of grammatical representation, deriving transformationally from S-structure (surface structure) and revealing explicit scope relationships among quantifiers such as *all*, *every*, and *some* (see chapter 2 for the notion of scope). Rules that yield the semantic interpretation of the sentence apply directly to logical form (May 1985; Chierchia and McConnell-Ginet 1990). In Lexical-Functional grammar, translation rules map the f-structure (functional structure) of a sentence to a semantic structure that represents the scope of quantifiers; semantic structure, in turn, maps onto a formula of a specific logical system, intensional logic, that directly indicates scope for adverbials (e.g., *necessarily*), tense, and negation (Halvorsen 1983). This is also somewhat similar to Montague's (1973) approach in which categories of a syntactic description of English are translated into those of an intensional logic.

A distinct strategy is to try to downplay the notion of logical form as a separate grammatical level and to represent scope ambiguities in other ways. This is the approach offered in Situation Semantics and related proposals (see Barwise 1987a, Cooper 1983, and Fodor's critique (1987)).

2. A typical passage: "'Now look here, Ulysses,' shouted the sheriff, 'you're just trying to complicate my deduction! Come on, let's play checkers!'" (McCloskey 1943).

3. This use of "deductive reasoning" does not directly tie it to any formal system of logic. For example, we can count the mental step from *Mike is a bachelor* to *Mike is unmarried* as an instance of deductive reasoning, even though the corresponding argument is not sanctioned in any standard logic.

4. A possible qualification is that there might be some level of comprehension—perhaps the level at which individual sentences are initially understood—that is inference free. Or, perhaps, any inferences that affect this level are highly specialized and distinct from more general inference processes operating on a higher cognitive level (Fodor 1983). The centrality claim, however, does not contradict these possibilities. What examples like (6) show is that deduction is part of the global process of extracting the speaker's meaning from text or spoken discourse. This notion of (global) comprehension is common to ordinary and scientific usage; hence, the evidence that deduction is central to comprehension isn't due to our taking "comprehension" in some unnaturally broad sense. For a defense of the view that deduction is part of every instance of verbal communication, see Sperber and Wilson 1986; for a discussion of different notions of comprehension, see Rips 1992.

5. Examples of syllogism and number-series problems appear in the next paragraph. Analogies include four-term verbal items such as *mayor : city :: captain : ?*. A sample arithmetic word problem is "When duty on a certain commodity decreases 30%, its consumption increases 60%. By what per cent is the revenue decreased or increased?" For verbal classification problems, the test takers might be asked to sort a set of words into two categories that are exemplified by separate word lists. As an example, if category 1 includes *lacerate, torture, bite,* and *pinch* and category 2 includes *suffer, ache, twinge,* and *writhe,* classify the following items as belonging to category 1 or 2: *wince, crucify, crush, smart, moan,* and *cut.* These simple examples don't do justice to Thurstone's brilliance as a test designer. See Thurstone 1937 for a list of his actual test items.

6. Aristotle's original use of "syllogism" in the *Prior Analytics* was apparently not limited to two-premise arguments (Corcoran 1974). In current writing, however, the two-premise format seems universal.

7. Among students of ancient logic, there is a debate on what Aristotle took to be the nature of a syllogism—whether he construed it as an argument, a proof, or a conditional. See Lear 1980 and Smiley 1973 for accounts of this controversy. There is also a disagreement about the total number of syllogisms and the number of deductively correct ones (Adams 1984), partly because Aristotle seems not to have considered as true syllogisms arguments with terms arranged as in (12). Neither of these historical controversies, however, has much impact on the claims psychologists have made about syllogistic reasoning, and we can safely ignore these issues in what follows.

8. See chapter 10 for an assessment of Johnson-Laird's (1983) claims about the extendability of his model of syllogisms.

Chapter 2

1. Pure axiomatic systems do not automatically allow the premises of an argument to be introduced as lines of the proof. Instead, an argument is deducible if the conditional sentence *IF p_1 AND p_2 AND ... AND p_k THEN c* is deducible from the axioms and modus ponens alone, where the p_is are the premises of the argument and c is its conclusion. The more direct method of table 2.2 is justified by the Deduction Theorem (Mendelson 1964, p. 32), which establishes that if the sentence *IF p_1 AND p_2 AND ... AND p_k THEN c* is deducible from the axioms then q is deducible from the axioms together with $p_1, p_2, ...,$ and p_k. This use of the Deduction Theorem is already a major step in the direction of natural deduction.

2. The second clause in this rule is logically redundant, since any argument that is deducible in the system is also deducible in a modified system in which this clause is omitted (see Jaśkowski 1934 for a proof). However, adding the second clause tends to make derivations simpler and seems a reasonable part of the informal reductio strategy. For example, the proof in (6) below requires two additional lines if the second clause is not available. By contrast, a system containing the second clause without the first is much weaker (i.e., is able to prove fewer theorems), as Jaśkowski also showed.

3. The relationship between the introduction and elimination rules for a connective is a prominent part of the literature on natural deduction in the philosophy of logic. This comes from attempts to use the structural characteristics of the proofs themselves as ways of defining the deductive correctness of arguments or defining the meaning of logical operators. (This project is an especially pressing one, of course, for those who regard with suspicion the semantic treatments of meaning and validity.) The issue can best be seen in terms of Prior's (1960) demonstration that it is possible to state introduction and elimination rules that define a bizarre connective (say, *) that would allow any sentence to be "deduced" from any other. In terms of table 2.3, the rules for * would be as follows:

* Introduction:
(a) If a sentence P holds in a given domain,
(b) then the sentence $P * Q$ can be added to that domain, where Q is an arbitrary sentence (cf. OR Introduction in Table 2.3).

* Elimination
(a) If a sentence of the form $P * Q$ holds in a given domain,
(b) then the sentence Q can be added to that domain (cf. AND Elimination)

Then from *Tin is elastic* it follows that *Tin is elastic* * *Fish float* (by * Introduction), and it follows in turn from the latter sentence that *Fish float* (by * Elimination). The upshot is that if the natural-deduction format is to define connectives or correct arguments, then some constraints have to be placed on potential rules (Belnap 1962). One possibility is to enforce "harmony" between the introduction and elimination rules so that the output of the latter don't go beyond the input to the former. See Dummett 1975 and Prawitz 1974 for attempts along these lines; see Sundholm 1986 for a review.

In the psychological literature, Osherson (1977, 1978) has claimed that logical connectives are natural for humans only if they can be formulated within a system in which their introduction and elimination rules are subject to certain constraints (e.g., that the sentences from the proof mentioned in the conditions of an introduction rule be no more complex than the sentence produced by the rule). The approach to constraints on rules in the present book depends on global features of the system I will propose: I seek constraints that conform to general properties of human reasoning, such as avoiding infinitely long proofs and generating all intuitively correct inferences. The nature of these constraints will become apparent in the statement of the deduction rules in chapters 4 and 6.

4. Gazdar (1979) follows Grice in defense of the OR of table 2.3. However, he abandons the IF of table 2.3 in favor of the conditional analysis of Stalnaker (1968). Braine (1978) advocates representing *if* in terms of the deducibility relation that holds between the premises and the conclusion of an argument. In his system, though, both of these reduce to a relation similar to that of the IF of the table. This means that any argument with false premises and a true conclusion is deductively correct. For example,

Spaghetti grows on trees.
Cows are mammals.

is deductively correct in this system—a result that seems much more counterintuitive than (11). Braine and O'Brien (1991) address the problem of (11) in a different way by placing further restrictions on IF Introduction. On this theory, a supposition for IF Introduction can be made only if that assumption is consistent with all earlier suppositions that hold in its domain. So, for example, the derivation in (12) will be blocked because the supposition in (12b) contradicts that in (12a). But although this analysis makes (11) nondeducible, the somewhat similar argument in (13) still goes through.

5. Another puzzle connected with the IF rules has to do with the tendency of some people to accept as correct an inference from sentences of the form *If P then Q* to *If Q then P* (or the

logically equivalent *If not P then not Q)*. For evidence, see the experiments on conditionals cited at the end of the first section of this chapter; see also Fillenbaum 1975, 1977. Such an inference is indeed correct when the original sentence is interpreted as a biconditional (that is, as *IF AND ONLY IF P THEN Q)*, but not when the sentence is interpreted as *IF P THEN Q* according to the rules of table 2.3. A related problem is the inference from *All x are y* to *All y are x*, which many investigators have identified as a source of error in syllogistic reasoning. The logical form of *All x are y* contains a conditional on the standard theory (as we will see momentarily), so these inferences may well have the same underlying source.

There is also a pragmatic theory that attempts to explain these tendencies. Geis and Zwicky (1971) claim that many conditionals "invite" such an inference, a phenomenon that they (1971) call "conditional perfection." For example, *If you lean too far out that window, you'll fall* certainly invites a hearer to suppose that if you don't lean too far then you will not fall. But, as Boër and Lycan (1973) point out, such inferences are warranted by the background information that we have about the subject matter (e.g., our knowledge about windows and falling) and may have little to do with conditionals *per se*. According to this account, conditional perfection is an inductive inference on the same footing as the inference from *Fred is a secretary* to *Fred can type*. Still, it can be said that subjects sometimes "perfect" a conditional in the absence of any supporting background information. Line e of table 1.1 contains an excellent example.

6. Some philosophers and linguists have also used quantifiers like *most* to motivate a change in representation from attaching quantifiers to single variables (in the way that *FOR ALL* attaches to *x* in *(FOR ALL x) P(x)*) to attaching them to phrases representing sets. As Barwise and Cooper (1981), McCawley (1981), and Wiggins (1980) point out, a sentence like *Most politicians whine* can't be stated in terms of *(MOST x) (Politician(x) * Whine(x))*, where * is a sentential connective. This is because the original sentence doesn't mean that something is true of most x, but instead that something (i.e., whining) is true of most politicians. This suggests an alternative representation that contains a *restricted* or *sortal* quantifier—for example, *(MOST: Politician x) Whine(x)*,—where *x* now ranges only over politicians. This also gives a natural better fit to the NP + VP shape of the English surface structure. However, see Wiggins (1980) for an argument against restricted quantifiers.

7. Harman's thesis that logic is not specially relevant to reasoning is based on the empirical assumption that people don't have the concept of logical implication and so can't recognize when one proposition logically implies another. He believes that people lack the concept of logical implication, in the sense that they don't distinguish purely logical implications from nonlogical ones. For example, they don't consistently divide implications like the following into logical and nonlogical types: (a) *P or Q* and *not P* imply *Q*; (b) $A < B$ and $B < C$ imply $A < C$; (c) *X is Y's brother* implies *X is male*; (d) *X plays defensive tackle for the Philadelphia Eagles* implies *X weighs more than 150 pounds* (Harman 1986, p. 17). However, being able to make a clear distinction between instances of one concept and instances of a complementary one is not a necessary condition for having the concept. People's inability to distinguish intermediate shades consistently as red or nonred does not entail that they have no concept of red. Perhaps Harman means that people do not consistently identify even clear cases such as (a) as logical implications, but the truth of this claim is far from evident. As Harman notes in an appendix, it may be impossible to decide whether or not logic is specially relevant to reasoning without independent criteria of logic and of immediate psychological implication.

8. This should not be taken to imply that such a system necessarily represents IF Elimination in the sense of containing a description of the rule in mentalese (in the way that table 2.3 contains a description of IF Elimination in English). One could also have a rule of IF Elimination in virtue of having a mental mechanism that produces tokens of *q* as output, given tokens of *p* and *IF p THEN q* as input. In other words, rules can be hardwired in a system, as well as represented symbolically and interpreted, as Fodor (1985), Smith et al. (1992), and Stabler (1983) have pointed out. Promoted rules seem more likely to be hardwired, whereas demoted rules seem more likely to be interpreted.

Chapter 3

1. The Traveling Salesman problem supposes there is a finite set of cities with a known distance between each pair of them. The problem is to find the shortest tour that passes through each city once and then returns to the first.

Cook's theorem demonstrated the NP-completeness of the problem of determining the satisfiability of an arbitrary sentence P in sentential logic, where P is said to be "satisfiable"if it is true in some possible state of affairs (see chapter 6). However, this theorem yields the NP-completeness of validity testing as a corollary. For if there were a decision procedure for validity testing that was *not* NP-complete, it could be used to establish satisfiability in a way that was also not NP-complete. This is because P is satisfiable if and only if $NOT\ P$ is not valid. Hence, to test P for satisfiability we would merely need to test $NOT\ P$ for validity. Since satisfiability testing is NP-complete, so is validity testing.

2. The literature in AI sometimes refers to theorem proving in the forward direction as "bottom-up"and theorem proving in the backward direction as "top-down." However, this terminology is somewhat confusing in the present context. Because arguments are conventionally written with the premises at the top and the conclusion at the bottom, it is odd to speak of the premise-to-conclusion direction as bottom-up and the conclusion-to-premise direction as top-down. For this reason, I will stick with the forward/backward terminology throughout this book.

3. The usual convention is to employ functions rather than subscripted temporary names. That is, instead of the name a_x in (4b), we would have $f(x)$. These are merely notational variants, however, and the use of subscripted temporary names is more in keeping with the discussion in chapter 2.

4. Of course, further information about the conditional's antecedent or consequent may cause you to withhold belief in the conclusion of a Modus ponens argument. Additional facts may convince you that the conditional is elliptical, specifying only some of the conditions that are sufficient for its consequent (Byrne 1989), or they may lead you to doubt the conditional outright (Politzer and Braine 1991). The present point, however, is that if P and $IF\ P$ $THEN\ Q$ occur to us simultaneously (or in close succession) then Q occurs to us too. (See the discussion of promoted and demoted rules in chapter 2.)

Chapter 4

1. An earlier version of this model, called ANDS (A Natural Deduction System), is described in Rips 1983, 1984. The new system deserves a new name, since it contains several improvements in its control structure and its memory representation.

2. Rules like IF Introduction deduce sentences on the basis of entire subdomains, as we have seen. For example, the conclusion of the proof in figure 4.1 depends on a derivation within a subdomain beginning with the supposition *Betty is in Little Rock* (see proof (2) below). In such cases, the deduction links run from the final sentence of the subdomains used by the rule to the sentence that the rule produces. For example, Backward IF Introduction produces the deduction link from *Ellen is in Hammond AND Sandra is in Memphis* to *IF Betty is in Little Rock THEN (Ellen is in Hammond AND Sandra is in Memphis)* in figure 4.1. The fact that the first of these sentences is part of a subdomain is indicated by dashed arrows.

3. This doesn't preclude the possibility that a person might forget a subgoal while retaining some of the assertions within the same proof. In the context of figure 4.1d, for example, there is nothing that would prevent forgetting of the subgoal *Ellen is in Hammond AND Sandra is in Memphis?* during the modus ponens step.

4. The Modus ponens rule in LT is discussed in chapter 3 above.

5. Another way to handle arguments (4)–(6) is to allow Double Negation Elimination to operate in a forward direction *inside* the conditional premise. A rule of this sort would immediately simplify the first premise of (4), for example, to *IF Calvin deposits 50 cents THEN Calvin gets a coke*, and Forward IF Elimination would apply directly to this new sentence. Although this seems a plausible hypothesis about (4)–(6), it doesn't solve the general problem, for we can find arguments analogous to these in which the antecedent of a conditional can't be deduced from the remaining premises by forward rules alone.

The difficulty inherent in (4)–(6) is also connected with another. Since both the antecedent and the consequent of a conditional can be arbitrarily complex, it is possible to create valid arguments that IF Elimination can't handle, even with the new backward rules. For example, PSYCOP can't prove the following argument, given only the rules of this chapter:

IF (P AND Q) THEN (IF R THEN S)
P
Q
R
————————————————————————
S

The point is that, if the conditional's consequent is sufficiently complex, it will keep PSYCOP from noticing that the consequent (plus other assertions) entails the conclusion and so prevents the program from attempting to prove the antecedent. The argument above is only the simplest example. A solution to this difficulty would be a generalized backward IF Elimination rule that first determines (in a subdomain) whether the consequent entails the current subgoal, setting up the antecedent as a new subgoal if it does. This rule would be an interesting mix between the IF Elimination and IF Introduction strategies, but it is not clear to me that the added complexity of such a rule is warranted by the facts about human inference.

6. Leon Gross suggested many improvements to the halting proof. Proof HP-III in its current form in the appendix is due to him.

Chapter 5

1. For this reason, it is unwarranted to conclude from a low score on a given problem that subjects weren't engaged in reasoning about the problem. In this vein, Braine et al. (1984, p. 360) point to problem B in table 5.1 as one in which "the conclusion seems to follow transparently from the premises," and state that the subjects' score on this item (66.7% "necessarily true" responses) "suggests that the experiment often failed to engage the reasoning procedure of subjects." It is unclear what rationale Braine et al. are applying in judging that this argument "transparently follows." The basic point, however, is that it is impossible to determine the extent to which subjects were engaged in reasoning from an absolute score without also knowing the response criterion the subjects were adopting. Fred Conrad and I (Rips and Conrad 1983) have replicated the experiment described here and found higher absolute scores (62% vs. 51% of subjects judged the classically valid arguments "necessarily true") but a very similar pattern of scores across problems.

2. Another method for estimating parameters is to include in the stimulus set an argument that turns on a single rule. The percentage of correct answers for that argument is then the estimate for that rule's availability (Braine et al. 1984; Osherson 1974, 1975, 1976). One difficulty with this procedure, for our theory, is that some of the rules, such as IF Introduction and NOT Introduction, can't be the sole rule used in the proof of an argument. Thus, the alternative method gives us no estimates for these items. Second, use of simple arguments to estimate parameters may sometimes spuriously inflate the fit of the theory. This is because the premise or the conclusion of a single-rule argument will often share the syntactic structure of the premise or conclusion of the argument that the investigator is trying to predict,

especially when the proof is short. Hence, any difficulties associated with comprehending the syntax will increase the correlation between the arguments' scores. See chapter 9 for further discussion.

3. This pattern of parameter values explains some observations about this experiment that Johnson-Laird, Byrne, and Schaeken (1992) have made. The low availabilities for OR Introduction and NOT Introduction mean that the model predicts a fairly low proportion of "necessarily true" responses on arguments that involve these rules and a fairly high proportion on arguments that don't.

Johnson-Laird et al. also claim that the scores for the problems in table 5.1 depend on whether or not the arguments "maintain the semantic information of the premises." By the amount of "semantic information," Johnson-Laird et al. mean the percentage of possible states of affairs that the premises eliminate. A possible state of affairs is, in turn, determined by an assignment of truth or falsity to each of the atomic sentences that appear in the argument (Johnson-Laird 1983, p. 36; Johnson-Laird et al. 1992, p. 423). For example, consider the simple argument

p AND q.
_____
p.

Since this argument contains just two atomic sentence types, the four possible states of affairs are one in which p is true and q is true, one in which p is true and q is false, one in which p is false and q is true, and one in which p is false and q is false. (Thus, the states of affairs are equivalent to the horizontal lines of a standard truth table for the argument.) In the sample argument, the premise rules out all but one of these states of affairs (the one in which p is true and q is true). However, the conclusion rules out only two states of affairs (the ones in which p is false). Of course, in any valid argument the conclusion must be true in all states of affairs in which the premises are true (see chapter 2), and this means that the amount of semantic information conveyed by the premise must be greater than or equal to the amount conveyed by the conclusion. Johnson-Laird (1983) talks of an argument "maintaining semantic information" if the premises and conclusion have the same amount of semantic information, and "throwing away semantic information" if the conclusion contains less semantic information than the premises. Thus, the argument above throws away semantic information.

According to Johnson-Laird et al.(1992, p. 428), "to throw away semantic information is to violate one of the fundamental principles of human deductive competence, and so we can predict that performance with these problems should be poorer." They then report a test comparing 16 arguments in table 5.1 that purportedly maintain semantic information with 16 arguments that don't. However, Johnson-Laird et al. apparently miscalculated the amount of semantic information in these arguments; according to the criterion of Johnson-Laird (1983), only three of the 32 arguments (C, O, and X) maintain semantic information. The percentage of "necessarily true" responses for these problems was 48.2%, nearly the same as the percentage for the entire problem set (50.6%). Instead, Johnson-Laird et al. seem to have decided which arguments maintained semantic information according to whether the conclusion contains an atomic sentence token that does not appear in the premises. (E.g., the conclusion of Argument A contains an r that does not appear in the premises.) Adding atomic sentences to the conclusion, however, is not the only way of reducing semantic information, as we have already seen with respect to the sample argument above.

In short, contrary to Johnson-Laird et al., there is no evidence from these data that "throwing away semantic information" hurts subjects' performance. What does seem to cause difficulty is the presence of atomic sentences in the conclusion that did not appear in the premises and may therefore seem irrelevant to those premises. This may be traced in turn to rules like OR Introduction (P; Therefore, P OR Q) that add sentences in this way.

4. This reinforces the conclusion from chapter 3 that resolution theorem proving, tree proofs, and other methods that rely on reductio as the central part of their proof procedure are probably not faithful to the deductive strategies of most human reasoners.

5. PSYCOP does not have any skill in producing or comprehending natural language. Its messages are limited to a few stock sentence frames that it fills with information relevant to the last processing cycle. The purpose is simply to give the user a signal about how it handled the input sentence. Similarly, its comprehension abilities are limited to the input propositions and to prompts ("suppose," "therefore," "... follows by Theorem 6," "... follows by means of OR Elimination," and so on).

6. Marcus (1982, experiment 2) also demonstrates that the embedding effect is not simply the result of the adverbial phrases ("Under that condition," "in that case") that introduce the embedded sentences in (7).

7. Of course, we still need to account for the second premise of (9a)–(9d), since it is unlikely that subjects have this sentence stored prior to the experiment. In the following chapter, however, we will see how this premise can be derived from general information (e.g., *IF Above(x,y) THEN NOT Above(y,x)*), which probably *is* part of subjects' knowledge base.

8. Further argument forms can be generated by substituting complex propositions for the antecedent and the consequent. For example, Evans (1977) explores the case in which the conditional can include a negative antecedent or a negative consequent.

9. This still leaves a puzzle as to why the 4-card is so frequently chosen in the selection task when converse interpretations seem to be relatively rare with similar materials in the conditional syllogism experiments. It is possible that the greater difficulty of the selection task encourages more converse interpretations. Alternatively, choice of the 4 card may reflect some more primitive strategy, such as matching the values named in the rule (Beattie and Baron 1988; Evans and Lynch 1973; Oaksford and Stenning 1992).

Chapter 6

1. A possible compromise is to distinguish between those conditional assertions to which the forward inference should apply and those to which it shouldn't. Hewitt (1969) incorporated this in his PLANNER in the form of what he termed "antecedent" and "consequent" theorems. It is possible to argue, however, that the appropriate direction for a conditional inference should be determined by the nature of the deduction environment rather than by intrinsic differences among conditionals. Moore (1982) suggests that the correct direction might be determined by the theorem prover itself as it reasons about its own inference abilities.

2. It may help to remember that the simplification we get from dealing with satisfaction rather than truth also occurs in CPL, though in slightly different ways. For instance, the usual semantics for CPL contains a clause like (b), specifying satisfaction of a conjunction in terms of satisfaction of the conjuncts. But, of course, it is not the case in CPL that $(\exists x)F(x)$ and $(\exists x)G(x)$ are true iff $(\exists x)(F(x) \text{ AND } G(x))$.

Chapter 7

1. To symbolize *No F are G*, we use $NOT(F(x) \text{ AND } G(x))$ in preference to the logically equivalent $IF\ F(x)\ THEN\ NOT(G(x))$ since the former seems closer to English syntax and should therefore be a more natural representation for English speakers.

2. See Boolos 1984 and Johnson-Laird and Bara 1984b for a discussion of this point. Apuleius was apparently the first to advocate these *subaltern* entailments (see Horn 1989).

3. In Aristotelian logic, All and Some-not sentences are "contradictories," as are No and Some sentences. The negative relations between these pairs aren't immediate in the traditional

All-Some-No terminology or in the quantifier-free notation of the b sentence in (1)–(4). This is due, in the latter case, to the implicit scope of the variables, mentioned in the previous chapter. In the case of All, we have *IF F(x) THEN G(x)* in (1b), which is equivalent to *(∀x)(IF F(x) THEN G(x))*, and its negation is *NOT((∀x)(IF F(x) THEN G(x)))* ≡ *(∃x) NOT (IF F(x) THEN G(x))* ≡ *NOT(IF F(b) THEN G(b))* ≡ *F(b) AND NOT G(b)*. This last sentence is our representation of Some-not in (4b). The same type of expansion also suffices to show that No and Some are contradictories.

4. Dickstein (1978a) reports data from two samples of subjects, both consisting of Wellesley undergraduates. The percentages we cite are based on the second sample, which contained more responses per premise pair.

5. One useful feature of syllogisms is that their syntactic complexity is approximately the same across the different argument types. Thus, the response distributions in the appendix are not due to variations in number of premises, number of connectives, and so on. In chapter 5 I argued on statistical grounds that the parameter estimates were not due to surface complexity; the similarity of the present estimates to those of chapter 5 lends some further support to this conclusion.

6. The data cited here are from experiment 3 of Johnson-Laird and Bara (1984a), in which subjects had as much time as they needed to produce a response. Those authors also report a separate study in which the response had to be made under a 10-second deadline. Since these data are less appropriate for assessing specifically logical processing, we will not consider them here. The tables in Johnson-Laird and Bara 1984a include only categorical responses that contained the end terms of the syllogism, plus the "no conclusion follows" responses. Johnson-Laird and Bara (1984a, p. 51) describe the remaining items as "idiosyncratic conclusions, e.g. the inclusion of a middle term instead of an end term as in 'Some A are B'." The statistics below that refer to the percentage of *reported* responses are based on this set. On the other hand, Johnson-Laird and Bara do tabulate conclusions in which the order of terms is opposite that of traditional syllogisms. (E.g., given premises ⟨All(G,H),All(F,G)⟩, they count the conclusions All(H,F), Some(H,F), etc., as well as All(F,H), Some(F,H), and the like.) The statistics that follow also include such responses. This means, in particular, that the number of premise pairs that yield valid conclusions is different from that in table 7.1 or the appendix.

7. The premise pairs for which forward processing is sufficient are all ones that have valid conclusions when the implicatures are accepted; however, of the 16 pairs that require backward processing, only four have valid conclusions under the implicatures. This means that the difference just reported may be partly due to subjects' accepting the presuppositions of the premises and the conclusion. Implicatures, though, can't be responsible for the entire effect. If we confine our attention to those four pairs, we still find only 42.5% of subjects producing a valid conclusion.

8. One fact about syllogisms is that the conclusions produced by the forward rules are also ones that have the dominant quantifier of the premises (as table 7.1 reveals); so responses in class a above are a subset of those in class b. Moreover, several of the conclusions in class d are also in class b. This raises the issue of whether we can't describe the results in a simpler way: Perhaps subjects skip logical processing altogether, either giving a conclusion that has the dominant quantifier or responding that nothing follows. The latter description, however, doesn't do full justice to the results, since subjects are more likely to produce a conclusion with a dominant quantifier when that conclusion is deducible than when it is not. Fourteen premise pairs have dominant conclusions that are deducible, and subjects produced these conclusions on 62.8% of trials; of the remaining 50 syllogisms, subjects produced dominant conclusions on only 44.2%.

9. The only important shortfall in PSYCOP's ability to prove the arguments in these exercises concerned ones whose premises had embedded conditionals. This is connected with the difficulties in dealing with conditionals by Backward IF Elimination that were discussed in

previous chapters (see especially note 5 to chapter 4). For example, PSYCOP cannot prove the following argument from the rules of chapter 6:

IF F(x) THEN (IF G(y) THEN H(y)).
_____
IF (F(z) AND G(z)) THEN (F(a) AND H(a)).

PSYCOP sensibly tries to prove this argument using IF Introduction, assuming the conclusion's antecedent and then attempting to prove its consequent. In order to establish $H(a)$, however, PSYCOP needs to use the premise information. Backward IF Elimination seems like the right strategy at this point, but the rule doesn't apply, since $H(y)$ is buried in the consequent of the premise's consequent. Of course, the proof would go through if we gave PSYCOP a generalized IF Elimination rule, such as the one discussed in chapter 4, that allowed it to work with these embedded conditionals; however, it is not clear whether such a rule would be psychologically plausible. McGee (1985) claims that IF Elimination sometimes gives results that are intuitively incorrect when applied to conditionals whose consequent is also a conditional. One possibility that McGee discusses (but doesn't necessarily endorse) is that people understand these embedded conditionals (ones of the form *IF P THEN (IF Q THEN R)*) as if they were logically equivalent conditionals with conjunctions in their antecedents (i.e., as *IF (P AND Q) THEN R*). This hypothesis both explains McGee's examples and allows PSYCOP to prove the arguments in question.

Chapter 8

1. I am assuming that the *Talk-to* links are one-way in order to keep the example simple. There are several ways to implement a version of the problem with two-way links. One is by substituting the following assertions for (1a) and (1b):

IF Talks-to(u,v) OR Talks-to(v,u) THEN Path(u,v)

IF (Talks-to(x,y) OR Talks-to(y,x)) AND Path(y,z) THEN Path(x,z)

A second simplification is that we are tacitly assuming that there are no closed circuits in the spy network (in fact, none of Hayes' problems contained circuits). Given just the information in (1a) and (1b), circuits will cause PSYCOP to loop endlessly. To prevent this, PSYCOP could keep a list of the spies who have already carried the message, preventing any such spy from receiving it twice. See chapter 7 of Clocksin and Mellish 1981 for an example of this sort.

2. Later research on memory for partial orders confirms some of these same effects. In experiments of this type, subjects learn relations between adjacent items in an ordering (e.g., *Tango is taller than China, Tango is taller than Tree*, etc.) and then answer questions about the adjacent pairs (*Is Tango taller than China?, Is Tree taller than Tango?*) or nonadjacent ones (*Is Tango taller than Larynx?, Is Larynx taller than China?*). (They are not required to trace each link in the chain.) Subjects tend to answer these questions faster for the adjacent than the nonadjacent items and faster for parts of the structure that contain no competing pathways (Hayes-Roth and Hayes-Roth 1975; Moeser and Tarrant, 1977; Warner and Griggs, 1980). However, the difference between adjacent and nonadjacent pairs decreases when metric information is included with the partially ordered items (Moeser and Tarrant, 1977), and the difference reverses for linearly ordered structures (Potts 1972; Scholz and Potts 1974). This disappearance or reversal is probably due to subjects' adopting a different representation from the pairwise relations that we have assumed in this example.

3. "Sufficiency" can have weaker or stronger interpretations. Much of the discussion about necessary and sufficient properties in the literature on categorization focuses on sufficiency in a modal sense in which the properties would have to guarantee category membership in all

possible worlds. It is usually easy to find sci-fi counterexamples to show that a proposed set of features is not modally sufficient for the category in question. (E.g., the possibility of a new type of mammal growing feathers would defeat feathers as a sufficient property for being a bird, if we take sufficiency in this strong way.) But (2) demands sufficiency in the weaker form that there is nothing (in the actual world) that satisfies the antecedent of the conditional that doesn't also satisfy the consequent. There could certainly be sufficient properties in this weaker sense, even though there are none in the modal sense.

One might argue that any useful classification procedure should be stronger than what is required by the conditional in (2). The procedure should be able to classify not only birds that happen to exist but also ones that *could* exist in some at least mildly counterfactual situations. Perhaps it should be able to classify all physically possible birds. Bear in mind, though, that what is at stake in this discussion is not a scientific theory of birds but a scientific theory of how people classify them. For the latter purpose, it is not clear to me exactly how strong the conditional should be.

4. And, of course, both (a) and (b) differ from

(c) George is a bird if there are causal relations of a certain sort.

Briefly put, (c) is a claim about the sufficiency of causal relations for category membership, (b) is a claim about people's belief in (c), and (a) is a claim about the sufficiency of the belief about causal relations for the belief about George's being a bird. Traditional arguments against sufficient properties for natural categories are directed against (c), and arguments against people's belief in sufficient properties are arguments against (b).

5. It is another question, and a much trickier one, whether we should identify our schemas or mini-theories with *concepts* of the same categories. There are good reasons, both philosophical (Putnam 1988) and psychological (Armstrong et al. 1983; Osherson and Smith 1981), for supposing that concepts and schemas are different creatures, although they are often run together in the psychological literature.

6. Rumelhart and Norman also mention as a fifth characteristic the fact that one schema can embed another; for example, the schema for *body* will include schemas for *head*, *trunk*, and *limbs*. It is not clear, however, whether this means that all of the information we have about heads is a physical part of our representation of bodies or rather that the representation of bodies can include a reference to heads. The latter notion, which seems the more plausible of the two, is surely within the compass of the logical forms we have been using.

7. Oaksford and Chater (1991) also note that the intractability (i.e., NP-completeness) of nonmonotonic logics make them unlikely as cognitive mechanisms for inductive inference. They use the intractability of these logics, however, as part of a general argument against classical representational approaches in cognitive science. Oaksford and Chater may be right that inductive inference will eventually be the downfall of these approaches. But, as the categorization example shows, the classical view isn't committed to nonmonotonic *logics* as a way of obtaining nondeductive belief fixation. This remains true even when the classical view is specialized so that all conclusions sanctioned in the system are deductively valid ones, because these systems can adopt a belief in ways other than making it the conclusion of an argument.

8. There is an echo here of the debate between Geis and Zwicky (1971) and Boër and Lycan (1973) on invited inference, which I touched on in chapter 2. The inference from *If you mow her lawn, Joan will pay you $5* to *If you don't mow her lawn, Joan won't pay you $5* might be taken as a type of nonmonotonic inference based on minimizing the possible circumstances in which Joan pays you $5 to those explicitly stated in the premise (i.e., those in which you mow her lawn). Obviously, if these circumstances coincide—if the paying-$5 cases are the same as the lawn-mowing cases—as this minimization predicts, then the conclusion follows. Thus, we can view Geis and Zwicky's "conditional perfection" as a special case of circumscription. The same goes for the tendency to perfect universals—to reason from *All X are Y* to *All Y are X*.

On one hand, it is clearly of interest that the same nonmonotonic mechanism might account both for these conditional and universal inferences and for the default inferences just discussed. On the other hand, perhaps this is merely a reflection of the fact that all these items are inductive and the fact that all inductive inferences require conceptual minimizing of some sort. We minimize the possibility that what is unforeseen or unlikely will turn out to be true.

Chapter 9

1. There are deontic logics that formalize permission and obligation and that are extensions of the basic CPL system (Føllesdal and Hilpinen 1971; Lewis 1974; von Wright 1971). These will be discussed below.

2. In order to handle some of these problems, PSYCOP needs a process that recognizes when the conclusion of an argument is inconsistent with the premises (as Braine et al. point out). In their experiments, subjects were required to determine whether the conclusion of an argument was "true" on the basis of the premises, "false" on the basis of the premises, or "indeterminate" (not just "follows" vs. "doesn't follow"). For example, the argument below should have a False response:

There is an F, and there's not an L.
There is an L.

PSYCOP can determine that an argument is false in a general way by proving that the negation of the conclusion follows from the premises. In some problems like this one, however, the negation of the conclusion is produced automatically in virtue of PSYCOP's forward rules, and PSYCOP could make an immediate "false" response if it detected the presence of such an assertion. Outcome measures in Braine et al.'s experiments suggest that subjects are able to do something like this. Braine et al. implement this through a separate inference rule; but since this monitoring seems to have a different status than the inference rules in chapters 4 and 6, it might be more appropriate as part of PSYCOP's response process.

3. In a later paper, Cheng and Holyoak (1989, p. 301) acknowledge that "looser versions of the memory-cuing view, which simply argue that remindings can influence reasoning, seem to us impossible to entirely rule out for any selection-task experiment conducted on adult subjects." But they note that "the critical weakness of looser formulations of the memory-cuing view ... is that they are not predictive; rather they provide only post hoc explanations of when facilitation is or is not obtained." Although an explanation based on specific experiences is certainly *post hoc* in the present context, it is not clear that it can't be developed in a way that makes testable predictions. One might start from the hypothesis that context is effective to the extent that it reminds subjects of (independently described) experiences that clearly identify violations. The current point, however, is not to develop such a theory, but simply to agree that it can't be entirely "ruled out."

4. Jackson and Griggs (1990) report that seemingly simple changes in wording can disrupt performance on abstract permission rules. For example, in their Experiment 4 they found only 15% correct responses when the problem was phrased as follows:

> Your task is to decide which of the cards you need to turn over in order to find out whether or not a certain regulation is being followed. The regulation is "If one is to take action 'A', then one must first satisfy precondition 'P'." Turn over only those cards that you need to check to be sure.

Cheng and Holyoak's (1985) wording was as follows:

> Suppose you are an authority checking whether or not people are obeying certain regulations. The regulations all have the general form, "If one is to take action 'A,' then one must first satisfy precondition 'P.'" In other words, in order to be permitted to do "A", one must first have fulfilled prerequisite "P." The cards below contain information on four people.... In order to check that a certain regulation is being followed, which of the cards below would you turn over? Turn over only those that you need to check to be sure.

Jackson and Griggs were able to replicate Cheng and Holyoak's effect if they repeated the *exact* wording, so presumably something about the pretense of the authority checking a regulation (Gigerenzer and Hug 1992) or the paraphrasing of the rule ("In other words ...") is crucial to the effect (Cosmides 1989). The checking context alone is not sufficient, however (Pollard & Evans 1987).

5. This is, of course, not to deny that people sometimes reason with principles (heuristics, inductive rules, plausible rules) that aren't deductively correct. We saw an example of heuristic reasoning of this sort in the context of categorization in chapter 8. It probably goes without saying at this point that a deduction system such as PSYCOP can incorporate these heuristics in the same way that production systems do. In fact, this suggests a third possibility for squaring the evidence on content effects with a deduction system such as ours: We can allow PSYCOP to apply (9a)–(9d) in order to solve the selection task, handling them in just the way we do any other conditional sentences. This would be an easy project, since there are only four sentences to worry about, and it would also avoid the need to postulate special deduction rules based on deontic concepts. In the text I have chosen to focus on the possibility of deontic deduction rules, since there do appear to be valid, productive relationships among sentences containing *PERMISSIBLE* and *OBLIGATORY*.

Manktelow and Over (1991) also note the possibility of construing pragmatic schemas in terms of a deontic deduction theory. They claim, however, that such a theory is not sufficiently general, since it could not account for why people come to accept deontic conditionals (e.g., *If you tidy your room, then I will allow you to go out to play*) in the first place. But although deduction can't always explain the rationale for deontic conditionals, it can explain certain relations among them. The situation is the same as the case of ordinary deductive inferences: Although a theory of deduction can explain why *Trump is rich AND Koch is famous* follows from the separate sentences *Trump is rich* and *Koch is famous*, it can't necessarily explain why you believe *Trump is rich (Koch is famous)* in the first place.

6. See chapter 2 above.

7. See also note 3 above.

8. See also Reiser et al. 1985.

9. I am using "obligation" and "permission" in a way that differs from Cheng and Holyoak's usage but that is more in keeping with their usage in deontic logic. See the above references to work on conditional obligation and permission. For Cheng and Holyoak, permission implies that a mandatory action (i.e., precondition) ought to be performed before the permitted action can be carried out, and obligation implies that an action commits a person to performing a later mandatory action. My use of PERMISSIBLE and OBLIGATORY carries no temporal restrictions. Rather PERMISSIBLE(P | Q) means that P can be the case given that Q is the case. OBLIGATORY(P | Q) means that P ought to be the case given that Q is the case. Thus, both permissions and obligations in Cheng and Holyoak's sense entail that some state of affairs is OBLIGATORY given some other state.

10. Another way to represent the dual obligation in this setup is to make the *OBLIGATORY* and *PERMISSIBLE* operators include an argument for the individual who is under the obligation or who is given permission.

11. Cosmides, following Manktelow and Over (1987), also notes disagreement among philosophers about exactly which arguments are deontically valid. But although there are differences

of opinion about the right set of rules or axioms for deontic logic (just as there are for sentential logic), systematic relations exist among the deontic systems, as Lewis (1974) demonstrates. Cosmides' comments seem to imply that these systems suffer from vagueness in their formulation ("similarities or differences [between deontic logic and social contract theory] will become clearer once deontic logic reaches the level of specificity that social contract theory has" (p. 233)). But just the opposite is the case; rival deontic systems emerged because of the need to formulate them at a detailed level. Moreover, the theoretical disagreements don't foreclose the possibility that some such system provides a good basis for human reasoning in this domain.

Chapter 10

1. Denise Cummins pointed this out (personal communication, 1992). Cohen (1981), Macnamara (1986), Osherson (1976), and Sober (1978) all develop similar analogies, as was noted in chapter 1.

2. Most of the work on believability derives from studies of categorical syllogisms, and most of the work on elaboration from studies of conditionals. There is no reason to suppose, however, that the results are peculiar to these paradigms. For example, content can change subjects' responses to syllogisms by causing them to interpret a universal premise (*All x are y*) as implying its converse (*All y are x*) in a way that parallels the findings with conditionals (Revlis 1975a). This is consistent with the structural similarity in the logical form of universals and conditionals.

There is also some evidence for a believability effect with conditionals. Fillenbaum (1975) found that subjects were somewhat more likely to conclude that a conditional implied its obverse when the obverse was factually true. For example, subjects were more willing to say that *If he goes to Paris he will visit the Louvre* implies *If he does not go to Paris he will not visit the Louvre* than to say that *If he goes to Paris he will get drunk* implies *If he does not go to Paris he will not get drunk*. The effect is rather small, however, as it often is in believability studies.

3. This research isn't invariably convincing, however. For example, Byrne and Johnson-Laird (1989) contrast their "mental models" with rule-based theories in predictions about the following problems:

(a) A is on the right of B.
   C is on the left of B.
   D is in front of C.
   E is in front of B.
   _____
   What is the relation between D and E?

(b) B is on the right of A.
   C is on the left of B.
   D is in front of C.
   E is in front of B.
   _____
   What is the relation between D and E?

According to these authors, there are two mental models that are consistent with (b), but only one that is consistent with (a). Since it is more difficult to keep track of two models than one, model theory predicts that (b) will lead to more errors than (a). Byrne and Johnson-Laird point out, however, that one can construct the same proof that D is to the left of E for both problems. (The first premise is irrelevant to the correct conclusion in both cases, and the remaining premises are identical; thus, any proof that will work with (a) will also work with (b).) Hence, they believe, rule-based theories are committed to predicting no difference between these items. Because subjects in fact have more difficulty with (b) than with (a), Byrne and Johnson-Laird conclude that model theory is right and rule theories are wrong.

There are multiple sources of difficulty, however, in interpreting this experiment. First, the instructions specifically requested subjects to form spatial arrays in solving the problems. This obviously biased the subjects to use an imaginal strategy that favored the mental-model predictions (or placed a strong task demand on them to respond as if they were trying to image the arrays—see Pylyshyn 1984). Second, there is no reason at all to suppose that the final length of a derivation is the only pertinent factor in rule-based accounts of this type of reasoning. In any realistic deduction system, searching for a correct proof can be sidetracked by the presence of irrelevant information, such as the first premise of these problems. In fact, we have already seen an example of how PSYCOP's problem solving becomes less efficient in the presence of irrelevant information for somewhat similar tasks (see the simulation of Hayes' spy problems in chapter 8). Of course, if a deduction system were able to ignore the first premise, it would produce equivalent performance for (a) and (b); but exactly the same is true for model theory. Third, Byrne and Johnson-Laird's method of counting models in these problems violate a policy that Johnson-Laird established elsewhere (Johnson-Laird and Bara 1984a, p. 37). In the case of the mental-model theory for other types of inferences (which will be discussed momentarily), a problem requires more than one model only if additional models rule out potential conclusions that are consistent with the initial model. In the relational problems, however, both of the purported models for (b) lead to precisely the same conclusion with respect to the relation between D and E. Thus, according to the former method of counting models, both (a) and (b) would be one-model problems.

4. These statistics are based on predictions and data in tables 9–12 of Johnson-Laird and Bara 1984a. Johnson-Laird and Byrne (1991) are less explicit about their predictions, but they are probably close to those of the earlier version.

5. I am assuming that *All green block are big* can't be eliminated on the basis of the bracketing in the second model of figure 10.3. But even if it can, predictions for the models theory will still depend on the order in which subjects consider these two models. In that case, if subjects first construct the model on the right of the figure, then the only potential conclusion would be the correct one (*Some big blocks are not green*), and syllogism (6) would be a one-model rather than a two-model, problem.

6. Polk and Newell (1988; see also Newell 1990 and Polk et al. 1989) have proposed a theory that combines aspects of mental models and proposition-based reasoning in the Soar framework and which may improve on Johnson-Laird and Bara's approach. The details of the theory in the published reports are too fragmentary to allow a complete evaluation. However, there are several facts about the scheme that are worth noting. One is that Soar's basic representational format consists of object-attribute-value triples. Both the mental models and the categorical propositions that Soar uses in solving syllogisms are constructed from these triples. In particular, Soar's mental models are not diagrammatic entities with inherent spatial properties; they are lists of attributes and values such as *(block-1 ^shape square ^color green)*. Second, use of mental models is extremely limited, at least in the single example that Polk and Newell provide. In fact, mental models seem restricted to determining the polarity of the conclusion (negative or positive); all other aspects of the conclusion (order of terms and quantifier) are determined entirely by the propositions. There seems to be no counterpart to Johnson-Laird's use of models to eliminate potential conclusions, which is the central component of his theory. Soar also allows new propositions to be produced from old ones. Finally, Soar makes errors because of simple biases in constructing the conclusion and because of conversion of premises. Number of models isn't the determining factor.

7. Johnson-Laird and Byrne (1991) revise this notation by eliminating the optional tokens (e.g., *0v*) and instead using the bracket convention as in the syllogism models. I have used the notation of Johnson-Laird et al. (1989) here, since their presentation is more complete. The two systems appear to make identical predictions, however.

8. Johnson-Laird et al. (1989) included some multiple-model premises that have no valid conclusion of the form Q_1 *of the X are related to* Q_2 *of the Y.* The correct response for these problems was "nothing follows," and for this reason their difficulty may be due to subjects' bias against responses of this sort (Revlis 1975a).

9. Some of the material in this section is drawn from Rips 1990b.

10. As support for models over rules, Johnson-Laird and Byrne (1991) cite earlier work (Oakhill et al. 1989) purportedly showing that believability of a tentative conclusion can affect the reasoning process. The notion is that rule theories can explain content effects only through the initial interpretation of premises or through the censoring of conclusions. Content does not affect the actual reasoning process, only its input and output. However, content can influence reasoning according to the "model" model by increasing subjects' willingness to consider more than one model of the premises. The evidence that supports the latter idea comes from syllogistic premises like these:

(a) All of the Frenchmen are wine drinkers.
 Some of the wine drinkers are gourmets.
                      ?

(b) All of the Frenchmen are wine drinkers.
 Some of the wine drinkers are Italians.
                      ?

These problems have the same form as (7b) (with the models in (8) and (9)), and neither has a valid categorical conclusion. However, for syllogism (a) the tentative conclusions that are consistent with model (8) are believable (e.g., *Some of the Frenchmen are gourmets*), whereas for syllogism (b) they are not (e.g., *Some of the Frenchmen are Italians*). If unbelievable tentative conclusions encourage subjects to persist in searching for alternative models, then subjects who receive (b) should be more likely to find model (9) and respond correctly that no conclusion follows. Oakhill et al. did indeed find more correct responses for (b) than for (a).

What Johnson-Laird and Byrne neglect to mention is that the evidence for mental models from Oakhill et al. is contradictory. If the believability of tentative conclusions affects subjects' performance on syllogisms with no categorical conclusions, it should also affect performance on multiple-model syllogisms that do have categorical conclusions. Oakhill et al. compare problems, such as (c) below, in which some of the tentative conclusions are unbelievable and in which the final correct conclusion is believable with problems, such as (d), in which both tentative and final conclusions are believable.

(c) Some of the houseowners are married.
 None of the houseowners is a husband.
                      ?

(d) Some of the houseowners are married.
 None of the houseowners is a bachelor.
                      ?

According to model theory, problem (c) has unbelievable tentative conclusions (including *None of the husbands are married*) and a believable final conclusion (*Some of the married people are not husbands*). Problem (d) has believable tentative conclusions (such as *None of the bachelors are married*) and a believable final conclusion (*Some of the married people are not bachelors*). Since unbelievable tentative conclusions should motivate subjects to search for further models, Oakhill et al. predict that problems of type (c) should produce better performance than ones of type (d). In three experiments, however, Oakhill et al. found no significant difference between these problems; in two of three, the trend was in the direction opposite to the mental-model predictions.

The generate-and-test account for syllogism production that I outlined in chapter 7 is quite consistent with these data. For problems (such as (a) and (b)) that have no categorical conclusion, PSYCOP will end up either responding "no conclusion follows" or guessing (incorrectly) the generated conclusion. If subjects are more likely to guess if the generated conclusion is believable, subjects' accuracy should be higher with (b) than with (a), as obtained. Now consider problems (such as (c) and (d)) that do have valid categorical conclusions. Since PSYCOP's forward rules are not sufficient to produce the correct conclusions, the program should again generate the tentative conclusion *None of the husbands are married* or its converse (in the case of (c)) and *None of the bachelors are married* or its converse (in the case of (d)). Neither of these conclusions is derivable, and most subjects will give up at this point, responding "no conclusion follows" or guessing at the conclusions just mentioned. Guessing more often for (d) than for (c) will produce no difference in accuracy this time, since both "no conclusion follows" and the guess (*None of the bachelors are married*) are incorrect. Thus, subjects' accuracy should be low and approximately equal for (c) and (d)—which is what Oakhill et al. observed.

11. These considerations do not show that there is anything wrong with the idea that people possess mental representations that integrate information across sentences or that integrate information from sentences and from perceptual sources. For example, many investigators have posited representations in which coreferring expressions in a text or discourse are associated with a common node or symbol. Although these representations are sometimes also called "mental models," "situation models," or "discourse models" (e.g., Just and Carpenter 1987; Kintsch 1988), their proponents do not claim that these models possess special representational powers that are in principle different from those of standard representations (mental networks or mental sentences). The same is true of theories in which "mental model" is used to mean a collection of beliefs about some scientific domain, such as electricity or temperature. (See the papers collected in Gentner and Stevens 1983.) These theories clearly differ from Johnson-Laird's (1983, 1989) conception of mental models, since he believes these models go beyond what standard representations can accomplish.

Chapter 11

1. The difference between architectural and strategic deduction may be related to Grice's (1977) contrast between "flat" and "variable" concepts of rationality. The first is the concept involved in the notion that people are rational beings, whereas the second allows some people to be more rational than others.

2. Many investigators fail to realize that parameter fitting is also part of the more standard statistical techniques, such as analysis of variance (ANOVA) and regression, that they use for hypothesis testing. For example, it comes as a surprise to many psychologists, including ones who have taken graduate-level statistics courses and who use statistics on a daily basis, that ANOVA involves parameter estimation for effect sizes. This goes unnoticed because different estimation techniques lead to the same choice of parameters unless the design is a complex one (e.g., involves an unbalanced number of observations).

3. I use "logicist" here, as Birnbaum and other AI researchers do, to mean a cognitive scientist who uses methods of formal logic as one of his or her main research tools. For connections between logicism of this sort and the older logicist program in the foundation of mathematics, see Thomason 1991.

4. What may have led to confusion about OR Introduction is the claim in an earlier paper (Rips 1984) that there are individual differences in subjects' use of this rule, and that such differences might constitute variations in reasoning competence. I was using *competence* in this context to refer to stable aspects of subjects' deduction abilities, as opposed to such temporary *performance* factors as inattention and motivation. Stable differences in

susceptibility to pragmatic influences, such as ones that affect OR Introduction, would be differences in competence on this approach. However, the term "competence" may have suggested that subjects who consistently refrained from applying OR Introduction were somehow "incompetent" in their reasoning. This, of course, was not the intent of the argument. Differences in reasoning between two individuals, even differences in their reasoning competence, needn't imply that either is thinking irrationally. (An analogy: Native English speakers who haven't learned Chinese—who have no competence in Chinese—aren't thereby defective in their linguistic abilities.)

5. It is possible for someone to claim that PSYCOP's incompleteness with respect to classical logic is itself evidence that the theory attributes to people a kind of systematic irrationality. No one supposes, however, that the incompleteness of arithmetic demonstrates the irrationality of finite axiom systems in classical logic. Thus, a critic would need some additional arguments to show why PSYCOP's incompleteness is especially culpable.

Another argument along these lines concerns the distinction between architectural and strategic levels. If the necessary deduction rules are built into the architecture, it may seem as though replicating these rules for strategic purposes is just introducing an unnecessary source of error. Once a deduction problem has been entered in memory, why doesn't the system simply deal with it at the architectural level? Our original motive for separating these two modes of deduction, however, was to keep the system from committing itself to conclusions that it was then powerless to retract. We need to be able to override some uses of deduction, and one way to do this is to separate the overridable uses from the overriding ones. Although this may seem unnecessary duplication and a possible source of mistakes, its purpose is to eliminate much more serious catastrophes. (There might also be a question about how the system could *keep* the architectural rules from applying to the overridable cases. One approach would be to tag sentences for architectural use; another would be to store them in a separate location, such as the production-rule memory of Anderson (1976, 1983).)

References

Adams, E. (1965) The logic of conditionals. *Inquiry* 8: 166–197.

Adams, M. J. (1984) Aristotle's logic. In G. H. Bower (ed.), *Psychology of Learning and Motivation*, volume 18. Academic Press.

Adkins, D. C., and Lyerly, S. B. (1952) *Factor Analysis of Reasoning Tests.* University of North Carolina Press.

Ajjanagadde, V., and Shastri, L. (1989) Efficient inference with multi-place predicates and variables in a connectionist system. *Program of the 11th Annual Conference of the Cognitive Science Society.* Erlbaum.

Anderson, A. R., and Belnap, N. D., Jr. (1975) *Entailment: The Logic of Relevance and Necessity*, volume 1. Princeton University Press.

Anderson, J. R. (1976) *Language, Memory, and Thought.* Erlbaum.

Anderson, J. R. (1983) *The Architecture of Cognition.* Harvard University Press.

Anderson, J. R. (1990) *The Adaptive Character of Thought.* Erlbaum.

Anderson, J. R., Greeno, J. G., Kline, P. J., and Neves, D. M. (1981) Acquisition of problem solving skill. In J. R. Anderson (ed.), *Cognitive Skills and Their Acquisition.* Erlbaum.

Armstrong, S. L., Gleitman, L. R., and Gleitman, H. (1983) What some concepts might not be. *Cognition* 13: 263–308.

Au, T. K.-F. (1983) Chinese and English counterfactuals: The Sapir-Whorf hypothesis revisited. *Cognition* 15: 155–187.

Bach, E. (1986) Natural language metaphysics. In R. Barcan Marcus, G. J. W. Dorn, and P. Weingartner (eds.), *Logic, Methodology, and Philosophy of Science*, volume 7. North-Holland.

Barwise, J. (1979) On branching quantifiers in English. *Journal of Philosophical Logic* 8: 47–80.

Barwise, J. (1986) The situation in logic-II: Conditionals and conditional information. In E. C. Traugott, C. A. Ferguson, and J. S. Reilly (eds.), *On Conditionals.* Cambridge University Press.

Barwise, J. (1987a) Unburdening the language of thought. *Mind and Language*, 2: 82–96.

Barwise, J. (1987b) Noun phrases, generalized quantifiers, and anaphora. In P. Gärdenfors (ed.), *Generalized Quantifiers: Linguistic and Logical Approaches.* Reidel.

Barwise, J., and Cooper, R. (1981) Generalized quantifiers and natural language. *Linguistics and Philosophy* 4: 159–219.

Beattie, J., and Baron, J. (1988) Confirmation and matching bias in hypothesis testing. *Quarterly Journal of Experimental Psychology* 40A: 269–289.

Begg, I., and Denny, J. (1969) Empirical reconciliation of atmosphere and conversion interpretations of syllogistic reasoning. *Journal of Experimental Psychology* 81: 351–354.

Begg, I., and Harris, G. (1982) On the interpretation of syllogisms. *Journal of Verbal Learning and Verbal Behavior* 21: 595–620.

Belnap, N. D. (1962) Tonk, plonk, and plink. *Analysis* 22: 130–134.

Benacerraf, P. (1967) God, the devil, and Gödel. *Monist* 51: 9–32.

Bergmann, M., Moor, J., and Nelson, J. (1980) *The Logic Book.* Random House.

Beth, E. W. (1955) Semantic entailment and formal derivability. *Mededelingen van de Koninklijke Nederlandse Akademie van Wetenschappen* 18: 309–342.

Birnbaum, L. (1991) Rigor mortis: A response to Nilsson's "Logic and artificial intelligence." *Artificial Intelligence* 47: 57–77.

Bledsoe, W. W. (1977) Non-resolution theorem proving. *Artificial Intelligence* 9: 1–35.

Bledsoe, W. W., and Bruell, P. (1974) A man-machine theorem-proving system. *Artificial Intelligence* 5: 51–72.

Bledsoe, W. W., Boyer, R. S., and Henneman, W. H. (1972) Computer proofs of limit theorems. *Artificial Intelligence* 3: 27–60.

Boër, S. E., and Lycan, W. G. (1973) Invited inferences and other unwelcome guests. *Papers in Linguistics* 6: 483–505.

Boolos, G. (1984) On 'syllogistic inference.' *Cognition* 17: 181–182.

Boolos, G. S., and Jeffrey, R. C. (1974) *Computability and Logic*. Cambridge University Press.

Borkowski, L., and Słupecki, J. (1958) A logical system based on rules and its application in teaching mathematical logic. *Studia Logica* 7: 71–106.

Bower, G. H., and Morrow, D. G. (1990) Mental models in narrative comprehension. *Science* 247: 44–48.

Brachman, R. J., and Schmolze, J. G. (1985) An overview of KL-ONE knowledge representation system. *Cognitive Science* 9: 171–216.

Braine, M. D. S. (1978) On the relation between the natural logic of reasoning and standard logic. *Psychological Review* 85: 1–21.

Braine, M. D. S. (1990) The "natural logic" approach to reasoning. In W. F. Overton (ed.), *Reasoning, Necessity, and Logic: Developmental Perspectives*. Erlbaum.

Braine, M. D. S., and O'Brien, D. P. (1991) A theory of If: A lexical entry, reasoning program, and pragmatic principles. *Psychological Review* 98: 182–203.

Braine, M. D. S., and Rumain, B. (1983) Logical reasoning. In P. H. Mussen (ed.), *Handbook of Child Psychology*, volume 3. Wiley.

Braine, M. D. S., Reiser, B. J., and Rumain, B. (1984) Some empirical justification for a theory of natural propositional reasoning. In G. H. Bower (ed.), *Psychology of Learning and Motivation*, volume 18. Academic Press.

Brooks, L. (1978) Nonanalytic concept formation and memory for instances. In E. Rosch and B. B. Lloyd (eds.), *Cognition and Categorization*. Erlbaum.

Burt, C. (1919) The development of reasoning in children—I. *Journal of Experimental Pedagogy* 5: 68–77.

Byrne, R. M. J. (1989) Suppressing valid inferences with conditionals. *Cognition* 31: 61–83.

Byrne, R. M. J., and Johnson-Laird, P. N. (1989) Spatial reasoning. *Journal of Memory and Language* 28: 564–575.

Carey, S. (1985) *Conceptual Change in Childhood*. MIT Press.

Carpenter, P. A., and Just, M. A. (1975) Sentence comprehension: A psycholinguistic processing model of verification. *Psychological Review* 82: 45–73.

Carroll, J. B. (1989) Factor analysis since Spearman: Where do we stand? What do we know? In R. Kanfer, P. L. Ackerman, and R. Cudeck (eds.), *Abilities, Motivation, and Methodology*. Erlbaum.

Carroll, J. B. (1993) *Human Cognitive Abilities: A Survey of Factor-analytic Studies*. Cambridge University Press.

Carroll, L. (1895) What the tortoise said to Achilles. *Mind* 4: 278–280.

Ceraso, J., and Provitera, A. (1971) Sources of error in syllogistic reasoning. *Cognitive Psychology* 2: 400–410.

Chang, C. C., and Keisler, H. J. (1973) *Model Theory*. North-Holland.

Chapman, L. J., and Chapman, J. P. (1959) Atmosphere effect re-examined. *Journal of Experimental Psychology* 58: 220–226.

Cheng, P. W., and Holyoak, K. J. (1985) Pragmatic reasoning schemas. *Cognitive Psychology* 17: 391–416.

Cheng, P. W., and Holyoak, K. J. (1989) On the natural selection of reasoning theories. *Cognition* 33: 285–313.

Cheng, P. W., Holyoak, K. J., Nisbett, R. E., and Oliver, L. M. (1986) Pragmatic versus syntactic approaches to training deductive reasoning. *Cognitive Psychology* 18: 293– 328.

Cherniak, C. (1986) *Minimal Rationality.* MIT Press.

Chierchia, G., and McConnell-Ginet, S. (1990) *Meaning and Grammar: An Introduction to Semantics.* MIT Press.

Chomsky, N. (1957) *Syntactic Structures.* Mouton.

Chomsky, N. (1965) *Aspects of a Theory of Syntax.* MIT Press.

Church, A. (1936a) A note on the Entscheidungsproblem. *Journal of Symbolic Logic* 1: 40–41.

Church, A. (1936b) An unsolvable problem of elementary number theory. *American Journal of Mathematics* 58: 345–363.

Clark, H. H. (1969) Linguistic processes in deductive reasoning. *Psychological Review* 76: 387–404.

Clark, H. H., and Chase, W. G. (1972) On the process of comparing sentences against pictures. *Cognitive Psychology* 3: 472–517.

Clement, C. A., and Falmagne, R. J. (1986) Logical reasoning, world knowledge, and mental imagery: Interconnections in cognitive processes. *Memory and Cognition* 14: 299–307.

Clocksin, W. F., and Mellish, C. S. (1981) *Programming in PROLOG.* Springer-Verlag.

Cohen, L. J. (1981) Can human irrationality be experimentally demonstrated? *Behavioral and Brain Sciences* 4: 317–370.

Cohen, L. J. (1986) *The Dialogue of Reason.* Clarendon.

Collins, A. M., and Loftus, E. F. (1975) A spreading-activation theory of semantic processing. *Psychological Review* 82: 407–428.

Collins, A., and Michalski, R. (1989) The logic of plausible reasoning: A core theory. *Cognitive Science* 13: 1–50.

Cook, S. A. (1971) The complexity of theorem-proving procedures. In Proceedings of the Third Annual ACM Symposium on the Theory of Computing.

Cooper, R. (1983) *Quantification and Syntactic Theory.* Reidel.

Copi, I. M. (1954) *Symbolic Logic.* Macmillan.

Copi, I. M. (1973) *Symbolic Logic,* fourth edition. Macmillan.

Corcoran, J. (1974) Aristotle's natural deduction system. In J. Corcoran (ed.), *Ancient Logic and Its Modern Interpretations.* Reidel.

Cosmides, L. (1989) The logic of social exchange: Has natural selection shaped how humans reason? *Cognition* 31: 187–276.

Cummins, D. D., Lubart, T., Alksnis, O., and Rist, R. (1991) Conditional reasoning and causation. *Memory and Cognition* 19: 274–282.

Davidson, D. (1970) Mental events. In L. Foster and J. W. Swanson (eds.), *Experience and Theory.* University of Massachusetts Press.

Davis, M., and Putnam, H. (1960) A computing procedure for quantification theory. *Journal of the Association for Computing Machinery* 7: 201–215.

DeJong, G. (1988) An introduction to explanation-based learning. In H. E. Shrobe (ed.), *Exploring Artificial Intelligence.* Morgan Kaufmann.

de Kleer, J. (1986) An assumption-based TMS. *Artificial Intelligence* 28: 127–162.

Dennett, D. C. (1971) Intentional systems. *Journal of Philosophy* 68: 87–106.

Dennett, D. C. (1978) *Brainstorms*. Bradford Books.

Dennett, D. C. (1981) True believers: The intentional strategy and why it works. In A. F. Heath (ed.), *Scientific Explanation*. Clarendon.

DeSoto, C. B., London, M., and Handel, S. (1965) Social reasoning and spatial paralogic. *Journal of Personality and Social Psychology* 2: 513–521.

Dickstein, L. S. (1978a) The effect of figure on syllogistic reasoning. *Memory and Cognition* 6: 76–83.

Dickstein, L. S. (1978b) Error processes in syllogistic reasoning. *Memory and Cognition* 6: 537–543.

Dowty, D. R. (1993) *Categorial grammar, reasoning, and cognition*. Paper presented at the 29th regional meeting of the Chicago Linguistics Society.

Doyle, J. (1979) A truth maintenance system. *Artificial Intelligence* 12: 231–272.

Dummett, M. (1973) The justification of deduction. *Proceedings of the British Academy* 59: 201–231.

Dummett, M. (1975) The philosophical basis of intuitionistic logic. In H. E. Rose and J. Shepherdson (eds.), *Logic Colloquium '73*. North-Holland.

Dummett, M. (1977) *Elements of Intuitionism*. Clarendon.

Embretson, S., Schneider, L. M., and Roth, D. L. (1986) Multiple processing strategies and the construct validity of verbal reasoning tests. *Journal of Educational Measurement* 23: 13–32.

Erickson, J. R. (1974) A set analysis theory of behavior in formal syllogistic reasoning tasks. In R. L. Solso (ed.), *Theories in Cognitive Psychology*. Erlbaum.

Erickson, J. R. (1978) Research on syllogistic reasoning. In R. Revlin and R. E. Mayer (eds.), *Human Reasoning*. Winston.

Ericsson, K. A., and Simon, H. A. (1984) *Protocol Analysis: Verbal Reports as Data*. MIT Press.

Evans, J. St. B. T. (1977) Linguistic factors in reasoning. *Quarterly Journal of Experimental Psychology* 29: 297–306.

Evans, J. St. B. T. (1982) *The Psychology of Deductive Reasoning*. Routledge & Kegan Paul.

Evans, J. St. B. T. (1989) *Bias in Human Reasoning*. Erlbaum.

Evans, J. St. B. T., and Lynch, J. S. (1973) Matching bias in the selection task. *British Journal of Psychology* 64: 391–397.

Evans, J. St. B. T., Barston, J. L., and Pollard, P. (1983) On the conflict between logic and belief in syllogistic reasoning. *Memory and Cognition* 11: 295–306.

Fikes, R. E., and Nilsson, N. J. (1971) STRIPS: A new approach to the application of theorem proving to problem solving. *Artificial Intelligence* 2: 189–208.

Fillenbaum, S. (1975) *If:* Some uses. *Psychological Research* 37: 245–250.

Fillenbaum, S. (1977) Mind your *p*'s and *q*'s: The role of content and context in some uses of *and, or,* and *if.* In G. H. Bower (ed.), *Psychology of Learning and Motivation*, volume 11. Academic Press.

Fine, K. (1985a) Natural deduction and arbitrary objects. *Journal of Philosophical Logic* 14: 57–107.

Fine, K. (1985b) *Reasoning with Arbitrary Objects*. Blackwell.

Fitch, F. B. (1952) *Symbolic Logic: An Introduction*. Ronald.

Fitch, F. B. (1966) Natural deduction rules for obligation. *American Philosophical Quarterly* 3: 27–38.

Fitch, F. B. (1973) Natural deduction rules for English. *Philosophical Studies* 24: 89–104.

Fitting, M. (1983) *Proof Methods for Modal and Intuitionistic Logics.* Reidel.

Fodor, J. A. (1975) *The Language of Thought.* Crowell.

Fodor, J. A. (1981) *Representations.* MIT Press.

Fodor, J. A. (1983) *The Modularity of Mind.* MIT Press.

Fodor, J. A. (1985) Fodor's guide to mental representation: The intelligent auntie's vademecum. *Mind* 94: 76–100.

Fodor, J. A. (1987) A situated grandmother? *Mind and Language* 2: 64–81.

Fodor, J. A., and Pylyshyn, Z. (1988) Connectionism and cognitive architecture. *Cognition* 28: 3–71.

Føllesdal, D., and Hilpinen, R. (1971) Deontic logic: An introduction. In R. Hilpinen (ed.), *Deontic Logic: Introductory and Systematic Readings.* Reidel.

Fong, G. T., Krantz, D. H., and Nisbett, R. E. (1986) The effects of statistical training on thinking about everyday problems. *Cognitive Psychology* 18: 253–292.

Forbus, K. D., and de Kleer, J. (1993) *Building Problem Solvers.* MIT Press.

Ford, M. (1985) Review of *Mental Models. Language* 61: 897–903.

Frege, G. (1964) *The Basic Laws of Arithmetic.* University of California Press. (Original work published 1893.)

Frege, G. (1977) Thoughts. In P. T. Geach (ed.), *Logical Investigations.* Yale University Press. (Original work published 1918.)

Galotti, K. M. (1989) Approaches to studying formal and everyday reasoning. *Psychological Bulletin* 105: 331–351.

Gardner, M. (1958) *Logic Machines and Diagrams.* McGraw-Hill.

Garey, M. R., and Johnson, D. S. (1979) *Computers and Intractability: A Guide to the Theory of NP-Completeness.* Freeman.

Gazdar, G. (1979) *Pragmatics: Implicature, Presupposition, and Logical Form.* Academic Press.

Geis, M. L., and Zwicky, A. M. (1971) On invited inferences. *Linguistic Inquiry* 2: 561–566.

Gelman, S. A., and Markman, E. (1986) Categories and induction in young children. *Cognition* 23: 183–209.

Genesereth, M. R., and Nilsson, N. J. (1987) *Logical Foundations of Artificial Intelligence.* Morgan Kaufmann.

Gentner, D. (1983) Structure-mapping: A theoretical framework for analogy. *Cognitive Science* 7: 155–170.

Gentner, D., and Stevens, A. L. (1983) *Mental models.* Erlbaum.

Gentzen, G. (1969) Investigations into logical deduction. In M. E. Szabo (ed.), *The Collected Papers of Gerhard Gentzen* (Originally published as Untersuchungen über das logische Schliessen, *Mathematische Zeitschrift* 39 (1935): 176–210, 405–431.)

Gick, M., and Holyoak, K. J. (1983) Schema induction and analogical transfer. *Cognitive Psychology* 15: 1–38.

Gigerenzer, G., and Hug, K. (1992) Domain specific reasoning: Social contracts, cheating, and perspective change. *Cognition* 43: 127–171.

Gilhooly, K. J., Logie, R. H., Wetherick, N. E., and Wynn, V. (1993) Working memory and strategies in syllogistic-reasoning task. *Memory and Cognition* 21: 115–124.

Ginsberg, M. L. (1987) Introduction. In M. L. Ginsberg (ed.), *Readings in Nonmonotonic Reasoning.* Morgan Kaufmann.

Goldman, A. (1986) *Epistemology and Cognition.* Harvard University Press.

Goodman, N. (1965) *Fact, Fiction, and Forecast.* Second edition. Bobbs-Merrill.

Grandy, R. E. (1977) *Advanced Logic for Applications.* Reidel.

Green, C. (1969) Theorem proving by resolution as a basis for question-answering systems. In D. Michie and B. Meltzer (eds.), *Machine Intelligence 4.* Edinburgh University Press.

Green, C. (1980) *The application of theorem-proving to question-answering systems.* Garland. (Doctoral dissertation, Stanford University, 1969.)

Green, R. F., Guilford, J. P., Christensen, P. R., and Comrey, A. L. (1953) A factor-analytic study of reasoning abilities. *Psychometrika* 18: 135–180.

Greene, S. B. (1992) Multiple explanations for multiply-quantified sentences: Are multiple models necessary? *Psychological Review* 99: 184–187.

Grice, H. P. (1977) "Some Aspects of Reason." Immanuel Kant Lectures, Stanford University.

Grice, H. P. (1978) *Studies in the Way of Words.* Harvard University Press.

Griggs, R. A. (1983) The role of problem content in the selection task and THOG problem. In J. St B. T. Evans (ed.), *Thinking and Reasoning: Psychological Approaches.* Routledge.

Griggs, R. A., and Cox, J. R. (1982) The elusive thematic-materials effect in Wason's selection task. *British Journal of Psychology* 73: 407–420.

Guttenplan, S. D., and Tamny, M. (1971) *Logic: A Comprehensive Introduction.* Basic Books.

Guyote, M. J., and Sternberg, R. J. (1981) A transitive-chain theory of syllogistic reasoning. *Cognitive Psychology* 13: 461–525.

Haack, S. (1974) *Deviant Logic.* Cambridge University Press.

Haack, S. (1976) The justification of deduction. *Mind* 85: 112–119.

Halvorsen, P.-K. (1983) Semantics for lexical-functional grammar. *Linguistic Inquiry* 14: 567–615.

Hamill, J. F. (1990) *Ethno-Logic: The Anthropology of Human Reasoning.* University of Illinois Press.

Harman, G. (1986) *Change in View: Principles of Reasoning.* MIT Press.

Harman, H. H. (1976) *Modern Factor Analysis.* Third edition. University of Chicago Press.

Hastie, R., Schroeder, C., and Weber, R. (1990) Creating complex social conjunction categories from simple categories. *Bulletin of the Psychonomic Society* 28: 242–247.

Haviland, S. E. (1974) Nondeductive Strategies in Reasoning. Doctoral dissertation, Stanford University.

Hayes, J. R. (1965) Problem typology and the solution process. *Journal of Verbal Learning and Verbal Behavior* 4: 371–379.

Hayes, J. R. (1966) Memory, goals, and problem solving. In B. Kleinmuntz (ed.), *Problem Solving: Research, Method, and Theory.* Wiley.

Hayes, P. J. (1979) The logic of frames. In D. Metzing (ed.), *Frame Conceptions and Text Understanding.* Walter de Gruyter.

Hayes, P. J. (1985) The second naive physics manifesto. In J. R. Hobbs and R. C. Moore (eds.), *Formal Theories of the Commonsense World.* Ablex.

Hayes, P. J. (1987) A critique of pure treason. *Computational Intelligence* 3: 179–185.

Hayes-Roth, B., and Hayes-Roth, F. (1975) Plasticity in memorial networks. *Journal of Verbal Learning and Verbal Behavior* 14: 506–522.

Henle, M. (1962) On the relation between logic and thinking. *Psychological Review* 69: 366–378.

Henle, M. (1978) Forward. In R. Revlin and R. E. Mayer (eds.), *Human Reasoning*. Winston.

Hewitt, C. (1969) PLANNER: A language for proving theorems in robots. In Proceedings of the International Joint Conference on Artificial Intelligence.

Heyting, A. (1956) *Intuitionism: An Introduction*. North-Holland.

Higginbotham, J. (1987) On semantics. In E. LePore (ed.), *New Directions in Semantics*. Academic Press.

Hintikka, J. (1974) Quantifiers vs. quantification theory. *Linguistic Inquiry* 5: 153–177.

Hintzman, D. L. (1986) "Schema abstraction" in a multiple-trace memory model. *Psychological Review* 93: 411–428.

Hitch, G. J., and Baddeley, A. D. (1976) Verbal reasoning and working memory. *Quarterly Journal of Experimental Psychology* 28: 603–621.

Holland, J. H., Holyoak, K. J., Nisbett, R. E., and Thagard, P. R. (1986) *Induction: Processes of Inference, Learning, and Discovery*. MIT Press.

Horn, L. R. (1973) Greek Grice: A brief survey of proto-conversational rules in the history of logic. In C. Corum, T. C. Smith-Stark, and A. Weiser (eds.), *Papers from the Ninth Regional Meeting of the Chicago Linguistic Society*. Chicago Linguistic Society.

Horn, L. R. (1989) *A Natural History of Negation*. University of Chicago Press.

Huttenlocher, J. (1968) Constructing spatial images: A strategy in reasoning. *Psychological Review* 75: 550–560.

Israel, D. J. (1980) What's wrong with non-monotonic logics? In *Proceedings of the First Annual National Conference on Artificial Intelligence*. Morgan Kaufmann.

Jackson, S. L., and Griggs, R. A. (1990) The elusive pragmatic reasoning schemas effect. *Quarterly Journal of Experimental Psychology* 42A: 353–373.

James, W. (1890) *Principles of Psychology*, volume 2. Dover.

Janis, I. L., and Frick, F. (1943) The relationship between attitudes toward conclusions and errors in judging logical validity of syllogisms. *Journal of Experimental Psychology* 33: 73–77.

Jaśkowski, S. (1934) On the rules of suppositions in formal logic. *Studia Logica* 1: 5–32.

Jeffrey, R. C. (1967) *Formal Logic: Its Scope and Limits*. McGraw-Hill.

Johnson-Laird, P. N. (1975) Models of deduction. In R. J. Falmagne (ed.), *Reasoning: Representation and Process in Children and Adults*. Erlbaum.

Johnson-Laird, P. N. (1983) *Mental Models*. Harvard University Press.

Johnson-Laird, P. N. (1989) Mental models. In M. I. Posner (ed.), *Foundations of Cognitive Science*. MIT Press.

Johnson-Laird, P. N., and Bara, B. G. (1984a) Syllogistic inference. *Cognition* 16: 1–61.

Johnson-Laird, P. N., and Bara, B. G. (1984b) Logical expertise as a cause of error. *Cognition* 17: 183–184.

Johnson-Laird, P. N., and Byrne, R. M. J. (1991) *Deduction*. Erlbaum.

Johnson-Laird, P. N., Byrne, R. M. J., and Schaeken, W. (1992) Propositional reasoning by model. *Psychological Review* 99: 418–439.

Johnson-Laird, P. N., Byrne, R. M. J., and Tabossi, P. (1989) Reasoning by model: The case of multiple quantification. *Psychological Review* 96: 658–673.

Johnson-Laird, P. N., and Steedman, M. J. (1978) The psychology of syllogisms. *Cognitive Psychology* 10: 64–99.

Johnson-Laird, P. N., and Tagart, J. (1969) How implication is understood. *American Journal of Psychology* 82: 367–373.

Johnson-Laird, P. N., and Wason, P. C. (1970) Insight into a logical relation. *Quarterly Journal of Experimental Psychology* 22: 49–61.

Just, M. A., and Carpenter, P. A. (1987) *The Psychology of Reading and Language Comprehension.* Allyn and Bacon.

Kahneman, D., Slovic, P., and Tversky, A. (eds.) (1982) *Judgment under Uncertainty: Heuristics and Biases.* Cambridge University Press.

Kahneman, D., and Varey, C. A. (1990) Propensities and counterfactuals: The loser that almost won. *Journal of Personality and Social Psychology* 59: 1101–1110.

Kalish, D. (1967) Review of Copi. *Journal of Symbolic Logic* 32: 252–255.

Keil, F. C. (1989) *Concepts, Kinds, and Cognitive Development.* MIT Press.

Kintsch, W. (1988) The role of knowledge in discourse comprehension: A construction-integration model. *Psychological Review* 95: 163–182.

Kintsch, W., Kozminsky, E., Streby, W. J., McKoon, G., and Keenan, J. M. (1975) Comprehension and recall of text as a function of content variables. *Journal of Verbal Learning and Verbal Behavior* 14: 196–214.

Klaczynski, P. A., Gelfand, H., and Reese, H. W. (1989) Transfer of conditional reasoning: Effects of explanations and initial problem types. *Memory and Cognition* 17: 208–220.

Koedinger, K. R., and Anderson, J. R. (1990) Abstract planning and perceptual chunks: Element of expertise in geometry. *Cognitive Science* 14: 511–550.

Kowalski, R. (1979) *Logic for Problem Solving.* North-Holland.

Kripke, S. (1972) Naming and necessity. In D. Davidson and G. Harman (eds.), *Semantics of Natural Language.* Reidel.

Kunda, Z., Miller, D. T., and Clare, T. (1990) Combining social concepts: The role of causal reasoning. *Cognitive Science* 14: 551–578.

Lakoff, G. (1970) Linguistics and natural logic. *Synthèse* 22: 151–271.

Lakoff, R. (1971) If's and's and but's about conjunction. In C. J. Fillmore and D. T. Langendoen (eds.), *Studies in Linguistic Semantics.* Holt, Rinehart & Winston.

Larkin, J., McDermott, J., Simon, D., and Simon, H. A. (1980) Expert and novice performance in solving physics problems. *Science* 208: 1335–1342.

Lea, R. B., O'Brien, D. P., Fisch, S. M., Noveck, I. A., and Braine, M. D. S. (1990) Predicting propositional logic inferences in text comprehension. *Journal of Memory and Language* 29: 361–387.

Lear, J. (1980) *Aristotle and Logical Theory.* Cambridge University Press.

Lear, J. (1982) Leaving the world alone. *Journal of Philosophy* 79: 382–403.

Leblanc, H., and Wisdom, W. A. (1976) *Deductive Logic.* Allyn and Bacon.

Lefford, A. (1946) The influence of emotional subject matter on logical reasoning. *Journal of General Psychology* 34: 127–151.

Legrenzi, P. (1970) Relations between language and reasoning about deductive rules. In G. B. Flores D'Arcais and W. J. M. Levelt (eds.), *Advances in Psycholinguistics.* North-Holland.

Lehman, D. R., Lempert, R. O., and Nisbett, R. E. (1988) The effects of graduate training on reasoning. *American Psychologist* 43: 431–442.

Lehman, D., and Nisbett, R. E. (1990) A longitudinal study of the effects of undergraduate education on reasoning. *Developmental Psychology* 26:952–960.

Lemmon, E. J. (1965) *Beginning Logic*. Nelson.

Levesque, H. J. (1988) Logic and the complexity of reasoning. *Journal of Philosophical Logic* 17: 355–389.

Levinson, S. C. (1983) *Pragmatics*. Cambridge University Press.

Lewis, C. (1981) Skill in algebra. In J. R. Anderson (ed.), *Cognitive Skills and Their Acquisition*. Erlbaum.

Lewis, C. I., and Langford, C. H. (1932) *Symbolic Logic*. Dover.

Lewis, D. (1973a) *Counterfactuals*. Harvard University Press.

Lewis, D. (1973b) Causation. *Journal of Philosophy* 70: 556–567.

Lewis, D. (1974) Semantic analyses for dyadic deontic logic. In S. Stenlund (ed.), *Logical Theory and Semantic Analysis*. Reidel.

Lewontin, R. C. (1990) The evolution of cognition. In D. N. Osherson and E. E. Smith (eds.), *An Invitation to Cognitive Science*, volume 3. MIT Press.

Li, J. (1993) Effects of Expectation in the Assessment of Covariation and Conditionals. Masters Thesis, University of Chicago.

Lifschitz, V. (1985) Computing circumscription. In *Proceedings of the Ninth International Joint Conference on Artificial Intelligence*. Morgan Kaufmann.

Liu, L. G. (1985) Reasoning counterfactually in Chinese: Are there any obstacles? *Cognition* 21: 239–270.

Lucas, J. R. (1961) Minds, machines, and Gödel. *Philosophy* 36: 112–127.

Luria, A. R. (1971) Toward the problem of the historical nature of psychological processes. *International Journal of Psychology* 6: 259–272.

Macnamara, J. (1986) *A Border Dispute: The Place of Logic in Psychology*. MIT Press.

Manktelow, K. I., and Evans, J. St B. T. (1979) Facilitation of reasoning by realism: Effect or non-effect? *British Journal of Psychology* 70: 477–488.

Manktelow, K. I., and Over, D. E. (1987) Reasoning and rationality. *Mind and Language* 2: 199–219.

Manktelow, K. I., and Over, D. E. (1990) *Inference and Understanding*. Routledge.

Manktelow, K. I., and Over, D. E. (1991) Social roles and utilities in reasoning with deontic conditionals. *Cognition* 39: 85–105.

Marcus, S. L. (1982) Recall of logical argument lines. *Journal of Verbal Learning and Verbal Behavior* 21: 549–562.

Marcus, S. L., and Rips, L. J. (1979) Conditional reasoning. *Journal of Verbal Learning and Verbal Behavior* 18: 199–224.

Markovits, H. (1987) Incorrect conditional reasoning: competence or performance. *British Journal of Psychology* 76: 241–247.

Markovits, H. (1988) Conditional reasoning, representation, and empirical evidence on a concrete task. *Quarterly Journal of Experimental Psychology* 40A: 483–495.

Mates, B. (1986) *The Philosophy of Leibniz*. Oxford University Press.

May, R. (1985) *Logical Form: Its Structure and Derivation*. MIT Press.

McAllester, D. A. (1978) *A Three-Valued Truth Maintenance System*. Memo 473, MIT Artificial Intelligence Laboratory.

McAllester, D. A. (1982) *Reasoning Utility Package User's Manual*. Memo 667, MIT Artificial Intelligence Laboratory.

McCarthy, J. (1968) Programs with common sense. In M. Minsky (ed.), *Semantic Information Processing*. MIT Press.

McCarthy, J. (1977) Epistemological problems of artificial intelligence. In Proceedings of the Fifth International Joint Conference on Artificial Intelligence.

McCarthy, J. (1980) Circumscription—a form of non-monotonic reasoning. *Artificial Intelligence* 13: 27–39.

McCarthy, J. (1986) Applications of circumscription to formalizing common sense knowledge. *Artificial Intelligence* 28: 89–116.

McCawley, J. D. (1981) *Everything That Linguists Have Always Wanted to Know about Logic But Were Ashamed to Ask*. University of Chicago Press.

McCloskey, R. (1943) *Homer Price*. Viking.

McDermott, D. (1987) A critique of pure reason. *Computational Intelligence* 3: 151–160.

McGee, V. (1985) A counterexample to modus ponens. *Journal of Philosophy* 82: 462–471.

McNamara, T. P., and Sternberg, R. J. (1983) Mental models of word meaning. *Journal of Verbal Learning and Verbal Behavior* 22: 449–474.

Medin, D. L. (1989) Concepts and conceptual structure. *American Psychologist* 44: 1469–1481.

Medin, D. L., and Schaffer, M. M. (1978) Context theory of classification learning. *Psychological Review* 85: 207–238.

Mendelson, E. (1964) *An Introduction to Mathematical Logic*. Van Nostrand Reinhold.

Mendelson, E. (1990) Second thoughts about Church's thesis and mathematical proofs. *Journal of Philosophy* 87: 225–233.

Meyer, B. J. F. (1975) *The Organization of Prose and Its Effects on Memory*. North-Holland.

Minsky, M. (1985) A framework for representing knowledge. In R. J. Brachman and H. J. Levesque (eds.), *Readings in Knowledge Representation*. Morgan Kaufmann. (Originally published as Memo 306, MIT Artificial Intelligence Laboratory, 1975.)

Minton, S., Carbonell, J. G., Knoblock, C. A., Kuokka, D. R., Etzioni, O., and Gil, Y. (1990) Explanation-based learning: A problem-solving perspective. In J. G. Carbonell (ed.), *Machine Learning: Paradigms and Methods*. MIT Press.

Moeser, S. D., and Tarrant, B. L. (1977) Learning a network of comparisons. *Journal of Experimental Psychology: Human Learning and Memory* 3: 643–659.

Montague, R. (1973) The proper treatment of quantification in ordinary English. In J. Hintikka, J. Moravcsik, and P. Suppes (eds.), *Approaches to Natural Language*. Reidel.

Moore, O. K., and Anderson, S. B. (1954) Modern logic and tasks for experiments on problem solving behavior. *Journal of Psychology* 38: 151–160.

Moore, R. C. (1982) The role of logic in knowledge representation and commonsense reasoning. *Proceedings of the American Association for Artificial Intelligence* 1: 428–433.

Morgan, J. J. B. (1945) Attitudes of students toward the Japanese. *Journal of Social Psychology* 21: 219–227.

Morgan, J. J. B., and Morton, J. T. (1944) The distortion of syllogistic reasoning produced by personal convictions. *Journal of Social Psychology* 20: 39–59.

Morris, M. W., and Nisbett, R. E. (1993) Tools of the trade: Deductive schemas taught in psychology and philosophy. In R. E. Nisbett (ed.), *Rules for Reasoning*. Erlbaum.

Mueller, I. (1974) Greek mathematics and Greek logic. In J. Corcoran (ed.), *Ancient Logic and Its Modern Interpretations*. Reidel.

Murphy, G. L., and Medin, D. L. (1985) The role of theories in conceptual coherence. *Psychological Review* 92: 289–316.

Murray, N. V. (1982) Completely non-clausal theorem proving. *Artificial Intelligence* 18: 67–85.

Nevins, A. J. (1974) A human oriented logic for automatic theorem-proving. *Journal of the Association for Computing Machinery* 21: 606–621.

Newell, A. (1973a) You can't play 20 questions with nature and win. In W. G. Chase (ed.), *Visual Information Processing*. Academic Press.

Newell, A. (1973b) Production systems: Models of control structures. In W. G. Chase (ed.), *Visual Information Processing*. Academic Press.

Newell, A. (1980) Reasoning, problem solving, and decision processes: The problem space as a fundamental category. In R. S. Nickerson (ed.), *Attention and Performance VIII*. Erlbaum.

Newell, A. (1990) *Unified Theories of Cognition*. Harvard University Press.

Newell, A., and Simon, H. A. (1972) *Human Problem Solving*. Prentice-Hall.

Newell, A., and Simon, H. A. (1976) Computer science as empirical inquiry: Symbols and search. *Communications of the ACM* 19: 113–126.

Newell, A., Shaw, J. C., and Simon, H. A. (1957) Empirical explorations with the Logic Theory Machine: A case study in heuristics. In Proceedings of the Western Joint Computer Conference.

Newstead, S. E. (1989) Interpretational errors in syllogistic reasoning. *Journal of Memory and Language* 28: 78–91.

Newstead, S. E., and Griggs, R. A. (1983) Drawing inferences from quantified statements: A study of the square of opposition. *Journal of Verbal Learning and Verbal Behavior* 22: 535–546.

Nilsson, N. J. (1991) Logic and artificial intelligence. *Artificial Intelligence* 47: 31–56.

Nisbett, R. E., Fong, G. T., Lehman, D. R., and Cheng, P. W. (1987) Teaching reasoning. *Science* 238: 625–631.

Nisbett, R. E., and Wilson, T. D. (1977) Telling more than we can know: Verbal reports on mental processes. *Psychological Review* 84: 231–259.

Norman, D. A., and Bobrow, D. G. (1979) Descriptions: An intermediate stage in memory retrieval. *Cognitive Psychology* 11: 107–123.

Nosofsky, R. M. (1986) Attention, similarity, and the identification-categorization relationship. *Journal of Experimental Psychology: General* 115: 39–57.

Notturno, M. A. (1982) Frege and the psychological reality thesis. *Journal of the Theory of Social Behavior* 12: 329–344.

Oakhill, J. V., and Johnson-Laird, P. N. (1985) The effects of belief on the spontaneous production of syllogistic conclusions. *Quarterly Journal of Experimental Psychology* 37A: 553–569.

Oakhill, J., Johnson-Laird, P. N., and Garnham, A. (1989) Believability and syllogistic reasoning. *Cognition* 31: 117–140.

Oaksford, M., and Chater, N. (1991) Against logicist cognitive science. *Mind and Language* 6: 1–38.

Oaksford, M., and Stenning, K. (1992) Reasoning with conditionals containing negated constituents. *Journal of Experimental Psychology: Learning, Memory, and Cognition* 18: 835–854.

Osherson, D. N. (1974a) *Logical Abilities in Children*, volume 1. Erlbaum.

Osherson, D. N. (1974b) *Logical Abilities in Children*, volume 2. Erlbaum.

Osherson, D. N. (1975) *Logical Abilities in Children*, volume 3. Erlbaum.

Osherson, D. N. (1976) *Logical Abilities in Children*, volume 4. Erlbaum.

Osherson, D. N. (1977) Natural connectives: A Chomskyan approach. *Journal of Mathematical Psychology* 16: 1–29.

Osherson, D. N. (1978) Three conditions on conceptual naturalness. *Cognition* 6: 263–289.

Osherson, D. N., and Smith, E. E. (1981) On the adequacy of prototype theory as a theory of concepts. *Cognition* 9: 35–58.

Osherson, D. N., Smith, E. E., and Shafir, E. B. (1986) Some origins of belief. *Cognition* 24: 197–224.

Osherson, D. N., Smith, E. E., Wilkie, O., Lopez, A., and Shafir, E. (1991) Category-based induction. *Psychological Review* 97: 185–200.

Peacocke, C. (1987) Understanding logical constants: A realist account. *Proceedings of the British Academy* 73: 153–200.

Pelletier, F. J. (1977) Or. *Theoretical Linguistics* 4: 61–74.

Politzer, G., and Braine, M. D. S. (1991) Responses to inconsistent premises cannot count as suppression of valid inferences. *Cognition* 38: 103–108.

Polk, T. A., and Newell, A. (1988) Modeling human syllogistic reasoning in Soar. In *Proceedings of the Tenth Annual Conference of the Cognitive Science Society*. Erlbaum.

Polk, T. A., Newell, A., and Lewis, R. L. (1989) Toward a unified theory of immediate reasoning in Soar. In *Proceedings of the Eleventh Annual Conference of the Cognitive Science Society*. Erlbaum.

Pollard, P. (1982) Human reasoning: Some possible effects of availability *Cognition* 12: 65–96.

Pollard, P. (1990) Natural selection for the selection task: Limits to social exchange theory. *Cognition* 36: 195–204.

Pollard, P., and Evans, J. St B. T. (1987) Content and context effects in reasoning. *American Journal of Psychology* 100: 41–60.

Pollock, J. L. (1987) Defeasible reasoning. *Cognitive Science* 11: 481–518.

Pollock, J. L. (1989) *How to Build a Person: A Prolegomena*. MIT Press.

Posner, M. I., and Keele, S. W. (1968) On the genesis of abstract ideas. *Journal of Experimental Psychology* 77: 353–363.

Potts, G. R. (1972) Information processing strategies used in the encoding of linear orderings. *Journal of Verbal Learning and Verbal Behavior* 11: 727–740.

Potts, G. R., and Scholz, K. W. (1975) The internal representation of a three-term series problem. *Journal of Verbal Learning and Verbal Behavior* 14: 439–452.

Prawitz, D. (1960) An improved proof procedure. *Theoria* 26: 102–139.

Prawitz, D. (1965) *Natural Deduction: A Proof-Theoretical Study*. Almqvist and Wiksell.

Prawitz, D. (1974) On the idea of a general proof theory. *Synthèse* 27: 63–77.

Prawitz, D., Prawitz, H., and Voghera, N. (1960) A mechanical proof procedure and its realization in an electronic computer. *Journal of the Association for Computing Machinery* 7: 102–128.

Prior, A. N. (1960) The runabout inference-ticket. *Analysis* 21: 38–39.

Putnam, H. (1975) The meaning of "meaning." In K. Gunderson (ed.), *Language, Mind, and Knowledge*. University of Minnesota Press.

Putnam, H. (1988) *Representation and Reality*. MIT Press.

Pylyshyn, Z. (1984) *Computation and Cognition: Toward a Foundation for Cognitive Science.* MIT Press.

Quine, W. V. (1936) Truth by convention. In O. H. Lee (ed.), *Philosophical Essays for A. N. Whitehead.* Longmans.

Quine, W. V. (1969) Existence and quantification. In *Ontological Relativity and Other Essays.* Columbia University Press.

Quine, W. V. (1970) *Philosophy of Logic.* Prentice-Hall.

Quine, W. V. (1950) *Methods of Logic.* Holt, Rinehart & Winston.

Quine, W. V. (1972) *Methods of Logic.* Third edition. Holt, Rinehart & Winston.

Reed, S. K. (1972) Pattern recognition and categorization. *Cognitive Psychology* 3: 382– 407.

Reed, S. K., McMillan, W., and Chambers, B. (1979) Usefulness of syntactic and semantic information in constructing logical derivations. Paper presented at meeting of Psychonomic Society, Phoenix.

Reichenbach, H. (1966) *Elements of Symbolic Logic.* Free Press.

Reiser, B. J., Black, J. B., and Abelson, R. P. (1985) Knowledge structures in the organization and retrieval of autobiographical memories. *Cognitive Psychology* 17: 89–137.

Reiter, R. (1980) A logic for default reasoning. *Artificial Intelligence* 13: 81–132.

Reiter, R. (1987) Nonmonotonic reasoning. *Annual Review of Computer Science* 2: 147–186.

Reiter, R., and Criscuolo, G. (1981) On interacting defaults. In Proceedings of the Seventh International Joint Conference on Artificial Intelligence.

Rescher, N. (1988) *Rationality: A Philosophical Inquiry into the Nature and the Rationale of Reason.* Clarendon.

Revlin, R., and Leirer, V. O. (1978) The effect of personal bias on syllogistic reasoning: Rational decisions from personalized representations. In R. Revlin and R. E. Mayer (eds.), *Human Reasoning.* Winston.

Revlin, R., Leirer, V., Yopp, H., and Yopp, R. (1980) The belief-bias effect in formal reasoning: The influence of knowledge on logic. *Memory and Cognition* 8: 584–592.

Revlis, R. (1975a) Syllogistic reasoning: Logical deductions from a complex data base. In R. J. Falmagne (ed.), *Reasoning: Representation and Process in Children and Adults.* Erlbaum.

Revlis, R. (1975b) Two models of syllogistic reasoning: Feature selection and conversion. *Journal of Verbal Learning and Verbal Behavior* 14: 180–195.

Rips, L. J. (1983) Cognitive processes in propositional reasoning. *Psychological Review* 90: 38–71.

Rips, L. J. (1984) Reasoning as a central intellective ability. In R. J. Sternberg (ed.), *Advances in the Psychology of Human Intelligence,* volume 2. Erlbaum.

Rips, L. J. (1986) Mental muddles. In M. Brand and R. M. Harnish (eds.), *The Representation of Knowledge and Belief.* University of Arizona Press.

Rips, L. J. (1989a) The psychology of knights and knaves. *Cognition* 31: 85–116.

Rips, L. J. (1989b) Similarity, typicality, and categorization. In S. Vosniadou and A. Ortony (eds.), *Similarity and Analogical Reasoning.* Cambridge University Press.

Rips, L. J. (1990a) Reasoning. *Annual Review of Psychology* 41: 321–353.

Rips, L. J. (1990b) Paralogical reasoning: Evans, Johnson-Laird, and Byrne on liar and truth-teller puzzles. *Cognition* 36: 291–314.

Rips, L. J. (1991) Similarity and the structure of categories. In D. J. Napoli and J. Kegl (eds.), *Bridges between Psychology and Linguistics: A Swarthmore Festschrift for Lila Gleitman.* Erlbaum.

Rips, L. J. (1992) Conceptualizing. Unpublished manuscript, University of Chicago.

Rips, L. J., and Collins, A. (in press) Categories and resemblance. *Journal of Experimental Psychology: General.*

Rips, L. J., and Conrad, F. G. (1983) Individual differences in deduction. *Cognition and Brain Theory* 6: 259–285.

Rips, L. J., and Marcus, S. L. (1977) Suppositions and the analysis of conditional sentences. In M. A. Just and P. A. Carpenter (eds.), *Cognitive Processes in Comprehension.* Erlbaum.

Roberge, J. J. (1970) A reexamination of the interpretations of errors in formal syllogistic reasoning. *Psychonomic Science* 19: 331–333.

Robinson, J. A. (1965) A machine-oriented logic based on the resolution principle. *Journal of the Association for Computing Machinery* 12: 23–41.

Rogers, H. (1967) *Theory of Recursive Functions and Effective Computability.* McGraw-Hill.

Rosch, E. (1978) Principles of categorization. In E. Rosch and B. B. Lloyd (eds.), *Cognition and Categorization.* Erlbaum.

Rumelhart, D. E. (1975) Notes on a schema for stories. In D. G. Bobrow and A. M. Collins (eds.), *Representation and Understanding.* Academic Press.

Rumelhart, D. E. (1989) Toward a microstructural account of human reasoning. In S. Vosniadou and A. Ortony (eds.), *Similarity and Analogical Reasoning.* Cambridge University Press.

Rumelhart, D. E., and Norman, D. A. (1988) Representation in memory. In R. C. Atkinson, R. J. Herrnstein, G. Lindzey, and R. D. Luce (eds.), *Stevens' Handbook of Experimental Psychology*, volume 2. Wiley.

Rumelhart, D. E., Smolensky, P., McClelland, J. L., and Hinton, G. E. (1986) Schemata and sequential thought processes in PDP models. In J. L. McClelland, D. E. Rumelhart, and the PDP Research Group (eds.), *Parallel Distributed Processing: Explorations in the Microstructure of Cognition*, volume 2. MIT Press.

Sadock, J. M. (1977) Modus brevis: The truncated argument. In W. A. Beach, S. E. Fox, and S. Philosoph (eds.), *Papers from the Thirteenth Regional Meeting, Chicago Linguistic Society.* Chicago Linguistic Society.

Salmon, W. (1967) *Foundations of Scientific Inference.* University of Pittsburgh Press.

Salmon, W. (1989) *Four Decades of Scientific Explanation.* University of Minnesota Press.

Schank, R. C. (1982) *Dynamic Memory.* Cambridge University Press.

Schank, R., and Abelson, R. (1977) *Scripts, Plans, Goals, and Understanding.* Erlbaum.

Schank, R. C., Collins, G. C., and Hunter, L. E. (1986) Transcending inductive category formation in learning. *Behavioral and Brain Sciences* 9: 639–686.

Scholz, K. W., and Potts, G. R. (1974) Cognitive processing of linear orderings. *Journal of Experimental Psychology* 102: 323–326.

Scribner, S. (1977) Modes of thinking and ways of speaking: Culture and logic reconsidered. In P. N. Johnson-Laird and P. C. Wason (eds.), *Thinking: Readings in Cognitive Science.* Cambridge University Press.

Sells, S. B. (1936) The atmosphere effect: An experimental study of reasoning. *Archives of Psychology* 29: 1–72.

Seltman, M., and Seltman, P. (1985) *Piaget's Logic: A Critique of Genetic Epistemology.* Allen & Unwin.

Singer, M., Halldorson, M., Lear, J. C., and Andrusiak, P. (1992) Validation of causal bridging inferences in discourse understanding. *Journal of Memory and Language* 31: 507–524.

Singer, M., Revlin, R., and Halldorson, M. (1990) Bridging-inferences and enthymemes. In A. C. Graesser and G. H. Bower (eds.), *Inferences and Text Comprehension*. Academic Press.

Skolem, T. (1967) On mathematical logic. In J. van Heijenoort (ed.), *From Frege to Gödel: A Source Book in Mathematical Logic, 1879–1931*. Harvard University Press. (Reprinted from *Norsk matematisk tidsskrift* 10 (1928): 125–142.)

Smalley, N. S. (1974) Evaluating a rule against possible instances. *Quarterly Journal of Experimental Psychology* 65: 293–304.

Smiley, T. J. (1973) What is a syllogism? *Journal of Philosophical Logic* 2: 136–154.

Smith, E. E. (1989) Concepts and induction. In M. I. Posner (eds.), *Foundations of Cognitive Science*. MIT Press.

Smith, E. E., Langston, C., and Nisbett, R. (1992) The case for rules in reasoning. *Cognitive Science* 16: 1–40.

Smith, E. E., and Medin, D. L. (1981) *Categories and Concepts*. Harvard University Press.

Smolensky, P. (1990) Tensor product variable binding and the representation of symbolic structures in connectionist systems. *Artificial Intelligence* 46: 159–216.

Smullyan, R. M. (1965) Analytic natural deduction. *Journal of Symbolic Logic* 30: 123–139.

Smullyan, R. M. (1968) *First-Order Logic*. Berlin: Springer.

Smullyan, R. (1978) *What Is the Name of This Book? The Riddle of Dracula and Other Logical Puzzles*. Prentice-Hall.

Soames, S. (1985) Semantics and psychology. In J. J. Katz (ed.), *Philosophy of Linguistics*. Oxford: Oxford University Press.

Sober, E. (1978) Psychologism. *Journal for the Theory of Social Behavior* 8: 165–191.

Sober, E. (1981) The evolution of rationality. *Synthèse* 46: 95–120.

Sperber, D., and Wilson, D. (1986) *Relevance: Communication and cognition*. Harvard University Press.

Springston, F. J., and Clark, H. H. (1973) *And* and *or*, or the comprehension of pseudo-imperatives. *Journal of Verbal Learning and Verbal Behavior* 12: 258–272.

Stabler, E. P., Jr. (1983) How are grammars represented? *Behavioral and Brain Sciences* 6: 391–402.

Stalnaker, R. C. (1968) A theory of conditionals. In N. Rescher (ed.), *Studies in Logic Theory*. Blackwell.

Stalnaker, R. C. (1976) Indicative conditionals. In A. Kasher (ed.), *Language in Focus: Foundations, Methods, and Systems*. Reidel.

Staudenmayer, H. (1975) Understanding conditional reasoning with meaningful propositions. In R. J. Falmagne (ed.), *Reasoning: Representation and Process in Children and Adults*. Erlbaum.

Stenning, K. (1992) Distinguishing conceptual and empirical issues about mental models. In Y. Rogers, A. Rutherford, and P. A. Bibby (eds.), *Models in the Mind*. Academic Press.

Sterling, L., and Shapiro, E. (1986) *The Art of Prolog*. MIT Press.

Sternberg, R. J. (1977) *Intelligence, Information Processing, and Analogical Reasoning: The Componential Analysis of Human Abilities*. Erlbaum.

Sternberg, R. J. (1980) Representation and process in linear syllogistic reasoning. *Journal of Experimental Psychology: General* 109: 119–159.

Stich, S. P. (1981) Dennett on intentional systems. *Philosophical Topics* 12: 39–62.

Stich, S. P. (1990) *The Fragmentation of Reason: Preface to a Pragmatic Theory of Cognitive Evaluation*. MIT Press.

Störring, G. (1908) Experimentelle Untersuchungen über einfache Schlussprozesse. *Archiv für die Gesamte Psychologie* 11: 1–127.

Strawson, P. F. (1952) *Introduction to Logical Theory*. Methuen.

Stroud, B. (1981) Evolution and the necessities of thought. In L. W. Sumner, J. G. Slater, and F. Wilson (eds.), *Pragmatism and Purpose*. University of Toronto Press.

Sundholm, G. (1986) Proof theory and meaning. In D. Gabbay and F. Guenthner (eds.), *Handbook of Philosophical Logic*, volume 3. Reidel.

Suppes, P. (1957) *Introduction to Logic*. Van Nostrand.

Sussman, G. J., and McDermott, D. V. (1972) Why Conniving Is Better Than Planning. Memo 255A, MIT Artificial Intelligence Laboratory.

Tanenhaus, M. K., Carroll, J. M., and Bever, T. G. (1976) Sentence-picture verification models as theories of sentence comprehension: A critique of Carpenter and Just. *Psychological Review* 83: 310–317.

Taplin, J. E. (1971) Reasoning with conditional sentences. *Journal of Verbal Learning and Verbal Behavior* 10: 218–225.

Taplin, J. E., and Staudenmayer, H. (1973) Interpretation of abstract conditional sentences in deductive reasoning. *Journal of Verbal Learning and Verbal Behavior* 12: 530–542.

Tarski, A. (1956) The concept of truth in formalized languages. In *Logic, Semantics, Metamathematics*. Oxford University Press. (Originally published as Der Wahrheitsbegriff in den formalisierten Sprachen, *Studia Philosophica* 1(1936): 261–405.)

Thomason, R. H. (1970a) *Symbolic Logic: An Introduction*. Macmillan.

Thomason, R. H. (1970b) A Fitch-style formulation of conditional logic. *Logique et Analyse* 52: 397–412.

Thomason, R. H. (1991) Logicism, AI, and common sense: John McCarthy's program in philosophical perspective. In V. Lifschitz (ed.), *Artificial Intelligence and Mathematical Theory of Computation*. Academic Press.

Thurstone, L. L. (1937) Tests for Primary Abilities. Unpublished manuscript, University of Chicago Library.

Thurstone, L. L. (1938) *Primary Mental Abilities*. University of Chicago Press.

Thurstone, L. L., and Thurstone, T. G. (1941) *Factorial Studies of Intelligence*. University of Chicago Press.

Touretzky, D. S. (1984) Implicit ordering of defaults in inheritance systems. In Proceedings of the Fifth National Conference on Artificial Intelligence.

Trabasso, T., Rollins, H., and Shaughnessy, E. (1971) Storage and verification stages in processing concepts. *Cognitive Psychology* 2: 239–289.

Tversky, A., and Kahneman, D. (1971) Belief in the "law of small numbers." *Psychological Bulletin* 76: 105–110.

Tversky, A., and Kahneman, D. (1973) Availability: A heuristic for judging frequency and probability. *Cognitive Psychology* 5: 207–232.

Tversky, A., and Kahneman, D. (1974) Judgment under uncertainty: Heuristics and biases. *Science* 185: 1124–1131.

Tversky, A., and Kahneman, D. (1983) Extensional versus intuitive reasoning: The conjunction fallacy in probability judgments. *Psychological Review* 90: 293–315.

Tversky, B., and Hemenway, K. (1983) Categories of environmental scenes. *Cognitive Psychology* 15: 121–149.

Ungar, A. M. (1992) *Normalization, Cut-Elimination, and the Theory of Proofs*. Center for the Study of Language and Information.

van Benthem, J. (1985) *A Manual of Intensional Logic*. Center for the Study of Language and Information.

van Fraassen, B. C. (1971) *Formal Semantics and Logic*. Macmillan.

van Fraassen, B. C. (1980) *The Scientific Image*. Clarendon Press.

Vendler, Z. (1967) *Linguistics in Philosophy*. Cornell University Press.

von Wright, G. H. (1971) Deontic logic and the theory of conditions. In R. Hilpinen (ed.), *Deontic Logic: Introductory and Systematic Readings*. Reidel.

Wang, H. (1960) Toward mechanical mathematics. *IBM Journal for Research and Development* 4: 2–22.

Warner, S. A., and Griggs, R. A. (1980) Processing partially ordered information. *Journal of Experimental Psychology: Human Learning and Memory* 6: 741–753.

Wason, P. C. (1966) Reasoning. In B. M. Foss (ed.), *New Horizons in Psychology*. Penguin.

Wason, P. C. (1968) Reasoning about a rule. *Quarterly Journal of Experimental Psychology* 20: 273–281.

Wason, P. C., and Evans, J. St. B. T. (1975) Dual processes in reasoning. *Cognition* 3: 141–154.

Wason, P. C., and Green, D. W. (1984) Reasoning and mental representation. *Quarterly Journal of Experimental Psychology* 36A: 597–610.

Wason, P. C., and Johnson-Laird, P. N. (1972) *Psychology of Reasoning: Structure and Content*. Harvard University Press.

Westerståhl, D. (1989) Quantifiers in formal and natural languages. In D. Gabbay and F. Guenthner (eds.), *Handbook of Philosophical Logic*, volume 4. Reidel.

Wetherick, N. E., and Gilhooly, K. J. (1990) Syllogistic reasoning: Effects of premise order. In K. J. Gilhooly, M. T. G. Keane, R. H. Logie, and G. Erdos (eds.), *Lines of Thought*, volume 1. Wiley.

Whitehead, A. N., and Russell, B. (1910–1913) *Principia Mathematica*. Cambridge University Press.

Whitely, S. E. (1980) Latent trait models in the study of intelligence. *Intelligence* 4: 97–132.

Wiggins, D. (1980) 'Most' and 'all': Some comments on a familiar programme, and on the logical form of quantified sentences. In M. Platts (ed.), *Reference, Truth, and Reality*. Routledge & Kegan Paul.

Wilkins, M. C. (1928) The effect of changed material on ability to do formal syllogistic reasoning. *Psychological Archives* 16: no. 102.

Winograd, T. (1972) *Understanding Natural Language*. Academic Press.

Winograd, T. (1975) Frame representations and the declarative/procedural controversy. In D. G. Bobrow and A. M. Collins (eds.), *Representation and Understanding: Studies in Cognitive Science*. Academic Press.

Woodworth, R. S. (1938) *Experimental Psychology*. Holt.

Woodworth, R. S., and Sells, S. B. (1935) An atmosphere effect in formal syllogistic reasoning. *Journal of Experimental Psychology* 18: 451–460.

Wos, L., and Henschen, L. (1983) Automatic theorem proving 1965–1970. In J. H. Siekmann and G. Wrightson (eds.), *Automation of Reasoning*, volume 2. Springer-Verlag.

Wos, L., Overbeek, R., Lusk, E., and Boyle, J. (1984) *Automated Reasoning: Introduction and Applications*. Prentice-Hall.

Index

Abelson, R. P., 290, 413n8
Abstraction, 254. *See also* Instantiation; Generalization; Matching
Acquisition of logical principles. *See* Learning; Innateness
Adams, E., 125
Adams, M. J., 232, 239, 402n7
Additivity requirement, 312–314, 317
Adkins, D. C., 16
Ajjanagadde, V., 186, 300
Algorithm for proofs. *See* Computer theorem proving; PSYCOP/PSYCOP+; Resolution theorem proving; Tree proof
Analogical inference, 11, 389, 391
A Natural-Deduction System (ANDS), 150
Anderson, A. R., 48–50, 383
Anderson, J. R., 60, 68, 109, 276, 281, 300, 418n5
Anderson, S. B., 307
Argument, definition of, 3
Argument evaluation, 3, 18, 19, 149, 261
  with categorical syllogisms, 233–239
  with multiple variables, 254–260, 265
  with sentential connectives, 150–157, 160, 170, 184, 310, 311
  task difficulty of, 312–313, 317
Argument reversal, 201, 202, 209
  and resolution system, 213
  and semantics, 207
  soundness of, 209–213, 218–220
Arguments, of predicates, 51. *See also* Permanent/Temporary names; Variables
Aristotelian syllogism. *See* Syllogism
Aristotle, 19, 25, 57, 58, 176, 195, 233, 239, 380, 402n6, 402n7, 408n3
Armstrong, S. L., 411n5
Artificial intelligence. *See also* Algorithm for proofs; Programming language
  and computer theorem proving, 64–66
  and deductive problem solving, 97–99
  and nondeductive inference, 269, 270, 389, 390
  and syllogistic reasoning, 23
Assertions (of a proof). *See also* Domain/subdomain/superdomain; Goal/subgoal; Inference rule; Supposition
  definition of, 68
  intermediate, 73
  working memory for, 111, 112
Assertion sensitivity, 72, 74
Associates, paired, 271
Atmosphere effects. *See* Syllogism
Atomic sentence
  definition of, 51

token/type, 141, 142
  in tree proofs, 75–77, 131
Au, T. K.-F., 401n2
Automated deduction. *See* Artificial intelligence; Computer theorem proving; Resolution theorem proving
Availability, of rules, 153–156, 242, 243, 260, 265, 407n3
Availability heuristic, 246, 339–347
Axiomatic system. *See* Logic

Bach, E., 390
Backward chaining, 71. *See also* Backward rule; Transitivity
Backward/forward distinction. *See* Forward/backward distinction
Backward rule
  definition of, 68
  in PSYCOP/PSYCOP+, 105, 115–121, 129–131, 140, 195–202, 209–213
  and self-constraint/promotion, 84–90, 404n9
Baddeley, A. D., 112
Bara, B. G., 23, 232, 234, 244–247, 349, 352, 356, 358, 361, 408n2, 409n6, 415n3, 415n4, 415n6
Baron, J., 408n9
Barston, J. L., 21
Barwise, J., 57, 93, 94, 186, 214, 345, 401n1, 404n6
Beattie, J., 408n9
Begg, I., 56, 228, 229, 231, 244, 303
Belief, 344, 389–390. *See also* Believability effect
  and categorization, 278, 279, 289, 292, 296–297, 300, 301, 391, 411n4
  coherence of, 11, 12, 298
  and deduction, 99, 300, 301
  and nonmonotonic logic, 411n7
Belief revision, 58–62
Believability effect, 21, 22, 238, 340, 342, 343, 371, 414n2, 416–417n10
Belnap, N. D., 48–50, 383, 384, 403n3
Benacerraf, P., 214
Bergmann, M., 203, 254, 351
Beth, E. W., 74
Bever, T. G., 176
Biconditional, 91, 178, 179. *See also* Conditional
Binding, of variables, 186, 187, 227, 269, 300, 399. *See also* Generalization; Instantiation; Matching
Binet test, 15
Birnbaum, L., 65, 389, 417n3